6th International Forum on Industrial Design (IFID 2018)

MATEC Web of Conferences Volume 176 (2018)

Luoyang, China
18 - 20 May 2018

Editors:

Changde Lu
Xuesheng Pei
Jianning Su

ISBN: 978-1-5108-6599-0

Printed from e-media with permission by:

Curran Associates, Inc.
57 Morehouse Lane
Red Hook, NY 12571

Some format issues inherent in the e-media version may also appear in this print version.

Printed by Curran Associates, Inc. (2018)

For additional information, please contact EDP Sciences – Web of Conferences at the address below.

EDP Sciences – Web of Conferences
17, Avenue du Hoggar
Parc d'Activité de Courtabœuf
BP 112
F-91944 Les Ulis Cedex A
France

Phone: +33 (0) 1 69 18 75 75
Fax: +33 (0) 1 69 28 84 91

contact-edps@webofconferences.org

Additional copies of this publication are available from:

Curran Associates, Inc.
57 Morehouse Lane
Red Hook, NY 12571 USA
Phone: 845-758-0400
Fax: 845-758-2633
Email: curran@proceedings.com
Web: www.proceedings.com

TABLE OF CONTENTS

Preface

Industrial Design is important in the development of global industrialization. In order to boost the development of Industrial Design, the 2018 6th International Forum on Industrial Design (IFID 2018) was held at the Urban Lounge in Luoyang International Exhibition Center during 18-20 May, 2018 to gather the scientists, scholars, engineers and students from the Universities all around the world and the industry together to present ongoing research activities, and hence to foster research relations between the Universities and the industry. IFID2018 is hosted by Luoyang Government, organized by Luoyang Science and Technology Bureau, Luoyang Productivity Promoting Center, Luoyang Creative Industry Design Center and Guangdong Academy of International Academic Exchange, co-organized by Northwestern Polytechnical University, Lanzhou University of Technology, Henan University of Science and Technology, GOTH DESIGN Co., Ltd., Low Carbon Design Society of Hong Kong, Xihua University, North Minzu University, Zhengzhou University of Aeronautics, Zhengzhou University of Light Industry, Nanchang University, Xi'an University of Science and Technology, Xi'an Jiaotong University, Hebei Agricultural University, and Tropical Agricultural Machinery Research Institute of Chinese Academy of Tropical Agricultural Sciences are the co-organizers. The forum is held every year to make it an ideal platform for people to share views and experiences in Industrial Design and related areas. In this edition, IFID2018 is providing a venue of high quality state-of-the-art research papers in the following areas of interest:

- Intelligent design and Computer Technology
- Design education and Design innovation development
- Information technology and Cloud design service platform
- User experience and Human-computer interaction

More than 200 submitted papers were received, which were reviewed by appropriately qualified experts in the field selected by the Conference Committee. After that tight selection procedure, only 95 papers were accepted for oral presentation and publication in this proceeding.

On behalf of the organizing committee and scientific committee of the IFID 2018, we would like to express our gratitude to all the participants, presenters, technical reviewers, and all collaborative partners for their contributions to the conference. We would like also thank the contributing authors for submitting papers and for being very patient to revise them multiple times based on the recommendations of the assigned reviewers.

As well, we would like to thank the technical committee members, who get the papers from the contributors being reviewed by suitable experts. We have received valuable feedbacks from all the participants, which will help us in organizing such conference in a better way in the coming future. Additionally, we place on record our sincere gratitude to the chairperson of each and every conference session, for decently conducting the oral presentation of the technical papers and coordinating the discussions among the participants. The discussions and deliberations during the sessions are sure to be valued by the participants.

Finally, we are deeply indebted to EDP Sciences for excellently bringing out this conference proceedings through the MATEC Web of Conferences.

The Committee of IFID2018

Committees

Chairman:
Prof.Changde Lu, Xi'an design Federation, China

Vice-chairman:
Prof.Jianning Su, Lanzhou University of Technology, China
A.Prof.Xuesheng Pei, Henan University of Science and Technology, China

Members:
President.JEONG SUKJUNE, GOTH DESIGN Co.LTD, Korea
Commander.Guanxian Zhi, Low Carbon Design Society of Hongkong, China
Prof.Kaining Meng, Xihau University, China
Prof.Chunyang Mo, North Minzu University, China
Prof.Zhongyan Hu, Zhengzhou University of Aeronautics, China
Prof.Jianjun Ren, Zhengzhou University of Light Industry, China
Researcher.Xuan Wang, Nanchang University, China
Prof.Dengkai Chen, Northwestern Polytechnical University, China
A.Prof.Qing Feng, Xi`an University of Science and Technology, China
A.Prof.Hongwei Li, Xi'an Jiaotong University, China
A.Prof.Xiyin Gao, Hebei Agricultural University, China
Prof.Linghao Zhang, China Industrial Design Association/ School of Design of Jiangnan University, China
Anil R. Kumar,Associate Professor,San Jose State University, USA
Ari Widyanti, Ph.D. , Bandung Institute of Technology, Indonesia
Chih-Yung Tsai , Ph.D. , University of Taipei, China
Jaehyun Park, Ph.D. , Incheon National University (INU), Korea
A.Prof.Rui Gou, Southwest Jiaotong University, China
Prof.Que Weimin, Peking University, China
Prof.Tongzheng Song, National Taiwan University of Science and Technology, China
Dr.Kaida Xiao ,School of Design, University of Leeds
Prof.RUNGTAI LIN, National Taiwan University of Arts, China
Prof.Bernhard E. Bürdek, University of Art and Design Offenbach am Main, Germany
A.Prof.Mehdi Toloo, Technical University of Ostrava, Czech Republic/ Editor in Computers&Industrial Engineering at ELSEVIER
Prof.Bin He,Shanghai University, China
Ph.D.Shih-Wen Hsiao,National Cheng Kung University, China
A.Prof.Lifang Yang,Harbin Institute of Technology, China
Dr.Chanprapha Phuangsuwan,Rajamangala University of Technology Thanyaburi, Thailand

Statement of Peer review

In submitting conference proceedings to *Web of Conferences*, the editors of the proceedings certify to the Publisher that

1. They adhere to its **Policy on Publishing Integrity** in order to safeguard good scientific practice in publishing.
2. All articles have been subjected to peer review administered by the proceedings editors.
3. Reviews have been conducted by expert referees, who have been requested to provide unbiased and constructive comments aimed, whenever possible, at improving the work.
4. Proceedings editors have taken all reasonable steps to ensure the quality of the materials they publish and their decision to accept or reject a paper for publication has been based only on the merits of the work and the relevance to the journal.

Title, date and place of the conference

2018 6th International Forum on Industrial Design

May 18-20, 2018

Luoyang International Exhibition Center,China

Proceedings editor(s):

Prof.Changde Lu, Xi'an design Federation, China

A.Prof.Xuesheng Pei, Henan University of Science and Technology, China

Prof.Jianning Su, Lanzhou University of Technology, China

Date and editor's signature

MATEC Web of Conferences **176**, 01001 (2018) https://doi.org/10.1051/matecconf/201817601001
IFID 2018

Research on the Improvement of Shared Massage Chair Based on User Journey Map[i]

JI Qian [1], ZHENG Jiayu [1,a], ZHANG Yu[1]

[1]Huazhong University of Science and Technology,430074 Wuhan

Abstract. In this paper, the User journey map is an oriented graph to visualize the user's interaction with products and services. It helps designers to understand the user's feelings, thoughts, and behaviours at a specific time and look for the pain and opportunity points. The rapid development of shared massage chairs in recent years has been chosen as a typical case among a large number of shared products in this paper. According to the earlier survey, we noticed that users always had poor experience when use them. The user journey map has been used as a tool to analyze the experience of using a shared massage chair based on the observation and investigation of users in order to proposes new directions for its improvement.

1 Introduction

The shared massage chair allows everyone to enjoy a massage services at anytime anywhere by scanning the two-dimensional code. It is convenient to use for rest [1] when people are prone to experience physical and mental fatigue and most likely to have the need of rest, it helps users take advantages of their fragmented time to relax timely as well as provide users relatively accurate massage services. The Research Report on the 2017 Shared Massage Chair Market released by the Speed Research Institute pointed out that at present, China's massage apparatus market is in an ascending stage, and the health care population has increased by a large margin year by year [2].

User Journey Map is a design tool for carding user scenarios and experience problems [3]. It can disassemble fuzzy requirements into user behaviours, user feelings, usage scenarios and other elements visual expression, user behaviour indicates the pain and opportunities points [4]. It describes the user's experience through storytelling and presents information in a visual way [5].

Based on the user journey map of the interaction between users and shared massage chair, this paper summarizes the opportunity(O) and pain(P) points through the observation and interview, then focuses on the O and P points to find the breakthrough of the improvement, which will lead to the final design direction.

2 Overview of the research process

This paper conducts research preparation through literature review, analysis of existing products, conducting user surveys and collation of interviewee data through records and interviews. All interviewees data are aggregated into the user journey map and the O and P points are enumerated. Finally, the P and O points of shared massage chairs are analysed to propose design directions and plans. The main research methods and processes of this paper include those shown in Fig. 1

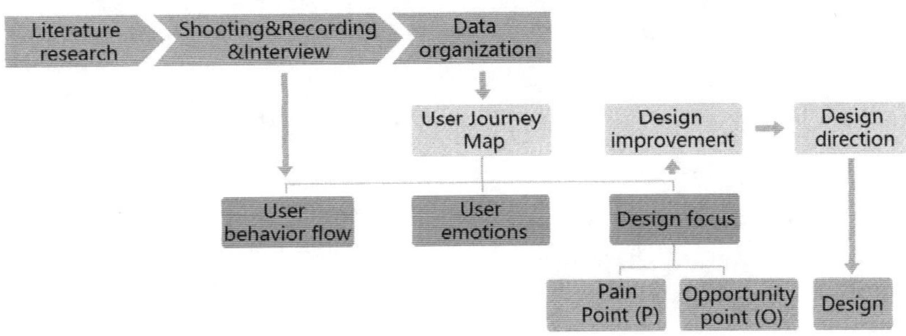

Figure 1. Main research methods and processes.

*Corresponding author: [a] 1104508815@qq.com

3 Preliminary investigation

(1) Literature review

By analysing the current research status, related documents, the characteristics of shared massage chairs as well as the structure and appearance design of massage chairs. The purpose of literature research is to understand the research status, and to look for opportunities of existing research to find research space in this field.

As the "shared massage chair" is a relatively new product, academic search through various channels found, including CNKI, Google, etc., Wu Yan-jun elaborated on the design ideas of the payment board between the cloud server and the massage chair sharing the massage chair, introduced the realization methods of each function, and improved the stability and reliability[6].Some researchers have analysed the problem of shared massage chairs and system components based on the development status of shared massage chairs. This area of research is relatively new, although it will bring difficulties to the research, but it will also become a suggestion for a better development of the massage chair in the future.

(2) Existing product analysis

At present, the most popular brands of shared massage chairs are MOMODA and LEMOBAR. There are 6 features mainly as following: simple to use, cheap, providing massage services timely, occupying no private space, meeting the needs of health pursuit and leisure consumption, consumption upgrade in line with the needs of the times.

(3) User research

Through field investigation, 50 users were surveyed to analysed and organize more comprehensive and objective user experience data. In order to restore the authenticity of the observations, this research conducts field research at crowed places, where people flow is high and users are prone to fatigue, such as the airports, high-speed rail stations, cinemas, gymnasiums, beauty salons, shopping malls, supermarkets and stations. The main methods used in the main phases of the investigation include tracking shots, recordings and user interviews. The specific user survey process is shown in Fig. 2.

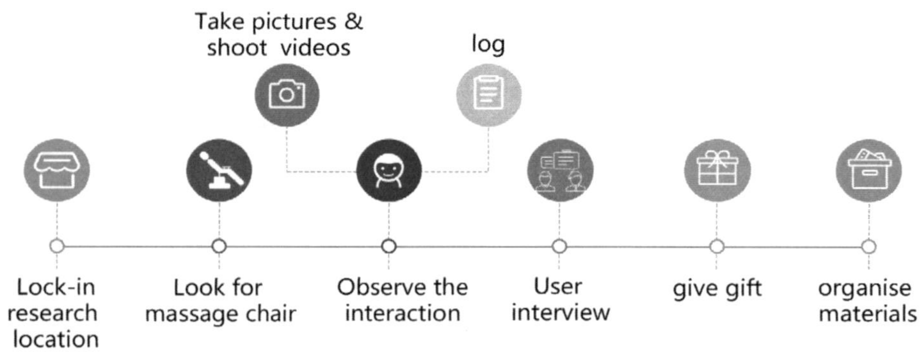

Figure 2. Specific user survey process.

The process of user research consists of two researchers. One is responsible for shooting, the other is responsible for observing and recording notes, and the researcher need not interrupt the users' normal behaviour when using products. After the filming is completed, the researcher will conduct about 15 minutes of interviews with the users. The main problems have been observed and the cause of the problems will be explored.

4 User Journey Map

The user journey map helps researchers to understand the needs and emotions of the target users through the entire interaction of the products, so as to achieve a better product and service. It can integrate the fragmentary observation and determine the P and O points for improvement. Different user journey maps are drawn for each typical user role or each type of user group, and the typical users' experience will be integrated to form a final user journey map. Compared to the user experience stage, the user behaviour is more micro-level, which is the flow of steps of specific user experience. As Fig.3 has shown, P and O points indicators to help identify opportunities for improvement. It is a design tool for combing user scenarios and experience problems. A requirement is presented horizontally according to user behaviour, and each behaviour node is rendered vertically. This process can disassemble the fuzzy requirements into user behaviours and user emotions, usage scenarios, etc.

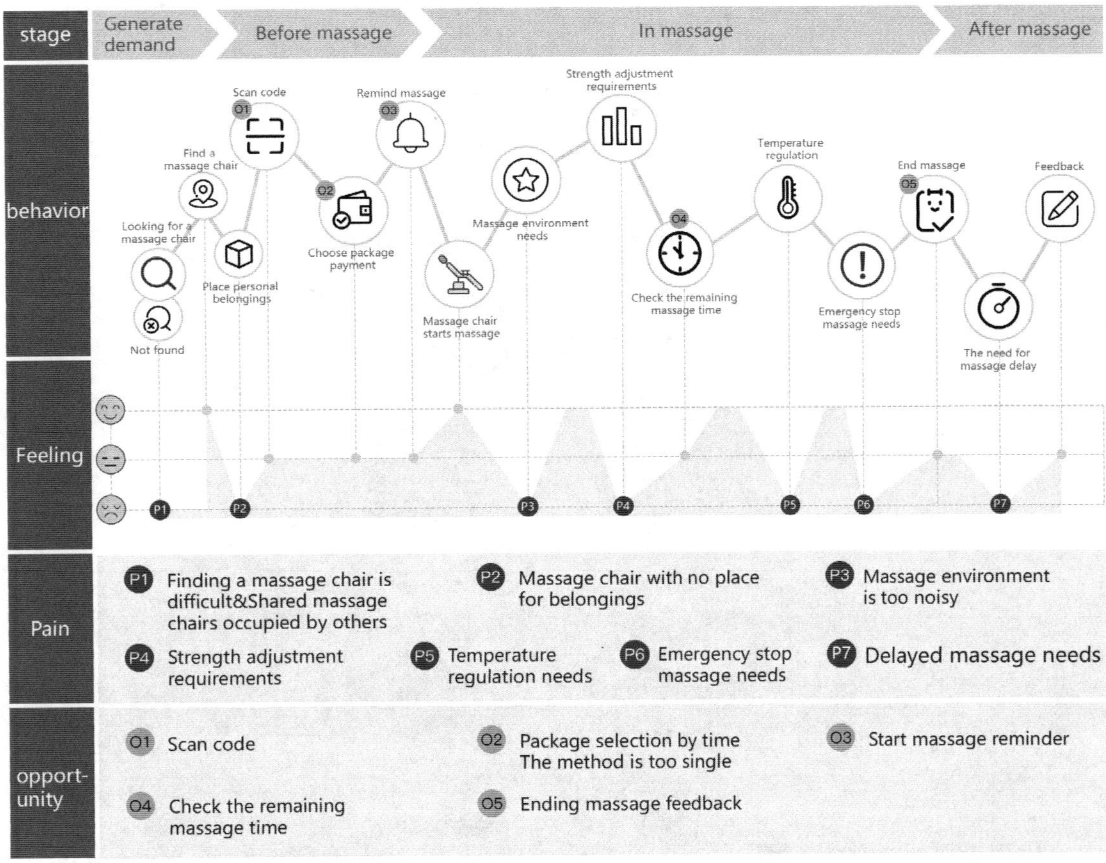

Figure 3. User journey map of shared massage chair.

5 Problems and Improve design ideas

Throughout the survey process of the shared massage chair, the output of each research process, the discovery of O and P and the transformation of the design of the research results have played a key role in the convergence. Tab.1 has shown improvement advice based on O and P points. Fig 4 has shown the improved design concepts.

Tab 1. Improvement points.

point	Question of investigation	reason	Improvement direction
P1	Difficult to find a massage chair	not evenly distributed, no navigation to locate through current positioning system	Add increase navigation function by GPS positioning function and assist App
P2	No place to lay belongings	No design for this function	Add storage space, ensure the safety of property, and reminders after the service
P3	Environment is too noisy	Mainly distributed in crowed places	Create an "immersive" relaxed massage atmosphere
P4	Massage intensity adjustment requirements	No massage adjustment during massage	Add the strength adjustment function mode, including “strong”, “medium” and “soft” grades, and choose massage techniques, including kneading, hammering, massage, and foot vibration function.
P5	Temperature adjustment needs	Feel cold during massage	Increase far-infrared heating function
P6	Emergency stop massage needs	Massage without emergency stop button	Add emergency stop massage button next to hands to meet the need for quick pause
P7	Delayed massage needs	Unable to continue massage when time is up	Simplify re-payment process and extend massage time at any time
O1	Scan code	After scanning the massage chair, the massage chair is started immediately without prompting, causes	Remind users to scan code

		uncomfortable experience	
O2	Limited selection mode	Only 3 types of service mode	Provide more types of service mode
O3	No start massage reminder	Instant massage after successful payment	Tips and reminder before massage
O4	Check the continuing massage time	Display the continuing massage time by mobile phone App	Increase continuing remaining massage time function
O5	No preparation at the end of service	No feedback after massage chair ends massage	End the massage through music or atmosphere

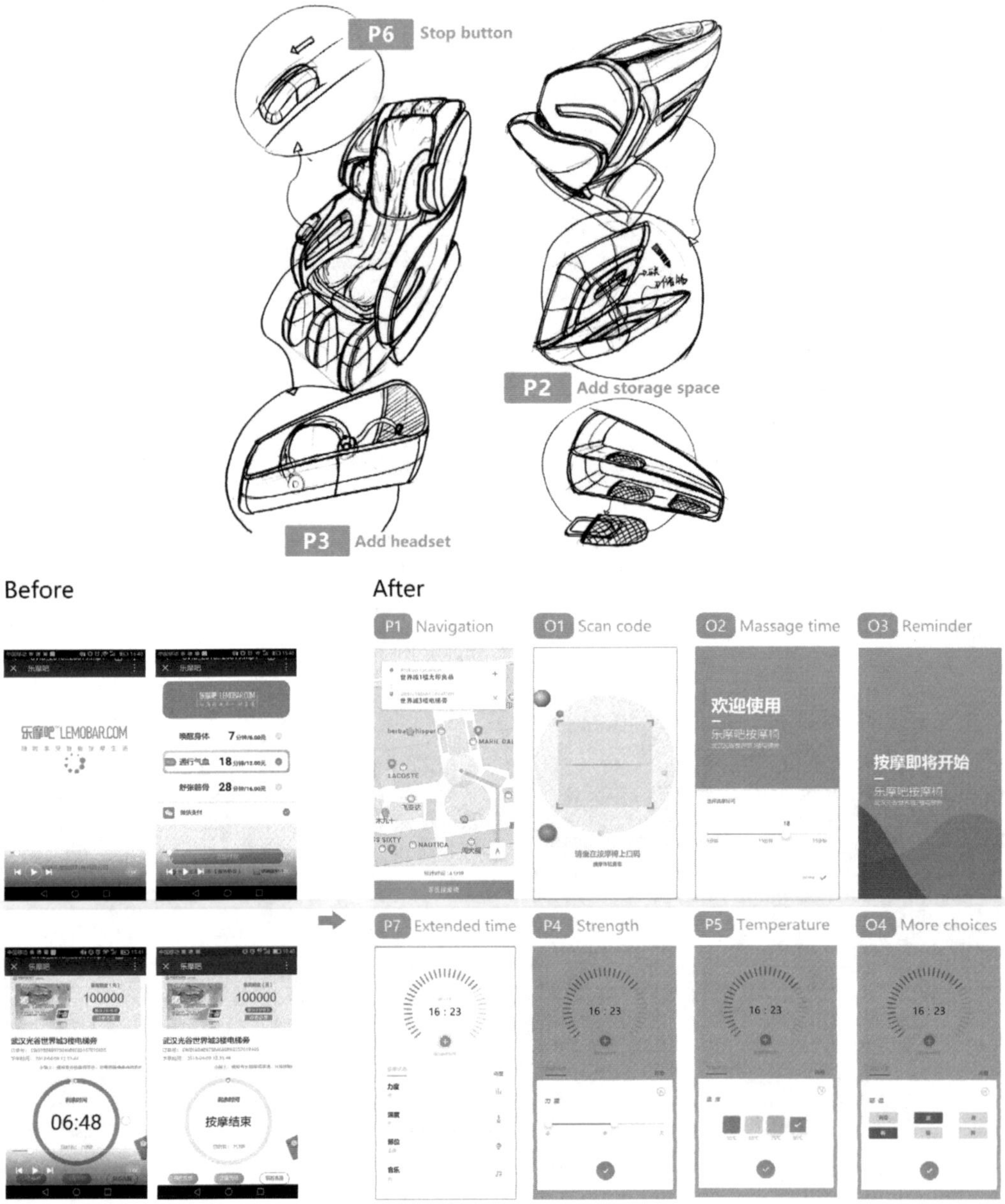

Figure 4. Improved design concepts.

6 Conclusion

The user journey map is a reflection of the emotions generated by the user's use of the product's behaviour. This paper aims to analyse the users' P and O points through user research and user journey maps, and further tap into potential opportunities for users in shared massage chairs and improve the current sharing of massage chairs. The current status of the product provides users with personalized service. The plan for the improvement of the later period will need to be further improved.

Acknowledgment

Supported by National Natural Science Foundation of China (Grant No: 51708236)
Supported by Fundamental Research Funds for the Central Universities (Grant No: 2016YXMS273)

References

1. Jiang Han. Where are the profitability points of the sharing economy?[J]. Money, 2017(8):10-11.
2. Lei Xuan. Shared Massage Chair: The new consumer style before the opening of the film [J]. China Quality Travel, 2017(8):78-80.
3. Xin Xiangyang. Interaction Design: From Physical Logic to Behavioral Logic [J]. Decoration, 2015(1):58-62.
4. Wang Yumei, Hu Weifeng, Tang Jin, et al. Travel postcard service design based on user experience journey[J]. Packaging Engineering, 2016(22):158-163.
5. Lei Xuan. Shared Massage Chair: The new consumer style before the opening of the film [J]. China Quality Travel, 2017(8):78-80.
6. Wu Yanjun. Internet-based Shared Massage System[J]. Internet of Things Technology, 2017, 7(11):74-76.

Analysis of Direction on Product Design in the Era of the Internet of Things

Baozhen Tian[1,a], Suihuai Yu[1],Jianjie Chu[1] and Wenhua Li[1]

[1]Shaanxi Engineering Laboratory for Industrial Design, Northwestern Polytechnical University, Xi'an,710072, China

Abstract. Internet of things (IoT) as a new revolution in science and technology will bring new vitality to the design. IoT has become the third revolution of the world industry information development after the world experienced the computer and the Internet. With the development of industry information, IoT as Internet service and applications expand through intellisense, identification technology, pervasive computing and ubiquitous network convergence applications. IoT era is the era of intelligent products. This article elaborates on the aspects of design content, design objects, design procedures and methods, means of obtaining design requirements, design tools, and changes in design direction. In the era of IoT, industry designers should focus on the interaction between humans and smart products and the interaction between smart products.

1 Introduction

The Internet of Things (IoT) has become a hot topic. Some applications in IoT are exploiting in healthcare, transportation, automotive industries, & electronic meters and so on[1]. "IoT is an emerging network superstructure that connects physical resources and people together with software"[2]. Like any information system, the IoT will rely on a group of hardware, software and architectures. The basic idea of IoT is to connect all things in the world to the internet [3]. Through the IoT, different types of goods, sensors, and facilities can communicate and form pervasive networks that convenient our daily lives [4]. What the IoT represents is an evolution of the application of these existing technologies according to several of facilities as well as the interconnection of networks of these devices across the Internet [5]. Although there is no general definition for the IoT, the core concept is that everyday objects can be equipped with identifying, sensing, networking and processing capabilities that will allow them to communicate with each other and with other devices and services over the internet to achieve some useful objective [6]. With the help of intelligent and reliable, IOT connected things wirelessly. Objects with this facility will be able to communicate without any human interference[7-8].The IoT consists of objects, sensor devices, communication infrastructure, computational and processing unit that may be placed on cloud, decision making and action invoking system[9].As a new scientific and technological revolution, it will bring new vitality to the design.

According to predictions of relevant experts, the future trend is the globalization of information resources, and global management will rely on various information resources [10-11]. Iot will control these information network resources. With the developments in the internet technologies, technologies in sensor networks and near field communication using RFID (radio frequency identification devices) tags have also been evolving [12]. Therefore, some developed countries (such as the United States, the European Union, Japan, etc.), enterprises and academic groups have invested human resources, material resources, and financial resources to conduct in-depth research on the IoT and have sought to make breakthroughs in this area.

Industrial design is bound to undergo profound changes as an important link closely connecting science and technology in the era of IoT. With the emergence of the IoT, it is a daunting task how to use the IoT technology better for design service, is suspends in front of the current industrial designer. It is not just combination the technology of IoT with the aesthetic knowledge simply, which need to test the ability and wisdom of a designer. Design as an initial impulse of humanity is the most fundamental human wisdom. This article puts forward some suggestions on issues that should be noted in the industrial design of IoT.

2 Product design in the era of the internet of things

"Intelligent type" is the characteristic of the IoT. How to design the intelligent products is worthy of further study to the industrial design researchers. The IoT is a paradigm where everyday objects can be configured with identifying, sensing, net-working and processing abilities that will allow them to interact with each other and with other facilities and services over the Internet to finish

* Corresponding author: [a] tbz246@ mail.nwpu.edu.cn,

some functions. The core concepts underlying the IoT are not new. For years, technologies such as RFID （radio frequency identification devices） and sensor networks have been applied in industrial and manufacturing contexts for tracking large ticket items such as cranes and livestock. The IoT can find its utilizations in almost every aspect of our daily life such as: prediction of natural disasters; industry applications; water scarcity monitoring; design of smart homes; medical applications; agriculture application; intelligent transport system design; design of smart cities; smart metering and monitoring and smart security[13]. The literature [5] showed that "Intelligent" products can understand people's intentions and make judgments, to reason, to execute instructions issued by humans and to make proper handling of items in a certain extent. Intelligence is based on artificial intelligence, and given by designers and engineers. It is an intelligent and internet-linked product that belongs to a higher level of smart products. In the environment of IoT, the term "intelligent item" is often used. In addition, the smart item can be a single product, such as a smart book, or it can be a system composed of a number of products, such as a smart public transportation system, smart security facilities, and so on. Future lives should be leaded by designing, which requires the simplest way to achieve the ultimate goal. The scope of research required to achieve IoT at the scale envisioned future customers' needs requires significant research along many directions.

2.1 Changes of design content

Traditional design content includes functions, structures, forms, surface treatments, materials, colors, etc. Tremendous development will be acquired based on the content in the future of the IoT. In functionality, they will be greatly improved with the development of IoT technology. The complexity of the function will complicate the design. In the structure, the rapid prototyping equipment interacts with the computer intelligently to realize the design of analog structures and to complete the production process of the structure's hand boards by itself. Integrating smart objects into physical infrastructure can improve flexibility, reliability and efficiency in infrastructure operation. These benefits can reduce cost and manpower requirements as well as enhance safety. As trillions of things (objects) are connected to the Internet, it is necessary to have an adequate architecture that permits easy connectivity, control, communications, and useful applications. In form, with the change of functionality and structure design, the form will also change accordingly. Smart products must be equipped with intelligent form. As a result, various "wisdom" solutions have been emerged. For example, smart transportation, smart logistics, and smart healthcare systems are all based on the IoT at the core of technology. In the future, the realization of these "wisdom" solutions can solve many problems facing humanity's sustainable development such as shortage of resources, energy waste, and inefficiencies [7].

2.2 Changes of design object

The serviceability of design is the basic attribute of industrial design, which serves people's survival life relying on the design of various products. Industrial designers take charge of enhancing the user experience of a product by developing its outside shape and its user interface. The Internet has tremendously evolved in the last few years connecting billions of things globally. These things have different sizes, capabilities, processing and computational power and support different kind of applications. Therefore, with the development of science and technology, changes will be occurred in design requirements and design objects. In the IoT era the object of product design has changed from the original design of a lifeless product to the design of items with individualized intelligence and the networks behind the items. The products in traditional design involved human, machines, and the environment. In the era of IoT, they will become human, machines (under the network), environments, which increase the complexity of design. Because in the environment of network, designers will face a variety of needs since design is to serve the needs. There will be born new demands and new products every second, and in turn, a variety of new products will lead to the emergence of new requirements. New demands and new products are intertwined with each other to promote the upgrading of products constantly.

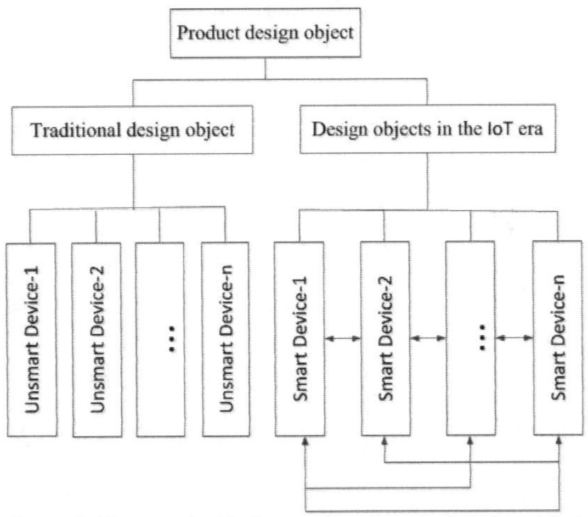

Figure 1. Compared with the traditional product design objects and IoT era design objects

Traditional product design objects must exchange information with the help of people. Where there is no information exchange between products. While in the IoT era, product design objects are devices with intelligence. With the advancement in technology, the devices processing power and storage capabilities significantly increased while their sizes reduced. These smart devices are usually equipped with different type of sensors and actuators. Large quantities of data were collected in the IoT environment. One future vision for the IoT is the Web of Things. The Web of Things proposes the use of web standards to fully integrate smart objects into the Worldwide Web. Using web technologies can make it easier for developers to build applications using smart objects and existing web protocols can more easily enable the interoperability and communication of different devices. Not only can these objects exchange information with people, but also can devices directly exchange information. As shown in Figure 1.

2.3 Changes in the means to obtain design requirements

Design requirements are the basis for creating excellent designs. Engineering and marketing models of product design and the product design process emphasize the importance of customer requirements. Ideally, companies that develop products ought to understand customer needs so that they can develop products that will sell. Assessments of customer needs are then used to specify functional requirements of the product. The functional requirements in turn are used to determine product design parameters. These three steps, from customer needs to functional requirements to design parameters are common for many established design methods including quality function deployment and axiomatic design. The product that has demand only has vitality. In the past, design requirements were obtained through observation, research, investigations, and interviews. In the IoT era, they can be obtained through the products themself. In the process of using the product (smart product), the user's demand for the product (smart product) will be reflected to the product (smart product). In the interaction between products (smart products), the demands between products (smart products) will also be generated. Through the IoT network, designers can obtain a variety of needs from users and smart products. In the IoT environment, all kinds of information can be fed back between smart products. Designers can obtain this information through certain means to analyze new potential needs and design more products that meet the needs of users. As shown in Figure 2.

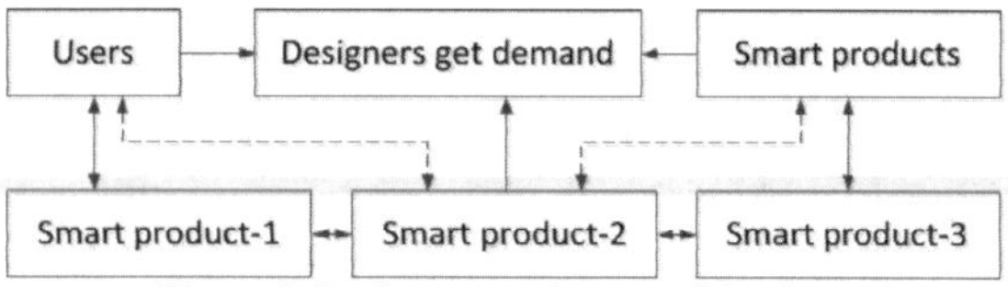

Figure 2. Designers get the way of the demand

2.4 Changes in design procedures and methods

Generally speaking, the design process mainly includes several stages, which are the previous market research and analysis, design and evaluation based on analysis, functional structure design, and production. The preliminary market survey analysis obtained problems during using product by face-to-face communication with users and potential users. While in the IoT era, it is only necessary to interact with existing products and enable real-time information exchange between products, which make design surveys more straightforward. Since this process more accurately reflects the user's applying at the time, the reliability of the information is high. In the IoT environment, a more objective assessment can be obtained and the assessment of design options and assessment methods can be carried out flexibly due to the scope of personnel involved in the assessment is very large and the smaller constraints on geographical and time.

2.5 Changes in the design tool be applied

Current design tools are limited to paper, pens, computers, etc. Future design tools will not be limited to these tools. It can also through various intelligent devices. These devices include personal computers, laptops, tablets, smart phones, PDAs and other hand-held embedded devices. The numbers of Internet connected devices are increasing at the rapid rate. These intelligent tools with intelligent information collection technology, sensor technology, sensing technology, thus can be used as industrial designers design tools. Under the IoT environment, human-machine interaction is no longer limited by time and place with the further development of technology, and it can realize remote-controlled computer aided industrial design, which can bring great convenience to designers. If our vision is correct, many IoT applications will be based on a deployed sensing, actuation, and communication platform (connecting a network of things). In these deployments, it is common for the devices to know their locations, have synchronized clocks, know their neighbor devices when cooperating, and have a coherent set of parameter settings such as consistent sleep/wake-up schedules, appropriate power levels for communication, and pair wise security keys.

2.6 Change of design direction

Since the IoT has not yet been realized, it might seem precocious to forecast the future directions of the IoT. However, future visions of the IoT will affect its current development and must therefore be considered. With the continuous development of IoT technology, industrial design direction will also undergo tremendous changes. Design on human-computer interaction will be the main design direction in the future. Given that IoT devices are likely to be connected to many objects and even to people themselves, examining the potential societal and personal impacts of the IoT is absolutely essential. Industrial design will play a more important role in the application of new technologies. In an IoT world, there exists a vast amount of raw data being continuously collected. It will be necessary to develop techniques that convert this raw data into usable knowledge. For example, in the medical area, raw streams of sensor values must be converted into semantically meaningful activities performed by or about a person such as eating, poor respiration, or exhibiting signs of depression. How to be safe and effective operation and avoiding misoperation, or even if the misoperation happened, but will not cause any damage, which need to be carefully studied for designers. Intelligent human-computer interaction will become an important design direction in the future.

3 Challenge for product designers

How to satisfy the users' requirements to the greatest extent will be a great challenge for product designers in the future of the IoT. With the development of IoT technology, various people will have a variety of requirements. Some of these requirements are meaningful to designers and users, some are meaningless, how to filter, and how to translate these requirements into products need the wisdom of designers. Industrial designers must have such ability and take on this responsibility.

The products and features of the IoT are mainly reflected in the following: 1) the frequency of information interaction is greatly increased. The previous information exchange needs to be carried out by people. In the IoT environment, products and products can be directly carried out, greatly reducing the burden on people, and to a certain extent, the transition from liberating physical strength to emancipating the mind. 2) The interaction between products and people is no longer limited by the spatial distance. 3) The product has certain wisdom. With a variety of advanced technologies, users can effectively use and manage products. At the same time, the ubiquity and interactions involved in IoT will provide many conveniences and useful services for individuals, but also create many opportunities to violate privacy. To solve the privacy problem created by IoT applications of the future, the privacy policies for each (system) domain must be specified. Once specified, either the individual IoT application or the IoT infrastructure (e.g., the utility capability) must enforce privacy. Consequently, the IoT paradigm must be able to express users' requests for data access and the policies, such that the requests can be evaluated against the policies in order to decide if they should be granted or denied. A new language is required to express privacy policies because the requirements not easily expressed in current privacy languages. It is needed to represent different types of data owners and request subjects in the system as well as external users and their rights when domains interact.

4. Conclusions

The IoT era will be the age of information explosion; the interaction of information will be frequent between products, and between people and products. By bringing existing technologies together in a novel way, the IoT has the potential to reshape our world. The IoT embeds intelligence in the sensor devices to autonomously communicate, exchange information and take intelligent decisions. Simply, IoT transitions human-human communication to human-human, human-device and device-device communication. The IoT holds the promise of improving people's lives through both automation and augmentation. The capabilities offered by the IoT can save people and organizations time and money as well as help improve decision making and outcomes in a wide range of application areas. In this context, "design" will be more reflected in "integrity" and "integration" aspects. Industrial designers need to grasp the frontiers of design, focus on exploring ways of innovation in the "goods, processes, and services", pay more attention and research on the IoT, and apply the IoT technology, using various design methods, and thus better service to the user, better to provide higher quality design services for this era. This article put forward some suggestions on issues in the era of IoT that industrial designers should pay attention. It elaborates on the aspects of design content, design objects, design procedures and methods, means of obtaining design requirements, design tools, and changes in design direction. Subsequent research will focus on the interaction between humans and smart products in the IoT environment and the interaction between smart products.

Acknowledgment

This work was supported by National Key Technology R&D Program, China (Grant No. 2015BAH21F01) and the 111 Project, (Grant No.B13044).

References

1. S. Nath, S. Som, Indian J. Sci. Technol., **10** (3), 1–5 (2017)
2. T. Kramp, R. van Kranenburg, S. Lange, *Introduction to the internet of things* (2013)
3. C. W. Tsai, C. F. Lai, M. C. Chiang, L. T. Yang, IEEE Commun. Surv. Tutorials, **16** (1), 77–97 (2014).
4. S.Balasubramaniam, J. Kangasharju, Computer (Long. Beach. Calif)., **46**(2), 62–68 (2013)
5. T. Jenkins, I. Bogost, the *32nd* annual ACM conference on Human factors in computing systems - CHI EA'14, 731–740 (2014)
6. A. Whitmore, A. Agarwal, and L. Da Xu, Inf. Syst. Front., **17** (2), 261–274 (2015)
7. F. Khodadadi, A. V. Dastjerdi, R. Buyya, *Internet of Things: Principles and Paradigms*, 3–27 (2016)
8. S. Li, L. Da Xu, S. Zhao, Inf. Syst. Front., **17** (2) 243–259 (2015)
9. Y. Yu, J. Wang, G. Zhou, ICDLE 2010 - 2010 *4th* International Conference on Distance Learning and Education, Proceedings, 74–77 (2010)
10. J. A. Stankovic, IEEE Internet Things J., **1** (1), 3–9 (2014)
11. A. Al-Fuqaha, M. Guizani, M. Mohammadi, M. Aledhari, M. Ayyash, IEEE Commun. Surv. Tutorials, **17** (4) 2347–2376 (2015)
12. Y.-K. Chen, *17th* Asia and South Pacific Design Automation Conference,383–388 (2012)
13. R. Khan, S. U. Khan, R. Zaheer, S. Khan, *10th* International Conference on Frontiers of Information Technology, FIT 2012, 257–260 (2012)

Design optimization method of line-of-sight with JACK for bulldozer operator

GUO Mei-ni[1]

Department of the Ideological and Political Theory, Xi'an Physical Education University , Xi'an Shaanxi, 710068, China

Abstract. The objective of this article is to investigate the line-of-sight (LOS) and visual areas in order to provide a lower risk of accident and a best available view for the operator of industry machine. This paper presented a method of simulating an bulldozer operation in a virtual environment for the sake of analyzing LOS of the operator during conditions of load and unload respectively. Coverage zone tool in the JACK software was utilized to calculate the percentage of visible zones from the virtual operator's position. At the same time, the modification of design with additional cameras was proposed based on the results of LOS analysis, which significantly improved compared with original design. The results of this study proved that the modifications (with visual monitoring system) could improve visibility of bulldozer operators to some extent according to the optimization method.

1 Introduction

Work conditions of blue-collar are typically adverse, strenuous, and precarious conditions (e.g., monotonous, highly repetitive, long-duration sitting) [1]. At present, several studies have examined how to make operators more comfortable that mainly focused on the aspect of structural design [2] and accessories [3]. Nowadays, line-of-sight (LOS) issues for industry equipment is a growing focus of research. Patrick et al. [4] presented a method for assessment of degradation of task visibility from operator cabins of field machines. Alison Godwin et al. [5] studied on the implications of articulating machinery on operator line of sight and efficacy of additional camera locations. Three assessment test were utilized to identify forklift truck design factors for influencing visibility of operators [6]. As mentioned above, several studies have been done to improve the structure and shape of bulldozer. Hence, this paper investigated the potential utility of using computer simulation to evaluate image of line of sight and percentage of visible area during the operation of industry equipment. And some modifications to the visual area have been done to improve the LOS of operator in order to ensure workers' safety.

2 Methods

2.1 Design procedures

JACK software was offered by Siemens to analyze workplace environments with virtual people that can scale to match different population characteristics. It could be used to test designs and operations for a wide variety of human factors, including injury risk, timing, user comfort, reachability, lines-of-sight, energy expenditure, fatigue limits and other important parameters [11]. The coverage zone feature in JACK associated with the computer simulation program were utilized in this study enabled us to use obscuration zones.

Virtual computer analysis was integrated into the design process of industrial machines, and a design optimization method of LOS based on JACK was proposed to evaluate the potential use of a camera intervention on bulldozer. A flow chart describing the optimization procedure for LOS analyzing of operating movement was proposed (see Figure 1).

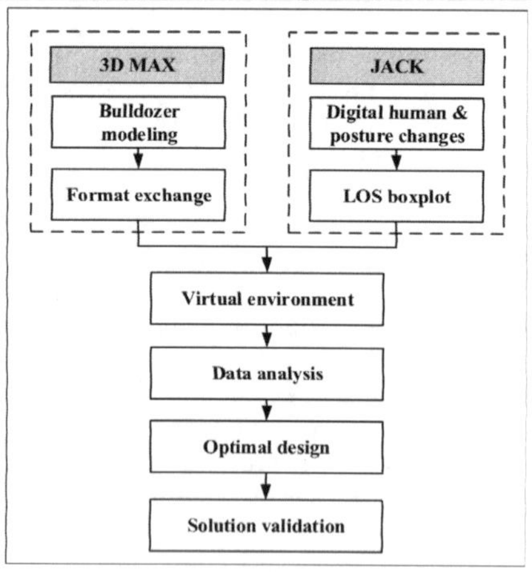

Figure 1. Flow chart of the study.

* Corresponding author: [1]957386089@qq.com

2.2 Vehicle design

Developing animations of machines using the key frame method in Jack is time consuming [10]. JACK software is a ergonomic tool to assess and compute lines-of-sight impairments of operator, while there is a disadvantage to build 3D modelling. Thus, the accurate 3D files of bulldozer machine, which modelling by 3D MAX software, were imported into a computer simulation environment (JACK) as vrml format.

From the observation of the tasks carried out by bulldozer operators, there were a battery of operations including, in turn, digging, loading, driving, dumping. Observing working condition should be performed effectively in a short time. Two conditions, that is, load and unload should be taken into account. Therefore, the digital model of bulldozer is presented in Figure 2, illustrating the sequence of events and various operations in which investigation were made.

(a) Unload

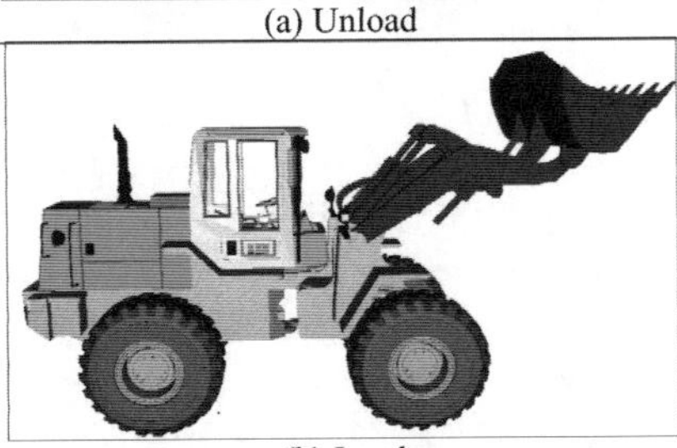

(b) Load

Figure 2. Digital model of bulldozer.

2.3 Human models

JACK software including nine digital human models[12]. Every default human figure has five percentile population, along with twenty-six body parameters to be chosen and adjusted depending on subjects' anthropometry. A 95th percentile male virtual human was chosen from CHINESE database, as a bulldozer operator, to simulate interactive operation tasks in which 3D models of bulldozer.

2.4 LOS boxplot

The LOS boxplot provides visual and non-visible images on coverage plane respectively, in which red indicating non-visible zones and green indicating visible zones. The program calculated the percentage of area that is visible/non-visible to the operator. LOS boxplot has been used previously in studies evaluating of LOS impairments in industrial machines [13].

The present study used the method already conceived by Jeffkins et al. [9]. Coverage planes representing visual attention locators for any vehicle under any operating scenario could be evaluated with this method. A rectangular box areas with 20m width, 10m length and 4.5m height was generated by utilizing coverage tool, and it was divided into 11 separate panels in which a 0.1m nodal space was set up.

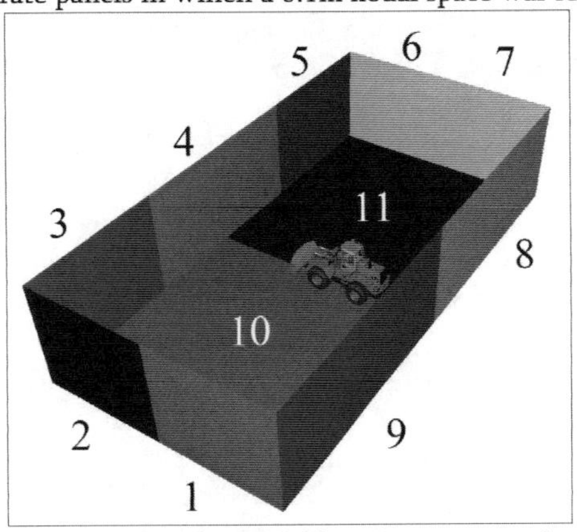

Figure 3. A LOS boxplot divided into 11 separate panels.

3 Results and design optimization

3.1 Data analysis

The data collection for the computer simulation method was performed by using the coverage zone tool in the JACK program to determine LOS from the virtual operator's position. Figure 4 displayed the image about which LOS of operator are to be made in condition load and unload operating, as it showed the green and red areas were behalf of visible and non-visible zones respectively.

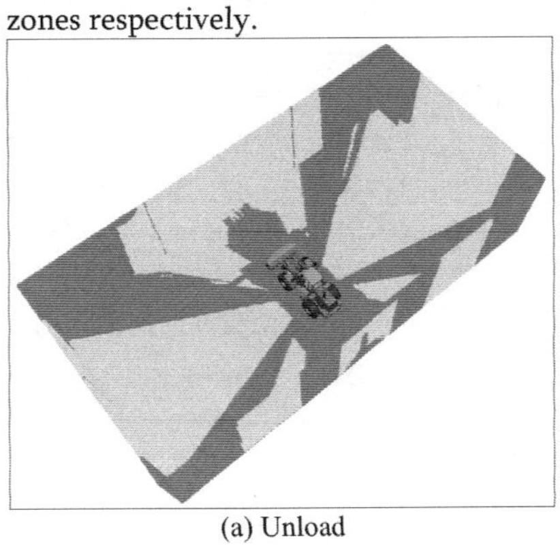

(a) Unload

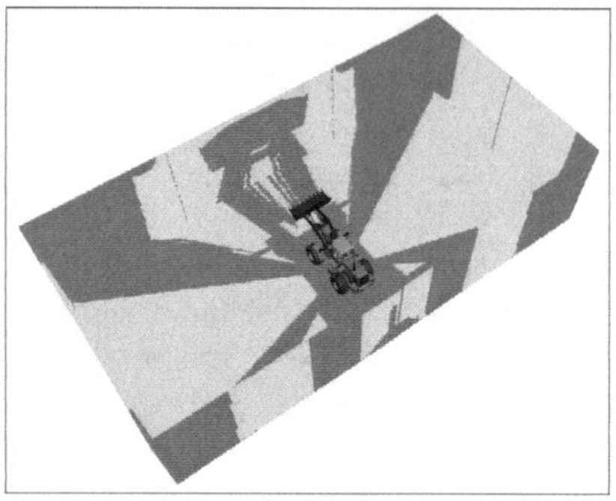

(b) Load

Figure 4. Restricted LOS for original design.

3.2 Design optimization

As shown above, the front and back view of operator was primarily obscured by rear-view mirror and structures of cabin under unload condition, and bucket principally restricted the front of LOS severely under load condition. Therefore, after above testing, the bulldozer design was modified based on the results of line-of-sight analysis. Compared structure of original and modified bulldozer, given as below, were illustrated in Figure 5. First of all, the dimensions of rear-view mirrors were narrowed. Secondly, the parts of support structure of original bulldozer were redesigned as well. Thirdly, the placement of four searchlights were relocated. Finally, the frame of windows were adjusted slightly. All of which were non-changing with original structure of the bulldozer cab.

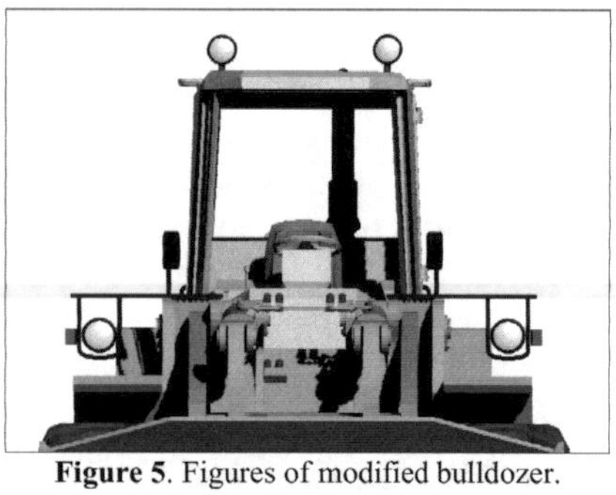

Figure 5. Figures of modified bulldozer.

The LOS boxplot and data presented in Figure 4 demonstrated that the operator had virtually no visual information available from the front of view when loading due to bucket and rack mainly. On the other hand, the severely restricted areas of back-side resulting from power system and balance weight that were loaded on the rear of vehicle. Hence, other than improving the original bulldozer as mentioned above (fig. 5), visual monitoring system was also installed on the front and rear side of modified vehicle in order to ameliorate the line-of-sight as fig. 6 depicted. The monitoring system was able to provide more visual information to operator towards front and rear side of vehicle. Consequently, reductions in pilot errors and improvements of decision-making with low accident rate will be made by operator [14].

(a) Camera 1

(b) Camera 2

Figure 6. Figures of original and modified bulldozer.

The 3-D file of modified industry machine was imported into JACK software and the LOS boxplot analysis of unload and load condition were repeated one more time to give best assessment.

Data collection was performed for original and modified design with two camera perspectives by using the coverage zone tool in JACK to analyze LOS area of operator (Table 1).

Comparison of LOS boxplot area for the original and modified design were presented in Table 2 and Figure 7. In the present study it was proved that, in general, the modified design of bulldozer with camera system provided more than 80% visual area of LOS in these key zones under both operating conditions (unload and load) with the exception of ground-level LOS (zones 10 and 11).

Table 1. Percentage of LOS boxplot area visible for original and modified design with cameras.

	Zones (%)	Area (m^2)

	1	2	3	4	5	6	7	8	9	10	11	
Unload- modified	75.43	97.91	30.71	98.28	33.96	99.31	85.15	47.03	53.38	59.98	59.11	297.62
Load- modified	74.87	98.01	29.13	53.48	36.98	99.23	77.30	47.60	52.73	58.62	59.98	279.47
Camera 1	1.14	22.87	87.34	98.29	88.32	22.54	1.15	0.00	0.00	17.01	19.03	129.59
Camera 2	96.14	3.33	0.00	0.00	0.00	0.88	92.38	98.38	98.95	8.11	8.06	148.33

Table 2. A comparison for percentage of LOS boxplot area visible with original and modified design.

	Zones (%)											Area (m^2)	Ratio (%)
	1	2	3	4	5	6	7	8	9	10	11		
Unload-modified	96.14	97.91	30.71	98.28	33.96	99.31	92.38	98.38	98.95	59.98	59.11	347.52	73.94
Unload-original	70.61	61.38	25.57	98.28	29.08	66.40	65.87	43.16	40.50	54.14	55.34	256.72	54.62
Load-modified	96.14	98.01	87.34	98.29	88.32	99.23	92.38	98.38	98.95	58.62	59.98	377.01	80.21
Load-original	72.86	60.97	24.75	50.25	19.05	54.50	75.26	39.46	43.50	52.95	54.22	233.73	49.73

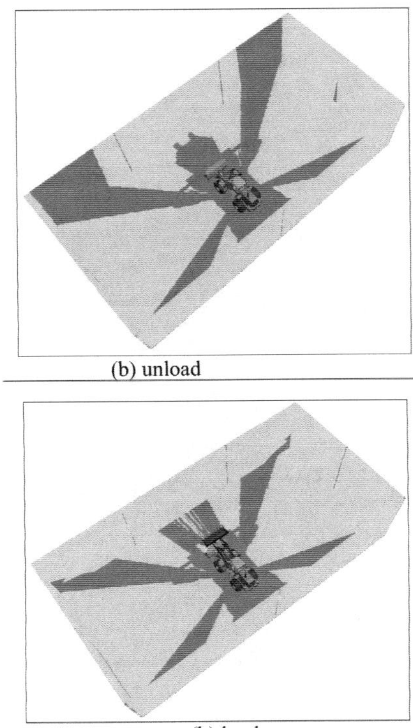

(b) unload

(b) load

Figure 7. LOS boxplot area for modified design.

4 Conclusions

This paper has presented a method of developing an integrated system including modeling software (3D MAX software) and LOS boxplot assessment (JACK software) that enabled researchers to objectively investigate the visual monitoring system locations on an industry machine that could best improve LOS of operators. As described, the coverage plane tool could preferably provided both a visual and a quantitative method of LOS evaluation. With reference to the results of the percentage of visible area at various zones, a targeted optimization was performed for improving the visible areas of a bulldozer. The methods discussed in this paper presented the recommendations for the improvement of ergonomic aspects of product design of the industry machines, so as to offering the best LOS for potential vehicle operator.

Acknowledgment

Fund Project: Shaanxi Culture Creative Industry Innovation policy Research（2018 Shaanxi Science and Technology Plan Soft Science Research Project）

References

1. O. HÃOmmig. Front. Public Heal. **2**, (2014)
2. X. Yu, L. Lijuan. Constr. Mach. Equip. **47**, 23-26,7 (2016)
3. J. Youchang. Des. &Manu. **4**, 248–52 (2015).
4. P.J. Barron, P.M.O. Owende, K.P. McDonnell, S.M. Ward. Int. J. Ind. Ergon. **35**, 665–73 (2005)
5. N. Schwabe, A. Godwin. Safety **3**, 17 (2017)
6. C.B.Choi, P. Park, Y.H. Kim, M. Susan Hallbec, M.C. Jung. Appl. Ergon. **40**, 280–5 (2009)
7. L. Sheming, W. Xiaoping, C. Dengkai, W. Shuxia. Comput. Mod. **8**, 106–10 (2013)
8. T. Zhengwen, X. Hongjun, S. Rune. Aeronaut. Comput. **40**, 79–81,106 (2010)
9. A. Jeffkins, T. Eger, A. Salmoni, R. Whissell. Ergon. Des. **12**, 12–7 (2004)
10. S.C. Puthenveetil, C.P. Daphalapurkar, et al. Virtual Real. **19**, 119–28 (2015)
11. Siemens PLM Software. https://www.plm.automation.siemens.com/en/products (2018)
12. Y. Qingsong, L. Qianfang, Z. Qianxiang, et al. Sp. Med. & Med. Eng. **29**, 440–5 (2016)
13. A. Godwin, T. Eger. Int. J. Ind. Ergon. **39**, 146–51 (2009)
14. Y. Ke, G. Mingyu, C. Jifeng. J. Hangzhou Dianzi Univ. **27**, 1–4 (2007)

https://doi.org/10.1051/matecconf/201817601004

Design and evaluation of silage equipment control panel based on the theory of emotional design and Kansei Engineering

Jie Yan, Bing Lv[a], Jianqiang Wang, Derong Duan, Mengjia Chen and Zequn Li

University of Jinan, School of Mechanical Engineering, 250022 Jinan Shandong, China

Abstract. In order to make the silage equipment control panel meet user needs better and translate user requirements into product design elements, this paper puts forward the design model of silage equipment control panel based on the theory of emotional design and Kansei Engineering. Firstly, qualitative and quantitative analyses of silage equipment control panel were conducted according to the results of the user survey. Then, the prior design elements and the "Feature-Vocabulary" correspondence were obtained, which were applied to the design of silage equipment control panel. Finally, the design plan was evaluated using semantic differential method. As a result, it is initially verified that the design model has certain feasibility for translating user requirements into product design elements.

1 Introduction

Today, the "people-oriented" design concept is gradually accepted by people and is successfully verified on more and more product designs. With the rapid development of science and technology and the continuous improvement of the quality of life, the factors that determine whether a product can fully reflect its value are gradually changing from functions to satisfying user's aesthetic appeal and a higher level of emotional appeal. Therefore, it requires designers to fully study user needs in the early stage of product design and design process in order to meet user's appeal. Starting from the theory of emotional design and Kansei Engineering can make us better understand user needs and provide guidance for emotional design. The theory of emotional design emphasizes the design research based on user's spiritual needs. The layers of instinct, behavior, and reflection play different roles in the use of products. Moreover, each layer was achieved using different methods [1], which provides designers with a vast creative space [2]. Scholars tried to convert user's psychological and emotional needs into specific design elements starting from the perspective of users [3-8]. In terms of human-machine interaction of silage equipment, the control panel, as an important part of the operated device, integrates the main control components of the silage equipment. This paper combines the theory of emotional design and Kansei Engineering to conduct the user emotional survey of silage equipment control panel. Moreover, the analysis results were applied to the design plan. Finally, the plan was evaluated to prove the feasibility of the research method.

2 Research Methods

Qualitative and quantitative research methods are basic and important methods in the field of social science and scientific research [9]. Qualitative and quantitative research methods were used comprehensively to put forward the design model of silage equipment control panel (as shown in Figure 1). Firstly, qualitative and quantitative analyses of silage equipment control panel were conducted according to the results of the user survey. Then, the existing problems of design elements, the prior design elements and the "Feature-Vocabulary" correspondence were summarized, which were applied to the design of silage equipment control panel. Finally, the design plan was evaluated using semantic differential method.

The first author: Jie Yan E-mail: jiejie_1488@qq.com *Corresponding author: [a]Bing Lv E-mail: me_lvb@ujn.edu.cn

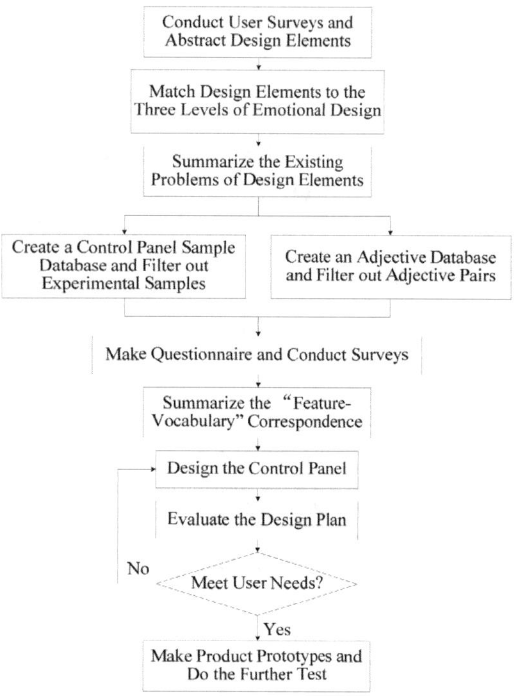

Figure1. Design Model of Silage Equipment Control Panel

3 Qualitative Research of Control Panel

Before the quantitative research, the qualitative research is necessary. The purpose is usually to make hypotheses or determine the stimuli of the study. Its depth and breadth of problem description are beyond quantitative research. The results of user surveys were combined with three-layer of emotional design to extract and classify the design elements of the control panel. Then the existing problems of the design elements were summarized.

3.1 Control Panel Design Elements Extraction and Classification

The emotional design proposed by Norman believes that when users use the product, they will have three layers of sensibility which are instinct layer, behavior layer, and reflection layer. They have different characteristics, factors and research methods. The design of the instinct layer is related to human's first reaction. The physiological characteristics such as vision, feeling, and sound play the main roll. The influencing factors include the shape, color, touch and weight of the product. The design of the behavior layer is related to human's feelings when using the product. The influencing factors include function, ease of use, comprehensibility and feelings. Professor Norman believes that it is difficult for users to express their needs clearly, and the way to find these needs is observation. Designers are required to discover user needs and got solutions when the product is used naturally. The design of the reflection layer is related to the culture, information and meanings of the product, and emotion and self-image aroused by products. The influencing factors include product semantics, self-image, memories and so on. The real value of products lies not only in the realization of functions, but also in satisfying the emotional needs of users, establishing self-image, highlighting personal taste and social status.

First of all, the observation method was used to pay attention to the words, actions, eyes, expressions and postures of target users (farmers, professional silage workers and manufacturers), who were using different silage equipment control panels (different in forms, colors, location layouts, etc.) naturally. Then users' feelings and evaluations were asked and noted. After that, the design elements of each part of the control panel were extracted according to the principles from the whole to the part. Based on the definitions of the three-layer of the emotional design, the correspondence (as shown in Table 1) of the design elements of each part and the three-layer of emotional design was obtained for follow-up study.

3.2 Analyses of the Design Elements Problems

Data shows that silage equipment control panel lacks in human-machine interaction design. Users do not be satisfied enough with products which do not consider users physiological and psychological factors fully [10]. There are some requirements of design elements such as the shape and installation position of the control panel, the shape and layout of the hand manipulators, and the location and promptness of the icons (as shown in Table 2). The lack of these element designs leads to the decrease of users understanding and operating efficiency of products, resulting in misoperation, inconvenience and even hidden dangers to health and safety.

4 Quantitative Research of Control Panel

The quantitative study was conducted based on the above analyses of the control panel design elements and existing problems.

Image Scale Method is a quantitative research method commonly used, which can be used to measure and analyse people's cognitive psychology of products. Image Scale Method is based on semantic differential method. It requires the researcher to collect vocabularies that can describe style characteristics of the research object to make a semantic analysis scale. This scale contains pairs of adjectives that are antisense to each other as two poles. Each pair of adjectives divided into seven grades on average to form a seven-grade scale. The closer the grade to a vocabulary is, the closer it is to the description of the vocabulary. Users were required to choose a certain grade to express their own perceptions and feelings. Combining semantic differential method and questionnaire method in quantitative research, the user survey on silage equipment control panel was conducted. The prior design elements and the "Feature-Vocabulary" correspondence were obtained.

Table 1. Correspondence Between Control Panel's Design Elements and the Three-Layer of Emotional Design

Design Elements	Instinct Layer			Behavior Layer			Reflection Layer		
	Panel	Manipulator	Icon	Panel	Manipulator	Icon	Panel	Manipulator	Icon
Form	●	●	●	●	●	●	●	●	●
Color	●	●	●	●	●	●	●	●	●
Material	●	●	●				●	●	●
Function				●	●	●			
Location				●	●	●			

4.1 Early Preparation

4.1.1 Filtering out Experimental Samples

After collecting a large of samples of silage equipment control panel with high user satisfaction, the control panel database was established (as shown in Figure 2).material and layout was removed. Then the six experimental samples was filtered out for subsequent questionnaire surveys (as shown in Figure 3).

Table 2. Problems Analyses of Control Panel Design Elements

Contents	**Problems**
Control Panel	Single form Missing detail design Heavy use of metal
Functional Area Layout	Not obvious to distinct Confused
Manipulator Layout	Do not correspond with operations.
Icons	Not easy to observe. Difficult to identify and understand.

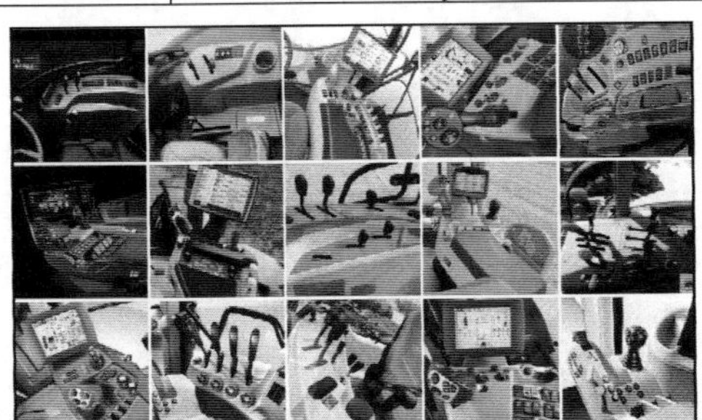

Figure2. Sample Database of the Control Panel (Partial)

4.1.2 Filtering out Vocabularies and Making Scale

After collating survey data and consulting documents, websites and magazines, the adjective database of the control panel containing descriptive vocabularies related to the control panel was created. The 15 pairs of bipolar adjectives recognized in the international consumer behavior field can define a product feature widely (as shown in Table 3).Then the neutral words and synonyms are removed through expert voting and discussion. Finally, 10 pairs of vocabulary words describing product feature of the control panel were filtered out. In addition, the "like-dislike" word pair was added for the investigation of the reflective layer to quantify the degree of resonance between the product image and user's emotion. The 11 groups of adjectives (as shown in Table 4) constituted a 7-grade scale for subsequent questionnaire survey.

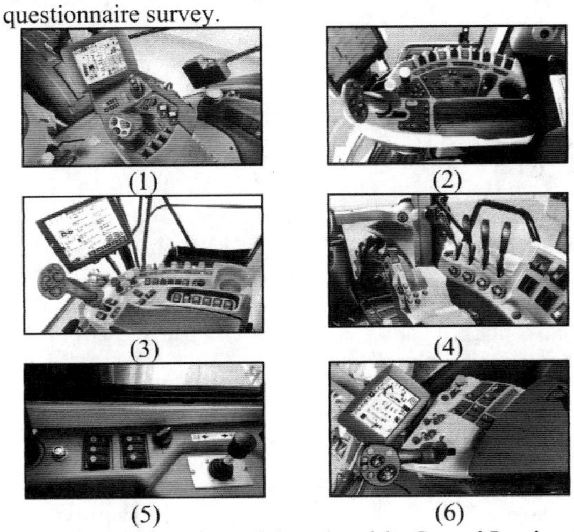

Figure3. Experimental Samples of the Control Panel

Table3. Bipolar Adjectives

1	2	3	4
Clever Rough	Peaceful Fierce	Relaxed Intense	Delicate Tough
5	6	7	8
Implied Exaggerate	Funny Serious	Popular Outdated	Mainstream Alternative
9	10	11	12
Warm Cold	Mature Childish	Common Bizarre	Progressive Conservativ e
13	14	15	
Concise Complicated	Gorgeous Pure	Realistic Fantasy	

4.2 Questionnaire Production and User Survey

First of all, the questionnaire was set up a user feature question to determine whether the user who are filling in the questionnaire understands or has used the control panel.

Then the questionnaire was set up a question of the design elements priority. The user was required to select four most important factors when using or purchasing products in order to obtain the prior design elements of the control panel.

Finally, the questionnaire was set up a question of 7-grade scales of control panel samples. One scale was next to one sample (as shown in Figure 4).

Table4. Experimental Adjectives

Form		**Color**	
1	2	3	4
Conservative Progressive	Stiff Gentle	Cold Warm	Intense Relaxed
Material		**Function**	
5	6	7	8
Rough Delicate	Single Diverse	Simple Abundant	Incompre-hensible Understand-able
Location		**Preference**	
9	10	11	
Complicated Concise	Confused Clear	Dislike Like	

Questionnaires were distributed to the target users, and users are provided with a brief explanation such as the questionnaire's structure and the rule to fill.

As a result, 41 questionnaires was collected. After removing invalid questionnaires (the user is unfamiliar with silage equipment control panel, 40 valid questionnaires was obtained.

4.3 Statistics and Analyses of Survey Results

Each grade in the 7-grade scale was counted from one to seven points. Then the average scores was calculated. As a result, the user's cognitive adjectives of each sample was obtained. Such as "conservative-progressive", if the average score is less than 4 points, it is conservative. If the average score is 4 points, it is neutral. If the average score is more than 4 points, it is progressive.

Statistically, adjectives of sample 1 are "progressive and stiff", "cold and relaxed", "delicate and diverse", "abundant and understandable" and "complicated and clear". Adjectives of Sample 2 are "progressive and gentle", "warm and intense", "delicate and diverse", "abundant and understandable" and "concise and confused". Adjectives of Sample 3 are "progressive and gentle", "warm and relaxed", "delicate and diverse", "abundant and incomprehensible" and "complicated and confused". Adjectives of Sample 4 are "progressive and stiff", "warm and relaxed", "delicate and single", "abundant and understandable" and "concise and confused". Adjectives of Sample 5 are "conservative and stiff", "cold and relaxed", "delicate and single", "abundant and complicated" and "concise and clear". Adjectives of Sample 6 are "progressive and gentle", "warm and relaxed", "delicate and single", "abundant and complicated" and "concise and clear".

User's favorite sample is sample 1. The most important elements are the function of the control panel and the layout of the manipulators. These two elements were considered first in the design process.

4.4 Feature-Vocabulary Correspondence

According to the user's favorite sample and corresponding adjectives, the line diagram of the layout was extracted. In accordance with "point-line-surface-body" and "details - the whole" orders, the "Feature-Vocabulary" correspondence of other design elements was summarized (as shown in Table 5). The following work was based on this.

1. Are you familiar with silage equipment control panel?
very familiar/use it frequently☐ familiar/use it occasionally☐ unfamiliar/rarely use it☐
2. How old are you?
younger than 18 years old☐ 18-30 years old☐ 30-45 years old☐ over 45 years old☐
3. What are your top concerns when using or buying it? (Select 4 items)
Control panel's Form☐ Color☐ Material☐ Function☐ Layout☐
Manipulator's Form☐ Color☐ Material☐ Function☐ Layout☐
Icon's Form☐ Color☐ Material☐ Function☐ Layout☐
4. Please observe the following 6 products, and check the box according to your feelings. (√)

(1)

		1	2	3	4	5	6	7	
Form	conservative	☐	☐	☐	☐	☐	☐	☐	progressive
	stiff	☐	☐	☐	☐	☐	☐	☐	gentle
Color	cold	☐	☐	☐	☐	☐	☐	☐	warm
	intense	☐	☐	☐	☐	☐	☐	☐	relaxed
Material	rough	☐	☐	☐	☐	☐	☐	☐	delicate
	single	☐	☐	☐	☐	☐	☐	☐	diverse
Function	simple	☐	☐	☐	☐	☐	☐	☐	abundant
	incomprehensible	☐	☐	☐	☐	☐	☐	☐	understandable
Location	complicated	☐	☐	☐	☐	☐	☐	☐	concise
	confused	☐	☐	☐	☐	☐	☐	☐	clear
Preference	dislike	☐	☐	☐	☐	☐	☐	☐	like

Figure4. Questionnaire Sample (Partial)

Table5. "Feature-Vocabulary" Correspondence of User's Favorite Sample

Adjective		Feature		
		Control Panel	Manipulator	Icon
Form	Progressive	Small rounded corners; Straight lines; Large curved surfaces; Facets; Squares	Square; Round; Polygonal; Polyhedron; Conform	Pattern; Scale; Direction
	Stiff			
Color	Cold	Gray; White; Color embellishment	Black; Gray; Orange; Color distinguish	White
	Relaxed			
Material	Delicate	Plastic; Cloth; Rubber	Plastic; Rubber; Polishing; Matte	Screen printing
	Diverse			
Function	Abundant	Integration; Partitioning	Push; Pull; Press; Screw; Ergonomic	Correspondence; Tip
	Understandable			
Layout	Complicated	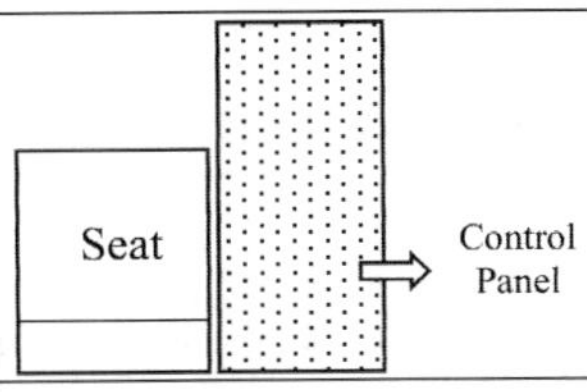	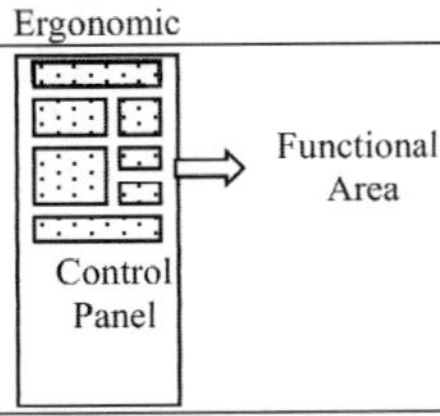	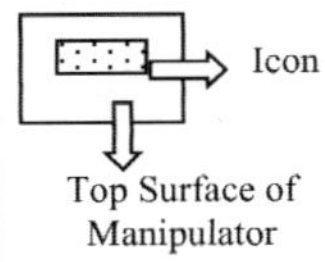
	Clear			

5 Design Plan and Evaluation

Based on the questions summarized in the qualitative research and the results of quantitative research, the following plan was put forward (as shown in Figure 7):

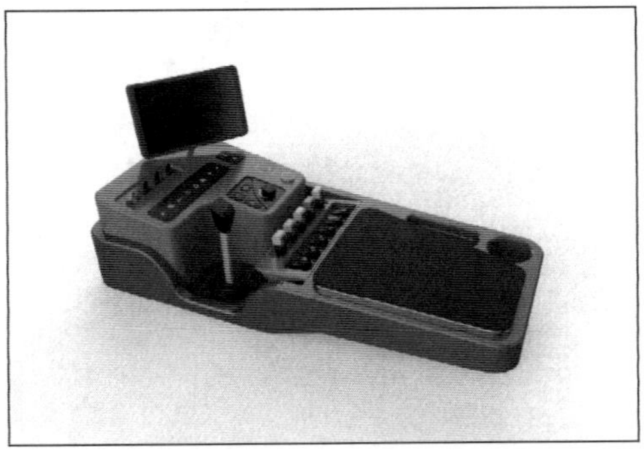

Figure7. Plan of Control Panel

The plan and the 7-grade scale were placed on the same page. The 40 target users were invited to judge the design plan and check each item. Statistically, the corresponding adjectives of the plan are "progressive and gentle", "cold and relaxed", "delicate and single", "abundant and understandable" and "concise and clear". The average score of the preference is 4.725. It showed that the plan meets emotional needs of users and has a high degree of preference.

6 Conclusion

In this paper, the design model of silage equipment control panel was put forward based on the theory of emotional design and Kansei Engineering. Firstly, the observation method was adopt to extract the design elements of silage equipment control panel, then the problems existing in design elements were analysed qualitatively. Secondly, user research was conducted using semantic differential method and questionnaire method, then the prior design elements and the "Feature-Vocabulary" correspondence were obtained, which were applied to the design of silage equipment control panel. Finally, the design plan was evaluated using semantic differential method. Due to space limitations, this paper only discussed methods, processes, results and conclusions of study. The complete statistical results were not listed in full. Moreover, the investigation of the reflection layer focused on the preference only. In the follow-up work, quantifying product semantics and user self-images will be further studied. Product prototype will be created to conduct user testing.

Acknowledgment

Fund Project: 2017 Shandong Province Agricultural Machinery Research and Development and Innovation Plan Funding Project (2017YF004-10)

References

1. D.A. Norman, *Emotional Design* (China CITIC Press, Beijing, 2015)
2. H.X. Zhu, Y.Y. Zhang, B.W. Xu, J. Mach. Des, 4, 122-124 (2016)
3. J. Huang, D.H Xiao, Packag. Eng, 4, 218-222 (2017)
4. Z.Y. Wang, H.S. Liu, J. Graph, **30**, 2, 126-129 (2009)
5. Y.F. Bi, N.W. Wang, Y.W. Zhu, Packag. Eng, 2, 160-165 (2018)
6. L.L. Sun, F.S. Kong, Y. Zhou, X.Y. Liu, Chinese J. Ergonom, **19**, 2, 60-62 (2013)
7. J.Q. Zhang, Q.W. Hu, M. Ding, Ind. Des, 10, 63-64 (2015)
8. X. Meng, J.C. Wang, Journal of Donghua University(Natural Science), **34**, 3, 299-302 (2008)
9. B.B. Li, *Product Design Psychology Evaluation Research*. (China Light Industry Press, Beijing, 2013)
10. B. Lv, J. Yan, J.Q. Wang, B. Yang, Z.Q. Li, J. Mach. Des, **34**, S2, 122-124 (2017)

Ecological optimization design of silage equipment key components based on innovation method theory

Jianqiang Wang, Bing Lv[a], Jie Yan, Yingjun Li, Zequn Li and Mengjia Chen

School of Mechanical Engineering, University of Jinan, 250022 Jinan Shandong, China

Abstract. Ecological environmental issues are constantly threatening the survival and development of human society and has been concerned by all walks of life. The seven ecological efficiency factors proposed by the WBCSD are the basis for improving the ecological performance. Through the mapping relationship between ecological efficiency factors and 39 engineering parameters, the ecological issues will be transferred to engineering problems. It is guided by the corresponding design concepts. Furtherly the TRIZ problem solving tools will be applied. Thereby, the optimized solution will be obtained. It can not only effectively reduce the environmental impact of products, but also can shorten the development cycle of green products while satisfying functional requirements. The development of China's agricultural machinery is extensive. This method is used to implement ecological optimization design of the bundling device mounting frame for silage equipment, which has important guiding significance for the development of China's agricultural machinery.

1 Introduction

Since the industrial development of our country to date, great changes have taken place in human society: science and technology have advanced by leaps and bounds, economic strength has been continuously enhanced, and material conditions have greatly improved. At the same time, as the rapid development of society, people have to face more and more serious resource and environmental problems [1]. The ratio of industrial output capacity and resource-environmental cost are low in China, especially in the field of agricultural machinery. At present, the development of large-scale agricultural machinery, high cost, energy-consuming supplies, but the low utilization rate, does not meet China's crop planting patterns and farmers' income levels.

The construction of ecological civilization is related to everyone. The traditional development model of development-pollution-government has failed in China. In the 1960s, when the book "*The Silent Spring*" was published, people began to pay attention to the ecological value of design. Z.F. Liu et al. [2] combined CBR with TRIZ to summarize the green product design model; F. Fei et al. [3] proposed 8 environmental parameters, and then transformed them into TRIZ problems through the relationship with engineering parameters; L. Zhang et al [4] obtained the product green design process by making up for the lack of TRIZ and patent analysis. In the conceptual design phase of the product, we take into account the ecological impact combining innovation method theory with ecological design. It can shorten the development cycle of green product.

With the adjustment of agricultural structure and the continuous development of animal husbandry, the acreage of silage crops has been expanding year by year. The demand for silage equipment is also increasing. However, the development of silage equipment is still in the traditional stage of development. This paper introduces ecological design into the field of agricultural machinery. It applies further an ecological design model based on the innovation method theory to analyze silage equipment so that silage equipment can improve its ecological performance while fulfilling its functions and meeting customer needs.

2 Ecological design based on innovation method theory

2.1 Theoretical basis

The innovation method is an auxiliary tool for improving people's innovative skills based on a large number of case studies and practices. It includes TRIZ, SIT and QFD [5]. Particularly, TRIZ is a powerful methodology for solving invention problems. Eco-design theory is mainly used to guide the direction of product development. The innovation method theory and the ecological design theory have become more mature. The method of ecological design based on innovation method theory has emerged.

The first author: Jianqiang Wang E-mail: 1391991303@qq.com [a] Corresponding author: Bing Lv E-mail: me_lvb@ujn.edu.cn

2.1.1 TRIZ theory

G.S. Altshuller from the former Soviet Union and a group of researchers led by him analyzed and studied 2.5 million patents from countries in the world [6]. In turn, they proposed TRIZ theory. TRIZ has three basic solutions [7]: conflict resolution principles, effects, and 76 standard solutions. Conflict includes technical conflict and physical conflict. Technical conflicts apply invention principles to solve problems by conflict matrix, and the physical conflict apply invention principles to solve problems by the separation principle. The effect is to solve problems with the scientific principles of physics, chemistry, and mathematics. The application of the 76 standard solutions is to establish the material-field problem model and then find the corresponding solution model.

2.1.2 Ecological design

Ecological design refers to not only considering the performance, price, market and appearance of the product in the conceptual design stage of the product, but also considering the ecological performance of the product from the entire life cycle. It maximizes the use of product resources and minimizes ecological impact [8].

As part of the product's overall design, eco-design is not a specific method or tool, but rather a way of thinking and analysing. It is a necessary precautionary measure. Eco-design sometimes provides users with an exciting need. It is not as easy to discover as basic needs and expected needs. Once it is realized, it will greatly increase the market competitiveness of products.

2.2 Ecological design method based on TRIZ

In order to further improve the level of sustainable development and strengthen the awareness of ecological environmental protection, the World Business Council for Sustainable Development (WBCSD) has proposed 7 ecological efficiency factors [9]: reducing the material intensity of products and services; reducing the energy intensity of products and services; reducing the spread of toxic substances; improving the recyclability of raw materials; promoting the sustainable use of renewable resources; improving the durability of products; increasing the service intensity of goods. In order to facilitate the use of operations, they are represented by A, B, C, D, E, F, G respectively. The introduction of ecological efficiency factors also provides a basis for the ecological design of products.

Chen et al. [10] summarized the mapping relationship between 7 ecological efficiency factors of WBCSD and 39 engineering parameters of TRIZ. In addition, a association table of ecological efficiency elements and engineering parameters was established, as shown in Table 1. Through this table, we will quickly turn ecological issues into TIRZ engineering problems. So it provides method and theoretical guidance for problem solving. And products can quickly and effectively improve the ecological efficiency factors.

Table 1. Ecological efficiency factors and engineering parameters association table.

Ecological efficiency factors	TRIZ engineering parameters
A	1, 2, 3, 4, 5, 6, 7, 8, 12, 14, 23, 26, 32, 39
B	1, 3, 5, 7, 17, 18, 19, 20, 21, 22, 32, 39
C	13, 23, 26, 28, 30, 31
D	9, 10, 11, 28, 29, 32, 36
E	14, 30, 31, 34
F	13, 14, 15, 16, 27, 30, 34
G	9, 24, 25, 27, 33, 34, 35, 37, 38, 39

Because an ecological efficiency factor does not correspond to an engineering parameter. In order to facilitate the selection of engineering parameters, the design concept corresponding to the ecological efficiency factors is summarized for the ecological design of product structure in the mechanical field, as shown in Table 2. This is based on the relationship between ecological design concepts, environmental demand characteristics and green attributes [11]. It guides the selection of TRIZ engineering parameters. Ecological design analyzes one of the seven factors that affect ecological efficiency. But it does not mean that ecological efficiency factors can be isolated. Conversely, the impact on other factors must be fully considered in designing.

Table 2. Ecological efficiency factors and design concepts.

Ecological efficiency factors	Design concepts
A	Minimal design, Lightweight design
B	Energy-saving design
C	Minimal pollution design
D	Modular design, Design for recyclability, Design for disassembly
E	Resource best use design, Resource regeneration design
F	Long life design, Balanced life design
G	Reduced design, Modular design

Ecological efficiency factors can guide products to reduce negative impacts. TRIZ theory can provide a more direct and easier-to-operate theoretical basis. Integrating eco-efficiency factors and TRIZ, the ecological design model based on innovative method theory is obtained. Figure 1 shows. It not only guides the design direction but also provides method theory.

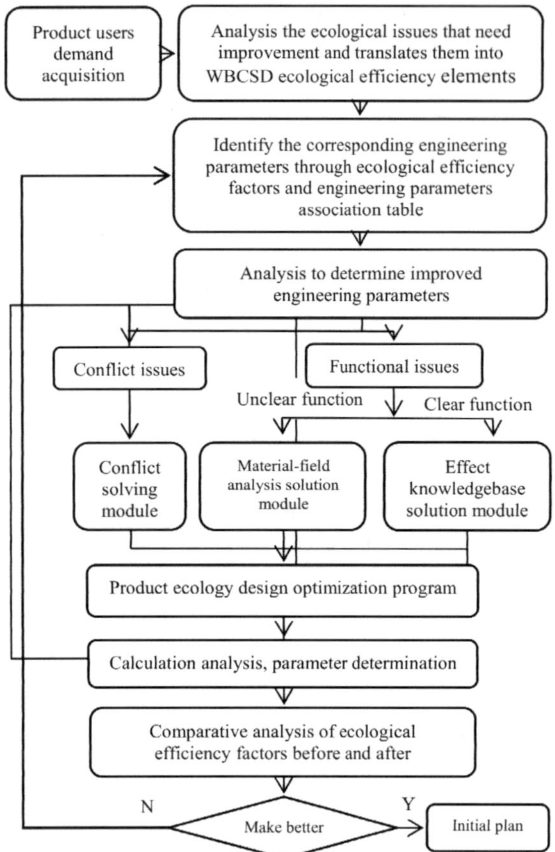

Figure 1. Ecological design model based on innovation method theory.

The ecological design model mainly includes six parts: demand analysis, ecological analysis, problem solving, preliminary program, parameter determination and program evaluation. The solution to the problem is to turn the actual problem into a model problem. And then selecting the corresponding solution principle, problem solving model or scientific effect applies to the specific problem.

Eco-design based on the innovation method theory can not only improve the product's environmental friendliness, but also improve the market competitiveness of products and shorten the development cycle of green products while satisfying the needs of customers. Therefore, the application of ecological design method based on TRIZ theory is of great significance for the optimization design of products.

3 Ecological optimization design of silage equipment

In 2017, the total sown area of grain was 112,220 thousand hectares in China, which was 815 thousand hectares less than last year. The increase in feed grain poses a threat to Chinese food security. It also restricts the development of animal husbandry in China [12]. Silage expands the source of feed and can solve the above problems. Therefore, the research on silage equipment is of great significance.

3.1 Overall structure of silage equipment

China is a big country in agriculture and animal husbandry. However, it is insufficient that agricultural machinery is suitable for hilly areas. The existing knapsack silage equipment has a relatively single functi-on. But power resources are wasted and the cost of material transportation is high in each step. There is a difference in process time, which affects the silage effect. In order to overcome the shortcoming of the current silage machinery. We developed modular knapsack silage equipment that integrates cutting, smashing, baling, and wrapping. It mainly includes a header device, a throwing device, a bundling device, a wrapping device, a lifting device, a telescopic device, and a power device.

This equipment is small and medium-sized and harvests two rows. The width of the header device is 1.4 m. The working speed is 5 km/h. The main working parameters are determined as follows:

(1) straw quality per hectare

We calculate corn yields at 6000 kg/hm^2. the ratio of corn straw material quality and corn kernel quality is 1.2:1. So we calculated the straw quality to be 7200 kg per hectare. 80% of the corn stalks are recycled and 20% of the crop stalks are returned to the field. The straw quality collected was 5760 kg per hectare. Therefore, the quality of the grain and straw collected was:

$$m = 6000 + 5760 = 11760\ kg.$$

The moisture content of silage straw is generally 40% to 60%. If we take 50%, straw quality per hectare was:

$$m_g = m/0.5 = 23520\ kg.$$

(2) Working time per hectare

The row spacing of corn is 0.6 m and the harvest width is 1.2 m. The working time per hectare was:

$$t_g = \frac{1000}{\frac{5000}{3600} \times 1.2} = 1.667\ h.$$

(3) Stem harvesting productivity

The theoretical calculation of stem harvesting productivity [13] was:

$$Q_j = 0.1 q_j W v_j \quad (1)$$

Where: W = width of work, m; q_j = stem yield, kg/hm^2; and v_j = machine travel speed, km/h.

Calculated:

$$Q_j = 0.1 \times 1.2 \times 23520 \times 5 = 3.92\ kg/s.$$

3.2 Installation structure design

In order to make full use of resources and improve the utilization of equipment, mounting frame for bundling device play a key role in the modular design. The ecological optimization design of the mounting frame can improve the use performance and ecological performance of the entire equipment.

3.2.1 Demand analysis

The existing mounting frames are tailored to the tractor and can only be adapted to the specific model tractor. When the power unit is replaced, it cannot be used. The bundling device is difficult to install on the mounting frame and requires engineering equipment.

3.2.2 Ecological analysis

The adaptability of the mounting frame is poor. It needs to be re-customized for different tractors. Thus this wastes material. And it cannot achieve self-handling so much that it needs to use engineering equipment. Thus this wastes resources. We model the actual problem. It corresponds to the eco-efficiency factor: increasing the service intensity of goods (G). According to Table 1, TRIZ engineering parameters corresponding to ecological efficiency factor G are 9, 24, 25, 27, 33, 34, 35, 37, 38, and 39. Based on reduced design concept, the improvement project parameters 33 are selected after the analysis. Operability: the operations to be completed require fewer operators and steps, and the use of tools are as simple as possible.

3.2.3 Problem solving

After the ecological analysis, it is known that the engineering parameters that need to be improved are operability. In other words, the mounting frame can achieve as many functions as possible with as little manpower and time as possible. Whether it is the installation of the bundling device or the installation of the mounting frame, their displacements are realized, which is a function problem. And the function is clear. Therefore, the effect is used to solve the problem. According to the function code table, its corresponding function code is F6 (controlling the displacement of the object). The recommended scientific effects include magnetic force, electronic force, pressure and inertia force. Pressure is applied to the movement of the mounting frame, which make the mounting frame scalable. Inertial force is used for the movement of the bundling device, which save human effort.

3.2.4 Preliminary plan

In order to facilitate the installation and adjustment of the mounting frame, we use square tube nesting and install the hydraulic cylinder inside the square tube. So the installation frame is adjustable and controllable in the three-dimensional space. In order to achieve the self-loading and unloading of the bundling device, a slide rail is provided on the support plate. Slides are used with the slider on the bundling device. Of course, the lifting device for mounting the wrapping device is also fully utilized to achieve self-loading and unloading. Figure 2 shows a retractable mounting frame.

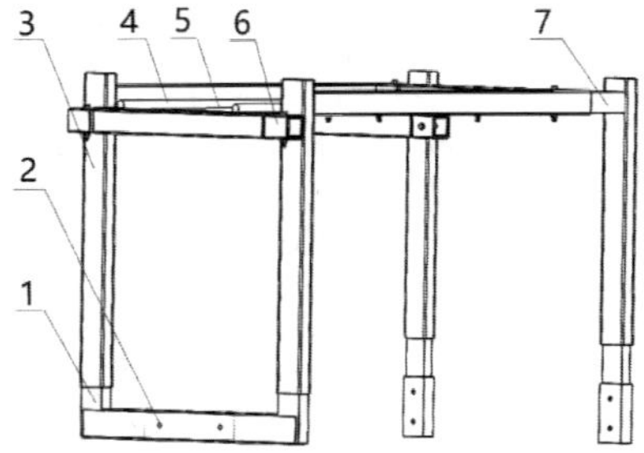

1. corner tube 2. mounting hole 3. hydraulic cylinder 4. slide rail 5. support plate 6. connection tube 7. built-in tube

Figure 2. the retractable mounting frame

3.2.5 Determination of main parameters

The equipment is small or medium sized. Mounting frame is mainly suitable for tractors of 50/60/70/80 horsepower different brands. It is mounted on the hood of the tractor. The design length can be adjusted in the range of 1400-1800 mm; the width can be adjusted in the range of 600-1000 mm; the height can be adjusted in the range of 800-1300 mm.

4 Summary

(1) This paper applies the ecological design method based on innovation method theory to optimize the key components of silage equipment. The ecological performance analysis and the working performance analysis of silage equipment will be completed in the follow-up work.

(2) The model integrated innovation method theory and eco-design method was applied to the field of agricultural machinery, which is of great significance to the healthy and effective development of agricultural machinery.

Acknowledgment

Fund Project: 2017 Shandong Province Agricultural Machinery R&D and Innovation Plan Funded Project (2017YF004-10)

References

1. Z.F. Liu, *Green Design Method Technology and Its Application* (Nat. Def. Ind. Press, Beijing, 2008)
2. Z.F. Liu, Y. Gao, D. Hu, J.D. Zhang, China. Mech. Eng, **23**, 9: 1105-1116 (2012)
3. F. Fei, L.W. Zhong, Precis. Manufa. Automat, 2: 47-56 (2008)

4. L. Zhang, W.W. Zhang, S.X. Jiang, Mech. Des. Res, **32**, 5: 1-3 (2016)
5. C.Y. He, Y. Li, W.Q. Li, J. Jiang, J. Eng. Des, **18**, 3: 153-158 (2011)
6. R.H. Tan, Q.H. Zhang, Ind. Eng. Manage, 1: 34-36 (2003)
7. M. Zhao, W.C. Zhang, G.S. Wang, *TRIZ Advanced and Practical* (Mech. Ind. Press, Beijing, 2016)
8. J.N. Liu, G. Jiang, W.J. Lu, X.D. Zhang, J. Mech. Eng, **52**, 5: 12-20 (2016)
9. L.D. Desimone, F. Popoff, *Eco-efficiency: The Business Link to Sustainable Development* (MA. Inst. Techn, Cambridge, 1997)
10. J.L. Chen, C.C. Liu. J. Sustain. Prod. Des, **1**, 4: 263-272 (2003)
11. G.C. Ren, Y.L. Tang. Mech. Des. Manu, 12: 61-63 (2016)
12. Z.Q. Wang, S.M. Teng, M. Zhao. Chinese Cow, 2: 43-44 (2007)
13. China Academy of Agricultural Mechanization, *Agricultural Machinery Design Manual* (Mach. Ind. Press, 1988)

Research and Experimental Application of Family Holographic Projection Entertainment Equipment

Anzhuo Li[1], Fan Li[2] and Dayong Ma[a]

[1]School of Design Art, Shenyang Aerospace University, Shenyang 110000, China
[2]School of Design Art, Shenyang Aerospace University, Shenyang 110000, China

Abstract. This paper introduces a kind of family entertainment equipment based on holographic projection technology and optical principle. It can achieve 3D viewing of video effect without wearing any head display equipment, with a sense of immersion and substitution. The equipment is mainly composed of external stereo structure and internal specific source. The results can be used for family entertainment. In the process of using, it can be visualize, embodied and effectively reduce the damage of digital devices to users' eyes.

1 Introduction

In recent years, with the development of science and technology, digital entertainment products such as VR and AR have gradually entered into people's lives. But at present, most of VR and AR products are inseparable from the participation of smart phones, televisions, tablet computers and other hardware devices. It is still necessary to be able to experience by mean of an external equipment and not to achieve a full 3D naked eye experience. This shortcoming will bring physical harm to users, especially to children. However, with the help of the technology of holographic projection, the naked eye can be viewed 360 degrees in all directions. The biggest advantage is that it does not need to wear any equipment. This paper aims at the entertainment demand of ordinary users, the learning and cognitive needs of the young children and the entertainment experience needs of the cartoon enthusiasts, and develops a set of holographic projection entertainment products with full naked eyes.

2 Function and principle

2.1 Equipment Function

The family holographic projection entertainment equipment is mainly composed of two parts of the external stereoscopic structure and the internal specific source, and the external stereoscopic equipment converges the specific sheet source picture to the center. Making use of holographic projection technology to make two-dimensional audio-visual broadcasting become three-dimensional. Through this holographic rendering, the user's horizons can be planed and stereoscopic. Giving them a deep sense of immersion also greatly reduces the damage to the eyes of digital products, and thus has a better user experience.

2.2 Fundamental principle

Holographic projection technology is the technique of recording and reproducing the real three-dimensional image of the object by the principle of reflection, refraction and diffraction of light. The projected image is the intensity distribution of the Fraunhofer diffraction image produced by the pure phase hologram. In this paper, we use the iterative Fourier transform algorithm, which is the most commonly used in the process of simulating optical diffraction, and use Fourier lens to realize Fraunhofer diffraction of plane images. The schematic diagram is shown in Figure 1.

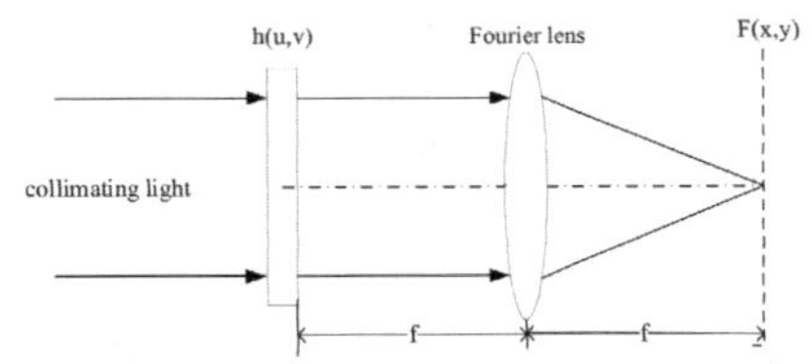

Figure 1. Schematic diagram of holographic projection.

Assuming that the hologram input formula is expressed by $h(u,v) = \exp(i\varphi_n)$, when the collimating light source is irradiated, the complex amplitude distribution F(x, y) of the Fourier lens is equal to the Fourier transformation of the hologram.

$$F(x,y) = \mathfrak{L}\{h(u,v)\}$$

h(u,v) is the amplitude distribution, φ is the phase function, and $\mathfrak{L}$ is Fourier transform.

3 Structural analysis

The structural design of the equipment is shown in Figure 2. The outer structure is embedded with a four pyramid in the cube border. The surface of the four pyramids is composed of four isosceles triangle with 70.5 equal angles

* Corresponding author: [a] 381772091@qq.com

at the top angle of 70.5 degrees, and the angle is 45 degrees from the ground.

Figure 2. Overall schematic diagram of equipment.

The source of the equipment plays from the front, back, left, right four angles of the object, using video editing software to recombine the video into a video source file with four surfaces at the same time. When the equipment is used, each of the four pyramids reflects the image of the corresponding plane, and the video of each surface is synthesized into three-dimensional imaging by reflection, refraction and diffraction of light. Because the distance between the light and the eyes of different faces is different, the video will form a certain time difference between the users, and the stereoscopic image that is accepted has a deep sense. In brief, the holographic projection entertainment equipment is to process the captured video into four video sources (as shown in Figure 3). The four overlapping images which are reflected by the four pyramids are combined into a three-dimensional picture, so that the original plane sense image has a three-dimensional sense.

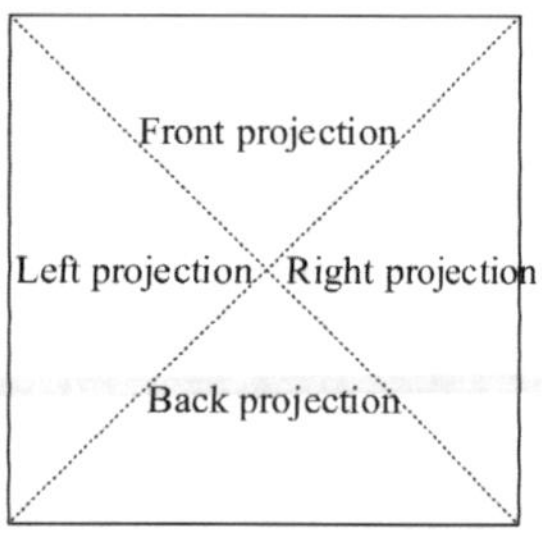

Figure 3. Projection video source distribution map.

Only when the bottom and waist length reach a certain proportion can the best playing effect be achieved. Based on certain experimental calculations and repeated argumentation, the optimal data obtained in this paper are as follows.

Bottom length = screen width

The height of isosceles triangle = bottom edge length /0.5= bottom edge length *0.707

Isosceles triangle oblique side length = bottom edge length /2cos54 degrees 75 '= bottom side length *0.866

4 Implementation results

4.1 Film production process

In the production of film source, we mainly use 3D model software and later software to obtain holographic projection sources.

(1) Use 3D software such as Autodesk Maya or 3ds MAX to model the roles, and export the models in obj. format.

(2) Brush the weight for the role model, that is, adjust the influence of the skinned bones on the fixed-point of the object.

(3) Use Autodesk MotionBuilder to create the connection relationship between the captured action and the bound bones, and map the data to the virtual skeleton of the role.

(4) Use 3D software such as 3ds MAX to create cameras at four angles of view around the role model, and maintain a fixed distance to follow the role model movement.

(5) The moving images are rendered, and the different images of the four cameras are presented, and the video is synthesized by the synthetic software to match the music according to a certain structure.

4.2 System implementation

Figure 4 are special film sources based on the process, which collect the real time images of the four sides of the object and processes them.

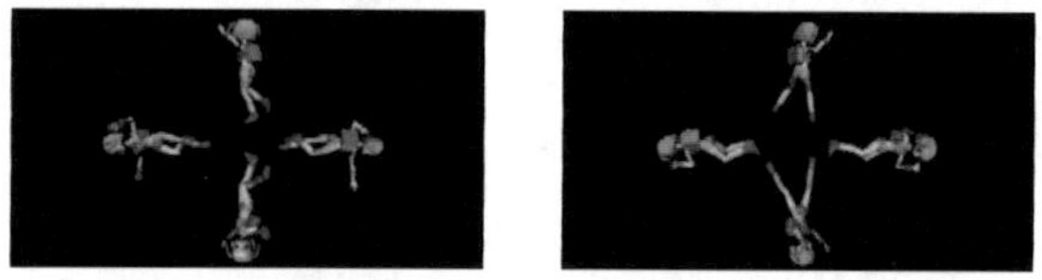

Figure 4.

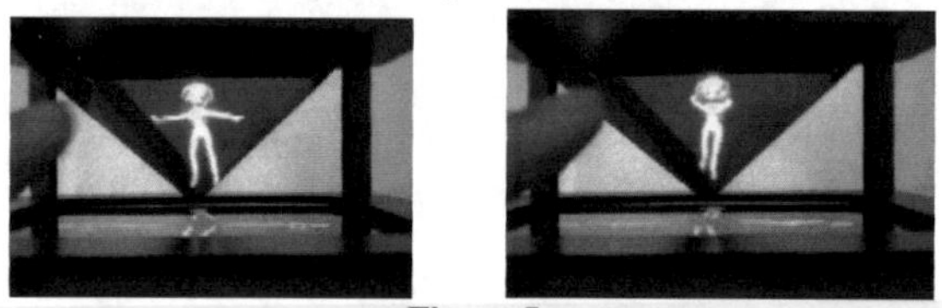

Figure 5.

Figure 5 are experimental verifications of a equipment playback source. It can play the source picture clearly and clearly, and can view the angle at any angle at 360 degrees. This shows that the family holographic projection entertainment equipment can achieve the effect of naked eye stereoscopic display.

5 Conclusion

Through the realization of the external three-dimensional structure of the equipment and the production of the internal chip source with the aid of holographic projection and optical principle. Then it reaches the stereoscopic display effect. The creative solution in the research has solved the problem that the moving subject cannot acquire the large image information during the previous production of the holographic chip source. Break through the technical bottleneck that the image cannot do complex motion and can only do the original motion around the center point. On this basis, the use of motion capture method can be more efficient action information. In addition, in the aspect of source production, it can be targeted to combine the users with high-quality output.

It is worth pointing out that holographic equipment is more motivate by low-child user group cognitive learning than traditional entertainment equipment in view of them. Users can view the source from multiple angles to get a more vivid experience. Besides, it also can be used to create atmosphere. For example, if you tell your child a story about the ocean at night, you can open the source of the underwater world's holographic video and dim the lights. Follow-up studies can be combined with other practical applications in many ways.

Acknowledgments

This work was financially supported by Study on the application of Manchu image design to promote the development of Liaoning culture tourism (Project number: W2015313).

References

1. X.Wu, W.Liao, H.G.Liu, CJL, 417-420 (2009)
2. Q.H.Wang, A.H.Wang, D.Liang, H.Deng, VE, 1-6 (2011)
3. Y.Yang, ES&CM, 94,98 (2013)
4. Q.Wang, Scientific advisory, 64-65 (2014)
5. G.B.Fang, Q.Q.Zhu, Y.H.Shen, G.J.E.Hu, Wireless interconnected technology, 140-141(2015)

Research on Industrial Design Laboratory with Service Design Concept

WANG Qiang[1], ZHANG Hai-chao[2], WANG Li[2]

[1]Dalian Jiaotong University, China
[2]Dalian Institute of Science and Technology China

Abstract: In industrial design teaching, the laboratory is an important teaching space for cultivating students' innovative spirit, practical and creative ability. Laboratory space construction, teaching link design, service and management mechanism directly determine the quality of teaching. The paper explores how to redesign laboratory teaching of industrial design professional through the concept and method of service, which enhances the service experience on the service contact and uses participatory service design tools in the teaching process to improve the teaching process and quality.

1 What is the service design?

There has not been a clear definition of service design as a professional rise so far, but the attention on user usability, ease of use, and enjoyment is recognized and focused by all, and the focus on service providers has also been paid attention. Therefore, there are obvious differences between service design and interaction design and experience design. Service design is more about system design. Service providers and users participating in the service are audiences. The application of service design is very extensive. A series of teaching activities can be carried out by service design thinking, from teaching system design to performance management. Service design is the design of behavioral systems. The four major elements are stakeholders, contact points, services, and processes. The five principles are user-centered, collaborative innovation, orderliness, tangibility, and integrity.

2 The background of laboratory construction

The Internet era of information technology has a certain impact on the whole social structure and relationship. The impact on traditional university education not only brings new knowledge, but also raises new challenge on the organizational form and education methods of university education. new challenge. The paper mainly discusses the study on the redesign of industrial design professional laboratory construction and teaching with the concept and method of service design. For industrial design teaching, face-to-face knowledge transfer can no longer meet the training of talents' innovative practical ability. It breaks the limitation of time and space. Enhancing the interaction between teachers and students can stimulate students' initiative in learning and promote the personalized development of student characteristics. More open laboratory teaching can cultivate students' innovative ability and practical ability.

Service design is a design activity that aims at improving service quality users experience, which plans and organizes the person, things, information communication and other related factors involved in the service so that all the system activities could be reasonable and effective. Service design provides users and servers with reasonable, easy-to-use, satisfied, trustworthy services for the user, which could be both tangible and intangible. Service design is always people-oriented, allowing high-level integration of communication, materials, environment and behavior.

With the development of service design, more and more areas are applying the concept and method of service design, and the education industry has begun to adopt it in various teaching tasks. Many educational experts also realize that the service design thinking is helpful for the laboratory construction and teaching.

3 The redesign of laboratory space and teaching services

Try to use the concept and method of service design to design a new learning space, studies the teaching behavior of industrial design laboratory, redesigns the existing space environment to make the use of the laboratory more efficient to adapt to new learning needs.

3.1 Investigation stage

The users' experience is not usually generated spontaneously but is guided by the designer. Therefore, the students have expecting experience on laboratory, and it must provide them with the appropriate environment and facilities. To understand the students' needs for space and service, research on teaching and research personnel and students to investigate students' needs for laboratory space and services.

3.2 User portraits

The portrait of the user is one of the important methods of service design. Through in-depth research on the user, it investigates and analyzes the behavior characteristics and needs of different users and portrays a representative user to represent the motivation of the general user, behaviors and expectations to accurately express the user's core needs.

3.3 Service route map

After establishing the persona model, the next step is to use the model to experience the space and services of the laboratory. It combines the role feelings and better design the space of the laboratory by simulating the sequences of users' actions and emotions that the user may have at the service contact point.

When determining the user's portrait, the user can experience the laboratory space and experimental teaching process. Based on the user's feelings, it simulated the actions and emotions of the users generated in the service contact point, and to better design the laboratory space and the experimental teaching process. The road map is only a part of the system behavior design. During the entire design process, it should be considered of different actions, experiences, and feelings in different scenarios of different users. The more different users being analyzed, the laboratory space and teaching process that meet the needs of most users could be designed.

3.4 Strengthen the coordination and communication of stakeholders

While applying service design to design education, the students are the ultimate audiences and the most important focus. The student's learning experience is an entirety rather than a single process in the service. Focusing on service learners, students, teachers, knowledge and the environment are the stakeholders of the entire design project, which treats the entire teaching process as an interactive service system. It should concern about students' learning experience and emphasizes the connection and interaction between teachers and students.

It focuses on the openness of space management, emphasizes direct conversations and communication between individuals with fully dialogues. It emphasizes practicing in the form of observations and drills under the guidance of teachers, mixes discussions, rest and cooperation to break the class mode that the teachers teach and students listen to. It encourages students to operate independently in the teaching method that teachers and students discuss together.

3.5 Enhance the service at contact points

There exists the problem that limited space with a large number of students for many laboratories in the industrial design profession. During the service design process, all contact points must consider the overall arrangement to create a clear and efficient experience.

In the communication with the lab technicians, it has been discovered that whether it is the mechanical operation of the basic model laboratory or the electronic operation of the rapid prototyping laboratory, the human nerves are in tension, long hours of work and noisy environment can easily affect the human emotions. So, it is very important to design the laboratory environment space so that the teachers and students can have a relaxed and happy attitude in the space.

The overall process of service is the interaction among space, people and their behaviors. Interesting design at the contact points can change the machine's sense of coldness and tension, allowing students who do not have engineering background knowledge to understand the space, notes, reminders, warnings and other information service instructions better.

3.6 Use participatory service

The purely experimental hands-on operation is not enough to arouse students' interest, nor can it practically implement practical operations. It can introduce enterprise resources into schools, integrate them into the teaching of the laboratory according to the needs of the enterprises and the company's projects, and stimulate students' autonomy and curiosity. Under the joint guidance of corporate designers and professional teachers, it conducts scientific research training (open experimental projects) and play a role in serving the society with innovation.

3.7 Change the rhythm of the process to bring new experiences

It will analyze uniformly all laboratory courses according to the industrial design professional course, make learning service process in the laboratory during the university, which will be dynamically demonstrated in a variety of media so that students can understand the experiment at any time in a variety of channels, to ensure the maximum openness of information.

Based on the conventional teaching process, it selective changes the conventional teaching process, such as the time limit for the transfer of laboratory keys, you can use it before application.

4 Enlightenment from Redesign of Laboratory Space and Teaching Services

4.1 Develop the diversified functions of the laboratory

From the process of designing space and services for industrial design laboratories, it has been found that the students' needs for laboratories have greatly changed. The wide spreading of network information technology and mobile devices has also been widely used in the laboratory space. To expand the spatial functions of laboratories, the needs in teaching behavior must be studied to realize the diversification of laboratory spatial functions.

4.2 Strengthen the social service function of the laboratory

In more and more teaching behaviors, the exchanges between teachers and students depend on information-based social behaviors. Therefore, it is necessary to add network technologies and various application tools in the laboratory. The rich social functions make teachers and students information acquired and socialization more convenient, not only improves the efficiency of learning, but also stimulates students' imagination.

4.3 Achieve the self-service of laboratory services

Simplification is one of the important service principles of the laboratory. Complex procedures can make students shrink back at the sight of using the lab. The important way to simplify services is self-service, which can improve resource utilization and work efficiency.

The self-service reduces the time of communication with management personnel firstly. Secondly, they can operate by individuals in the use process and can independently select what suit their own needs. Thirdly, it also reduces unnecessary waste of time for laboratory workers, who can focus more on more constructive work.

5 Conclusion

The rapid development and popularization of social networking and informatization still cannot replace the collective learning, mutual consultation and face-to-face communication between people, especially the entity emotions within a limited space that cannot be replaced by the Internet. So, it is still necessary to continue to research in-depth and create innovative learning spaces that are suitable for learners, and to make full use of the service design theory to continue designing more reasonable and effective emotional perceptions to adapt to the rapid changes in social patterns.

References

1. LIU Xin, LIU Ji-kun. Possible Opportunity: the Concept and Practice of Product Service System Design (J) . *Creation and Design*, **5** (2011)
2. LUO Shi–jian, HU Yi . Model Innovation Driven by Service Design [J]. *Packaging Engineering*, **14** (2015)
3. XU Yue- ren. Research on the Space and Service Design of NCSU Library [J]. *Library Forum*, **5** (2014)
4. GAO Bo, YIN Zheng-sheng, ZHANG Liang-jun. Design Practice of Service Design Applied to Innovative University Library (J) . *Packaging Engineering*, **1** (2016)
5. HONG Hua, TAN Xiang-lin, TAO Jin. Analysis of Influencing Factors of Situation Perception on Service Design [J]. *Packaging Engineering*, 33 (2012)

https://doi.org/10.1051/matecconf/201817601008

Research on the practical cross-curriculum system of product design specialty from the perspective of new engineering

WANG Li, ZHANG Hai-chao

Dalian Institute of Science and Technology

Abstract: The traditional economy has transformed into a new economy led by innovation and entrepreneurship, deepened the reform of engineering education and pushed forward the development of "new engineering" as a trend. In the face of "new economy" and "neo-engineering", the applied field of design science is rapidly rising and widening, and the paradigm of design science, teaching idea, intension and talent training mode should be changed. Carrying out the study of the practical cross curriculum system of the major of products design from the perspective of "new engineering", it is mainly discussed from the aspects of curriculum reform, innovation and entrepreneurship education, and directional personnel training between schools and enterprises.

1 The emergence and development of "new engineering"

1.1 How "New engineering" produce

At present, the country drives innovation to drive development, the implementation of "the Belt and Road", "Made in China 2025", "Internet +" and other major strategies, with new technologies, new industries, new models, new industries as the representative of the new economic development, the engineering and technological personnel put forward a higher demand, urgent need to accelerate the reform and innovation of engineering education. The original traditional education model cannot meet the needs of the new economic related fields, and the single ability structure does not conform to the requirement of talents. With the coming of the information age, all kinds of new economy are developing vigorously. The state has formulated and implemented the "The Belt and Road", " China manufacturing in 2025", "Internet plus" and a series of strategies to promote innovation driven economic development,which has put forward new requirements for engineering technology.And the corresponding talents ability and education must also be reformed and innovating.

In order to improve the mismatch of talent supply and demand, the education of "new engineering", which accords with the development of new economy, has emerged. In order to promote the construction and development of "new engineering", the research and practice of "new engineering" is carried out. In February 2017, the Ministry of Education issued the "new engineering" in the Department of Higher learning to carry out the study and practice of the notice, hope that universities around the "new engineering" research and practical activities, so as to deepen the reform of engineering education and promote the construction and development of "new engineering". The research and practice of "new engineering" is a new concept, new structure, new model, new quality and new system of engineering education reform. In order to promote the development of "new engineering course" to match the demand of talent supply and demand, the Ministry of Education issued "Notice on Department of Higher Education of the Ministry of Education Carry Out Research and Practice about "New Engineering Course" "It requires colleges and universities in all regions to carry out the "new engineering" education reform. The education of "new engineering" mainly revolves around the concept, structure, mode, quality and system of engineering education.

1.2 What is "New engineering"

There is no clear definition of "new engineering" at present, but the whole society has reached a consensus on the category of "new engineering". "New engineering" is faced with emerging industries, including large data, artificial intelligence, intelligent manufacturing, robotics, cloud computing, and traditional engineering professional upgrading. Compared with traditional engineering, "new engineering" emphasizes the practicality, crossover and comprehensiveness of the subject, especially the close combination of new technologies such as information communication, electronic control, software design and traditional industrial technology. The new engineering course has a higher requirement for the knowledge structure. It emphasizes the practicality and comprehensiveness of various disciplines, especially the application of information communication and electronic technology in traditional industrial technology.

1.3 The talent training of "new Engineering"

In order to adapt to the development of "new engineering", it is the consensus of the whole society to cultivate talent in advance, train the new economy in urgent need of talents, and cultivate the talents with innovative entrepreneurial consciousness, digital thinking and cross-border integration ability. "New engineering" talent not only proficient in a certain discipline, but also should have a knowledge of the integration of interdisciplinary disciplines, they have the ability to learn new knowledge, new technologies to solve future development problems, but also understand the economy, society and management, but also have the humanities. And they are comprehensive talents who are more concerned about society, humanities and art.

To put it simply, the goal of "new engineering" is to train new and innovative talents for new economy. New engineering appears in the new economic transition situation, its education system should also be changed. The difference between the "new engineering" education and the traditional engineering education is that the "new engineering" education promote the innovation and the deep change of the talent training system in many aspects, such as mechanism, idea, curriculum system, training route, quality evaluation standard and enterprise participation degree. Compared with traditional engineering course, the education of the "new engineering course" has put forward higher requirements."New engineering course" pays more attention to the cultivation of practical ability,which makes teaching more docking with enterprises. To strengthen the development of production, teaching and research, we need to reform and innovate teaching ideas, curriculum system, training methods and quality evaluation.

On the whole, the development of new economy calls for the "novel Engineering", and also puts forward new requirements for talent training. "New Engineering" is the general trend, will be to guide the direction of university personnel training, will become the education sector and the community has been the focus of attention.

1.4 Introduction on the development of "new engineering" in our school

Dalian University of Science and Technology joined the new Engineering Alliance in March 2018. Our school will use the new education concept, to create new engineering features, through the integration of various disciplines, the Dalian Institute of Science and Technology into a new engineering practical talent training cradle. Our school will create an educational concept that is consistent with the development of "new engineering course" and build Dalian Institute of Science and Technology into a university of training applied talents of "new engineering course". Our school has set up innovation and Entrepreneurship College, Robotics Institute, Ali cloud College and so on, build mobile cloud computing, network security, artificial intelligence, intelligent hardware, such as "new engineering" professional cooperation, training the current emerging industries in the urgent shortage of new talent, practice the implementation of new engineering construction. In the face of the current development of the new engineering education and the vision of our school to build the new engineering Stanford, as well as the new application fields that the design discipline Foundation is facing in the emerging economy, the paradigm of design discipline, teaching idea, intension and talent training mode should be changed. Therefore, under the background of the development of "new engineering" in Dalian Institute of Technology, the product design specialty of Design Art Institute has carried out the research on the reform of the cross-type curriculum system of product design specialty under the new engineering perspective.

2 Problems and solutions in the education of product design at present

The problems of the expansion of enrollment scale, the heavy workload of teachers ' scientific research and the emphasis on theory light practice are more prominent. It is necessary to reform and construct the direction of emphasizing the practical innovation ability, strengthening the teaching of professional design practice, and to build the practical cross course system of product design specialty on the basis of realizing the skill training and aiming at the result display and evaluation.

There is a certain gap between the students ' quality and the demand of the enterprise, and the disconnection between the new economy and the new engineering is serious, which reflects the problem of the current training mode. The practical cross curricular system needs to be closely integrated with the design industry. In addition to enabling students to master basic skills in design, it should also be developed to foster students' market thinking. So that their design works can meet the needs of the market and possess commodity attributes.. At the same time, also cultivate students ' vision and creative thinking ability, communication and collaboration ability, self-learning ability, can complete design services and business transformation needs. Through the practice of the cross-curriculum system, to achieve a student-centric, to increase the current economic needs and social needs of the curriculum content, especially the "new engineering" corresponding to the emerging professional, the allocation of interdisciplinary teachers, strengthen the construction of school-enterprise cooperation base. By changing the way of knowledge imparting in traditional classroom teaching and breaking the limitation of time and space in traditional management system, a more open teaching management system is established. This can truly teach students in accordance with their aptitude, so as to meet the needs of students of different levels and characteristics, and to maximize improve the students' ability to learn independently.

3 The main characteristics of the interdisciplinary and practical teaching

Interdisciplinary and practical teaching can cultivate students ' ability to analyze and solve problems. In order to guarantee the basic teaching requirement, we should turn from teacher-centered to student-centered, break the limitation of time, space and system, set up an open operation management mechanism to meet the students with different levels and different demands, and give full play to students ' autonomy and enthusiasm.

It will rearrange and combine the experimental hours originally dispersed in each course, form an independent and complete project design, carry on the comprehensive evaluation result from classroom report, design report to practice achievement, perfect the integrality of practice course, improve the efficiency and quality of experiment teaching.

We will vigorously carry out cooperation in research and development, cultivate students ' adaptability to society, and let students begin to accept various forms of design training and practical activities in universities. Cultivate the students ' autonomous learning ability and comprehensive practical ability. The practice-type cross course system, can orient the talented person's training and the occupation localization, impels the school and the enterprise the close connection, is divorced from the traditional classroom form, may promote to the design thought innovation also satisfies the enterprise need, may carry on the talented person "the order form" the training, increases the student employment rate Cross-curriculum system to cultivate special creative talents, improve students to cross and practice curriculum characteristics of the design concept and practical ability. The close connection with enterprises can cultivate special talents and make knowledge and ability more practical.

4 The model of practice-type cross-curriculum system in product design specialty

4.1 The cross-course system of product design specialty

The curriculum content organization and system construction takes the social environment and the economic demand as the direction, constructs "the 1+2+1" the teaching platform, guarantees the design science discipline systematic and the science, constructs the curriculum system, 1 year of Design Basic course, 2 year of specialized knowledge and the skill class, 1 year of specialized design curriculum. To increase the richness of the teaching staff, on the basis of the traditional product design teaching team, the interdisciplinary teachers' team and the Enterprise Designer are joined to promote the teachers' teaching, research and practical projects together, and the resources such as scientific. Research and practical projects are integrated to cultivate students' ability to discover and solve problems creatively.

The content of thematic design changed the form of specific product categories in the past. should be linked to social issues, cross-border cooperation to complete the development of new products, for enterprise projects to provide valuable results. The current research problems mainly include information and interactive experience design, health and medical problems design, intelligent products networking Home product design, transportation and travel experience design, cultural products innovation and development and other fields. Combined with the above issues, the curriculum, thematic research, practical curriculum integration, emphasizing the cross cooperation between different professions, strengthen interdisciplinary cooperation, pay attention to design in line with industry needs.

4.2 The teaching mode of the practice-type cross course of product design specialty

The teaching mode no longer emphasizes knowledge transfer, but focuses on students, combining teaching with scientific research, so as to achieve mutual benefit in scientific research and teaching activities. Cultivate students ' independent learning, innovative spirit and practical ability.Let teachers' scientific research and teaching be closely integrated, so that they are no longer limited to face to face teaching in class.And it can cultivate students' ability of independent learning and practice

The teaching of curriculum emphasizes inspiration and guidance, let the students out of the classroom facing the society, so that the enterprise designers and industry experts to participate in the design and process of teaching links, to meet the needs of enterprise oriented personnel training, the teaching results and industry docking, the quality of students and industry needs corresponding to the teaching links to achieve interdisciplinary, cross-field, which can let the teaching achievement have the innovation and the social value.

The construction of school-enterprise cooperation base is an important foundation of practical teaching, constructs a complete practice system, establishes the concept of equal emphasis on teaching, scientific research and practice, and allows students to understand social needs and participate in practical projects. Building a school enterprise cooperation platform is a necessary way to combine the scientific research, teaching and practice of teachers. School enterprise cooperation enables students to integrate learning and practice projects, thereby enhancing their in-depth understanding of economic and social needs.Including large data, cloud computing, network security, artificial intelligence, virtual reality and augmented reality, intelligent hardware and other cutting-edge science and technology, the industry's new ideas, new technologies, new knowledge and enterprise needs to integrate into the curriculum system construction. The school-enterprise cooperation can achieve a mutual win.

Through cooperation with the forefront of the field of enterprise, update the content of the course, to provide students with a rich teaching platform. In order to ensure the integrity of the teaching curriculum system, according to the needs of enterprises to train the corresponding ability of talent, directed for the enterprise training high-quality personnel, through cooperation with enterprises, to establish long-term research value of the subject content. The purpose of this study is to explore a new training mode of talents which is more in line with the new economic environment for the product design profession.

5 Conclusion

The practice-type cross course system of product design is combined with the disciplines and specialties of the new engineering, which is advantageous to the interdisciplinary development of multi-disciplinary, and the cooperation with the emerging enterprises is beneficial to the further development of the research, and the competitiveness of the product design professional. This research is a beneficial exploration to the reform of curriculum system and the cultivation of practical talents in product design specialty.

References

1. Wei Jie. Social Transformation and Design Education Reform: Exploration of “121 Integrated Innovation Talents Training Model” of School of Design, Jiangnan University [J]. *Decoration*. **7** (2016)
2. Xin Xiangyang. "New areas, new problems, new countermeasures." Lecture on International Conference on Design Education Redesign, (2013)
3. Qi Yongqi. “Design for Activism”, “Designing for Transformation”, (International Design Education Forum Presentation Record, 2016)
4. Lin Jian. "China's New Engineering Facing the Future". Education Research, Tsinghua University, **3** (2017)
5. Zhong Denghua. Connotation and Action of New Engineering Course Construction. *Social Sciences II. Higher Education*, **3** (2017)
6. Wu Aihua et al. "Accelerating Development and Construction of New Engineering Subjects to Actively Adapt to and Lead a New Economy." *Research in Higher Education*, **1** (2017)

Study on humanized design of intelligent charging device for electric bicycle

Shan liang Yao[1], Man Luo[2,a]

[1]EDP Sciences, Wuhan university of engineering, School of art design,China
[2]EDP Sciences, Wuhan university of engineering, School of art design, China

Abstract. According to the analysis of the classification and demand of electric bicycle charging device, and combining with the humanized concept, we can discuss the design method of electric bicycle charging device. In order to produce electric bicycle way of humanized design of intelligent charging device moved by appearance, with emotion, pleasure from color as three kinds of expression way, based on the appearance and structure, function and operation, interface and detail from three aspects, physiological needs to the person's psychology and spirit pursuit are so important, we should show more respect and satisfy it, while the demands of users are coming. Users will feel more comfortable, while using this product, then they will have an emotion and dependence on product.

1 Introduction

As the most widely used transportation, Electric bicycle has advantages on both side of environmental protection and energy saving. On the other hand, we can see that its matching chargers per charge up to 7-8 hours. Once the battery run out of energy while driving, users will be in trouble. Electric bikes are bulky and extremely difficult to move. However, the demand of e-bike is so great, electric bicycle charging problem is badly in need of solving. Electric bicycle humanized design of the intelligent charging device should be guided by technology and function, concentrating on user needs. We need to add technology, function, color, shape, material and other factors into product humanized design, after analyzing and studying of user demands. This paper analyzes the humanized design through example of electric bicycle charging device and its design.

2 Overview of electric bicycle charging device

2.1 classification of electric bicycle charging device

According to different classification criteria, electric bicycle charging devices can be divided into different types.

(1) Classification of electric bicycle charging device.We can classify the charging form as two modes, mainly in the form of fast charge and slow charge, in needs of users. When the user is in urgent need of the car and the battery is too low, it is suitable for fast charging mode, which is generally applicable to slow filling mode.

(2) Classification by placement.According to the resettlement form of electric bicycle charging device, it mainly includes quick charging station, box-type charging pile and embedded charging pile.

(3) Classification by structural features.The charging station adopts a site assembly, and then the whole movement can be carried out like a container. The internal equipment is modular and equipped with special maintenance equipment for regenerative batteries.

(4) Classification by means of payment.In addition to traditional cash, the payment method also has the current popular mobile payment.

(5) Classification by application site.According to the electric bike users of the main activities of the regional classification, it can be divided into residential areas, public parking lots, high-speed service area, large shopping plaza, the company and office buildings, parking open side of the road.

2.2 Demand analysis of e-bike charging device

To improve the function of electric bicycle charging device according to the existing problems provided by users.

(1)Voice operation.Most of the existing charging devices in the market are charging stations and charging piles, which are large in size, and can have innovative designs in the shape, color and material of charging devices.

(2)Display function.User demand for charging device is not only the charging, also include in the process of using parking demand, payment, and so on, the demand of users and convenient lifestyle are also affect the charging device design, which we consider as a great innovation of design point. In this way, the charging

*Corresponding author: [a] Man Luo: 471636092@qq.com

device is not only a product, but also a convenient system for users to travel, changing the way people live.

(3) Automatic adjustment.Considering the age on using the crowd, level of education, and the health situation are different, the charging unit operation should be simple, fast, clear, using process can be implemented by means of animation simulation display or voice prompt to release.

(4) Cooling system.The existing charging unit lack of consideration on the performance of man-machine engineering, so the innovation of the charging device design man-machine performance indicators should be comprehensive consideration, and on the basis of existing data and real-time test data to correct.

3 Humanized design of intelligent charging device for electric bicycle

In the process of electric bicycle intelligent charging device design based on the needs of people, human physiological and psychological characteristics, following the principle of respect and care, meeting the user in the physical, mental, physical, psychological aspects of requirements. To take the advantages of artificial intelligence to create a safe, comfortable, efficient electric bicycle intelligent charging device as the goal. Electric bicycle intelligent charging device design of human nature is the designer of form and function of "human" factor of injection, products with "human nature is changed" character, has the emotion, personality, temperament and life.

3.1 Expressions

The humanized expression of the intelligent charging device of electric bicycle means to carry and embody the invisible spiritual form in tangible material form. Generally speaking, there are three kinds of humanized expressions (table 1):

(1) Break the form design of the existing charging device on the market, through to the intelligent charging device modelling, colour, material, texture, such as the change of shape elements, bring psychological feelings and emotional experience to the user, namely "moved by appearance";

(2) With the design of product function development and mining, that an increasingly perfect the function and performance optimization of permeability in the process of the designer's personal feelings as well as to the care of the vulnerable group, make users feel more comfortable, convenient, make the person feel kind, warm and humanitarian care, respect just meet the demand of the people's physical and spiritual pursuit, namely "with emotion";

(3) A proper color for the interface will often become the finishing touch of the design, which comes from the deep processing of the interface and details, that is, " pleasure from color".

Table 1. The humanized design expression of electric bicycle intelligent charging device.

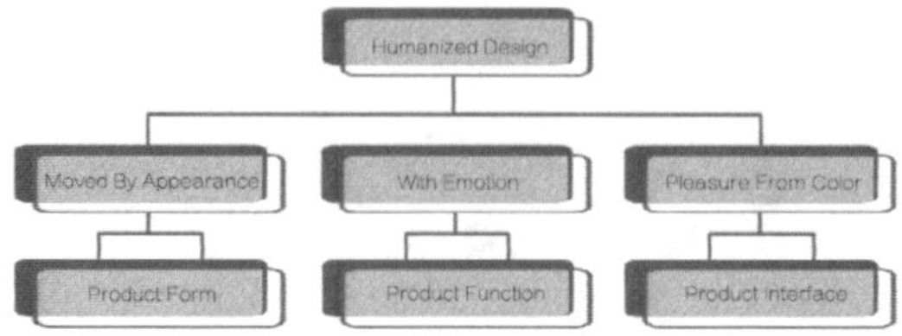

3.2 Design principles

Electric bicycle intelligent charging device design should be comprehensive with consideration of user requirements, technical support, material technology and so many other factors, there are huge differences between the humanized design of the electric bicycle intelligent charging device and the traditional charging device. Here comes the following design principles:

(1) Multi-functional design. Charging electric bicycle travel daily to remove this basic demand, is also important to stop a, and therefore should be integrated in the development of intelligent charging device design integration of multiple functions such as charging and parking, in order to effectively solve the user in the usual life of electric bicycle is disorderly parking place and charging the inconvenience;

(2) Green design. Electric bicycle intelligent charging device in design, saving of energy and materials should be considered, and the charging device material can choose in the recycling and facilitate the processing of materials, choose a kind of classic and timeless design on modelling, or by changing a few key components can be easily updated style, so as to prolong the service life of relative charging unit, achieve the goal of saving.Its payment method is paid offline by the device equipped with the app, which reduces the use of the real money and is another embodiment of green design.

(3) System design.Electric bicycle intelligent charging device solved a series of problems of the users in the daily, such as parking, charge, charge, weather, etc., to perfect on the function to the home from the trip to every step, is a set of system design.At the same time, the future business process of the intelligent charging device also has a relatively perfect specification, so that the product has a strong practical operation and becomes the user's intelligent travel steward.

4 Design example of intelligent charging device for electric bicycle based on human nature

4.1 Humanized design with attractive appearance and structure

Humanized design and product design are complementary and mutually reinforcing. The development of product design requires humanization, while humanized design needs the support of product design. Therefore, in the design, we not only seek the unity of beauty and practicality, but also seek the coordination of products and people and environment. This electric bicycle intelligent charging device abandons the common charging station appearance, charging pile on market with large volume, molding machine, and they are really not harmony with the surrounding environment, which is just designed by simple geometric shapes. Due to combined with charging the design of the device to lock the car in the parking lot, the lock and the charging device are just matched. At that time, the scene electric bike in a mess will pass away, the phenomenon such as security, reduces the waste of space, save material will come to us, and in the parking lot this particular environment, the charging device is subject to the environment, not only into the environment, also played the importance to the role of the environment, to achieve product consistent results in harmony with the environment. The overall design orientation is very strong, with neutral color as the main tone, and color on the details, which can remind the user.

Figure 1. Below the figure.intelligent charging device and parking space of electric bicycle.

4.2 Humanized design of function and operation with emotion

This electric bicycle into the intelligent charging device lock the car with multiple functions such as charging, using induction pressure plate is connected to the lock switch, when the device is still， switch will be closed, the charger contraction; When the electric bicycle wheel comes into contact with the device, the lock will open automatically according to the pressure and displacement direction; When the electric bicycle is parked, it will not move for a period of time, and the sensor pressure plate will not feel the change of pressure, then the lock will open automatically. At the same time, the charge line cover will be opened, and the charging cable can be freely telescoped by the spring line to recharge the electric bicycle. In addition,the function of charging device development and mining embodied humanistic care, parking information, positioning function, charging real-time feedback, additional features such as weather forecast will be added to the main body of charging device functions. Combining the main function with a matched app makes the product a completely reasonable device, which makes the function of the products more perfect, more convenient to users in every way out, solves the electric bicycle charging inconvenience, disorderly parking in residential area and a series of problems. It will be intelligent housekeeper in travels. Due to the perfection and humanization design of the device, the user is quite convenient in operation, for example, the voice prompt function of the intelligent charging device facilitates the operation of the user.

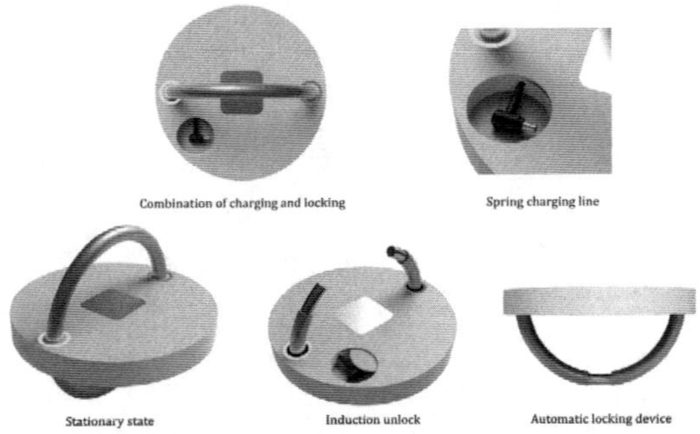

Figure 2. Function diagram of intelligent charging device for electric bicycle.

4.3The humanized design for the user - interface and details

Electric bicycle charging device should pay attention to man-machine interface and detail design, and ensure the operation more accuracy, efficiency and comfort for user. Different functions of the product buttons, knobs, and the layout of the operation panel and modelling has different design requirements. Product interface design fully embody the features of the product, such as charging icon design used in app charging interface is the shape of the electric bicycle charging line, then the user will be clear at a glance while using. In the matched app, its interface is concise, clear, charging device in addition to meet the parking charge and the two main functions without redundant design, also do not have too much decoration and color processing. Locked and unlocked as two states, which is designed into red and green to enhance display effect. The interface design of the supporting app adopts the fresh green, which gives the user a comfortable experience, and echoes the green transportation tool of electric bicycle.

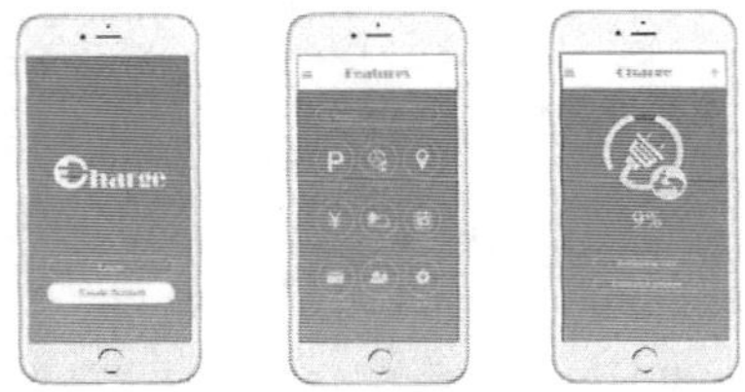

Figure 3. Main app interface of the smart charging device of electric bicycle.

5 Conclusion

The development and change of e-bike is not only driven by technology, but also by solving existing problems as an important force, as well as the design of external product charging device. The designer should pay attention to the object of the service, not only focus on the comfort level of product use, but also pay attention to the psychological satisfaction, and follow the trend of the current fashion. Then making a design maximally meets the needs of users, reflects electric bicycle charging unit, man-machine relationship, form and function, while using. Psychological aspects of the concern for people with respect, makes every effort to electric bicycle travel way of life, emphasize life, individuation, make electric bicycle intelligent charging device fully embodies the humanized design.

References

1. P qian, L zijian, S xia. Research on SOHO office furniture system design based on humanized concept ,Furniture and interior decoration. (2009)
2. S hui, H mi, Research on innovative design of bathroom products based on kansei engineering , Packaging engineering.(2011)
3. S miao. Exploration and research on humanized design in medical device products,Packaging engineering.(2007)
4. G wenzi,Design of an electric bicycle reverse charging device , China manufacturing informatization.(2011)
5. N shao qiang.,*Design history and theoretical research: inheritance and development.*(2007)
6. S zhiguo,Research on teaching and application of integrated equipment for the storage and charging of electric bicycles,Electromechanical information.(2017)
7. Donald a. Norman. Design psychology [M]. Xiao ke, translated. Citic press.(2015)
8. [8] jia xiaoxia. Analysis and visualization of user behavior based on e-bike data [D]. Zhejiang university.(2017)

Research on the Representation of Line- type of Digital Sketching in Product Design

Liu Ying[1] , Liu Xiaojing[1] and Chen Yi[2, a]

[1]Cnetral South University, Industrial Design Department, 410083 Changsha Hunan, China
[2]Guzhi Science and Technology Co., Ltd. 410083 Changsha Hunan, China

Abstract: The type of lines which from digital hand drawing representation is the central element to the constituted form. At present, there are a few special topics on the structural description of the type of lines. According to the classification of kind of lines which from the basis of painting, integrated using of various lines can create spatial illusions in the plane horizon to achieve the performance of three-dimensional entities. By clarifying features and characteristics of various lines, the digital technology can be quickly generated to design the representation effect and form the graphic design language.

1 Introduction

Digital hand drawing is not only synthesizes the effect characteristics of many drawing tools but also simulates the effect of paper hand drawing to realise paperless painting. The stored record function of the computer can also support the repeated modification of pictures, which is a kind of a closer expression means to combine technology and art [1]. The performance features which is fast and convenient can provide technical support for design representation and communication. At present, the research on hand drawing design is focused on the techniques of skill which from marker pen and the teaching curriculum system, while there are a few special topics for product structure representation [2-4]. The core of product form design is the continuation and reconfiguration of the form [5], so the structure analysis and structure of the type of lines are the research focus in digital design. The research of kind of lines classifies the function of the line, conducts differential effect processing in the picture, synthesises technical characteristic of digital representation, integrates the technical characteristics of the digital image to form the spatial perspective and designs diagram of the shape structure.

2 Classification of lines

Line is the soul of hand drawing representation [6]. As the design representation under the background of emerging technology, digital hand drawing is a technical extension derived which from the basis of structural sketch line. Highly generalised lines are needed by the plotter to describe the physical characteristics of the object. Objects can be presented intuitively in real space, but lines are not real, they are the space boundary between two objects or between object and environment under the condition of light. Spatial boundary of the object is formed by the reflection of light where on the boundary of object and
the environment, which is commonly referred to as the "contour line"; the reflection of the light between the object's own surface makes a difference in intensity, thus forming "light and dark line" which can be perceived by vision in objective. The die line is the overlapping edge which is caused by the need for production and splicing of blocks and surfaces, which is also the spatial boundary between each component. These three lines can be defined as solid lines by visual perception, that means, visual lines that actually exist on real objects.

2.1 Functional classification of lines

Several types of lines which are used in digital hand drawing cannot be visually seen. In order to describe characteristics of objects in detail, designers can use a large number of auxiliary lines, which are based on the cognitive framework of spatial thinking. Because of their difference in functional utility, they can be divided into structural lines, perspective lines, analytical lines, cross section lines, etc.

As shown in figure 1, the structural line is the characteristic line which used by the designer to describe the shape of objects. Being the structural component that determines the shape of the object, which can reflect the turning point, span an extension of the surface. The structure line is fixed compared to the object, and it does not move with the angle of perspective. The perspective line is used to assist the generation of spatial meaning, which is usually accompanied by indicator arrows to create visual direction and guide fabricate three-dimensional space in visual perception. In order to better explaining the structure and shape of the product, the

*Corresponding author: a 48316365@qq.com

cross-section line is a boundary formed by the designer's hypothetical cutting through the object, which can be used to explain the shape and structure of the object.

Figure 1. solid and dotted lines

All types of lines (as shown in Form 1) are comprehensively used in drawing representation and are not isolated. The description of the features of solid and dotted lines is not an absolute definition. The outline of an object usually refers to the continuous edge of a structural line under a fixed angle of view, and the profile line is often described as solid lines which is the outline in product decomposition map. The strength and weakness of types of lines should be treated with a specific situation. Virtual-actual transformation of visual perception is produced by differentiation of straight curve, thickness, softness and hardness, speed and weight of picture.

Form 1. Linear classification

Solid lines			Dotted lines			
contour lines	outlines	light and dark line	cross-section line	structural line	perspective line	analytical line
Emphasis on treatment		General treatment	Weakening treatment		Weakest treatment	

2.2 Differentiation of lines

According to the function of their pictures, the virtual-actual transformation of visual perception is produced by differentiation of straight curve, thickness, softness and hardness, speed and weight. Digital hand drawing inherits the line feature of structure sketch, and the representation of a line in picture is not only a single form expression. The computer can provide pressure-sensing function. The plotter only needs to emphasize the virtual-actual linear change through the difference of hand movement, and make full use of the thickness, weight, and extension of lines to create spatial illusions in near and far space in the plane horizon, thus achieving performance of three-dimensional entity. As shown in figure 2, the cube at perspective angle forms the contour lines with nine solid lines. In order to create the visual illusion in the far and near space, the contour lines should be drawn apart from the visual differences: line A from the nearest visual point has the heaviest color, then is line B and C, the contour line of the visual bottom is slightly influenced by projection, and the line D and E increases the width; visual level of the remote contour is on the back, the line G and I needs to be weakened in thickness and color; and longitudinal and horizontal structure of the object surface is used as the auxiliary line to further weaken the strength.

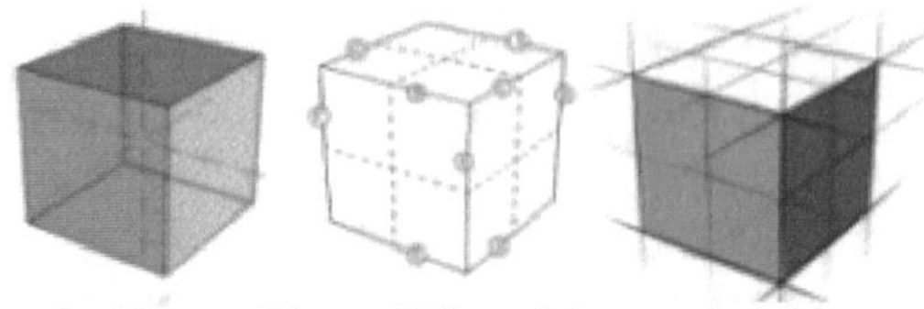

Figure2. Linear differential representation

Vision is a basic tool for thinking [7]. At the initial creation of the draft, the designer should always quickly to record the sporadic, fleet design inspiration, turn the vague intention into a visual representation and regard it as the original material for the idea. Compared with the rigorous perspective chart, the fast-recording drawing speed will increase the random degree of type of lines. However, in this painting stage, the representation of auxiliary line is still essential. Figure 3 shows a quick representation diagram in which we can see impromptu interest and certain design gesture [8]. There are a large number of structural lines that represent the bending of the body, cross section lines that indicate the variation of the area and perspective lines to assist space coordinate. The comprehensive application of multiple lines can enrich the structure of the picture and carry more structural design information so as to enhance communication and discussion of design.

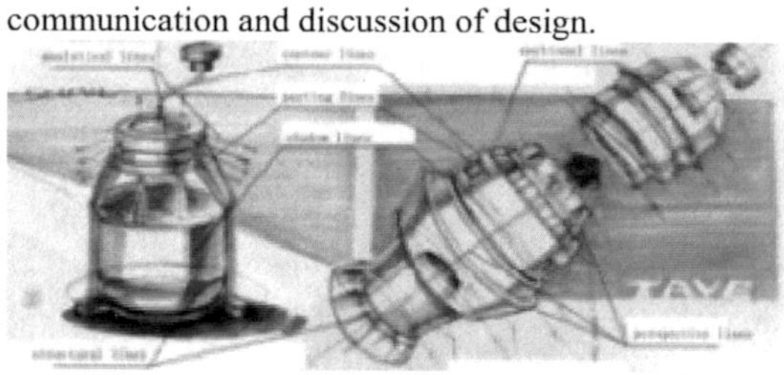

Figure 3. Application of type of lines in fast representation

2.3 Application of type of lines in comprehensive performance

When digital hand drawing is used to express the design effect, the line is the main representation factor of the form, and the structure mode of the design object plays a decisive role in the requirement of type of lines. The thickness, length, width, twists and turns of lines depend on the structure trend of the shape of the object. The technological advantage of the digital representation makes the line more fluent, directive and hierarchic, which makes designers easy to grasp the characteristics of line; solid lines are used to describe visual contour, while dotted lines assist the generation of spatial structure. As shown in Figure 4, lines are used to establish the basic structural characteristics of the form. In the representation of spatial effect, the digital technology can give full play to the technological advantages of the computer and help teachers and students to set up the structure quickly. The methods and technique of graphic language are used to express, communicate and evaluate various design information

 https://doi.org/10.1051/matecconf/201817601010

and design plans, as well as to transform creative ideas into graphic design language [9].

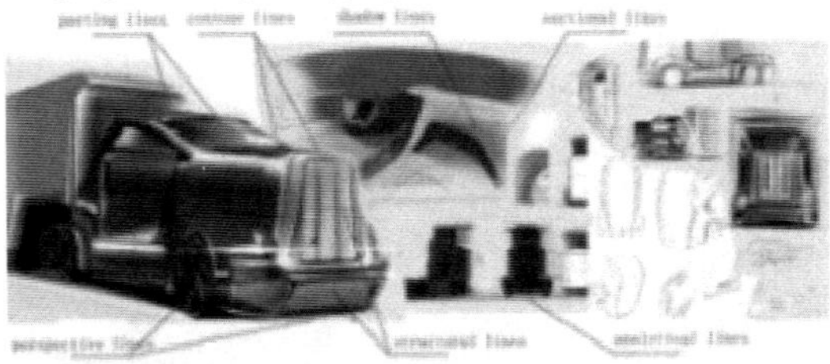

Figure 4. Application of type of lines in comprehensive representation

3 Conclusion

Digital hand drawing focuses on structural analysis and line formation. The designer should first distinguish the functional types of lines in the screen, then use the differential representation form to create visual level and make space effect, and finally to describe the structure composition and surface features of the design objects in detail through various auxiliary type of lines. The design drawings with distinct effect can highlight the key points of design, enhance visual language of the picture and enrich design information of drawings. In order to clarify difference of type of lines and analyze the modeling structure in detail, sustainable development of digital representation technology will provide more possibility for type of lines and synthetic technique.

Acknowledgment

The paper is the final supporting material for Hunan philosophy and social science foundation project "Industrial design value and performance evaluation research", Item No.: 16yba369

References

1. Xue Yanmin, Deng Binshuo, Wang Jiamin. The position and function of fast representation of hand drawing in product Design. Packaging Engineering, 08(2008)
2. Ren Min, Wu Lili. Creative performance of hand drawing products under the background of cultivating applied talents. Art Education Research ,19(2017)
3. Wang Xueqin, Zheng Yinfeng. Teaching of representation techniques of hand drawing for products. Mass literature and art, 03 (2017)
4. Liu Yang, Zhang Zhiming, Xia Lili. The representation technique of hand drawing. Beijing Arts and Crafts Press.(2016)
5. Chen Zhenyi. Analysis and reconstruction-exploration of the theory of typology in teaching of furniture improvement design in Ming and Qing dynasties. Adornment ,04(2016)
6. Li Yinxing. Discussion on the training model of students'ability in product hand drawing. Adornment, 09(2013)
7. Arnheim·Rudolph. Visual thinking. translated by Teng Shouyao, Guangming Daily Press. (1986)
8. Zhong Xuhui, Xu Lei. The role of hand drawing in teaching of ring art design. Packaging Engineering ,26(2005)
9. An Jingbin. The function of hand drawing in product design process. Industrial design 01(2017)

MATEC Web of Conferences **176**, 01011 (2018) https://doi.org/10.1051/matecconf/201817601011
IFID 2018

The design and research of the shared kitchen system in the hospital

YE Xin [1], JI Qian [1,a]

[1]Huazhong University of Science and Technology,430074 Wuhan

Abstract. The shared economy has been developing rapidly with low cost, low consumption and high environmental efficiency features under the background of internet waves. The shared economy model has emerged in housing, catering, and travel. As people look forward to high quality of life and their social interaction need, the shared kitchen platform arises at the right moment. This paper takes the shared kitchen as an example, focusing on the patients and their caregivers, the existing shared kitchens and its service platform as well as the space system design and human-computer interaction of the shared kitchen have been investigated and analysized. Taking the "high efficiency, the intelligence and the humanization" as the design principles, we are committed to exploring new directions for modular kitchen design under the background of shared economy.

1 The purpose and significance of research

There are four main dining types for patients in hospital: taking meals in a hospital or a restaurant, ordering take-out food and delivered by caregivers, while most patients would prefer the last two choices other than taking meals in a hospital or a restaurant.

The reasons for this phenomenon are as following: Firstly, the food in the hospital canteen does not meet with their taste. Secondly, caregivers are concerned about the freshness of the food as well as the clean cooking process. Thirdly, the price of the food in restaurant is relatively high, the service attitude and the environment would be poor in some cheaper canteens. [1]

Family meal delivery has become the most common way for patients and caregivers, however, through long-term observation and research, we find that it is difficult for those who live far away from hospital to enjoy family meal delivery. Therefore, this paper aims to propose solutions to the problems, which will not only meet the patients' needs of eating healthy food, but also not too much interruption of caregivers' daily life and work. It will also be able to dig out new commercial interests in line with the trend of economic development.

2 Preliminary investigation and analysis

Our objectives of investigation refer to inpatients, caregivers, and nursing staff.

For patients, hospitalization often brings some psychological pressure to them, so they are prone to have the feeling of anxiety, loneliness, fear, depression and pessimism, they hope that caregivers can give more care and companionship. At this time, family's help and care can effectively enhance the patient's confidence in receiving treatment and help improve the patient's quality of life.

In addition, for caregivers, it is found that they are also prone to feel anxious, tense, sad, and self-blamed, delivery meals will also increase the trouble in their lives. through on-site observation and investigation, we notice that there are 10 steps for the caregivers to cook and deliver meals to patients. (table 1)

Table 1. caregiver process analysis

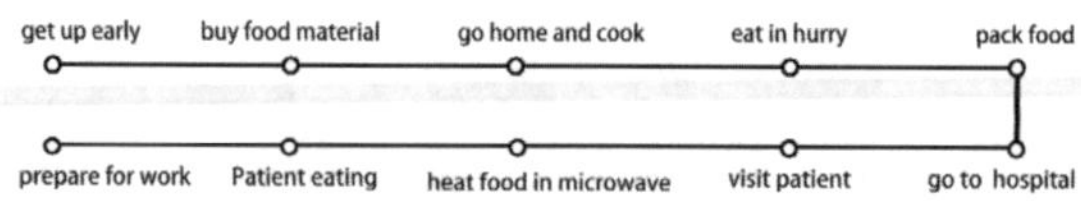

First of all, getting up early can easily lead to the lack of sleep and increase fatigue. Secondly, buy ingredients then go home cooking, caregivers should spend too much time on the preparing and cooking. Thirdly, the caregivers always finish the meal quickly to save time and then pack the food to the hospital, which will easily cause irregular diet and some healthy problems. Fourthly, packaged food will not provide the atmosphere of eating at home. Fifthly, traffic jam at rush hour will waste time. Sixthly, the packaged food always needs heating, but reheating will affect the taste of the food. Finally, caregivers will feel exhausted after the whole process. Many of these steps have negative impacts on caregiver's physical and

*Corresponding author: [a] author@e-mail.org

mental health, so problems can be revealed through the observation and analysis.

2.1 The development of shared kitchens and the concept of new shared kitchens

2.1.1 Existing shared kitchen platform research

The existing common kitchens are operated meeting the needs of two types of people, office workers who want to eat homemade dish and people who want to earn money through cooking skills. The representative shared kitchen platforms are two brands "I have a meal " and "Go home for dinner."

"I have a meal" belongs to the social sharing platform. It discovers the resources of the dinner in the city, regularly publishes dinner information, gathers customers together. It embodies the "Kitchen + Social" marketing model. The target group is the people who love food.

"Go home for dinner " is the “personal sentiment” style type. Its marketing mode is private kitchen cooking - delivery service - dining. The target group is the person who likes cooking and the office workers who are looking for " hometown taste". [8]

2.1.2 A shared kitchen design proposed in this paper

This paper puts forward a new direction for the development of shared kitchen platform in hospital. With "kitchen + health" as its marketing model, the target customers are patients who expect to recuperate health through diet and caregivers who want to spend more time with patients. The new type of shared kitchen advocates users to control the freshness of food ingredients, as well as food hygiene and safety, let the patient eat health.

As we all know, diet therapy plays an important role in restoring health for the patient. Due to the difference of the physical condition, patients' needs for food and nutrition are different. But caregivers often know very little about the practice and efficacy of food for patient. Previous research has found that there are few products with the function of healthy dietary guidance in the market, while patients' need for dietary therapy is very huge.

The new shared kitchen takes "dietotherapy" as an innovative point. By analyzing the diagnostic reports given by the hospital, the intelligent machine collate the trace elements and substances required by the patients. Based on the principles of comprehensive diversification, nutrition and equalization, specific recipes and diet matching are given. Caregivers can easily cope with the problem of "what to eat today".

2.2 Advantage and innovation of new shared kitchen

2.2.1 Food safety

In the operating mode of the new shared kitchen, users make an appointment to the shared kitchen through the hospital health card. The system intelligently analyses the patient's health status, give a variety of recipes for caregivers to select. And user can view the original material of food needed to be prepared. From food ingredients to production, all the process will be checked by users to ensure the safety of food.

2.2.2 The credit system of real name authentication

According to the survey, almost all hospitals have implemented real-name registration.

Compared with the existing shared kitchen platform which lacks credit system among customers, the new shared kitchen is bound to the user through the hospital health card, so it is easy to manage and maintain.

2.2.3 Healthy diet guidance as a marketing point

The existing shared kitchen platform does not Satisfy the rigid demand of the customers, but has grasped the characteristics of the customer with the "feeling" meal, the customer stickiness is not high [8]. It is easy to encounter bottlenecks in development.

The new shared kitchens focusing on "healthy eating," especially in hospitals, is urgent for patients to adjust their functions by using the characteristics of food. Therefore, dietary care and guidance are widely needed.

3 Related human-machine dimension research, spatial color and layout, and product HCI mode analysis

At present, most of the hospitals in China have limited environmental space, the whole decorated kitchen with large equipment and large area is not suitable for the shared kitchen in hospitals. This paper investigates and analyses the application of ergonomic parameters in kitchens and cabinets. Considered color matching, function partitioning and human-computer interaction, we propose a modular of future shared kitchen design scheme with small space and complete functions from the actual environment.

3.1. Study of man-machine size

According to the operation basis of ergonomics, we determined the dimensions of the cabinet plane and section to meet the user's operational requirements. The comfort data of different heights were obtained from the literature research as follows: [5] (table 2)

Table 2. Corresponding comfort heights

height	150cm	153cm	155cm	158cm	160cm	163cm	165cm	168cm	170cm
Comfortable operating height	79cm	80cm	81.5cm	83cm	84cm	85.7cm	86.5cm	88cm	89cm

At present, the height of most operating platform is 860mm. According to the national scale of the human body scale, the 10th percentile of the adult female height is 150.3cm, and the 90th percentile of the adult female height is 164cm. Therefore, the height of the corresponding console is from 79cm to 86.5m [5] (Figure 1)

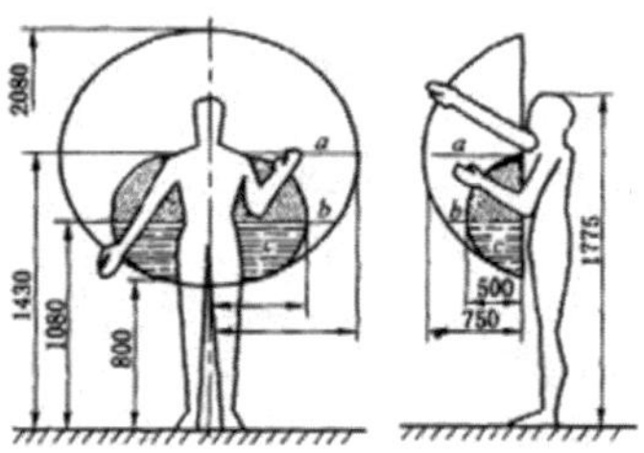

Figure 1. the height for standing position

The width of a person in standing operation is 660mm, and the male is 700mm. In addition, the size correction should also be considered. Through man-machine data analysis, we know that when the angle between the arm and the body is 15 degrees, the work is relatively easy. So the width of the operation surface should be 760mm. And the width of the console should be greater than or equal to 760mm if conditions permit. [5] (Figure 2)

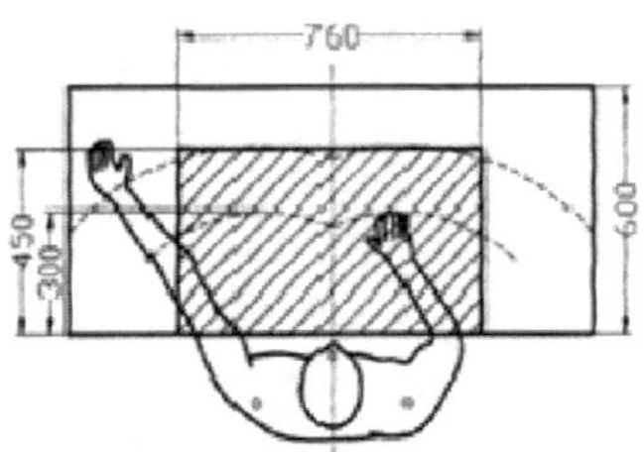

Figure 2. the width of operating platform for standing position

3.2 Color collocation and research

Color matching has a certain effect on visual perception and space size [4]. Generally speaking, high-brightness colors have the characteristic of retreat, it can make the space look more spacious. Moreover, under the pressure of tension, warm and bright environment can give people some psychological support and comfort.

3.3 Functional partition and layout

Under normal circumstances, the kitchen is mainly divided into four major areas: operating area, washing area, cooking area and storage area. Because the use environment is in the hospital, and user has uncertainty, the material does not need to be stored. Therefore, the main functional areas can be divided into three parts: operation area, washing area and cooking area.

There are four common kitchen layouts, One-line layout, L-type, U-type layouts, and island-type layouts. Among these layouts, the L-shaped layout is also called a semi-enclosed layout. Since a triangular area is formed between the washing area, the operation area and the cooking area, user can make full use of the blue triangle area shown in figure 3. So it is a more practical and space-saving kitchen layout design. [7] (figure 3)

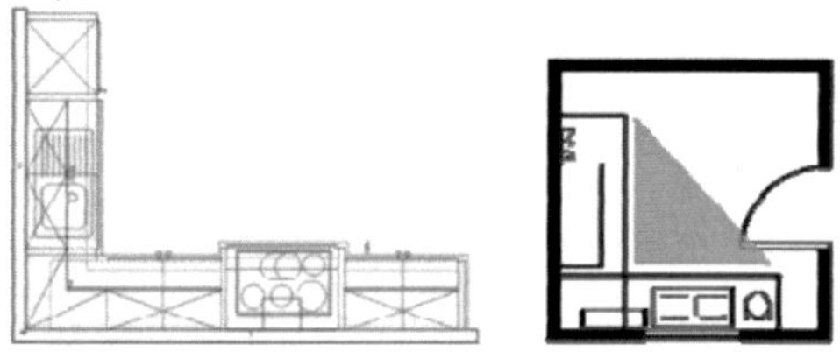

Figure 3. Layout and design of L type kitchen

4 Design scheme

The design of shared kitchen system should not only focus on space layout planning, but also consider the interaction between users and products in the pre - use, use, and post - use stages. Make the product easy to use by simplifying the operation. (Figure 4)

User experience is embodied in three aspects: form, content and behavior. The form is the appearance of the kitchen and the interface of the interactive graphics; the content is shown on the function and information of the product, and the behavior refers to the human-computer interaction [6]. In the design process, we need to focus on the specific form and interaction model of the product in order to enhance the user experience. [6]

Before use: user is bound to the new shared kitchen platform on the mobile phone. According to the medical record information and the inspection

https://doi.org/10.1051/matecconf/201817601011

report, system provides a number of recipes guidance for the recovery of the body function. User can view the corresponding list of Food material after selecting a recipe.

In use: After the user makes an appointment for the free kitchen, the smart door lock has a verification code, user unlocks the shared kitchen through the verification code. Then the system starts charging, and the application guides the user to cook until the end of use.

After use: cleaning is the most important problem that public facilities need to pay attention to. Especially in the hospital, besides the basic cleanliness, it must be sterilizing. Therefore, after the end of the use, system reminds the user to clean, and it ends the billing until the cleaning is finished.

In addition to the ultraviolet bactericidal in the kitchen, the wavelength 240-270nm ultraviolet rays can destroy the DNA and RNA of the bacteria within the 1.2M, and make it lose the reproduction ability and achieve the purpose of the death of the disease bacteria. And the UV specific wavelengths can make the air chemical reaction to produce ozone that can destroy the protein of the pathogen. This disinfection method can kill the hepatitis virus, Escherichia coli and other daily bacteria, effectively ensuring the cleanliness and hygiene of the kitchen.

Figure 4. New design scheme of shared kitchen

5 Concluding remarks

With the development of information age, intelligent technology has been widely used in household kitchen and toliet. The new way of interaction and experience brought by technological progress has become the key factor to enhance the competitiveness of products. With the advancement of science and technology, the sharing of kitchen systems in the future will be able to satisfy people's increasingly high-level needs.

Acknowledgment

Supported by National Natural Science Foundation of China（Grant No：51708236）

Supported by Fundamental Research Funds for the Central Universities（Grant No：2016YXMS273）

References

1. C.W.Sun, X.P.Lu. Focus on a Center to Solve the Problem of Inpatient Patient's Difficulties in Four Ways [J]. Jiangsu Health Management, 1997(05):32-33.

2. S.H.Yu. Composite kitchen design based on indoor man-machine environment [J]. Automation and Instrumentation,2014(11):56-58.
3. Y.M.Mou. Research on Kitchen Humanization Design Based on Low-carbon Life [D]. Shenyang Aerospace University,2012.
4. X.Mao. Talking about the Importance of Color Matching in Interior Design [J]. Art Technology,2017,30(12):340.
5. D.Y.Li, B.Chen, Y.F.Li. Overall kitchen man-machine design [J]. Shanxi Architecture,2008(02):45-46.
6. J.H.Li, S.J.Liu. Research on Intelligent Kitchen Design in Information Age [J]. Art Grand View,2017(09):122-123
7. D.W.Zhang. Research on Application of Kitchen Space Structure Design for Affordable Housing [D]. He Bei University,2017.
8. W.C.He. The Development Status and Countermeasures of Sharing Kitchen in Sharing Economy [J]. modern commerce,2017(18):157-158.

Research on Parametric Form Design Based on Natural Patterns

X Li[1], JN Su[2,a]

[1]School of Mechanical & Electronical Engineering, Lanzhou University of Technology,730050 Lanzhou Gansu, China
[2]School of Design Art, Lanzhou University of Technology, 730050 Lanzhou Gansu, China

Abstract. Parametric form design method based on natural patterns is proposed for the design schema of the traditional form bionics. Firstly, the concepts of natural patterns are analyzed, concluded and summarized. Secondly, the parametric design thinking is elaborated from three aspects: thinking mode, design flow, tools and scripts. It is also proposes a parametric logo design method. This paper takes logarithmic spiral pattern as an example to describe the process from the law of natural pattern to logo design, which includes nature pattern analysis, control rules of from and color, algorithm research and generating design.

1 Introduction

The aesthetic laws of statistical aesthetics, most of which are based on the structure and growth of plants and animals in the natural world[1]. Learning in nature exists at every stage of design development. Different stages of development have different understandings. From the initial appearance simulating to rational creation born out of the inside, humans gradually increase the integration of design and nature. Design absorbs nourishment from nature and helps to create beauty actively and regularly, including new forms and new structures. The design pursues the realm of natural harmony between man and nature.

Parametric technology has been widely used in architectural design, industrial product design, landscape design, fashion design, jewelry design and other design fields[2]. The goal of parameterization is to construct an automatic design system that can be edited at any time. Parametric technology provides infinite creativity for design[3]. It can obtain several design schemes at one time, thus improving the design efficiency.

For the design schema of the traditional bionic form, this paper focused on the mathematical logic behind natural patterns, and studied the parametric form design method based on natural patterns.

In the following Section II, we provide a brief introduction to the concept of natural pattern, including analysis and induction. Section III discusses the parametric design, including process, thinking model, tools and scripts. Section IVstudies the method of parametric logo design. Case study in Section V. The last part is the conclusion.

2 Natural Pattern

The term pattern is not unfamiliar and covers a wide range of fields, such as biology, economics, computer science and technology, physics.

We are in nature. Human exploration of natural patterns began as early as ancient Greek philosophers. Plato, Pythagoras, and Empedocles had tried to reveal the order of the natural world, and established the philosophical foundation for the study of natural patterns. In 1202, Leonardo Fibonacci published his famous book *Liber Abaci*, and raised the Fibonacci numbers on the issue of rabbit breeding[4]. In the 19th century, the Belgian physicist Joseph Plateau studied the soap film, prompting him to propose the concept of minimal surface [5]. The Scottish biologist and molecular mathematician D'Arcy Thompson took the lead in researching the growth patterns of plants and animals. In 1917, he published a book *On Growth and Form*. In his book, Thompson proposed to associate phyllotaxis with the Fibonacci sequence[6]. He showed that complex spiral growth can be explained by simple equations. In the 20th century, the British mathematician and the "father of artificial intelligence" Alan Turing pushed the study of natural patterns to a climax. In 1952, he wrote *The Chemical Basis of Morphogenesis*[7], and the seemingly complex and irregular pattern of spots and stripes could be described by the Turing equation. Then, in 1968, Hungarian biologist Aristid Lindenmayer developed the L- system to simulate the fractal of plant growth pattern[8]. The scientific research results of these natural patterns are the premise of 'design research based on natural patterns'.

Patterns in nature are visible regularities of form found in the natural world[6]. Symmetry patterns are ubiquitous in nature. Humans and animals are mainly mirror-symmetrical and plants usually have radial or rotational symmetry. Non-living bodies also have symmetrical patterns, such as snowflakes, ice crystals, crystals and so on. Spirals is undoubtedly the most

*Corresponding author: [a] sujn@lut.cn

beautiful universal pattern, the initial pattern of life system. From the inanimate spiral galaxy to the genetic material of life the double helix of DNA molecule, petals, fingerprints, eddy currents, cochlea, the tendrils of plants and so on. Insects and animals show the extremes of the spots and stripes pattern. For example, leopards, cows and ladybugs are full of spots, zebras and angelfish have distinctive stripes, butterflies blend spots and stripes. Meanders are common in nature and life, such as the whereabouts of animals, brain gyrus, artificial mazes, and pedestrian trails. Branches and fractals are widespread in nature and have infinite self-similarity. Such as lightning, mountains, coastline, the body's nervous system and blood vessels branch, etc. Alongside fractals, chaos theory ranks as an essentially universal influence on patterns in nature. Mathematics tries to discover and explain various abstract patterns and rules. The visual model of nature can find explanations in logarithmic spirals, fractals, topology, chaos theory, and other mathematics, which lays a mathematical foundation for parametric design.

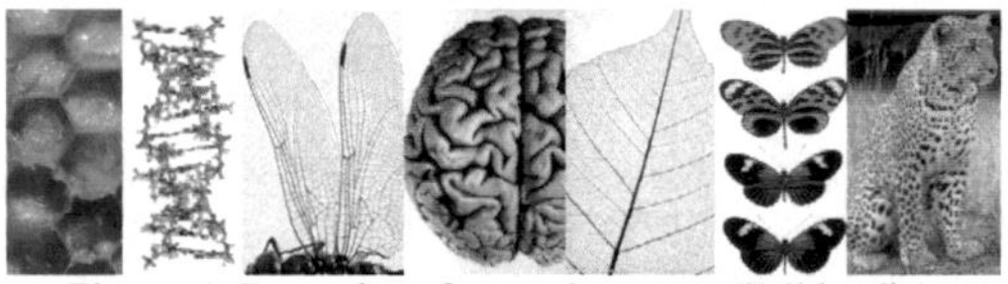

Figure 1. Examples of natural patterns (Wikipedia).

Patterns organizes and defines the relationship of nature, and can be applied to practical design to enhance and support visual communication[6]. This article attempted to develop the intersection between natural patterns and design sciences, and tried to combine natural patterns with the form design through computer programming techniques to explore a new form-aided design approach.

3 Parametric design

Parametric design originated from mechanical design[9]. The fundamental difference in parametric design is the application of computer programming techniques, compares to a typical sketch-manual modeling design schema. Its purpose is to construct an automated generative design system that can edit and modify parameters at any time. Therefore, the parametric design has changed in three aspects: Design Processes (DP), Design Thinking (DT) and Design Tools (DT). This also leads to the design cognitive model of designers to be changed.

3.1 Parametric design thinking(PDT)

Hugh Whitehead thinks that parameterization is more about a way of thinking[10]. Rivka Oxman[11] claims that this is mainly due to the intersection of three areas of knowledge: professional design knowledge, computer programming knowledge, and mathematical knowledge. Parametric design does not deal directly with the form, but rather studies the mathematical logic behind the form. Computer programs are used to calculate the various elements that affect the styling (parameter variables).

Robert Woodbury[10], in his book *Elements of Parametric Design* (2010), proposed that Parametric Design Thinking(PDT) has three main characteristics - abstract thinking, mathematical thinking, algorithmic thinking. Parametric design thinking processes shown in Figure 2 can also prove this view. Abstract thinking is the basis of parametric design, abstracting design ideas or concepts into symbols, data, variables, functions, etc. Mathematical thinking mainly involves how to translate mathematical theorems and data structures into useful algorithms [12]. The essence of algorithmic thinking is the step-by-step problem solving. In parametric design, algorithmic thinking means writing functions in scripting languages. Functions are part of the digital form, the editing function is to edit digital form.

In traditional paper-based design, designers mostly reduce the distance from the ideal design scheme by drawing sketches and making models (digital or physical models). At the beginning, however, parametric design schema need to transform concepts into data. Compared with traditional paper-based design, parametric schema emphasizes systematic design process and the geometry logic of form.

The organic management of data is the key for designers to form designs by programming technology. That is: data flow driven form, data structure organize form. All of this is accomplished by data transfer between the various functions written in a scripting language. In computers, form is represented by data. Designers achieve design goals through 'design' code while the code records the thought process of the designer. The design process of the human brain is no longer a black-box operation.

Therefore, the parametric thinking schema can be understood as a process of integrating abstract thinking, mathematical thinking and algorithm thinking in order to realize the design goal of organic automation under the guidance of design knowledge.

3.2 Parametric design process

Whether there is a specific thinking process in parametric design, there is no definite conclusion yet[12]. However, no matter what type of design has its own general design process. Figure 2 is a typical parametric design thinking process. First of all, consider concepts and ideas based on customer needs and design tasks, and present them in sketches, text, or data. Secondly, designers constantly abstract and digitizes ideas and concepts, explore the geometric logic rules, and include evaluation rules[13]. Gradually, designer establish an associative set of algorithmic rules and data structure. In the third step, the designer must standardize all parameters, including the definition, coding, and naming of the parameters, and further clarify the relationship between the design input and the design response (design output)[3]. Further, designers need to consider the internal data stream transfer parameters to form a control parameter of the organic system. Step Four: designer writes the script code in the script environment according to the algorithms, rules and data structure, runs and debugs the program, and checks the design response. Finally, the designer evaluates the output and communicates with the customer to provide timely feedback. However, the design is not a linear process, especially the process of parameterization. Modifying rules, algorithms, and code is a regular job.

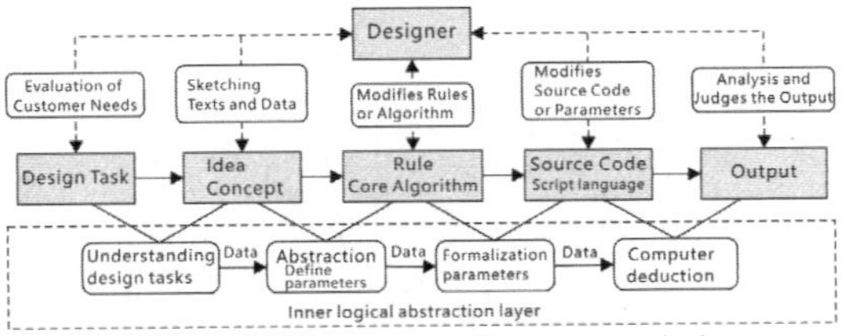

Figure 2. The process of parametric design.

3.3 Parametric design tool and scripts

The core work of parametric design is algorithm research and programming. The design of parametric digital form by programming technology requires graphic design platform and script environment. For example, CorelDraw is a graphic design platform, VBA can be used as a scripting language. However, this is not a secondary development in the general sense, which is a branch or direction of design method and design technology development. In script environment, form is driven by algorithm and code. Program statements and the definition of functions and classes can express the form logic construction process[14].

Grasshopper is the most popular parametric design tool, and is a visual scripting language. It has been built into Rhino6.0. Grasshopper itself supports multiple scripting languages such as Python, C#, and VB. It is often used in architecture design, industrial design, jewelry and so on. Illustrator supports multiple scripting environments (VB, JavaScript, AppleScript). Processing is an extension of the Java language, which can be used for visual communication design, interactive media art design, and information visualization[15], such as the logo designed by the Danish design studio NR2154 for United Nations Climate Change Conference in Copenhagen. Mathematica and Matlab can be used for the calculation of parametric form design[16]. The features of parametric tools and scripts are listed in Table 1.

Table 1. Tools and scripts for parametric design.

Tools and scripts	Language type/ Futures	Scope of application
Rhino / Grasshopper /Python[14]	Visual scripting code / Code and model in parallel	Architecture/ Product etc.
CorelDRAW / VBA[17]	Macro scripting language	graphic design
Illustrator/ JavaScrip[18]	scripting language	graphic design
Processing (JavaScrip)[15]	Graphic design language	Interactive/Visual Art/Information Visualization
Mathematica (wolfram)[19]	symbolic language	2D/3D design calculation

The parametric algorithmic schema has been completely different from the traditional paper-based design schema. However, this does not mean that the designer must become a programmer, or that the programmer can replace the work of designer. In the process of parametric design, therefore, designers need to constantly balance programming techniques and the understanding of design knowledge [11].

4 The method of parametric logo design

As a typical form, the logo is the core of enterprise brand image. A good logo is both attractive and meaningful. It is an important bridge between the public and the company. The core steps of the parametric logo design based on the natural mode are as follows.

Firstly, designers must have a deep understanding of the culture, market environment and core values of the enterprise, and extract core demand and key visual elements [20].

Secondly, we need to find natural patterns that match the design requirements. The natural patterns that match the enterprise image can be crossed and merged in several natural patterns. For instance, symmetry and rotation can be fused with spiral pattern. After the match is successful, the visual constituent laws and associated logic of the selected natural patterns can be studied, especially the geometric logic relations. At this point, designer can initially define the parameter set of the logo form: $\{s_1, s_2, s_3, \ldots, s_n\}$.

Then, according to the geometrical logic relation and the form association logic, designers can construct the transformation rule of the form, and transform all the rules into the transform algorithm of the logo form. On the other hand, the overall image of the logo is also affected by other factors, such as proportion, location, text, etc. This requires the construction of some additional rules for systematic coordination. In addition, designers should define color control parameter set: $\{c_1, c_2, c_3, \ldots, c_n\}$ and color transformation rules based on the color design scheme of the logo and color space. In order to facilitate the color transformation and algorithm implementation, it is necessary to map the value range of the color space to the interval of [0, 1]. Sometimes, in order to show better results, it is necessary to associate the color parameters of the logo with the form parameters of the logo.

Finally, according to design requirements, we need to define the font control parameter set: $\{f_1, f_2, f_3, \ldots, f_n\}$ and font control rules.

The process of studying natural patterns is also the process of studying algorithms. Parametric form design is a process of parametric experiment. It constantly adjusts rules and modifies parameters to satisfy the visual demand of the customer based on design responses.

5 Case study

The design task from Gansu ZBloom Culture Media Co. Ltd. and its core philosophy: the culture spread to the

https://doi.org/10.1051/matecconf/201817601012

hearts of the people, the spirit of sustainable artisans. The spiral pattern is radially scattered from the center to the outside, implying the infinite transmission of the energy of cultural media, which coincided with the core philosophy of ZBloom Cultural Media. This case, therefore, applied a logarithmic spiral pattern to the parametric form design.

5.1 Logarithmic spiral pattern

Logarithmic spiral, also known as isometric spiral or growth spiral, is a self-similar spiral curve and it is a common pattern in nature. Logarithmic spiral was first described by Descartes and later extensively investigated by Jacob Bernoulli, who called it 'the marvelous spiral'[5]. The Fibonacci spiral also known as the 'golden spiral' in geometry. It is a special case of logarithmic spiral and is also the most perfect classic gold proportion in nature. The logo design of this case used a logarithmic spiral pattern which comes from Nautilus and seed head of sunflower (Figure 3).

The head of sunflower is spiral. Its seeds are Fibonacci spiral arrangement, and there are two groups of spiral in the opposite direction. This arrangement is described by any spiral, wherein the spiral of Archimedes easiest. The definition of Archimedes spiral line: $r(\theta)=a\theta$ (polar equation). Generally, there are 34 to 55 spiral lines from inside to outside. 34 and 55 are two consecutive numbers in the Fibonacci sequence.

Figure 3. The classical logarithmic spiral in nature: Seed head of sunflower and Nautilus (Wikipedia)

The polar coordinate definition of logarithmic spiral is

$$r(\theta) = ae^{b}\theta \tag{1}$$

where $a, b \in R$, and $a \neq 0$. In order to facilitate the implementation of the algorithm, the formula (1) must be converted into a parametric equation as shown in formula (2).

$$\begin{cases} x(t) = r(t)cos(t) = ae^{bt}cos(t) \\ y(t) = r(t)sin(t) = ae^{bt}sin(t) \end{cases} \tag{2}$$

5.2 The control rules of form and color

The parametric design of the logo includes three aspects: parametric form, parametric color, and parametric text. In this case, we used disks instead of sunflower seeds for parametric logo design.

The sine function was selected as the radius transformation function of disks. The radius changes with the number of disks, but the radius of the disk cannot be negative. So we defined the disk radius transformation function as shown in formula (3).

$$\text{Disks\_Radius}(n) = \begin{cases} a\sin(bn) + c & \text{if } n \geq 0 \\ 0 & \text{if } n < 0 \end{cases} \tag{3}$$

where a, b and c are positive real numbers, and a ≤ c. The independent variable n is the number of disks, $n \in [0,+\infty)$. The function image is shown in Figure 4.

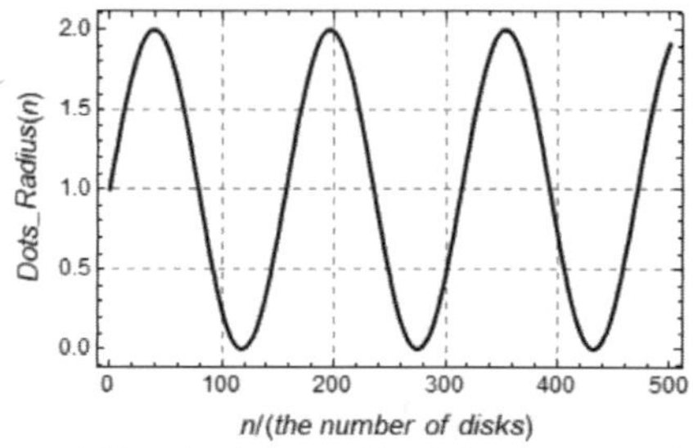

Figure 4. Function image of the disks radius transform.

RGB, HLV, CMKY and other color spaces can be parameterized by logo colour. The value of the color space was converted to [0, 1] according to the script environment and programming needs. Therefore, the color transformation function can be defined by the hyperbolic tangent function, which is the quotient of the hyperbolic sine and the hyperbolic cosine. Its definition process is as follows:

$$\sinh(x) = (e^{x}-e^{-x})/2 \tag{4}$$

$$\cosh(x) = (e^{x}+e^{-x})/2 \tag{5}$$

$$\tanh(x)=\sinh(x)/\cosh(x) = (e^{x}-e^{-x})/(e^{x}+e^{-x}) \tag{6}$$

From the formula (6), we have $x \in (-\infty,+\infty)$ and $\tanh(x) \in (-1,+1)$. But the color values cannot be negative. Therefore, we defined the following function:

$$\text{Color\_Transform}(n) = \begin{cases} \tanh(kn) & \text{if } n \geq 0 \\ 0 & \text{if } n < 0 \end{cases} \tag{7}$$

where $k \in R^{+}$, $n \in [0,+\infty)$, and the independent variable n is the number of disks. The value of constant k determines the quality of the color transformation. The process of the color change is shown in figure 5.

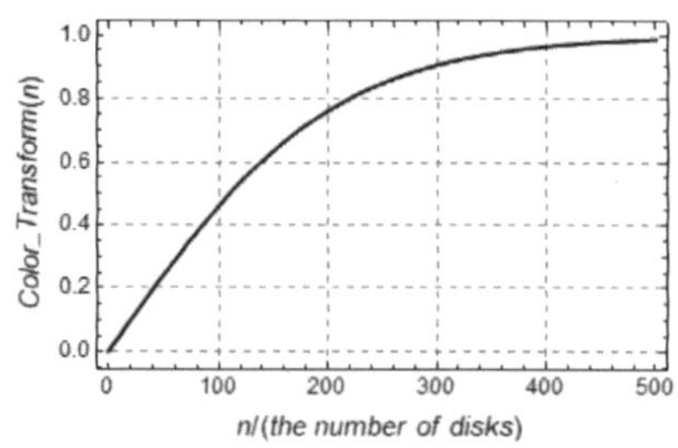

Figure 5. Function image of color transformation.

The combination of the blending colour algorithm and the color transformation function can present multicolour nonlinear gradient of the color design. In this case, the mixture of the three colors is defined as the color scheme of the logo.

5.3 Core algorithm

Firstly, the logarithmic spiral arrangement of disks is implemented according to formula (2), where the parameters are the radius and the angle. [0, a + c] is the domain of the radius changes of disks, where a and c are constants in equation (3). [0°, 360°] is the domain of angle changes. Secondly, according to the formula (3) to achieve the control algorithm of the change of disks radius, the range of the number of disks is [0, N], where N is a constant. The constant N is determined according to the design response and can be modified at any time. Thirdly, three color nonlinear gradient design is achieved by the blending colour algorithm and the formula (7). The color change of the logo with the number of disks n change. Finally, we can achieve the function of calling and selecting fonts by calling the standard font of the Window system and the Font library of the script environment.

5.4 The generator of parametric logo design

This article developed a generator of parametric logo design (Figure 6) with Wolfram language in mathematica for Gansu ZBloom Cultural Media. The left side of the logo generator interface is the parameter control bar of the logo, and the right side is the logo browser. The form parameters of the logo includes four parameters: the angle, the radius of disks, the number of disks, and the size of the logo image.

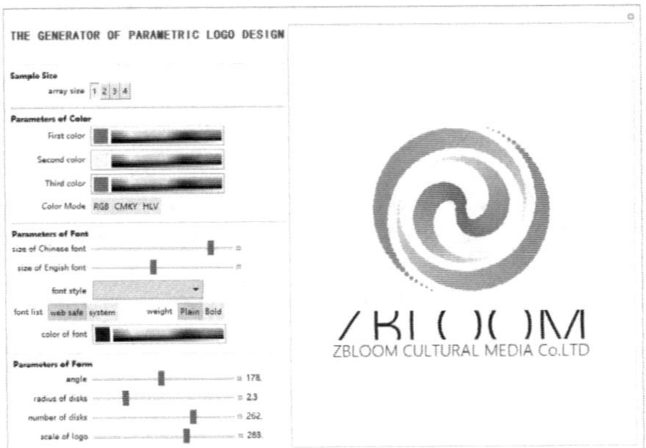

Figure 6. The generator of the parametric logo design.

Design results in Figure 7 selected out by the designers, which were selected in the first round. They were designed by the logo generator under different parameter values. The parameter values are shown in Table 2. Figure 7(c) was selected as the logo for the ZBloom Cultural Media judged by a evaluation group.

(a) **(b)** **(c)** **(d)**

Figure 7. The forms of logo in different parameters.

Table 2. Parameters of the logo form

Parameters	angle	Min radius Max radius	Number of disks	Image size	Color value (RGB)
(a)	2.3	0.1 1.75	271	390^2	(255, 0, 50) (230, 255, 30) (20, 128, 155)
(b)	119	0.31 3.11	261	272^2	(15, 128, 253) (250, 255, 15) (255, 0, 50)
(c)	178.33	0.25 5.41	164	374^2	(162, 0, 0) (255, 255, 23) (10, 150, 210)
(d)	195	0.6 3.5	165	348^2	(0, 128, 255) (255, 255, 10) (240, 20, 45)

6 Conclusions

Natural patterns has provided an unlimited source of design and can be effectively applied to form design. Parametric design can effectively enrich the content of form design. Finding the mathematical logic behind natural patterns has been a key step. The combination of natural patterns and parametric design technology will open up new design schema and methods for form design. This has been a fusion of aesthetics and technology. Parametric languages and scripting techniques will have an unprecedented impact on design thinking. Designers has been required to constantly update their knowledge structure. Parametric design has required designers to respect the mathematical and logical laws of the scripting environment. It has been difficult for designers to anticipate design results in a scripting environment. The combination of natural patterns and parametric thinking has prompted the form design becoming an generative system of organic closed-loop from design requirements to design results.

The next work of this article will study the parametric design method of complex product form based on natural patterns.

Acknowledgments

The project is sponsored by National Natural Science Foundation of China (51465037) and Hongliu Outstanding Talent Development Program of Lanzhou University of Technology (201406). In addition, Zbloom Culture Media also provided support for this project.

References

1. WJ Yue. The natural theorem of art and design. Shanghai Art & Crafts, 1, 82-83 (2011)

2. J Chen. Research and practice of product design based on parameterization. Art Journal, 3, 111-115 (2015)
3. WG Xu. Parametric design and algorithm generating. World Architecture, 6, 110-111 (2011)
4. DL Ma. *A study on Fibonacci's Liber Abaci* (PhD thesis). (ShangHai Jiao Tong University, Shanghai, 2009)
5. S Hildebrandt, A.J Tromba, S Sheng. *The Parsimonius Universe*. (ShangHai Education Press, Shanghai, 2004)
6. M Macnab, WB Fan. *Design by nature: using universal forms and principles in design* (China Machine Press, Beijing, 2013)
7. AM Turing. The chemical basis of morphogenesis. 1953. Bull Math Biol, **52**,153-197(1990)
8. A Lindenmayer. Mathematical models for cellular interactions in development. Journal of Theoretical Biology, **18**, 3, 280-315 (1968)
9. CRB Hernandez. Thinking parametric design: introducing parametric Gaudi. Design Studies, **27**, 3, 309-324 (2006)
10. R Woodbury. *Elements of Parametric Design* (Routledge, New York, 2010)
11. R Oxman, N Gu. Theories and Models of Parametric Design Thinking. eCAADe 33, **2**, 477-482 (2015)
12. R Oxman. Thinking difference: Theories and models of parametric design thinking. Design Studies, **52**, 4-39 (2017)
13. YC Liu. Parametric Design: Method, Thinking Strategy and Framework. Architecture Technique, Z1, 34-37 (2011)
14. RQ Bao. *Parametric Logic Design Process* (Phoenix Science Press, Nanjing , 2015)
15. L Tan. Application Research of Code Art Based on Processing. Art & Design, **2**, 104-105 (2012)
16. JN Su, JH Wu, Y Liu, QW Zhang. Research on 3D Product Shape Merging Technology Based on Spherical Harmonic Map. Journal of Graphics, **35**, 3, 417-422 (2014)
17. XJ Liu, YY Wu. The Research on Rapid Design of Fan Products by Computer-Aided Intelligence. Packaging Engineering, 10, 42-45+56 (2013)
18. M O'Neill, A Brabazon. Evolving a logo design using Lindenmayer systems, Postscript & Grammatical Evolution. Evolutionary Computation. IEEE, 3788-3794 (2008)
19. S Wolfram. *An Elementary Introduction to the Wolfram Language* (Wolfram Media Inc, Champaign, 2016)
20. DQ Jin. *The Brand Design 100+1* (Peking University Press, Beijing, 2017)

MATEC Web of Conferences **176**, 01013 (2018)
IFID 2018
https://doi.org/10.1051/matecconf/201817601013

Research and Application of Rubber Tree Quantitative Fertilization System Control Based on PLC

Yeqin Wang[1], Yuan Zhang[1*], Yiguo Deng[1*], Lijiao Wei [1],and Shengli Liu [1]

[1] Institute of Agricultural Machinery, Chinese Academy of Tropical Agricultural Sciences, China

Abstract. In this paper, the quantitative control method and system control process of the natural rubber forest quantitative fertilization system are introduced on the basis of the demand for the quantitative fertilization of natural rubber forest and the application process of the rubber forest fertilizing machine. The selection of PLC, frequency converter type selection and software design process are described in detail.

1 Introduction

In recent years, with the development of Internet technologies, computer technologies, and modern electronic information technologies, our country's agriculture has slowly been produced from traditional agricultural methods to precision agriculture.Quantitative fertilization is an important part of precision agriculture and has achieved significant economic and social benefits abroad. The research on quantitative implementation technology of rubber forest in China started relatively late. The development of fertilization control system for application of granular fertilizer or powdered fertilizer in China is not yet mature, and the degree of automation is relatively low. Therefore, according to the practical needs of fertilizing the trenches for rubber trees, a quantitative fertilizer application system for rubber fields was developed based on the existing fertilizer applicators.

2 Composition of quantitative fertilization system

Quantitative fertilization system hardware is to select the fertilizer with the disk rotation, row fertilizer baffle-type fertilizer, through the use of motor driven worm gear reducer to the power to the fertilizer turntable to achieve fertilization[1]. Quantitative fertiliser machine row fertilizer structure is shown in Figure 1, from the fertilizer barrel, fertilizer turntable, row fat hopper, row fertilizer baffle, worm gear reducer, motor, level sensor, speed sensor, fertilizer pipe, weighing sensor, etc. composition.

For quantitative fertilization control, the flow rate of the fertilizer is automatically calculated and the speed of the motor is adjusted according to the input weight and time of the row of fertilizer to achieve the set flow rate requirement. The fertilizing structure of the quantitative fertilization system is shown in Figure 1. Quantitative fertilization system gives the total weight and time of fertilization and power up, the motor starts to rotate, the microprocessor controls the motor speed according to the current operation; the motor rotates and transmits the power to the worm gear reducer worm gear; the reducer transmits power to the flange Fertilizer turntable. During the rotation of the fertilizer turntable, the fertilizer in the fertilizer tank is guided to the edge of the fertilizer turntable by the action of its own gravity; Fertilizer at the

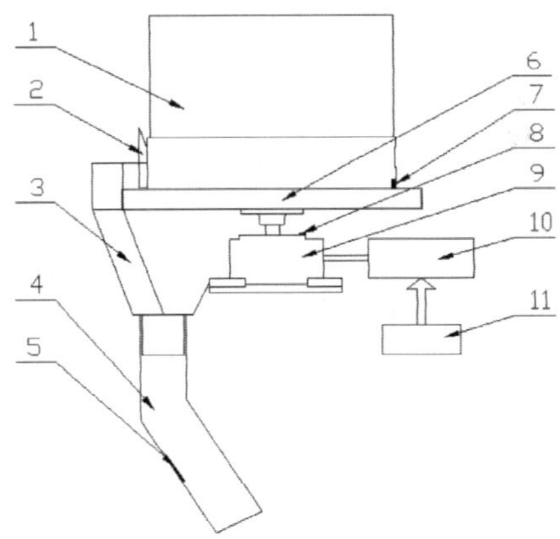

1. Fertilizer barrel; 2. Composting baffle; 3. Composting hopper; 4. Row fertilizer tube; 5. Load cell 6. Fertilizer turntable; 7. Level sensor 8. Speed sensor; 9. Worm gear reducer 10. Motor; 11. Inverter

Figure 1. Fertilizer system structure schematic

edge of the fertilizer turntable is scraped by a row of fat-retaining baffles into a row of fat hoppers; a load cell is weighed through a fat-feeding tube; a load cell outputs a voltage signal according to the magnitude of the applied force, and is amplified by the transmitter to output a measurement level signal proportional to the flow rate of the fertilizer.The signal is sent to the interface of the

*Corresponding author: Yeqin Wang: 441213852@qq.com

upper computer. After sampling and converted into a flow signal, the current flow value is displayed on the upper computer. At the same time, the flow signal is sent to the PLC interface and compared with the ratio of the total fertilization weight and time set by the upper computer, and then the adjustment operation is performed. The control amount is sent to the inverter to change the output value of the inverter. Change the speed of the drive motor. Adjust the given amount and make it equal to the set value to complete the quantitative fertilization process.

Flow is the weight of fertilizer that passes through the fertilizer pipe at a certain time. The weighing sensor is the instantaneous flow, the upper computer gives the ratio of the average flow rate, that is, the ratio of the total weight to the time, and the two are deviated in the real-time measurement. In the actual control of the flow, the most widely used PID regulation is used in the industrial control. According to the flow deviation, the control quantity is controlled by the proportion, the integral and the differential calculation. The relation between the input and output (error) of the control quantity is expressed as follows in the time domain.

$$u(t) = k\left[e(t) + \frac{1}{T}\int_0^t e(t)d(t) + \frac{Hde(t)}{dt}\right]$$

In the formula, e(t) denotes the error that is the controller input; u(t) is the controller output; k is the proportional coefficient; T is the integral time constant; H is the derivative time constant. Figure 2 shows the system flow PID closed-loop regulation structure. When the fertilization process is automatically adjusted, according to the fertilization requirements, the total amount of fertilizer and the time to adjust the fertilization flow are set by the upper computer. Flow measurement control is a combination of measurement deviation and frequency control. It has the advantages of simple structure, good stability, reliable operation and easy adjustment.

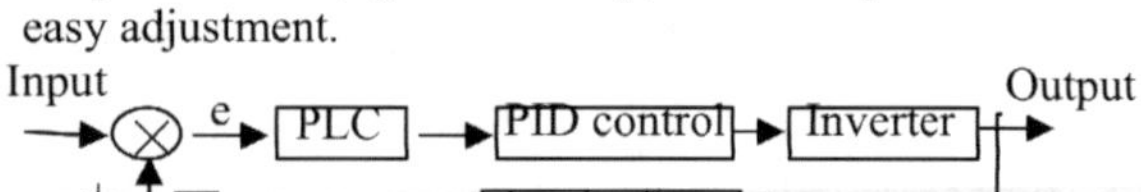

Figure 2. Flow PID closed-loop regulation

3 System control process

When the system begins to work, first step of the system program is initialized, and the total amount and time of input fertilization are set through the upper computer or the touch screen to check whether the fertilizer barrel has fertilizer material. If there is no fertilizer, fertilizer is sent to the fertilizer barrel, the quantitative fertilizer system is started, the weighing sensor is weighed and measured in real time, and the CPU calculates the real-time flow and the accumulated flow. If there is a deviation between the set flow and the actual flow, the regulator compares the deviation of the set value from the actual flow according to the system control requirements. The PID adjustment changes the output signal to control the speed adjustment of the inverter to the DC motor, thereby realizing constant flow control[2]. The main program control flow of the system is shown in Figure 3.

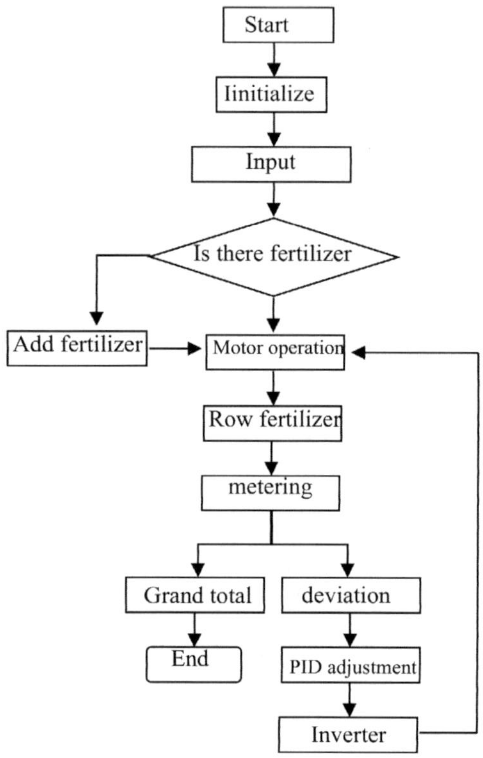

Figure 3. Control flow chart

4 PLC control system hardware settings

Quantitative fertilization in the system is controlled by the PLC and the upper computer. The system consists of a speed sensor, a load cell, and a frequency converter that form the controlled object. The start and stop of the motor is controlled by the switch quantity. The PLC digital output signal is used as the input signal of the control terminal of the frequency converter. After the frequency converter modulates and outputs the high frequency pulse to the motor, the speed sensor measures the speed of the motor. The system requires 3 digital input signals, 5 digital input signals and 5 digital output signals. The total number of I/O points is 13.

4.1 PLC selection Inverter selection

Since the number of I/O points of the system controlled object does not exceed 16 and the system process requirements, scanning speed, self-diagnosis function, etc., Mitsubishi FX2N-48 is selected. In addition to meeting the design requirements, the selected PLC has a certain margin[3]. Mitsubishi FX series can be connected to the expansion module in the basic unit, can be a flexible combination of 16-256 points input and output. It can be choosed 16/32/48/64/80/128-point host; can be used the minimum expansion module 8 points to expand, it can freely be choosed according to the power supply and output form[4]. Program capacity built-in 8k step can be expanded to 16k steps.

4.2 Inverter selection

The frequency converter is the hardware of the actuator of the quantitative fertilization system. It changes the frequency of the motor by changing its frequency, and thus changed the rotational speed of the row of fertilizer. The choice of frequency converter must be selected based on the power and current of the motor. According to the rated power of the drive motor of the fertilizer applicator 2KW, rated voltage 380V, speed 720r/min, FR-A540 series inverter, select the speed range 120 ~ 1200r/min. According to quantitative fertilization production process requirements for PID control[5].

5 Software design of PLC control system

This system control mainly includes PLC control program, PC control program and communication program. PLC control program as a lower computer control, the entire control system data acquisition and processing has an important role. It accepts external switch signals (buttons, relay contacts), collects speed data and weight data to determine the current system status and output signals to control contactors, relays and other devices to complete the corresponding control tasks. In addition, another important task is to accept the control commands of the PC (upper computer) for automatic quantitative control. The Mitsubishi PLC control program is divided into a main program and 6 subroutines, and the proportional integral derivative control program in the subroutine is the core of the quantitative fertilization system. The proportional integral derivative control command PID is used for analog closed-loop control, [S1·][S2·] each use a data register, [S1·] is used to store the set target value, [S2·] is used to set the current value to be measured , [S3·] is the first address defined by the user for the PID instruction. The range is D0 to D7975, and 25 continuous data registers starting from [S3·] are required, where [S3·]~[S3·] + 6 Set the control parameters[6]. [D·] uses a separate data register to store the output value. When the program is executed, the result of the operation is stored in [D·]. The function of PID instruction is to calculate the adjustment value according to PID algorithm after receiving one input data.

6 Conclusion

The system adopts the method of PLC control and PID adjustment to design a quantitative fertilization system. Through logical judgment, the speed of the variable worm gear reducer is adjusted to achieve a quantitative effect of fertilization, and the intelligence level of fertilization operations and the accuracy of fertilization are improved.

Acknowledgements

This work was financially supported by the Natural Science Foundation of Hainan Provincial(518QN279); Central Public-interest Scientific Institution Basal Research Fund for Chinese Academy of Tropical Agricultural Sciences(1630132017003);Public Welfare Research and Capacity Building of Guangdong Province (2017A02028012);2017 provincial agricultural development and rural work special "natural rubber processing of key technologies in Thailand application"(Yue Nongji [2017] No.39)and Collaborative innovation and platform environment construction special of Guangdong Province (2017A040406003).

I would like to thank the members of the research group for their selfless help, especially the communication author Zhang Yuan and Deng Yiguo,and the guangba farms in Hainan Province for the project test of strong support.

REFERENCES

1. Qin Chaomin, Liu Junhui. Study Design of Manure Distribution Parts for Centrifugal Manure Spreader[J]. Journal of Agricultural Mechanization Research, 2006,(10):100-102.
2. Sun Xiaoquan, Qian Shaoming. Design and Implementation of PID Controller Based on PLC[J]. Applied Science and Technology, 2008, 35(6):29-32

3. Wang Guohai, programmable controller and its application [M]. Beijing: China Labor Social Security Press, 2007:204
4. Yan Yingfu. PLC Practical Guide [M] Beijing: Beijing Normal University Press, 2011: 167-168
5. MITSUBISHI Mitsubishi FR-A540 Series Inverter Manual
6. Mitsubishi Automation Engineering Co., Ltd. Programmable Controller FX2N User's Manual [M]. Shanghai: Mitsubishi Automation Engineering Corporation, 2005.

Research on the Washing Machine Design Improvement of Specific Consumption Groups

Meina Wang[1,a]

[1] Sichuan University Jinjiang College, Chengdu, Sichuan, China

Abstract. This research focuses on the "Improved Product R&D Project" of Sichuan Chaochen Electric Co., Ltd, analyzing its market status from the life style of its main consumer groups, namely users of the secondary and tertiary markets. Through field observation and in-depth interview methods, the user's daily habits and demands for washing machines are closely looked into. Then the research comes up with some design elements aiming at the low-end markets, and also offers the corresponding specific design proposal. On this basis, it provides new ideas and fresh design methods for the appearance improvements of the secondary and tertiary market washing machines, from angels of external morphology, human-computer interaction and concept trends etc, thus in hopes of being referential to the actual product improvements of the mid-and-low-end washing machine markets.

1 Introduction

With the continuous improvement of people's living standards in the secondary and tertiary markets and the gradual saturation of the household appliance market in the first-tier cities, the household appliance companies would be focus on strategic layouts, because of the development of secondary and tertiary markets . For one thing, users in this market want household appliances to change their lives and improve their quality of life. For another thing, the lack of user-friendly household appliance designs leads to great frustration in their daily use. Therefore, the improvement of the household appliance designs in the secondary and tertiary markets， to make them more humane， is a manifestation of respect and concern for people of different living standards and levels.

2 Research Background

The survey has found out that there are significant differences in the living environment, economic conditions, education levels, and living habits between users in the mid-and-low-end markets and those in the first-tier cities, which leads to different aesthetic characteristics, perceptions, and preferences. However, currently, many household electrical appliance companies directly cut the price of those out-products from the first-tier cities and put them into these secondary and tertiary markets. This is an irresponsible approach that lacks humanistic care. The products needed in these markets should never simply be the "reduced version" but products that have core functions, in fit with the operating environment, well meet quality requirements, and are practical and cost-effective. Therefore, the improvement and optimization of household appliance product designs in the secondary and tertiary markets is imminent.

Although the Chinese washing machine market starts late, it has developed rapidly, and is currently at a mature stage. Being faced with an excess capacity and the gradual saturation in urban markets, many washing machine companies exploit the secondary and tertiary markets as their strategic goal. According to the National Information Center's statistic data, sales of major washing machine companies in these markets have increased significantly in recent years. For example, the sales of Haier washing machines in this market have maintained a growth rate of over 40% for three consecutive years; Little Swan enjoys a growth rate of up to 300%, compared with last year; that of Sanyo Washing Machine increased by more than 80% year-on-yea; and sales of Panasonic Washing Machine in this market grow by 20%. The explosive growth of secondary and tertiary market's washing machine sales allows the companies to notice the huge potential of this market. Meanwhile, Chinese Government's Consumer Electronics Subsidy Program (Home Appliances to the Countryside) is stimulating the release of consumer energy in the secondary and tertiary markets. The sinking of key enterprise's products and sales channels has also ensured the realization of this kind of consumer enthusiasm.

This research focuses on the "Improved Product R&D Project" of Sichuan Chaochen Electric Co., Ltd, analyzing its market status from the life style of its main consumer groups, namely users of the secondary and tertiary markets. Through questionnaires, field visits and in-depth interview methods, the user's daily habits and demands for washing machines are closely looked into. It then comes up with some design elements aiming at the low-end markets, providing a reference for improved design and

* Corresponding author: Meina Wang [a]Email Address: cimona@126.com

new product development in those markets.

3 Market Research Result Analysis

In the early stage of market research, questionnaire was mainly adopted, by dividing the samples into 10 research groups and independently choosing consumers from residential areas, supermarkets and electronic stores, meanwhile ensuring the sample number of each group is ≥100.

In addition with the sales data provided by the marketing department of Chaochen Company, the analysis of the survey results found out that in the secondary and tertiary cities, washing machines with large capacity is more popular. The first-time consumer as well as those households that owns multiple numbers of washing machines usually choose the ones of 4-6kg. And for the second-time buyers who need one for upgrading, the common option is a big capacity washing machine of 7-8kg or above, as in Table 1.

Table 1. The Survey Results of the Washing Machine Capacity Choices

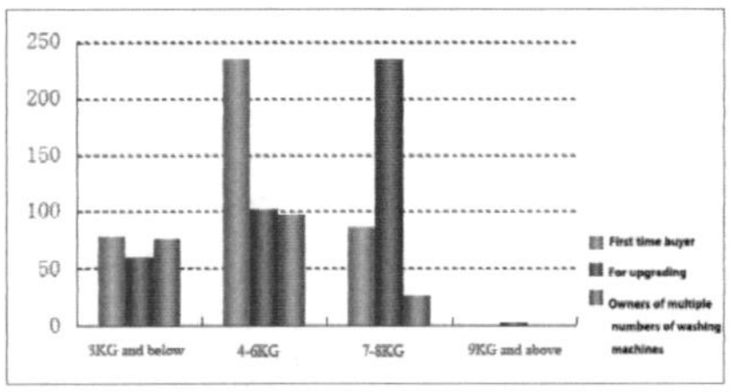

The survey of human-computer interaction interfaces reveals that users prefer touch screen operation interfaces. However, the touch screen interfaces are not always visualized. Along with the gradual increasement of washing machine functions, the most troublesome problem for the first time users is the lack of direct visual understanding of operational approach. Therefore, this design proposal attempts to design the operation interface as a soft interface—a touch-screen operation interface, focusing on improving the straightforwardness of the operation, enhancing the intelligence of the washing machine, and adopting the fuzzy processing of one simple touch as much as possible.

Besides, through field observation and user interviews, it is noticed that different positioning of the washing machines may sometimes leads to problems of moist or overlighting, and that some washing machines are too cumbersome to move or difficult to clean. Those find-outs have provided us with necessary information for our subsequent designs.

4 Specific Research and Research Results

After analyzing and summarizing the results of market research and research on people's life forms, we found that the following design elements can effectively guide this washing machine improved design practice.

4.1 Starting from the human-computer interaction interface, simplify the interface and the button, highlighting humanization design.

Low-end users usually cannot tolerate complicated operations. And the ease of use design should be visualized with easy-to-understand interface operation mode, realizing human-computer interaction to provide with a humanized design.

Figure 1. Human-machine interface of washing machines respectively under non-operating and working conditions

In this project design proposal, Plan One: "geometry" is to make innovative attempts on the interface and operation modes, as shown in Figure 1. This design makes full use of the oversized panel of a fully automatic washing machine, combined with current flat panel technology, to make the laundry process more joyful. At the same time, in design of the icon, the existing text-based format is abolished, being replaced by large icons with greater visibility, and one-click intelligent processing. In doing so, on the one hand, it facilitates visually impaired middle-aged and elderly people. On the other hand, it allows users to operate easily without instruction books, and is particularly suitable for consumer groups with low education levels in the middle-and-low-end markets.

Although the low-end market has limited consumption capacity, still its consumers eager to enjoy the convenience brought by high technology. Along with the rapid development of science and technology, the technical costs have been reduced greatly. According to the company's R&D (Research and Development) to production time cycle, for a product that would be put in market 3-5 years later, its design must fit into the future trend.

4.2 Being of high quality and low cost, the appearance of traditional washing machines should be improved with its cost been well controlled.

High-quality with low-cost is widely expected, especially by the low-end users. The designers found that with the stretching of lines and patches, the washing machine would appear more capaciousness without enlarging the inner cylinder. Such a tiny skill may increase the washing machine sales, while not causing any substantial increase in costs. This proposal has been unanimously approved by the Research and Development Department of Chaochen

Company.

4.2.1 Rejuvenate the traditional semi-automatic washing machine

While the market has gradually been occupied by the automatic washing machines, the semi-automatic washing machines survive with their own unique features. Compared with fully automatic washing machines, semi-automatic double-cylinder washing machines, although cannot realize one-button operation function, need less water, and the three functions of washing, rinsing and dehydration can be freely selected according to needs, and the detergent can also be reduced if needed. Therefore, in the secondary and tertiary markets, there are still many consumers who choose semi-automatic twin-cylinder washing machines. In order to maintain its competitive advantage of low-cost and manual-selective capacity, this time's design will focus on the appearance improvement, and most prominently on the main cover.

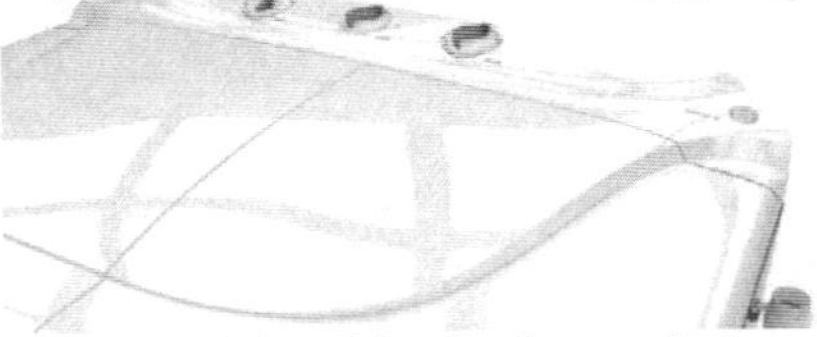

Figure 2. Overall plan of the "Yun" two-cylinder washing machine and its upper cover design details

Plan Two. The "Yun" washing machine chooses sea waves as its theme, having its upper cover been designed in curve, featuring the mobility of water, as in Figure 2. As for the operation area, integrated processing is performed, using level difference to segment each zone. Besides, innovation has been made on the button design, taking "wave" as its theme in modeling and texture. Thus, the washing machine seems more stylish, dispelling a sense of rigid simplification usually felt in low-end products. This represents humanistic care for the consumers' inner feeling. In addition, the smooth lines make the upper cover mellow and full, and it seems to be more solid, raising the customer's satisfaction while purchasing.

4.2.2 Create visual illusion of a large capacity without really changing the inner diameter of the cylinder, having the cost of mould in control.

Due to cost control restrictions, consumer preferences and the particularity of surroundings, automatic washing machines launched in the second and tertiary market are mostly pulsator type instead of roller ones. However, the space for mold shape improvement of the washing machine top cover is very limited. How to do the large-capacity designs for such products?

Mosaic gives people the feeling of delicacy and animation, with layers of rich colors. The integral treatment of the washing machine top cover may provide a sense of visual expansion. But the flat and monotonous design still gives customers bad user experiences. In such cases, the designer can make use of the active mosaic to add joy and avoid monotony, taking diverse mosaic display forms for different working modes. As shown in Figure 3.

Figure 3. Use the mosaic display to add joy

Also, the designer may get rid of the conventional pulsator washing machine design of separating the console and the cover plate. After integration, hide the control button and the circuit under the large cover plate. Such treatment may give the consumers the impression of a large capacity, with high quality and low cost, thus enhance their purchasing desire. This design concept and tactic has been approved in the marketing department of Chaochen company.

4.3 Conceptual Design Based on New Energy Technology

Along with the intensification of traditional energy crisis and the prominent pollution problems, the future technology would inevitably highlight natural clean energy or new energy technologies. Thus the dynamic design of washing machines would certainly follow the trend. It is found through the market research that some consumers prefer to use washing machines in the open yard. There comes this program of conceptual design on the utilization of solar energy. Also, it offers some trend forecasting options for the company's future product development.

The design of this washing machine adopts a large surface, smooth overall lines and chrome-plate frame, featuring its simple and elegant style, besides offering a sense of science and technology. There are hidden handles on its side to preserve the washing machines' integrated appearance. General design is adopted for its shell, and there are multiple colors available for the consumers to choose. The solar panel is on the outer surface to maximize the solar energy absorption, as well as its transforming into electrical energy storage. In addition, this washing machine is a home appliance product supported by Internet to Things technology. Manufacturers provide APP software application for users to download on their smart mobile terminals. Therefore this intelligentize design reduces the hardware cost as for remote-controller.

5 Conclusion

Design is a re-recognition and re-creation of artificial

objects. The key point of this scientific research is to shift the perspective of industrial design from the focus on things to the concern for relationships between things and people's behavior. Due to the specific environmental factors, human factors, habits, and cognition of the washing machine users in the secondary and tertiary markets, the external appearance, human-computer interaction, and concept trends must be different during design process. Some of the design elements proposed this time have been effectively applied in the actual product designs, and well approved by relevant developers in the company. I hope these design elements can provide references to the washing machine design improvement in the mid-and-low-end market.

Acknowledgment

Funded Program. Young teacher research fund project of Sichuan University Jinjiang College.
Item number: 12110106

References

1. Li Binbin. Design Psychology. *Beijing: China Light Industry Press*, (2009)
2. Xiong Xiqiu, Jiang Wenping. Research on Design of Smart Home Control Panel Based on Interactive Experience. [J] Mechanical Design, (2014)
3. Liu Jingyu. Conceptual Analysis of Product Appearance Design. M D, **02**(2013).
4. Yu Dongjiu, Feng Yajuan. Consumer-oriented Product Design Research [J] Mechanical design and manufacturing, (2007)
5. Mo Lian. Research on Product Design Method Based on Life Style. [J] Mechanical Design, (2013)
6. Lin Liang. Analysis of ergonomic application points in product modeling design, V E,**36**(2015) .
7. Yu Wenjun, Ling Zhihao. Research on the Internet of Things Smart Home System . [J] Automated Instrument.(2011)
8. Huang Sheng, Zhang Linghao. Research on VUX System Design Based on the Users' Visual Experience of Drum Washing Machines' Hard Interface, *Chongqing: Packaging Engineering*, (2015)
9. Plummer Jospeh T.The concept and application of lifestyle segmentation [J]Journal of Marketing, (1974)

Design and Implementation of Training Management Software for General Simulation Training System

Wei Xiang[1,*], Sun Chunsheng[1], and Dong Yanhong[1]

[1]Navy Submarine Academy, Qingdao 266199, Shandong Province, China

Abstract. The common simulation training system realizes the common design of hardware and software, and also increases the difficulty of group training management. In order to solve the problem of flexible group training of multiple training modes for general simulation training system of a certain type of naval combat system, this paper puts forward a formal description method of group training resources and group training programs based on an in-depth analysis of training management requirements. Design and implementation of a general simulation training system training management software.

1 Introduction

With the continuous development of simulation technology, the development of general simulator or simulation training system suitable for specific fields has played an important role in personnel training, playing a significant economic and social benefits [1-3]. Universal simulation training system to achieve a common hardware and software design[4-8], but also increased the difficulty of group training management.

The authors recently developed a general warship combat simulation training system, including four training platforms and three kinds of simulation software, which can realize three types of training modes, such as single professional multi-person training, multi-professional multi-person training, and whole system cooperative training.

In the process of development, a flexible group training management software based on group training resources and group training programs was designed and implemented. Practice has proved that the software can better solve the multi-mode flexible group training problem of general simulation training system.

2 A generic simulation training system group training resources

2.1 Hardware group training resources

Hardware group training resources mainly refers to various types of training platform used to meet the group training staff and trainee use. According to the structure and function of each training station, it can be divided into four types: universal teaching console, general virtual simulation console, general analog standard console and special analog console. Among them, the general virtual simulation console and general analog standard control console can run different professional equipment simulation software, so as to achieve different professional training functions.

Universal teaching console is used to run all kinds of teaching control software, from the control cabinet, mainframe, monitors, LCD electronic signage, keyboard and mouse, voice Mike interface and so on. General virtual simulation console used to run the professional equipment of the virtual simulation software, the control cabinet, mainframe, monitors, LCD electronic signage, keyboard and mouse components.The general analog standard console is used to realize the display and console simulation function of the electronic equipment, which is composed of cabinet, display, host, control panel, LCD electronic signboard and so on.The special analog console is mainly used to simulate the non-standard professional equipment. The special analog cabinet has no unified standard structure, which is consistent with the corresponding professional equipment's exterior structure.

2.2 Software group training resources

Software group training resources mainly refers to the various types of software running in the hardware platform. According to the function can be divided into teaching and control software, virtual simulation software, simulation software, three categories.

The teaching and control software is installed in the host of the general education console. It is used for online management of whole system equipment, training and setting of roles and functions, training director control, training operation process monitoring, training record and evaluation, training place audio-video monitoring and other functions. The virtual simulation software is installed and run on the host of the general virtual simulation platform, and simulates the appearance and operation flow of the corresponding

*Corresponding author: weix826@aliyun.com

equipment through software, and realizes the simulation of the equipment function and performance through the simulation model. The simulation software is installed and run on a common analog standard control console and a dedicated analog control console. The simulation signal is received according to the operation signal of the analog table component, and is calculated according to the simulation model. The display part of the analog table is driven to display the corresponding calculation result.

3 Group training management needs analysis

3.1 Group training mode

The common simulation training system for a certain type of warship operation system can realize three training modes including single-profession simultaneous multi-person training, multi-professional multi-person simultaneous training and system-wide collaborative training.

When organizing a single professional multi-person training at the same time, you need to configure and automatically start the virtual simulation platform, analog standard control console or the corresponding professional simulation software on the dedicated analog control console through the group training management software so as to achieve the same professional multi-person simultaneous training , A certain type of general combat training system for combat training system can achieve up to 36 cadets at the same time a professional training. In the organization of multi-professional and multi-people training at the same time, according to training needs through group training management software for the corresponding configuration, you can achieve any combination of multiple professional training at the same time. In the organization of system-wide collaborative training, all the professional equipment simulation software of the combat system needs to be activated through the configuration of the group training management software, and the information interaction among various professional simulation softwares is realized through the network so as to realize the system-wide collaborative training function of the combat system.

3.2 Group training resources allocation principles

In order to achieve different group training mode, it is necessary to assign corresponding teaching control software and simulation software to each training station through group training management software. Group training resource allocation refers to the group training needs to achieve the system hardware and software resource allocation process. The following principles need to be followed in the group training resource allocation process of the general simulation training system of a certain type of naval combat system.

1) The principle of pertinence. Group training resource allocation should be in accordance with the requirements of group training mode for each station assigned the appropriate software resources.

2) Integrity principle. When conducting system-wide collaborative training, you need to deploy a full suite of specialized equipment simulation software for your combat system.

3) The principle of feasibility. The software that each type of hardware platform can run is limited, so the resource allocation needs to consider the feasibility of the hardware platform. Universal teaching station can be assigned to run a variety of teaching control software, universal virtual simulation platform can be assigned to run a variety of virtual simulation software, universal analog standard console can be assigned to run a variety of standard console simulation software, dedicated analog console can be assigned to run the corresponding professional equipment simulation software.

4 Sets of training information description method

4.1 Group training resource description

Group training resources include system hardware resources and software resources. In order to implement flexible training management functions, all training resources need to be formally described. The definition of group training resource description is given below.

Definition 1: SimSub ships SimSub is made up of r model ships Sub, with independent functions and features that can be run alone.

$$SimSub=\{Sub_i,i=1,2,\ldots,r\} \tag{1}$$

Definition 2: A single type of sub-ship Sub is composed of s different professional analog equipment positions ProfessionE, in accordance with certain combinations to achieve naval cooperative training.

$$Sub=\{ProfessionE_i,i=1,2,\ldots,s\} \tag{2}$$

Definition 3: Single professional simulation equipment position ProfessionE is simulated by SimWay, equipment name EName, which type Type, equipment program ESoft.

$$ProfessionE=\{SimWay,Ename,Type,ESoft \tag{3}$$

According to the definition 1 design different types of ship configuration data, according to the definition 2 and the definition of 3 different types of equipment configuration data design. Finally, the ship configuration information and equipment configuration information generated by the combination of platform information description file.

4.2 Group training program description

Group training program description includes group training mode information, group training mode and equipment correspondence information as well as training equipment attribute information.

Definition 4: Group training mode The OrgTModel is composed of three training modes TModel, each training mode has an independent training function.

$$OrgTModel=\{TModel_i, i=1,2,3\} \quad (4)$$

Definition 5: Each training mode TModel is composed of n training equipment TE.

$$TModel=\{TE_i, i=1,2,\cdots,n\} \quad (5)$$

Definition 6: Each training equipment TE is composed of the host name of the simulator, SHost, the electronic nameplate access server name CName, the equipment name EName, the type of the equipment, and the equipment program ESoft.

$$TE=\{SHost, Cname, Ename, Type, ESoft \quad (6)$$

5 Training management software design

The main functions of the training management software include: reading the training station information configuration file, realizing the flexible configuration of the hardware and software resources, monitoring the network status in real time, and sending the station configuration information. The main interface of the software is shown in Fig. 1.

Fig.1 Training Management Software Interface

This article is based on object-oriented technology design training management software, using C ++ programming.

(1) The left tree view class CLeftView

This class is mainly used to complete the read, record, display group training resource information and hardware and software resource configuration operations, the main methods are ReadIniFile and DisposeE.

ReadIniFile method is used to read the station information configuration file and display the analog device. The input parameter is the location information profile path. The output parameter is an array of structures for all station information.

DisposeE method to configure the simulation device. Input parameters for analog devices and their related information. The output is a Boolean type that identifies whether the configuration was successful.

(2) List box view class CFormViewEx

This class is used to complete the reading, recording, display each group training configuration file information and send analog device information, the main method is ReadIniFile, SndOrder.

ReadIniFile method used to read the group training configuration file and display it in the interface. Input parameters for the group training configuration file path. The output parameter is an array of structures that record all the training configuration files.

(3) The main form of class CMainFrame

This class is used to complete the network connection and its detection, display station information and each group training configuration file information, the main method is HandleNetWork. This method realizes the network connection, the network receives the data.

6 Conclusion

In this paper, the software of group training management is designed and realized,which was based on the formal description method of group training resources and group training programs. The practice has proved that the software can solve the flexible group training problem of the general simulation training system. At the same time, the group training management solution is also applicable to other similar general simulation training systems.

References

1. CHEN Lei, WANG Song, ZHANG Feng. Demand Analysis of Universal Simulator [J] .Computer Science and Modernization, 2012 (8): 166-169.
2. Fan Cheng, Zhou An-dong, Yang Lu-gang.A universal simulator LCD display scheme design [J]. Computer and Digital Engineering, 2010,38 (5): 163-165.
3. ZOU Xian-Yang, HU Wei-Biao, WANG Qi.Design of Embedded System Radar Electronic Interference Simulator [J]. Process Automation Instrumentation, 2012,33 (6): 70-72
4. Wang Q, Hao M A, Rong X, et al. Design and Implementation of the Directing and Adjusting Control of Environment in a Common Simulation Training System[J]. Fire Control & Command Control, 2012.
5. Yang J. Design of Artillery Fight Training Simulation Directing and Adjusting System Based on Information System[J]. Command Control & Simulation, 2011.
6. Guangzhou. Design of Directing & Adjusting Frame in Combat Simulation Training System[J]. Ship Electronic Engineering, 2008.
7. Wang X, Wang W, Liu Q, et al. Design and Realization of Naval Air Combat Simulation System's Director Platform[J]. System Simulation Technology, 2010.
8. Sheng D H, Qiu X G. Design and Realization of Directing and Adjusting Federate Member and Its Surroundings in Fight Simulation[J]. Computer Simulation, 2004, 21(10):14-17.

Modeling and analysis of medium speed maglev vehicle network based on CPN

Yibo Jiao[1], Xiangqian liu[1], Xiaoyong Chen[2]

[1]Beijing Jiaotong University, School of Computer and information Technology, Beijing, China
[2]China Railway Jinan Group Co., Ltd., General engineer room, Jinan, China

Abstract. With the upsurge of magnetic levitation construction and research in China, in order to improve the running speed of mid-low-speed maglev train, the 13th Five-Year Science and Technology Major Proposal put forward a medium speed maglev solution with long stator synchronous traction. According to this new plan, the magnetic levitation subsystem, including the control system, needs re-co-ordination design, and the car network system must be changed accordingly. In this paper, based on the original scheme, a new magnetic levitation vehicle network system is designed to meet the needs of localization. In this paper, colored Petri nets are used to model and analyze the original scheme and the improved scheme. It proves theoretically that the improvement scheme is superior to the original scheme in failure rate and can meet the actual project requirements.

1 Introduction

Maglev is the recent rise of transport, with fast, small impact on the environment and so on[1]. With the maglev line in Changsha and Beijing "S1 line" have been opened up operations, set off a boom in magnetic levitation and research. In order to improve the running speed of medium and low speed maglev train, the 13th Five-Year Science and Technology Major Proposal put forward a long-stator synchronous traction medium speed maglev program. For this new scheme, all subsystems including the control system need to re-co-ordinate the design, While the on-board operation control system also needs to be changed accordingly as part of the operation control system. At the same time, it needs to be pointed out that in the process of localization, it follows the technical route of foreign countries or combines with the latest technological trends. There are many disputes over adopting new architecture and agreement. The purpose of this paper is to use the method of formal analysis, Research, for a new generation of medium-speed magnetic levitation vehicle control system to do some design.

2 Scheme Introduction

2.1. Origin Scheme

Figure 1 is a schematic diagram of the maglev vehicle communication network in the original solution. In the scheme, there is one communication antenna at the rear of the car, two MRCU modules are placed on the front of the car, the rear of the car is connected to the MRCUB via the RS232 bus, the MRCUA and MRCUB are connected to The vehicle safety computer1(VSC1) is connected and VSC1 and VSC2 are connected via Ethernet[2].

The original design has a serious flaw that VSC1 and VSC2 have different effects. VSC1 receives the message of two MRCU modules and then forwards the message to VSC2. In this scenario, VSC1, as the main vehicle-mounted security computer, plays a much greater role than VSC2. Some control signals such as "1st brake current cut-off", "2nd brake current cut-off", "free flow receiver" and other commands are controlled by VSC1 and VSC2 at the same time, but for some control signals such as " Right Door "," Open Left Door "and other instructions are only controlled by VSC1. This design will cause some interference to the safe operation of the train. If VSC1 fails during operation, VSC2 can not take over the operation of VSC1 because it does not have all the functions. What VSC2 can do is guide the safety of the maglev train.

In addition, the original program there are several drawbacks: One of them is to place MRCUA and MRCUB in the front of the car. If MRCUA and MRCUB are damaged in the same way as a whole or other accidents occur, the maglev vehicle loses contact with the decentralized control system or with the central control system. The basic functions of the whole car may be damaged, which is not in line with the principle of redundant design; In addition, due to the technical limitations of the time did not use real-time performance better Ethernet, such as Industrial Ethernet Ethernet Powerlink and other technologies.

* Corresponding Yibo Jiao: jyb_haha@163.com

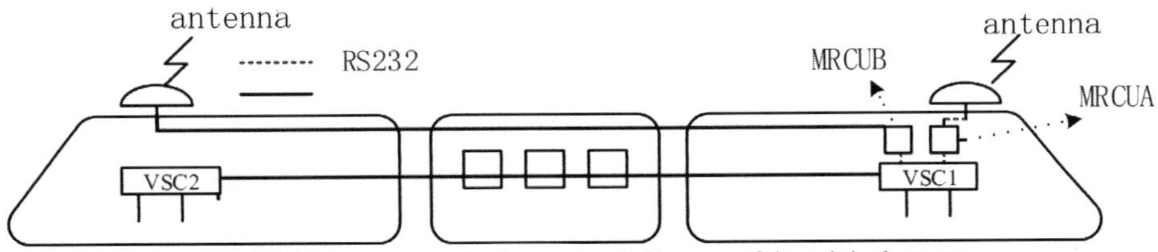

Fig. 1. Maglev communication network diagram of the original progra

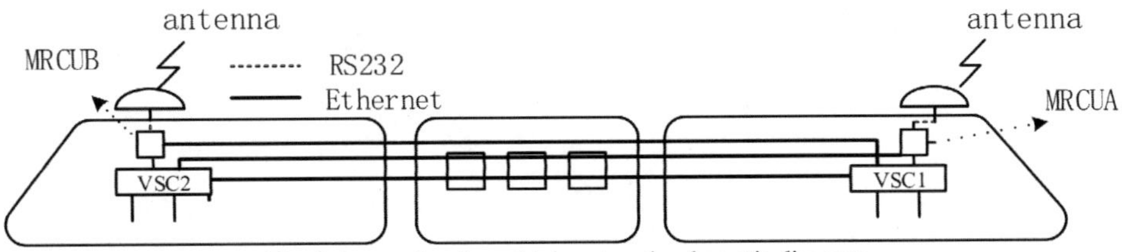

Fig. 2. improving the vehicle network schematic diagram

2.2 Improve Scheme

Place the figure as close as possible after the point where it is first referenced in the text. If there is a large number of figures and tables it might be necessary to place some before their text citation. If a figure or table is too large to fit into one column, it can be centred across both columns at the top or the bottom of the page.
Affiliation(s) should appear aligned to the center including organisation, address and e-mail.

The linespace must be of exactly 11-point with 9-point of font size and the font style set to italic.

In order to overcome the shortcomings of the original vehicle network system, this paper discusses the design of a new vehicle network system based on the original vehicle network system, the schematic diagram of improved vehicle network shown in Figure 2.

Relative to the original scheme, this article made the following modifications in the car network:

(1) The MRCUA and MRCUB are placed on the front and the rear respectively, so that even if the front of the car is severely damaged, a complete set of equipment for parking spaces can work safely.

(2) Connect MRCUA and MRCUB with two VSC1 and VSC2 on-board safety computers, respectively, and add 4-channel communication based on the original two-channel communication, so the security is higher.

(3) Replacement of outdated technologies in the in-vehicle network, such as replacing the traditional Ethernet with real-time better industrial Ethernet.

(4) The VSC2 at the rear of the vehicle communicates with both MRCUs not as a secondary computer system. As long as one of the two on-board safety computers is in operation, the entire maglev train can run safely.

(5) The two VSCs can still communicate with each other, which is mainly used to compare the obtained information and leave the correct information frame with the minimum delay.

3 CPN Modeling

3.1 Origin Scheme

CPN is a kind of advanced Petri nets. On the basis of Petri nets, the concept of color set is added to facilitate the analysis of discrete events such as concurrency and synchronization, which greatly reduces the model complexity[3].

The CPN is represented by a nine-tuple: CPN=$(\Sigma, P, T, A, N, C, G, T, I)$ (Wei, Z. 2012) where

Σ: limited non-empty color collection;

P: limited place collection;

T: limited transition collection;

A: limited arc collection, satisfies $P \cap A = P \cap T = T \cap A = \varnothing$;

N: node function, defined as mapping: $A \rightarrow P \times T \cup T \times P$;

C: color function;

G: security function;

E: arc expression function;

I: initialize function;

In this paper, the executable model of Maglev communication system is constructed by CPN.

3.1.1 The Original Scheme Top Model

In order to verify whether the improved scheme is better than the original scheme and whether it meets the project requirements, under the Windows10 operating system, the CPN Tools tools were used to model the original scheme and the improved scheme, respectively, to compare whether the failure rate meets the requirements.

The form should be completed and signed by one author on behalf of all the other authors.

Figure 3 is the use of CPN principle of the original program network system to establish the top model, Where the circular element is the place and the square element is transitions.

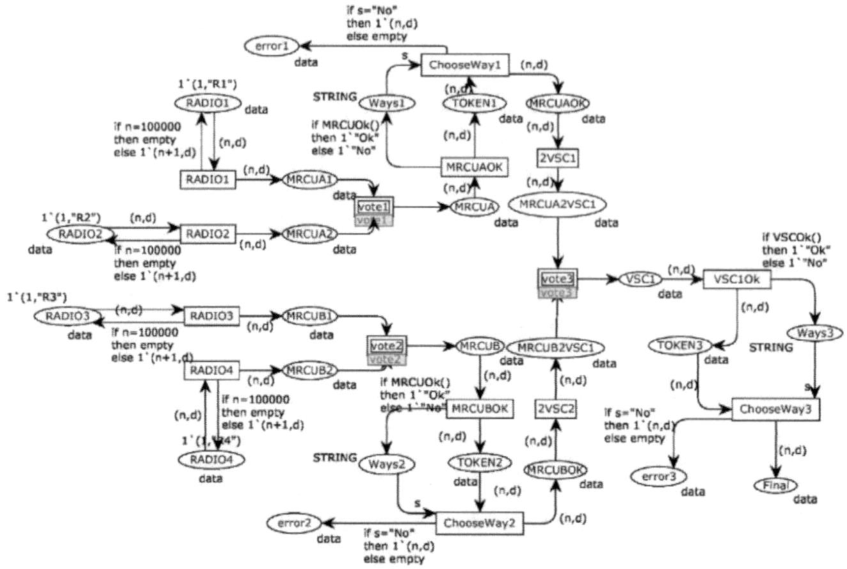

Fig. 3. the top layer model of the original scheme of the vehicle network system

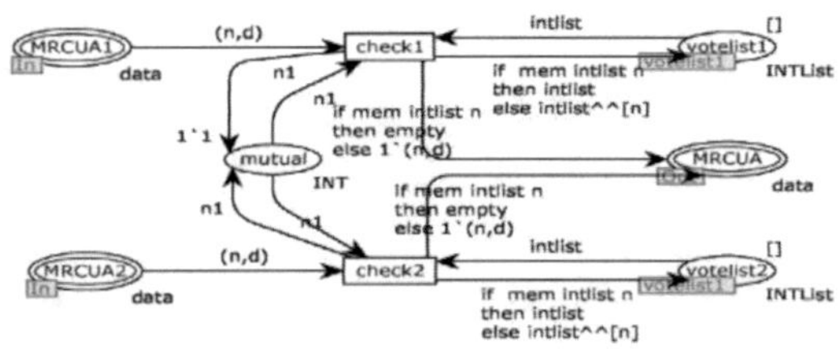

Fig. 4. improved voting submodel for vehicle network system

The data frame is sent redundantly from the four channels by the car wireless communication system. Two identical data are sent to the place MRCUA, and two identical data are sent to the place MRCUB. After the two data reach the MRCU module, the tokens are triggered by the transition vote1(vote1, vote2, vote3 are sub-transitions, which will be introduced in later articles). If the MRCU module is working normally, the MRCUAOk transition causes the data frame to be sent again. Otherwise, the data frame is sent incorrectly. After two transitions 2VSC1 and 2VSC2 firing, the data frame is sent to the VSC1. There are two channels, MRCUA to VSC1 and MRCUB to VSC1 respectively. Next, VSC votes the information obtained from MRCUA and MRCUB by transition vote3, leaving the correct first-arrival information frame and finally judging whether VSC1 is working properly. If normal Work, the information frame flows normally into the place Final.

It is worth mentioning that, in the figure MRCUOK() and VSCOK() are two functions, used to calculate whether the corresponding equipment is working.

3.1.2 The Original Scheme Vote Sub-Model

vote1, vote2, vote3 Several voting sub-models are almost completely structurally straightforward, taking the vote1 vote sub-model here as an example in figure 4.

Voting submodel data frame flow as follows: When there is a data frame to enter the model, the transition check will be triggered. First check whether there is the current data frame serial number in the place votelist, if not, store the serial number in the votelist and output the data frame to the output place; if the serial number already exists in the place votelist, it means the data Frames are arrived after the data frame, to be discarded. Place mutual play a mutually exclusive role to prevent the two channels at the same time. Place votelist1 and votelist2 are fusion place, they represent the same place.

3.2 Improve Scheme

3.2.1 The improve Scheme Top Model

Layered model, Figure 5 is to improve the program top-level model.

The data frame is sent redundantly from the four channels by the car wireless communication system. Two identical data are sent to the MRCUA, and two identical data are sent to the MRCUB. After the two data reach the MRCU module, the trasition is triggered by the vote1. If the MRCU module is working normally, the transition MRCUAOk fires to send data frame. Otherwise, the data frame is sent incorrectly. After two transitions of 2VSC1 and 2VSC2, the data frame is sent to the VSC1 and the VSC2, respectively Four channels MRCUA to VSC1, MRCUB to VSC1, MRCUA to VSC2, MRCUB to VSC2; then VSC is triggered by vote3 and vote4, voting information from MRCUA and MRCUB, leaving the correct first arriving message frame, the last two The information in a VSC initiates the correct first-arrived frame of information when fired by the vote5 transition.

in the figure MRCUOK() and VSCOK() are two functions, used to calculate whether the corresponding equipment is working[5]. Vote1, vote2, vote3, vote4 and vote5 are vote sub-model just as the original scheme.

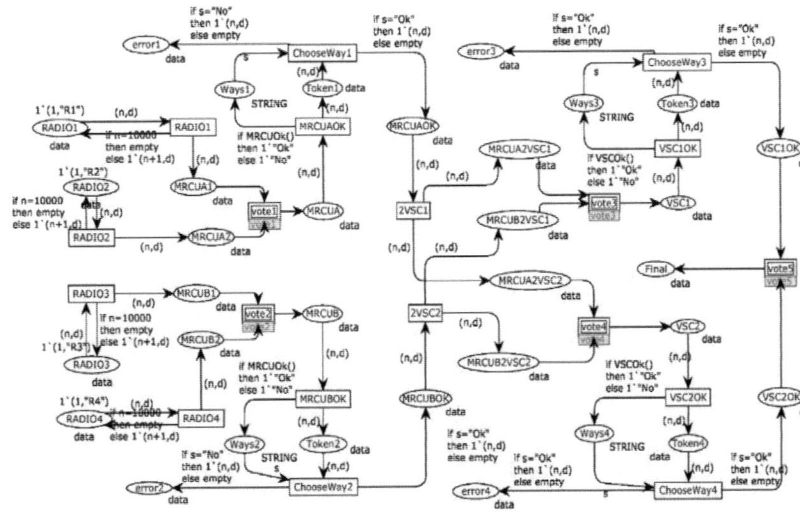

Fig. 5. improving the top layer model of the vehicle network system

Table 1 comparison test results

	90	91	92	93	94	95	96	97	98	99
Original scheme	8868	9008	9080	9162	9265	9354	9572	9697	9790	9881
Improve scheme	9787	9836	9866	9902	9933	9946	9955	9987	9994	9999

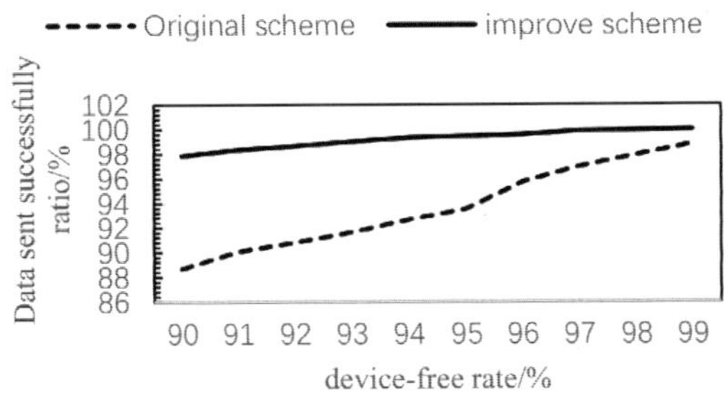

Fig. 6. contrast test data folding diagram

4 Experimental Analysis

By simulating the vehicle network model running in the original scheme and the improved scheme, the simulation sends 10000 data frames, starting from the RADIO place and ending with the final place. A number of independent experiments found that the stability of the model is better, and there is not much difference in the data between groups of experiments. Now, taking one of the groups as an example, Table 1 compares the results of the experimental data with the device-free rate of 90%, 91% , 92%, 93%, 94%, 95%, 96%, 97%, 98%, 99%, etc. The resulting data frame is obtained from the model (in this experiment, the pros and cons, in the actual project in general the failure rate of equipment is much better than this).

Generally believed that the packet loss rate of more than 99.95 in the network is considered to be applied in the project. It can be seen from Table 3-9 that the original solution still fails to meet the 99.95% standard when the device-free rate is 99%; and the improved solution can achieve packet loss rates greater than 99.95% when the device-free rate is 99% Send data packet. In order to more intuitively show the improved performance of the program, the use of line chart display data, as shown in Figure 6.

5 Conclusions

The train network system project of this project fully considered the project "Twelve Five" key project "research and development of key technologies of high-speed maglev operation control"[6] and medium-speed maglev vehicle network architecture in the past, designed the maglev train network system in this paper, then using colored Petri nets to simulate the original scheme and the improved scheme separately, the conclusion is drawn that the performance of the improved scheme is obviously better than the original scheme on the performance of no-fault rate. This article has certain reference meaning for the future research of maglev rail transit.

This research is supported by the key technology research and equipment development of high speed maglev operation control system with grant number 2016YFB1200602-26, and key technology research and equipment development of medium speed maglev operation control with grant number 2016YFB1200601-B24.

References

1. Cao Guangzhong. Maglev system control algorithm and implementation, Tsinghua University Press. (2013)

2. Chen, Q., Y. Tan, Q. Yang, J. Li, I. Mareels, Q. Chen, Y. Tan, Q. Yang, J. Li and I. Mareels. Centralized control implementation using distributed observer for Meglev systems. Chinese Control Conference(2017).
3. Rakkay, H. and H. Boucheneb. Security Analysis of Role Based Access Control Models Using Colored Petri Nets and CPNtools, Springer-Verlag(2009).
4. Wei, Z. "Petri net model of maglev train running across different control systems." Journal of Traffic & Transportation Engineering. (2012)
5. CAO Yuan, ZHANG Yuzhuo, MA Lianchuan, SUN Yaqing and MU Jiancheng. "DSPN-Based High-Speed Maglev System Switching Model." Journal of Traffic and Transportation Engineering (2). (2014)
6. Balko, P. and D. Rosinova. Modeling of magnetic levitation system. International Conference on Process Control. (2017)

Generalized Labeled Multi-Bernoulli Extended Target Tracking Based on Gaussian Process Regression

Luo-jia Chi, Xin-xi Feng and Lu Miao

School of Information and Navigation, Air Force Engineering University, Xi'an, China

Abstract. For the problems that Gamma Gaussian Inverse Wishart Cardinalized Probability Hypothesis Density (GGIW-CPHD) filter cannot accurately estimate the extended target shape and has a bad tracking performance under the condition of low SNR, a new generalized labeled multi-Bernoulli algorithm based on Gaussian process regression is proposed. The algorithm adopts the star convex to model the extended target, and realizes the online learning of the Gaussian process by constructing the state space model to complete the estimation of the extended target shape. At the same time, in the low SNR environment , the target motion state is tracked by the good tracking performance of the generalized label Bernoulli filter. Simulation results show that for any target with unknown shape, the proposed algorithm can well offer its extended shape and in the low SNR environment it can greatly improve the accuracy and stability of target tracking.

1 Introduction

In an extended target tracking problem, target measurements collected by the sensor are no longer one point for one target, but a set of points. By obtaining the extended form of the target from measurement sets, we can achieve better tracking and recognition performance. The extended target form can be modelled as circle, rectangle, ellipse, star convex and other geometric shapes. In 2008, Koch first proposed the random matrix[1] which modelled the target as ellipse and estimated the motion state and extended form of the target. In 2012, Granstrom applied the random matrix to the extended target probability hypothesis density(PHD) filter and proposed the Gaussian Inverse Wishart PHD (GIW-PHD)filter[2] , then he applied it to the Cardinalized probability hypothesis density (CPHD) filter and got Gamma Gaussian inverse Wishart CPHD (GGIW-CPHD)filter[3]. However, in low SNR environment, the tracking performance of above RFS algorithm is greatly reduced. In 2008, Baum proposed an extended target tracking method based on random hypersurfaces[4]. Then he modelled the targets as star-convex[5] and realized the tracking of irregular shape targets. In 2015, Gaussian process regression of machine learning is proposed to estimate extended target shape[6], avoiding complex calculation problems of the above algorithm due to excessive parameters, and achieving the accurate estimation of the target of any unknown shape.

A new generalized labeled multi-Bernoulli algorithm based on Gaussian process regression is proposed to solve the problem that GGIW-CPHD filter cannot accurately estimate the extended target shape and has a bad tracking performance under the condition of low SNR. The algorithm improves the accuracy and stability of target tracking in low SNR environment and realizes the accurate estimation of the unknown extended target shape using the Gaussian process regression.

2 Star convex model for extended target based on Gaussian process

2.1. Gaussian process regression

At present, Gaussian process is widely used in machine learning, statistics and communication processing to classify and identify signals[7-9]. In simple terms, the Gaussian process can be regarded as a distribution function $f(u)$ and can be defined by means functions $\mu(u)$ and covariance function $k(u,u')$.

$$f(u) \sim GP(\mu(u), k(u,u')) \tag{1}$$

which

$$\mu(u) = E\left[f(u)\right] \tag{2}$$

$$k(u,u') = E\left[(f(u)-\mu(u))(f(u')-\mu(u'))^T\right] \tag{3}$$

The Gaussian process learns the unknown function through the input training data. The measurement model is given below:

$$z_k = f(u_k) + e_k \tag{4}$$

Corresponding author: 592255820@qq.com, fengxinxi2005@aliyun.com, 1766584727@qq.com

The learning process mainly is: given a set of measurement $z \triangleq [z_1, \ldots, z_N]^T$ and their corresponding input $u \triangleq [u_1, \ldots, u_N]^T$, then learning the function f by Gaussian process so that we can estimate the corresponding function values $f \triangleq [f(u_1^f), \ldots, f(u_{N^f}^f)]^T$ when the input is $u^f \triangleq [u_1^f, \ldots, u_{N^f}^f]^T$. According to literature 6, it is known that the measurement value z_k and function value f are subject to the joint Gaussian distribution.

$$\begin{bmatrix} z_k \\ f \end{bmatrix} \sim N\left(0, \begin{bmatrix} k(u_k,u_k)+R & K(u_k,u^f) \\ K(u^f,u_k) & K(u^f,u^f) \end{bmatrix}\right) \quad (5)$$

From the above joint Gaussian distribution, it is easy to obtain the likelihood function and the initial prior probability:

$$p(z_k \mid f) = N(z_k; H_k^f f, R_k^f) \quad (6)$$

$$p(f) = N(0; P_0^f) \quad (7)$$

which

$$H^f(u_k) = K(u_k,u^f)[K(u^f,u^f)]^{-1} \quad (8)$$

$$R^f(u_k) = k(u_k,u_k) + R - K(u_k,u^f)[K(u^f,u^f)]^{-1}K(u^f,u_k) \quad (9)$$

$$P_0^f = K(u^f,u^f) \quad (10)$$

Through (6) the likelihood function is obtained, then establish the state space model, and the Gaussian process regression can be realized using the Kalman filter.

$$f_{k+1} = F^f f_k + Q^f, \quad w_k^f \sim N(0,Q^f) \quad (11a)$$

$$z_k = H^f(u_k) f_k + e_k^f, \quad e_k^f \sim N(0,R^f(u_k)) \quad (11b)$$

$$f_0 \sim N(0,P_0^f) \quad (11c)$$

which

$$F^f = e^{-\alpha T} I \quad (12)$$

$$Q^f = (1-e^{-2\alpha T})K(u^f,u^f) \quad (13)$$

2.2 Star convex model for extended target based on Gaussian process

In this paper, the extended target shape is modeled by star convex, and the estimation of it is realized by combining the learning characteristics of Gaussian process regression. According to the definition of star convex model, the shape of the target can be represented by the radius function $r = f(\theta)$. When the measurements from the sensor come from target surface, we model the measurement equation as

$$z_{k,l} = c_k + s_{k,l} p(\theta_{k,l}) f(\theta_{k,l}) + e_{k,l} \quad (14)$$

the location of the object at time k is c_k, $\{z_{k,l}\}_{l=1}^{N_{z,k}}$ is the measurement set at time k, $\{\theta_{k,l}\}_{l=1}^{N_{z,k}}$ and $f(\theta_{k,l})$ are respectively measured corresponding angles and radius, $p(\theta_{k,l})$ is the direction vector, $s_{k,l}$ is the scaling factor, $e_{k,l}$ is the Gaussian noise with zero mean and covariance R.

The radius function of the target shape can be learned through the Gaussian process

$$f(\theta) \sim GP(\mu(\theta), k(\theta,\theta')) \quad (15)$$

For each measurement value $z_{k,l}$, it corresponds to an angle $\theta_{k,l}^L$. Taking into account the initial direction ψ_k of the target, the expression of $\theta_{k,l}^L$ is:

$$\begin{aligned} \theta_{k,l}^L(c_k,\psi_k) &= \angle(z_{k,l} - c_k) - \psi_k \\ &= \theta_{k,l}^G(c_k) - \psi_k \end{aligned} \quad (16)$$

Put the formula (11) and (16) in(14), the standard measurement equation can be obtained, and its expression is:

$$\begin{aligned} z_{k,l} &= c_k + s_{k,l} p_{k,l}(c_k) f(\theta_{k,l}^L(c_k,\psi_k)) + e_{k,l} \\ &= c_k + s_{k,l} p_{k,l}(c_k)\left[H^f(\theta_{k,l}^L(c_k,\psi_k)) f_k + e_{k,l}^f\right] + \bar{e}_{k,l} \\ &= \underbrace{c_k + s_{k,l}\tilde{H}_l(c_k,\psi_k) f_k}_{h(c,\psi,f)} + \underbrace{s_{k,l} p_{k,l}(c_k) e_{k,l}^f + \bar{e}_{k,l}}_{e} \\ &= h_{k,l}(c_k,\psi_k,f_k) + e_{k,l}, \qquad e_{k,l} \sim N(0,R_{k,l}) \end{aligned} \quad (17)$$

which

$$\tilde{H}_l(c_k,\psi_k) = p_{k,l}(c_k) H^f(\theta_{k,l}^L(c_k,\psi_k)) \quad (18)$$

$$h_{k,l}(c_k,\psi_k,f_k) = c_k + \tilde{H}_l(c_k,\psi_k) f \quad (19)$$

$$R_{k,l} = p_{k,l} R_{k,l}^f p_{k,l}^T + R \quad (20)$$

$$p_{k,l} = p_{k,l}(c_k) = p(\theta_{k,l}^G(c_k)) = \frac{z_{k,l} - c_k}{\left\| z_{k,l} - c_k \right\|} \quad (21)$$

$$R_{k,l}^f = R^f(\theta_{k,l}^L(c_k,\psi_k)) \quad (22)$$

$$s_{k,l} \sim N(\mu_s, \sigma_s^2) \quad (23)$$

3 Generalized labeled multi-Bernoulli algorithm based on Gaussian process regression

3.1. Generalized labeled Multi-Bernoulli filter

In multiple target tracking problem, filtering methods based on traditional RFS theory cannot provide target track, therefore, Vo introduced label into RFS and put forward the general labeled multi-Bernoulli filter (GLMB)[10][11]. In the process of Bayesian recursion, the posterior probability density of GLMB RFS has the characteristics of maintaining the same form, which can avoid the complicated integral solving process in traditional algorithm. The posterior probability density can be expressed as follows:

$$\pi(X)=\Delta(X)\sum_{(I,\xi)\in F(L)\times\Theta}\omega(I,\xi)\delta_I[L(X)][p(\cdot\,;\xi)]^X \quad (24)$$

$X=\{(x,l)_i\}$, $(i=1,2,\cdots,|X|)$ represents the labeled RFS; $\Delta(X)$ is the labeled indicator function; L is the discrete labeled space, $F(L)$ represents the track set; Θ is the discrete association space; Each pair of (I,ξ) represents an association hypothesis , $\omega(I,\xi)$ is the corresponding weight; $p(x,l\,;\xi)$ is the single target probability distribution; $[p(\cdot\,;\xi)]^X=\prod_{(x,l)\in X}p(x,l\,;\xi)$.

Now assuming that the posterior probability density at time $k-1$ has the form of formula (24), then the prediction step and update step of GLMB can be expressed as follows:

Prediction step:

$$\bar{\pi}_+(X)=\Delta(X)\sum_{\xi,J,L_+}\bar{\omega}_+(\xi,J,L_+)\delta_{J\cup L_+}[L(X)][\bar{p}_+(\cdot;\xi)]^X \quad (25)$$

which

$$\bar{\omega}_+(\xi,J,L_+)=1_{F(B_+)}(L_+)r_{B,+}^{L_+}[1-r_{B,+}]^{B_+-L_+}\times\sum_{I\in F(L)}1_{F(I)}(J)[\bar{P}_S(\cdot\,;\xi)]^J[1-\bar{P}_S(\cdot\,;\xi)]^{I-J}\,\omega(I,\xi) \quad (26)$$

$$\bar{P}_S(\cdot,l;\xi)=\langle p(\cdot,l;\xi),P_S(\cdot,l)\rangle \quad (27)$$

$$\bar{p}_+(\cdot;\xi)=1_L(l_+)\frac{\langle P_S(\cdot,l_+)f_+(x_+\,|\,\cdot,l_+),p(\cdot,l_+;\xi)\rangle}{\bar{P}_S(\cdot,l_+;\xi)}+1_{B_+}(l_+)p_{B,+}(x_+,l_+) \quad (28)$$

$\xi\in\Theta, J\in F(L), L_+\in F(B_+)$, B_+ is the new target labeled space and $L\cap B_+=\varnothing$; $r_{B,+}$ and $p_{B,+}(x_+,l_+)$ are the birth probability and probability distribution of newborn target respectively; $f_+(x_+\,|\,\cdot,l_+)$ is the Markov state transition function and the label of the survival target remains unchanged in prediction step. $P_S(\cdot,l_+)$ is the survival probability for the target.

Update step:

$$\pi_{Z_+}(X)\propto\Delta(X)\sum_{\xi,J,L_+,\theta_+}\omega_{Z_+}(\xi,J,L_+,\theta_+)\delta_{J\cup L_+}[L(X)][p_{Z_+}(\cdot;\xi,\theta_+)]^X \quad (29)$$

which

$$\omega_{Z_+}(\xi,J,L_+,\theta_+)=1_{\Theta_+(J\cup L_+)}(\theta_+)[\bar{\psi}_{Z_+}(\cdot;\xi,\theta_+)]^{J\cup L_+}\bar{\omega}_+(\xi,J,L_+) \quad (30)$$

$$\bar{\psi}_{Z_+}(\cdot,l_+;\xi,\theta_+)=\langle\bar{p}_+(\cdot,l_+;\xi),\psi_{Z_+}(\cdot,l_+;\theta_+(l_+))\rangle \quad (31)$$

$$p_{Z_+}(\cdot;\xi,\theta_+)=\frac{\bar{p}_+(\cdot;\xi)\psi_{Z_+}(\cdot;\theta_+(l_+))}{\bar{\psi}_{Z_+}(\cdot,l_+;\xi,\theta_+)} \quad (32)$$

$$\psi_{Z_+}(\cdot;\theta_+(l_+))=\begin{cases}\dfrac{P_D(x_+,l_+)g(z_{\theta_+(l_+)}\,|\,x_+,l_+)}{\kappa(z_{\theta_+(l_+)})}, & \theta_+(l_+)>0\\ 1-P_D(x_+,l_+), & \theta_+(l_+)=0\end{cases} \quad (33)$$

$\theta_+\in\Theta_+$ represents the correlation mapping of targets to measurements; $g(z_{\theta_+(l_+)}\,|\,x_+,l_+)$ is the measurement likelihood function; $P_D(x_+,l_+)$ is the target detection probability.

3.2 Generalized labeled multi-Bernoulli algorithm based on Gaussian process regression

According to the derivation of section 2.2, the extended target is modeled as

$$x_{k+1}=Fx_k+w_k,\qquad w_k\sim N(0,Q) \quad (34a)$$

$$z_k=h_k(x_k)+e_k,\qquad e_k\sim N(0,R_k) \quad (34b)$$

$$x_0\sim N(\mu_0,P_0) \quad (34c)$$

The state vector of the target is expressed as $x_k\triangleq[\underbrace{(c_k)^T,(c_k')^T,\psi_k}_{x_k^n},(f_k)^T]^T$, including the target's motion state $x_k^n=\{(c_k)^T,(c_k')^T,\psi_k\}$ and the target expansion state f_k . The extended target measurements of each moment is $z_k=[z_{k,1}^T,\ \ldots,\ z_{k,n}^T]^T$.

which

$$R_k=diag[R_{k,1},\ \ldots,\ R_{k,n}] \quad (35)$$

$$h_k(x_k)=[h_{k,1}(x_k)^T,\ \ldots,\ h_{k,n}(x_k)^T]^T \quad (36)$$

$$F=diag(F^n,F^f) \quad (37)$$

$$Q=diag(Q^n,Q^f) \quad (38)$$

F^f 、 Q^f are determined by formula (12) and (13) which related to the movement of the target. The specific parameters are given in the simulation experiment.

The main steps for the generalized labeled multi-Bernoulli algorithm based on Gaussian process regression are that firstly using generalized labeled multi-Bernoulli filter to obtain the target motion state, then according to formula (17) derived in this paper, Gaussian process regression is realized by using kalman filter to complete the estimate of the target extended shape. The joint posterior probability density is

$$p(f_k,x_{0:k}^n\,|\,z_{1:k})\approx p(f_k\,|\,x_{0:k}^n,z_{1:k})p(x_{0:k}^n\,|\,z_{1:k}) \quad (39)$$

$p(f_k\,|\,x_{0:k}^n,z_{1:k})$ is obtained by Gaussian process learning, $p(x_{0:k}^n\,|\,z_{1:k})$ is given by generalized labeled multi-Bernoulli filter.

4 Simulation result and analysis

4.1. Parameter setting

This paper makes a comparative analysis of the proposed algorithm and GGIW-CPHD algorithm. we verify the performance of the proposed algorithm in the two following aspects:

(1) shape estimation: whether the target of any unknown shape can be well studied and given its extended form;

(2) tracking performance: whether it has good tracking accuracy and stability under low SNR environment.

Our experiment assumes that the extended target is shaped like a star. The new target random set can be represented by the labeled Bernoulli parameter set $\left\{r_{B,k}(l_i), p_{B,k}(l_i)\right\}_{i=1}^{4}$. The probability density of new target is $r_{B,k}(l_i)$=0.04 which is subject to Gaussian distribution $p_B(l_i)$=$N(x;m_B^{(i)},P_B)$. The initial state of the four new targets is $m_B^{(1)}$=[40,2.5,40,2.5]^{T}, $m_B^{(2)}$=[18,-2.5,20,1.5]^{T}, $m_B^{(3)}$=[30,3,130,0]^{T}, $m_B^{(4)}$=[120,2,190,-3]^{T}. P_B=diag([10,5,10,5]^{T})^2. Target survival probability $P_s = 0.98$, detection probability $P_D = 0.8$. The background clutter number obeys the Poisson distribution with a mean value of 20 and evenly distributed in the monitoring area. The maximum Gaussian number $H_{\max} = 1000$. Target position and rotation direction are modeled as the uniform velocity model:

$$F^n = \begin{bmatrix}1 & T\\ 0 & 1\end{bmatrix}\otimes I_3, Q^n = \begin{bmatrix}\frac{T}{3} & \frac{T}{2}\\ \frac{T}{2} & T\end{bmatrix}\otimes\begin{bmatrix}\sigma_q^2 & 0 & 0\\ 0 & \sigma_q^2 & 0\\ 0 & 0 & \sigma_{q^\psi}^2\end{bmatrix} \quad (40)$$

Assuming the position process noise $\sigma_q^2 = 1$, rotation direction process noise $\sigma_{q^\psi}^2 = 0.1$, sampling period $T = 1$. The covariance function of Gaussian process[6] is

$$k(\theta,\theta') = \sigma_f^2 e^{-\frac{2\sin^2\left(\frac{|\theta-\theta'|}{2}\right)}{l^2}} + \sigma_r^2 \quad (41)$$

The radius prior variance $\sigma_r^2 = 1$, output prior variance amplitude $\sigma_f^2 = 2$, length scale of the function $l = \frac{\pi}{4}$ and the measurement noise covariance $R = 0.1^2 I_2$. The whole tracking process continuous 100s and 100 Monte Carlo experiment is conducted. The initial state of the target is shown in table 1.

Table 1 Target initial state

Target	State		
	· Initial state	Appearing time	Disappearing time
Target 1	[40 2.5 40 2.5]	1s	60s
Target 2	[180 −2.5 20 1.5]	21s	80s
Target 3	[30 3 130 0]	31s	100s
Target 4	[120 2 190 -3]	41s	100s

4.2. Analysis of simulation result

In this paper, the simulation results are shown in figure 1-4. Fig.1 shows the extended target real tracks and filtering results of GGIW-CPHD and our proposed algorithm.

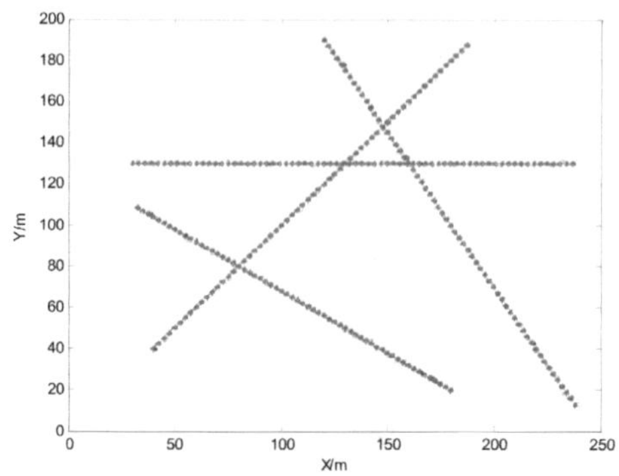

Fig. 1. Target real trails and filtering results.

Fig.2 shows the local amplification of filtering results. The black line , blue line and red line are respectively stand for target real tracks and real shape of the extension、 GGIW-CPHD filtering results and shape estimation 、 our proposed algorithm filtering results and shape estimation. We can see intuitively from Fig.1、 2 that in a low SNR environment, our proposed algorithm can effectively suppress clutter measurement interference and get better and sustained tracking results. Meanwhile, the proposed algorithm is more precise in shape estimation than GGIW-CPHD.

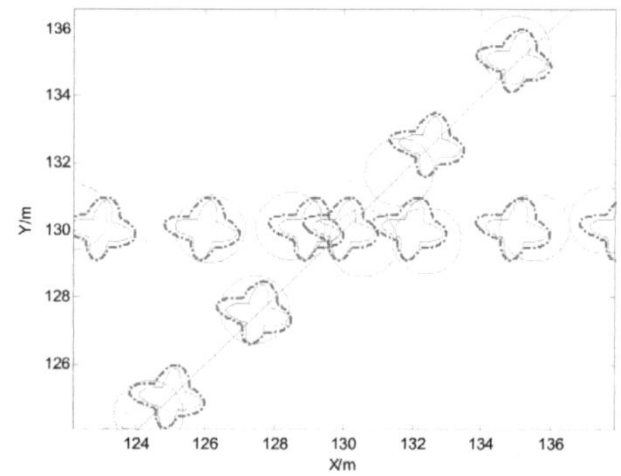

Fig. 2. Local amplification of filtering results.

Fig.3 shows target estimation number of GGIW-CPHD and the proposed algorithm. Yellow, green shadows respectively stand for target number statistical standard deviation of GGIW – CPHD and the proposed algorithm. We can see that GGIW - CPHD and the proposed algorithm both carry on the unbiased estimation, but the standard deviation of GGIW-CPHD is bigger than the proposed algorithm which verifies that in low SNR environment, our proposed algorithm has better tracking accuracy and stability.

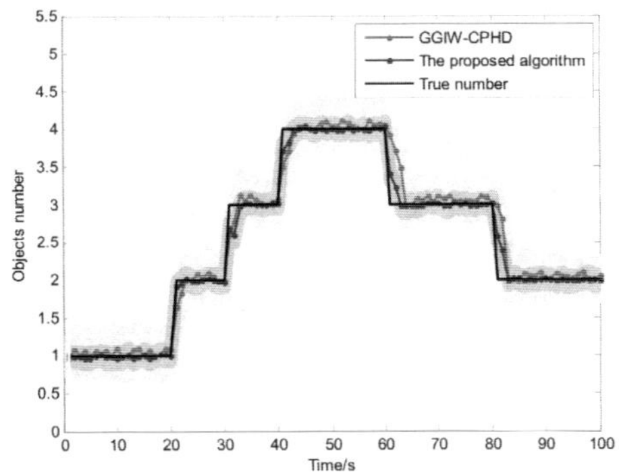

Fig. 3. Estimation of target number.

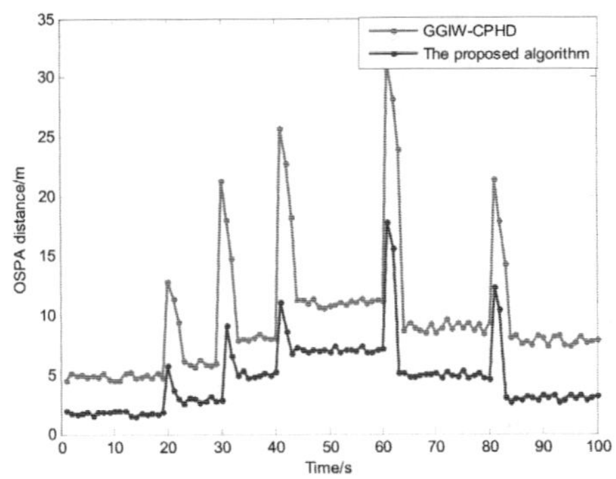

Fig. 4. OSPA distance contrast.

Fig.4 shows OSPA distance contrast of GGIW-CPHD and the proposed algorithm. It can be seen from the figure, when target number changes, the filtering effect of both algorithm has varying degrees of decline, but the proposed algorithm is smaller on the whole and proves to have a higher filtering accuracy and stability.

5 Conclusions

This paper presents a generalized labeled Bernoulli algorithm under Gaussian process regression. The proposed algorithm uses Gaussian process of machine learning to learn extended target shape, avoiding the existing algorithms' excessive parameters calculation complex problems, then tracking the targets based on the generalized labeled Bernoulli filter good tracking performance under low SNR environment. The experimental results show that the proposed improved algorithm can effectively track the extended target in the low SNR environment, which also has better stability and more accurate shape estimation.

References

1. J .W .Koch. Bayesian approach to extended object and cluster tracking using random matrices[J]. *IEEE Transactions on Aerospace and Electronic Systems*, 2008, 44(3): 1042-1059.
2. K. Granstrom, U. Orguner. A PHD Filter for Tracking Multiple Extended Targets Using Random Matrices[J]. *IEEE Transactions on Signal Processing*, 2012, 60(11): 5657-5671.
3. C. Lundquist, K. Granström, U. Orguner. An Extended Target CPHD Filter and a Gamma Gaussian Inverse Wishart Implementation[J]. *Journal of Selected Topics in Signal Processing*, 2013, 7(3): 472-483.
4. M. Baum, U. D. Hanebeck. Random Hypersurface Models for Extended Object Tracking[C]. *IEEE International Symposium on Signal Processing and Information Technology*. IEEE, 2010: 178-183.
5. M. Baum, U. D. Hanebeck. Shape tracking of extended objects and group targets with star-convex RHMs[C].*Proceedings of the, International Conference on Information Fusion. IEEE*, 2011: 1-8.
6. N. Wahlström, E. Özkan. Extended Target Tracking Using Gaussian Processes[J]. *IEEE Transactions on Signal Processing*, 2015, 63(16): 4165-4178.
7. C. E. Rasmussen, C. K. I. Williams. *Gaussian Processes for Machine Learning* [M]. Cambridge, USA :The MIT Press, 2005.
8. J. Ko, D. Fox. GP-BayesFilters: Bayesian Filtering Using Gaussian Process Prediction and Observation Models[J]. *Autonomous Robots*, 2009, 27(1): 75-90.
9. E. Özkan, N. Wahlström, S. J. Godsill. Rao-Blackwellised particle filter for star-convex extended target tracking models[C]. *International Conference on Information Fusion*. IEEE, 2016.
10. B. T. Vo, B. N. Vo. Labeled random finite sets and multi-object conjugate priors[J]. *IEEE Transactions on Signal Processing*, 2013, 61 (13): 3460-3475.
11. B. N. Vo, B. T. Vo, Phung D. Labeled random finite sets and the Bayes multi-target tracking filter[J]. *IEEE Transactions on Signal Processing*, 2014, 62 (24): 6554-6567.

Super resolution DOA estimation with incomplete single snapshot data via matrix completion and compress sensing

Dong Zhang[1,*], Qin Zhang[1], Baojun Song[1], Guimei Zheng[1], and Yongshun Zhang[1]

[1]Air and Missile Defense College, Air Force Engineering University, Xi'an 710051, China

Abstract. A method of super resolution DOA estimation with incomplete single snapshot data via matrix completion (MC) and compress sensing (CS) is presented. First, the incomplete single snapshot data is reshaped into a low-rank Hankel matrix form and the complete data can be reconstructed through matrix completion. Then, super resolution DOA estimation can be got through CS algorithm using these constructed complete data. Numerical simulations demonstrate that this method can get high accuracy DOA estimation with less number of array elements.

1 Introduction

DOA is a very important parameter in Radar system and its estimation accuracy will seriously affect the performance of Radar system. DOA estimation of maneuvering targets is usually difficult because the available snapshot number is usually rare. So the DOA estimation with short snapshots is receiving more and more attention and many literature devote to it [1]. More recently, DOA estimation based on CS (CS-DOA) becomes a hot field because of its advantage in fully exploiting the inherent sparseness of the DOA [2] and reducing the observation.

As we know, matrix completion is a novel technique which emerges on the heels of compress sensing[3]. It can recover a low-rank matrix which is incomplete and perhaps even corrupted. So it has the potential of reducing the array number. In this paper, we proposed a novel DOA estimation method which combines matrix completion with compress sensing under the condition of incomplete single snapshot. First, we reshape the incomplete single snapshot data into a low-rank Hankel matrix form and we can get the complete data through matrix completion. Then, we can get super resolution DOA estimation via CS algorithm using the reconstructed complete data. The matrix completion theory ensures that we can get the accurate complete data with the array number reducing to a certain extent. The compress sensing theory ensures that we can get super resolution estimation with the reconstructed complete data. Thus, this method can obtain super resolution DOA estimation with less array number.

2 Signal model

Assume there is a uniform linear array (ULA)which has N receivers. The interval between array elements is d .The signal of targets are incoming from M different direction which are θ_i, $i = 1,2,...,M$. And $f_i = d\cos(\theta_i)/\lambda$ are the normalized DOA. In the rest of the paper, we will directly refer to it as DOA for simplicity.

Then the complete output of the receive array with single snapshot can be expressed as

$$\boldsymbol{x}_C = \boldsymbol{A}(\theta)\boldsymbol{s} + \boldsymbol{w} = \sum_{i=0}^{M-1} \boldsymbol{a}(\theta_i)s_i + \boldsymbol{w} \quad (1)$$

where $\boldsymbol{x}_C = [x_0, x_1, ..., x_{N-1}]^T$ denotes the received complete data of N receivers with single snapshot. $\boldsymbol{w} = [w_0, w_1, ..., w_{N-1}]^T$ refers to the noise vector. $\boldsymbol{s} = [s_0, s_1, ..., s_{M-1}]^T$ denotes incident signal of M targets. $\boldsymbol{a}(\theta_i) = [a_0(\theta_i), a_1(\theta_i), ..., a_{N-1}(\theta_i)]^T = [1, ..., \exp(\mathrm{j}(N-1)2\pi f_i)]^T$ are receive steering vectors corresponding to the DOA *of* i^{th} target and $\boldsymbol{A}(\theta) = [\boldsymbol{a}(\theta_0), \boldsymbol{a}(\theta_1), ..., \boldsymbol{a}(\theta_{M-1})]$.

Discretize the range of DOA to $N_L >> N$ resolution grids. The CS theory ensures that, under certain conditions, we can get the super resolution of DOA by solving a sparse reconstruction problem.

But we want to reduce the number of array elements as more as possible. For example, we only want to use N_S array elements. And we assume that they are randomly picked from N array elements. If we continue use the CS method, the performance will decrease for the reduction of observation.

Note that the CS method theory utilizes the inherent sparseness of targets to get high resolution. But, in addition to sparsity, the received signals have the property of low rank. It ensures that we can use the partial data (we determine it as incomplete data)to recovery the full data(we determine it as complete data)

* Corresponding author: zhangdongtougao@163.com

via matrix completion theory. So the combination of matrix completion with compress sensing will bring the advantage of get higher resolution estimation of DOA with less array elements.

3 MC-CS algorithm

According to Equation (1),the received complete data of N receivers with single snapshot is $\boldsymbol{x_C} = [x_1, x_2, ..., x_N]^T$ and the output of the receive array element n ($n = 0,1,..., N-1$) can be expressed as

$$x_n = \sum_{i=0}^{M-1} a_n(\theta_i) s_i + w_n, n = 0,1,..., N-1 \quad (2)$$

where $a_n(\theta_i) = \exp[jn2\pi f_i]$ .Then we randomly pick N_S array elements from the ULA and $N_S < N$ .The incomplete data is $\boldsymbol{x_{IC}} = [x_1, x_2, ..., x_{N_S}]^T$ .Let $\boldsymbol{x_{ZP}}$ represents the zero-padding result of incomplete data $\boldsymbol{x_{IC}}$. Then we can regard $\boldsymbol{x_{ZP}}$ as an incomplete measurement of $\boldsymbol{x_C}$

$$[\boldsymbol{x_{ZP}}]_l = [\boldsymbol{x_C}]_l, l \in \Omega \quad (3)$$

where $[\cdot]_l$ stands for the lth item of the vector. Ω denotes a subset of $[0: N-1]$ and it represents the array elements which are random picked. Another form of Equation (5) is $\boldsymbol{x_{ZP}} = \mathrm{P}_\Omega(\boldsymbol{x_C})$ .Where $\mathrm{P}_\Omega(\cdot)$ stands for the operation of randomly selection.

Based on complete data $\boldsymbol{x_C} = [x_1, x_2, ..., x_N]^T$, a Hankel matrix can be constructed as follows

$$\boldsymbol{Hank}(\boldsymbol{x_C}) = \begin{bmatrix} x_0 & x_1 & \cdots & x_{N-d} \\ x_1 & x_2 & \cdots & x_{N-d+1} \\ \vdots & \vdots & \vdots & \vdots \\ x_{d-1} & x_d & \cdots & x_{N-1} \end{bmatrix} \quad (4)$$

where d is a positive integer which is often set as $d = \frac{N}{2}$ or $d = \frac{N+1}{2}$ .According to Equation (2),we can decompose the Hankel matrix into the following form

$$\boldsymbol{Hank}(\boldsymbol{x_C}) = \boldsymbol{U\Sigma V} \quad (5)$$

where $\boldsymbol{U} = \begin{bmatrix} a_0(\theta_0) & a_0(\theta_1) & \cdots & a_0(\theta_{M-1}) \\ a_1(\theta_0) & a_1(\theta_1) & \cdots & a_1(\theta_{M-1}) \\ \vdots & \vdots & \vdots & \vdots \\ a_{d-1}(\theta_0) & a_{d-1}(\theta_1) & \cdots & a_{d-1}(\theta_{M-1}) \end{bmatrix}$,

$\boldsymbol{V} = \begin{bmatrix} a_0(\theta_0) & a_1(\theta_0) & \cdots & a_{N-d}(\theta_0) \\ a_0(\theta_1) & a_1(\theta_1) & \cdots & a_{N-d}(\theta_1) \\ \vdots & \vdots & \vdots & \vdots \\ a_0(\theta_{M-1}) & a_1(\theta_{M-1}) & \cdots & a_{N-d}(\theta_{M-1}) \end{bmatrix}$ and

$\boldsymbol{\Sigma} = \mathrm{diag}(s_0, s_1, ..., s_{M-1})$.

It obvious that $\boldsymbol{rank}[\boldsymbol{Hank}(\boldsymbol{x_C})] \le M$.

Then, according to the matrix completion theory, the estimation result $\tilde{\boldsymbol{x}}_C$ of $\boldsymbol{x_C}$ can be estimated through solving the problem as

$$\min \ \|\mathrm{Hank}(\boldsymbol{x_C})\|_*, \ \mathrm{s.t.} \mathrm{P}_\Omega(\boldsymbol{x_C} - \boldsymbol{x_{ZP}}) \le \varepsilon \quad (6)$$

where $\|\cdot\|_*$ denotes the nuclear norm. This matrix completion problem can be solved by many algorithms, like the inexact augmented Lagrange multiplier algorithm [4] which possess high computational efficiency and adequate precision.

After get the estimation result $\tilde{\boldsymbol{x}}_C$, we can use the CS method to get super resolution DOA estimation. Discretizing the range of DOA to $N_L >> N$ resolution grids, the estimation data can be expressed as

$$\begin{aligned} \tilde{\boldsymbol{x}}_C &= \boldsymbol{\Phi}(\theta) \boldsymbol{s}_{sparse} + \boldsymbol{w} \\ &= \sum_{i=0}^{N_L} \boldsymbol{a}(\theta_i) s_i + \boldsymbol{w} \end{aligned} \quad (7)$$

where $\boldsymbol{\Phi}(\theta) = [\boldsymbol{a}(\theta_0), \boldsymbol{a}(\theta_1), ..., \boldsymbol{a}(\theta_{N_L-1})]$ is the super resolution DOA dictionary, $\boldsymbol{s}_{sparse} = [s_0, s_1, ..., s_{N_L-1}]^T$ is the sparse vector whose non-zero elements' position represent the super resolution DOA estimation result. The CS theory shows that [5], if $\boldsymbol{A}_{new}(\theta)$ possess the restricted isometry property(RIP), then $\boldsymbol{s}_{sparse}$ will be reconstructed precisely according to $\tilde{\boldsymbol{x}}_C$ via solving a optimization problem as

$$\min \|\boldsymbol{s}_{sparse}\|_1 \ \ \mathrm{s.t.} \|\tilde{\boldsymbol{x}}_C - \boldsymbol{\Phi}(\theta)\boldsymbol{s}_{sparse}\|_2 \le \delta \quad (8)$$

Among the reconstruction methods, OMP is usually seemed as the more suitable method for application because of its fast computation speed and satisfactory accuracy. So we solve Equation (8) by OMP algorithm.

https://doi.org/10.1051/matecconf/201817601018

Input:

Radar received incomplete signal $\mathbf{X}_{IC}$, the remaining array set Ω , the super resolution grids N_S and the number of targets *M*.

Output:

Estimated DOA f_m of *m*th (*m*=1,2,...,*M*) target.

Procedure:

- step1: Get $\mathbf{X}_{ZP}$ by zero-padding to the incomplete signal $\mathbf{X}_{IC}$.
- step2: Get the reconstructed complete data $\tilde{\mathbf{X}}_C$ by solving the Equation (6).
- step3: Get super resolution DOA estimation f_m by solving the Equation (8).

Figure 1: MC-CS algorithm

This method is termed as the matrix completion-compress sensing (MC-CS) algorithm in this paper. Using this method, we can get high resolution estimation of DOA with less number of array elements. In summary, the MC-CS algorithm consists of three main steps is obtained which is given in Fig. 1.

4 Simulation results

of mth target are $f_m = 0.2m - 0.66$. We made three kinds of simulation. In all the simulation, we set $N = 50$ and $N_L = 150$, i.e. the number of complete array and discretizing grids are 50 and150 respectively. And all the simulation are conducted in the environment of additive white Gaussian noise.

For the first simulation, we set SNR=15dB. Then we randomly pick 38 array elements and the DOA estimation performance of the proposed MC-CS algorithm is shown in Fig. 2 which indicates that our method can obtain satisfactory estimation performance.

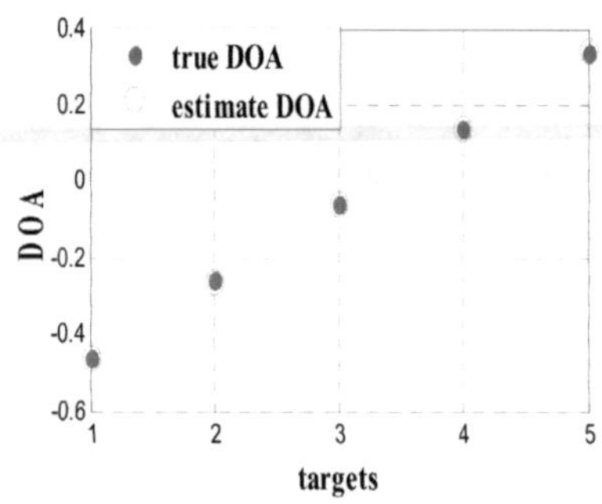

Fig.2 DOA estimation result of the proposed method

For the second simulation, we contrast the variation of average root-mean-square error (RMSE) of estimated DOA of all five targets with different SNR for the proposed MC-CS algorithms. The contrast test is the CS method using the incomplete data. The SNR varies from 0dB to 30dB. 200 trails Monte Carlo simulations are performed for each given SNR. The other parameters are same with the first simulation. And the result is presented in Fig. 3 which indicates that the result of the proposed MC-CS algorithm is better than the CS method. Especially when SNR<-15dB, the proposed method is better than the CS which indicates that the proposed method have better performance in low SNR.

In the third simulation, we compare the RMSE of estimated DOA of all five targets with the picking number of array elements for CS method and the proposed MC-CS algorithm. The SNR is 15dB.Fig. 4 shows the comparison result with picking number from27 to47.It obviously that the proposed MC-CS method is better than the CS method. We can see that with the decreasing of picking number, the CS method decrease significantly. While when the picking number is large than 41, the estimation performance of MC-CS method is constant. It indicates that our method have a tolerant limit of the picking number. If the picking number is in the tolerant limit, our method will not be affect by the picking number. This property can help us to reduce the array elements.

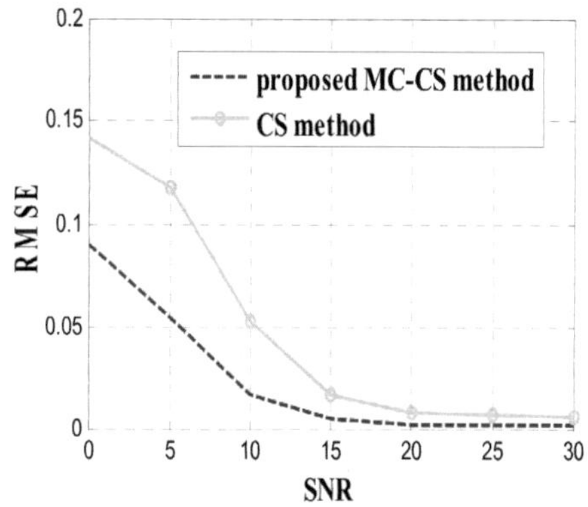

Fig. 3 Average RMSE of DOA estimation with different SNR

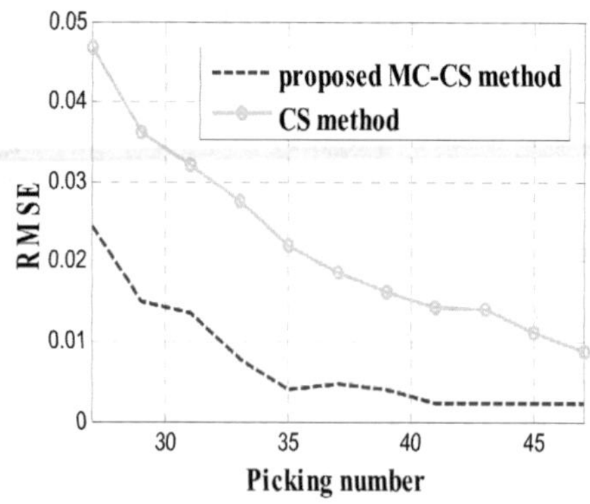

Fig. 4 Average RMSE of DOA estimation with different picking number

5 Conclusions

A super resolution DOA estimation with incomplete single snapshot data via matrix completion and compress sensing is proposed in this paper. Numerical simulations verify that the proposed MC-CS method can get super resolution estimation performance meanwhile reduce the array number to a certain.

Acknowledgements

This work was supported by the National Natural Science Foundation of China under grant 61571459， 61372166.

References

1. B. Radich, K. Buckley,. IEEE SPL, **4,** 4(1997)
2. S. Fortunati, R. Grasso, F. Gini, M. Greco, In Proc. 39th IEEE ICASSP, (2014)
3. E. Candes, Y. Plan, Proc. IEEE. **98**, 6 (2010).
4. D. Yang, G. Liao, S. Zhu, X. Yang, X. Zhang, IEEE GRSL, **11**, 9 (2014).
5. M. Davenport, M. Wakin, IEEE TIT, **56**, 9(2010).

An Improved K-means Method with Density Distribution Analysis

Huiwen Xue[1,*], Haochen Li[1], and Yanfei Wang[1]

[1]College of Science, China Agricultural University, Tsinghua East Road, Beijing, China

Abstract. In this paper, a novel K-means clustering algorithm is proposed. Before running the traditional K-means, the cluster centers should be randomly selected, which would influence the time cost and accuracy. To solve this problem, we utilize density distribution analysis in the traditional K-means. For a reasonable cluster, it should have a dense inside structure which means the points in the same cluster should tightly surround the center, while separated away from other cluster canters. Based on this assumption, two quantities are firstly introduced: the local density of cluster center ρ_i and its desperation degree δ_i, then some reasonable cluster centers candidates are selected from the original data. We performed our algorithm on three synthetic data and a real bank business data to evaluate its accuracy and efficiency. Comparing with Traditional K-means and K-means++, the results demonstrated that the improved method performs better.

1 Introduction

Today we are living in a world full of data. To store and manage the information we obtain every day, a large amount of dataset is generated. Thus, data analysis technology is needed. Cluster analysis plays an important and indispensable role in understanding data and has a long and rich history in variety of research fields. It is defined as "a statistical classification technique for discovering whether the individuals of a population fall into different groups by making quantitative comparisons of multiple characteristics according to Webster [1]'' One of the most popular and simplest clustering algorithms is K-means. It is proposed in 1955 and has been extended in many different ways in the past 50 years [2]. Although thousands of clustering algorithms have published today, traditional K-means is still wildly used in many fields. Easily implementation, simplicity and empirical success are the main reasons for its popularity [1-3].

The traditional K-means method is a typical partitioned algorithm. It can work very well for compact and hyper spherical clusters. However, despite its wide application, K-means suffers from a serious limitation. Before running the algorithm, there are three parameters: the number of clusters, cluster centers initialization and distance metric, have to be determined firstly [1, 4]. Mostly, K-means is utilized with the Euclidean metric to compute the distance between points and cluster centers. This is why K-means perform well in detecting spherical or ball shape clusters while perform poorly in grouping arbitrary shape data. Although Minkowski distance, Hamming distance, sup distance and Person correlation are also applied in some research field, the experimental and practical results are not satisfied [2]. The reason is the researchers have not considered the relationship between different features in the data, but assume they are orthogonal. It makes the distance compute only based on the difference in the same features while not in different features. This kind of assumption is not reasonable sometimes because in real data different features usually always have connection with each other. To solve this problem, proper prior process "distance metric learning" is needed [4]. Mahalanobis distance is a kind of metric used to detect hyper ellipsoidal cluster, covariance matrix of different features has to be calculated. Although for different data, it can learn its own Mahalanobis distance, this comes at high computational cost. Meanwhile, covariance describes the linear relationship between two variables, it is not universally for all kinds of data [2, 5].

Another important shortage that restricts the application of K-means is the initial cluster centroids and the number of clusters K must be decided before analysis [1-8]. The analysis results heavily depend on the initial positions of the cluster centers, thus if a bad initialization is chosen the objective function is easily getting trapped in poor local minima [7, 8]. In the meantime, cluster analysis is unsupervised learning which means there are no any category labels that tag objects with prior identifiers, thus it is very hard to find a proper K. For this issue,several heuristic methods have been given. However, the most widely used method is running the algorithm independently for different values of K and to find the most meaningful partition [5, 6, 7, 8]. It is a kind of dynamic strategy. The data is clustered from 1 group to N groups, here N is the total number of data points. When K is set differently, the partition is different. A reasonable K would be select according to domain knowledge or based on the evaluation criterion of the original data.

In this paper, we will focus on how to determine the parameter K in K-means. Equivalently, we will find the correct cluster centroids before applying K-means method for analysis of dataset. The ideal inspired from Rodriguez and Laio's brilliant clustering method which is based on fast search and find of density peaks [3]. In the next section, we will introduce the basic idea about how to determine the cluster centers. Then, in section 3 we will perform our new method on two benchmark dataset to test it efficiency and effectiveness. Finally, we apply this improved algorithm on a real bank business data to detect the underlying group structure.

2 Methods

2.1 Detection of cluster centers

As we mentioned above, the cluster centers should be the points that surrounded closely by their neighbors, this property describes the inside structure of a group is compact and the centers have very high local density [9, 10]. Meanwhile, centers in different clusters should be far away from each other which means they have a large relatively distance from each other. Based on this assumption, Rodriguez and Laio proposed clustering method by fast search and find of density peaks [3]. Here we introduce its basic idea and apply it to detect the cluster center. Let $X= \{x_i\},\ i = 1,2\ldots.\ n$, be the set of n dimensional points to be grouped. For each data point x_i, two quantities would be compute: its local density ρ_i and the distanceδ_I from other points with higher density. To obtain these two values, we have to compute the distances d_{ij} between data points and set a threshold d_c. It's clear that varying d_c would affect ρ_i and δ_i. Empirically, we choose d_c so that the average number of neighbors of a point is 2% of the total number of points in the dataset. The local density ρ_i of point x_i is defined as:

$$\rho_i = \sum \chi(d_{ij} - d_c) \tag{1}$$

Here $\chi(x) = 1$ if $x<0$ and $\chi(x) = 0$ otherwise. From this definition, ρ_i is actually equal to the number of points that are closer than d_c to point x_i. δ_i is obtain by computing the minimum distance between point x_i and any other point with higher density, the definition is as followed:

$$\delta_i = \min_{j:\rho_j>\rho_i}(d_{ij}) \tag{2}$$

We give both two values to each data point and plot them in a plan, then we will find the cluster centers [3]. The proper cluster centers should have peak values in both two quantities.

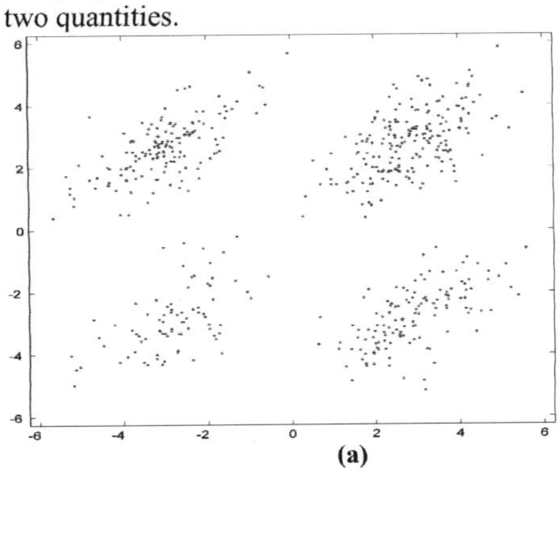

(a)

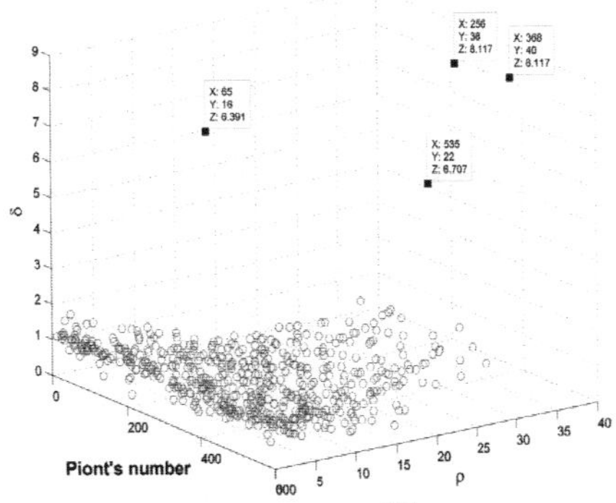

(b)

Fig.1. Four clusters centers in K-means data from MATLAB.

We use K-means data in MATLAB to show how powerful this method is. In "Fig. 1(b)", clearly the four black squares have significantly high value in local density ρ and distance from other points with higher density. Thus, we decide that there are four cluster centers and the data should be grouped into four parts. The result is reasonable according to the introduction in MATLAB about this dataset which is shown in Fig. 1(a).

2.2 K-means algorithm

K-means is a typical partitioned algorithm. In this section we will introduce its basic idea. K-means algorithm finds a partition via minimizing the squared error between the empirical mean of a cluster and the points inside the cluster. Here, Let $C = \{c_k,\ k = 1,2\ldots.\ K\}$ be the set of K clusters. Let v_k be the center of cluster c_k and usually it is computed as the mean of the all points in c_k. The squared error between v_k and all points is defined as an objective function:

$$J(c_k) = \sum_{x_i \in X} a_{ik}\|x_i - v_k\|^2 \tag{3}$$

where a_{ik} is equal to 1 if x_i is a point in cluster c_k and a_{ik} is 0 otherwise. The sum of the squared error over all K cluster is defined as:

$$J(C) = \sum_{k=1}^{K} \sum_{x_i \in X} a_{ik}\|x_i - v_k\|^2 \tag{4}$$

The goal of K-means is minimizing the sum of the squared error via finding the best a_{ik} for every point x_i. Minimizing the objective function above is known as a NP-hard problem. It can only converge to a local minimum. Usually, K-means begin with an initial partition with K clusters via select cluster centers randomly and then assign points to clusters so as to reduce the squared error. The main steps of K-means are as follows [1, 10]:

1) Select K initial cluster centers and begin computing J(C)
2) Generated a new partition via assigning each point to its closest cluster center.
3) Compute new mean of every cluster as the new cluster centers.
4) Repeat steps 2 and 3 until cluster centers do not move.

2.3 Silhouette value

We utilize silhouette measure [11] to assess the quality of clusters. To calculated the silhouette value $s(i)$ of anyone point, firstly we must estimate two scalars $a(x_i)$ and $b(x_i)$. Suppose point x_i belong to cluster A, when cluster A contains other genes apart from x_i, then we can compute:

$$a(i) = average\ distance\ of\ x_i\ to\ all\ other\ points\ of\ cluster\ A. \quad (5)$$

Then we consider any other cluster C which is different from A, and compute:

$$d(i, C) = average\ distance\ of\ x_i\ to\ all\ points\ of\ cluster. \quad (6)$$

After computing d(i,C) for all cluster $C \neq A$, we select the smallest of those values and denoted it by:

$$b(i) = \min\{d(i, C)\}, C \neq A \quad (7)$$

Suppose cluster B is the cluster which this minimum is obtained, that is, $d(i,B)=b(i)$, then we call it the neighbor of point x_i. Now $s(i)$ can be obtained by combining $a(i)$ and $b(i)$ as follows:

$$s(i) = \frac{[b(i) - a(i)]}{\max\{b(i) - a(i)\}} \quad (8)$$

From the above definition we can easily see that s(i) locates in [-1,1], when s(i) is close to 1, it implies that the 'within' distance $a(i)$ is much smaller that the smallest 'between' distance $b(i)$. There for, we can consider x_i is tight with its cluster and it is 'well-clustered'. Another situation is $s(i)$is around 0 which means $a(i)$ and $b(i)$are almost equal, hence it is not clear whether x_i should belong to either cluster A or B. This situation is considered as an 'intermediate case'. However, the worst situation is $s(i)$ is close to -1. It shows $a(i)$ is much larger than $b(i)$, thus gene x_i is much closer to B than to A. Therefore, we consider this is a "bad cluster".

3 Results and discussion

In this part, we firstly test our combined method on three UCI clustering analysis benchmark data: Iris, Wine, Seed which are widely test in different clustering method [12-14] and make a comparison with traditional K-means and K-means++. Then we apply our method on a real bank business data: aiming to detect its potential group structure. Because the clustering structure of the bank business data is unknown, therefore we just analysis the data distribution itself while do not consider its real background.

3.1 Testing on benchmark data

We firstly test our approach on the four popular benchmark data. Specially, we will focus on the clustering analysis on Iris data and illustrate the analysis results in Fig. 2. As we know that Iris data is one of the most classical datasets for analysis of pattern recognition, classification and clustering. There are 150 samples and divided into 3 groups. Every sample has four features. In this analysis, we pretend that the number of clusters k is unknown in advance, thus we have to estimate its value by calculating ρ and δ for every sample. As shown in Fig. 2 (a), there are three extreme values of δ and these three samples are the three centers of the clusters. It is much clearly in Fig 2 (b) that the three cluster centers are sample 50, sample 70 and sample 121 respectively. Fig. 2(c) is the final cluster center position we obtained after running the traditional K-means method and our combined approach just for one time. Here, we pick two features sepal length and sepal width as the coordinates in the plane. The three different color points represent three different three clusters. The red round points are cluster center computed by our approach while the dark triangle points are cluster center obtain by the traditional K-means method. Apparently, as cluster centers, the red round points are more reasonable because they are located in the central position of the three groups. On the contrary, it is obviously wrong if the dark triangle points are considered as the center of cluster because two of the centers are the same group and it is unacceptable. Meanwhile, in Fig 2(d), the evaluation obtained from the distribution of silhouette value of each cluster suggests this improved K-means method is more effective because all silhouette value of samples is over zero. On the view of data distribution, there are no wrong groups.

Table 1 is the detail of analysis on the three benchmark data. We compared the three center initialization algorithm: traditional K-means algorithm、K-means ++ algorithm and the improved algorithm. The results suggest the new improved K-means algorithm perform much better than the two previous K-means algorithms. Firstly, in terms of computing time, compared with the traditional K-means algorithm, the improved algorithm saved about three quarters of the computing time; At the same time, improved algorithm also increased accuracy (especially in Wine data).

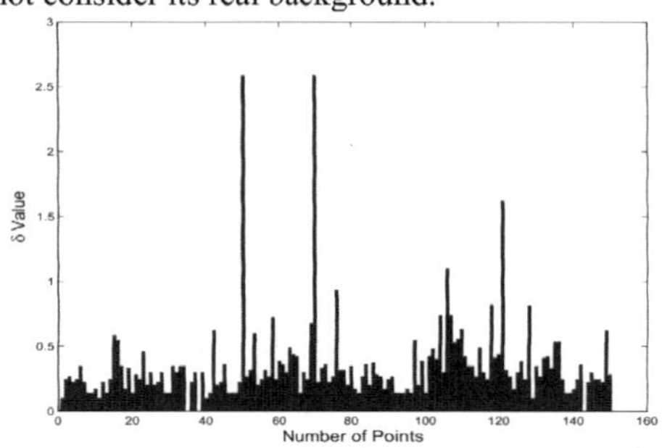

(a)

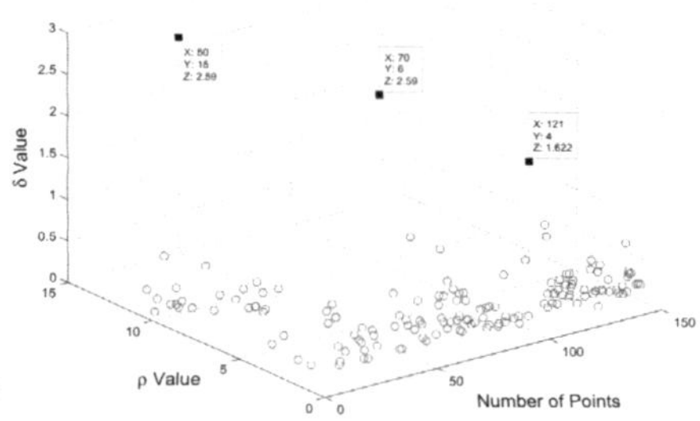

(b)

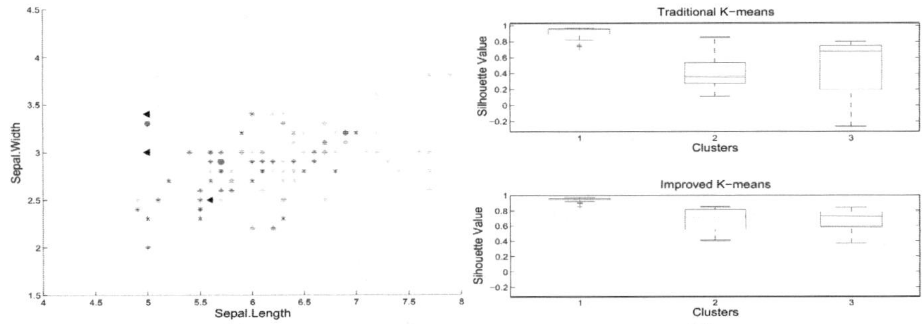

(c) (d)

Fig. 2. Analysis on Iris Data

Table 1. Clustering analysis on four benchmark dataset

Data Sets	Size	K	Time(s) (Traditional/Kmeans++/Improved)	Accuracy (Traditional/ Kmeans++/Improved)	Silhouette Value (Traditional/ Kmeans++/Improved)
Iris	150	3	0.866/0.697/0.149	88.67% /89.33%/88.67%	0.7342/0.7355/0.7342
Wine	178	3	0.603/0.126/0.147	38.20%/38.20% /70.22%	0.7274/0.7274/0.7323
Seed	210	3	0.468/0.113/0.119	89.05% / 89.05%/89.52%	0.6584 /0.6584/0.6632

3.2 Analysis on bank customer data

Clustering analysis is widely applied in financial economics. In this part, we apply the improved K-means on bank business data to classify bank customer. In this data, 40 bank card customers are selected. Considering that when banks classify customers, they are more concerned with the features that can play a key role in cluster analysis. So, the following six features are selected to segment: age, gender, education, monthly income, monthly transaction amount and monthly transactions.

Table 2. Different values of the features

Age	Sex	Education	Monthly income	Monthly transaction amount	Monthly transactions
30	male	undergraduate	5000	3000	6
3	2	6	4	3	4

Firstly, for convenience, we combine the different values of the features in the range of 1-10. (Table 2) After the actual experiment, we find that the survey data divided into four groups is better than three ones, and the classification of the description data is also more detailed, so we suppose that the number of clusters is 4. Secondly, we still use the above improved ideas ---selecting the cluster center first, (Fig3 (a)) and then clustering the 40 samples. At last, the results were tested using the silhouette value method and the box-plot. In Fig3 (b), there is no silhouette value less than 0, so the classification of four clusters are very good, especially the third cluster and the fourth one , silhouette values of which are above 0.5, showing that the clustering results in theory is very reasonable.

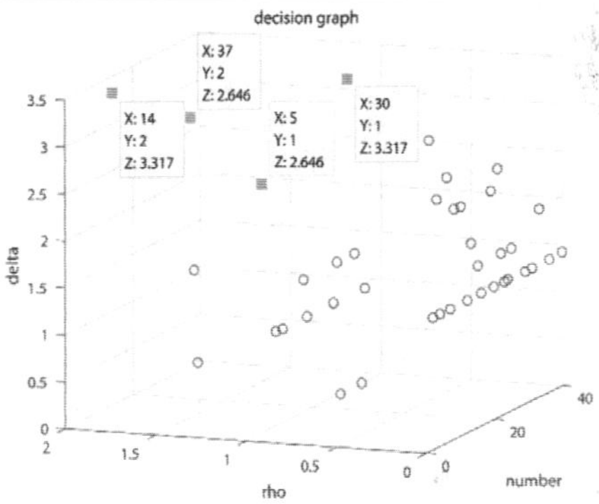

(*a*)

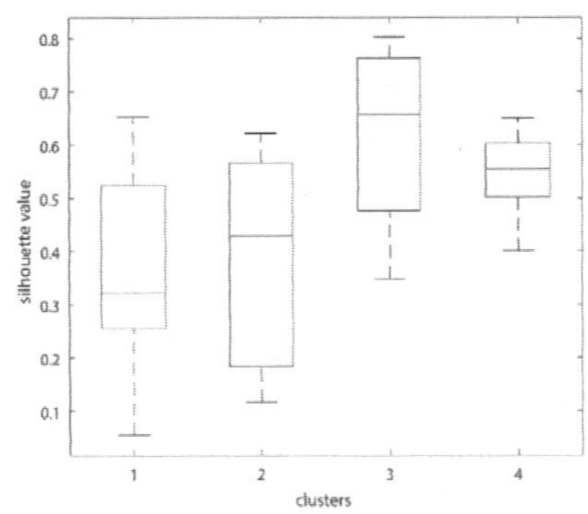

(*b*)

Fig 3. Analysis on bank business data

For banks, the first cluster of customers belongs to the middle-aged groups. They are mostly well-educated with bachelor or master degrees; monthly income is stable in the 3000-8000 yuan and the monthly transaction amount are less than 5,000 yuan. The proportion of the first category is very large, which is the mid-range customer groups. Banks need to pay more attention to their directions. The second cluster of customers belongs to the older groups. They are mainly male with high academic qualifications, high income and frequent transaction; however, their monthly amount of consumption is still less than million. The proportion of the second category is not high, which is the potential customer groups with the potential to rise to high-end customers. Banks may take measures to facilitate their conversion to high-end. The third cluster of customers are not high academic qualifications, their monthly income is very low, the amount of monthly transaction are about 3,000 yuan and the number of transaction is more than small. They belong to low-end customers. Although there is no potential value at present, the proportion of the group is still in a large number, so banks can be more publicity for this group. The fourth group of customers are highly educated with middle-age. Their monthly incomes are more than 20,000 yuan, the monthly transaction amount are more than 10,000 yuan, and monthly transaction are more than 10 times. They are high-end customers, although the proportion of the group is smaller, the banks should focus on providing them with personalized service.

4 Conclusions

In K-means cluster analysis, it is crucial to choose a proper cluster number K and proper cluster centers before applying the clustering algorithm. A proper K and correct cluster centers can make the iteration of the algorithm faster and more precise. To solve this issue, we propose an improved K-means method combine with the distribution analysis of dataset. The core idea of this approach is finding good cluster centers via computing two value of each point: its local density ρ_i and the distance δ_i from other points with higher density. For a good cluster center, we have the assumption that it should have both high values of ρ and δ. By this simple method, we find the number of clusters which also show the potential group structure of a dataset. We test this approach on three machine learning benchmark datasets. The experiment results suggest the improved method perform much better than the traditional K-means and K-means++. Meanwhile, we apply our method on clustering analysis of bank business data, it also performs well. Using this improved method, we successfully help the bank to classify the customers and give the bank some advice to manage the customers.

Acknowledgment

This work is supported in part by the University Students Innovation Fund of China Agricultural University.

References

1. Jain, A.K., "Data clustering: 50 years beyond K-means" *Pattern Recongnition letters 31*, pp. 651-666 (2010)
2. Xu, R. and Wunsch, D., "Survey of Clustering Algorithms", IEEE Transactions on Neural Networks, Vol.**16**, No.3, pp:645-677 (2005)
3. Rodriguez, A. and Lai, A., "Clustering by fast search and find of density peaks", Science Vol **344** Issue 6191, pp. 1492-1496 (2014)
4. Schwammle V. and Jensen O. N., "A simple and fast method to determine the parameters for fuzzy c-means cluster analysis", Bioinformatics, Vol. **26**, No.22, pp: 2841-2848 (2011)
5. Tzortzis, C., and Likas, A., "The Min-Max k-Means clustering algorithm", *Pattern Recognition*, Vol. **47**, pp. 2505-2516 (2014)
6. Ball, G and Hall, D., "ISODATA, a novel method of data analysis and pattern classification.", *Technical report NTIS AD* 699616. Stanford Research Institute, Stanford, CA, 1965.
7. Kleinberg, J. "An impossibility theorem for clustering", In: NIPS **15**, pp. 463-470. (2002)
8. Wallace, C.S and Freeman, P.R., "Estimation and Inference by compact coding" JRSSB, **49**, , pp.240-251 (1987)
9. Fukuyama, Y. and Sugeno, M. "A new method of choosing the number of clusters for the fuzzy c-means method." Proc. *5th fuzzy syst.* Symp., PP. 247(1989)
10. MacQeen, J., "Some methods for classification and analysis of multivariated observations" In: *Fifth Berkeley Symposium on Mathematics, Statistics and Probability.* University of California Press, pp: 281-297 (1965)
11. Kaufman, L. and Rousseeuw, P.J. "Finding groups in data: an introduction to cluster analysis." Wiley series in Probability and Statistics (2005)
12. Mao, J. and Jain, A.K., "A self-organizing network for hyper-ellipsoidal clustering (HEC)", IEEE Transactions on Neural Networks, Vol. **7**, pp. 16-29 (1996)
13. Figureueredo, M. and Jain, A.K., "Unsupervised learning of finite mixture models" IEEE Transaction on Pattern Analysis and Machine Intelligence, Vol **24**, No. 3, pp. 381-396 (2002)
14. Tavazoie, S., Hughes, J.D., Compbell, m.J., Cho, R.J. and Church, G.M., "Systematics determination of genetic network architecture", Nature Genetics, Vol. **22**, 281-285 (1999)

MATEC Web of Conferences **176**, 01020 (2018) https://doi.org/10.1051/matecconf/201817601020
IFID 2018

Regional Load Balancing Circuitous Bandwidth Allocation Method Based on Dynamic Auction Mechanism

Wang Chao[1], Zhang Dalong[2], Ran Xiaomin[1]

[1]National Digital Switching System Engineering and Technological Research Center,ZhengZhou, China;
[2] College of Information Engineering, Zhengzhou University, Zhengzhou ,China

Abstract. Aiming at the problem of link congestion caused by the shortage of network bandwidth resources at the user end, this paper first proposes a regional load balancing idea. Then, for the problem of bandwidth resource allocation in regional load balancing, a bandwidth allocation model is established and a dynamic auction algorithm is proposed. The algorithm calculates the link quality and stability by constructing a link model, and introduces the auction bandwidth to the auctioneer's incentive degree to obtain the auction bidding function. The simulation results show that the algorithm can effectively improve the user's network status, reduce the service response delay, increase the throughput, and at the same time can effectively prevent the auction user's false bidding behavior, so that the auction quote quickly converges to the maximum quote, reduces the number of auctions, and reduces Communication overhead.

1 INTRODUCTION

The rapid development of the Internet has put higher demands on the bandwidth. Although the link capacity is quite adequate, overconsumption of link congestion and bandwidth is still widespread in the Internet. Therefore, it is of great significance to efficiently use the available bandwidth resources in the network.

For the allocation of limited resources, the price control mechanism is an effective solution (Song Qizhu, 2010). The most typical control mechanism based on price is to set a static price for each unit resource, the most obvious advantage of this method is simple and easy to implement (Odlyzko A, 1997). However, the static pricing model can not adapt to the dynamic changes of network traffic in the network environment where the resource's demand changes dynamically. In order to solve the problem of bandwidth resource allocation in dynamic network environment better, a dynamic pricing model is proposed. A classical dynamic pricing model uses the auction way to price the network bandwidth for maximum benefit (Semret N, 1999). Dramitinos M (2007) proposed a distributed network bandwidth auction mechanism for Dutch multi-unit auctions by setting a sufficiently high bidding price for each link's bandwidth and conducting price reduction auctions based on variable price reduction rules until the first bidder appears. The method uses different bidding prices to reflect the imbalance of link's bandwidth requirements, meanwhile, the pricing method using VCG (Vickrey-Clarke-Groves) mechanism ensures the bidding behavior of the bidders. However, this mechanism requires bidders to monitor bidding progress at all time, which leads to large communication costs. Tipsuwan Y (2009) comparatived the advantages and disadvantages of three bandwidth allocation methods, and proposed a centralized auction mechanism based on game theory and dynamic bandwidth allocation method.As bidders initially submitted price may be different from the final payment price, bandwidth utilization and initial offer is used to determine its final offer and avoid fake quotations.

Link evaluation is a way to improve routing performance through link quality (Chan K P, 2003 and Lin-Yuan L, 2010). To solve the problem of network congestion caused by multiconcurrency services, this paper first proposes a solution of regional load balancing, then proposes a dynamic bandwidth auction method. Based on the centralized dynamic auction mechanism, the classification of bandwidth resources is firstly refined by evaluating the link's quality to meet the needs of different bidders. The pricing rules based on link's quality can effectively inhibit bidding's fake bidding behavior. At the same time, this paper also proposes auction incentive value mechanism, which determines the degree of stimulation or suppression of bandwidth resources to the bidders in each round of auctions, it avoids the communication overhead of multiple interactive interactions between auction parties, not noly

Corresponding author: ok135246sdu@163.com, ttengzhang@163.com ensures that the auction ends within limited rounds, but also makes auction quotes quickly tend to the maximum. Finally, the problem is simplified by separately solving the maximum benefit of each unit instead of calculating the global maximum benefit.

The rest of this paper is organized as follows.In Section 2,we introduce the concept of regional load balancing.In Section 3,we describe the model of bandwidth allocation and link quality.Then we describe the bandwidth auction algorithm in Section 4.Extensive simulations are discussed in Section 5.Section 6 concludes this paper.

2 REGIONAL LOAD BALANCING

In a multi-ISP (Internet Service Providers) network, the traditional multi-WAN router only considers the load balance within the device and does not consider the load balancing within the region, it easily leads to the user's data transmission between different ISPs. However, the bridge bandwidth between different ISP servers is often difficult to meet the demand of large amount of data transmission, which limits the implementation of load balancing. Meanwhile, due to massive data forwarding between ISP bridges, the transmission delay of user services under the load balancing policy increases, making it difficult to satisfy users' QoE.

In order to solve the above problem, this paper presents a regional load balancing technology - through multiple gateways (the gateway needs more than two WAN ports) to collaborate with each other, and to complete the round robin forwarding of the services of the congested gateways within a certain spatial domain. That is, using the corresponding WAN ports and links of idle gateways in the local area to implement detouring and forwarding of the congested links, and avoiding the preemption of load balancing services on the bridge bandwidth between ISPs. Enabling multiple users to reuse access band-width resources of a certain WAN port on demand to improve network access rate and throughput so as to complete distributed traffic balance at the bottom and enable efficient access to data, video, and other services on different ISP servers.

Regional load balancing is a load balancing technology that enables cooperative forwarding and traffic transfer among multiple devices within a certain spatial domain to round off congested links. Forwarding user's data on the congestion side by borrowing the links of other idle gateways, the load of the congested links and nodes can be release and the service response time of the congested gateway can be reduced, so as to achieve distributed traffic balance. The principle is shown in Figure 1. When multiple gateways in a network cooperate with each other to complete bandwidth renting and link bypassing, traffic load of the congested nodes is transferred to idle nodes. Adopting this circuitous strategy can avoid the transmission pressure of traffic between two different ISPs and implement the underlying multi-network convergence.

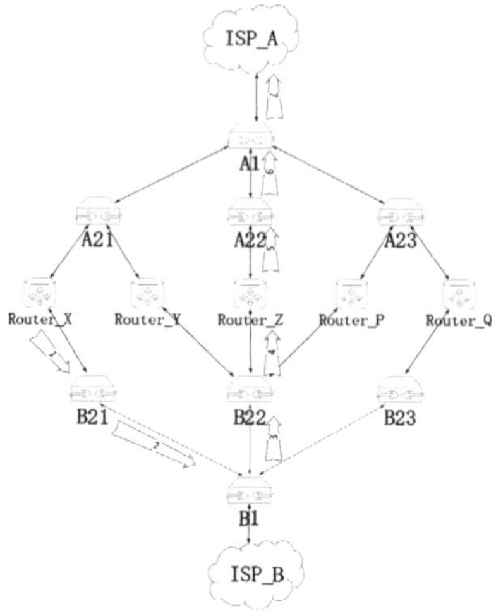

Figure 1: Regional load balancing principle diagram

3 MODEL BUILDING

3.1 Auction Model

Although the link capacity is sufficient, as the network user base and the user's level of network quality requirements increase dramatically, the user's demand for bandwidth is far greater than the bandwidth resources provided by the operator. While centralized allocation algorithm is easy to form a "heat island" effect, and the central server is easy to become a performance bottleneck, and there is a delay in the interaction and update of the information, which can not well adapt to the network with frequent dynamic changes. To rationally allocate resources on demand and ensure the fairness of resource allocation as well as the benefit of resource providers, this paper adopts the auction method for the band-width allocation of users with the same bandwidth requirements.

For the allocation of bandwidth resources to users requesting the same bandwidth, this paper describes the auction model as a optimization problem. According to bidders submit the offer information to determine the bandwidth allocation program. The model defines participants as three types: participants with free bandwidth resources are auctioneers, participants who request bandwidth resources are bidders, agents who decide on bandwidth allocation results and payment rules for both bidders.

During the auction, the total revenue obtained by defining N auctioneers is $\sum_{i=1}^{N} W_i$, where W_i is the revenue obtained by the auctioneer i , so the auction model can be abstracted as follow:

$$\max \sum_{i=1}^{N} W_i$$
$$s.t. \quad \sum_{j=1}^{M} B_j \le C,\ B_j \ge 0,\ j = 1,\ldots,M \tag{1}$$

Where B_j is the bandwidth requirement of bidder j .

In order to solve the maximum value, the above optimization problem is decomposed to solve the optimal value of each auctioneer so as to opt-imize the overall return. Therefore, Eq. (1) can be decomposed into the following formula:

$$\max W_i$$
$$s.t. \quad \sum_{j=1}^{M_i} B_j \le B_i,\ B_j \ge 0,\ j=1,\ldots,M_i \qquad (2)$$

Where B_i is the free bandwidth resource pro-vided by the auctioneer i and M_i is the total number of bidders owned by the auctioneer i.

3.2 Link Quality

The purpose of the region load balancing stra-tegy is to realize the traffic transfer from the congested node to the idle node, that is to select a better-quality path for data transmission. In the transmission of the service, the congestion status of the link is more important than the number of hops to affect users' QoS .

To achieve regional load balancing, you need to measure the quality of the path between the client and the server. In the end-to-end multi-hop link topology shown in Figure 2 , D is a server, S is a client gateway, and the others nodes are routers. For the client, the effect of the neighbor node on it's QoS is higher than that of the remote node. Therefore, the link weight vector is introduced as the impact value of each link quality on the client. The weight of link k is:

$$\omega(k)=\frac{1}{N+1-k} \qquad (3)$$

Where N is the total number of end-to-end hops, k is the link number, and the closer it is to the client k, the larger it is.

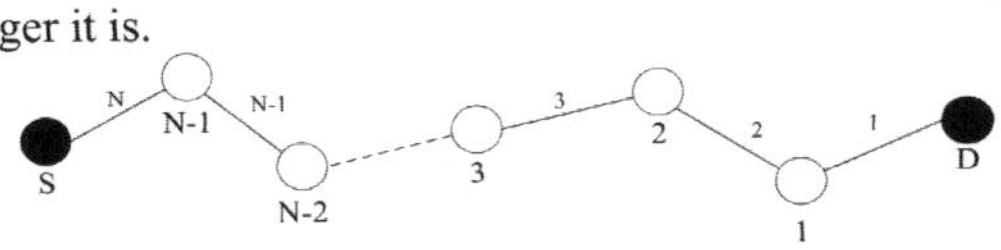

Figure 2: End-to-end multi-hop forwarding link

In this paper, the round-trip delay of packets is the main parameter of link quality. In normal con-ditions, we define the average roundtrip delay is $\overline{RTT_0}$, then the quality of link k is:

$$Q(k)=\left[\frac{\overline{RTT_0}}{\overline{RTT_k}}\right]\omega(k) \qquad (4)$$

Where $\overline{RTT_k}$ is the average round-trip delay of link k in the quality calculation period. Therefore, the client's port τ to the operator's server path quality Q^τ is:

$$Q^\tau=\sum_{k=1}^{N}\left[\frac{\overline{RTT_0}}{\overline{RTT_k}}\right]\omega(k) \qquad (5)$$

In the multi-hop path from the user terminal to the server, there may be multiple links with the same quality. In order to distinguish the quality of the links, a link's stability parameter is introduced. Assume that the end-to-end path performs m mea-surements within one RTT calculation period., so the link RTT matrix $\mathbf{R}$ is obtained:

$$\mathbf{R}=\begin{bmatrix} RTT_{11} & \cdots & RTT_{1m} \\ \vdots & \ddots & \vdots \\ RTT_{N1} & \cdots & RTT_{Nm} \end{bmatrix} \qquad (6)$$

Where RTT_{ij} represents the jth RTT measurement of link i. Therefore, the link's stability S^τ is the vari-ance of matrix $\mathbf{R}$:

$$S^\tau = D(\mathbf{R}) \qquad (7)$$

4 BANDWIDTH AUCTION ALGORITHM

As the bidder often requests more bandwidth than the actual demand in bidding, in order to avoid the bidding behavior of the bidder and result in the waste of resources, the bidding party's payment function P_{bid} is defined, indicating that the re-quested link quality is Q_{bid} and the bandwidth is B_{bid} ,the bidder's payment function is defined by the following formula:

$$P_{bid}=\alpha(Q_{auc}-Q_{bid})B_{bid}-\beta S_{auc} \qquad (8)$$

Where α and β are unit price coefficient constants of link quality and bandwidth. If a bidder requests a bandwidth greater than the actual demand, the cost to be paid by the bidder increases with a certain difference in the quality of the link, thereby suppressing the bidder's fake bidding behavior. If the bidder needs a certain bandwidth, the higher the bidding link quality is, the higher the cost will be borne.

Bidding process, different bidders may be different, set a quotation in the highest offer is $F_{\max}$, then the next quotation, the last highest bid is the reserve price of the offer. Suppose the nth bid quotation of bidder i is $F_i(n)$, the highest quotation of the bid is $F_{\max}(n)$, in order to reduce the bidding process information interaction, making bidding quickly converge to the highest quotation, we propose a incentive function $\theta_i(n)$, said the item is attractive or repulsive to the bidder in the quote. The incentive value is determined by the attraction generated by the ratio of the quality of the bidding object to the bidder's own network quality and the price increase per bidding quote, as follows:

$$\theta_i(n)=\begin{cases}\dfrac{Q_{auc_i}}{Q_{bid_i}} & ,n=0\\[2ex] \theta_i(n-1)-\dfrac{\mathrm{F}_{\max}(n-1)-\mathrm{F}_i(n-1)}{\mathrm{F}_i(n-1)} & ,n\ge 1\end{cases} \qquad (9)$$

When $\theta_i(n)>0$, bidder i will conduct the next bid, when $\theta_i(n)\le 0$, bidder i will give up bidding. From Eq.(9), we can see that when $n\ge 1, \theta_i(n)$ is a decreasing function, that is the bidding enthusiasm of bidders will gradually decrease as the number of bidding increases. After limited rounds of bidding, $\theta_i(n)\le 0$, bidding participants give up auction and the auction ends.

From Eq.(8), we know that the maximum that an auctioneer can obtain in each round auction is

$\max P_{bid}\left(B_{bid}\right) \approx \alpha[\ln(n)+C]\cdot B_{bid}$, where C is the Euler's constant and $C = 0.57722...$. In the case of the same bandwidth request and the number of hops between the client and the operator's server, B_{bid} and n is a constant. In order to make the bidding price quickly converge to the maximum bidding price, we set up bid L times per round. When $\theta_i(n) > 0$, the bidder bid increases to be $\Delta P(n)$, so the bidding round of bidder i is:

$$P'_{bid}(n) = \begin{cases} P_{bid} & , n = 1 \\ F_{\max}(n-1) + X_{\theta(n)} \cdot \Delta P(n), & n \geq 2 \end{cases} \quad (10)$$

In the Eq.(10), where $X_{\theta(n)} = \begin{cases} 0, \theta_i(n) \leq 0 \\ 1, \theta_i(n) > 0 \end{cases}$ and $0 \leq \Delta P(n) \leq \max P_{bid}\left(B_{bid}\right)$. From Eq.(10),we can see that each round of bidding the quote is higher than the the highest quote of last round of bidding, combined with Eq.(9), it can be obtained within limited rounds of auctions, the quotation will quickly converge to the highest final price.

5 SIMULATION ANALYSIS

In order to verify the advantages and dis-advantages of the proposed bandwidth allocation algorithm, NS2 is used to design the following experiment.

The experimental results are shown in Figure 3, There were six users who made fake quotes and compared the performance and cost before and after their quotes.

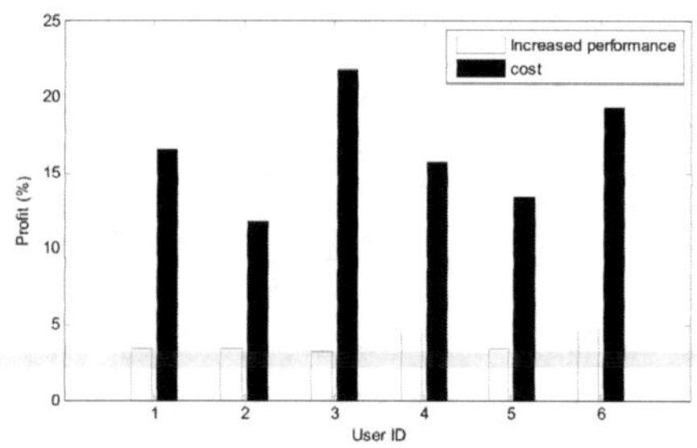

Figure 3: Fake quote profit contrast

We can see from the Figure 3 that when users make fake quotes, their performance improvement ratio is far less than the increase in cost, so the pricing rules provided in this paper can effectively avoid the problem of false quotes.

In order to evaluate the impact of the proposed algorithm on the performance of networks, the effect of link quality and bandwidth on users is simulated under two scenarios respectively: Case 1 is the effect on performance of users leasing different band-widths under the same link quality; case 2 is the effect on the user's performance under the condition that the bandwidth of the user is the same and the link quality is different. In the case 1, the delay of three users and the throughput result are shown in Figure 4 and 5; In the case 2, the delay and through-put results shown in Figure 6 and 7.

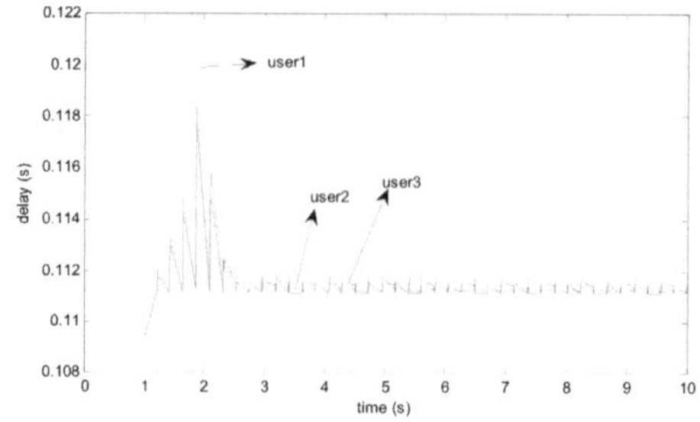

Figure 4: User's delay in case 1

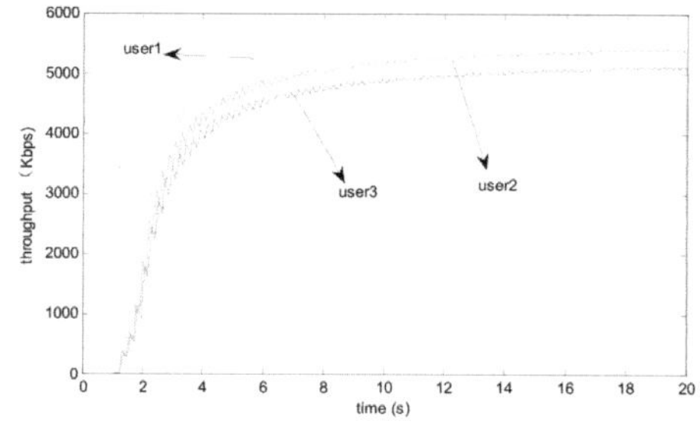

Figure 5: User's throughput in case 1

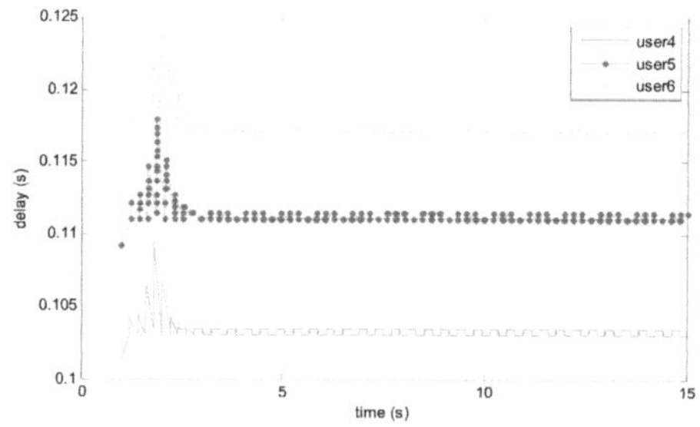

Figure 6: User's delay in case 2

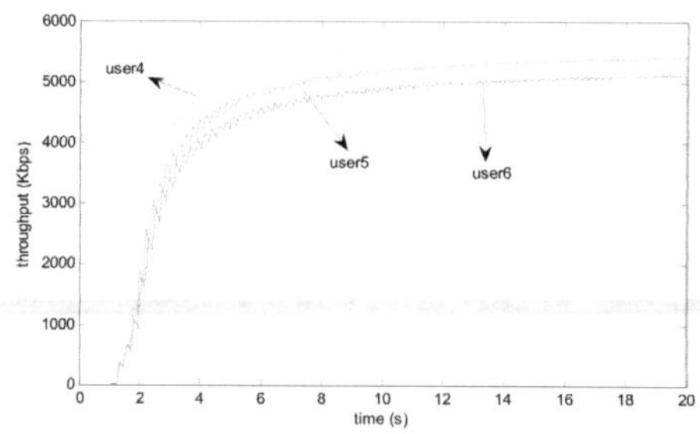

Figure 7: User's throughput in case 2

Comparing Figure 4 and 6 shows that after the transmission is stable, when the link quality is different and the bandwidth is the same, the better the link quality is, the lower the delay is. As can be seen from the comparison between Figure 5 and 7, the throughput of the client is related to the band-width and the link quality. When the bandwidth is the same, the better the link quality is, the larger the throughput is. In the case of a certain link quality, the larger the bandwidth, the greater the throughput. Because the method proposed in this paper improves the link quality and increases the logical bandwidth at the same time, so can better improve user's QoE.

To verify the advantages and disadvantages of the proposed algorithm, we simulate the bidding situation of bidders under the same bandwidth and bidding under different bandwidth requests by multiple bidders. The simulation results are shown in Figure 8 and Figure 9.

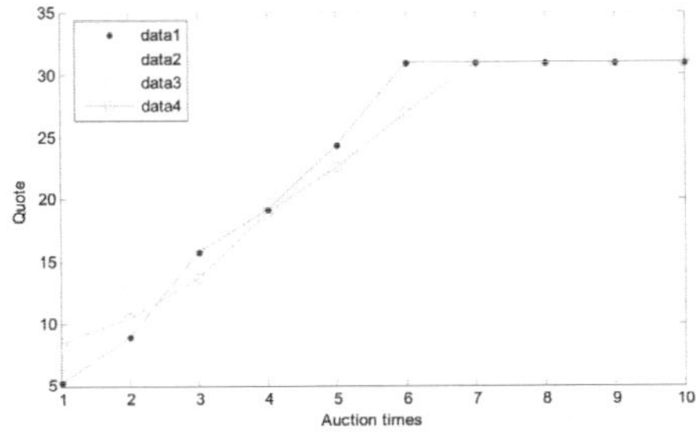

Figure 8: The same bandwidth's quote

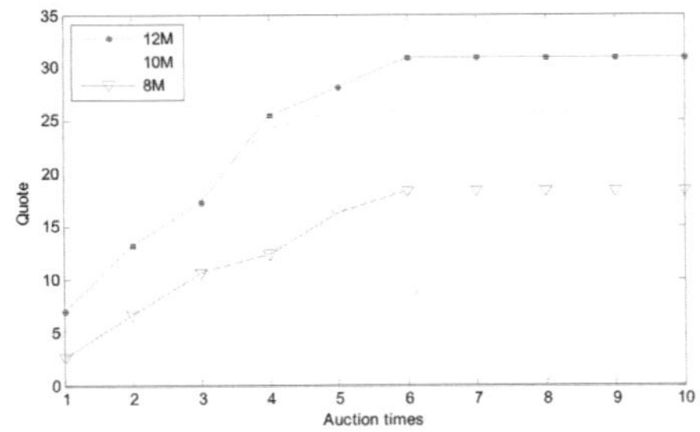

Figure 9: Different request bandwidth's quote

Where Figure 8 is a bidding result of four bidders bidding simultaneously with a bandwidth of 12M. From Figure 8, it can be seen that in the case of a bidding bandwidth of a certain size, bidders' initial quotations are not necessarily the same. In the bidding process, each Therefore, the bidders bid in the next round of bidding is also different, and the highest bid of the last bid is the lowest bid of the next round of bidding. Within the limited rounds of bidding, the quotation reaches the highest quotation of the bandwidth, When a bidder first reached the maximum quotation, the auction ended. As can be seen from Figure 9, for different auction bandwidths, the initial bidding price is different and the highest bidding price is also different. The price difference of bidding for two adjacent bidding rounds has nothing to do with the bidding bandwidth, but both reach the highest quotation within the limited bidding times. Therefore, when the highest bid price is obtained for each round of quotations, the total auction proceeds reach the maximum.

6 CONCLUSION

In this paper, we propose a regional load balancing scheme based on dual WAN routers from the perspective of users and propose an auction-based bandwidth allocation strategy for the link congestion in the network and the uneven allocation of bandwidth resources. Based on the idle state and link quality of the client routers in the logical area, the bandwidth resources are auctioned and allocated dynamically. The simulation results show that the bandwidth allocation strategy proposed in this paper can effectively ensure that the auctioneer can obtain greater benefits while improving bidder QoS.

References

1. Song Qizhu. Research on Market Allocation Mechanism of Radio Spectrum Resources [D]. Beijing University of Posts and Telecommunications, 2010.
2. Odlyzko A. A Modest Proposal for Preventing Internet Congestion[M]. Center for Discrete Mathematics & Theoretical Computer Science, 1997.
3. Semret N, Liao R F, Campbell A T, et al. Market pricing of differentiated Internet services[C]// Seventh International Workshop on Quality of Service. IEEE, 1999:184-193.
4. Dramitinos M, Stamoulis G D, Courcoubetis C. An auction mechanism for allocating the bandwidth of networks to their users[M]. Elsevier North-Holland, Inc. 2007.
5. Tipsuwan Y, Kamonsantiroj S, Srisabye J, et al. An auction-based dynamic bandwidth allocation with sensitivity in a wireless networked control system[J]. Computers & Industrial Engineering, 2009, 57(1):114-124.
6. Chan K P, Fu W C, Yu C. Haar Wavelets for Efficient Similarity Search of Time-Series: With and Without Time Warping[J]. Knowledge & Data Engineering IEEE Transactions on, 2003, 15(3):686-705.
7. Lin-Yuan L. Link Prediction on Complex Networks[J]. Journal of University of Electronic Science & Technology of China, 2010, 39(5):651-661.

Design and Implementation of HD Video Encoding System Based on HDMI

Wanjia Gao[1], Baohai Sun[2], Qingqing Peng[3], Huixin Zhang[1*]

[1]National Defense Key Laboratory for Electronic Measurement Technology, North University of China, Taiyuan, China;
[2]Tianjin 712 Communication and Broadcasting Group Co. LTD (TCB), Tianjin, China;
[3]North Automatic Control Technology Insititute,Taiyuan, China

Abstract. Focus on the problem that TI's dedicated video processor TMS320DM8148 cannot directly collect video data from HDMI interface, this paper presents a video coding system based on H.264.The system used DSP+FPGA architecture, FPGA is responsible for collecting video data of HDMI interface and caching. And then send to DM8148 through GPMC, DM8148 completes video encoding and decoding through the interaction of internal modules. The results show that video is displayed clearly and smoothly, without distortion or error. It successfully realizes the collection of the video data of HDMI interface obtained with DM8148.

1 Introduction

In recent years, digital image technology has been widely used in security, medical treatment, education, and monitoring, which has led to a great development and attention. With the continuous improvement of video quality, the storage speed and the bandwidth growth speed cannot meet its requirements. So the video encoding technology is becoming increasingly important. With the continuous popularization and application of advanced video compression coding standards, such as H.264, HD video is rapidly entering into people's daily life. HDMI HD video interface not only has the features of higher bandwidth and higher resolution, but also integrates video transmission and audio transmission, which greatly simplifying the cable connection settings.

The DSP of TMS320DM8148 of TI is a special chip with rich video image processing module and low power consumption. It can achieve the processing of 1 channel 1080P/60fps or 4 channels 720P/60fps, and the speed is fast. However, the video data information transmitted by HDMI HD video interface cannot be directly collected.

In view of this, this paper designs and implements a high definition video coding system based on HDMI interface.

2 Overall system design

The overall system adopts FPGA+DSP architecture, and the overall scheme design structure is shown in Fig 1. FPGA sends control signals and clock synchronization signals to the forward HDMI interface to control the beginning and end of video information collection. The received high definition video information is cached in the internal FIFO of FPGA, then be sent to the FIFO of GPMC though the data logic control unit. Then the information is sent to DSP by GPMC data bus. The DSP of the system is the TMS320DM8148 of TI scheme. After receiving video information, the DSP will encode and decode video according to the program control process. Finally, the video data is output by the HD interface, which is displayed by the special display.

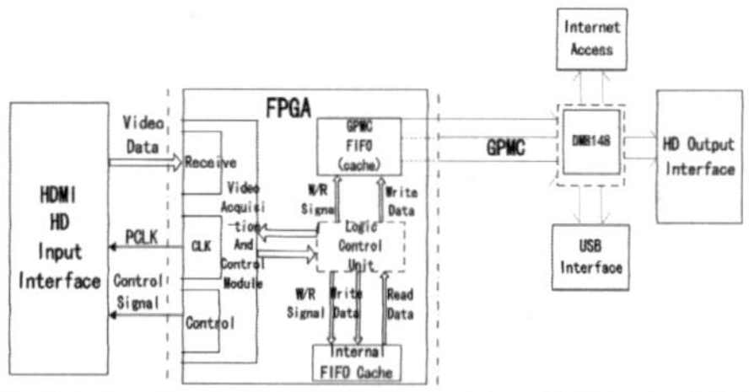

Fig. 1. General block diagram of the system structure.

3 HD interface design

3.1. High definition interface hardware design

High definition interface design includes video data input interface and video data output interface. The output interface is interlinked with DSP, and the input interface can be interlinked with FPGA or DSP. Because the DSP integrates the high definition control module, it is easier to handle the data collection and interface controlling than the FPGA. However, the internal integration of DSP is high, and when the utilization rate is high, it will have a certain effect on the internal running speed. Therefore, when the internal resource utilization rate of DSP is high, FPGA can be used to

* Corresponding author: author@e-mail.org

collect data and reduce the DSP burden. When the usage rate is low, it can be collected directly by DSP.

3.1.1 High definition input interface design

The system uses ADV7619 and IP4776CZ38 as the video decoding and receiving chip. ADV7619 is a high quality, double-input, single-output(2:1) multiplex HDMI receiver with a maximum clock frequency of 170MHz. And it supports all mandatory 3D extension formats that specified in the (HDMI®) 1.4a specification, named sYCC601, Adobe RGB, Adobe YCC 601, xvYCC color range. IP4776CZ38 can provide high quality ESD protection for TMDS signals. It can also perform a level conversion to protect HDMI's DDC channel. It is used to prevent the system from collapsing or sending errors due to excessive static electricity. Fig 2 shows the high definition interface.

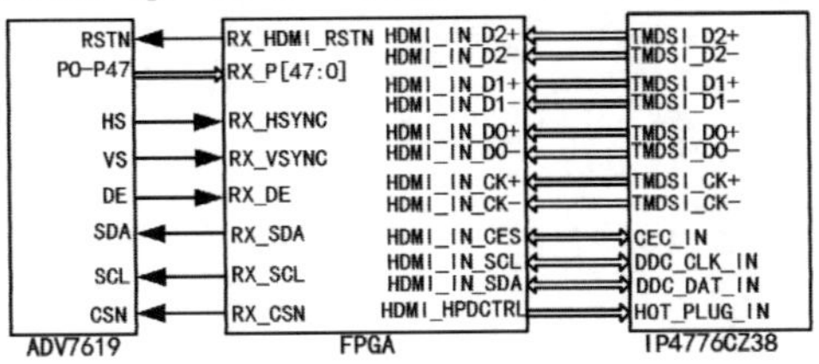

Fig. 2. High definition interface schematic.

3.1.2 High definition output interface design

The HD output interface is TPD12S016. It is a multimedia interface conversion chip that integrates low capacitance direction protection diode, and it contains a conversion buffer that automatically induces the I2C level. TPD12S016 supplies the HDMI power line with the 55mA limited stream 5V. The CT_PHD pin manages the 5V output and hot plug control, which is independent of the LS_OE pin, enabling the activation detection to run between the start of the HD link SDA, SCL, and CEC lines are pulled to VCCA on side A. The I2C control signal SCL and SDA can drive load capacitance higher than 1.4 version of HDMI specification, which can reach 750pF. When the HDMI mechanical interface is inserted into the socket, it may cause error detection. However, the PHD_B port integrated burr pulse filter can solve this problem. The reverse current protection function is integrated internally to prevent the reverse current from burning the chip during a power outage. Features include: Compatible with HDMI test without other external devices; Hold 1.4 version HDMI data transmission rate; Four differential pairs for 8-channel transmission channels are used to prevent electrostatic discharge by using low differential capacitors; 5V output pin integrated chip load switch, current is limited to 50mA; Long HDMI cables use single trigger circuit driver, in line with the HDMI specification on the integration of pull-up resistors and drop-down resistors, also provide reverse drive protection in mechanical interface, this is the direction of automatic induction I2C level converter. Fig 3 shows the high definition output schematic diagram.

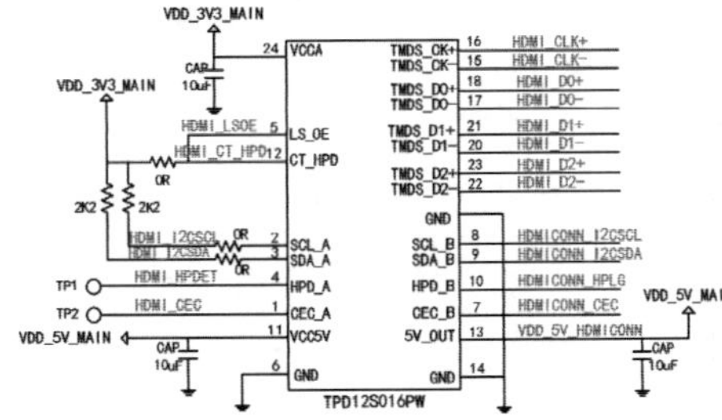

Fig. 3. High definition output interface schematic diagram.

3.2. High definition interface collection timing

The data collection of HD interface is mainly control of ADV7619. Fig 4 is the ADV7619 sequence diagram. And (a) is I2C sequence diagram, it includes eight parts: t1-t8. (b) is pixel port and SDR output control sequence diagram. It consists of two parts: clock output and data, control output. The details are shown in Table 1

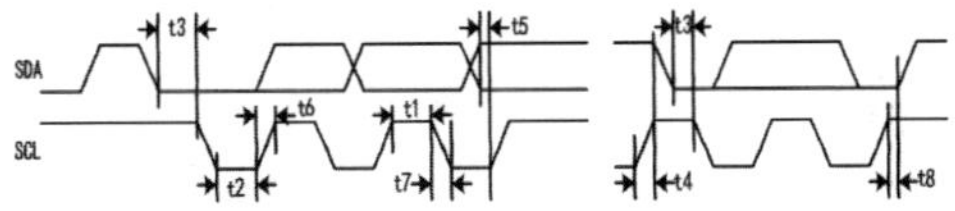

(a) I2C Port timing.

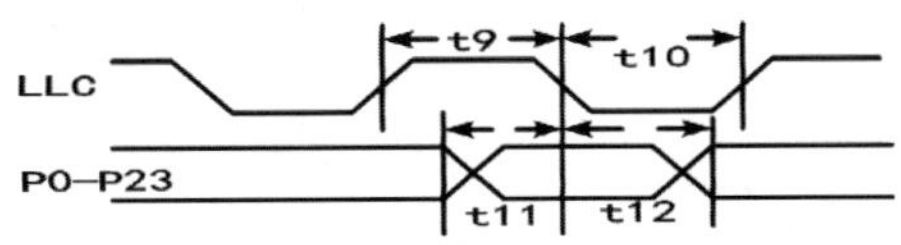

(b) Pixel port and SDR control output timing..

Fig. 4. Sequence diagram.

Table 1. Details of sequence diagram.

Parameter		Time
I2C Port	SCL Min Pulse Width High	t1
	SCL Min Pulse Width Low	t2
	Start Condition Holding Time	t3
	Start Condition Setting Time	t4
	SDA Building Time	t5
	SCL and SDA Rising Time	t6
	SCL and SDA Falling Time	t7
	Stop Condition Building Time	t8
CLK Output	LLC Space Ratio	t9; t10
Data and Control Output	Data Output Conversion Time.	t11
		t12

In Table 1, t11 is the time of effective data end to negative clock edge, t12 is negative clock edge to effective data begin time.

Fig 5 is the I2C control sequence diagram, which controls the beginning and end of data exchange. Combining the data reading and writing sequence of Fig 6, it can be seen that the state of the stop bit is always changing. It is needless for stop bit when writing data, but is needed when reading.

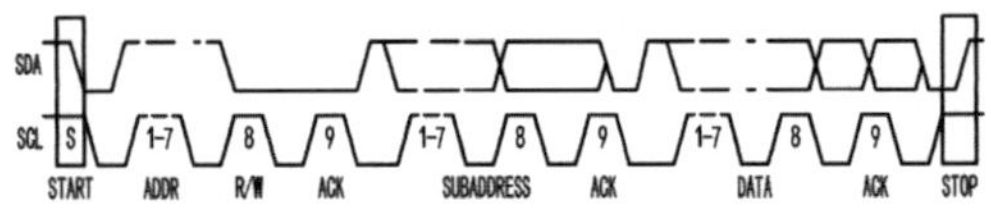

Fig. 5. I2C control timing

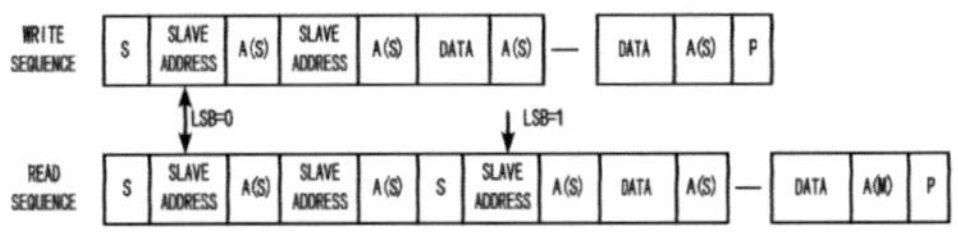

Fig. 6. Data read-write sequence

4 Software coding and decoding

4.1. Software coding design

FPGA collects video information transmitted by HD interface, and caches the information in the internal FIFO. The cached data is transmitted to GPMC FIFO through logical control unit. Then send to DM8148 by GPMC data bus. After receiving video information, the coding and decoding of video is followed by the software process. Finally, it is output by the HD interface and displayed by the display. The interaction between the internal threads involved in the video encoding process is shown in Fig 7.

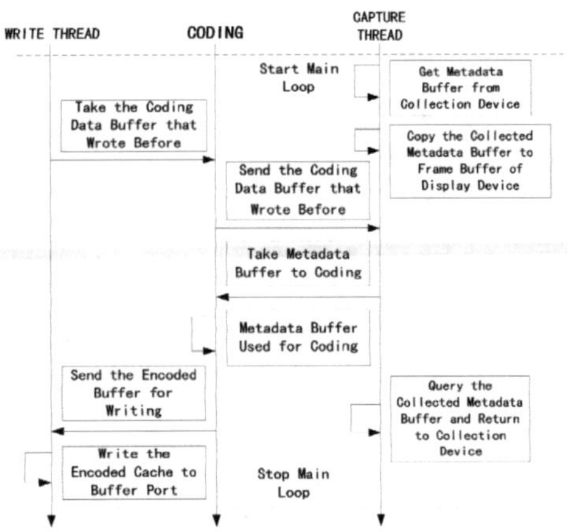

Fig. 7. Video interactive thread.

First, the capture thread takes the video data from the data collection buffer. At the same time, the encoding thread takes out the I/O buffer that has been written to the file from the write thread. Then giving the encoded data buffer to the capture thread to populate the new video frame data. To encode the video frame that is being processed, the encoding thread needs to obtain video source data from the capture thread. At this point, the encoding thread takes the source data cache from the capture thread through FIFO_get () for encoding. After that, the encoding thread calls the internal encoding function on the DSP, encodes the received source video, and stores it in the I/O cache. Setting the collection data cache as read-only to avoid modifying the source data in the encoding process. When the video encoder running on the DSP will code the data in the cache to the I/O cache, the latter will use the FIFO_put () function to send to the write thread. In this way, it ensures that the three threads interact with each other, successfully completing data collection, encoding data, and caching data.

4.2. Video decoding design

The encoded video information cannot be displayed normally without decoding. So when the encoded video data file loading thread is correctly loaded into the buffer, the video file needs to be decoded to ensure its normal display. The thread is mainly divided into four aspects. The process is shown in Fig 8.

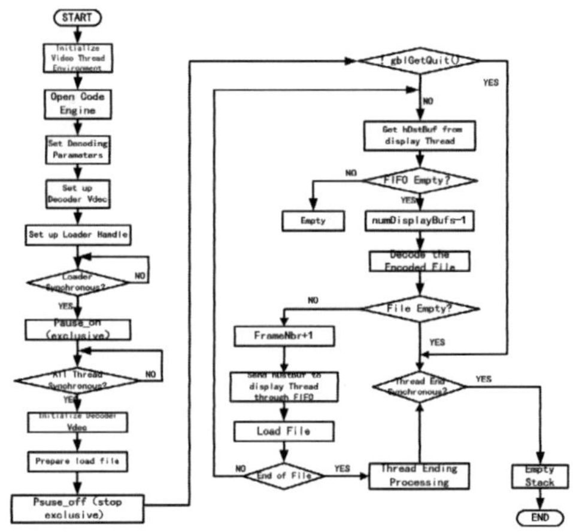

Fig. 8. Decoding process

First, the video thread preparation work. Initialize the video thread environment, and establish the interface API between the decoding thread and the underlying algorithm interface SPI and the high-level application, so that the underlying codec algorithm is transparent to the decoding thread.

Second, run the interrupt service function to store the image data in the appropriate file. When all threads are in sync, initialize the decoder Vdec, then start the interrupt service function to read the image data and store it in the file, using the Pause_off () function to terminate the system resource exclusive.

Third, the main loop, decoding video files. Check if the pipe is empty, and if not, perform the appropriate pipe cleanup operation. Using the Vdec_process () function to perform the decoding operation of the file. If the file is empty, exit the main loop and wait for the end of the other threads. Instead, continue and add 1 to the decoded data frame until all the files have been decoded.

Fourth, finish the document. When all the files have been decoded, to ensure the continuity of the image, the last frame of the image is always displayed on the screen

answer and question, this paper proposes a new deep learning model Att-BiRNN-Att based on two attention mechanisms for the medical answer selection problem. Different from the previous studies, we perform two attention mechanisms to calculate the answer features. One joins the representation before the input of BiRNN. Another is after the output of BiRNN. The combination of the two attention mechanisms can better generate the answer feature representation based on the question. The Att-BiRNN-Att model is tested with other four baseline deep learning methods on the HealthTap database.

The rest of the paper is organized as follows: Section2 describes the related work for deep learning in the answer selection; Section3 provides the details of the proposed models; Experimental setting and results of HealthTap database are discussed in section4; finally, we draw conclusions in section5 and acknowledgments in section6.

2 RELATED WORK

Traditional answer selection methods usually rely on language processing tools or other external methods. In this paper(Wang and Manning, 2010), the answer selection problem was transformed to a syntactical matching between the question/answer parse trees. Some work tried to fulfill the matching using minimal edit sequences between dependency parse trees(Heilman and Smith, 2010). Recently, discriminative tree-edit features extraction and engineering over parsing trees were automated in(Severyn and Moschitti, 2013).

Handling the answer selection task by using deep learning approaches has been very mature in recent years. Deep learning models convert text into vectors and model them in the vector space. There are several common deep learning models: Convolutional Neural Network (CNN)(Yin et al., 2015), Recurrent Neural Network (RNN)(Socher et al., 2013) and so on. When RNN processes the long-time dependence it will bring the gradient disappearance problem while the deformation of RNN---LSTM(Graves, 1997; Wang and Jiang, 2016) and GRU(Gated Recurrent Unit)(Cho et al., 2014) can solve this problem effectively, so they have good performance in the text.

There are several ways to resolve the answer selection tasks as follows: constructed a joint feature vector based on question and answer and then transformed the task into a classification or sorting problem(Wang and Nyberg, 2015). What's more, Bahdanau, et.al(Bahdanau et al., 2014) applies the idea of text generation model to answer selection task. Papers (Yu et al., 2014; Feng et al., 2015; Santos et al., 2016; Tan et al., 2016; Wang et al., 2016)learned the features of the question and answer, and then match them used similarity measures. The papers (Feng et al., 2015; Tan et al., 2016; Wang et al., 2016) used the deformable models of LSTM to deal with the problems. Single direction LSTM cannot use context information in the future while BiLSTM is able to use the past and future context information and process the text in two directions. Most papers (Mnih et al., 2014; Wang and Nyberg, 2015; Mueller and Thyagarajan, 2016; Neculoiu et al., 2016; Tan et al., 2016) are modeled by BiLSTM.

Even though BiLSTM can take the relation of word order into account, the effect of distance words is reduced after long distance calculations. The attention mechanism is introduced to enhance the weight of the associated words and reduce the weight of the less associated words.

Recent studies show that models based on the attention mechanism improve the performance of the deep learning models(Mnih et al., 2014; Zheng et al., 2015). However, these models separated the question from the answer, which ignored the question's relevant information corresponded with answer. Such as, Tan et al(Tan et al., 2016) tried to add the attention mechanism to the RNN structure. It dynamically aligned the parts of answers relevant to the questions. The paper applied attention mechanism after the feature extraction. Nevertheless, when RNN processes the sequence the state of the t moment contains all the information from the start to the t moment. When we add the question attention information to find the most useful information, the features closer to the end of the sequence are easier to pick out because it contains all of the previous information. Therefore, the attention mechanism is more biased towards the latter state features. In order to deal with the problem caused by the above computation, paper(Wang et al., 2016)proposed to add attention mechanism before the feature extraction.

In view of the fact that the representation of answer has not fully utilized the relevant information about the question and answer in the previous researches, we propose a model Att-BiRNN-Att to deal with this problem in this paper. The model uses two attention mechanisms with BiRNN, which avoids the output features tending to the back state features and gives full consideration to the relationship between questions and answers.

3 APPROACH

The answer selection problem in medical field solved in this paper can be expressed as follows: Given a question and an answer candidate pool for a question, the goal is to find the best answer candidate. If the selected answer is inside the ground truth set (one question could have more than one correct answers) of question, the question is considered to be answered correctly, otherwise it is answered incorrectly.

Our model combines two attention mechanisms with BiRNN to better produce the feature representation of the answer. The algorithm framework is shown in figure 1. After obtaining the question features by BiRNN and the max pooling, attention1 are calculated by combining the answer input and the question features. Then, we utilize the output of BiRNN in answer and the question features to calculate attention2 and obtain the answer features by max pooling. Finally, we employ the cosine function to match the question and answer. The combination of two attentions can get the answer features expressed with the relevant the question information.

until a new decoding task arrives or the main thread ends synchronously, emptying the corresponding cache stack space content.

5 System testing and analysis

The HD video encoding system sends the decoded video files to the display thread for final processing, which can be displayed on the displayer. Through the real-time online debugging function of CCS, the video data on the host with the resolution of 1920*1088 and the YUV format is transmitted to DM8148 by using the network port. After coding, the H.264 format video data will be sent back to the upper computer through the network interface. And the coding effect and encoding multiple of DM8148 can be verified. In Fig 9, (a) shows that program initialization, starts to read the configuration file, completes the reading configuration file, and starts to frame the process. The encoding of each frame will be shown, and frames it while passing it back. (b) shows the frame will end when all frames are encoded.

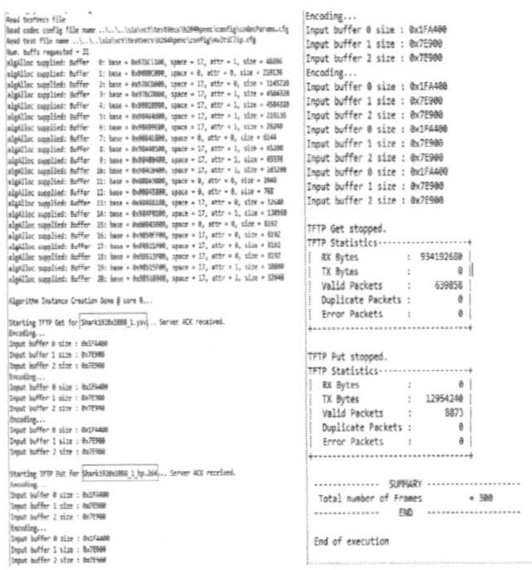

Fig. 9. (a) Program coding beginning (b) Program coding end

Before coding, video information is YUV format video, and video information after coding is hp.264 format video. Compared to video before and after the coding, the coding multiple is about 79 times. The comparison of video screenshots before and after the coding is shown in Fig 10

Fig. 10. Comparison of video screenshots before and after encoding

By comparing to two videos before and after coding, we can find that there is little difference in sharpness, and there is no distortion or disorder in the recognition of human eyes. It indicates that the system works normally and meets the overall design index of the system.

6 Conclusion

In this paper, a high definition video coding system based on HDMI is successfully designed. The system can process the high definition video with a resolution of 1920*1088. And it adopts DSP+FPGA framework. FPGA realized the function of collecting video information, caching data and communicating with DM8148.DSP receives video information from FPGA, encodes and decodes it, and finally uploads to the upper computer, and displays the decoded video information through the displayer. The system uses the coding system of TI scheme. It encodes and decodes the source video information collected by the hardware interface. It successfully solves the video data problem that TMS320DM8148 cannot directly collect the video data from HDMI interface.

Acknowledgement

This paper is supported by the National Natural Science Foundation for Distinguished Young Scholars (NO. 51425505).

References

1. Key Digital Systems; Boscov's Department Store achieves success with 100 HD Displays (2011, 4) HDMI Sources, and custom HDMI Distribution Solutions from Key Digital. In Leisure and Travel Week..
2. Chao Zhang; Li Jun Yun; Jun Sheng Shi; Kun Wang; Zhi Hui Deng (2013), Design and Implementation of the HDMI HD Image Acquisition System Based on FPGA. In Advanced Materials Research.
3. Jiang Xiong; Qing Ming Yi; Min Shi; Ting Ting Li (2013),HDMI Data Transmission System Design. In Applied Mechanics and Materials.
4. J Xiong; Q Yi; M Shi; T Li. Research and Design of Data Transmission System Based on HDMI. (ICCSEE-13 ,2013).
5. S Cho; ST Chung; N Binh; VQ Do (2014), Design and implementation of an embedded multimedia live streaming decoder system. In International Conference on Advanced Technologi.
6. Ming Kui Zheng; Kai Xiong Su; Xiu Zhi Yang (2011), A Scheme of H.264 HD Encoding/Transcoding System Based on ASIC. In Applied Mechanics and Materials.

Integrated Development of Communication Technology and Computer Technology

Daijiancong[1]

[1]Tianjin University of Technology, College of Art, China

Abstract. As the information age comes, new technology has become an important backbone for global economic development. Economic globalization has made all countries and regions value the research and development of new technology. They will rely on new technologies systematically to enhance their economic status and improve the market competency. Therefore, the penetration and integration between different kinds of technologies has seen unprecedented boom. Among them, the development and combination between communication and computer technology is a typical example and has witnessed outstanding performance. At present, computer and telecom computerization equipment has become indispensable communication tools in social life. As a result, a new technology called network communication technology comes into being. This paper mainly discusses computer and communication technology based on existed facts. In the meantime, the integration between the two has been specifically interpreted. At last, it is expected that breakthroughs will be made in science and technology through effective cooperation methods.

1 Introduction

With the accelerated world economy and civilization integration and the in-depth reform and opening-up, good communication in study, life, and work will stimulate the overall science and development level of our country and the world. Information can meet the demands for sharing through computer technology. Communication technology can guarantee the message transfer and delivery between people. No matter it is communication technology or computer technology, it will facilitate the development of social civilization. The paper will discuss the technical concepts integrating these two technologies, to realize the function of sharing and treatment methods of informatization and show the convenience and safety the high technology brings to life.

2 Technology related to electronic computer

2.1 System technology is the core technology of electronic computer

In electronic computer technology, system technology is the core to maintain the completeness of computer system. It mainly includes structure, management, maintenance and application technology. Different system technology will have different functions and fulfill different tasks. The purpose of structure technology is to guarantee the process speed and replace humans in computation. It stands out in terms of performance. Management technology exists in the operation system and shall be completed through operational procedures. This technology will greatly enhance the computation level of the computers and come up with the calculation results very quickly. Therefore, much labor and costs will be reduced. The function of maintenance technology is to carry out all-round examinations of the computer programs to locate and solve the troubles in time. Application technology covers a large range, which is mainly about the automation in design and the development and application of related software.

2.2 Machine piece technology is the basis for electronic computer technology

Machine piece technology is consisted of various electronic components. They have different functions and locations. But they all form an integrated device. Only a complete set of electronic equipment can give rise to complete computer technology. Therefore, when designing the computer, advanced electronic equipment and device will be introduced, so as to make sure the computer is safe and effective. In this way, the corresponding data analysis will be more scientific and make more sense. According to related researches, the complexity of computer programs mainly comes from the complicated logic. And the completeness and perfection of logic is the result of the coordination by advanced electronic equipment. Therefore, the exploration to computer requires good knowledge of advanced electronic equipment and corresponding research and development.

2.3 Component technology is an indispensable part of computer technology

The structure of computer is very complicated. It not only contains the electronic devices mentioned above, but also components. Similar to the features of electronic devices, each component has its own unique functions. Therefore, component technology is a significant part for computer technology. It will benefit the stable and fast operation of the computer.

2.4 Installation technology is the key technology for computer

As the electronic device and component technology continues to develop and upgrade, higher requirements have been posed on installation technology. The effective coordination between installation technology and electronic device and components is essential to the improvement of computer technology.[1] From current condition, it can be said that computer tends to become smaller and smaller. Therefore, related departments should invest more in installation technology and try every effort to reach the international level.

2.5 Integrated analysis technology is the development direction of computer technology

Computer technology under knowledge economy is not only limited to the improvement in calculation speed and accuracy. Nowadays, what computer technology pursues is the stable operation of computer and the diversified application of computer technologies. Current technologies cannot meet the demands by economy and society. In order to meet the new requirements posed by the time and society, innovation and improvement in computer technology is very necessary. To find a comprehensive analysis technology to realize the transfer from data information to knowledge graphs and tables and to enable computer to voluntarily sort and summarize the data is of great importance. It will analyze the data based on the requirements of the clients so as to meet the demands by the users.

3 Communication technology

The current business range of communication industry in our country is very broad, while the communication methods is also diversified. But to certain extent, communication technology is about transferring and delivering all kinds of information through the network and realize the fast transfer of information in time and space. First of all, the main goal of communication technology is to effectively and quickly deliver messages in different forms. In other words, network serves a medium during the transferring process and communication is realized through the network; second, the continuous development of communication technology is mainly shown by the upgrade and perfection of data transmission technology and signal path. For data transmission technology, in recent years, technologies like the data exchange, and frequency and band transmission have been developed. The improvement of signal path is mainly about progress in optical fiber and satellite communication, etc.; lastly, digital communication technology and other advanced multi-media technologies has to some extent facilitated the research and development of communication technology.

4 Integration of computer and communication technology

4.1 Development trend of communication technology and computer technology

As a matter of fact, from the perspective of current science and technology level, the integration of communication technology and computer technology has gained outstanding achievements. It has become dominant part in the information time. The development of science and technology is infinite. In the future, the integration between communication and computer technology will only be strengthened. The corresponding results will be applied to more areas. Based on the exited integration achievements concerning these two technologies, there will be shocking findings, which will bring many surprises and exciting moments to people's life through the development of science and technology. In this way, in production and life, the utilization efficiency of resources will be improved and the competition will become fiercer, which will highlight the comprehensiveness of science and technology.

4.2 Performance of the integration of communication and computer technology

4.2.1 Computer communication technology

The realization of communication and computer technology is a technical innovation combining the features of these two technologies. Among them, computer communication technology is the major content of their integration. In computer communication technology, the computer terminals can be used to calculate the data and fulfill the tasks. The exchange and integration of information technology will then be realized. To be specific, printing technology, mobile telephone technology, cable technology and many others are examples of the application of computer communication technology. Through computer communication technology, the resources can be cleverly shared and analyzed to realize the obstacle-free circulation of information. Moreover, the computer communication technology has been applied to multiple computers for connection, so more complicated technical calculations and resource-sharing will be performed through such technology. All in all, computer communication technology can give the best play to the resources of each computer and make the process of information transmission and message delivery smooth.

4.2.2 Information technology

Under the time of big data, the society lays more emphasis on the collection, processing and analysis of information, the timely and accurate transfer of data, and reliable analysis by computer. These factors directly impact the social and economic development. Information technology is the technology to effectively process systematic and complex information. It involves many kinds of advanced science and technology to process the data. For example, it combines telecommunication technology to process the data in accordance with the user needs and presents the outcome in the form of pictures, texts, tables, and so on, to meet different demands in data by various users.

4.2.3 Bluetooth technology

Bluetooth technology is the effective form for current integration of communication and computer technology.[2] It is also a technology that is widely applied. First of all, Bluetooth technology can realize short-distance transmission of documents, pictures, information data without any other costs. Through wireless connection, data transmission will be realized; besides, Bluetooth is convenient while the technical requirements are not high. The smaller the distance is, the higher the efficiency will be. It can realize the transmission between one user and the other, or between one user and some others, which benefit the users a lot. The main content of Bluetooth technology is shown in the following diagram:

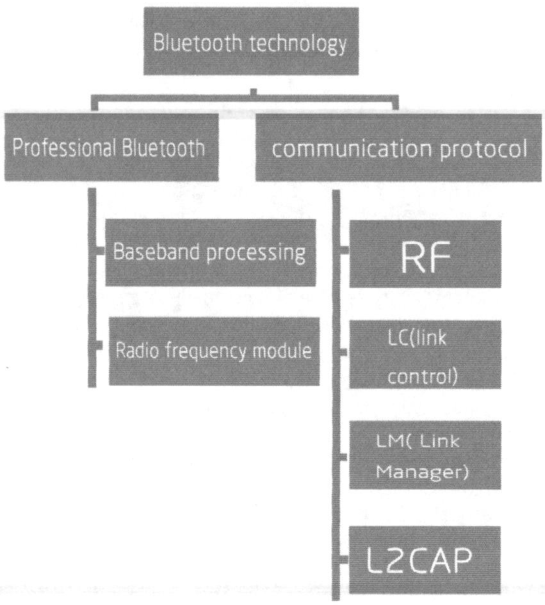

Among them, professional Bluetooth, the hardware structure of Bluetooth, is mainly for receiving the data. Communication protocol is about the safety and effectiveness of the system processor. Currently, Bluetooth technology has wide application. Many enterprises have come up with regulations and standards to regulate, update and manage this technology. From this, we can see that Bluetooth technology is development rapidly and the novel technical market centering on the integrated communication and computer technology is currently under exploration.

4.2.4 Multi-media communication technology

Multi-media communication technology is mainly about using computer technology to collect, summarize, categorize the information and to transfer the data. There are many technical approaches. These solve the following problems: the multi-media content should be sent in which format to occupy the least storage, how to achieve strong fault-tolerant capacity during transmission; how to fast transmit, and how to save the most resources. Multi-media communication technology has shortened the distance between computer and communication technology. The interaction of computers and distribution of communication has been connected to satisfy the requirements by some people.

4.3 Advantages in technical integration of communication and computer technology

4.3.1 Obstacle-free space communication

With the continuous progress of the time, the integration process of the world's economy and culture has been accelerated. People are having higher and higher requirements for communication beyond space. In order to realize this purpose, the integration between communication and computer technology can substantially realize the purpose of long-distance communication. The application of wireless computer network promotes the communication beyond time and space, through which good service can be provided using communication technology.

4.3.2 Multimedia information support system

Computer technology integrates traditional communication technology and provides more superior service system to help with the high-quality and non-stop transmission of data and information. During the process of transmission or delivery, in order to make people feel the dimensions of the data, data programing has been made to effectively deliver the information and data through voice, impact and texts. In this way, people's life quality can be leveled up. There are many examples for the application modern communication technology in daily life: to have an online conference in the company, long-distance education between students and teachers, and sending electronic contracts for the world trade

https://doi.org/10.1051/matecconf/201817601022

business, and so on. There are also many inventions based on communication technology, for example, the popularization and application of Bluetooth, etc.

5 Conclusion

The economic time has brought opportunities for the integrated development of communication technology and computer technology. The outcome of information technology, computer communication technology and other technologies will be the main production force. The development and innovation in high technology industry requires continuous research on computer technology, communication technology and other modern scientific technologies.

References

1. W.B. Wan. Research on the role of computer technology in the promotion and development of communication technology,Digital technology and application,(2015)
2. L.Z.C.Liu. The integration of communication technology and computer technology under the market economy environment. Knowledge economic,(2015)

Image recognition of individual cow based on SIFT in Lαβ color space

Feng Lv[1], Chunmei ZHANG[1,*] ,and Changwei Lv [1]

[1]School of Computer Science and Engineering, North Minzu University, No.204 Wen Chang Street,Yin Chuan , China

Abstract. Using image recognition technology to identify individual dairy cattle with her biological features shows strong stability. This kind of non-contact, high precision and low cost individual recognition methods based on image processing are more and more popular recently to replace the electronic tag and ear mark which can hurt the cattle's psychology and physical health and can affect cattle's behavior. By comparing the various color space transformations, he proposed a scale-invariant feature transform algorithm based on the Luminace of Lαβ color space. With this algorithm, a biological features recognition and management system of Holstein cow has been developed. The identification accuracy is higher than 98%, which is the best result than all the similar reports for cows' identification.

1 Introduction

The biological characteristics of cows, with strong stability and obvious individual difference, are their intrinsic attributes, which can be used for individual identification of dairy cows. Recently, studies have shown that the back patterns of cows vary from other patterns, and the back patterns will remain stable throughout their lives[1]. The cow's biometric identification is not optional by using the RFID, and the cow's e-ear tag may fall off due to cattle's bite and rubbing for long time. Besides, the e-ear tag can be taken off from one cow and then put on another, so it is not reliable to just use the RFID. As for the cow's life insurance, it is of extreme importance to study the biometrics identification by applying the image processing.

With the rapid development of computer information technology, pattern recognition technology has begun to permeate the animal husbandry, and many researchers have studied animal identification and management using image processing technology. Xia[2]et al. proposed a dairy cow's face description model based on the binary pattern texture feature, which identifies cow's facial features by extracting features, using principle component analysis method, combing with the sparse coding classification. Unfortunately, the recognition system is sensitive to the angle of the face image because of the fixed photo graphing position, which makes it difficult to realize the automatic identification. Wang Rui[3] proposed a matching algorithm based on the combination of pole constraint and edge recognition. However, this method can not deal with object occlusion, angle difference and deformation, and the recognition rate is not high. Jin Yichu[4] proposed a homomorphic filtering algorithm based on wavelet transform in YCbCr color space and a region growing algorithm based on sub block region. The sample data of the experiment was 50 groups, and each cow was composed of four pictures, 200 pictures of cows in total, finally the algorithm recognition rate is 84%. But this algorithm cannot solve the problem of image affine tilt. Liu Jun[5]proposed a dairy image recognition algorithm based on multi-feature fusion. The experiment consists of 23 sets of sample data. Each group of cows is composed of 2-10 different pictures, about 200 cow pictures, and the algorithm recognition rate is 93.33%. The background of the images of the experimental data was removed by photoshop software, causing a large number of workload, while the characteristic points that on the edge of the cow's body will be affected, which may have direct effect on the recognition result.

In view of the above problems, we propose a new SIFT[6](Scale-invariant feature transform) algorithm based on the Luminace of Lαβ color space to identify individual cow. The scheme took advantage of the local characteristic in scale space of the SIFT algorithm, improved and designed the feature descriptor which is able to rotate, scale and keep brightness, with stable character to view changing, transforming and noise influence. On the other hand, the algorithm process and identification method were given, and the experimental verification and result analysis are carried out.

2 Algorithm Introduction

2.1. Feature extracting steps based on SIFT algorithm

(1) Scale Space Extreme Value Detection in Scale Space: Search the image position on all scales, finding out

* Corresponding author: chunmei66@hotmail.com

potential points of interest for rotation and scale invariance by using the Gaussian differential function.

(2) Key point positioning: At each candidate location, the scale and position are determined by fitting the fine model. The choice of key points depends on their stability.

(3) Direction determination: Based on the gradient direction of the local image, one or more directions are assigned to each key point.

(4) Description of Key point: the local gradient of the image is measured at the selected scale within the perimeter of each key point.

2.2 Matching method

Image matching in essence is a feature matching. Firstly, the Euclidean distance of feature vectors of critical points is used as the similarity measure of the key points in the two images. Secondly, the error matching points are eliminated to improve robustness. The Brute Force Matcher algorithm always tries all possible matches so that it always finds the best match. In this paper, we use the force matching algorithm to match the features.

2.3 Choice of color space

The color of the cow's skin is one of the most distinctive features of the cow's appearance, which is not sensitive to displacement, rotation, and scale changes.Therefore, color features are more stable than other features. As there is a big difference of the dairy cow's colors in different color space clustering[7], the conclusion of whether there being an optimal color space is still not uniform according to the current conclusions of the various researchers. At present, the common color spaces include RGB, HSV, YUV, YCrCb and Lαβ[8]. Based on this, the color of the dairy cow was changed in each color space, as was shown in Figure 1(a) ~ (r) for the same cow image on different color components.

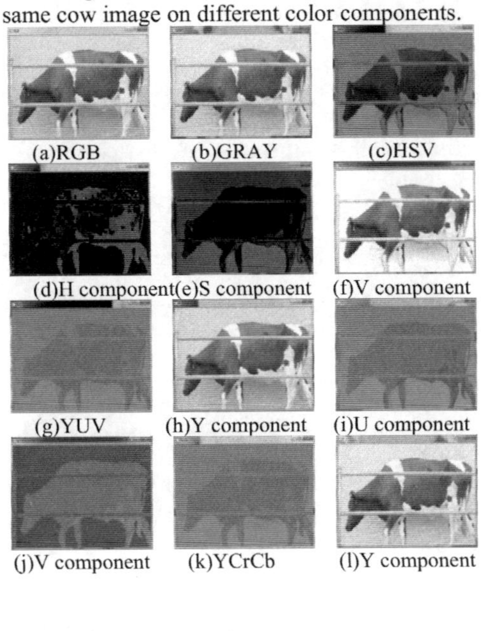

(a)RGB (b)GRAY (c)HSV

(d)H component(e)S component (f)V component

(g)YUV (h)Y component (i)U component

(j)V component (k)YCrCb (l)Y component

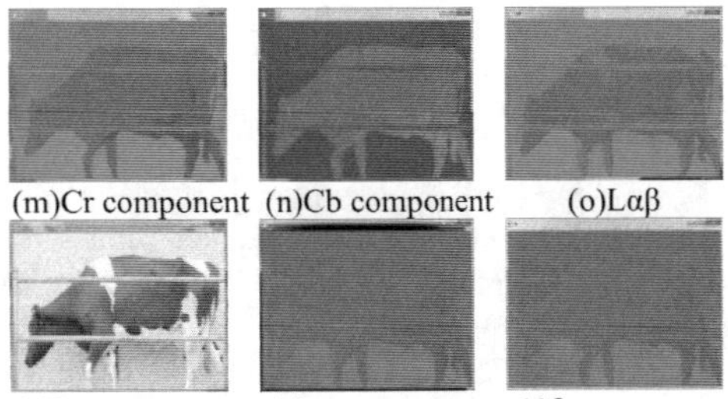

(m)Cr component (n)Cb component (o)Lαβ

(p)L component (q)α component (r)β component

Fig. 1. shows the same cow in different color spaces

In order to study whether there is an optimal color space or spatial component, we first randomly extracted 20 cows' images from the gallery, and each cow randomly selected 6 pictures, a total of 120 pictures as a group, a total of 6 sets of data. Each picture is identified with the other images in different color space components. It is found that GRAY and V components in HSV space, Y components in YUV space, Y components in YCrCb space, and L components in L space can distinguish friesian cow, which is consistent with human visual perception. The results of the experiment are shown in Table 1.

Table 1. Accuracy and time consuming in each color space component for SIFT algorithm

No.	Component	Accuracy(%)	Total time(s)	Average time(s)
1	GRAY	99.03	200.568	1.671
2	Y(YUV)	98.19	203.267	1.694
3	U	5.14	121.411	1.012
4	V	21.53	123.097	1.026
5	Y(YCrCb)	99.03	203.680	1.698
6	Cr	5.98	128.173	1.068
7	Cb	14.18	131.355	1.095
8	H(HSV)	55.89	197.978	1.671
3	S	53.61	222.955	1.858
4	V	93.89	213.393	1.778
11	L(Lαβ)	99.31	204.794	1.707
12	α	0	--	--
13	β	13.33	143.609	1.197

Note: The system accuracy is defined as: Accuracy = Identify the correct number of dairy images / Number of cow images that are involved in the identification.

3 Experiment and result analysis

3.1 Image acquisition and processing

The video was collected from the dairy farm of Ruifeng garden professional cooperatives in Yongning County, Yinchuan, the Ningxia Hui Autonomous Region. It was collected at 13:00 to 17:00 January 3, 2017, and the healthy Chinese Holstein cows were collected. The cow goes through a fixed narrow road to the barn as it comes out of the milking parlor, where a blue cloth was hung in the wall as shot background meanwhile a SLR camera was placed on a tripod whose mode function was adjusted to take videos and whose visual width is larger than 1 cattle's length. There is a fence foreground mask between the dairy target and the camera, and the grid size is 0.5m×2.0m.The three view of the cow image acquisition is shown in Figure 2.

The data acquisition environment for no fog, no haze weather, when individual cows appear in the camera view right at the start of acquisition, continued to collect a number of dairy cows until the last walk to view the left edge of a video segment, the total acquisition gets 5 videos. The video is captured in AVI format and stored in the camera local storage card. The frame rate is 24 fps, the total bit rate is 39813kbps, and the resolution is 1280 pixels (horizontal) x 720 pixels (vertical).

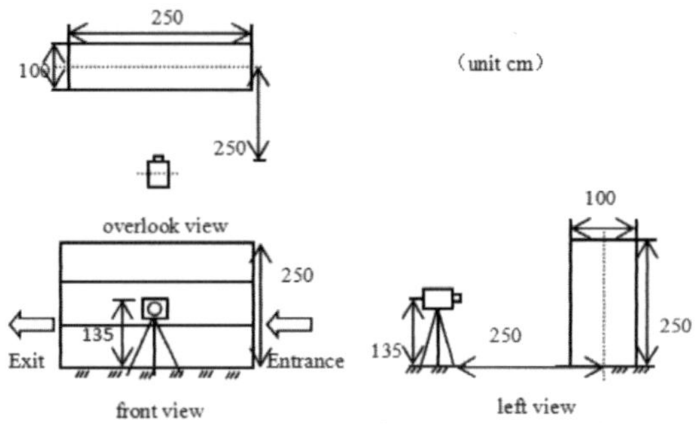

Fig. 2. the three view of cow image collection

The CPU, Intel(R) Core(TM) I7-2600k,was used as the subsequent video processing platform whose main frequency is 3.4GHz,memory 4GB,hard drive 1TB with Microsoft Visual Stdio 2010 being the development platform.Opencv2.4.11;database for SQL Server 2008; The program is written in C++, using MFC as the framework for development. The videos were translated into pictures at a rate of 24 frames per second by Total Video Converter, excluding the ones into which the cow followed, paused or showed less than 50% of body parts, forming about 1500 pictures of 60 cows. Figure 3 shows the changes in the posture, blurred, occlusion, and position of the pictures of some dairy cows, and puts forward some challenges to the recognition algorithm.

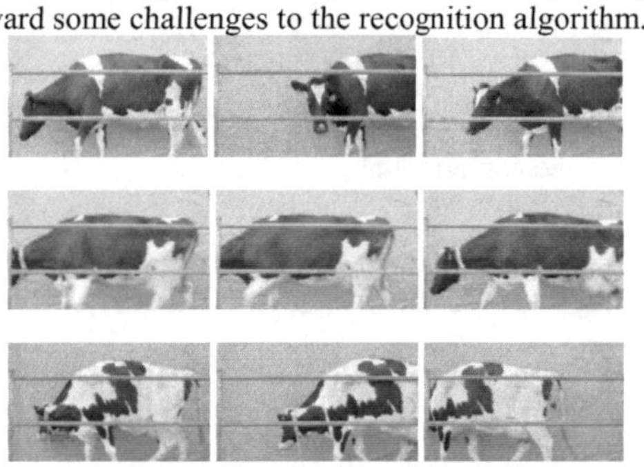

Fig.3. sample of cow images

60 cows were numbered from 1 to 60, and each cow was about 15~30 pictures. In order to improve the efficiency of the program, all the original image sizes are compressed to 192*108 pixels.

3.2 Experimental scheme

From the above experiments, it is found that under the same sample and the same conditions, the L component of Lαβ color space has a higher recognition rate. In this paper, the L component of Lαβ color space is used as the best component of cow recognition. Figure 4 is a process flow chart for the experiment of the identification system.

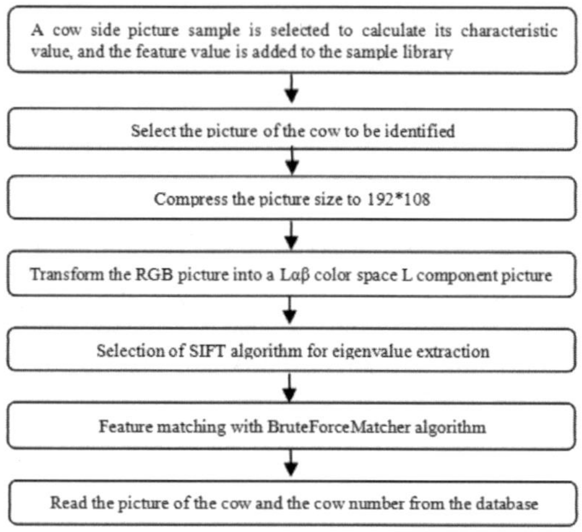

Fig.4. cow identification process chart

3.3 Experimental results and analysis

In the experiment, each cow was selected a complete picture of the cow body as the sample library in the database from 15 to 30 pictures of 60 cows, and each cow was randomly selected 10 pictures (except for a sample picture selected outside) as the test images, a total of 600 test images as a group, the 6 groups randomly the data of experiment, the experimental results are shown in Table 2, the average recognition rate of 98.33%.The results of this paper are compared with other algorithms for detecting local features of the same type, as shown in Table 3. ORB[9] (Oriented FAST and Rotated BRIEF) is a fast feature point extraction and description algorithm. SURF[10](Speeded-Up Robust Features) is an improvement to the SIFT algorithm, which solves the shortcoming of high complexity and time-consuming.

Table 2. Experimental recognition rate

Experimental group	Match the correct number	Recognition rate
1	586	97.667%
2	587	97.833%
3	588	98.000%
4	592	98.667%
5	592	98.667%
6	595	99.167%
Average	590	98.330%

Table 3. Recognition rate of several cow image recognition algorithms

Recognition algorithm	Recognition rate
ORB	80.917%

SURF	83.833%
SIFT	97.694%
Algorithm in this paper	98.330%

4 Conclusion

In view of the special nature of the cow body pattern, this paper proposes a SIFT recognition method based on the L component of Lαβ color space, this method can overcome the posture, position, the unfixed size of the cow in the picture and other issues with a strong detail extraction ability, so it can be easily used for fast matching in large data set. Through the experiment, the recognition rate of 98.33% is obtained by this method. The research and development of cow image recognition management system can overcome many problems such as the high cost of RFID, non-uniform technical standard as well as the difficulties of large-scale promotion and so on. Therefore, it is necessary to realize the individual cow no contact, high accuracy and low cost identification and to improve the safety of dairy products, dairy modernization, as well as the intelligent optimization management by the image recognition technology.

Acknowledgments:

This work is supported by Ningxia first-class discipline and scientific research projects (electronic science and technology), NO. NXYLXK2017A07; "the innovation team of National People's Liberation Committee" project funding (NO. PY1608).

References

1. Shinji Umeyama. Least-Squares estimation of transformation parameters between two point patterns[J]. IEEE T PATTERN ANAL,**13**(4):376-380,(1991)
2. Xia M,Cai, C (Cai, Cheng),Li, JQ (Li, Jianqiao) Cattle Face Recognition Using Local Binary Pattern Descriptor. IEEE T PATTERN ANAL,1-4,(2014)
3. Wang Rui. Research on cow insurance system based on image recognition and matching technology [D]. Inner Mongolia University, 2011.
4. Jin Yichu.Research on cow recognition algorithm based on Wavelet Moments[D],Shanghai Normal University,2011.
5. Liu Jun. Research on image recognition system of dairy cows based on multi feature fusion [D]. Shanghai Normal University, 2013.
6. David G. Lowe. "Distinctive image features from scale invariant keypoints",INT J COMPUT VISION,**60**,91-110, (2004)
7. Xu Zhanwu, Zhu Miaoliang. A review of color based skin detection [J]. Chinese Journal of image and graphics, **3**,377-388,(2007)
8. Chai D, Bouzerdoum A. A Bayesian Approach to Skin Color Classification in YCbCr Color Space[J].IEEE TENCON,**2**, 421-424.(2000)
9. Ethan Rublee, Vincent Rabaud, Kurt Konolige, Gary R. Bradski: ORB: An efficient alternative to SIFT or SURF[J]. ICCV,2564-2571(2011)
10. H. Bay, T. Tuytelaars, and L. Van Gool. Surf: Speeded up robust features[J]. ECCV,**1**, 404-417,(2006)

Medical Answer Selection Based on Two Attention Mechanisms with BiRNN

Jiajia Ma, Chao Che and Qiang Zhang*

Key Laboratory of Advanced Design and Intelligent Computing Ministry of Education, Dalian University, Dalian, China

Abstract. The contradiction between the large population of China and the limited medical resources lead to the difficulty of getting medical services. The emergence of question answering (QA) system in the medical field allows people to receive timely treatment at home and alleviates the burden on hospitals and doctors. To this end, this paper proposes a new model called Att-BiRNN-Att which combines the Bidirectional RNN (Recurrent Neural Network) with two attention mechanisms. The model employs BiRNN to capture more information in the context instead of the traditional directional RNN. Also, two attention mechanisms are used in the model to produce better feature representation of the answer. One attention is used before the input of BiRNN, and the other is used after the output of BiRNN. The combination of two attentions makes full use of the relevant information between the answer and question. The experiment on the HealthTap medical QA dataset shows that our model outperforms four state-of-the-art deep learning models, which confirm the effectiveness of Att-BiRNN-Att model.

1 INTRODUCTION

The difficulty of getting medical services is a hot and difficult issue in China. It is also a major livelihood problem that the masses of people want to solve urgently. China's large population and the limited medical resources is the main reason for the problem of "the difficulty of getting medical services". However, "many people always want to go to the hospital regardless of their illness state," this also increases the pressure of hospitals and doctors. Moreover, answering the same question every day to different patients is sure to consume the doctors' energy of treating patients. Automatic QA system allows patients describe their situations on the Internet directly and get doctor's professional advice. Patients can be treated promptly at home which decreases the amount of outpatients and alleviates the burden on hospitals and doctors. An important module in the medical automatic QA system is the answer selection. Once a patient asks a question about his illness, lots of answers related to the question are found. Finding the correct answer what the patient really needs exactly is a very difficult task.

Traditional answer selection methods usually rely on the language processing tools or other external methods(Wang and Manning, 2010). Because many steps need to be carried out before the text data are input into the models, semantic information may be easily lost and mixed. But the imprisonment of the traditional approaches have been broke by deep learning methods, which do not rely on language processing tools and input the data into the models directly. The deep learning methods convert a sentence into a vector space and extract its features to represent the sentence, which is then implemented to accomplish a task. For example, Feng, et.al(Feng et al., 2015) extracted the features of the questions and answers by difficult CNN models and adopted the cosine function to measure their similarity. In recent years, attention mechanism(Bahdanau et al., 2014; Luong et al., 2015; Yin et al., 2015) has good performance in many areas of Natural Language Processing, and more and more studies have applied the attention mechanism to the answer selection task. Candidate answers in medical selection task usually are very long and contain a lot of words that are not related to the question. If we calculate the question and answer features separately, the answer will be affected by the similar phrases or noise words thus the relevant semantic information to the question and answer will be ignored, which is undoubtedly very serious for patients with consulting questions. Attention mechanism can solve this problem by assigning different weights to different part of the answers when calculating the answer features. Attention mechanism gives a bigger weight to the parts of answer associated with the question, while assigns a smaller weight to the parts of answer not related to question so the representation of the answer features will have better correlation with the question.

In order to generate better answer feature representation take advantage of the relationship between

Corresponding author: jiabao6861@163.com, chechao101@163.com, zhangq26@126.com

https://doi.org/10.1051/matecconf/201817601024

3.1 Recurrent Neural Network (RNN)

RNN have been widely exploited to deal with variable-length sequence input. The long-distance history is stored in a recurrent hidden vector which is dependent on the immediate previous hidden vector. LSTM and GRU are the popular variations of RNN to mitigate the gradient vanishing problem of RNN.

In this paper, BiLSTM and BiGRU are used to calculate the question and answer features. Because BiLSTM/BiGRU is the improved model based on the LSTM/GRU, we first introduce LSTM/GRU, and then introduce BiLSTM/BiGRU.

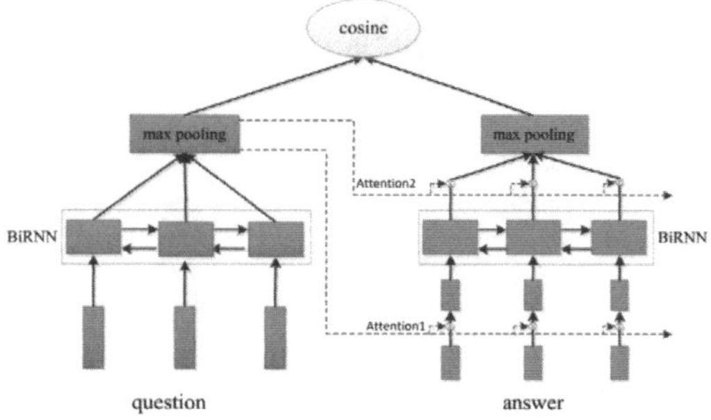

Figure 1: Algorithm framework in this paper.

Given a sentence $X=\{x_1,x_2......x_n\}$, x_t is k dimension vector which is 100 dimensions in this paper. LSTM hidden vector h_t at the time step t is updated as follows:

$$i_t = sigmoid(W_i x_t + U_i h_{t-1} + b_i) \quad (1)$$

$$f_t = sigmoid(W_f x_t + U_f h_{t-1} + b_f) \quad (2)$$

$$o_t = sigmoid(W_o x_t + U_o h_{t-1} + b_o) \quad (3)$$

$$\tilde{C}_t = \tanh(W_c x_t + U_c h_{t-1} + b_c) \quad (4)$$

$$C_t = i_c * \tilde{C}_t + f_t * C_{t-1} \quad (5)$$

$$h_t = o_c * \tanh(C_t) \quad (6)$$

There are three gates, i.e. input gate i, forget gate f, output gate o and a cell memory C in the LSTM architecture. The input gate can determine how incoming vectors x_t alter the state of the memory cell. The output gate can allow the memory cell to have an effect on the outputs. Finally, the forget gate allows the cell to remember or forget its previous state. The formula (4) is an input transformation, and formula (5) is an update of the cell state.

GRU is formulated as follows:

$$z_t = sigmoid(W_z x_t + U_z h_{t-1}) \quad (7)$$

$$f_t = sigmoid(W_f x_t + U_f h_{t-1}) \quad (8)$$

$$h_t = \tanh(W_h \tilde{x}_t + U_h (f_t \odot h_{t-1})) \quad (9)$$

$$h_t = (1 - z_t) \odot h_{t-1} + z_t \tilde{h}_t) \quad (10)$$

Where W_z, W_f, W_h, U_z, U_h are weight matrices and $\odot$ stands for element-wise multiplication.

LSTM/GRU only uses the information about the past, while Bidirectional LSTM/GRU can take the past and future sequence information into account. Bi LSTM/BiGRU utilizes both the previous

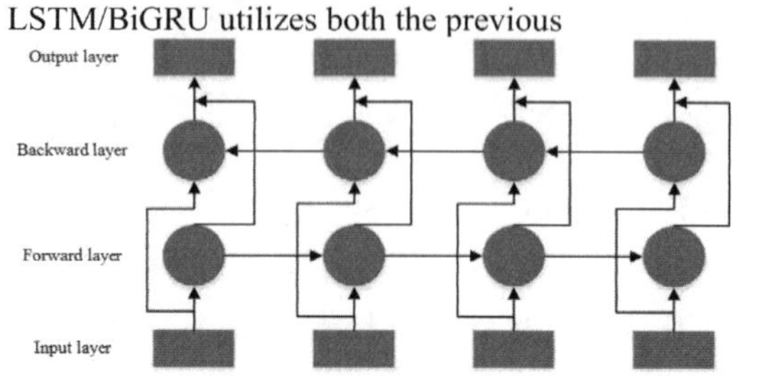

Figure 2: Bidirectional LSTM/GRU architectures.

and future context by processing the sequence on two directions, and generates two independent sequences of LSTM/GRU output vectors. One processes the input sequence in the forward direction, while the other processes the input in the reverse direction. The output at each time step is the concatenation of the two output vectors from both directions, i.e., $h_t = \overrightarrow{h_t} \,||\, \overleftarrow{h_t}$ 。

3.2 Attention mechanism

When quickly read long text, our attention is focused on key events or entities; when looking for an answer, we make use of the information of the question to find the most relevant answer in the answer pool. The attention mechanism is designed to take advantage of the information about questions and answers. In this paper, the two attention calculations we use are as follows:

Attention1 : It is performed before the input of BiLSTM/BiGRU. Attention1 can adjust the effective information parts of question corresponding to the answer and find the link between question and answer, which was then applied to feature representation of the answers.

$$\alpha_t = sigmoid(r_q^T M_{qi} x_t) \quad (11)$$

$$\tilde{x}_t = \alpha_t * x_t \quad (12)$$

M_{qi} is a attention matrix that converts the question into word embedding space.

Attention2 : BiLSTM/BiGRU can take the word orders into consider, but when the sentence is very long, BiLSTM/BiGRU may be influenced by the less important words in the candidate answers. So we introduce attention2 to increase the weights of strong associated words, and reduce the weight of weak associated words in the output of BiLSTM/BiGRU. In BiLSTM/BiGRU, a word at each time step is added and the hidden state is updated recurrently, those hidden states near the end of the sentence are expected to capture more information. Consequently, when the attention2 information is added to the time sequence hidden representations, the near-the-end hidden variables will be more easily selected because of the abundant semantic accumulation, which may lead to a biased attentive weight towards the later coming words in RNN.

Attention1 calculation also has carried on the correction. The combined use of the attention mechanism produces a better answer representation. Attention function F_a calculation methods and answer features are calculated as follows:

$$m(t) = \tanh(W_{hm} h_a(t) + W_{qm} r_q) \quad (13)$$

$$F_a(r_q, h_a(t)) = \exp(w_{ms}^T m(t)) \quad (14)$$

$$S_t \propto F_a(r_q, h_a(t)) \quad (15)$$

$$\tilde{h}_a(t) = h_a(t) * S_t) \quad (16)$$

$$r_a = \sum_{t=1}^{m} \tilde{h}_a(t) \quad (17)$$

Among them, $h_a(t)$ is the hidden state of the answer at the t moment, W_{hm}, W_{qm} is the attention weight matrix, and w_{ms} is the attention weight vector. It can be argued that when the hidden state of answer is not related to the question, it will play a very small role in the final feature representation, and conversely, it contributes greatly to the representation of the answer.

3.3 Objective function

The model is constructed in the form of (q , a_+ , a_-). Q stands for questions, a_+ stands for positive answers, and a_- stands for negative answers. The negative answers are chosen randomly in training, and are combined into the form of (q , a_+ , a_-). We use the objective function L as follows:

$$L = \max\{0, M - \cos(q, a_+) + \cos(q, a_-)\} \quad (18)$$

The cosine function calculates the similarity of the question and answer and compares it with the range M., $M - \cos(q,a_+) + \cos(q,a_-) > 0$ the similarity of positive answer is less than the negative answer. If $M - \cos(q,a_+) + \cos(q,a_-) \le 0$ there is no need to update the parameters and we will train a new negative example until the margin is less than M.

4 EXPERIMENTAL RESULTS AND ANALYSIS

4.1 Setup

We evaluate the proposed model on the HealthTap database. HealthTap is the first world's global health care platform. It allows users to access via the video, text, or voice all day, with more than 108000 top doctors online. HealthTap's answers all come from real doctors, and basic questions can be answered free. We use a part of this data(Nie et al., 2017). Among it, there are 11915 questions in the training data, and 1601 problems in the test data. The creation format of test data are same with paper(Feng et al., 2015). The answer pool for each question are composed of positive answers, and then randomly select the answers from all the answer pool until the total number of answers to 500. The length of the question and answer sentences are 100.

Our method is implemented by the Tensorflow framework. Word2vec is used for training the word vector and the vector dimension is 100. The optimization method is Stochastic Gradient Descent (SGD), batch size is 256, and learning rate is 0.01. The value of margin is set as 0.05. Hidden size is 220. We use the Top1 accuracy (P@1)to evaluate the effectiveness of our method.

We calculate the matching scores of question with 500 answers in the answer pool. If the tag of the answer with the highest matching score is 1, answer selection is right. Otherwise, it is wrong.

4.2 Comparison algorithms and experimental results analysis

We employed four state-of-the-art algorithms to compare with our method in this paper:

1.BiLSTM(Tan et al., 2016): The model does not use the attention.

2.QA-LSTM(Tan et al., 2016): The model employs bidirectional LSTM model and uses the attention after the feature extraction.

3.IARNN-WORD(Wang et al., 2016) and IALSTM-WORD: Add attention information before RNN hidden representation. IARNN-WORD and IALSTM-WORD employ bidirectional GRU and LSTM model to perform feature representation, respectively.

Our proposed model is also tested using BiLSTM and BiGRU, which is called Att-BiGRU-Att and Att-BiLSTM-Att for short, respectively. The experimental results and analysis are in Table 1:

Table 1: Experimental results

	Model	**P@1**
1	BiLSTM	60.39
2	QA-LSTM	62.46
3	IARNN-WORD	61.64
4	IALSTM-WORD	61.71
5	Att-BiGRU-Att	63.58
6	Att-BiLSTM-Att	**63.83**

As we can see from table 1, LSTM model performs slightly better than the GRU model, and the performance of the model based on two attention mechanisms is superior to other models. QA-LSTM and IARNN-WORD outperform the model BiLSTM, which demonstrates the importance of the attention mechanism in the answer representation. For the non-attention models, the features of question and answer are represented individually, and the similarity scores of questions and answers represent their correlation. In the model with attention, the answer feature is calculated with the question feature. Answer representation is related to the question information. So the similarity scores contain relevant information.

Two attention mechanisms are applied in our model. The model using two attentions can generate better answer representation according to the question. Compared with models with one attention, Att-BiLSTM-Att model can extract more question

Table 2: Examples (questions, correct and wrong answers) selected in the HealthTap dataset.

Q: I am having extreme pain and burning in my index finger and morning stiffness in other fingers. It gets better after the morning. It is only in one hand and iblood work. Does it indicate rheumatoid arthritis or not?
Answer 1: Carpal tunnel is Associated with altered sensation in the thumb, index, middle and part of the ring. It can affect the muscles of the thumb. Symtoms can be intermittent, occasional or severe and long standing. Testing such as a nerve study/emg is often used to aid diagnosis and gauge severity. Treatment can range from splinting to injections and even surgery. A very common disorder; many functions well despite it.
Positive Answer: Many possibilities. This could be carpal tunnel syndrome, or another form of arthritis associated with psoriasis or other diseases, or could even be early rheumatoid arthritis. Ask your doctor for help with diagnosis and consider physical therapy if prescribed.

to represent answer, and makes the answer representation more targeted when selecting answer. As shown in Table 2, with regard to the questions Q, we should answer "Does it indicate rheumatoid arthritis or not". QA-LSTM and IALSTM-WORD with one attention pay more attention to the symptoms, and there is no clear answer to the question. Although answer1 has a relationship between the question and answer, the question needed to be answered is only mentioned as "A very common disorder". While the model with two attention focus more attention on the correlation between question and answer, such as "Many possibilities. This could be" and "or could even be" are all interrelated with "whether rheumatoid arthritis" in the correct answer. Therefore it has a better prediction effect.

5 CONCLUSIONS

In this paper, we propose a bidirectional RNN model with two attentions to perform answer selection for the healthcare QA. The two attentions is embedded before the input and after the output of BiRNN respectively based, which gives full consideration to the relation between the questions and answers. The experiment results on the HealthTap database show that the model performs better than several models. In the future work, we would like to study the answer ranking in health QA.

ACKNOWLEDGEMENTS

We acknowledge the support from the National Natural Science Foundation of China (No.91546123), Program for Changjiang Scholars and Innovative Research Team in University (No. IRT15R07).

References

1. Bahdanau, D., Cho, K. and Bengio, Y., 2014. *Neural Machine Translation by Jointly Learning to Align and Translate*. Computer Science.
2. Cho, K., Merrienboer, B. V., Gulcehre, C., Bahdanau, D., Bougares, F., Schwenk, H. and Bengio, Y., 2014. Learning Phrase Representations using RNN Encoder-Decoder for Statistical Machine Translation. *In EMNLP, 2014 Conference on Empirical Methods in Natural Language Processing* (pp.1724–1734). ACL.
3. Feng, M., Xiang, B., Glass, M. R., Wang, L. and Zhou, B., 2015. Applying deep learning to answer selection: A study and an open task. *In ASRU, Automatic Speech Recognition and Understanding* (pp.813-820).
4. Graves, A., 1997. *Long Short-Term Memory*. Neural Computation. 9(8), p.1735.
5. Heilman, M. and Smith, N. A., 2010. Tree edit models for recognizing textual entailments, paraphrases, and answers to questions. *In Human Language Technologies, The 2010 Annual Conference of the North American Chapter of the Association for Computational Linguistics* (pp.1011-1019). ACL.
6. Luong, M. T., Pham, H. and Manning, C. D., 2015. Effective Approaches to Attention-based Neural Machine Translation. *In Proceedings of the 2015 Conference on Empirical Methods in Natural Language Processing*. ACL.
7. Mnih, V., Heess, N., Graves, A. and Kavukcuoglu, K., 2014. Recurrent models of visual attention. *In Proceedings of the 27th International Conference on Neural Information Processing Systems* (pp.2204-2212). MIT Press.
8. Mueller, J. and Thyagarajan, A., 2016. Siamese recurrent architectures for learning sentence similarity. *In AAAI-16, 3th AAAI Conference on Artificial Intelligence* (pp.2786-2792). AAAI Press.
9. Neculoiu, P., Versteegh, M. and Rotaru, M., 2016. Learning Text Similarity with Siamese Recurrent Networks. *In ACL2016, 1st Workshop on Representation Learning for NLP.*
10. Nie, L., Wei, X., Zhang, D., Wang, X., Gao, Z. and Yang, Y., 2017. *Data-Driven Answer Selection in Community QA Systems*. IEEE Transactions on Knowledge & Data Engineering. 29(6):1186-1198.
11. Santos, C. D., Tan, M., Xiang, B. and Zhou, B., 2016. *Attentive Pooling Networks*. Computer Science.
12. Severyn, A. and Moschitti, A., 2013. Automatic feature engineering for answer selection and extraction. *In EMNLP, 2013 Conference on Empirical Methods in Natural Language Processing* (pp.458-467). ACL.
13. Socher, R., Perelygin, A., Wu, J. Y., Chuang, J., Manning, C. D., Ng, A. Y. and Potts, C., 2013. Recursive deep models for semantic compositionality over a sentiment treebank. *In EMNLP, Conference on Empirical Methods in Natural Language Processing* (pp.1631-1642). ACL.
14. Tan, M., Santos, C. D., Xiang, B. and Zhou, B., 2016. Improved Representation Learning for Question Answer Matching. *In ACL, 54th Annual Meeting of the*

Association for Computational Linguistics (pp.464-473). ACL.

15. Wang, B., Liu, K. and Zhao, J., 2016. Inner Attention based Recurrent Neural Networks for Answer Selection. *In ACL, 54th Annual Meeting of the Association for Computational Linguistics* (pp.1288-1297). ACL.
16. Wang, D. and Nyberg, E., 2015. A Long Short-Term Memory Model for Answer Sentence Selection in Question Answering. *53rd Annual Meeting of the Association for Computational Linguistics and the 7th International Joint Conference on Natural Language Processing* (pp.707-712). ACL.
17. Wang, M. and Manning, C. D., 2010. Probabilistic tree-edit models with structured latent variables for textual entailment and question answering. *23rd International Conference on Computational Linguistics* (pp.1164-1172). Coling 2010 Organizing Committee.
18. Wang, S. and Jiang, J., 2016. Learning Natural Language Inference with LSTM. *2016 Conference of the North American Chapter of the Association for Computational Linguistics: Human Language Technologies*. ACL.
19. Yin, W., Schütze, H., Xiang, B. and Zhou, B., 2015. *ABCNN: Attention-Based Convolutional Neural Network for Modeling Sentence Pairs*. Transactions of the Association of Computational Linguistics.
20. Yu, L., Hermann, K. M., Blunsom, P. and Pulman, S., 2014. *Deep Learning for Answer Sentence Selection*. Computer Science.
21. Zheng, Y., Zemel, R. S., Zhang, Y. J. and Larochelle, H., 2015. *A Neural Autoregressive Approach to Attention-based Recognition*. International Journal of Computer Vision. 113(1):67-79.

Research on Embedded Multi-task Balancing Scheduling Algorithm

Han Zhuangzhi[1], Ma Tianlin[2]

[1]Information and Communication Engineering, Shijiazhuang Campus, Army Engineering University, No. 97 Heping West Road, Shijiazhuang City, Hebei Province, China
[2]Information and Communication Engineering, Shijiazhuang Campus, Army Engineering University, No. 97 Heping West Road, Shijiazhuang City, Hebei Province, China

Abstract. For embedded systems, there are two cases of using an operating system and not using an operating system. When the real-time task is accomplished by the embedded system of the operating system, the task needs to meet certain conditions and occupy part of the processor's resources. Therefore, based on the method of event interruption, timed interruption and task decomposition, the real-time performance of the completion of the task of the embedded system is achieved. Finally, an embedded radar track compression scheduling algorithm is designed. It is proved through experiment that the track data can be compressed and transmitted in real time.

1 INTRODUCTION

The problem of multitasking processing lies mainly in the scheduling among different tasks [1]. According to the characteristics of the task and the requirements for completing the task, the method of scheduling is also different [2]. According to the nature of the task can be divided into static scheduling and dynamic scheduling. Static scheduling assigns priorities to tasks based on the static attributes of tasks, which can reduce the storage and computational costs, but has poor flexibility [3]. Dynamic Scheduling According to the priority of dynamic task assignment during task execution, EDF (Earliest Deadline First) is a typical dynamic scheduling algorithm that schedules tasks based on task deadline [4]. Its advantage is that it can be performed according to the task. Dynamic execution of tasks requires the use of resources such as processor memory and computational resources. According to the real-time requirements of task completion, it can be divided into hard real-time scheduling and soft real-time scheduling. Hard real-time scheduling is used for tasks with high real-time requirements. Immediate processing is required when tasks occur. Soft real-time scheduling can delay task execution time appropriately when the load is heavy. According to whether the task is preempted during execution, scheduling can be divided into preemptive scheduling and non-preemptive scheduling. Preemptive scheduling means that during the execution of a task, if a task with a higher priority needs to be executed, the processor will suspend the current task and execute the task with a higher priority [5]. The flexibility is high, but the switch of the task will occupy the resources of the processor. For non-preemptive scheduling algorithms, they will not be preempted during the execution of the task. Relative to preemptive tasks, its real-time performance has certain limitations. The current scheduling algorithms are mostly used directly in the operating system, but the use of the operating system often requires tasks to meet certain requirements in terms of periodicity, execution time, etc. [6], and the operation of the operating system itself also requires a certain amount of processor resources. . This also limits the application of real-time operating systems in some projects. By analyzing the method of task scheduling in the operating system, it is directly applied in the embedded system to achieve real-time balanced scheduling of tasks. And it is used in target track compression. Experiments have proved that real-time compression of the target track can be achieved.

2 REAL-TIME BALANCED SCHEDULING ALGORITHM

For embedded program tasks, it is mainly divided into periodic tasks, acyclic tasks, and auxiliary tasks. The significance of scheduling is to equalize periodic tasks while ensuring real-time completion of real-time tasks.

2.1 Task Equalization

Equalization of tasks means that the tasks are divided equally in time to avoid the occurrence of tasks and bursts of computation. Tasks can be divided into two types, cycle and event.

Cyclic tasks are executed in the order of tasks. If a task is not completed, the next task will not be executed.

Unbalanced tasks will result in the limited operational efficiency of the program. The task in the loop is an executable task that is not real-time and can be used to perform tasks in a circular schedule. For some unpredictable execution time tasks, event interrupt scheduling is used. Avoid wasting processor resources due to waiting tasks. For a periodic task, the task is divided equally over the entire period, avoiding that the calculation of the task is performed only at a certain moment in the processor, while the resources of the processor are relatively left at other times. Therefore, a recursive algorithm is used to perform periodic tasks so that the computational load is equalized throughout the entire cycle.

The processor can only be executed serially during the execution of the task. In order to improve the resource utilization efficiency of the processor, it is necessary to reduce the delay between tasks and tasks [7]. Task decomposition can be used to decompose complex tasks into simple tasks, as shown in Fig. 1. Divide these simple tasks into loops and interrupt tasks. For real-time periodic tasks, tasks that are in urgent need of processing are completed during the interruption, to avoid waste of resources and time delays caused by calls between tasks. Fig.2 .shows the scheduling structure of the task.

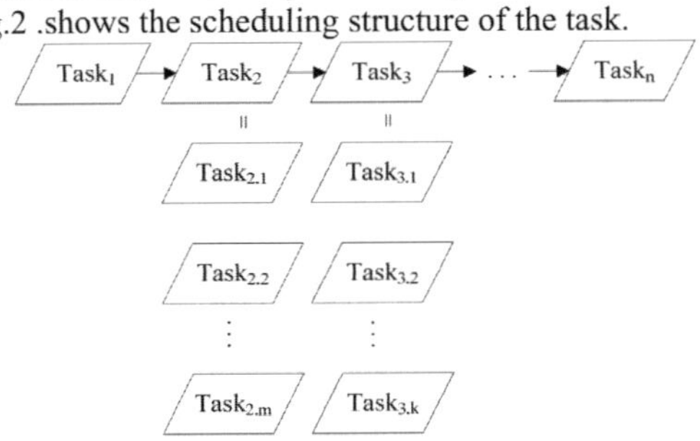

Fig. 1. Decomposition structure of the task

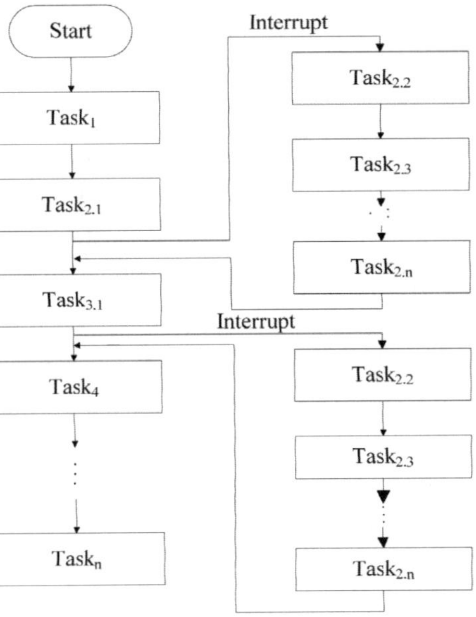

Fig. 2. Task Scheduling Structure

From Fig. 1 we can see that the processor needs to complete Task1, Task2, Task3...Taskn a total of n tasks. Among the complex tasks are Task2 and Task3. And the execution time of these two tasks is unpredictable. In order to increase the utilization efficiency of the processor, these two tasks are set as interruption events. The effective allocation of single-core processors over time is completed [8]. For a complex task Task2, it can be decomposed into m tasks for Task2.1, Task2.2...Task2.m. Task2.3...Task2.m can be executed in round robin scheduling. Put it in the loop event, put Task2.1, Task2.2 in the interrupt event, complete the decomposition of the complex task. The decomposition in task Task3 is similar to the task Task2 decomposition.

2.2 Real-time Mission

One of the advantages of an embedded system is its ability to complete tasks in real time. The real-time execution of tasks is mainly accomplished through event interrupts. For tasks that require high real-time performance such as data acquisition and data reception, hard real-time interrupts are required. The deadline for the task will lead to data receiving errors.

During the execution of a cyclic task, considering that multiple interrupt events may occur at the same time, it is necessary to set priorities for all interrupt events. According to the execution time, real-time and urgency of the event, the priority of the interrupt event is set. For tasks with higher real-time requirements, such as Task2.1 and Task2.2, real-time processing is required. For non-emergency interrupt events, such as Task2.3...Task2.m, flag bits are set in the interrupt to pass through the main program. Query flags to perform tasks.

For real-time periodic tasks, such as data acquisition, data reception, etc., there is a certain gap between the received data, so the task is set to hard real-time interrupts. The data needs to be processed after receiving the data. Decompose complex data processing into simple tasks. If the interrupt task is not processed when the next interrupt arrives, data reception will be lost. As shown in Fig. 1. The tasks that need to be processed after receiving are placed in interrupts, such as Task2.1, Task2.2, etc., and the processing time is not guaranteed to be greater than the interval between two interruptions. That is, the real-time nature of the interrupt task is guaranteed, and the resources of the processor due to the scheduling between tasks are also avoided.

3 COMPRESSED RADAR TRACK SCHEDULING ALGORITHM

The scheduling algorithm is applied to the radar track compression algorithm. Experiments show that the data can be received and compressed in real time. The main task of the algorithm is five parts. Respectively receive data in real time, data batch, threat judgment, data compression and data upload. Through the task decomposition, receive interrupts to achieve real-time data reception and balanced execution of tasks.

3.1 System Structure

Real-time data is uploaded from the radar to the processing terminal according to the RS232 protocol. Since the appearance of the target is uncertain and the radar detects that the target needs to be uploaded in real time, otherwise the data will be lost, so the data will be received.

Set to interrupt reception and set the highest priority. And in the cyclic task enable receive interrupt (NVIC_EnableIRQ()).

The terminal receives radar data in bytes. The target track ultimately consists of a series of fixed-form traces, each of which represents the motion parameters of the target at the corresponding time [9]. The first thing you need to do is divide the received bytes into standard format radar traces. Radar track data compression is performed using feature points. Before the compression, it is necessary to acquire the points of a certain period of time of the batch of the target, and batch the received point data according to the target batch number in the fixed data format.

The interval between radar upload bytes is the same. Framing of data can be completed within this interruption interval. Due to the relatively long time required for data batching, placing batches in receiving interrupts will result in the omission of target receiving points. Batching data in cyclic tasks. Set the flag. Query the flags in the cyclic task and batch the data.

Threat judgment is the screening of different batches of targets. By querying the new target flag, the threat assessment function is used to calculate the new target threat degree. For the radar to obtain the track, it needs a certain period. In order to balance the operation, a recursive algorithm is used to calculate the threat degree of the target. Query the time period flag to perform data compression tasks. When the data is compressed, the compressed data is uploaded through the serial port. A simple flow chart for a compressed radar track scheduling algorithm is shown in Fig. 3.

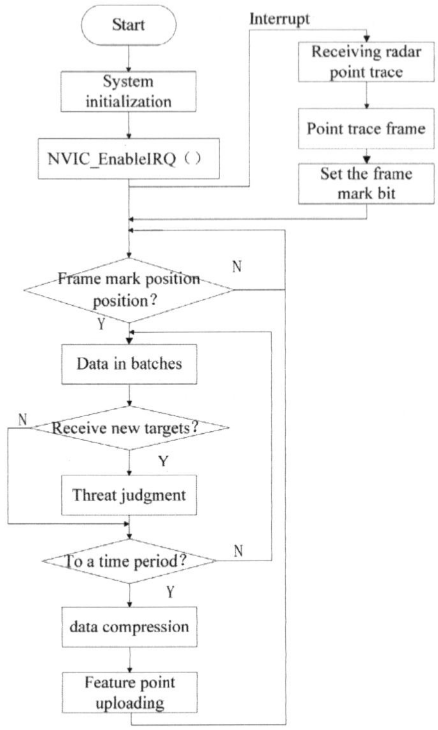

Fig. 3. Simple flow chart of compressed radar track scheduling algorithm

3.2 System Implementation

The system is implemented according to the designed system structure. The main functions, subfunctions, and flag bits of the system are shown below. The main program contains two while loops, querying the frame flag bit in the first while loop, completing batches of points. Query the new target flag to complete the threat assessment of the target. After the time period, jump out of the first while loop. The trajectory is compressed based on linear prediction. The feature points of the target track are uploaded and the related flag bits are cleared to complete the target track compression and upload for one cycle.

```
Int main(void)
{SystemInit(); //System and variable initialization
UART1_Init(); // Serial port initialization and setting receive interrupt
{if(flag1==1) // Received radar track
BD_date[Date_qdbnew][j++]=ch; // Framing the points
... }
While (1)
{while (1)
{if(flag2==1) //Data receive and frame flag
For (i = 0; i < 20; i++) // batches the framing points
{if(get_same_pi[i][0][5]==BD_date[t][5]) }
If(flag4==0) //new track is a new target
If(flag4==0) //new track is a new target
{wei[n]=DATEHANDLE(n); //Calculate the threat of the new target}
MAO(wei[n]); //Bubble sorts the target's threat
```

```
If(timer0_counter>=6000 && n!=0 )
 Break; //out of cycle at 1 minute of set time period}
A0=fana0(0,0, julix, juliy); // Call function calculation coefficient (batch number, starting point of fitting)
A1=fana0(0,0, julix, juliy);
For(i=3;i<dian_num;i++) //Finding feature points based on linear prediction
For(j=0;j<76;j++)
{ UART3_SendByte(dispose_date[j]);//Upload feature points
Dispose_date[j]=0x00;}
 Timer0_counter=0; // Clear the relevant flag bit
  ...} }
```

3.3 Effect of Operation

The designed scheduler was put into operation in LPC1768. Experiments showed that the data uploaded by radar can be processed in real time. And it can screen out high threat targets through threat judgment. Can effectively compress the target track and upload data effectively. Due to the large amount of target track data, it is easy to lose the target data and cannot effectively screen high-threat targets. Through the interrupt call, the program execution time is reasonably allocated. By decomposing complex tasks, framing of radar traces can be completed within the interval of received bytes. Reduced system delays and improved processor efficiency.

4 CONCLUSION

With the increasing complexity of tasks handled by embedded processors, the ability of processors to efficiently schedule tasks for execution has become a key factor in determining the efficient use of processors. Through the decomposition of the complex tasks into simple tasks proposed in this paper, simple tasks can be completed within the interval of the processor performing other tasks, reducing the system delay, thereby improving the efficiency of the processor. At the same time, the reasonable scheduling of interrupt tasks and cyclic tasks completes the reasonable time allocation of the processor, avoids the system delay caused by the waiting tasks, and then increases the speed of executing the tasks of the processor.

REFERENCES

1. Zhou Lei. Research and implementation of event-driven embedded system scheduling kernel [D]. *Jilin University: Jilin University,* 2015.
2. Sun Juan. Design and implementation of task scheduling algorithm based on service quality [D]. *Dalian University of Technology: Dalian University of Technology,* 2016.
3. Jiang Jianchun. Research on key issues of heterogeneous multi-core embedded software [D]. *Chongqing University: Chongqing University,* 2012.
4. Cheng Yi, Zhao Hongwei, Long Manli, Li Yucui,. Improvement of the earliest deadline scheduling algorithm [J]. *Journal of Jilin University (Engineering Science),* 2013, (5).
5. Jiang Lei,. Research on preemptive scheduling algorithm and preemption threshold scheduling algorithm [J]. *Modern Computer,* 2013, (12).
6. Li Zhe, Mu Dejun, Guo Lantian, Huang Xingli, Li Liutao. Research on Mixed Scheduling Mechanism of Embedded Multiprocessor Systems[J]. *Journal of Northwestern Polytechnical University,* 2015, (1).
7. Xiao Hong, Zhou Puxiong,. Embedded Multi-core System Software Design and Development [J]. *Modern Computer (Professional Edition)*, 2008, (5).
8. Wang Liang. Research on large-scale grid platform modeling and scheduling algorithm [D]. *Xidian University: Xidian University,* 2005.
9. Song Yan, Liu Limin, Han Zhuangzhi,. Research on Radar Track Data Compression Method[J]. *Electrooptics and Control*, 2017, (4).

MATEC Web of Conferences 176, 01026 (2018) https://doi.org/10.1051/matecconf/201817601026
IFID 2018

DDoS Attack Detection Based on Self-organizing Mapping Network in Software Defined Networking

Chanchan Zhao[1,2,*] and *Feng* Liu[1]

[1]School of Computer and Information Technology, Beijing Jiaotong University, 100044 Beijing, P.R. China
[2] College of Information Engineering, Inner Mongolia University of Technology, 010051 Hohhot, P.R. China

Abstract. The software defined networking is a new kind of network architecture, the programmability of SDN enables hackers to easily launch DDoS attack on the network through software programming. To solve the problem, a DDoS attack detection scheme based on self-organizing mapping network in the software defined networking was proposed. The first is to give an early warning according to the probability of occurrence of Packet_In event. If the threshold value is exceeded, the characteristics of the flow are calculated and the self-organizing mapping network is used for clustering of eigenvalues to finally detect the DDoS attack flow. The experimental results showed that the DDoS attack detection scheme based on self-organizing mapping network was superior to the comparison scheme in detection rate and false alarm rate.

1 Introduction

The software defined networking(SDN) is a new kind of network architecture that can meet the needs of the future Internet, and its emergence makes it possible to break through the bottlenecks of existing network architecture. The software defined networking separates the control plane and the data plane, shielding the complexity of the underlying network infrastructure, making the management of the whole network more convenient and efficient. At the same time, the centralized management, openness and programmability of SDN make it a good support for the innovation of future new business.

SDN separates the data plane and the control plane, to realize high efficient centralized management of the network. However, this architecture also brings security risks. Because of the existing communication path between the controller and the network device, attackers can send attack packets frequently and the controller are always busy deciding how to forward these packets, but unable to provide services to the legitimate users, which belongs to the control layer DDoS attacks. Similar DDoS attacks can also be launched at the infrastructure level. Flooding of the flow table will deplete the memory resources and make the network unable to provide normal resource access or services, resulting in network collapse. In addition, DDoS attacks may also cause rule modification or fraudulent rules to be insert.

The remainder of this paper is organized as follows. Section 2 reviews some related studies. In Section 3, we propose a attack detection scheme in the software defined networking. The analysis is further validated by extensive simulation experiments introduced in Section 4. Finally, Section 5 concludes this research work.

2 Related work

In the past few years, the size, number and type of DDoS attacks have been increasing year by year. In order to adapt to this situation, the academe and the industry have devoted a lot of research efforts in the detection of DDoS attacks. DDoS attack detection has become a research hotspot in the field of network security.

In SDN, in order to reduce the harm of DDoS attacks, researchers have proposed a series of different solutions. Flow detection and analysis[1] is an effective means of detecting attacks in SDN. Tsinghua University Network Research Center [2] presents a flow analysis method, trigger a "not found" event during each check of the flow table, and then encapsulate the data packet to the controller to send the message, and then check the data packet IP address, however, this method will drain a large number of load to the controller, causing great burden to the controller.

* Corresponding author: cczhao@imut.edu.cn

In order to alleviate the overload of SDN controller, National Technical University of Athens network management and optimization design laboratory (Netmode) [3] adopt In Mon Company's network flow monitoring technology sFlow based on packet sampling to be in charge of the collection of information flow, and reduce the communication between the switch and the control device by lookup the forward flow table. Then analyze the flow variation characteristics of the anomaly module, use the algorithm based on information entropy to detect the anomaly, and generate the rule of flow table to issue to the switch. However, the method of anomaly detection based on information entropy needs to be combined with other technologies to determine the threshold.

In addition to the above detection method based on flow variation characteristics, there is also a method based on the connection migration mechanism. Based on the connection migration mechanism, literature[4] extends the data plane of SDN, designs a security architecture AVANT-GUARD that can defend against DoS attacks, adding the connection migration module and encouraging the trigger module.

In this paper, we argue that a new scheme for DDoS Detection based on SOM to reduce resource consumption, improve detection ratio and false alarm ratio.

3 Attack detection

3.1. SDN flow processing

In the software defined networking, the controller creates rules for each flow. There are two modes in the setting of flow rules: active and passive. In the first model, flow table rule is pre-installed in the flow table, and the flow table rules have been set up before the first packet arrives at the switch; in the second mode, only if the table rules of the corresponding flow in the flow table items do not exist, then the controller can set up rules for such flow table, that is when the first packet arrives at the switch the flow table rules are set up. The software defined networking discussed in this paper takes the second mode by default.

3.2 Packet_In trigger probability

When the flow of the main switch does not have corresponding flow table rules to match with, the Packet_In event is triggered. Based on this, during the time of DDoS attacks, the proportion of Packet_In event data packets triggering is called Packet_In event triggering probability, is $P(v_a)$, v_a is denoted as the rate of DDoS attack flow.

Let $v_n\mu_d=N$, $v_a\mu_d=A(v_a)$, which represents the number of data packet sent by the normal flow and attack flow in μ_d .The Packet_In proportion of normal flow triggering is:

$$\frac{\varphi}{N}=\frac{\sum_{i=1}^{v_n\mu_d} C(i)}{v_n\mu_d} \tag{1}$$

It can be deduced that the average probability of Packet_In is:

$$P(v_a)=\frac{\sum_{i=1}^{v_n\mu_d} C(i)+\sum_{j=1}^{v_a\mu_d} C_a(j)}{v_n\mu_d+v_a\mu_d} =\frac{\varphi+\xi(v_a)}{N+A(v_a)} \tag{2}$$

3.3 Flow feature

The feature vector of flow table is highly abstract to the state information of normal flow and abnormal flow, and the attack flow will show certain regular patterns. We can get the flow table information and analyze the change of network flow distribution characteristics in a certain period of time to detect malicious attacks. Therefore, the selection of flow feature is a necessary part of the DDoS attack detection scheme. In this paper, the following feature parameters are proposed as the basis for detecting DDoS attacks.

(1) Number of source IP address

DDoS attacks generally use IP address fraud and other attacks methods to send a large number of attack packets in a relatively short time to consume the resources of the flow table.

(2) Source IP address Generating Speed

When DDoS attacks occur, an attacker generates a large number of source IP addresses to send data packets to the injured host, and the Source IP address Generating Speed generally starts to change significantly. It can be expressed by the difference between the number of source IP addresses in two adjacent cycles $Src\_Num(T_{t+1})-Src\_Num(T_t)$.

(3) Destination port number

In a cycle, the number of ports will fluctuate normally, but DDoS attackers will scan ports and choose different ports to attack. The destination port number will change significantly.

(4) Ports Generating Speed(PGS)

Under normal circumstances, the Ports Generating Speed will be relatively stable within a certain range. When DDoS attack occurs, it will choose port randomly, so the growth rate of ports will also increase. To indicate as:

$$PGS = Port\_num / interval \quad (3)$$

Where $Port\_num$ is number of ports, $interval$ is the time interval.

(5) Median of Bytes per flow(MBF)

In order to enhance the intensity of malicious attacks, the data packets sent by the DDoS attack are generally very short and contain less bytes. Take the number of bytes per flow as a sample, and each item in the flow table should be sorted in ascending according to the number of bytes, calculated as follows:

$$MBF = \begin{cases} b_{i+1/2} & i \bmod 2 \neq 0 \\ (b_{i/2} + b_{(i+1)/2})/2 & otherwise \end{cases} \quad (4)$$

Where b_i stands for item i of the sample set $B = \{b_1, b_2, ..., b_i ..., b_n\}$ composed by the number of bytes in each packet, n is the number of samples, and when $\forall j$ makes $i < j$, $b_i \leq b_j$ still holds.

3.4 Detection scheme

The DDoS detection scheme is described as follows, as shown in Fig. 1.

1)Following the flow procedure specified in 3.1 section, for a packet entering the switch OFS_i which fails to match with flow table and does not know how to operate on, OFS_i will encapsulate such data in Packet_In to send to SC_j. According to the analysis of 3.2, the increase of flow will increase the occurrence probability of Packet_In in the DDoS attack. According to this, when the occurrence probability $P(v_a)$ of Packet_In reach to certain threshold $\frac{\varphi}{N}$, the alarm can be predicted.

2)Carry out the feature extraction according to 3.3 section, the SOM clustering method is used to deal with the data. When an attack is detected, the injured host is located according to the flow table information.

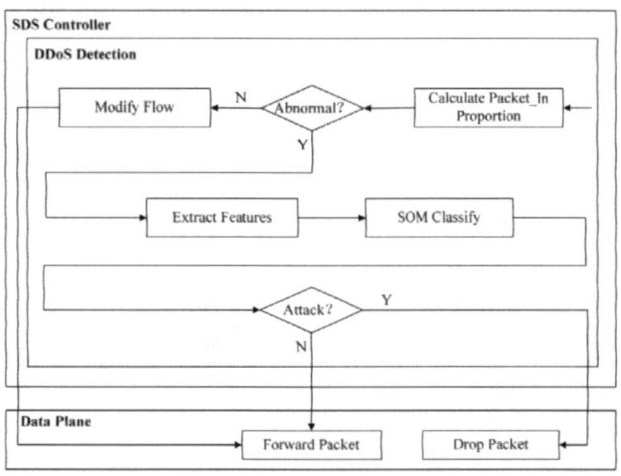

Fig. 1. Flow chart of DDoS attack detection.

4 Experimental results and analysis

The experimental data used in this paper consists of two parts, one part of which is normal flow, which is collected from WIDE project[5] and has typical representativeness. According to literature [6], 50.8% of normal flow adopts TCP protocol, 47.24% adopts UDP protocol, and 1.96% adopts ICMP protocol. The other part of the attack data is released by MIT Lincoln Laboratory. At present, it is still a classic dataset used to study network attacks, and its network environment is close to the real environment, having certain authority.

In this section, the results of the DDoS attack detection scheme in the designed software defined network are analyzed by simulation experiments. The simulation experiment is carried out in the Matlab2010b environment, the parameters used are set according to literature[7].

In this section, two quantitative indicators of Detection Ratio and False Alarm Ratio to judge the detection effect. They are expressed as R_d and R_f respectively, and the formulas are as follows:

$$R_d = \frac{A_a}{A_a + A_n} \quad (5)$$

$$R_f = \frac{N_a}{N_a + N_n} \quad (6)$$

Where A_a is the number of attacks being correctly detected in attack samples, A_n is the number of attacks mistakenly detected as normal in attack samples, N_a is the number of attacks mistakenly detected in normal samples, N_n is the number of attacks correctly detected in normal samples.

As a contrast, this paper carries out a comparative experiment in accordance with the method in literature [7]based on the same data. The result is shown in Fig. 2 and Fig. 3. From the figures, we can see that the detection rate of the proposed scheme is higher than that of the contrast scheme, and the false alarm rate is lower than the corresponding false alarm rate of the comparison scheme.

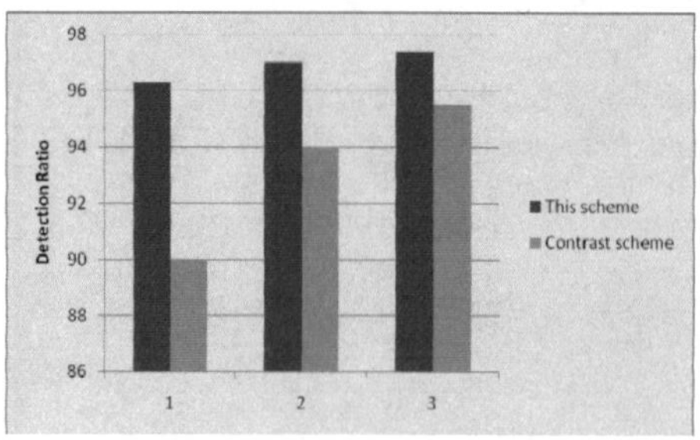

Fig. 2. Comparison of attack and detection results.

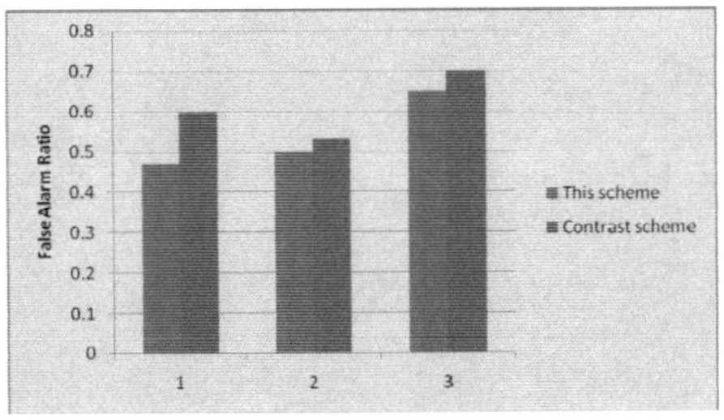

Fig. 3. Comparison of attack and detection results.

5 Conclusions

To solve the issue of the DDoS attack, a DDoS attack detection scheme based on self-organizing mapping network in the software defined networking was proposed. The first is to give an early warning according to the probability of occurrence of Packet_In event. If the threshold value is exceeded, the characteristics of the flow are calculated and the self-organizing mapping network is used for clustering of eigenvalues to finally detect the DDoS attack flow. The experimental results showed that the DDoS attack detection scheme based on self-organizing mapping network was superior to the comparison scheme in detection rate and false alarm rate.

Acknowledgment

This work is supported by the National Key R&D Plan (No. K17B500071), the Natural Science Foundation of Inner Mongolia (No. 2016MS0706, No. 2017MS0702), the Science and Technology R&D Plan of China Railway Corporation (No. 2016J007-B), the Institution of Higher Learning Science Research Project of Inner Mongolia (No. NJZY078) and the Science Research Project of Inner Mongolia University of Technology (No. ZD201522).

References

1. Z.A.Qazi, J.Lee, T.Jin, G.Bellala, M.Arndt, G.Noubir, Comp. Com. **43**,4 (2013)
2. G. Yao, J. Bi, P. Xiao, *In IEEE International Conference on Network Protocols*. (2011)
3. K. Giotis, C. Argyropoulos, Androulidakis G, D.Kalogeras, V.Maglaris, Comput Netw. **62**,5(2014)
4. S.Shin, V.Yegneswaran, P.Porras, G. Gu, *ACM Sigsac Conference on Computer & Communications Security* . (2013)
5. C. Kenjiro, MAWI working group traffic archive[OL]. 2016[2016-12-8].http://mawi.wide.ad.jp/mawi/.
6. D. E.Taylor, J. S.Turner, *Conference of the IEEE Computer and Communications Societies*. (2005)
7. R. Braga, E. Mota, A.Passito, *In Conference on Local Computer Networks*. **8** (2010)

A Novel Algorithm For Radar Target Feature Extraction

Shen Limin[*]

The PLA University of Information Engineering Luoyang Campus Luoyang, Henan, 471009, China

Abstract. Due to the aspect sensitivity of High Resolution Range Profile (HRRP), traditional radar target recognition methods usually use average HRRP within some aspect region.Actually,the amplitude fluctuation property of HRRPs also represents some feature information of target.According to the scattering center model , a new feature extraction method using the amplitude fluctuation property of HRRPs is proposed in this paper. The new algorithm mainly extracts the features of the effective distance unit according to the distribution of the target scattering points to improve the recognition efficiency.The experimental results based on the SVM classifier show that the novel feature extraction method can improve recognition performances greatly .

1 Introduction

Radar target recognition based on High Resolution Range Profile (HRRP) is the mainstream of modern war environment perception and recognition. Radar target recognition based on HRRP avoids complicated motion compensation and can greatly improve the target interception ability to meet the requirements of real-time guidance. HRRP recognition is an important method for the identification of complex military targets and has received extensive attention and in-depth research. Anti-noise performance, azimuth sensitivity, and training-set size sensitivity are important indicators of the overall performance of the HRRP classifier[1][2].

Feature extraction is the most critical for radar target recognition. The recognition ability of target recognition system depends greatly on the selection of feature vectors and the accuracy of feature extraction. Most of the radar observations are in the optical scattering region, the target can be equivalent to a set of multiple isolated scattering centers. The scattering center contains features such as position, amplitude, and geometry type. Extracting these features accurately has important application value in the fields of automatic target recognition and self-focusing. At present, the feature extraction method based on HRRP is mainly divided into non-parametric methods and parameterized methods[3-5].

The typical representation of non-parametric methods is the direct use of HRRP. Li and Yang elaborated the feasibility of directly using HRRP as feature vectors, and proposed a recognition method based on matching degrees The typical representation of the parametric method is the Relax algorithm based on the simple scattering point model, this algorithm is based on the Clean algorithm. Based on the Relax algorithm, this paper presents an improved feature extraction method, which uses the position and intensity of the scattering center as the target feature to extract the geometric parameters of the target structure.

2 Data model of Echo signal

The simple scattering point model theory is that when the radar work in optical region, the target can be composed of several discrete scattering points, and the radar target echo is the vector sum of the sub-echo formed by the backscattering of the emission point by each scattering point[6-8]. Relax algorithm is a nonlinear least squares relaxation algorithm for solving simple scattering point model parameters.In this paper, by using the average distance of the Relax algorithm for radar echo as feature extraction. Formula (1) is the simple scattering point model of radar target withe noise[9].

$$y_n = \sum_{k=1}^{K} \alpha_k e^{j2\pi f_k n} + e_n \quad (1)$$

k represents the number of scattered points of radar exposure at a specific target azimuth; α_k is the complex envelope of the kth scattering point echo, which is a function of time and represents the radar target intensity; f_k is the kth sine wave frequency, which means the distance to the position information. Assuming e_n is white noise, in the Relax algorithm, the noise relaxation is the self-regression process. as follows:

$$e_n = \sum_{m=1}^{M} a_m e_{n-m} + w_n \quad n = 0,1,\cdots N-1 \quad (2)$$

w_n represents a zero-mean complex Gaussian white noise process

[*] Corresponding author: shenlimin1996@163.com

$$w(f_k)=\left[1,e^{j2\pi f_k},e^{j2(2\pi f_k)},\cdots,e^{j(N-1)2\pi f_k}\right]^T \quad (3)$$

Rewrite the above model in matrix form

$$Y = A\alpha + e_n \quad (4)$$

The problem becomes to solve the parameters based on the above model and radar data

$$\{f_k,a_k\} = \arg\min \arg\min_{\{f_k,a_k\}} \|Y - A\alpha\| \quad (5)$$

3 Radar target feature extraction

Radar HRRP recognition is mainly divided three steps: Gaining HRRP; Feature Extraction for Radar target; Classifier, Flow chart shown in Figure 1.

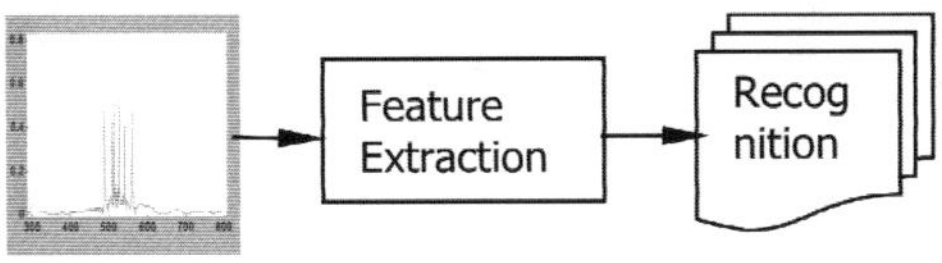

Fig. 1. Flow chart of Radar HRRP Recognition

3.1. Pre-processing of HRRP

Pre-processing method of HRRP is introduced in order to strengthen useful information and restore the degenerated phenomenon which was caused by the other factors. The following pre-processing method was used in this paper.

3.1.1 Power Transformation

HRRP is obtained through the absolute duplicate value of HRRP data, regarding the Γ positive solidly vector process, every variable can obey the distribution approximately, correspondingly, Γ distribution can transform the kind of Gaussian distribution through power transformation. The power transformation is defined as:

$$y = x^v, 0 < v < 1 \quad (6)$$

Where v are coefficients of power transformation.

3.1.2 Normalization

The centre of goal scattering position and the relative scope is emphasized of HRRP classification, normalizations each goal's HRRP according to the biggest peak value is not only eliminate dependence of he goal but also simplify hunting zone of the parameters σ . If specify it has n samples in pattern classes, Normalized processing as following equation (7).

$$x^{-(i)} = \frac{x_j^{(i)}}{\left\|x_i^{(i)}\right\|} \quad \{i=1,2,\cdots c; j=1,2,\cdots N\} \quad (7)$$

3.2. A Novel Algorithm Based on Relax

Improved algorithm focuses on the selection of effective distance units, it can be considered from two aspects: firstly there are almost no scattering point echoes on some distance units, or there are only some very weak clutter and noise; Secondly, there are many scattering points in some distance unit distribution, but there is no obvious effect. an improved algorithm is proposed to solve the above problems, Figure 2 is a flowchart of an improved algorithm. Assuming the parameters $\{a_k, f_k\}$ have been estimated, Signal $\sum_{i=1,i\neq k}^{K} a_i w(f_i)$ reconstructed from a simple scatter point model has a residual signal .

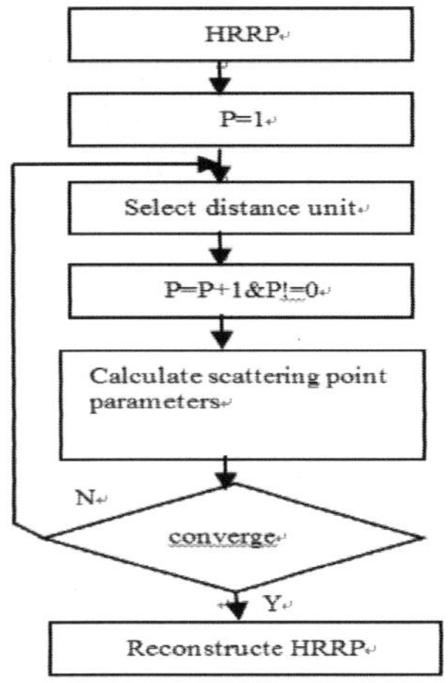

Fig.2 The flow chart of the improved algorithm

$$y_k = Y - \sum_{i=1,i\neq k}^{K} a_i w(f_i) = Y - wa + w(f_k)a_k \quad (8)$$

$$a_k = \frac{w^T(f_k)y_k}{N} = \frac{DFT(y_k)}{N} \quad (9)$$

$$f_k = \arg\max_{f_k} \arg\left\|DFT(y_k)\right\|^2 \quad (10)$$

4 Simulation and analysis

Support Vector Machines(SVM) are used as classifiers to perform training classification to verify the effectiveness of the proposed algorithm. HRRP of the radar target V-22 with pitch angle and horizontal azimuth spacing is simulated.The simulation parameters are carrier frequency 10GHz,bandwidth150MHz (corresponding distance resolution 1m), sampling points 200, signal to noise ratio 10Db,A novel Relax algorithm convergence threshold set to 10-3.The influence of the number of scattered points and the data processing speed are verified.

4.1 Influence of Number of Scattering Points on Reconstructed HRRP

The experimental results are shown in Fig.3, as follows (a), (b), (c), and (d) are reconstructed from the scattered points of 18, 15, 8 and 6 respectively.

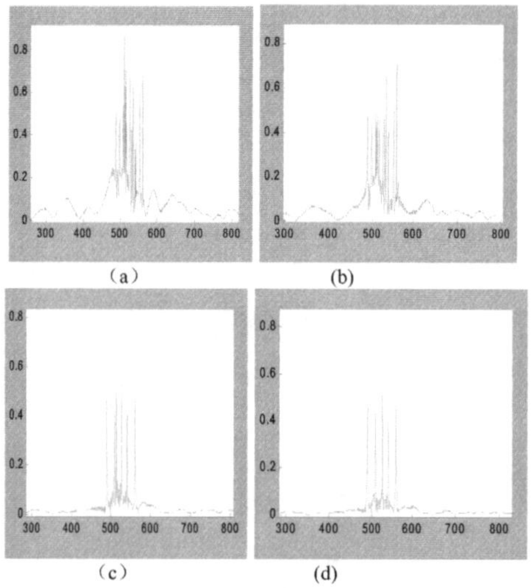

Fig.3 The restructuring HRRP of choosing different scattering spots

It can be seen from the Fig.3 that the target scattering point parameters extracted by the RELAX algorithm can reflect the scattering point distribution of the original range profile. From the simulation diagram, the more the scattering points are extracted from the target echo, the closer the reconstruction range profile is to the original range profile, and more beneficial to the design of the classifier. It can be seen from Fig. 3 (c) and (d) that when the number of scattered points is less than 10, the complete distance image cannot be constructed. Fig. 3(a), (b) When the number of scattering points are greater than15, the reconstructed range profile has a small difference from the original range profile.

4.2 Recognition rate

Table 1 shows the simulation results from correct recognition rate. It can be seen from Table 1 that the improved algorithm has considerable advantages.

Table 1. Compared the performance with Relax and improved Relax.

	scattering points	18	15	8	6
Relax algorithm	Correct recognition rate	0.97	0.96	0.96	0.93
improved Relax	Correct recognition rate	0.98	0.97	0.97	0.95

5 Conclusions

This paper first analyzes the data model of the target echo signal. Based on this model, the Relax algorithm is deeply analyzed. The characteristics of the radar target HRRP are initialized. With the improved Relax algorithm, the characteristics of the scattering point parameters are extracted from the measured data of the target V-22 radar echo. The simulation system based on MATLAB is established and the distance profile is reconstructed. Finally, the simulation results show that the improved algorithm is effective in selecting the number of scattered points and data processing speed.

References

1. Li H, Yang S. Using range profiles as feature vectors to identify aerospace object[C]. IEEE Trans. on AP. 41 (3):261-280 (1993).
2. Huang Deshuang, Technology of Intelligent Signal Processing Based On High Resolution Radar[M]. Beijing: Publishing Of Machinery Industry(2001).
3. H-J.Li,Y.D,Wang,L-H.Wang,Matchingscore properties between range profile of high resolution radar targets, IEEE Antennas and Propagation Magazine[J]. 44(4)： 444-452 (1996).
4. Xing M，Wu R，Lan J，et al.Migration Through Resolution Cell Compensation in ISAR Imaging[J].IEEE GRS.Letters， 1(2)： 360-400,(2004).
5. BAO zheng,Xing Mengdao,Wang tong. Radar Imaging Technique[M] Beijing: Publishing Of Electronics Industry,(2015).
6. Pan mian. Study of Radar Target Recognition using Range Profiles Based on Time Frequency Features and Kernel Methods [D],ChengDu: University of Electronic Science and Technology of China.(2017)
7. ZHANG xuefeng. Study on Radar HRRP Target Recognition[D]. XI AN : Xidian University.(2015)
8. ZHU jiehao Research on Radar Target High Resolu- tion Range Profile Simulation and Recognition [D]. NANJING: Nanjing University of Aeronautics.(2012)
9. ZHANG zhongming. Research on Radar Target High Resolution Range Profile Simulation and Recognition [D]CHANGSHA: National Defense University,(2014)

MATEC Web of Conferences 176, 01028 (2018) https://doi.org/10.1051/matecconf/201817601028
IFID 2018

Understanding of the Coherent Demodulation with Phase-Locked Loop

Bingcong Zhai[1]

[1] School of Information Engineering Beijing, Institute of Petrochemical Technology, North Qingyuan Road, Daxing District, Beijing, China

Abstract: The phase-locked loop (PLL) technology is a very important technology in the communication field. With the development of electronic technology toward digitalization, the phase-locked processing of signal needs to be realized in digital way. Therefore, more and more attentions have been paid to the research and application of all digital phase-locked loops. This paper serves as an introduction about the basic background of PLL, the basic characteristics and structure of PLL, and the basic principles of modulation and demodulation. It provides a concise application about the basic principle and main design process of modulation and demodulation of FSK signal, which are realized by using phase-locked loop chip NE564.

1 INTRODUCTION

In 1932, De Bellescize invented the first phase-locked loop and presented the theory of synchronous detection. People were constantly exploring the application of PLL technology. Until 1970s, because of the rapid development of integrated circuit technology, the integrated phase-locked loop technology gradually rose. The cost of phase-locked loop gradually was reduced and the function was gradually improved, which provided widely space for PLL technology application development. Up to now, PLL has been widely applied in communication, radar, instrumentation, spaceflight, navigation, computer, industry, geology and other technology fields.

With the development of digital electronic technology, the digital phase-locked loop (PLL) is also rising. A large number of digital phase locked loops are widely used in the fields of digital carrier signal transmission synchronization, bit synchronization, coherent demodulation and so on. But the start appearance of the digital phase locked loop is a half analog circuit which still has some analog devices in the circuit. The analog devices will be influenced by temperature and voltage. In order to solve these problems, an all-digital phase-locked loop technology has appeared. All-digital phase-locked loop has high accuracy and is not affected by voltage and temperature. It can preset the central frequency and loop bandwidth of phase-locked loop and is easy to construct high-order phase-locked loop. With the development of integrated circuit technology, the frequency of PLL is increasing and the whole system can be made into system on chip. The phase-locked loop circuit is made into a function IP core, which is embedded in SOC to form in chip phase locked loop. At the same time, with the rapid development of Field − Programmable Gate Array and Complex Programmable Logic Device technology, the performance index of an all-digital phase-locked loop have also been rapidly developed and greatly improved.

Although the development of PLL technology has more than 80 years, the application of phase-locked loop technology is constantly expanding. Because of the development of the high-tech product, People need to improve the index of PLL. So many domestic and foreign engineers in the circuit design of the phase-locked loop technology continued their research to get the new PLL structure which can be satisfied in different occasions. This paper is going to talk about the coherent demodulation with phase-locked loop. The first section is the structure of PLL. The second section is the introduction of modulation and demodulation. The third section is the application about the FSK signal using PLL chip.

2 BACKGROUND

PLL is the fusion of automatic frequency control and automatic phase control technology. In 1930s, scientists built synchronous control theory and the French engineer Bellescize published a mathematical description of PLL and Synchronous detection theory in 1932. But the circuits were complex and the cost was high. Thus, the PLL was not widely available. In 1943, the phase-locked loop was firstly used in black and white TV receiver. It can suppress the external noise which could disturb the synchronous signal. Then, the phase-locked loop circuit was used to synchronize the color pulse string in the color TV receiver. Since then, the phase-locked loop has

*Corresponding author: 18601167058@163.com

been applied and developed rapidly.

In 1950s, with the development of space technology, Jaffe and Rechtin successfully used phase-locked loop filter as the tracking missile beacon. It was the first time that they published the article about the analysis of the linear theory of phase-locked loop on noise effect and solved the problem about optimal design of phase-lock loop. The development of space technology promoted the further discussion of the phase-locked loop and its theory and greatly promoted the development of phase locked technology.

In the early 60s, Viterbi studied the nonlinear theory of the noiseless phase-locked loop and published a paper about the principle of coherent communication. With the development of semiconductor technology, the phase-locked loop chip has been widely applied in various fields as a low-cost multi-functional component.

In 1970s, Undsy and Chanes researched the nonlinear analysis theory of noise of one order, two order and high order PLL. With the extensive research on the theory and application of phase-locked technology and the development of digital circuit, the phase detector was partly replaced by digital circuit and the rest part was still analog circuit, which was the first digital phase-locked loop. The exact name of it was the Mixed-single PLL. With the continuous development and perfection of the digital mode, Hybrid PLL technology and theory became the mainstream of the phase-locked loop.

Now, with the demand of low cost, low power consumption and high data transmission rate, the integrated circuit is developing towards the direction of high integration and low power consumption. Phase-locked loop technology has become a systematic theoretical science. It has been widely applied in communication, radar, aerospace, precision measurement, computer, infrared, laser, atomic energy, stereo, motor control and image technology departments.

America nation Semi-Conductor announced launching the LMx243x series phase-locked loop chip in June 2003. Its operation frequency was higher than 3GHz. It was suitable for WLAN, 5.8GHz indoor cordless phone, mobile phone and base station. Low power and ultra-low phase noise (the normalization phase noise can reach - 219dBcmz) makes it prominent.

In China, Haokai Microelectronics (Shanghai) Co. Ltd research and development high performance clock phase-locked loop which own completely independent intellectual property rights. Now the series of products have been pass the Multi Project Wafer silicon verification. The PLL with a new structure, unique and differential charge pump Voltage Controlled Oscillator design, can make ensure that PLL has very low noise. The unique design of the differential VCO can maintain the 50% duty cycle of the output clock. Power consumption can be reduced to 1/4 of conventional design.

3 STRUCTURE OF PLL

In this section, we will talk about the structure of PLL.PLL is a feedback circuit, which can make one signal to track another one. Since PLL has a tricking function, it is usually used in closed loop tracking circuit. When the frequency of output signal is equal to the frequency of input signal, the output voltage and input voltage maintain a fixed phase difference. It means that the phase of output voltage and input voltage is locked, which is the origin of phase-locked loop name. PLL keeps an output signal synchronizing with a reference input signal in frequency as well as in phase. It is widely applied in the fields of communication, radar, measurement and automatic control.

The PLL in Fig 1 consists of a phase detector (PD), a loop filter (LF), and a voltage-controlled oscillator (VCO). This structure is just like driving cars. When we drive on the road, our eyes like a discriminator, which has the same function as phase detector. Our eyes responsible for distinguishing the direction of the car (feedback) and the road ahead (input) whether there is a difference. And then our brain judges the difference and command the hands rotate the steering wheel to make sure our car going straight. In this construction direction, the car is like the feedback and the loop filter and the voltage-controlled oscillator are like our brain to filter some useless signal and deal with some useful signal.

Firstly, we discuss about the Phase detector. The function of Phase detector is like an institution of phase monitor, which can find the phase difference between the input signal and the feedback signal and then expressing the difference in a reasonable way. This difference can be expressed by voltage form. The function of the relationship between the phase difference and the output voltage is called Phase discrimination characteristics. Phase detector is one of the basic components of phase-locked loop.

The characteristics of the Phase detector are expressed in $U_{d(t)} = K_d f[\theta_{e(t)}]$. K_d is the gain coefficient of the phase detector and $\theta_{e(t)} = \theta_{1(t)} - \theta_{2(t)}$. This function indicates the phase difference between the two input signals. The function $f(x)$ represents the Phase discrimination characteristics, which reflects the relationship between the output voltage of the phase detector and the phase difference. The common characteristics of phase discrimination are cosine, sawtooth and triangle and so on. If the input is X_i and the VCO signal is X_0 , the expressions will be as $X_{i(t)} = Acos(w_{it} + \theta_i)$ and $X_{0(t)} = Bcos(w_{0t} + \varphi_0)$ where and are angular frequencies of the input signal and the VCO; and are their phase constants. If the loop is initially unlocked and the phase detector has a sinusoidal characteristic, the significant output signal at the PD is given by $V_{e(t)} = K_d\{cos[(w_i - w_0)t + \theta_i - \varphi_0] + cos[(w_i + w_0)t + \theta_i + \varphi_0]\}$, where K_d is the gain of the PD.

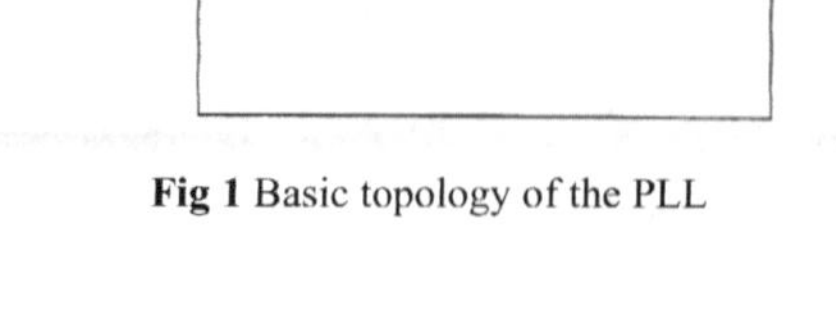

Fig 1 Basic topology of the PLL

Secondly, we talk about the loop filter. In fact, loop filter is one type of filters, which is used in the loop circuit. Therefore, people name it loop filter. It is an important part of the PLL circuit. In order to understand it, you must firstly understand the principle of PLL. The low-pass filter has two functions: one is that the loop circuit can suppress high frequency error components at the output of the Phase detector, which improves the anti-jamming performance. The other is that when the loop filter is out of lock state, the loop filter can be stored in a short time and recover the signal quickly.

A loop filter is usually a linear circuit that consist of a linear element resistance, a capacitor and an operational amplifier. The loop filter is used for attenuation phase error caused by the input signal noise and high frequency components leaked by a smooth phase detector. The order of the loop filter and the noise bandwidth determine the dynamic response of the loop filter.

Last but not least, we talk about voltage-controlled oscillator. The definition of voltage-controlled oscillator (VCO) is the unit controlling the corresponding relationship between the output frequency of the oscillation circuit and the input control voltage. Its frequency equals to the function of input voltage. The work condition of VCO or Component parameters of oscillation circuit is influenced by the input control voltage. The characteristics of VCO is represented by the relation curve between the output angle frequency and the input control voltage U_c (Figure 1). In the diagram, the angular frequency of U_c at zero is called the free oscillation angle frequency and the slope of the curve of is called the control sensitivity. In a communication or measuring instrument, the input control voltage is a signal intending to be transmitted or desired. The voltage-controlled oscillator is usually called a fequency modulation by the most of people, which is used to produce FM signals. In the automatic frequency control loop and the phase-locked loop, the input control voltage is the error signal voltage and the voltage-controlled oscillator is controlled parts in the loop.

The types of VCO are LC voltage-controlled oscillator, RC voltage-controlled oscillator and crystal voltage-controlled oscillator. The VCO requires good frequency stability, high control sensitivity, wide FM range, linear relationship between frequency offset and control voltage, suitable for integration and so on. The crystal voltage-controlled oscillator has high frequency stability while the FM range is narrow. The frequency stability of RC VCO is lower and the FM range is wide. The characteristic of LC voltage-controlled oscillator between the crystal voltage-controlled oscillator and the RC VCO.

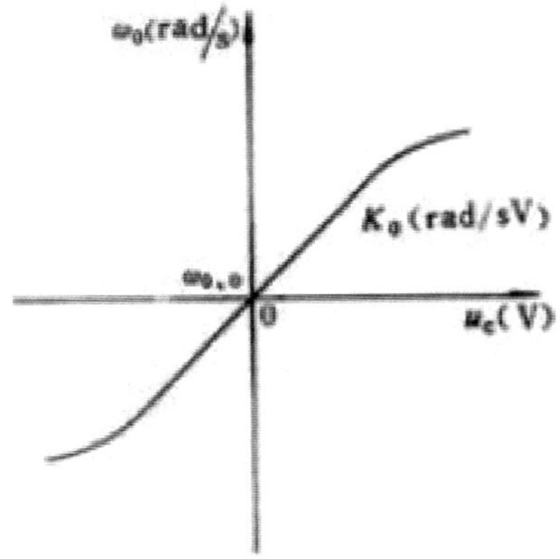

Fig 2 control characteristics of a voltage-controlled oscillator

4 MODULATION AND DEMODULATION

In order to realize long-distance information transmission, people usually used to modulate the signal at the transmitter. After receiving the signal, the receiver will demodulate to restore the original signal. In fact, the modulation is a parameter which can carry the information of input signal to control the carrier signal. The parameters of the carrier signal have amplitude, frequency and phase, so there are three kinds of ways to modulate the signal: amplitude modulation (AM), frequency modulation (FM) and phase modulation (PM).

The characteristics of amplitude modulation wave is that the frequency- is equal to the frequency of the carrier signal and the amplitude varies with the change of the amplitude of the input signal. The characteristics of FM wave is that the amplitude is equal to the amplitude of the carrier signal and the frequency varies with the change of the amplitude of the input signal. The characteristic of phase modulation wave is that the amplitude is equal to the amplitude of the carrier signal and the phase varies with the change of the amplitude of the input signal.

Demodulation is the inverse of modulation, which can restore the modulation wave into the original signal.

There are many types of modulation and the classification methods that are not consistent. In the form of modulated signal, it can be divided into analog modulation and digital modulation. The process using analog to modulation is called analog modulation. And the process using data or digital modulate signal is called digital modulation. Corresponding to the classification of modulation, the demodulation can be divided into sine wave demodulation (sometimes also called continuous wave demodulation) and pulse wave demodulation. Sine wave demodulation can also be divided into amplitude demodulation, frequency demodulation and phase demodulation.

According to the modulation method, there are two types: linear modulation and nonlinear modulation. Linear modulation includes amplitude modulation (AM), suppression of carrier amplitude modulation (DSB-SC),

https://doi.org/10.1051/matecconf/201817601028

band amplitude modulation (SSB), residual band amplitude modulation (VSB) and so on. The nonlinear modulation of anti-interference performance is stronger than linear modulation and the nonlinear modulation includes frequency modulation (FM), frequency shift keying (FSK), phase shift keying (PSK), differential phase shift keying (DPSK) etc. The linear modulation will not change the original signal spectrum structure, while the nonlinear modulation.

Coherent demodulation is also called synchronous demodulation and it is suitable for all the demodulation of linear modulation signals. The key to realize the coherent demodulation is to restore a coherent carrier that is strictly synchronized with the modulation carrier. Coherent demodulation usually uses a multiplier to multiply the input a reference signal that is coherent with the carrier frequency and the carrier frequency.

5 APPLICATIONS

In this part, we discuss the design of modulation and demodulation circuit for FSK signal using PLL chip.

Firstly, we talk about the Phase-locked loop chip NE564 and CD4046. High frequency analog phase-locked loop NE564 is produced by Philips Semiconductor (Holland Philip Company). The highest working frequency of NE564 can reach 50MHZ, which is powered by +5V single power supply. It is especially suitable for the FM signal of modulation and demodulation in high speed digital communication and 2FSK shift keying signal without external complex filter. CD4046 PLL is used in model RC voltage-controlled oscillator, which characteristic is a wide range of power supply voltage between 3V18V, dynamic power consumption is small, power consumption is only 600 W at the center frequency of F0 10kHzm and belongs to a micro power device

Secondly, we discuss the basic concepts and characteristics of FSK. Digital modulation refers to the process of using digital baseband signals to control the carrier and transform the digital baseband signals into digital band-pass signals (adjusted signals). Using the discrete values of digital signals, the technology of realizing digital modulation is called the key control method by opening the key control carrier. Digital frequency modulation is also called frequency shift keying (FSK - Frequency Shift Keying) and binary frequency shift keying is recorded as 2FSK. It is one of the key control methods, which uses the frequency change of the carrier to transmit digital information. The expression and waveform diagram of the 2FSK signal are shown as follows:

In the 2FSK signal, the frequency of the carrier changes with the binary baseband signal between the two frequency points of 1F and 2F

$$e_{2FSK(t)} = \begin{cases} A\cos(w_1 t + \phi_n) \\ A\cos(w_2 t + \theta_n) \end{cases}$$

If the binary sequence s (T) is l01001, the waveform of the 2FSK signal is shown in the Fig3.

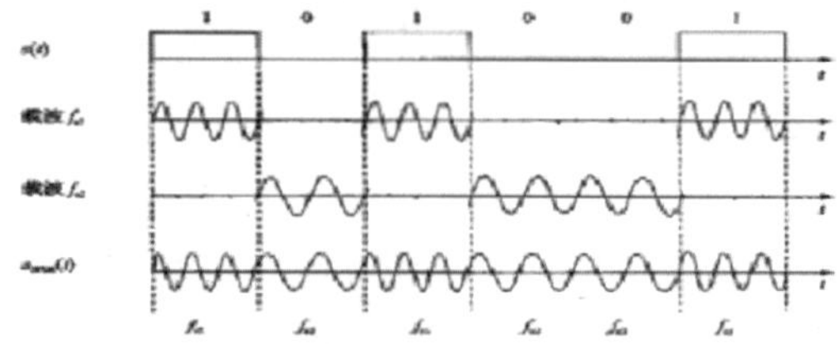

Fig 3 the waveform of 2FSK

Thirdly, we talk about the basic principle of FSK signal modulation. The digital frequency modulation signal can be divided into two cases, the phase continuity and the phase discrete. If the two signals are provided by different independent oscillator, the phase between them are not related. We usually name discrete phase digital FM signal. If two signals are provided by the same oscillation signal source, the phase of two carrier frequency is a continuous digital frequency modulation signal.

Then here is an introduction about the design of FSK signal modulation circuit by NE564.The circuit diagram is a FSK modulation circuit composed by NE564 and so on. In the circuit, NE564 is an analog PLL integrated circuit, which use two-state signal to control CD4016 and simulate FSK modulation switch. The two foot voltage of the NE564 is converted between 1.42V to 5V by CD4016.Therefore, in the case of continuous phase, the output of the voltage-controlled oscillator (VCO) can be changed. When the VCO center frequency capacitance is fixed, the offset between the FSK frequencies can be adjusted by R_1 and R_2 .

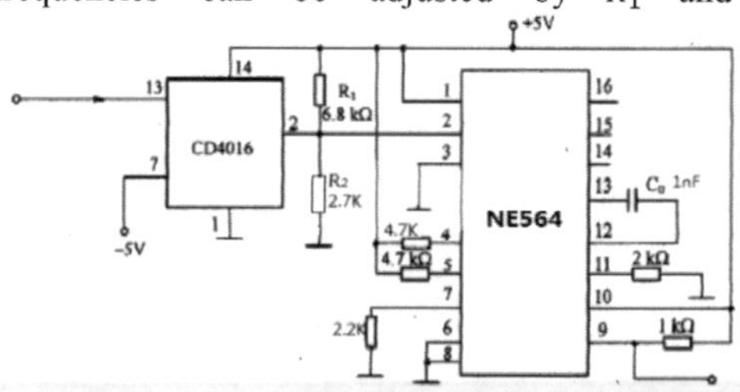

Fig 4 Demodulation of FSK signal by phase-locked loop chip

There are many ways to demodulate FSK signals. In this paper, we use the integrated phase-locked loop CD4046 to demodulate the FSK, which is shown in Fig4. When designing the phase-locked loop, we should fix the phase-locked loop on a carrier frequency 1F of FSK and output the high level and unlock the carrier frequency 2F and output the low level. Then the output of phase locked loop filter can get baseband signal sequence. When inputting the FSK signal, PLL is locked. When inputting the frequency of signal, the low pass filter will output at high level. When inputting the frequency of signal, the low-pass filter will output at low level. Thus, we complete the demodulation of FSK signal. The principle block diagram of demodulation circuit of FSK signal is realized by CD4046.

6 CONCLUSION

This paper gives a concise review of the PLL, as well as modulation and demodulation. The status of the PLL technology and its applications have been discussed. A summary of the PLL technology and its development tends are also included. In the future, I believe that the PLL will become more and more important and popular.

REFERENCES

1. Blanchard, Phase-Locked Loops: Application to Coherent Receiver Design. New York: Wiley, 1976.
2. F. M. Gardner, Phaselock Techniques, 2nd ed. New York: Wiley, 1979. [17] J. A. Afonso, A. J. Quiterio, and D. S. Arants, "A phase-locked loop with digital frequency compare for timing signal recovery," in Conf. Rec., 1979 Nat. Telecommun. Conf., paper 14.4.
3. W. C. Lindsey and C. M. Chie, "A survey of digital phase-locked loops," Proc. IEEE, vol. 69, pp. 410-431, Apr. 1981.
4. Zongsheng Lee, 2FSK modulation and demodulation circuit [J] (phase-locked loop NE564) [J]. Shijia science and technology Career Technical College 2009:6 ~ 7
5. Hong Li, Demodulation of binary frequency shift keying signal based on CMOS integrated phase-locked loop [J]. Guangdong University of Technology.2009:41～42.
6. Chongyi Zheng, The application of phase-locked loop in frequency modulation and demodulation circuit [J]. Hunan School of Building Materials.2003:36～37.
7. Ricai Tian, Wengui Liu, Research on modulation and demodulation of FSK signal by CMOS PLL chip [J]. Harbin Institute of Technology.1996:65～67.
8. Yingna Guo, Design of a modulation and demodulation circuit for FSK signal [J]. Xi'an petroleum of University.2006:4～10

https://doi.org/10.1051/matecconf/201817601029

The fast recognition of vehicle license plate based on the improved template matching

Zhixin Jiang[1], Zhengkui Lin[1,2], Jing Tang[1], Hao Li[1] and Menglu You[1]

[1]Information Science and Technology Department, Dalian Maritime University, No1. Linghai Road, Dalian, 116026, China

Abstract. In order to solve the problem of low accuracy and slow speed in vehicle license plate recognition, a method of number-plate recognition using template matching is proposed. It can effectively recognize low quality and fuzzy number-plate image in real system .The accuracy is 95%, and the recognition time is close to 0.14s.

1 Introduction

Vehicle license plate recognition (VLPR) system is a typical application of remote digital video monitoring and image recognition technology. The fast and accurate recognition of vehicle license plate is important to the function of automatic traffic violation detection systems. Many factors will influence the recognition accuracy and speed, such as uneven brightness, inclination of image shooting, complex background, stained plate and different plate styles. In order to solve these problems, an improved template matching method is proposed in this paper. This method will improve the recognition accuracy and speed for images with different resolution and interferences.

2 Methodology

In this study, the improved recognition method consists of three steps: location of license plate, character segmentation and recognition of character, which is shown in Figure 1.

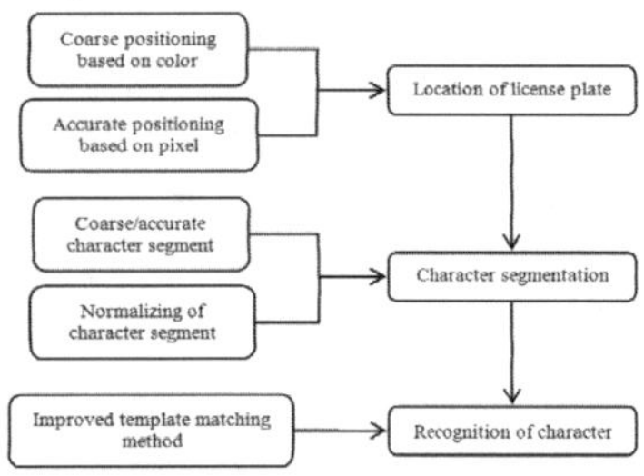

Fig.1. Procedures of character recognition method.

3 Characteristics Of License Plate

Before choosing the method, the characteristics of license plate are analyzed. In this study, the Chinese vehicle license plate is chosen as a sample to be recognized. The size of Chinese vehicle license plate is 440mm×140mm with 7 characters. The width and strokes of each character is 45mm and 10mm respectively. What's more, the distance between the second and third character is 34mm.The distances of other characters are all 12mm.The typical Chinese vehicle license plate are shown in Figure 2.

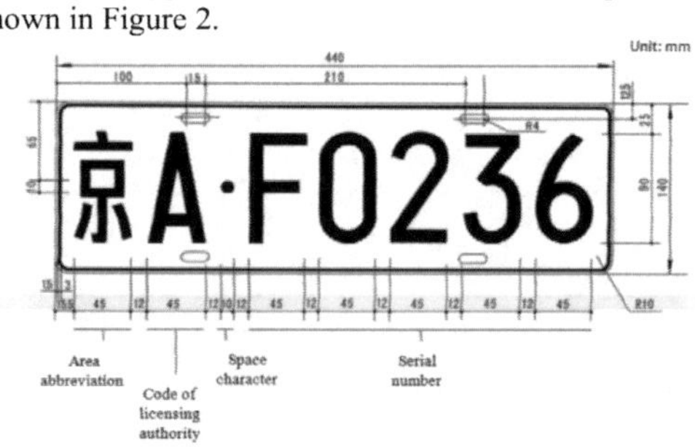

Fig.2. Standard license plate style.

3.1 Coarse and accurate positioning

The color features of license plate are important factors that influence the selecting of recognition methodology. The color of Chinese vehicle license plate consists of five styles: white characters with blue background, black characters with yellow background, white characters with black background, black characters with white background and white characters with green background([1]). Specific color features can be found in

*Corresponding author: [2]dalianjx@163.com

area ratio, vertical projection and characters strokes uniformity of each character.

Based on the features described above, the location of license plate is divided into two steps .Firstly, the coarse positioning of plate is conducted by color spaces; secondly, the accurate positioning of plate is completed by statistical analysis of pixel.

(1) Coarse positioning of license plate

OpenCV is used to process the data in captured image and coarse positioning of license plate is accomplished based on the color features. Taking the license plate of white characters and blue background as example ,firstly, the white-blue color is converted from RGB to HSV color space; secondly, the image is scanned completely, and binarization process is conducted for the H, S and V value of HSV image according to the pixel range; finally, the three image intersect byte by byte. Then the blue color is obtained. The primary location of license plate can be obtained after denoising process.

Several images containing the license plate are selected as samples to have the coarse positioning treatment, which are shown in Figure 3.The value of HSV components are H (94, 115), S (90, 255), V (36, 255) respectively. Experimental results show that the coarse positioning method can obtain the position of plate with fast speed which is shown in Figure 4.

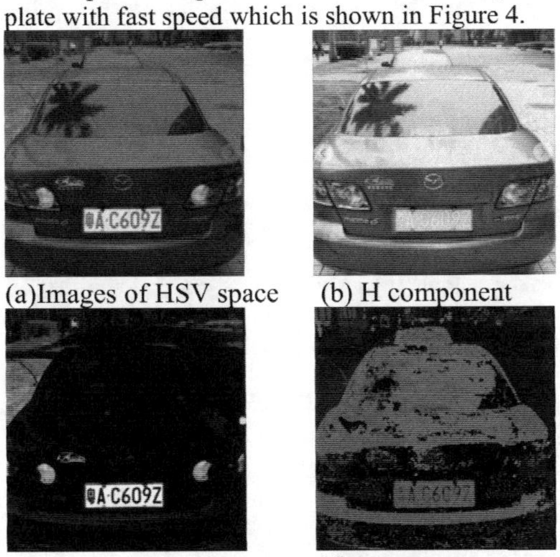

(a)Images of HSV space (b) H component

(c) S component (d) V component

Fig.3. RGB、HSV color space conversion.

Fig.4. Coarse positioning results based on color space.

(2) Accurate positioning of license plate

The accurate positioning of license plate is accomplished based on the statistical analysis of pixel. As for the license plate with white characters and blue background, rank scanning is used to capture the information of blue pixel. The line scanning is used to detect the upper and lower boundary of license plate, and the threshold of pixel is chosen as Th=5; while row scanning is used to detect the left and right boundary, and the threshold of pixel is chosen as Th=3([2]).

Then the additive operation is made between the line and row blue pixel matrix, then the whole license plate can be extracted, which is shown in Figure5.

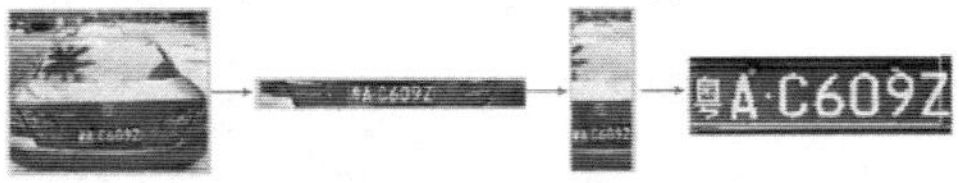

Fig.5. License plate extraction process.

3.2 Character segmentation and character size normalization

The purpose of the license plate character segmentation is to separate the seven characters in the license plate using the characteristics of each character and character spacing. In order to improve the anti-interference ability of character segmentation, this paper uses the method of combining prior knowledge and vertical projection to realize the segmentation of license plate characters.

(1) Coarse Character segmentation

The position of each character in the license plate image is determined by the position of each character in the character segmentation template. According to prior knowledge analysis, ordinary license plate consists of Chinese characters, English letters, and numbers. If the total length of the character area on the license plate is T_Length, the width of a single character is approximately 7.5-1 of the total length (T_Length·7.5-1). In an actual license plate binary image, the character width and character spacing are about 1 to 2 pixels apart from the theoretically estimated value. The first two characters are divided from left to right, and then the remaining five characters are divided from right to left. This avoids the problem of splitting the second and third characters consecutively. This method could minimize the impact of weather factors such as characters and lighting.

(2) Precise segmentation of license plate characters

The license plate candidate region image is preprocessed to obtain a binary image. The matching degree of vertical projection and character segmentation template are calculated to achieve more accurate license plate character segmentation. The equation is shown in equation 1:

$$P_T(b,a)=\sum_{i=0}^{6}\sum_{j=b_i}^{a_{i+1}} V(j) \qquad (1)$$

represents the character interval template matching degree, V(j) represents the vertical projection of the license plate area which is shown in Figure 6. As a result, the incorrect segmentation points that still exist in the rough segmentation are removed, and the accurate character segmentation result is obtained, which is shown in Figure 7.

Fig.6. License plate binary image and vertical projection.

Fig.7. Character segmentation results.

(3) Character size normalization

In general, compared with the standard character library, large inconsistencies in the characters size could exist during character dividing procedure. In order to facilitate the subsequent processing, the character size must be normalized before the character recognition. In this article, the characters are uniformly normalized to the size of 40×20 pixels, as shown in Figure 8.

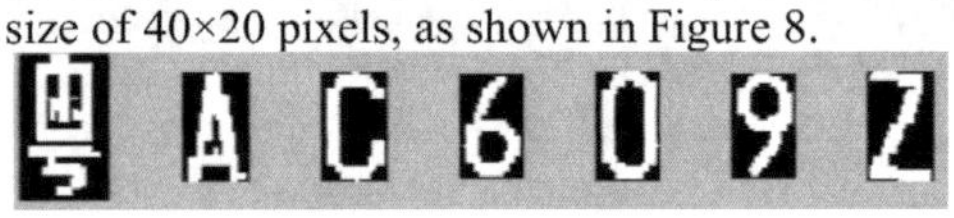

Fig.8. Normalization.

4 Character recognition method based on template matching

Deformation and rotation of images could cause severe interference to the recognition results. To solve this problem, many studies on character recognition introduce neighborhood distances based on template matching method. This paper improves a template matching method based on Hausdorff distance to identify the license plate characters. The character recognition template used is shown in Figure 9 below.

Fig.9. Standard character template.

4.1 General method of template matching based on Hausdorff distance

The Hausdorff distance is the method to analyze the similarity degree between two sets of point sets. The smaller the value, the better the matching, between the set of points([3]). The Hausdorff distance between two sets of points is defined as equation 2:

$$H(A,B) = \max(h(A,B), h(B,A)) \quad (2)$$

$$h(A,B) = \max(a \in A)\min(b \in B)\|a-b\| \quad (3)$$

$$h(B,A) = \max(b \in B)\min(a \in A)\|b-a\| \quad (4)$$

||.|| is the distance paradigm between set A and set B. The equation (2) is the bi-directional Hausdorff distance, which is the basic form of the Hausdorff distance. The h(A,B) in equation (3) is called the unidirectional Hausdorff distance from set A to set B. By equation (2), the bidirectional Hausdorff distance H(A, B) is the max value of the one-way distances h(A, B) and h(B, A). When using Hausdorff distance for template matching, edge features of the image are usually selected as the matching basis. Firstly, the edges of the template image and the to-be-matched image are extracted to obtain the corresponding edge image. Then the edge image is converted to a binary image. The edge pixel grayscale value is set to 1 (or 0) and the non-edge pixel grayscale value is set to 0 (or 1)([4]). Each edge point is represented by its coordinate position in the binary image. Finally, the edge binary image of the sample and the image to be identified is calculated.

The Haursdorff distances for edge binary images and perform template matching are calculated in the following procedure: Firstly, the parameter A and B are defied as $A=\{x_1,x_2,......,x_m\}$ $B=\{y_1,y_2,......,y_n\}$; then, the Hausdorff distance is calculated in both directions. The parameter cmax is defined as the max value. The loops always traverse all points, therefore, the calculating time of algorithm1 is O(mn).The two loops are called the outer loop and the inner loop, respectively.

4.2 Improved Hausdorff distance template matching

In the general algorithm, calculating the one-way distance directly always requires all points to be traversed, which takes a long time to complete the calculation. In fact, the scanning in the inner loop does not always have to be fully executed. The goal of the algorithm is to find the unidirectional Hausdorff distance cmax ([5]). In the inner loop, When d<cmax is found, cmax will not change. This means that the algorithm can end the inner loop and continue with the next outer loop. Here, the idea of Early Interruption is proposed. The improved algorithm is shown in Table 1.

Table 1. algorithm based on Early Interruption.

Algorithm1.One-way Hausdorff Distance Calculation Based on Early Interruption
1: cmax ← 0
2: E← $A\setminus(A\cap B)$
3: Er←randomize(E)
4:Br←randomize(B)
5:**for all** $x \in E_r$ **do**
6:cmin←∞
7:**for all** $y \in B_r$ **do**
8:d ← ||x,y||
9:**if** d<cmax **then**
10:break
11:**end if**
12:**if** d<cmin **then**
13:cmin←d
14:**end if**
15:**end for**

```
if cmin>cmax then
cmax←cmin
end if
end for
return cmax
```

B represents all the random list which is used to iterate through the inner loop. In the same way, E represents all random list in the outer loop. Since picking a random candidate set in a loop does not ensure all points are traversed, it is necessary to prepare a random set in advance. It is possible to generate a random sequence by swapping each point in the set randomly selected. Random scan eliminate the effect of spatial locality in point concentration. The improved algorithm is shown in Table 2.

Table 2. Random sequence selection

Algorithm2.Random sequence selection

Algorithm requirements:： Finite set S
result： Random sequence Sr
Sr←S
for all $p_1 \in S_r$ **do**
p2←randompoint(Sr)
swap(p1,p2)
end for
return Sr

Table 3. Character recognition time comparison

Character recognition method	Correctly identify	Accuracy	Recognition time (s)
Hausdorff distance template matching	335/357	94.05%	0.25
Improved Hausdorff distance template matching	339/357	95.16%	0.14

In order to make template matching apply to the condition of slight character rotation, deformation, etc. When calculating the distance metric, the minimum distance of the 3×3 neighborhood will be considered([6]). The main steps of the improved character recognition method based on the Hausdorff algorithm are as follows.

(1) Initializing the character template distance.

(2) Scanning the binary edge image of the character to be recognized pixel by pixel from left to right and from top to bottom. If it is 1, recording the position information of this point. If it is 0, skip it.

(3) In the template edge image, searching 1 in the 3×3 domain centered on *Px*. Finding the nearest point to *Px* and calculating the closest distance between Px and that point. This distance is the minimum distance between the image to be identified and the template image at this point.

(4) Adding the calculated distance to the one-way Hausdorff distance $D(X, T_i)$.

(5) Calculating $D_i = \max(D(X, T_i), D(T_i, X))$. Traversing all the template to be identified, when *Di* is the minimum, the corresponding template character is the result of the recognition.

4.3 Experimental results and analysis

This article selects 357 vehicle images from the video image of the car camera. The image size is mostly 720×576, 1920×1080, and 556×390 pixels. The experimental example is shown in Figure 10. The experimental results presented in this paper are compared with the experimental results of the original method as shown in Table 3.

Fig.10. License plate recognition examples.

The experimental results show that, the average accuracy of license plate recognition reached 95% in the improved method, and the average execution time is about 0.14s. The experimental results show that the method proposed in this paper has improved the character recognition accuracy and recognition efficiency of the license plate, which is better than the original method.

5 Conclusion

In order to solve the problem of low accuracy and slow speed in vehicle license plate recognition, a fast recognition method based on the improved Template matching is proposed .The experimental results show that this method can improve the accuracy and effectiveness of vehicle license plate recognition.

References

1. Chang,J.,Ryoo,S.&Lim,H,Journal of Supercomputing, **65(1)**, 353(2013)
2. Jiang,X.,&Huang,Y.D,IEEE, 15(2012)
3. Margarito,J.,Helaoui,R.,Bianchi,A.M.,Sartor,F.,&Bo

nomi,A.G,IEEE Transactions onBiomedical Engineering,**63(4)**, 788(2016)
4. Guada, C., Gómez, D., Rodríguez, J. T., Yáñez, J., & Montero, J,International Journal of Computational Intelligence Systems,**9(sup1)**, 43(2016)
5. Taha, A. & Hanbury, A,IEEE Transactions on Pattern Analysis and Machine Intelligence, **37(11),** 2153(2015)
6. Yang,X.W.,Feng,Z.Q.,Huang,Z.Z.,&He,N.N,Applie dMechanics&Materials,**713-715(3)**, 2156(2015)

Evaluation Model for Protocol Conformance of BDS D1 Navigation Messages

Menglan Wang[1], Zhicheng Lv[1,*], Jing Peng[1], Weihua Mou[1], and Gang Ou[1]

[1]Engineering Research Center for Position, Navigation and Time, College of Electronic Science, National University of Defense Technology, Deya Road 109, Changsha, China

Abstract. Navigation messages are the basic data for navigation and positioning calculations in satellite navigation systems. Nowadays, there is a growing need to evaluate the protocol conformance of navigation messages. In this paper, the evaluation model and the calculation method for protocol conformance of BDS D1 navigation messages are proposed, and the example analysis of actual BDS D1 navigation messages is presented. The evaluation model is described from three aspects, including formatting conformance, verification conformance and quantization unit conformance. Every aspect is considered carefully with calculation and analysis. The results show that the model can evaluate the protocol conformance of BDS D1 navigation messages reasonably.

1 Introduction

Navigation messages are broadcasted by navigation satellites, containing spatial references and time bases that can be used for navigation and positioning. They are the basic data for navigation and positioning calculations in satellite navigation systems.

Interface Control Document (ICD) is a set of agreed rules for senders and receivers to generate and interpret navigation messages, **which is one of the protocols in a satellite navigation system. O**nly by implementing the same protocol can navigation messages be transmitted properly and effectively. Therefore, it is necessary to evaluate protocol conformance of navigation messages in the process of product development.

At present, research on navigation messages at home and abroad focuses on analyzing the quality of observation data [1-3] and error correcting design [4]. The research on the evaluation model for protocol conformance of navigation messages is still rare.

In this paper, the evaluation model and the calculation method for protocol conformance of BDS D1 navigation messages are proposed, and the example analysis of actual BDS D1 navigation messages is presented.

2 Evaluation model for protocol conformance of BDS D1 navigation messages

2.1 Frame structure of BDS D1 navigation messages

The frame structure of BDS D1 navigation messages is shown in Fig. 1 [5].

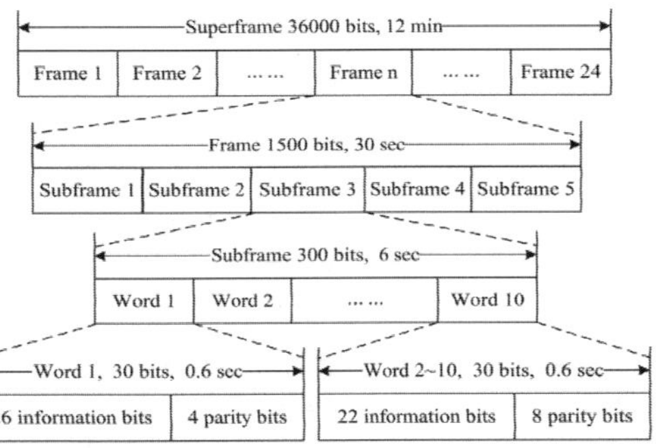

Fig. 1. The frame structure of BDS D1 navigation messages.

Each frame is composed of 5 subframes. Each subframe is composed of 10 words. Each word has 30 bits. Each word consists of navigation message data and parity bits. In the first word of every subframe, the first 15 bits are not encoded and the following 11 bits are encoded in BCH (15,11,1) for error correction. Each of the other 9 words contains two blocks of BCH codes with22 information bits in it.

2.2 Evaluation model for protocol conformance of BDS D1 navigation messages

Protocol conformance reflects the level of satisfaction of generated navigation messages with ICD.

By studying the requirements in ICD, the evaluation model for protocol conformance of navigation messages is described from three aspects, including formatting

* Corresponding author: lvzhicheng@chinauninav.com

conformance, verification conformance and quantization unit conformance, as is shown in Fig. 2.

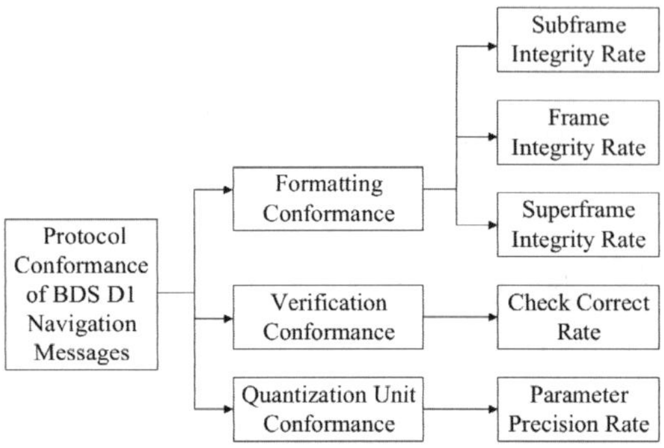

Fig. 2. The evaluation model for protocol conformance of BDS D1 navigation messages.

Formatting conformance is defined as formats of navigation messages comply with the ICD, requiring that messages are complete without any duplication or loss. There are three indicators to describe formatting conformance of navigation messages, including the subframe integrity rate, the frame integrity rate, and the superframe integrity rate.

Verification conformance is defined as check results of error correction decoded navigation messages are correct. The indicator to describe verification conformance of navigation messages is the check correct rate.

Quantization unit conformance is defined as calculated values of parameters solved from navigation messages are close to their true values determined when messages are generated. The indicator to describe quantization unit conformance of navigation messages is the parameter precision rate.

3 Calculation method for protocol conformance of BDS D1 navigation messages

3.1 Calculation method for formatting conformance of BDS D1 navigation messages

Formatting conformance of BDS D1 navigation messages is described by three indicators, including the subframe integrity rate, the frame integrity rate, and the superframe integrity rate. Since the calculation method of each indicator is the same, this subsection uses the calculation of the subframe integrity rate as an example.

Each subframe of BDS D1 navigation messages consists of 10 words. Each word has 30 bits. The subframe integrity rate of the *i*th word IR_{sbfi} is calculated as

$$\begin{cases} IR_{sbfi} = \sum_{i=1}^{10} \alpha_i \cdot \frac{v_i}{30} \\ \sum_{i=1}^{10} \alpha_i = 1 \end{cases} \tag{1}$$

Where α_i is the weight of the *i*th word and v_i is the number of valid bits of the *i*th word. Moreover, α_i reflects the importance of the *i*th word and should be considered carefully.

3.2 Calculation method for verification conformance of BDS D1 navigation messages

Verification conformance of BDS D1 navigation messages is described by the check correct rate.

It is necessary to detect whether navigation messages are reversed before verification [6] because of phase ambiguity. It is assumed that this step has already been done at the time of frame synchronization earlier. Then verification of BDS D1 navigation messages can be performed as follows.

Step 1: Take the first 22 information bits from each word of navigation messages. Divide it into two groups of 11 bits each. Then take the other 8 parity bits.

Step 2: According to the BCH (15,11,1) encoding process, calculate the 4 parity bits of each group with 11 information bits respectively. Connect the 2 sets of parity bits into 8 bits. It is worth noting that the one calculated by the first 11 information bits are placed in front, and the others are placed behind.

Step 3: Compare the 8 parity bits calculated in step 2 with the parity bits taken in Step 1. If they are the same, the first 22 information bits from the word of navigation messages are correct.

For the first word of each subframe, the first 15 bits are not encoded, while the following 11 bits are encoded. Therefore, if a word of the navigation message is verified to be the first word of the subframe, then it is feasible to take the 11 bits with number from 16 to 26 and the corresponding 4 parity bits with number from 27 to 30 in Step 1. Then in Step 2, only one encoding calculation is needed to get the 4 parity bits. Compare the two sets of parity bits in Step 3.

There are 1200 words in a superframe. The check correct rate of a superframe *CCR* is calculated as

$$\begin{cases} CCR = \sum_{j=1}^{1200} \beta_j \cdot v_j \\ \sum_{j=1}^{1200} \beta_j = 1 \end{cases} \tag{2}$$

where β_j is the weight of the *j*th word, which reflects the importance of the word and should be considered carefully. If the check is correct, v_j equals to 1. Otherwise, it equals to 0.

3.3 Calculation method for quantization unit conformance of BDS D1 navigation messages

Quantization unit conformance of BDS D1 navigation messages is described by the parameter precision rate.

The parameter precision rate *PPR* is calculated as

$$PPR = 1 - \left| \frac{v_t - v_c}{v_t} \right| \times 100\% \tag{3}$$

where v_c is the calculated value of the parameter solved from the navigation message, and v_t is the true value of the parameter determined when the navigation message is generated earlier. Both v_c and v_t are floating point numbers.

The calculated value of the parameter solved from the navigation message v_c can be calculated as

$$v_c = n_b \times f \tag{4}$$

where n_b is the number of bits and f is the scale factor.

There are some parameters of navigation messages to be considered, including ephemeris parameters, almanac parameters, ionospheric delay correction model parameters, clock correction parameters, BDT-UTC time offset parameters, and BDT-GNSS time offset parameters. Although the number of parameters is large, the calculation method is the same.

4 Example analysis for protocol conformance of BDS D1 navigation messages

4.1 Example analysis for formatting conformance of BDS D1 navigation messages

Taking a group of actual BDS D1 navigation messages as example to evaluate the formatting conformance. The data was selected from the International Satellite Navigation System Monitoring and Evaluation Service (iGMAS) in BJF1 station on September 28, 2017 from 0:00.

Since the weights need to be considered carefully, this subsection uses the same weights to calculate. To simplify the expression, this subsection takes the calculation of a superframe and its first subframe and first frame as an example, as is shown in Table 1.

Table 1. Calculation results of the formatting conformance of the actual BDS D1 navigation messages.

PRN	6	7	8	9	10
IR_{sbf1}	100.00%	100.00%	100.00%	100.00%	100.00%
IR_{f1}	100.00%	100.00%	100.00%	100.00%	99.87%
IR_{spf}	98.92%	100.00%	100.00%	100.00%	95.88%

In Table 1, PRN is the number of the satellite, IR_{sbf1} is the subframe integrity rate of the first subframe, IR_{f1} is the frame integrity rate of the first frame and IR_{spf} is the superframe integrity rate of the superframe.

For Satellites 7 to 9, they have good formatting conformance. For Satellites 6, a bit loss may occur to other frames, which affects the superframe integrity. For Satellites 10, a bit loss may occur to other subframes of the first frame, which affects the frame integrity and the superframe integrity.

It does not make sense to look at the percentage simply. It is necessary to know where the bit loss occurs so that the correction will reach 100% of the integrity rate eventually, instead of simply calculating. It is unreasonable that the integrity rate reach 99.9% while the key bit is wrong.

4.2 Example analysis for verification conformance of BDS D1 navigation messages

The data is the same as the previous subsection.

The verification conformance is described by the check correct rate. This subsection uses the same weights to calculate. Table 2 shows the check correct rate of superframes of the actual BDS D1 navigation messages.

Table 2. The check correct rate of the actual BDS D1 navigation messages.

PRN	Error number	*CCR*
6	0	100.000000%
7	0	100.000000%
8	0	100.000000%
9	1	99.999071%
10	0	100.000000%

In Table 2, *CCR* is the check correct rate of a superframe with 1200 words. All satellites except Satellites 9 have good verification conformance. For Satellites 9, it indicates that 1 bit error may occur to a word during transmission or baseband processing and the error may be an information bit error or a parity bit error. Where the bit error occurs should be figured out and the error should be corrected.

4.3 Example analysis for quantization unit conformance of BDS D1 navigation messages

The data is the same as the previous subsection. Take the ephemeris parameters of Satellite 6 as an example. The result is as shown in Table 3.

Table 3. The parameter precision rate of the ephemeris parameters of Satellite 6.

Par.	v_c	v_t	*PPR*
t_{oe}	1.008000000000E+05	1.008000000000E+05	100.000000000000%
$\sqrt{A}$	6.493335044815E+03	6.493335046823E+03	99.999999969076%
e	1.543931746171E-04	1.543931746172E-04	99.999999999935%
ω	1.963504892640E-01	1.963505038930E-01	99.999992549548%
Δn	6.255604791828E-10	6.259186369169E-10	99.942778867254%
M_0	8.003448350212E-01	8.003448351777E-01	99.999999980446%
Ω_0	2.130725946031E+00	2.130725960318E+00	99.999999329477%
$\dot{\Omega}$	-1.794837407355E-09	-1.794837407356E-09	99.999999999944%
i_0	9.607569219780E-01	9.607569228630E-01	99.999999907885%
IDOT	-7.549361580454E-11	-7.549361580455E-11	99.999999999987%
C_{uc}	-1.298283539894E-05	-1.298494698940E-05	99.983738166496%
C_{us}	2.650808174265E-05	2.650808174266E-05	99.999999999962%
C_{rc}	-5.815928831984E+02	-5.815928831984E+02	100.000000000000%
C_{rs}	-3.932218439467E+02	-3.932218439467E+02	100.000000000000%
C_{ic}	-1.298623569240E-07	-1.298623569241E-07	99.999999999923%
C_{is}	-1.133883942967E-07	-1.133883942968E-07	99.999999999912%

In Table 3, v_c is the calculated value of the parameter solved from the navigation message, and v_t is the true value of the parameter determined when the navigation message is generated earlier, and *PPR* is the parameter precision rate. As can be seen from Table 3, all ephemeris parameters have good quantization unit conformance.

5 Conclusion

In this paper, the evaluation model for protocol conformance of BDS D1 navigation messages is described from three aspects, including formatting conformance, verification conformance and quantization unit conformance. Each aspect is considered carefully with calculation and analysis. The results show that the model can evaluate the protocol conformance of BDS D1 navigation messages reasonably.

Acknowledgment

This work is supported by the National Science Foundation of China (Nos. 41604016).

References

1. F. Bai, Bull. Surv. Map. **6**, 72 (2010)
2. W. Yu, W. Dai, Z. Yang, J. Geod. Geodyn., **30**, 81 (2010)
3. H. Liu, S. Tang, H. Cui, Geom. Spat. Info. Tech., **1**, 5 (2014)
4. S. Lian, L. Yan, Comp. Meas. Cont. **18**, 2344 (2010)
5. China Satellite Navigation Office, *Beidou Navigation Satellite System Signal In Space Interface Control Document Open Service Signal B3I (Version 1.0)*, **1**, 18 (2018)
6. S. Chen, D. L. Donoho, ION, **55** (1999)

Reconstruction Method of Electrical Capacitance Tomography Based on Wavelet Fusion

Zhou Lei[1,2,*],Yan Jiangbao[2,3], Zhu Feng[1] , Tan Xiangyu[2],and Zhang Lifeng[1]

[1]Department of Automation, North China Electric Power University,071003,China
[2]Yunnan Electric Power Research Institute,Kunming,650217,China
[3]College of Information Engineering and Automation, Kunming University of Science and Technology, Kunming, 650500, China

Abstract. The accuracy of reconstructed images of Electrical Capacitance Tomography (ECT) is a bottleneck concerning the successful application of ECT. An image data fusion algorithm based on wavelet transform was proposed in this paper to improve the accuracy of reconstructed images. First, reconstructed images were obtained using conjugate gradient least square algorithm and Landweber iterative algorithm, respectively. Secondly, reconstructed images were decomposed by wavelet. After that, the approximate component was processed according to the weighted average fusion rule. The detail component was processed according to the maximum fusion rule of absolute value. Finally, the new reconstructed images were obtained by wavelet reconstruction. Simulation and static experimental results showed that the reconstructed images with higher accuracy can be obtained after fusion and the artefacts were decreased obviously.

1 Introduction

Electrical capacitance tomography (ECT) is a kind of process tomography technique that was developed during the late 1980s. The ECT technique has been investigated extensively during the past decades as a visualization technique for measurement and imaging of two-phase flows in real time in industrial process monitoring. ECT is considered to be one of the most attractive process imaging technology with wide developing prospect due to its advantages of non-invasion, high-speed, safety and low cost [1, 2].

The task of image reconstruction for ECT is to determine the permittivity distribution and hence material distribution over the cross-section using the capacitance measurements which were obtained by data acquisition system (DAS) from different viewing angle via array electrodes which are mounted circumferentially around an industrial flow pipe or receptacle and relies on changes in capacitance between electrodes owing to the change in permittivity of flow components.

ECT image reconstruction is a typical ill-posed problem and its solution is unstable. Image algorithms of ECT can be divided into non-iterative and iterative algorithms [3]. Non-iterative algorithms are commonly fast in speed. The most commonly used non-iterative algorithms are linear back projection (LBP) and Tikhonov regularization algorithms. On the other hand, the most commonly used iterative algorithms contain Landweber iterative algorithm and conjugate gradient least square (CGLS) iterative algorithm. Non-iterative algorithm is simple and fast, but the algorithm is poor in image quality and is generally used for qualitative analysis.

Landweber iterative algorithm is similar to the steepest gradient method, and its convergence is poor for the complicated flow patterns, which limits its application [4]. CGLS algorithm is ideal for simple flow patterns and complex flow patterns [5]. In order to further improve the accuracy of the reconstructed images, an image fusion method based on wavelet decomposition was presented. First, reconstructed images were obtained by Landweber iterative algorithm and CGLS algorithm, respectively. Secondly, wavelet transforms were carried out on these reconstructed images and the corresponding image fusion method was applied on it. Finally, images were obtained using wavelet reconstruction. Simulation and static experiments were carried out and the results showed that the quality of reconstructed images was improved.

2 Principle of ECT

2.1. ECT System

The diagram of a16-electrode ECT system is shown in Fig. 1. Capacitances are measured between different electrode pairs and the measurements obtained are used to reconstruct a cross sectional distribution of flow components.

*Corresponding author: Zhou Lei: zhouleiect@163.com

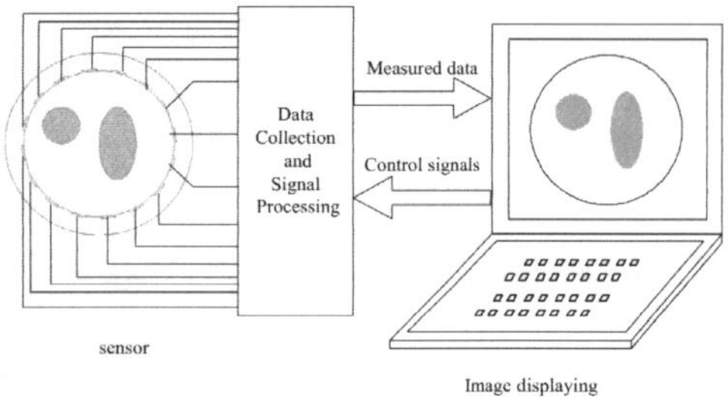

Fig. 1. Structure of 16-electrode ECT system

For a 16-electrode system, the number of independent capacitance measurements is 120. ECT is composed of forward problem and inverse problem. The forward problem is to determine capacitance measurements given the permittivity distribution and the boundary condition. The inverse problem is also called image reconstruction.

2.2 Image Reconstruction Algorithm of ECT

ECT image reconstruction algorithms are based on the linear model of the mapping of permittivity distribution to capacitance values. After being discrete, linearized and normalized, the model is shown in (1):

$$\mathbf{C} = \mathbf{S}\mathbf{G} \tag{1}$$

Where $\mathbf{C}$ is the normalized capacitance vector, $\mathbf{S}$ is the sensitivity matrix of normalized capacitance with respect to normalized permittivity and $\mathbf{G}$ is the normalized permittivity vector.

In this paper, Landweber iterative algorithm and CGLS algorithm are selected to obtain the initial reconstructed images.

2.3 Landweber Iterative Algorithm

The steepest descent method selects the negative gradient direction as the iterative direction, and the iterative formula of the Landweber iterative algorithm is shown in (2):

$$\begin{cases} \mathbf{G}_{k+1} = \mathbf{G}_k + \alpha \mathbf{S}^T(\mathbf{C} - \mathbf{S}\mathbf{G}_k) \\ \mathbf{G}_0 = \mathbf{S}^T\mathbf{C} \end{cases} \tag{2}$$

Where α is the step length and $\mathbf{G}_k$ is the normalized image grey in the kth iteration. $\mathbf{G}_0$ is the initial value of the image grey.

2.4 CGLS Algorithm

Conjugate Gradient Least Squares (CGLS) is developed by Conjugate Gradient (CG) algorithm. It is an excellent iterative algorithm for solving large dimensionality ill-posed systems and the system matrix can be asymmetric and singular. The basic idea of the CGLS iterative regularization algorithm is to apply the conjugate gradient method to solving the problem of the minimum (3):

$$\min_{\mathbf{G}_m} \|\mathbf{C} - \mathbf{S}\mathbf{G}_m\|_2 \tag{3}$$

It is required for the CG iterative algorithm that the sensitivity matrix must be symmetric positive definite. We multiply the two sides of (3) to obtain the normal equation:

$$\mathbf{S}^T\mathbf{S}\mathbf{G} = \mathbf{S}^T\mathbf{C} \tag{4}$$

And then, the sensitivity matrix $\mathbf{A} = \mathbf{S}^T\mathbf{S}$ is symmetric positive definite. Conjugate gradient method is used for CGLS algorithm to solve the asymmetric problem and hence the normal equation can be obtained. The CGLS algorithm is carried out according to the following steps.

Initialization: $\mathbf{G}_0 = 0$, $r_0 = \mathbf{C} - \mathbf{S}\mathbf{G}_0$, $d_0 = \mathbf{S}^T r_0$, $m = 1$

step 1: $$\alpha_m = \frac{\|\mathbf{S}^T r_{m-1}\|_2^2}{\|\mathbf{S} d_{m-1}\|_2^2} \tag{5}$$

step 2: $$\mathbf{G}_m = \mathbf{G}_{m-1} + \alpha_m d_{m-1} \tag{6}$$

step 3: $$r_m = r_{m-1} - \alpha_m \mathbf{S} d_{m-1} \tag{7}$$

step 4: $$\beta_m = \frac{\|\mathbf{S}^T r_m\|_2^2}{\|\mathbf{S} r_{m-1}\|_2^2} \tag{8}$$

step 5: $$d_m = \mathbf{S}^T r_m + \beta_m d_{m-1} \tag{9}$$

$$m = m + 1 \tag{10}$$

Where m is the iteration step, α_m is the iteration step size, r_m is the residual vector, β_m is the conjugate coefficient and d_m is the iteration search direction, respectively.

It can be seen from the above algorithm steps that the CGLS iteration process involves only the product of the vector and the sensitivity matrix or the transposed matrix, and the iteration step m is used as the regularization parameter. As the CGLS algorithm has a semi-convergence, the inappropriate iterative step size will cause "under estimate" or "over estimate" results.

3 Image Reconstruction Method for ECT Based on Wavelet Fusion

The reconstructed images have artefacts or noise, and the spatial resolution is not high. In order to further improve the image quality, the reconstructed image is processed by wavelet fusion. Wavelet analysis is a tool for signal multiresolution analysis, which has good properties in both time and frequency domain.

3.1 Wavelet Transform for the Reconstructed Images

To fulfill the wavelet fusion for the reconstructed images which were used as the source images, wavelet decomposition for the source images was carried out. After that, high and low frequency coefficients of each source image can be obtained. And then, image fusion based on the regional features of the decomposed wavelet coefficient matrix was adopted. Finally, the new reconstructed images are obtained by inverse wavelet transform. After wavelet transform, the total data of the image will not increase. The wavelet transform is non-redundant and wavelet transform is directional, which makes it widely used in the field of image fusion [6].

Assuming the function $f(t) \in L^2(R)$, the wavelet transform is defined as (11):

$$W_f(a,b) = \int_{-\infty}^{+\infty} f(t)\phi_{a,b}(t)dt = \int_{-\infty}^{+\infty} f(t)\frac{1}{\sqrt{a}}\phi(\frac{t-b}{a})dt \quad (11)$$

Where $\phi_{a,b}(t)$ is the basis function, a is the scale parameter ($a>0$) and b is the translation parameter, respectively.

In the image processing, it is necessary to discretize the continuous wavelet, which is also known as discrete wavelet transform (DWT). In general, the discrete formula of the scale parameter a and the translation parameter b in the continuous wavelet transform are taken as $a = a_0^m$ and $b = na_0^m b_0$ ($m \in Z$, $a_0 > 1$). And then, the corresponding discrete wavelet function $\phi_{m,n}(t)$ can be written as (12):

$$\phi_{m,n}(t) = \frac{1}{\sqrt{a_0^m}}\phi(\frac{t-nb_0a_0^m}{a_0^m}) = a_0^{-m/2}\phi(a_0^m t - nb_0) \quad (12)$$

The corresponding discrete wavelet transform coefficients can be defined by (13):

$$C_{m,n} = \int_{-\infty}^{+\infty} f(t)\phi_{m,n}^*(t)dt = < f, \phi_{m,n} > \quad (13)$$

Reconstruction formula of wavelet transform is (14):

$$f(t) = \alpha\sum_{-\infty}^{+\infty}\sum_{-\infty}^{+\infty} C_{m,n}\phi_{m,n}(t) \quad (14)$$

Where α is a signal-independent constant.

3.2 Image Fusion Rules

Three are three levels in image fusion: pixel level, feature level and decision level. In this paper, pixel level image fusion method was used to improve the accuracy of the reconstructed images [7]. The process of this image fusion method is as follows:

step 1: source images are obtained using Landweber iterative algorithm and CGLS algorithm, respectively.

step 2: filtering processing: a mean filter is used to the image pixels.

step 3: The wavelet decomposition is carried out by choosing the appropriate wavelet basis function and decomposition level.

step 4: The fusion process of the approximate component and the detail component is made beads on the corresponding fusion rule, respectively.

step 5: Wavelet reconstruction based on the wavelet coefficients after fusion is completed and the final reconstructed images can be obtained.

Fig. 2 shows the structural diagram of the image fusion method based on wavelet transform.

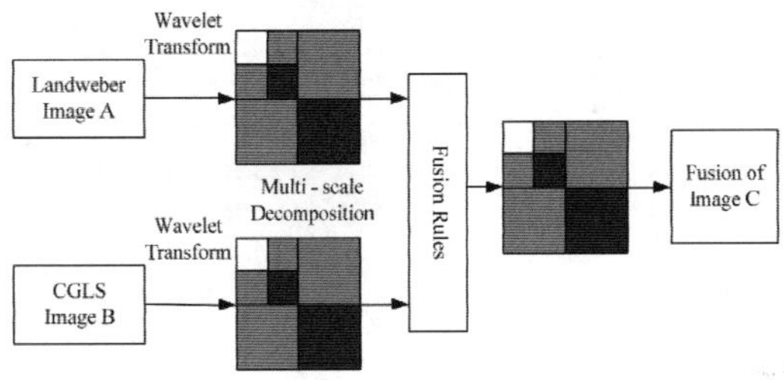

Fig. 2. Image Fusion Process Based on Wavelet Transform

In this paper, the fusion rules and fusion algorithms used are as follows:

Rule 1: The approximation component of the fusion image is processed by the improved logic filter algorithm fusion rule, as shown in (15):

$$\mathbf{X_M}(x,y) = \theta\mathbf{M}_1(x,y) + (1-\theta)\mathbf{M}_2(x,y) \quad (15)$$

Where θ is the weighting coefficient and let θ=0.5. $\mathbf{M}_1(x,y)$ and $\mathbf{M}_2(x,y)$ is the approximate component of the wavelet decomposition of the reconstructed images obtained by Landweber iterative and CGLS algorithm, respectively. The approximate component contains the main information of the image. The average characteristics of the source images can be reflected by this part, which reflects the overall outline of the image. The low frequency part is fused by the weighted averaging operator.

Rule 2: The detail component of the fusion image is processed by the fusion rule with the largest absolute value of the coefficient, as shown in (16):

$$\mathbf{Y_N}(x,y) = \max\{|\mathbf{N}_1(x,y)|, |\mathbf{N}_2(x,y)|\} \quad (16)$$

Where $\mathbf{N}_1(x,y)$ and $\mathbf{N}_2(x,y)$ is the detail component of the wavelet decomposition of the reconstructed images obtained by Landweber iterative and CGLS algorithm, respectively. The details of source images such as edges and regional boundary features are mainly reflected by the detail component part. And hence the dealing for the high frequency part is the key of the whole fusion process. The fusion rule based on the largest absolute value of the coefficient is adopted for the detail component part.

4 Experimental Results and Analysis

4.1 Simulation Experiment

In the simulation experiment, oil-gas two-phase flow was selected as the research object and 4 typical flow phantoms were studied. The relative permittivity of the oil and gas is set to 3 and 1, respectively. The COMSOL finite element software was used to obtain the simulated capacitance measurement data and the ECT image reconstruction was completed by Matlab software. The imaging area is divided into 812 pixels.

In simulation process, the Landweber algorithm and the CGLS algorithm are used as the image reconstruction algorithm to obtain the initial reconstructed image, and then the wavelet transform theory is used as the image fusion algorithm to further improve the image precision. Among them, the Landweber algorithm and the CGLS algorithm take 100 and 25 iterations respectively. In this process, the "bior3.7" function is chosen as the base function of the wavelet transform, and the decomposition level is 3. The simulation results are shown in Fig3.

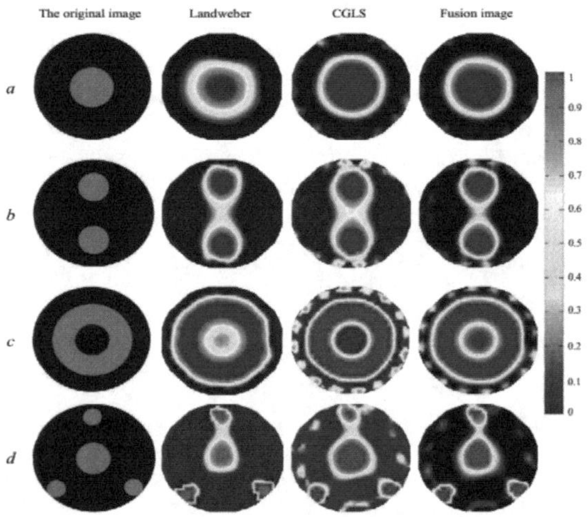

Fig. 3. Image reconstruction results

The image quality is calculated for quantitative evaluation, and the relative error and correlation coefficient are calculated. The definition is shown in Ref. [3].

The quantitative index RE and CC of the reconstructed images of the reconstructed images in Fig. 3 are calculated, which can be seen in Table 1 and Table 2, respectively.

Table 1. Image relative error

Flow Phantom	Landweber	CGLS	Fusion image
a	0.7931	0.5454	1.5543
b	0.7532	0.7106	1.1342
c	0.5821	0.6130	1.3169
d	0.4288	0.5341	0.9540

Table 2. Correlation coefficients

Flow Phantom	Landweber	CGLS	Fusion image
a	0.5957	0.8749	0.3130
b	0.7488	0.7666	0.4345
c	0.9277	0.7156	0.2963
d	0.8817	0.7657	0.4234

It can be seen from Fig. 3 and Tables I and II that the quality of reconstructed images after wavelet fusion is improved for the selected 4 flow phantoms. As to phantom b, the two objects can be separated clearly after image fusion and have better shape fidelity, while there are artefacts in the reconstructed images using Landweber iterative or CGLS algorithm. For phantom c, the reconstructed image was greatly improved with fewer artefacts and better fidelity. Due to the low sensitivity on the center of the pipe, the reconstructed images of phantoms a and d after wavelet fusion is slightly improved. But it still can be seen that for the complicated distribution phantom d, objects also can be separated more clearly and better shape fidelity can be obtained compared with that of Landweber iterative or CGLS algorithm.

4.2 Static Experiment

Static experiment was carried out using the digital ECT system developed by Tianjin University [8], which can be seen in Fig. 4. The ECT system contains 24 channels, which was designed for two plane of 12-electrode sensor. It also can be used according to custom-defined scheme. In our static experiment, we use 16 channels for the 16-electrode sensor.

In the static two-phase flow experiment, a 16-electrode sensor pipe with the inner diameter of 125 mm was used. In low pattern I, the pipe is divided into two parts with a plastic plate, half of which is filled with plastic particles. As to flow pattern II, there are two hollow plastic rods with the diameter of 15 mm. The image area is also divided into 812 pixels.

The static experimental sensor and the results were showed in Fig. 5.

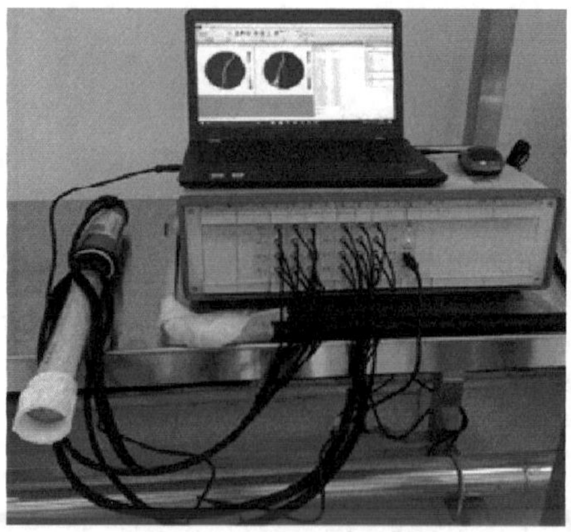

Fig. 4. Digital ECT system

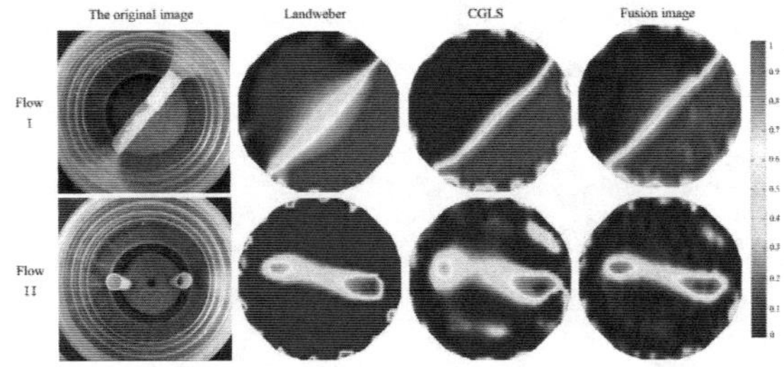

Fig.5. Experimental imaging results

For the flow pattern I, the separation of gas and plastic particles in the reconstructed image after image fusion is much clearer and more accurate than that of Landweber iterative or CGLS algorithm. As to flow pattern II, the two plastic tubes can be clearly distinguished and the image artefacts can be reduced obviously, which fully demonstrates the effectiveness of the fusion method based on wavelet transform.

5 Conclusions

In this paper, an ECT image fusion method based on wavelet transform is proposed. Landweber iterative and the CGLS algorithms were used to obtain the source images, which were used for image fusion using wavelet transform. Simulation and static experiments were carried out. Experimental results showed that the accuracy of reconstructed image is improved and the higher edge fidelity of the object can be obtained, which provides a new method for the study of ECT image reconstruction.

Acknowledgment

The author would like to thank Dr. Lifeng Zhang for his helpful suggestions on the use of ECT DAS during the static experiments.

References

1. H. S. Tapp and R. A. Williams, "Chemical engineering applications of electrical process tomography," Chem. Eng. J., vol. 77, pp. 119-125, 2000.
2. I. Ismail, J. C. Gamio, S. F. A. Bukhari and W. Q. Yang, "Tomography for multi-phase flow measurement in the oil industry," Flow Meas. Instrum., vol. 16, pp. 145-155, 2005.
3. W. Q. Yang and L. H. Peng, "Image reconstruction algorithms for electrical capacitance tomography," Meas. Sci. & Technol., vol. 14, pp. R1-R13, 2003.
4. W. Q. Yang, D. M. Spink, T. A. York and H. McCann, "An image-reconstruction iteration method for electrical-capacitance tomography," Meas. Sci. & Technol., vol. 10, pp. 1065-1069, 1999.
5. H. X. Wang, X. M. Zhu and L. F. Zhang, "Conjugate gradient algorithm for electrical capacitance tomography," Journal of Tianjin University, vol. 38, pp. 1-4.
6. P. J. Zheng and J. W. Huang, "Discrete Wavelet Transform and Data Expansion Reduction in Homomorphic Encrypted Domain," IEEE Trans. Image Process., vol. 22, pp. 2455-2468, 2013.
7. P. F. Chai, X. Q. Luo and Z. C. Zhang, "Image Fusion Using Quaternion Wavelet Transform and Multiple Features," IEEE Access, vol. 5, pp. 6724-6734, 2017.
8. H. X. Wang and L. F. Zhang, "Identification of two-phase flow regimes based on support vector machine and electrical capacitance tomography," Meas. Sci. & Technol., vol. 20, pp. 114007(8 pp), 2009.

An Improved Normalized Model of Electrical Capacitance Tomography

Yan Jiangbao[1,2,*], *Zhou* Lei[2,3], *Zhu* Feng[3], *Tan* Xiangyu[2],and *Zhang* Changsheng[1]

[1]College of Information Engineering and Automation, Kunming University of Science and Technology, Kunming, 650500, China;
[2]Yunnan Electric Power Research Institute, Kunming, 650217, China
[3]Department of Automation, North China Electric Power University, 071003, China

Abstract. Electrical capacitance tomography (ECT) technology is a process tomography, which is based on medical CT technology and develops together with computer and sensor technology. The measured capacitances by ECT system are usually normalized at the high and low permittivity for image. Parallel normalization model is commonly used during normalization process, which assumes the distribution of materials in parallel. And thus, the normalized capacitance is a linear function of measured capacitance. The usage of series normalization model results in the normalized capacitance as a nonlinear function of measured capacitance. The research on parallel, series normalization model and hybrid normalization model. In this paper, we propose a method based on the center electric field line to determine the model weighting factor for the hybrid normalization model. The simulation and static test results show that the reconstructed image quality is improved obviously by the hybrid normalization model based on the center electric field line.

1 Introduction

Electrical capacitance tomography (ECT) is a non-intrusive and non-destructive image reconstruction technique in industrial processes for obtaining information about the contents of closed pipes or vessels by measuring variations in the dielectric property of material inside the vessel. This technique determines the permittivity distribution using capacitance measurements obtained by applied voltages through the electrodes mounted on the periphery of the domain of interest. One can also obtain information about volume fraction and velocities of the contents of pipes for a two-phase system. With the aid of ECT, it is possible to image materials such as oils, plastics, image flames and combustion .The ECT system can measure the characteristic parameters of a two-phase fluid consisting of a medium with different dielectric properties. Using the array capacitive sensor, the combination of the various measurements between the electrodes can reflect the multi-phase fluid concentration and the distribution of the tube in the cross-section, the capacitance measurement as the projection data, through a certain image reconstruction algorithm , It is possible to reconstruct the phase distribution of the fluid flowing through the pipe at a certain moment.

The system of ECT consists of three parts: a sensor, a data acquisition and signal processing unit, and an image reconstruction computer, as shown in Fig1. Electrical tomography is one kind of non-intrusive and visible measurement technique. Electrical tomography has wide applications in clinical monitoring and industrial multi-phase flow measurement for the advantages of being fast in response, nondestructive and low cost[1].

The system of ECT can measure the characteristic parameters of a two-phase fluid consisting of a medium with different dielectric properties. Using the array sensor, the combination of the various measurements between the electrodes can reflect the multi-phase fluid concentration and the distribution of the tube in the cross-section, the capacitance measurement as the projection data, through a certain image reconstruction algorithm. It is possible to reconstruct the phase distribution of the fluid flowing through the pipe at a certain moment.

Theoretically, the capacitance between the electrodes can be obtained through a Poisson equation, which is given by

$$\nabla \cdot [\varepsilon(x,y)\nabla\phi(x,y)] = -\rho(x,y) \quad (1)$$

Where $\varepsilon(x,y)$ is the permittivity distribution in the sensing field, $\phi(x,y)$ is the potential distribution and $\rho(x,y)$ is the charge distribution, which is the source of the electrical field. Since there are no sources, i.e. no charge inside the sensor, (1) can be rewritten as

$$\nabla^2\phi(x,y) + \frac{1}{\varepsilon(x,y)}\nabla\varepsilon(x,y)\nabla\phi(x,y) = 0 \quad (2)$$

Where the electric field $E(x,y) = -\nabla\phi(x,y)$ .In general, it is impossible to solve (2) for an inhomogeneous permittivity distribution. The

*Corresponding author: Yan Jiangbao: 120958764@qq.com

potential $\phi(x, y)$ can be calculated numerically by applying the finite element method (FEM).

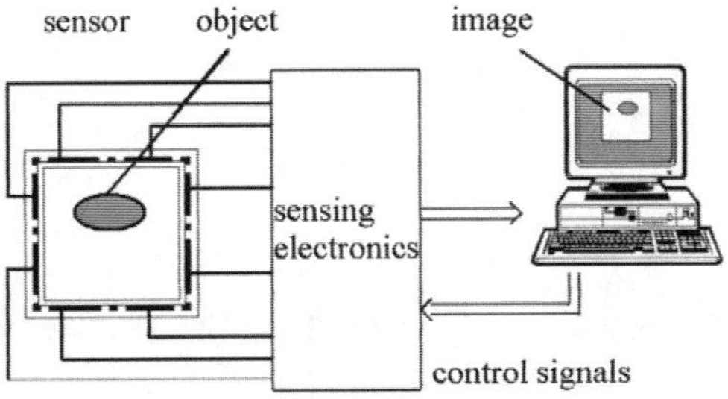

Fig. 1. Layout of the ECT system

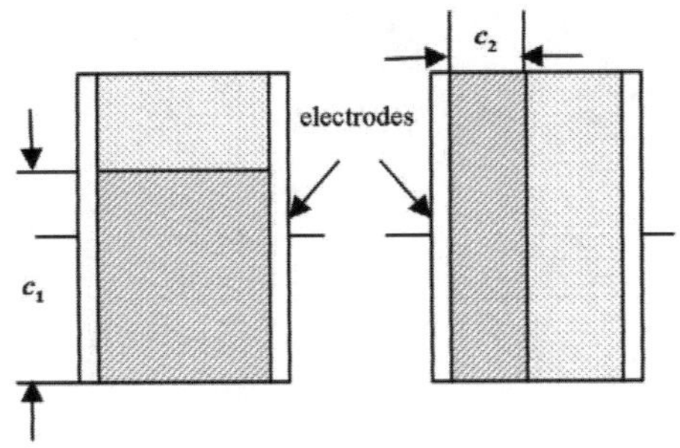

Fig. 2. Normalized model

If the potential $\phi(x, y)$ is known, the charge Q of an electrode can be calculated using Gauss' law[2]:

$$Q = -\oint_{\Gamma} \varepsilon(x, y) \cdot \nabla \phi(x, y) d\Gamma \tag{3}$$

Where Γ is the electrode surface. Using the charge Q at each detector electrode, the electrical capacitance C can be calculated as

$$C = \frac{Q}{V} = -\frac{1}{V} \oint_{\Gamma} \varepsilon(x, y) \nabla \phi(x, y) d\Gamma \tag{4}$$

Where is V the potential difference between the source and detector electrode.

2 The normalized model

For the ECT system, the actual measurement is usually carried out empty and full tube calibration, that is, the capacitance value C^h and C^l .For the actual two-phase mixed media, the capacitance measurement data C^m should be normalized before calibration using the calibration data. Normalization needs to be met:

$$\lambda = f(C_m, C_h, C_l) \tag{5}$$

$$f(C_m, C_h, C_l) = 0, C_m = C_l \tag{6}$$

$$f(C_m, C_h, C_l) = 0, C_m = C_h \tag{7}$$

The advantage of normalizing the capacitance measurement data is that the measurement data can be dimensionless, facilitated for mathematical processing and associated with digital images and reduced measurement errors. For the same capacitance measurements, different normalized models will affect the quality of the reconstructed image[3].

2.1. Parallel and Series Normalization Model

Since the electrode capacitances strongly depend on the sensor electrodes geometric configuration besides permittivity distribution, the capacitance responses between different electrode combinations present a great distinction in magnitude and distribution profile. In order to eliminate the effect and reduce systematic errors in the measurement system, before being applied reconstruction algorithm, the measured capacitances, sensitivity and permittivity in need to be normalized. The parallel and series normalization models are the most widely used in ECT. Both of them treat each pair of measuring electrodes as an ideal parallel plate capacitance sensor, and assume that the distribution of the two types of materials is in parallel or series arrangement. Fig. 1 shows the parallel and series models in (a) and (b) respectively. The oblique portion represents a higher permittivity and the blank portion represents a lower permittivity. C_1 and C_2 represent the percentage of thickness for the higher permittivity material.

For the parallel model, the measured capacitance can be expressed as

$$C^m = (1 - C_1)C^l + C^h C_1 \tag{8}$$

For the series model,it is given by

$$1/C^m = 1/[(1 - C_2)C^l] + 1/(C^2 C^h) \tag{9}$$

Rearranging (8) and (9), λ^p and λ^s represent the normalized capacitances in addition to being the volume fraction between the electrode pair i, j corresponding to parallel and series models, and then are given by

$$C_1 = \frac{C^m - C^l}{C^h - C^l} = \lambda^p \tag{10}$$

$$C_2 = (1/C^m - 1/C^l)(1/C^h - 1/C^l) = \lambda^s \tag{11}$$

Normalizing with (10) is called as conventional normalization model and the normalized capacitance is a linear function of the electrode capacitance, in contrast to the series normalized capacitance being a nonlinear function.

The sensitivity of the electrode pair i, j with respect to the kth element in FEM mesh, an entry of S can be defined as

$$S_{i,j}(k) = u(k) \cdot \frac{C_{ij}^m(k) - C_{ij}^l}{C_{ij}^h - C_{ij}^l} \cdot \frac{1}{\varepsilon_h - \varepsilon_l} \tag{12}$$

Where $C_{ij}^m(k)$ is the capacitance value between electrode pair i, j when the kth element is filled with higher permittivity material in the lower permittivity background and $u(k)$ is an area correction factor, which is assigned to the ratio of the area of the largest element to the area of the kth element .

2.2 Hybrid normalized model

Multiphase flow patterns are complex and variable, and for ECT array electrodes, the distribution of capacitance and dielectric between any pair of pairs cannot be simply expressed in parallel or in series model. For the hybrid model, it is given by

$$\lambda^c = (1-\beta)\lambda^p + \beta\lambda^s = (1-\beta)\frac{C^m - C^l}{C^h - C^l} + \beta\frac{1/C^m - 1/C^l}{1/C^h - 1/C^l} \quad (13)$$

Where λ^c the normalized capacitances of hybrid model. β is the model weighting factor.

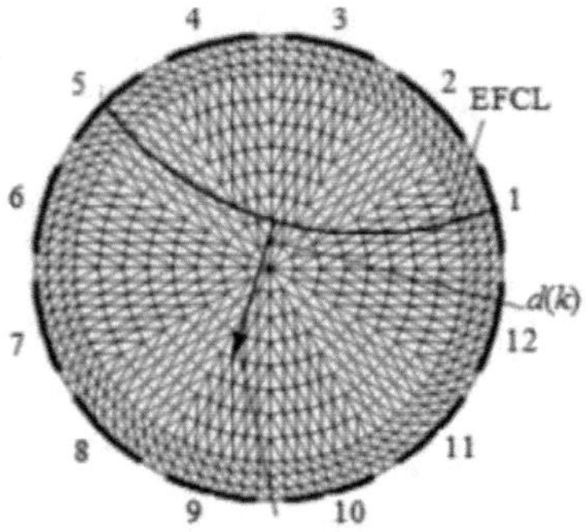

Fig. 3. Electrical field center line between electrode1and 5

When $\beta = 1$,that is, the series normalization model.

$$\lambda^c = \lambda^s = \frac{1/C^m - 1/C^l}{1/C^h - 1/C^l} \quad (14)$$

When $\beta = 0$,that is, the parallel normalization model.

$$\lambda^c = \lambda^p = \frac{C^m - C^l}{C^h - C^l} \quad (15)$$

The hybrid model is the weighted sum of the parallel model and the series model. Sensitivity matrix of hybrid normalized model，it is given by

$$S_{ij}(k) = u(k)\cdot[(1-\beta(k))(\frac{C_{ij}^m(k) - C_{ij}^l}{C_{ij}^h - C_{ij}^l}) + \beta(k)(\frac{1/C_{ij}^m(k) - 1/C_{ij}^l}{1/C_{ij}^h - 1/C_{ij}^l})]\cdot\frac{1}{\varepsilon_h - \varepsilon_l} \quad (16)$$

It is necessary to determine the value of $\beta(k)$ for the sensitivity of the split grid of each cell

3 Model weighting factor calculation

In this paper, based on electrical field center line method to determine β ,thus determining the hybrid normalized model.The idea of the center electric field line was first proposed by Loser .In this paper, 12 electrode ECT as the object of study, 1-5 electrode center line as shown in Figure 3. Figure 3 shows the distance $d(k)$ between the k unit and the electrical field center line. The model weighting factor is determined using the maximum of the distance between k and each pixel element to the center electric field line. As a result，model weighting factor is formulated as

$$\beta(x) = \frac{d_{ij}^k}{d_{max}} \quad (17)$$

Where d_{ij}^k is the distance between the k th element and EFCL of the electrode pair i, j , and d_{max} is the maximum distance.

In 1999, Landweber iterative algorithm was first proposed by Yang .Subsequently, Liu et al. Optimized the iterative factors of the algorithm, accelerated the iteration speed, and reconstructed the image[5-6].The parallel normalization model is taken as an example. The algorithm is shown as follows:

$$\begin{cases} G_{k+1} = G_k + \eta_k S^T(\lambda^P - SG_k) \\ G_0 = S^T\lambda^P \\ \eta_k = \|S^T e_k\|^2 / \|SS^T e_k\|^2 \end{cases} \quad (18)$$

Where $e_k = \lambda^P - SG_k$. η_k is the k step of the iteration factor. G_k is the image gray scale matrix of step k .

For the hybrid normalization model, since the normalized capacitance value is related to the model weighting factor, the optimal model weighting factor needs to be determined, and the optimal iteration factor is obtained. At this time, the Landweber iterative algorithm is as follows:

$$G_{k+1} = G_k + \eta_k S^T(\lambda^c - SG_k) \quad (19)$$

$$\begin{aligned} e_{k+1} &= \lambda^c - SG_{k+1} \\ &= \lambda^c - S(G_k + \eta_k S^T e_k) \\ &= e_k - \eta_k SS^T e_k \\ &= (I_M - \eta_k SS^T)[(1-\alpha_k)\lambda^p + \alpha_k\lambda^S - SG_k] \end{aligned} \quad (20)$$

The square of the norm of e_{k+1} is

$$\begin{aligned} J(\eta,\alpha) &= \|e_{k+1}\|^2 \\ &= \|(I_M - \eta_k SS^T)[\lambda^p + \alpha_k(\lambda^s - \lambda^p) - SG_k]\| \end{aligned} \quad (21)$$

M is the number of independent measurements

Let $\frac{\partial J(\eta,\alpha)}{\partial \eta} = 0$ and $\frac{\partial J(\eta,\alpha)}{\partial \alpha} = 0$,there is

$$\eta_k = \frac{\|S^T[\lambda^p + \alpha_k(\lambda^s - \lambda^p) - SG_k]\|^2}{\|SS^T[\lambda^p + \alpha_k(\lambda^s - \lambda^p) - SG_k]\|^2} \quad (22)$$

$$\alpha_k = [A^T B^T BSG_k + (A^T B^T BSG_k)^T - A^T B^T B\lambda^P - (A^T B^T B\lambda^P)^T]/(2A^T B^T BA) \quad (23)$$

Where $A = \lambda^s - \lambda^p$, $B = I_M - \eta_k SS^T$.

4 Experimental results and analysis

In this paper, we use Core i5 Windows 10 4G running memory notebook. In Matlab, we write the software package to realize the hybrid model, and realize the functions of finite element method and Landweber iterative algorithm to reconstruct the image. The ECT system with 12 electrodes, 66 independent measurements, the diameter of the pipe is 125mm, and the finite element grid is 768. In this paper, the Landweber iterative method is used, the iterative factor is chosen as 2, and the reconstructed image is iterated 300 times. The four simulation models are selected as one object, two objects, three objects and five objects. The reconstructed image is shown in Figure 4.

It can be seen from Fig. 4 that the image obtained by the parallel normalization model is blurred, 2, 3 and 5 objects, the imaging effect of the center object is poor and the reconstructed image near the tube wall is connected, and the series model is better. The model obtained by the mixed model is closer to the true object distribution. The model reconstructed by the mixed model is better than the conventional model in the vicinity of the wall and the central region.

To evaluate the performance, the relative image error(RE) and the correlation coefficient (CC) between estimated permittivity vector $\hat{g}$ and the original permittivity vector g are used and defined as[7]

$$RE = \frac{\left\| \hat{g} - g \right\|}{\left\| g \right\|} \tag{24}$$

$$CC = \frac{\sum_{i=1}^{N} (\hat{g} - \bar{\hat{g}}) \cdot (g_i - \bar{g})}{\sqrt{\sum_{i=1}^{N} (\hat{g} - \bar{\hat{g}})^2 \cdot \sum_{i=1}^{N} (g_i - \bar{g})^2}} \tag{25}$$

Where $\bar{g}$ and $\bar{\hat{g}}$ are the mean values of g and $\hat{g}$, respectively. A smaller RE and CC closer to 1 are considered to be better performance indices. It can be seen from Table 1 that the relative error of reconstruction images based on mixed normalization model is smaller than that of parallel and series normalization model.

Static test using the latest development of Tianjin University FPGA dual-mode (capacitance / resistance) imaging system. Using the Landweber iterative algorithm, reconstructing the image as shown in Fig5.

As can be seen from Figure 5, the first distribution of an organic glass rod in the center of the pipe, another plexiglass rod close to the wall. The reconstructed image of the parallel model can not distinguish between two rods. The reconstructed image of the series model roughly distinguishes two rods, but the edges of the image are not clear. The reconstructed image of the mixed model is very clear to distinguish between two plexiglass rods. The second distribution, the mixed model of the reconstructed image effect is much better than the parallel, series model. The object is clearly distinguished and the edges of the image are clear.

Original parallel series hybrid

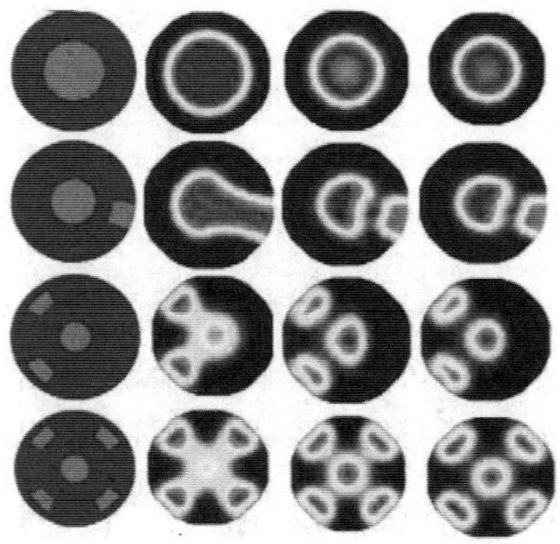

Fig. 4. Reconstructed images

Table 1. Image relative error at 300th iteration

Original	Parallel	Series	Hybrid
one object	0.7502	0.3134	0.2396
two objects	0.7877	0.5368	0.4548
three objects	0.7297	0.7104	0.6306
five objects	0.7740	0.7707	0.6709

Original parallel series hybrid

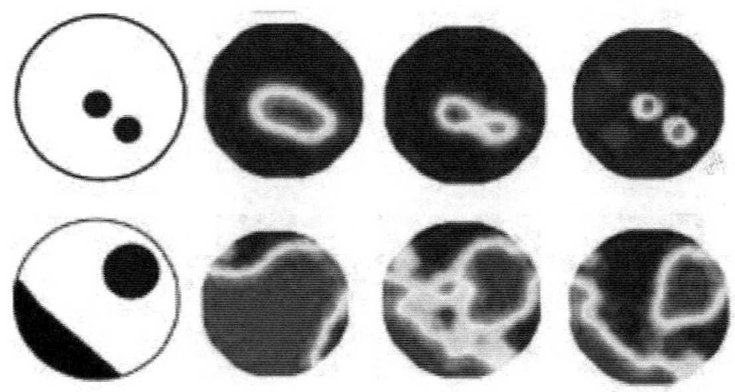

Fig. 5. Static test results

5 Conclusions

In this paper, the hybrid normalization model based on the center electric field line is applied to ECt image reconstruction, which improves the quality of image reconstruction. Simulation and results show that the normalized model provides a new method and approach for ECT image reconstruction

In the following research, we propose a method based on the center electric field to determine the model weighting factor of the mixed model. The ECT image reconstruction was performed by using parallel, series and mixed normalization models. Simulation and static tests show that the mixed model can distinguish the complex flow pattern of multiple objects, the edge of the image is clear and the relative error is small. It can be seen that the hybrid model is more accurate than the conventional model and can be used as a better equivalent model for the distribution of objects. Simulation results have given superior image quality. It shows that the sensitivity based on the new model is suitable for common iterative algorithms, and achieves a better reconstruction performance.

Acknowledgment

The author would like to thank Mr. Zhou Lei for his helpful suggestions on the use of ECT DAS during the static experiments.

References

1. Yong S K, Seong H L, Bong Y C, et al. Sensitivity map generation in electrical capacitance tomography using mixed normalization models[J]. Measurement Science and Technology, 2007, 18 (7):2092-2102.
2. Y.T. Makkawi, P.C. Wright, luidization regimes in a conventional Fluidized bed characterized by means of electrical capacitance tomography[J].Chemical Engineering Science, 2002, 14(4):2411-2437
3. D. L. Donoho. "Compressed sensing," IEEE Transactions on Information Theory, 2006, 52, 1289-1306.
4. Dong X Y and Guo S Q. Image reconstruction method for electrical capacitance tomography based on the combined series and parallel normalization model[J]. Measurement Science and Technology, 2008, 19 (4) : 1032-1039.
5. Yang W Q, Peng L H. Image reconstruction algorithms for electrical capacitance tomography[J]. Measurement Science & Technology, 2003, 14(1):R1-R13.
6. Zhang L F, Wang H X. Identification of oil-gas two-phase flow pattern based on SVM and electrical capacitance tomography technique[J]. Flow Measurement & Instrumentation, 2010, 21(1) : 20-24.
7. Yang WQ, Nguyen T, Betting M, Chondronasios A, Okimoto S, Okimoto FT,McCann H. Imaging wet gas separation process by capacitance tomography.IS&T/SPIE 14 Symp. Electron Imag 2002. p. 34-58.
8. M. A. T Figueiredo, R. D Nowak, S. J. Wright. "Gradient Projection for Sparse Reconstruction: Application to Compressed Sensing and Other Inverse Problem," IEEE Journal of Selected Topics in Signal Processing, 2007, 1(4): 586-597.

The research of regression model in machine learning field

Shen Rong[1] Zhang Bao-wen[2]

[1] School of information engineering of Ningxia University, YIN Chuan, China,750021
[2] School of mathematics and statistics,YIN Chuan,China,750021

Abstract: The paper herein will analyze the sale of iced products affected by variation of temperature. Firstly, we will collect the data of the forecast temperature last year and the sale of iced products and then conduct data compilation and cleansing. Finally, we will set up the mathematical regression analysis model based on the cleansed data by means of data mining theory. Regression analysis refers to the method of studying the relationship between independent variable and dependent variable. Linear regression model that corresponds to the practical situation is proposed in the paper, which is to set up simple linear regression model based on practical problem and then to implement the following with the help of the latest and most popular Python3.6. Python3.6 boasts the features of pure object-oriented, platform independence and concise and elegant language. So we will call the corresponding library function to predict the sale of iced products according to the variation of temperature, which will provide the foundation for the company to adjust its production each month, or even each week and each day. As a result, the situation of over-production can be avoided. Moreover, the other situation as the profit will be affected by the lack of production since the rise of temperature will also be avoided. So the regression model also has reference value for the other fields of marketing.

1 INTRODUCTION

With the increasing growth of the Internet, various kinds of data have been increasing in an explosive way. For example, twitter produced the data at the volume of 8TB each day[1] in 2011, Facebook produced the data at the volume more than 500TB a day in 2012[2] and moreover as the biggest Internet company, Google might work on the data at the volume of 20PB each day in 2008[3]. So, it will be so important to collect, analyze and model a large amount of data in order to conduct valuable prediction in various fields. Nowadays many machine learning systems running in data center have emerged continuously, such as Graph Lab[4] , Mahout[5] , Mad LINQ[6] and so on. Among them, Mahout based on distributed machine learning library has been widely used by lots of corporations such as Yahoo, Twitter, Linked In and so on. Under this background, Python, as the most popular programming language in the field of machine learning, has been used more and more widely. The paper herein will conduct the programming analysis on the model based on the latest Python3.6.

Python3.6 is a generalized programming language with strong function, that has been widely used and is easy to learn at the same time. Moreover, it fits for software programming of various scale [7]. Nowadays Python3.6 has mainly been used in fields of data mining, analysis and some others. Python boasts the features of unified writing form , strong readability, diverse algorithms and rich data structures, which means it can package both data structures and general algorithms. With its various advantages, it can not only integrate with other programming languages but also maximum its advantage of mixed programming language, leading to its great convenience of utility. Prediction analysis is one problem that has to be solved in data mining field. Generally speaking, we can choose the most suitable algorithm and model to conduct the analysis according to the practical case. The paper herein will mainly study on how to define the fitting relations between independent and dependent variables and then confirm parameters of the model, finally go back to the assumed equation to predict the variation tendency of dependent variable based on the typical linear regression model of predicting the sale of iced products according to the temperature variation. In the paper, we will establish linear regression model of one-variable with the help of Python3.6, which may predict the effect of temperature variation on the sale of iced products ideally.

2 PYTHON 3.6

2.1 Introduction

In recent years, further study [8-9] has gradually been the research focus of machine learning field, which may give rise to the prevailing of the object-oriented programming, Python3.6 in the field of machine learning and being well-received by learners.

There have been many new features added to Python3.6 on the basis of Python 2.7, such as formatting string and literals, variable comment syntax, underlining literals, asynchronous generator, asynchronous derivation and so on. Python3.6 has showed its great advantage on data analysis and data mining. Python3.6 has attracted great attention because of its convenience of learning and strong functions and boasted great advantage in data analysis and data mining.

2.2 Advantage

Python3.6 is an object-oriented language design program with pure script, which combines essence and designing rules of various design languages showing the features of interactive connections and type of explanation. Python has been focused by researchers due to its concise, elegant and clear language. Google was the first to use the Python as the development tool of network applications.

Python3.6 is a pure object-oriented language that can be used in the development of large-scale software due to its object-oriented mechanism, efficient execution and platform independence. It can express almost every comprehensive object with advanced data of tuple, list, dictionary and so on.

Python3.6 can write codes while running and each code can be tested immediately after being finished, which can dramatically improve the efficiency of engineers. Moreover, procedures written by c/c++ can be easily changed into the expansion mode of Python due to its strong expansibility. Python3.6 simplifies the duplicated codes in the software giving rise to the feature of permitting dynamic construction and execution of procedure.

The paper herein will predict the sale of iced products affected by the variation of temperature based on the library function such as linear regression by concise programming language.

3 DATA MINING

3.1 Introduce

The Huge amount of data triggers the swift development of data mining in the age of big data. One experienced data analyst will collect data first and then cleanse, analyze, and model it, which may have a close relation with data mining theory. The classic examples of application of data mining are the influenza trend forecast service pushed out by Google and "election of big data" [11] of Obama team. Domestic scholars also start related researches such as Meng Xiaofeng who systematizes and concludes the concepts, technologies and challenges of big data management; Hou Jingchuan who studies the quotation of data in the age of big data and has a deeper analysis and discussion on its current situation, latest development and future improvement.

Nowadays commonly used algorithms of data mining can be divided into several kinds of classification, cluster, association rules and time series prediction. Data mining may mainly be used in aspects of banking service, telecommunication, information security and scientific study. Furthermore, the popular tools of data mining are Weka, statistical analysis software Spass, Clementine, Rapidminer, Orange, Knime, Keel, Tanagra and so on.

Sorting algorithms that are often used in data mining are mainly linear regression algorithm, logistic regression algorithm, Bayesian decision theory and classifier, Support Vector Mouhime proposed by Cortes and Vupnik in 1995. Among these SVM algorithms, they can also be divided into several kinds according to its linear situation and the kernel function is used in the widest way.

Clustering algorithms commonly used in data mining are mainly hierarchical clustering algorithm, partition clustering algorithm, clustering algorithm based on density, clustering algorithm based on network, clustering algorithm based on model which may also include statistical method and neural network method.

3.2 Trend

Data The paper herein may mainly propose the linear regression algorithm belonging to sorting algorithm, including data collecting, data cleansing. We will set the forecast temperature as the independent variable and the sale of iced products as the dependent variable. The results of data analysis show that the factors which may influence the sale of the company are chosen totally correct.

4 LINEAR REGRESSION MODEL

4.1 Theoretical

Linear regression analysis can be divided into simple linear regression and multiple linear regression. The paper will mainly analyze simple linear regression model that is the analysis method of studying the relations between independent variable and dependent variable. We will set the model of dependent variable y and the independent variable x_i (i=1,2,3……) that will influence the variable y and the predict the development trend of y ,Simple linear regression model will be expressed as followed:

$$y = a_0 + a_1 x + e$$

y is the dependent variable and x is the independent variable. a_0 , the constant term, is the intercept of the regression line on the vertical axis and a_1 is regression coefficient that is the slope of the regression line. e is the random error which will be used to express the effect of random factors on dependent variable.

4.2 Methods

Regression analysis will evaluate a_0 and a_1 by observing the sample (x_i, y_i) in practical application. The paper will draw the scatter diagrams of dependent variable and independent variable by Python3.6 to evaluate the model parameter and establish regression model. After that, the regression equation and accuracy will be defined by the judgement of coefficient. For simple linear regression, coefficient of determination will be defined as:

$R^2 = cor^2(\hat{Y}, Y)$

$R^2 = ESS/TSS = 1 - ESS/TSS$

$$TSS = \sum(Y_i - \bar{Y})^2$$

$$TSS = \sum(\bar{Y}_i - \bar{Y})^2$$

$$TSS = \sum(Y_i - \bar{Y}_i)^2$$

$\hat{y}$ is the original value and y is the predicted value, so the equation will be showed here TSS is sum of squares for total and ESS is regression sum of squares. Moreover, RSS is residual sum of squares.

5 APPLICATION CASE ANALYSIS

5.1 Algorithm implementation

The paper will use Python3.6 to set up linear regression analysis model targeting at the effect of temperature variation on the sale of company. We introduce the unified operating system interface function in Python3.6 and all the functions in the numpy library that stores object variable. Moreover, we will also introduce Pandas analysis package and establish more advanced data structure and data analysis package of tool. The importing statements of Python3.6 will be showed as followed:

```
Import os;
Import numpy;
From pandas import  read_csv;
From matplotlib import pyplot as plt;
From sklearn linear_model import lineatRegression;
```

5.2 The comparison results

Draw the scatter diagram of the forecast temperature and sale of iced products after data cleansing, which will be showed as followed:

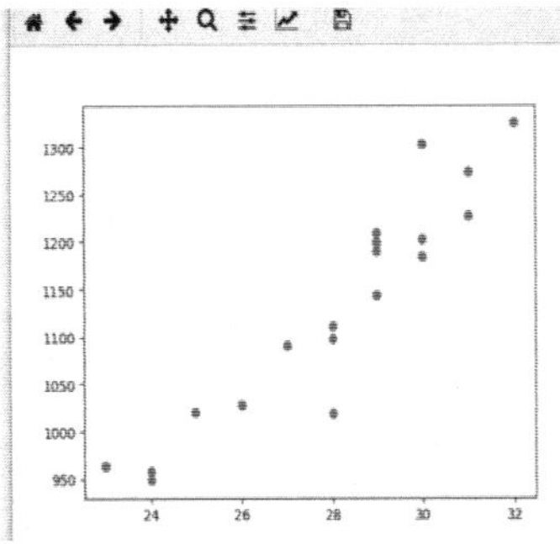

Fig.1 Scatter Diagram

Plt. ScatterEstimate model parameter andset up regression model, then introduce Linear regression function: LrModel=LinearRegression().

We can predict the linear relations between x and y by means of the sample of corresponding relations of variable x and variable y. The training model will be showed as followed: lrModel.fit(x, y) and lrModel.score(x, y), Test the regression model and the result will be showed in Fig.2.

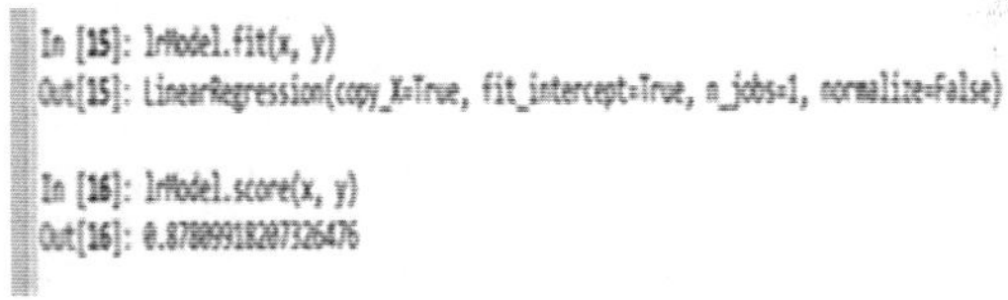

Fig.2 Test Result of Regression Model

Predict by the regression model
lrModel.predict([[50], [40], [30]])
Intercept and parameter will be showed in Fig.3.
alpha = lrModel.intercept_[0]
beta = lrModel.coef_[0][0]

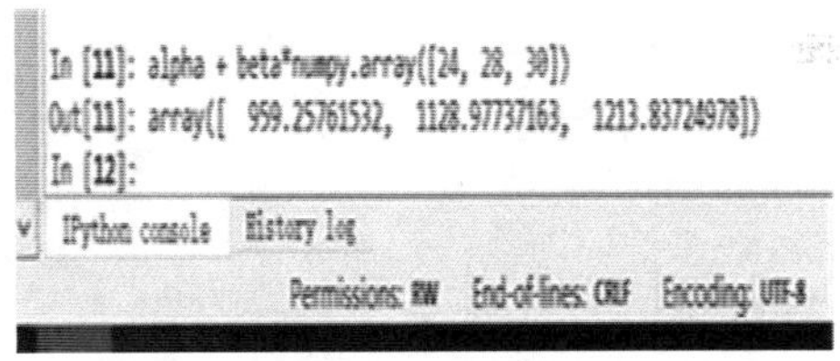

Fig.3 Intercept and Parameter

Output the predicted values of sale under different temperatures and results will be showed in Fig.4.
alpha + beta*numpy.array([50, 40, 30])
alpha + beta*numpy.array([55, 45, 35)

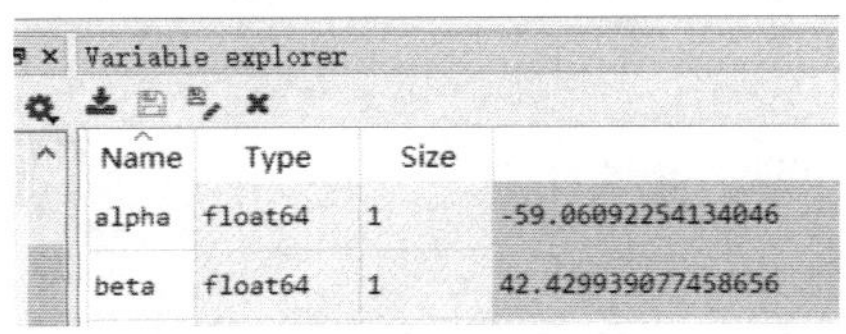

Fig.4 Temperature Variation and the Sale of Iced Products
3

The result shows when the temperature is 24 degrees, the predicted value of sale will be 959.25; when the temperature is 28 degrees, the predicted value of sale will be 1128.977; when the temperature is 30 degrees, the sale will be 1213.837. So, the company can adjust the production according to the predicted value of sale, which will have great effect on the company. At the same time, the linear regression model used in the paper can obtain greater imitative effect of the predicted value of product sale based on the temperature variation and boast strong practicality. The latest Python3.6 used in the paper also shows its concise and elegant statements that fits for mathematics model. Python3.6 in data mining will be the first choice of learners of machine learning field.

6 CONCLUSION

The paper herein introduces the algorithm and model of the field of machine learning. Linear regression model is used to analyze the sale of iced products of company and the effect of temperature variation on the sale. Firstly, we cleanse the data collected one year ago and analyze data at the same time. Then we choose forecast temperature as the independent variable and the sale of iced products as the dependent variable to establish simple linear regression model for analysis. We use the object-oriented programming language Python3.6 and introduce the linear regression function. Programming language can also make data analysis in the field of data mining easier. The final result correctly leads the company to adjust the production and sale of iced products flexibly according to the variation of temperature, which definitely provides great commercial value and offers crucial theoretical foundation for the sale of other companies who produce iced products.

Acknowledgment

Fund project: Ningxia high school science research project: NGY2017032;

REFERENCES:

1. Krikorian R. Twitter by the numbers. 2010. http://www.slideshare.net/raffikrikorian/twitter-by-the-numbers.
2. Tam D. Facebook processes more than 500 TB of data daily.2012. http://www.cnet.com/news/facebook-processes-more-than-500-tb-of-data-daily/
3. Wikipedia,Petabyte.2014. http://en.wikipedia.org/wiki/Petabyte
4. Low Y,Gonzalez J, Kyrola A, Bickson D, Guestrin C, Hellerstein JM. Graphlab: A new framework for parallel machine learning. ar Xiv preprint ar Xiv:1006.4990. 2010.
5. The apache software foundation, what is apachemahout. 2014. http://mahout.apache.org/
6. Qian ZP, Chen XW, Kang NX, Chen MC, YuY,Moscibroda T, Zhang Z. Mad LINQ: Large-Scale distributed matrix computation for the cloud. In: Proc.of the 7th ACM European Conf. on Computer Systems. ACM Press, 2012. 197210. [doi: 10.1145/2168836.2168857]
7. Sun Q, Li JH, Li SH. Research on the development of text classification system based on Python[J].Computer application software,2011,28(3):13-14.
8. Hinton GE,Osindero S,Teh Y W.A fast learning algorithm for deep belief nets[J].Neural computation,2006,18(7):1527-1554.
9. Arel I,Rose D C,Karnowski T P.Deep machine learning-A new frontier in artifical intelligence esearch[J].Computational Intelligence Magazine,IEEE,2010,5(4):13-18.
10. Google Flu Trends. [EB/ O L]. http:
// www.google.org/ flutrends.
11. M. Scherer. Inside the Secret World of the Data Crunchers Who Helped O bama Win. [EB/ O L]. (2012- 11- 07) [2013- 03- 06]. http:
//swampland.time.com/ 2012/ 11/ 07/ inside- the-secret- world- of- quants- and- data- crunchers- who-helped- obama- win/ .
12. Meng XF. Big data management: concept, technology and challenge.
[J]. Computer research and development, 2013,50 (1) : 146-169.
13. Hou JC, Fang JY. Data citation research: progress and prospect.[J]. Journal of Chinese library, 2013 (1) : 112-118.

Application of Extreme Learning Machine in GPS Positioning Process

Chengxin Li [1], Jing Peng [1,*], Zhicheng Lv[1], Mengli Wang[2], and Gang Ou[1]

[1]Engineering Research Center for Position, Navigation and Time, College of Electronic Science, National University of Defense Technology, Deya Road 109, Changsha, China
[2]Satellite Navigation Center, Beijing, China

Abstract. In the positioning process of GPS, the linear least squares algorithm and Kalman filtering algorithm are widely used but still have shortcomings. Application of extreme learning machine in this area is proposed in this paper, which breaks through the limitations of the traditional method of positioning based on mathematical models. Two simulation experiments of ELM in GPS positioning process are presented in this paper while the latter is a supplement to the former. Each one contains three phases, including simulation data generation, network training and network prediction, each of which is considered carefully. The feasibility of extreme learning machine is verified through experimental simulation. A more accurate positioning result can be obtained.

1 Introduction

In the positioning process of the global positioning system (GPS), the linear least squares (LS) algorithm and Kalman filtering (KF) algorithm are usually used [1]. The LS algorithm is sensitive to observation errors. The KF algorithm depends on the statistical properties of the noise of the state model and the measurement model, which may lead to the divergence of the filter [2, 3]. Although both algorithms have good performance practically, there are still some problems to solve.

Artificial neural network (ANN) is a nonlinear dynamic system composed of a large number of simple processing units (neurons) interconnected by a certain structure [4]. It is the simplification and simulation of human brain information processing mechanism. Neural networks have been shown to approximate continuous and differentiable functions with arbitrary accuracy [5]. Since GPS positioning equations are continuous and differentiable, which do not exist any analytic solution, the equations can be approximated by neural networks [6]. Including the back propagation (BP) neural network, the traditional single hidden layer feedforward neural network (SLFN) have some disadvantages, including the slow training speed, the poor generalization ability and the sensitivity to the learning rate.

Extreme learning machine (ELM) is one of SLFN with high precision and fast training speed [7]. ELM is applied to the GPS positioning process in this paper. The training data is composed of observation data from the simulation and real locations of nine receivers arranged in the grid. The network may predict the positions of the receivers, which move in a certain path in the area. The result of ELM is compared to that of least linear squares method and Kalman filtering method.

2 Positioning observation equation

Pseudo distance positioning observation equation [8] can be expressed as

$$Pr = |SV - U| + B + Er \tag{1}$$

where Pr is the observation pseudorange of the receiver, SV is the coordinates of the visible satellites in the earth-centered/earth-fixed (ECEF) coordinate system, U is the position of the receiver in the ECEF coordinate system, B is the clock error of the receiver, Er is the pseudorange measurement error, including the satellite clock error, the ephemeris error, the atmospheric delay error, the multi-path error, the noise of receivers and other unknown error.

In (1), SV and Pr is known, and the known part of Er can be calculated by models, while U and B are unknown. Without considering the unknown error, the essence of the traditional positioning algorithms is to solve the nonlinear equation set composed of (1). They are usually linearized and calculated by LS or KF method. It is obvious that the ignorance of the original nonlinear characteristics of the observation equations may result in a reduction in the accuracy. Meanwhile, the models of atmospheric delay error and other known errors are empirical models, so the true value of errors in one epoch are unknown.

From (1), the relationship among the observation pseudorange of the receiver Pr, the coordinates of the visible satellites SV and the position of the receiver U

* Corresponding author: jingpeng_nnc@163.com

can be considered to be a multi-input and multi-output nonlinear mapping F which has a fixed form as

$$U = F(SV, Pr) \tag{2}$$

There is no explicit expression for the nonlinear mapping F, which is continuous and differentiable. It can be approximated with arbitrary accuracy by the neural network with enough nodes of the hidden layer.

3 Extreme learning machine

ELM is one of SLFN, which have good learning ability. The typical SLFN structure can be seen in Fig. 1.

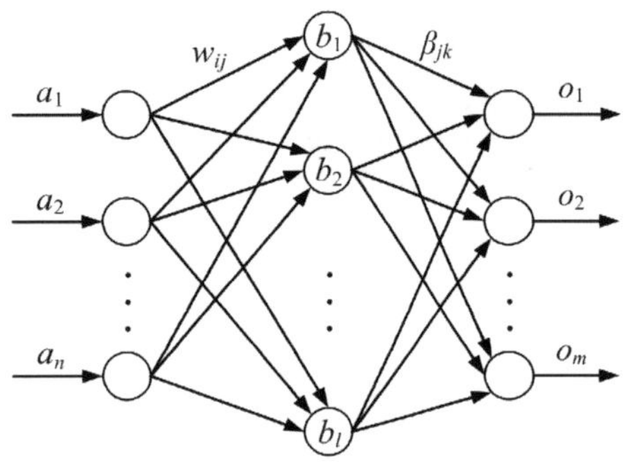

Fig. 1. The typical single hidden layer feedforward neural network structure.

Yet some learning algorithms of SLFN like BP algorithm have slow training speed and adopt the gradient descent method, leading to poor generalisation ability and sensitivity to the learning rate. ELM randomly generates weights w of connections between the input layer and the hidden layer, and the bias b of the neurons in the hidden layer. w and b keep the same in the training process. The weights β of connections between the hidden layer and the output layer can be obtained by solving the LS solution of the following equation as

$$\min_{\beta} \|\mathbf{H}\beta - \mathbf{T}'\| \tag{3}$$

where $\mathbf{H}$ is the output matrix of the hidden layer and $\mathbf{T}'$ is the transpose of the network output.

The solution is unique and its norm is minimal. Compared to other neural networks of SLFN, ELM has fast learning speed, good generalization performance and high training precision in theory. In the GPS positioning process, the coordinates of receivers are on the order of 10^7 meters. In order to achieve centimeter-level positioning accuracy, high training precision is required.

4 Application of ELM in GPS positioning process

There are two simulation experiments of application of ELM in GPS positioning process. The second one is a supplement to the first one. Each one contains three phases, including simulation data generation, network training and network prediction.

4.1 Simulation experiment I

4.1.1 Simulation data generation

In the simulation data generation phase, the simulation data is composed of the positions and corresponding observation data of receivers. Since the systematic errors can be basically eliminated by the known model, they are not considered, including the earth's rotation error, the relativistic effect and the satellite clock error. The positions of satellites are true value in one epoch. The ionosphere error obtained by the 8-Klobuchar model and the tropospheric error obtained by the Hopfield model is added to the true pseudorange as the observation pseudorange.

Nine receivers are arranged in the 3×3 layout, which can be seen in Fig. 2. The difference in latitude and longitude between adjacent nodes is 0.5', and the height of each node is 312 meters.

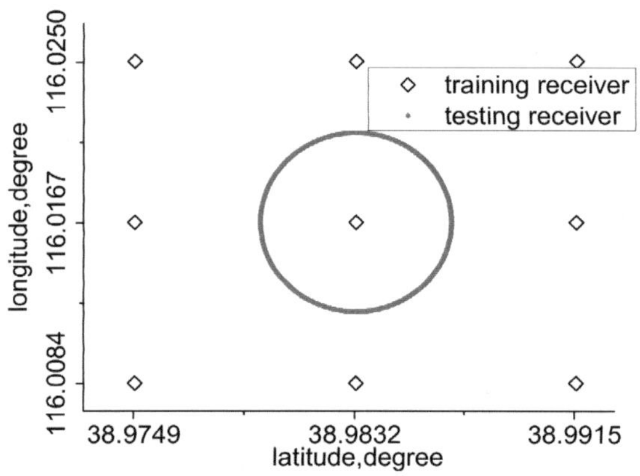

Fig. 2. The layout of 9 training receivers and the motion route of the testing receiver of the first simulation experiment.

The training data is the simulation data of the receivers in 40 minutes. Each epoch is one second. So the number of samples for the training set is 9×40×60=21600. The input of the network is composed of coordinates and the pseudorange of nine continuous visible satellites, of which the cut-off angle is five degrees. The input of ELM is a 36-dimensional vector, which can be expressed as (x1, y1, z1, p1, …, x9, y9, z9, p9). The output of the network is the exact location (x, y, z) of the receivers corresponding to the input.

4.1.2 Network training and prediction

In the network training phase, in order to achieve higher training precision and a larger network scale, the number of neurons in the hidden layer is taken as 2000, and the neuron activation function takes the 'sin' function.

In the network prediction phase, we consider the motion of the testing receiver. The input of the trained network is the observation data of the testing receiver that perform circular motion in the grid area. The circular motion route can be seen in Fig. 2. The output is the 3-dimensional coordinates of the receivers' position. The motion time of the receivers is ten minutes, and the line velocity of the motion is 6m/s.

With no noise, the result of network prediction performs high accuracy, which shows that ELM can approximate the nonlinear mapping of the input and the output, even if there is the existence of the ionospheric error and the tropospheric error.

Then the random noise is added to the pseudorange, of which the standard deviation is 5 meters and the mean value is 0. After prediction, we compare the 3-dimensional positioning error of the prediction result with that of LS method and KF method. The results are shown in Fig. 3.

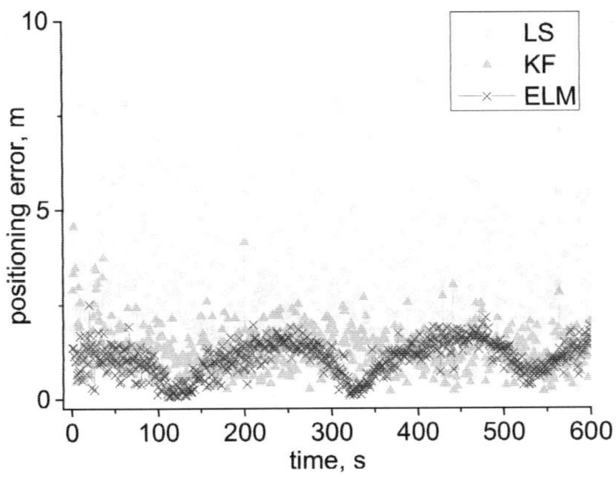

Fig. 3. The 3-dimensional positioning error of LS algorithm, KF algorithm and ELM.

Table 1. The mean square errors of 3-dimensional positioning error of LS algorithm, KF algorithm and ELM.

Positioning algorithm	LS	Kalman	ELM
Mean square error/m	2.83	1.33	1.06

As can be seen in Table 1, the mean value of the 3-dimensional error of LS algorithm is 2.83m, and that of KF algorithm is 1.33m, while that of ELM is 1.06m, which performs higher accuracy than the others.

We can also see in Fig. 3 that the curve of the error of ELM varies regularly with the circular motion of the testing receiver, which may be related to the position of the testing receiver in the area. This may be due to the lack of training data in the blank area of the 2×2 grid. So we conduct following simulation experiment.

4.2 Simulation experiment II

In the simulation data generation phase, 4 training receivers are newly added to the center of each grid, which can be seen in Fig. 4. Other experimental settings remain unchanged.

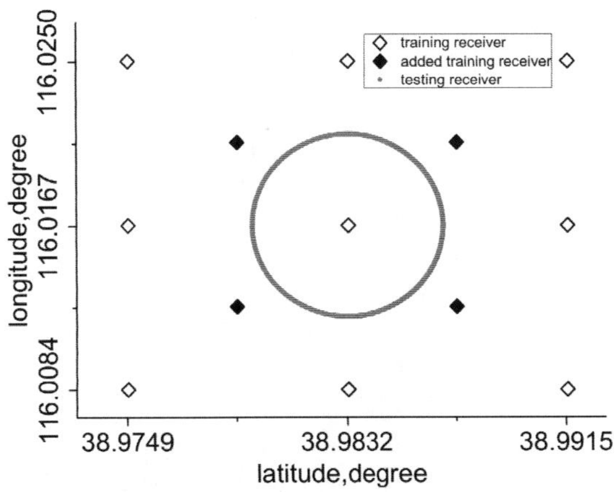

Fig. 4. The layout of 13 training receivers and the motion route of the testing receiver of the second simulation experiment.

As can be seen in Fig. 5 and Table 2, the 3-dimensional positioning error of 13 training receivers is smaller and more stable than Simulation Experiment I. The mean value of positioning error reduces to 0.0755m, which is acceptable.

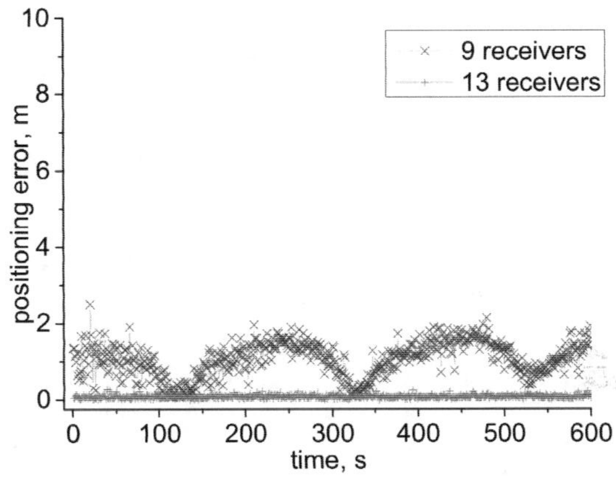

Fig. 5. The 3-dimensional positioning error of ELM with 9 receivers and 13 receivers.

Table 2. The mean square errors of 3-dimensional positioning error of ELM with 9 receivers and 13 receivers.

Number of receivers	9	13
Mean square error/m	1.06	0.0755

5 Conclusion

Applications of ELM in GPS positioning process are proposed in this paper. The results of simulation experiments are more accurate than LS and KF algorithms. The results of experiments show that the more complete the training data is, the more accurate and stable the positioning results are.

This work was supported by the National Natural Science Foundation of China (Nos. 61601485).

References

1. Mehra R. K., Auto. Cont. IEEE Trans., **5**, 693 (1972)
2. Gelb A., Proc. IEEE, **64**, 574 (1974)
3. Boutayeb M., Rafaralahy H., Darouach M., Auto. Cont. IEEE Trans., **42**, 581 (1995)
4. Haykin S., Neur. Netw. Comp. Foun., **1**, 71 (2008)
5. Hecht-Nielsen R., Inte. Join. Conf. Neur. Netw. IEEE, **1**, 445 (2002)
6. Chansarkar M., GPS Solu., **4**, 14 (2000)
7. G. Huang, Q. Zhu, Siew C. K., Neur., **70**, 489 (2006)
8. P. Axelrad, R. G. Brown, *GPS navigation algorithms* (1996)

An Novel Image Recognition method based on Three-way Decision

Jin Dai[1], Shuai Shao[1], Zu Wang[1] and Xianjing Zhao[1]

[1] School of Software Engineering, Chongqing University of Posts and Telecommunications

Abstract: The traditional recognition method takes the low-level information of the image as the foundation. The image recognition center of gravity is biased towards the typical features, and achieves the effect of recognition by region-dependent segmentation. Because the general image segmentation is a regular rectangle, easily lead to the same target is divided into different sub-blocks, ignoring the image of the fuzzy part, so the image recognition is not complete. An image recognition algorithm based on three-way decision is proposed. It takes full advantage of effective information in the image, improving the image recognition accuracy. First, this method divided the image into three regions: positive region, negative region and delay decision region. Second, an iterative process is performed on the region of the delay decision. Final, image recognition is performed on the positive sample region. Based on the basic theory of the three-way decision, the more obvious the decision result is, the more iterations are, and the information is added to the classifier until the blurred part of image cannot be divided. Finally, to achieve the realize effective image recognition. This method simulates the process of human cognition effectively, and makes the utilization of the effective information reach the maximum in the recognition process. The results of the experimental analysis showed that the method is more concise and efficient, and the recognition accuracy is more accurate.

1 INTRODUCTION

Image recognition refers to the use of computers to image processing, analysis and understanding to identify a variety of different models of the goals and the objects of the technology. Based on content of image recognition is a very active research field since the 1970s, its driving force is derived from two major research directions: database system and computer vision [1]. At present, the initial image recognition research focused on how to select the appropriate global features to describe the image content and what kind of similarity measure for image matching. Owing to the immaturity of computer vision and artificial intelligence, the further development of image recognition is affected. Because of the global image features, this method is only suitable for simple images or background images.

In recent years, based on image recognition related feedback technology has also become a research hotpot. At present, the computer vision and pattern recognition technology cannot achieve the object of high efficiency recognition, which makes it difficult to describe the semantic and abstract layer semantics of object layer. Therefore, the study of image semantic features is focused on the first layer of semantic feature mode [2]. Because the simple semantic feature extraction and analysis is based on the use of complex semantic information, and the computer's understanding of the image content generally refers to the image of the low-level visual features, such as color, texture, shape, etc... In fact, the human understanding of the content of the image far more than the visual features of the image. There is a large gap between the low-level and the high-level semantic features of the image, called the "semantic gap" [2,3].

In summary, the general image recognition methods are based on the image of the low-level semantics to study. Due to the computer's performance, can only be programmed to perform a single instruction, resulting in the general method of image recognition rate is low. How to improve the image recognition rate and understand the deep semantics of the image becomes the research direction which needs to be solved urgently.

At present, three-way decision theory is applied to solve complex problems and computer simulation of human thinking methods. Many scholars combined the three-way decision and particle computing in the study, and most scholars focused on image recognition research about describe the image content (low-level information), and it is still less that integrating the classifier to improve the classification performance of the method. Due to the complexity content of the image (high-level semantics),

*Corresponding author: { Jin Dai, Shuai Shao }daijin@cqupt.edu.cn, nandehutubai@hotmail.com

the image classification task is very difficult, and the three-way decision theory is generally used for fuzzy information, which can effectively classify the fuzzy information in the image in order to achieve the purpose of improving the image recognition rate. In this paper, we purposed an image recognition algorithm based on the three-way decision, and we improved the image classifier algorithm.

2 RELATED WORKS

Image recognition is to classify the processed image. First, the category name is determined. Then, the feature to be extracted is selected on the basis of the segmentation, and some parameters are measured. Finally, the image is classified according to the measurement result. In order to better recognition the image, we need to analyse the whole structure of the image, describing the image, so that the main information of the image to get an explanation and understanding, and through many of the structural relationship to deepen understanding of the image. So, the image recognition is in each of the parts after the division, to find its shape and texture and other characteristics, that is feature extraction (sometimes including image segmentation), in order to classify the image, and structural analysis the entire image.

At present, the mainstream image recognition process includes pre-processing, image segmentation, image feature extraction, image classification.

The three-way decision theory is developed in recent years, a method of dealing with uncertainty decision-making, is a complex human cognitive "Trisecting and Acting" model [6]. The three-way decision theory is a decision-making model based on human cognition [6,12]. Which argues that people can make quick judgments immediately in the course of actual decision-making, for those who have a good grasp of acceptance or rejection. Immediate decision-making things, people tend to postpone the judgment of the incident, that is delay decision [6]. In the process of practical decision-making, there are the complexity of the decision-making environment, the incompleteness of the information acquisition, the inconsistency of the expert opinions in the group decision-making [7]. The uncertainty of the knowledge and the ambiguity of the thinking situation, the decision-maker in most cases it is difficult to accurately give the specific value of the loss function. In general, the meaning of uncertainty is broad, including randomness, ambiguity, imperfectness, instability and inconsistency [8]. The three-way decision is divided into two modes: the double evaluation function and the single evaluation function [12].

Definition 1: The three-way decision based on the double evaluation function [6]

Definition 2: The three-way decision based on the single evaluation function [6]

Axiom 1: The more knowledge, the three-way decision is clearer [13]

The more information is known, the more likely it is to accept and reject the decision. The less likely it is to promise, the smaller the known information, the less likely to accept and reject, and the greater the likelihood of no commitment. The more the features of the set are extracted, the more the same or opposite properties can be determined. The less the different attributes are, the more accurate the degree of association is. The less the feature extraction is, the less the same or the opposite the more attributes, the degree of contact is rougher.

3 THE THREE-WAY DECISION IN IMAGE RECOGNITION

To improve the accuracy of image recognition has always been a difficult problem in the field of image recognition. In general, the research of image recognition focuses on the low-level visual features of images, which leads to a single image recognition algorithm, and the researchers focused on the research in the low-level visual feature points. It is easy to result in the recognition of the useful information in the image is not complete, thus reducing the image recognition rate. In this paper, we proposed an image recognition method based on three-way decision, which makes useful information in the image to make the image recognition more accurate.

- The main problem of existence

The image segmentation of the rules causes the same objects to be split into different sub-blocks.

At present, most scholars focus on the classification of image recognition in the description of image content (the low-level information), such as color, texture, shape, etc... In fact, the human understanding of the image semantic information expressed much more the visual features. The existing image segmentation usually divides the image directly into a regular rectangle, causing the same objects to be divided into different image sub-blocks, resulting in errors in the classification. Existing methods of identification for improved fusion of classifiers in order to improve image recognition performance are still less. Due to the complexity of the image information, the image classification task is difficult, and the image semantic classification is still a challenging subject in the field of image recognition and computer vision.

- The three-way decision in image recognition

In view of the above problems, this paper proposed an image recognition method based on three-way decision. The method uses three mechanisms to deal with fuzzy information. The uncertain regions of different sub-blocks in image segmentation will be judged again. Because this method divided the image by increasing the decision condition of the classifier, the images in different sub-blocks are divided into the same sub-blocks in the process of continuous iteration, which effectively avoids the problems in traditional method. Each of the three-way decision classifier to increase the conditions of the decision is from the existing conditions after the screening of information, so each increase in the information according to the current image of their own attributes, and constantly adjust the partition region, thus achieve accurate recognition purpose.

- Technological Scheme

In this paper, we used efficient image segmentation method to improve the recognition rate. We used the multi-feature, segmentation, detection, multi-classifier and other methods, the depth of the sample image training, in reducing the image loss at the same time, splitting the target region, and retraining the new information. The composite SVM used in this paper is an improved version based on SVM. The final detection and recognition is realized by fusion and segmentation. Aiming at the problem of low recognition rate of general method, this paper proposed an image recognition method based on three-way decision. According to the characteristics of human cognitive things. Because of the unique decision-making characteristics of the three-way decision, the new decision information is added to the decision-making condition in the initial judgment condition. After completion, the positive and negative regions that have been divided will be trained as a new training set, and a new judgment condition will be added to the region of the delay decision until the region of the delay decision cannot be divided. Finally, the image recognition is performed. As stated in Axiom 1, each training will add new decision conditions to make the classification of the three-way decision classifiers is clearer, the delay decision-making part of the smaller and smaller, until a certain critical value, and finally to achieve the image recognition.

According to the above method, put forward the technical roadmap, as shown in Figure 2.

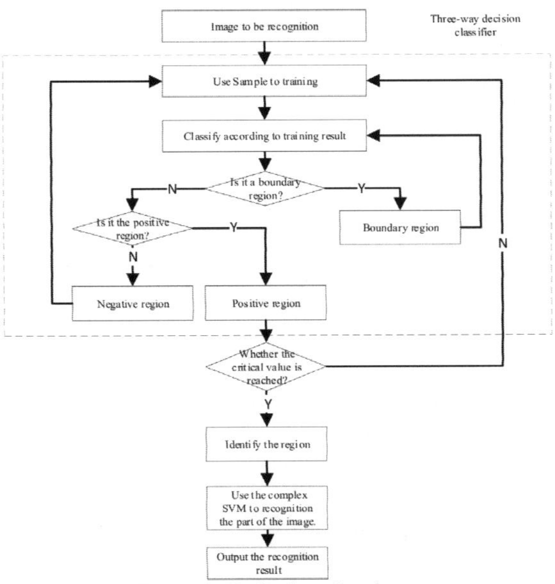

Figure 2: Technology Roadmap.

4 IMAGE RECOGNITION ALGORITHMS BASED ON THREE-WAY DECISION

Corresponding to the three-way decision, we use α , β and ξ , respectively, that acceptance, rejection and delay decision. Assuming that the evaluation function is defined as $P_r(X|[x])$, the risk function is $R(\Delta|x)$, where the decision action for x is Δ . Based on the cost matrix given in Tab 1, the following states can be estimated as follows:

Acceptable: $R(\alpha|x)=\lambda_{\alpha p}\cdot P_\beta(X|[x])+(1-P_\beta(X|[x]))$;

Refuse: $R(\beta|x)=\lambda_{\beta p}\cdot P_\beta(X|[x])+(1-P_\beta(X|[x]))$;

Delay decision: $R(\xi|x)=\lambda_{\xi p}\cdot P_\beta(X|[x])+(1-P_\beta(X|[x]))$.

In the decision-making process, based on the risk function, select the risk of the smallest decision-making action: When the condition $R(\alpha|x)\le R(r|x)\wedge R(\alpha|x)\le R(n|x)$ is satisfied, the acceptance is selected; when the condition $R(r|x)\le R(\alpha|x)\wedge R(r|x)\le R(n|x)$ is satisfied, the rejection is selected; when the condition $R(n|x)\le R(\alpha|x)\wedge R(n|x)\le R(r|x)$ is satisfied, the delay decision is selected. Assumed that the risk function satisfies the following conditions:

$\lambda_{\alpha p}\le\lambda_{\xi p}<\lambda_{\beta p}$, $\lambda_{\beta n}\le\lambda_{\xi n}<\lambda_{\alpha n}$,

$$\frac{\lambda_{\beta p}-\lambda_{\xi p}}{\lambda_{\xi n}-\lambda_{\beta n}}>\frac{\lambda_{\xi p}-\lambda_{\alpha p}}{\lambda_{\alpha n}-\lambda_{\xi n}}.$$

By substituting $R(\alpha|x)$, $R(r|x)$ and $R(n|x)$ into the above three inequalities, the following results can be obtained:

If $P_r(X|[x])\ge\alpha$, select accept; if $P_r(X|[x])\le\beta$, select reject; if $\beta\le P_r(X|[x])\le\alpha$, select delay decision.

Table 1: Two Kinds of State Decision Problem Matrix.

Decision action	Objective state	
	Satisfaction:	Dissatisfaction:
Acceptance: α	$\lambda_{\alpha p}$	$\lambda_{\alpha n}$
Rejection: β	$\lambda_{\beta p}$	$\lambda_{\beta n}$
Delay decision: ξ	$\lambda_{\xi p}$	$\lambda_{\xi n}$

Based on the above theory, the following algorithm is proposed. Algorithm 1 is an image classifier algorithm based on three-way decision. we purposed to divide the image into three regions, and did the preliminary work for the recognition of algorithm 2. Algorithm 2 is a recognition algorithm based on three-way decision, through the algorithm 1, the image segmentation of the part of the recognition.

Algorithm 1: Image Classification Algorithm based on Three-way Decision

Input: The image dataset ψ .

Output: An image classifier M based on three-way decision.

Begin

Step1: Input the image training dataset ψ .

Step2: According to the state condition in Table 1, classifier parameters $\lambda_{\alpha p}$, $\lambda_{\alpha n}$, $\lambda_{\beta p}$, $\lambda_{\beta n}$, $\lambda_{\xi p}$, $\lambda_{\xi n}$ are trained.

Step3: The positive sample region is obtained according to the value of formula: $\alpha=\dfrac{\lambda_{\alpha n}-\lambda_{\xi n}}{(\lambda_{\alpha n}-\lambda_{\xi n})+(\lambda_{\xi p}-\lambda_{\alpha p})}$,The negative sample region is obtained according to the value of formula: $\beta = \frac{\lambda_{\xi n} - \lambda_{\beta n}}{(\lambda_{\xi n} - \lambda_{\beta n}) + (\lambda_{\beta p} - \lambda_{\xi p})}$.

Step4: The delay decision region is obtained according to the value of μ, and $\beta < \mu < \alpha$.

Step5: Output the image classifier M.

End

Through this algorithm, the image dataset is trained to get an available classifier based on three-way decision.

Algorithm 2: Image Recognition Algorithm based on Three-way Decision

Input: Image C to be recognized.

Output: The Image Recognition Result N.

Begin

Step1: Input the image C.

Step2: Using the classifier M in algorithm 1, the image C is divided into three regions: positive region(P), negative region(N), delay decision region(B).

Step3: It is determined whether or not the delay decision region(B) has reached the recognition threshold value $\xi = \frac{\lambda'_{\alpha n} - \lambda'_{\xi n}}{(\lambda'_{\alpha n} - \lambda'_{\xi n}) + (\lambda'_{\xi p} - \lambda'_{\alpha p})}$, and if not, repeat step 2 for the B region.

Step4: If the ξ achieve the threshold, use the complex SVM to recognition the region of the image.

Step5: Output the image recognition result N.

End

Through this algorithm, the image is classified by the classifier obtained in Algorithm 1, and iterative processing is performed to obtain the image recognition result.

5 EXPERIMENT

- Multiple Objects Recognition Based on CIFAR-10 Dataset

The CIFAR-10 [14] is labeled subsets of the 80 million tiny images dataset. They were collected by Alex Krizhevsky, Vinod Nair, and Geoffrey Hinton. The CIFAR-10 dataset consists of 60,000 32×32 color images in 10 classes, with 6,000 images per class. There were 50,000 training images and 10,000 test images. The dataset is divided into five training batches and one test batch, each with 10,000 images. The test batch contains exactly 1,000 randomly-selected images from each class. The training batches contain the remaining images in random order, but some training batches may contain more images from one class than another. Between them, the training batches contain exactly 5,000 images from each class. The original dataset is a single target image. In order to verify the accuracy of the three-way decision classifiers, four images in the original dataset are synthesized in this experiment, each test item has four targets to be recognized.

The experimental results are shown in Tab 2, this experiment uses the 4,000 pictures provided in the dataset, test each type of random selection of 400 pictures, each experiment for 100 pictures, the final results take the average. As shown in the above table, the average accuracy rate of the method is 87.58% and the average F-Measure is 87.06% in the dataset CIFAR-10, and the recognition rate based on the three-way decision classifiers can get higher recognition rate and accuracy rate.

Table 2: Based on the three-way decision CIFAR-10 multi-target recognition rate.

Species	Airplane	Automobile	Brid	Cat	Deer	Dog	Frog	Horse	Ship	Truck
Quantity	100	100	100	100	100	100	100	100	100	100
Precision	86%	86.5%	90%	83.75%	81.75%	86%	89.5%	90.5%	90%	91.75%
Recall	91.68%	89.48%	92.08%	87.22%	84.61%	88.64%	81.55%	92.47%	89.78%	83.23%
F-Measure	88.75%	87.96%	91.03%	85.43%	83.16%	85.99%	85.31%	91.47%	89.89%	87.34%

- Multiple Objects Recognition Based on Car detection on UIUC Dataset

The UIUC dataset [15-19] captures images of side views of cars with resolution 40×100 pixels. The training set contains 550 positive samples and 500 negative samples. The test set is divide into two subsets: 170 single-scale test images, containing 200 cars at roughly the same scale as in the training set, and 108 multi-scale test images, containing 139 cars at various scales.

Table 3: Recognition rate comparison based on UIUC dataset.

Method	UIUC Dataset		
	Precision	Recall	F-Measure
CS-AdaBoost [15]	95.5%	95.1%	95.3%
AdaBoost+LDA [16]	97.8%	99.41%	98.6%
AdaBoost [17]	98.6%	98.6%	98.6%
Pruning [18]	97.8%	99.41%	98.6%
FD [19]	99.28%	97.8%	98.6%
3WD	99.41%	99.12%	99.26%

The experimental results are shown in Table 3, for the UIUC dataset, where the dataset in the image characteristics of which 3WD (three-way decision) for the proposed method, FD (fast detection framework) for the fast detection framework [19], all the data in the table is average, Figure 4 shown that the accuracy of image recognition based on three-way decision is higher than that of the fast detection framework (FD). The method of recognition rate of 99.41%, F-Measure of 99.26% slightly higher than the FD method.

- Multiple Objects Recognition Based on Car detection on KITTI Dataset

The KITTI dataset [19] was co-founded by the Karlsruhe Institute of Technology and the Toyota American Technology Research Institute. It is the largest computerized visual algorithm evaluation data set in the world. The dataset is a recently proposed challenging dataset which consists of 7481 training images and 7518 test images, comprising more than 80 thousand of annotated objects in traffic scenes. In this paper, the image of the car is used to experiment and compare, and the method of comparison is also used as the experimental object of the car information in the image. The experimental results as shown in Tab 4.

Table 4: Recognition rate comparison based on KITTI dataset.

Method	KITTI Dataset		
	Precision	Recall	F-Measure
mBoW [20]	36.02%	56.3%	43.93%
MDPM [21]	71.19%	65.05%	67.98%
DPM-C8B1[22]	74.33%	69.92%	72.06%
OC-DPM [23]	74.94%	69.53%	72.13%
AOG [24]	80.26%	74.23%	77.13%
SubCat [25]	81.94%	76.98%	79.38%
Regionlets [9,10]	84.75%	78.83%	81.68%
FD [18]	87.19%	80.85%	83.9%
3WD	89.27%	88.45%	88.86%

As shown in Tab 4, the recognition rate of the image recognition method (3WD) based on three-way decision is 89.27%, the F-Measure is 88.86%, higher than the fast frame method (FD). The methods used in this paper have higher accuracy and F-Measure than other methods.

6 CONCLUSION

In this paper, we proposed a novel method image recognition that based on three-way decision theory. firstly, we invoked the three-way decision method in the field of image recognition. Secondly, we improved the composite SVM algorithm that through the various of classifier. Finally, through these two methods, the image recognition rate is improved. The experimental results shown that in the case of the same experimental dataset, the image recognition based on three-way decision has a significant improvement in accuracy compared with the traditional image recognition method. To the future work, Optimization of the running time of image recognition is an important topic. And the same time, we will attempt on improve the image recognition method based on three-way decision classifier, and use a variety of recognition methods for image recognition to further improve the image recognition accuracy.

ACKNOWLEDGEMENTS

This work is supported by the National Natural Science Foundation of China (NSFC) under Grant (no. 61533020, 61309014); Major Science and Technology Project for "Innovation of Common Key Technology in Key Industries " of CQ under Grant (no. cstc2017zdcy-zdzx0046); Natural Science Foundation Project of CQ CSTC under Grant (no. cstc2017jcyjAX0408).

REFERENCES

1. Smith, J., 1998. *The book*, The publishing company. London, 2nd edition.
2. Xuelong Li, Zhengkai Liu. *An Efficient Semantic Image Classification Method [J]*. Journal of Circuits and Systems, 2002, 7(2):22-25.
3. Hao Zhang. Extraction and Analysis of Semantic Image Features[D]. Shanghai Jiao Tong University, 2006.
4. Yao Y. An Outline of a Theory of Three-Way Decisions[M]// Rough Sets and Current Trends in Computing. Springer Berlin Heidelberg, 2012:1-17.
5. Dun Liu. The three-way decision and granular computing[M]. China Science Pubic, 2013.
6. Liang Decui. The research of decision-making method based on decision-theoretic rough set under the fuzzy environment[D]. Southwest Jiaotong University, 2014.
7. Li Deyi, Liu Changyu, Du Yi, et al. Artificial Intelligence with Uncertainty[J]. Journal of Software, 2004, 15(11):1583-1594.
8. Wang X, Yang M, Zhu S, et al. Regionlets for Generic Object Detection[C]// IEEE International Conference on Computer Vision. IEEE, 2014:17-24.
9. Long C, Wang X, Hua G, et al. Accurate Object Detection with Location Relaxation and Regionlets Re-localization[C]// Asian Conference on Computer Vision. Springer, Cham, 2014:260-275.
10. Shao Xiaoyan, Li Yan, Li Lihong. Transformation of no-commitment decision of three-way decision based on the maximization of income[J]. Microcomputer its Applications, 2017, 36(8):79-82.
11. Yin Ye, Ke Deying, Liu Chuanyong. Throry of trinary decision and its application[J]. Journal of Shanghai Normal University (Natural Sciences), 2015, 44(1):95-104.
12. Liu Baoxiang, Li Yan, Sun Jie. Three-way decisions and related theoretical research[J]. Microcomputer its Applications, 2014(12):1-3.
13. Carvalho E F, Engel P M. Convolutional Sparse Feature Descriptor for Object Recognition in CIFAR-10[C]// Brazilian Conference on Intelligent Systems. IEEE Computer Society, 2013:131-135.
14. Masnadishirazi H, Vasconcelos N. Cost-sensitive boosting.[J]. IEEE Transactions on Pattern Analysis & Machine Intelligence, 2010, 33(2):294-309.
15. Wu J, Brubaker S C, Mullin M D, et al. Fast Asymmetric Learning for Cascade Face Detection[J].

IEEE Transactions on Pattern Analysis & Machine Intelligence, 2008, 30(3):369.

16. Viola P, Jones M. Robust real-time face detection[J]. International Journal of Computer Vision, 2004, 57(2):137-154.
17. Paisitkriangkrai S, Shen C, Hengel A V D. Asymmetric Pruning for Learning Cascade Detectors[J]. IEEE Transactions on Multimedia, 2014, 16(5):1254-1267.
18. Hu Q, Paisitkriangkrai S, Shen C, et al. Fast Detection of Multiple Objects in Traffic Scenes with a Common Detection Framework[J]. IEEE Transactions on Intelligent Transportation Systems, 2016, 17(4):1002-1014.
19. Behley J, Steinhage V, Cremers A B. Laser-based segment classification using a mixture of bag-of-words[C]// Ieee/rsj International Conference on Intelligent Robots and Systems. IEEE, 2013:4195-4200.
20. Forsyth D. Object Detection with Discriminatively Trained Part-Based Models[J]. IEEE Transactions on Pattern Analysis & Machine Intelligence, 2014, 47(2):6-7.
21. Yebes J J, Bergasa L M, Arroyo R, et al. Supervised learning and evaluation of KITTI's cars detector with DPM[C]// Intelligent Vehicles Symposium Proceedings. IEEE, 2014:768-773.
22. Pepikj B, Stark M, Gehler P, et al. Occlusion Patterns for Object Class Detection[C]// Computer Vision and Pattern Recognition. IEEE, 2013:3286-3293.
23. Li B, Wu T, Zhu S C. Integrating Context and Occlusion for Car Detection by Hierarchical And-Or Model[M]// Computer Vision – ECCV 2014. Springer International Publishing, 2014:652-667.
24. Ohn-Bar E, Trivedi M M. Fast and Robust Object Detection Using Visual Subcategories[C]// Computer Vision and Pattern Recognition Workshops. IEEE, 2014:179-184.

Bipolar Triangular Wave Current Pulse Inverter for Shallow TEM Survey

Zhao Yifu[1,2], Liu Lihua[1,*], Geng Zhi[1], and Liu Xiaojun[1]

[1]Institute of Electronics, Chinese Academy of Sciences Key Laboratory of Electromagnetic Radiation and Sensing Technology, Chinese Academy of Sciences, Beijing 100190, China
[2]University of Chinese Academy of Sciences School of Electronic, Electrical and Communication Engineering, Beijing 100049, China

Abstract. A bipolar triangular wave current pulse inverter for shallow TEM survey is described. It can generate a peak current more than 10A and the PRF of the bipolar current pulse is between 1Hz and 10kHz. The proposed inverter contains a high voltage source circuit for the rising edge and a Zener diodes circuit with constant voltage clamping for the falling edge. Measurement results are presented, which show the high quality triangular wave current pulse with linear rising edge and rapidly turnoff falling edge.

1 Introduction

Triangular wave current pulse can be used for mineral exploration, unexploded ordnance exploration, hydrogeological survey, engineering geological survey, geological mapping and so on[1]. It also has several merits against square wave in ground penetrating. It has the advantage that the primary field is simple and it is suitable for shallow low-resistivity target detection, as well as early signal acquisition and processing[2].

In this letter, a high voltage source circuit and inverter bridge circuit are designed to generate the bipolar triangular wave current pulse. For high voltage source circuit, five power modules are connected in series to provide the high power with stable DC voltage. For the inverter circuit, it has a full-bridge circuit of four MOSFETs, which are driven by four isolated PWM signals given by MCU. High and constant voltage clamping circuit is the essential part of this inverter to make the current pulse rise lineally to peak current and fall down rapidly to zero during the turn-off time. Finally, we can obtain periodic triangular wave current pulse with peak values more than 10A and PRF of 1Hz to 10kHz for different applications.

2 Theoretical Analysis

For a load such as small air-core coil, it is typically equal to a resistor and an inductor connected in series[3]. For a current pulse with linear edges, the corresponding voltage of the coil should be linear too. The reason will be described soon. A positive triangular wave current pulse is depicted in formula (1), and the negative cycle is the same to the positive one, except the polarity is different.

$$i(t) = \begin{cases} \frac{I_m}{t_r}t, & 0 \le t < t_r; \\ I_m\left(1 - \frac{t - t_r}{t_f}\right), & t_r \le t < t_r + t_f; \\ 0, & t_r + t_f \le t < \frac{T}{2}. \end{cases} \quad (1)$$

where t_r is the rising time of the current pulse and t_f is the falling time of the current pulse. I_m is amplitude of the peak current. T is the period of the current pulse. The corresponding equations of the coil is as following

$$\begin{cases} u_L(t) = L\frac{\mathrm{d}i(t)}{\mathrm{d}t} \\ u_R(t) = Ri(t) \\ u(t) = u_L(t) + u_R(t) \end{cases} \quad (2)$$

where $u(t)$ is the voltage of the coil. L and R are the inductance and resistance of the load respectively. According to the formula (1) and the formula (2), the $u(t)$ is shown as formula (3)

$$\mathrm{u(t)} = \begin{cases} \frac{LI_m}{t_r} + \frac{RI_m}{t_r}t, & 0 \le t < t_r; \\ \frac{LI_m}{t_f} + RI_m\left(1 - \frac{t - t_r}{t_f}\right), & t_r \le t < t_r + t_f; \\ 0, & t_r + t_f \le t < \frac{T}{2}. \end{cases} \quad (3)$$

In practical application, it is difficult to generate this kind of voltage, so an approximate solution is applied. For a small air-core coil, it can be inferred that $Ldi(t)/dt \gg Ri(t)$, that is $u_L(t) \gg u_R(t)$, so $u(t)$ can be simplified to a constant voltage in formula (4)

* Corresponding author: lhliu@mail.ie.ac.cn

$$u(t)=\begin{cases}\frac{LI_m}{t_r}, & 0\le t<t_r;\\ \frac{LI_m}{t_f}+RI_m\left(1+\frac{t_r}{t_f}\right), & t_r\le t<t_r+t_f;\\ 0, & t_r+t_f\le t<\frac{T}{2}.\end{cases} \quad (4)$$

With a constant voltage, the exact formula of the current is showed below. The time constant τ of the coil can be get from $\tau = L/R$, U_z is the constant clamping voltage of the falling edge.

rising edge

$$i_r(t)=\frac{U}{R}\left(1-e^{-\frac{t}{\tau}}\right),0\le t<t_r \quad (5)$$

Falling edge

$$i_f(t)=\left(I_m+\frac{U_Z}{R}\right)e^{-\frac{t-t_r}{\tau}}-\frac{U_Z}{R},0\le t<t_r \quad (6)$$

The value of t_r and t_f is shown in formula (7)

$$\mathrm{t_r}=\tau\ln\left(\frac{U}{U-RI_m}\right),t_f=\tau\ln\left(1+\frac{RI_m}{U_z}\right) \quad (7)$$

The derivative of the rising stage and the falling stage can be obtained by formula (8) and formula (9)

$$\frac{di_r(t)}{dt}=\frac{U}{L}e^{-\frac{t}{\tau}},0\le t<t_r \quad (8)$$

$$\frac{di_f(t)}{dt}=-\frac{1}{L}(RI_m+U_Z)e^{-\frac{t-t_r}{\tau}},t_r\le t<t+t_f \quad (9)$$

In general, if $e^{-\frac{t}{\tau}}>0.95$[4], that is $t/\tau<0.0513$, the $i_r(t)$ and $i_f(t)$ are deemed to be linear. The condition of the resistance of the coil can be simplified as (10)

$$\ln\left(\frac{U}{U-RI_m}\right)<0.0513,\ln\left(1+\frac{RI_m}{U_Z}\right)<0.0513 \quad (10)$$

3 Inverter Circuit

From the analysis above, it is obviously that how to provide a high and constant voltage is the key point of the circuit. For the triangular wave current pulse, high voltage can be applied to make the current rise up and fall down linearly. Therefore, we apply active constant voltage[5] clamping to the rising edge and passive constant voltage clamping to the falling edge. The high voltage generation circuit for active constant voltage clamping is shown in Fig. 1.

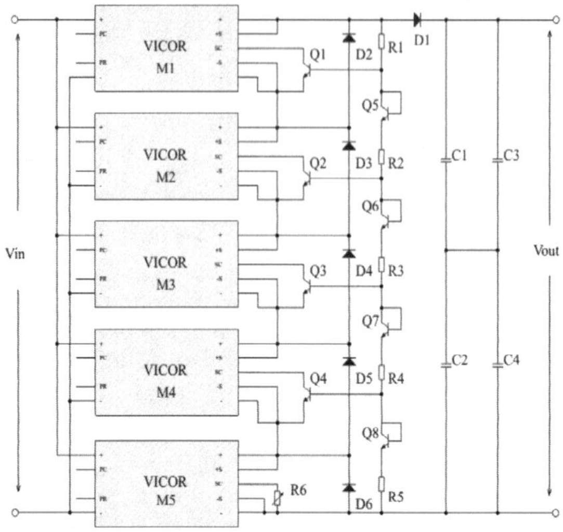

Fig. 1. Hight Voltage Generation Circuit.

VICRO module V24B48C250BL is chosen for the triangular wave pulse generation. It has input voltage of 24V, maximum output voltage of 48V. The power of this module is 250W and the maximum current output is 7A. 5 modules connected in series are needed to generate rising edge of the triangular wave. The total clamping voltage of the 5 modules is up to 240V. In this circuit, the diode D1 isolates the high voltage source and the inverter circuit. Diodes D2 to D6 protect each power module. Capacitors C1 to C4 are applied to store energy and increase the maximum current limit and their values are 220μF.

For this application, the output voltage of the module is required to be adjusted. The configuration of Fig. 1 provides a reliable and inexpensive solution to realize voltage adjusted by R6 with a value of 10kΩ. In this solution, resistors R1 to R5 are all equal and their values are 10kΩ. All the transistors Q1 to Q8 are 2N222. The effect of Q1 to Q8 is to adjust the voltage of each converter. When the output voltage of the converter M5 is adjusted, the voltages of convert M1 to M4 also change until they are all equal to the voltage of M5. Thus, the five converters have an effect on the total output voltage.

The full bridge circuit is shown in Fig. 2 and it has four MOSFETs[6]. The MOSFET module is SCT2280KE of ROHM Semicondctor. As mentioned above, a high-voltage passive clamping is used to the falling edge because the current must turn off as soon as possible to provide wide-band high frequencies for shallow TEM explorations.

When the power is supplied, QUL and QDR are turned on first, and the current passes D7, QUL, L, R and QDR to generate positive pulse[7]. Because the coil is inductive, the current rises in linear rule by the work of the high voltage circuit. When the current reaches the peak amplitude, QUL and QDR are turned off and QSW is turned on to let the current in the coil to go through the damping resistor RESn. At this time, the current has two ways to go. One way is to pass through the diode of QUR and QDL, diode D8 and Zener diodes circuit, the other one is to pass through QSW and RESn. The Zener diodes

 https://doi.org/10.1051/matecconf/201817601036

circuit form the high-voltage passive clamping circuit. The Zener diodes are 1N5369B which has Zener voltage of 51V, so the total clamping voltage of 10 diodes is about 510V. The capacitors C9 and C10 in parallel to the Zener diodes are used for protecting the Zener diodes from damage if the power is too large. The resistors R11 and R12 with value of 100kΩ are used to discharge the contour of C9 and C10. The effect of the damping resistor RESn is to suppress current overshoot when the current decays to zero. What the value of RESn is selected depends on the coil.

Due to stray parameters[8] of the entire system, there is a high frequency oscillation at the early part of the turn-off current when the switch is suddenly cut off. The oscillation will affect the early electromagnetic data, so a RCD circuit parallel to each MOSFET is added to absorb and decrease the oscillation current[9].

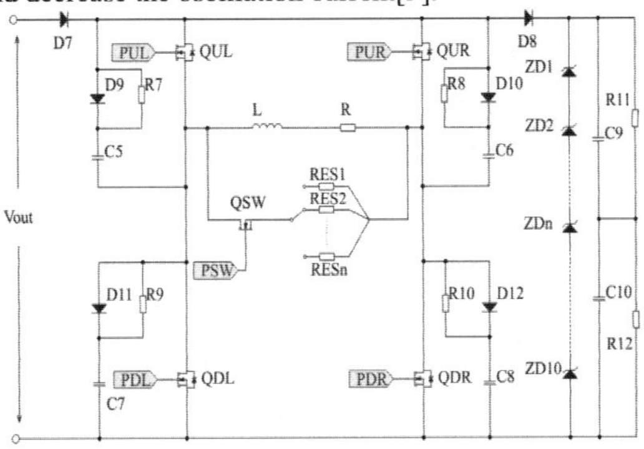

Fig. 2. Circuit Diagram.

4 Measurement

We use two different coils, the Coil A and Coil B to test the triangular wave current inverter. Both of the coils are 1m×1m square shape. The Coil A has 30 turns and the cross section of the wire is $2.5mm^2$. It is equal to a 2Ω resistor connected in series with a 3mH inductor. The Coil B has 25 turns and the cross section of the wire is $4mm^2$. It is equal to a 281mΩ resistor connected in series with a 1.65mH inductor. A high-accuracy current probe and high-voltage differential probe are used to measurement the current and the voltage waveforms of the coils.

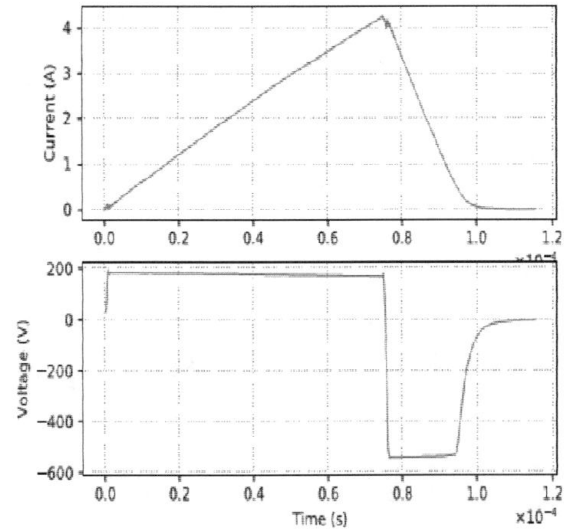

Fig. 3. Current and Voltage of Coil A.

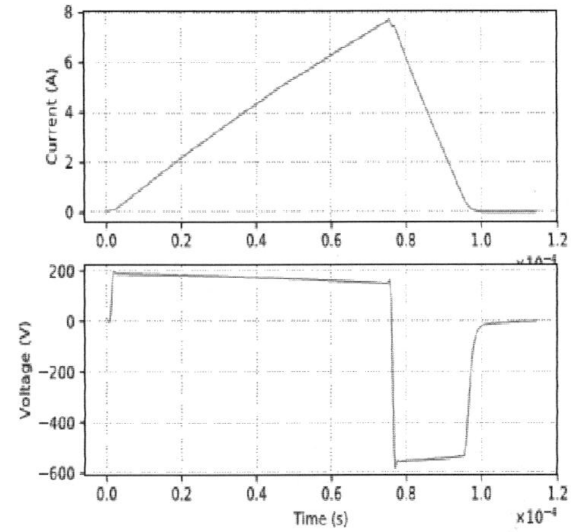

Fig. 4. Current and Voltage of Coil B.

The results of Coil A are shown in Fig. 3 and the results of Coil B is shown in Fig. 4. From Fig. 3 and Fig. 4, the current rises linearly to the peak in 75μs with the constant clamping voltage of 200V. The current in Coil A reaches 4.3A and decays to zero in 24.5μs. The current in Coil B reaches 7.7A and decays to zero in 22.6μs. The turn-off current in both coils decay linearly and rapidly with the constant clamping voltage of 510V. Because they both have high linearity rising edge and falling edge, the quality of the triangular wave current is very good for applications.

However, there is a flaw of small oscillation in the current waveform due to the stray parameters and the oscillation of Coil B is smaller than Coil A. The designed RCD circuit could reduce but cannot completely remove the oscillation, so there will be a future work to suppress the oscillation and further enhance the quality of the current waveform.

5 Conclusions

The key point of the present circuit is how to generate triangular wave pulse current in practical application. At all, the circuit present above is able to produce a high quality triangular wave pulse current with linear rising edge and linear and rapid falling edge. The peak current is more than 10A and its peak power is 1000W. The PRF of the pulse inverter is between 1Hz and 10kHz. It can completely meet the requirements of the practical application.

Acknowledgements

This work has been supported by Key Laboratory of Electromagnetic Radiation & Sensing Technology, Chinese Academy of Sciences.

References

1. G. Hodges, T. Chen, Exploration Geophysics, **46**, 58-63(2014)
2. B. Nikls, H. Garbe, M. Schaarschmidt, International Symposium on Electromagnetic Compatibility - Emc Europe, 1-6(2017)
3. B. K. Sternberg, S. L. Dvorak, W. Feng, Journal of Applied Geophysics, **136**, 211-218(2017)
4. K. Schoeman, P. Meyer, D. I. L. D..Villiers, Africon, 1-5(2013)
5. Y. Moursy, R. Iskander, M. M. Louërat, Mixed-Signal Testing Workshop, 1-6(2015)
6. B. Niklas, H. Garbe, M. Schaarschmidt, International Symposium on Electromagnetic Compatibility-Emc Europe. 1-6(2017)
7. H. S. Saini, J. M. Martinez, L. A. C. Lopes, Iet International Conference on Power Electronics, Machines and Drives IET, 1-6(2014)
8. J. A. Ferreira, Kane, I. J. Klinkert, IEEE Transactions on Industry Applications, **40**, 213-219(2017)
9. M. Stork, Radioelektronika. IEEE, 1-4(2017)

Research on Block-Based Blind Identification of High-rate Punctured Convolutional Codes

Hua Yan [1,*], *Ying* Huang [1], *Baoguo* Li [1] ,and *Jing* Lei [1]

[1] College of Electronic Science, National University of Defense Technology, Chang Sha, Hunan Province, China

Abstract. Aiming at the large amount of memory in high bit rate punctured convolutional codes, a soft recognition algorithm based on block Hadamard matrix (B-SWHT) is proposed. By using the idea of block Hadamard matrix operation, the soft WHT algorithm with excellent fault-tolerance performance is applied to the recognition of high-rate punctured convolutional codes. The simulation experiments show that the algorithm can effectively reduce the memory required for the recognition of high-rate punctured convolutional codes while maintaining high fault-tolerance performance. This paper provides a feasible solution for the identification of high bit rate punctured convolutional codes.

1 Introduction

In the face of poor and time-varying wireless communication channels, in order to ensure communication quality, a communication system is usually designed based on the worst-case channel conditions. However, this also causes a problem that the channel capacity cannot be fully utilized. Adaptive Modulation and Coding (AMC) can adjust the parameters of the transmitter (such as modulation method and coding method) in real time according to the change of channel quality, so as to ensure that the channel is fully utilized. Because the channel environment is constantly changing, the parameter information of the transmitter is limited by various aspects in practical applications and cannot be transmitted to the receiver in real time. Therefore, how to quickly identify the channel coding system based on the signal and data received by the receiver is the key to recovering the original information sequence. This shows that the analysis and identification of channel coding play an important role in practical communication applications.

Because of its simple structure, variable code rate, and strong versatility of decoding, punctured convolutional codes have been widely used in satellite communication systems, mobile communication systems, and deep space communication systems, and their identification methods have also become a hot topic. Literature [1] proposed a method of identifying punctured convolutional codes by using the constraint relationship between generator polynomial matrix and check polynomial matrix. The disadvantage of this method is that there are many unknowns in the process of solving the linear equations, and the number of iterations of the algorithm is larger, which leads to higher recognition complexity. A $1/n$ code rate convolutional code is divided into a number of $1/2$ code rate convolutional codes, and Walsh-Hadamard transform is used to solve the $1/2$ code rate convolutional code check matrix [2]. This realizes the blind recognition of a $1/n$ convolutional code at a high error rate. However, this method is limited by the memory space of the computer and cannot solve the high-dimensional check matrix. According to the soft information of the received sequence, the cumulative log-likelihood ratio of the code-word verification relationship is calculated, and the recognition accuracy is estimated [3]. This method fully utilizes the reliability information of the bit-symbols to improve the fault-tolerant capability of the code recognition. However, the problem with this method is that the soft decision algorithm is based on a specific set of code constraints to identify it, and it cannot perform full blind recognition. For the problem of hard-decision loss of a large amount of sequence information, it is proposed to introduce the sequence soft information into the frequency sequence to improve the fault-tolerant performance of the algorithm [4]. Due to the limitation of the memory space of the computer, using the WHT algorithm does not identify the punctured convolutional code with a higher code rate. In summary, the WHT algorithm is widely used. However, the algorithm requires a large amount of storage when it is used to identify high-rate punctured convolutional codes, which exceeds the range that the computer can handle. In this paper, based on the WHT algorithm of soft decision sequences, this paper proposes a blind recognition algorithm based on block Hadamard matrix for high bit rate punctured convolutional codes. While taking full advantage of the fault-tolerant performance of the WHT algorithm, the algorithm can effectively reduce the computational memory required for identifying high-rate punctured convolutional codes

* Corresponding author: 28113901@qq.com

through block-based Hadamard matrix operations. Therefore, it has good application value.

2 Punctured convolutional code

Punctured convolutional code can generally construct a punctured convolutional code of any $n-1/n$ code rate by a convolutional code with a code rate of $1/2$ [5].Therefore, in this paper, we focus on various optimal punctured convolutional codes generated by $1/2$ code rate convolutional codes, and illustrate the blind recognition algorithm based on block Hadamard matrix.

Let F be a binary domain, $F[D]$ be a polynomial ring, and $F(D)$ be a rational function domain. A convolutional code with a code rate of $1/2$ can be represented as any one-dimensional subspace C on $F(D)^2$. If $G(D)$ is a matrix of 1×2 on $F(D)$ and the row vector forms a set of bases of C, $G(D)$ is said to be A generator matrix for C. If $G(D)$ is a polynomial generator matrix and $G(0)$ is full rank, $G(D)$ is called an encoding matrix.

For a convolutional code C with a code rate of $1/2$, the information sequence $U(D)=\sum_{i=0}^{\infty}u_i D^i$ is input, and the coded output code sequence is $V(D)=\left(\sum_{i=0}^{\infty}v_{i,0}D^i,\sum_{i=0}^{\infty}v_{i,1}D^i\right)$. By constructing a high-rate punctured code by the $1/2$-rate convolutional code, it is first necessary to equivalently split the information sequence and the code sequence, and then delete the specific position of the output codeword. Finally, the code with the increased code rate is obtained. As shown in Figure 1.

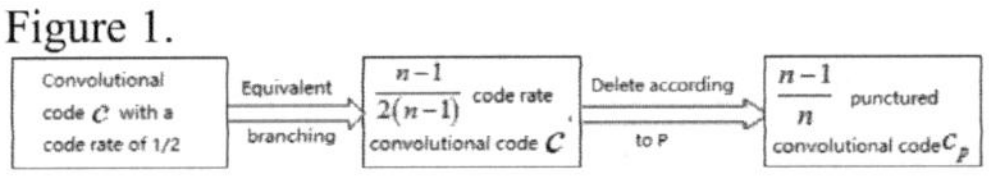

Fig. 1. Construction of a punctured convolutional code

3 Recognition of punctured convolutional codes based on B-SWHT

3.1 Walsh-Hadamard algorithm

According to the theorem of punctured convolutional codes, a punctured convolutional code with an arbitrary code rate $n-1/n$ has only a unique minimum check polynomial. Therefore, the classical Walsh-Hadamard transform algorithm can identify the simplest check polynomial of the punctured convolutional code of the equivalent code rate by using the conventional n-1/n convolutional code generating codeword. The recognition principle of WHT algorithm [2] is as follows.

Let $H_P(D)^T=(h_0(D),h_1(D),\cdots,h_{n-1}(D))$ be the check polynomial matrix of C_P, and use the relationship between the convolutional code generation matrix and the check matrix $G_P(D)\bullet H_P(D)^T=0$, when the received data length $N>n\times(m+1)$ (where m is the coding constraint degree).According to the received sequence $R_P(D)$ in the case of high bit error, a parity check matrix of C_P can be obtained by solving a set of solution vectors satisfying the largest number of equations in the system of the faulty linear equations in equation (1).

$$\sum_{j=0}^{m}\sum_{i=1}^{n}r_{i,j+s}h_{i,m-j}=0, s=0,1,\cdots,N \tag{1}$$

Convert (1) to a system of binary equations:

$$\begin{bmatrix} r_{1,0} & \cdots & r_{n,0} & \cdots & r_{1,\mathrm{m}} & \cdots & r_{n,\mathrm{m}} \\ r_{1,1} & \cdots & r_{n,1} & \cdots & r_{1,\mathrm{m}+1} & \cdots & r_{n,\mathrm{m}+1} \\ \vdots & & \vdots & & \vdots & & \vdots \\ r_{1,N} & \cdots & r_{n,N} & \cdots & r_{1,\mathrm{m}+N} & \cdots & r_{\mathrm{n},\mathrm{m}+N} \end{bmatrix} \begin{bmatrix} h_{1,\mathrm{m}} \\ \vdots \\ h_{n,\mathrm{m}} \\ \vdots \\ h_{1,0} \\ \vdots \\ h_{n,0} \end{bmatrix} = 0 \tag{2}$$

The equations (2) indicate that the received sequence $R_P(D)$ is grouped by lengths, each set of codeword vectors is expressed as a decimal number, and the resulting frequency sequence $\eta=\left[\eta_0,\eta_1,\cdots,\eta_{2^{n(m+1)}-1}\right]$ is constructed using the obtained decimal numbers. Then perform WHT operation on η:

$$z=\eta\bullet H_{2^{n(m+1)}} \tag{3}$$

In the formula, $z=\left[z_0,z_1,\cdots,z_{2^{n(m+1)}-1}\right]$ is a Walsh spectrum of η, and $H_{2^{n(m+1)}}$ is a Hadamard matrix of order $n(m+1)$. The binary vector i_{bin} corresponding to the position of the largest element z_i in the Walsh spectrum is the check sequence of the encoding.

3.2 Soft decision frequency sequence

The classical Walsh-Hadamard transform method is based on the hard-decision 0,1 sequence of the received sequence to construct the frequency coefficient, because the decision function has only 0,1 values, and the frequency coefficient can not reflect the size of the judgment probability, thus resulting in the loss of estimation performance. The soft decision frequency sequence is used in [3] to make full use of the reliability information of bit symbols to improve the fault tolerance of code recognition.

The model of the communication system is shown in Figure2. The information bit $b=[b_1,b_2,\cdots,b_k]$ is coded to generate a code sequence $c=[c_1,c_2,\cdots,c_n]$, and after adding a specific modulation method, it is transmitted through the channel. The received symbol can be represented as $r_i=s_i+n_i$, where s_i represents the BPSK modulation symbol (binary $0 \to +1, 1 \to -1$) and n_i represents additive white Gaussian noise (mean value 0, variance is $N_0/2$). Using the received sequence r, the soft information $\ell = [\ell_1, \cdots, \ell_n]$ of the codeword C can be calculated, where ℓ_i represents the posterior log likelihood ratio (LLR) of the codeword c_i:

$$\ell_i = \log\left(\frac{\Pr(c_i = 0|r)}{\Pr(c_i = 1|r)}\right) \tag{4}$$

Assuming that the BPSK signal is transmitted over the AWGN channel, the soft information can be expressed as:

$$\ell_i = \Lambda(c_i|r_i) = \frac{4r_i}{N_0} \tag{5}$$

At the same time, the received sequence r is grouped according to the length $n(m+1)$ and is composed of N decision equation coefficient vectors $r_0, r_1, \cdots, r_{N-1}$. We can define the sequence vector soft decision function as:

$$f_{soft}(r_i, k) = \begin{cases} \underset{\substack{j=0,\cdots,n(m+1)-1 \\ i=0,\cdots,N-1}}{\boxplus} \ell^i_j & , r_{i,dec} = k \\ 0 & , r_{i,dec} \neq k \end{cases} \tag{6}$$

among them

$$\ell_1 \boxplus \ell_2 = \text{sign}(\ell_1)\text{sign}(\ell_2)\min(|\ell_1||\ell_2|) + f(|\ell_1 + \tag{7}$$

The soft-decision frequency coefficients available for sequence vectors are:

$$\eta_k = \sum_{i=0}^{N-1} f_{soft}(r_i, k), k = 0, 1, \cdots, 2^{n(m+1)} - 1 \tag{8}$$

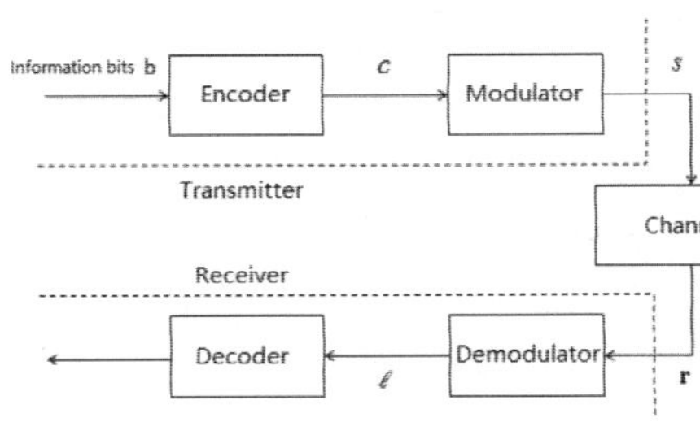

Fig. 2. Communication system model

3.3 Identify check polynomials based on block Hadamard matrix

The punctured convolutional code improves the code rate and the transmission rate, but its high dimensionality limits the application of the traditional WHT algorithm. For a $n-1/n$ punctured convolutional code generated by a $1/2$ source convolutional code. In the calculation of the traditional WHT algorithm, the Hadamard matrix has a size of $2^{n(m+1)} \times 2^{n(m+1)}$ and requires $4^{n(m+1)}$ memory to store it. When the code rate of the convolutional code is removed by 7/8 and the code memory m=6, the required memory reaches the order of $10^{34} bit$, which far exceeds the storable space of the computer. In this regard, this paper proposes an algorithm based on the block Hadamard matrix, which greatly reduces the required operating storage space, enabling the WHT algorithm to handle the identification of high-dimensional punctured convolutional codes. The algorithm identification process is as follows:

Step 1: Assume that the received sequence of the $(n, n-1, m)$ punctured convolutional code is $R_P(D)$, group $R_P(D)$ into $n(m+1)$ lengths, and represent each set of codeword vectors as a decimal number. The resulting N decimal numbers are used to construct the frequency sequence $\eta = [\eta_0, \eta_1, \cdots, \eta_{2^{n(m+1)}-1}]$.

Step 2: When $n(m+1)$ is an even number, divide the $n(m+1)$ -length vector of codewords into equal parts, that is, divide η by $2^{n(m+1)/2}$ to get $\eta_d = [\eta_{d_0}, \eta_{d_1}, \cdots, \eta_{d_{2^{n(m+1)/2}-1}}]$. Among them, $\eta_{d_0} = [\eta_0, \eta_1, \cdots, \eta_{2^{n(m+1)/2}-1}]$, $\eta_{d_1} = [\eta_{2^{n(m+1)/2}}, \eta_{2^{n(m+1)/2}+1}, \cdots, \eta_{2 \cdot 2^{n(m+1)/2}-1}]$, $\cdots$, $\eta_{d_{2^{n(m+1)/2}-1}} = [\eta_{(2^{n(m+1)/2}-1) \cdot 2^{n(m+1)/2}}, \eta_{(2^{n(m+1)/2}-1) \cdot 2^{n(m+1)/2}+1}, \cdots, \eta_{2^{n(m+1)}-1}]$. When $n(m+1)$ is odd, the difference is only that the separation length is different.

Step 3: According to the frequency sequence after the equalization, the $2^{n(m+1)}$ -order Hadamard matrix is correspondingly divided into $2^{n(m+1)/2}$ $2^{n(m+1)/2}$ -order Hadamard matrices, namely:

$$H_{2^{n(m+1)}} = \begin{bmatrix} H_{2^{n(m+1)/2}} & H_{2^{n(m+1)/2}} & \cdots & H_{2^{n(m+1)/2}} \\ H_{2^{n(m+1)/2}} & H_{2^{n(m+1)/2}} & \cdots & H_{2^{n(m+1)/2}} \\ \vdots & \vdots & & \vdots \\ H_{2^{n(m+1)/2}} & H_{2^{n(m+1)/2}} & \cdots & H_{2^{n(m+1)/2}} \end{bmatrix} \tag{9}$$

Step 4: Calculate the equidistant frequency sequence and the block Hadamard matrix to obtain the spectral coefficients of the block algorithm:

$$z_d^T = [z_{d_0}, z_{d_1}, \cdots, z_{d_{2^{n(m+1)/2}-1}}]^T = H_{2^{n(m+1)}}{}^T \cdot \eta_d{}^T \tag{10}$$

Step 5: Determine the position of the largest element in the entire Walsh spectral coefficient by comparing the largest elements in the $2^{n(m+1)/2}$ z_{d_i}, so that the check sequence can be obtained.

From the above algorithm identification process, it can be seen that once a block Hadamard algorithm reduces the Hadamard matrix operation that originally requires $2^{n(m+1)} \bullet 2^{n(m+1)} = 2^{2n(m+1)} bit$ storage space to only $2^{n(m+1)/2} \bullet 2^{n(m+1)/2} = 2^{n(m+1)} bit$, the algorithm can continue to perform secondary blocking and reduce the required storage space to $2^{n(m+1)/2} bit$ size. It can be seen that there is a significant reduction in operating storage requirements compared to the classic WHT algorithm.

4 Simulation and analysis

Consider the $1/2$ code rate convolutional codes of four different constraint degrees, ie, the $(2,1,2)$、$(2,1,3)$、$(2,1,4)$、$(2,1,5)$ convolutional codes, and perform the WHT algorithm operations on the soft and hard decision frequency sequences respectively. Through Monte Carlo experiments, the recognition performance of the two recognition algorithms for different convolutional codes is compared. The simulation results are shown in Figure 3.

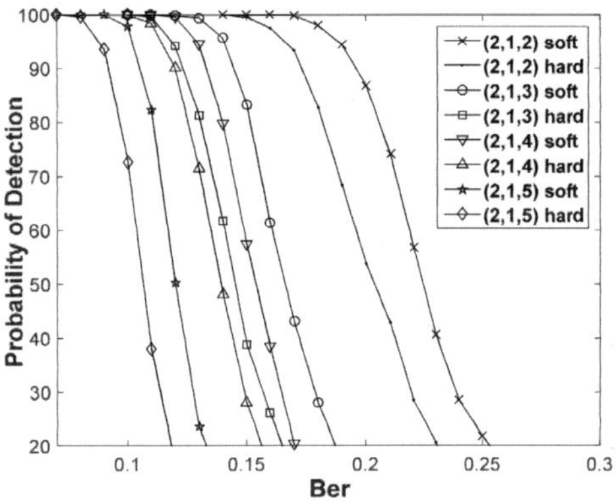

Fig. 3.WHT algorithm performance comparison of soft and hard-decision frequency sequences with 1/2 code rate convolutional code

Among them, the number of simulations is 1000, and the number of decision equations is $N = 1000$. Using BPSK modulation, the channel model is AWGN model. It can be seen from the experimental results that the performance of the WHT algorithm is significantly improved by the soft decision frequency sequence.For example, when the $(2,1,2)$ convolutional code is at a bit error rate of 0.2, the hard-decision-frequency sequence WHT algorithm can only achieve 50% correct recognition probability, and the soft-decision frequency sequence WHT algorithm can achieve more than 85% correct recognition probability.

The identification of punctured convolutional codes with $n-1/n$ code rate is based on a $1/2$ code rate source convolutional code. On the $1/2$ code rate convolutional codes that the classic WHT algorithm can handle, the block Hadamard matrix algorithm is used to reduce the running memory of the algorithm while not reducing the recognition performance. For the different code rate punctured convolutional codes generated on the basis of the $(2,1,6)$ convolutional code, when using the block Hadamard algorithm, the reduction of the running storage volume is shown in Figure 4 .As we can be seen from the figure, the algorithm based on the block Hadamard matrix reduces the amount of running memory required to identify high-rate punctured convolutional codes to the computer-processable range (10^9). For example, for a $7/8$ code rate convolutional code generated on the basis of a $(2,1,6)$ convolutional code, the running memory amount is reduced from $10^{33} bit$ to $10^8 bit$ after passing twice a block Hadamard algorithm.

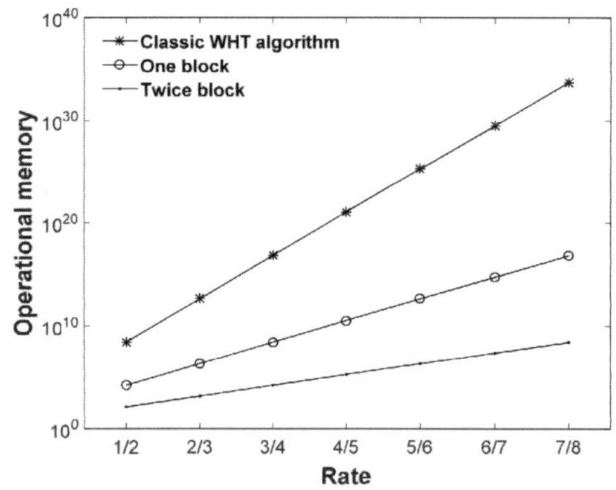

Fig. 4. Operational storage of different code rate punctured convolutional codes

The soft decision sequence algorithm based on block Hadamard matrix proposed in this paper identifies the syndrome relations of punctured convolutional codes. Figure 5 shows the recognition performance of the $2/3$ code rate convolutional code generated by the $(2,1,6)$ convolutional code when the received data amount is 21000. It can be seen from the figure that the soft decision recognition algorithm based on the block Hadamard matrix can not only reduce the running storage to the computer-processable range, but also maintain the recognition performance of the classic WHT algorithm at high bit error rate.

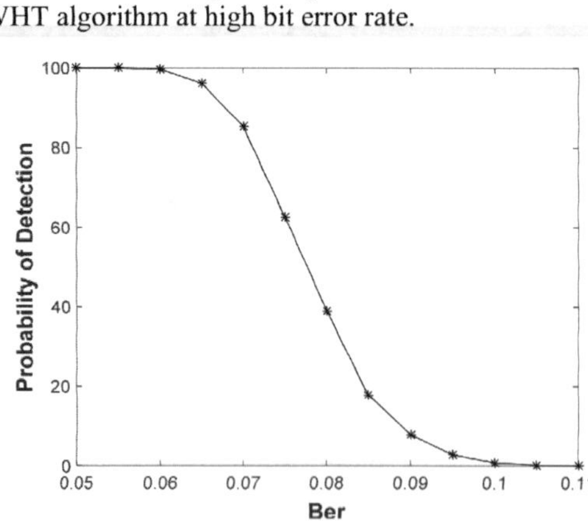

Fig. 5. The B-SWHT algorithm recognition performance of $2/3$ code rate punctured convolutional codes generated with $(2,1,6)$ convolutional codes

5 Conclusions

This paper proposes a punctured convolutional code recognition algorithm based on B-SWHT and compares the fault-tolerance performance of $1/2$ code rate convolutional codes with different constraint degrees under the WHT algorithm of soft and hard decision sequence, this verifies that the soft decision reliability information improves the fault-tolerant performance of the WHT algorithm. By introducing soft decision frequency sequences, the combination of soft information and the classic WHT algorithm is realized, which ensures the excellent fault tolerance of the algorithm. At the same time, the idea of block Hadamard matrix is used to solve the problem of high storage capacity for high-rate deconvolution. Based on the code rate punctured convolutional codes generated on the basis of $(2,1,6)$ convolutional codes, the reduction of the running storage capacity after using the block Hadamard algorithm is analyzed. The simulation performance of the $2/3$ code punctured convolutional code generated by the $(2,1,6)$ convolutional code is analyzed. It can be seen from the simulation results that using this algorithm, excellent fault tolerance can be guaranteed. And can reduce the amount of running storage to a range that the computer can handle. Therefore, this algorithm has important application value for the recognition of high bit rate punctured convolutional codes. With the increase of code rate, the time complexity of the classic WHT algorithm is an area that needs further research and improvement.

References

1. Lu Pei-zhong , Shen Li , Zou Yan , etal. Blind recognition of punctured convolutional codes[J].Science in china Ser Information Sciences,2005,48(4):484-498.
2. Liu Jian , Wang Xiao-jun, Zhou Xi-yuan, Blind Recognition of Convolutional Coding Based on Walsh-Hadamard Transform[J],Journal of Electronic and Information Technology, 2010,32(4):884-888.
3. R. Moosavi and E. G. Larsson ,"Fast blind recognition of channel codes," IEEE Trans. Commun., vol.62,no.5,pp.1393-1405,May 2014.
4. HUANG Kai-zhi, CHEN Song. A soft fast estimation method of PN sequence based on weighting Walsh- Hadamard transform (WHT) [J]. Journal of Electronic & Information Technology , 2013 , 35(1) : 74-79.
5. SHEN B Z, PATAPOUTIAN A, McEWEN P A. Punctured recursive convolutional encodes and their applications in turbo codes[J]. IEEE Trans on inform Theory,2001,47(5):2300-2320.
6. You Ling, Zhu zhong-liang, The application of Walsh Function in Resolving of F(2) equations[J].Signal Processing, 2000,16 (12) : 27-31.
7. J. G. Proakis and M. Salehi, Digital Communication, 5th ed. McGraw-Hill,2008.
8. Qi Lin, Hao Shi-qi, Wang Lei, Blind decoding algorithm of punctured convolutional codes based on improved WHT[J], Application Research of Computers, 2011,28（4）：1457-1459.
9. Yu Pei-dong, Li Jing, Peng Hua, A Novel Algorithm for Channel Coding Recogniton Using Soft-Decision[J], Acta Electronica Sinica,2013, 41（2）：301-306.
10. Peidong Yu, Hua Peng, Jing Li,"On Blind Recognition of Channel Codes Within a Candidate Set,"IEEE Commun.Lett.,vol.20,no.4,pp.736-739,Apr.2016.

Study on a Quantitative Analysis Method for Pulse Compression Results

MA Linzhi[1,*], Wang Min[1], WENG Chenxiang[1], and SHI Zhouyan[1]

[1] Air Force Early Warning Academy, Wuhan 430019, China

Abstract. In order to further improve the ability of detecting and evaluating the detection performance and interference effect of the integrated signal, a quantitative analysis method (K-means quantization) for pulse compression is proposed. The method is based on the amplitude analysis of the pulse compression results. By using the improved K-means clustering method, the recognition degree of the selected target points is obtained by induction and analysis. The simulation results show that the analysis of the detection performance or interference performance of the integrated signal is consistent with the traditional analysis conclusion by using K-means quantization method. It has better measurability, objectivity and independence, which can be used for automatic evaluation of the system..

1 INTRODUCTION

In the detection performance analysis of integrated signal, the quantitative parameters such as radar detection are commonly used as evaluation indexes. It plays an important role in evaluating the performance of integrated signal, and has the advantages of strong objectivity and high distinction. In the process of interference analysis, especially the related interference, the pulse compression diagram is often used for corresponding analysis and evaluation, which has the advantages of wide applicability and intuitive results. In view of the deception jamming effect of the pulse compression results, the quantitative analysis method of the peak to side lobe ratio (PSLR) [1] can achieve better results, but the ability of the coverage jamming effect is insufficient; the peak to average ratio (PAR)[3] is adopted for the coverage interference effect of the pulse compression results, but the analysis ability of deceptive jamming effect is insufficient; the subjective analysis[2,6]or subjective analysis with parameters[5,7] is more direct, but it is not conducive to the application of the evaluation system or to the comparative analysis, and the degree of subjective influence is heavier.

In order to synthesize the advantages of these methods, to improve the detection performance of the integrated signal and the ability to evaluate and analyze the interference effect, and to achieve the purpose of the performance of the automatic discriminant system, a method of quantitative analysis of the results of pulse compression (K-means quantization) is proposed. The quantitative parameters is obtained with the amplitude information of the pulse compression results, and it is used to evaluate the detection effect and interference effect, so as to improve the applicability and accuracy of the evaluation index[4].And the feasibility of the quantitative analysis method in signal performance analysis and jamming effect analysis is simulated.

2 PULSE COMPRESSION TECHNOLOGY

Usually, pulse compression technology is used for special radar signals, and the Linear Frequency Modulation (LFM) signal is more representative. It is used as an example to analyze the pulse compression process. The LFM signal can be expressed as:

$$s(t) = A\exp(j2\pi(f_0 t + \frac{1}{2}(\frac{B}{T})t^2)) \quad (1)$$

In the formula, is the amplitude of the signal, is the initial frequency, is the signal bandwidth, and is the signal pulse width. The response of the corresponding matched filter can be expressed as:

$$h(t) = s^*(-t) \quad (2)$$

In the formula, is a complex conjugate signal with time inversion. The output results of the pulse compression can be expressed as

$$p(t) = s(t) \otimes h(t) \quad (3)$$

In the formula, means convolution. Combined with (1) (2) and the formula (3) can be expressed as:

* Corresponding author: gbgzbz@163.com

$$p(t) = A\sqrt{D}\,\mathrm{sinc}(\pi Bt)\exp(\mathrm{j}2\pi f_0 t)$$

(4)

In the formula, D is the pulse compression ratio, $D = BT$. From the formula (4), it can be seen that the result of pulse compression is a function. Compared with the original LFM signal, the target response pulse width is reduced by D times and the amplitude has changed to D times. It is obviously that the result of pulse compression has higher amplitude in target corresponding position, while the amplitude of other locations is much lower than the target location. This characteristic is used to measure the detection ability of signals.

3 QUANTITATIVE ANALYSIS ALGORITHM

From the previous analysis results, it can be seen that the analysis often start with the peak value of the actual target. When analyzing the performance of integrated signal detection, it is generally considered whether the ratio between the peak value of the main-lobe and the side-lobe reaches the requirement. In the jamming effect evaluating, whether can the pulse compression results of the jamming signal effectively cover the response of the target position or form a higher false target response plays an important role in it. In order to realize evaluating the performance of the signal and the jamming effect automatically, a quantitative algorithm for this result is designed on the premise of not changing the information from the amplitude and it is designed based on the idea of K-means clustering algorithm. The K-means algorithm was first proposed by Macqueen in 1967, and it is a simple unsupervised learning algorithm[8]. The algorithm owns the advantages of fast convergence and good clustering effect.

Considering that the analysis of the results of pulse compression is based on the peak of the image and the cluster result of the K-means algorithm is easily affected by the initial selection. In order to reduce these effects, the algorithm is improved properly and the quantization result of the algorithm is called the recognition degree. The improved algorithm is designed as follows:

Step1: If the amplitude of all points in pulse compression image is recorded as $A = \{a_i\}$, $i = 1,2,3\ldots$, and the target point is a_x , $x \le i_{\max}$. For each point in the image, it will be selected when it satisfies $a_{i-1} < a_i < a_{i+1}$. All the selected points are recorded as b_i , whose collection is written as B .

Step2: If $a_x \notin B$, that means the target point is not one of the selected points, the target point will not be confirmed as the true target point, and the recognition degree will be 0; If $\{a_x\} = B$, that means only the target point is the selected point, the target point will surely be confirmed as the true target point, and the recognition degree will be 1. If these two conditions are not satisfied, the Step3 will be taken.

Step3: Cluster the selected points for analysis: Select 4 determined cluster initial centers as p_1 , p_2 , p_3 , p_4 . p_1 represents the amplitude of the target point, that is $p_1 = a_x$; p_2 stands for the high sidelobe cluster center, and $p_2 = a_x/2$; $p_3 = a_x/31$ according to the ratio 30dB of the main and sidelobes, which is set for the radar's clear recognition of target; As a low side-lobe clustering center, $p_4 = 0$ is taken. The result of cluster is recorded as C_1 , C_2 , C_3 , C_4 .

Step4: It is believed that the points of C_1 and C_2 have a strong influence on the detection of the target point. Therefore, all the points of C_1 and C_2 are taken as average values and recorded as m_1 and m_2 ; It is believed that the points of C_3 and C_4 have a little influence on the detection of the target point, so all points in C_3 and C_4 retain their maximum value , which are recorded as m_3 and m_4 .Finally, the recognition degree is calculated according to the calculation method of geometric probability. If the recognition degree is recorded as P , it can be expressed as:

$$P = \frac{a_x}{m1 + m2 + m3 + m4}$$

(5)

According to formula (5), it is obviously that if the recognition degree used for signal ability analysis, the higher the P value, the better the signal pulse compression results; If used for the assessment of interference effects, the lower the P value, the better the jamming effect. The algorithm process uses a flow chart as follows:

 https://doi.org/10.1051/matecconf/201817601038

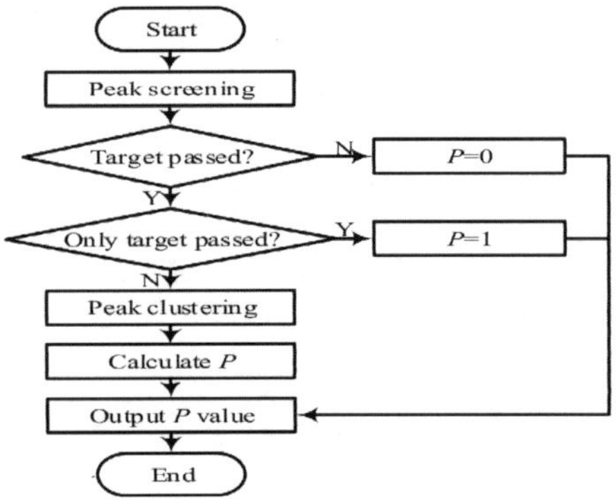

Fig.1, Algorithm flow chart

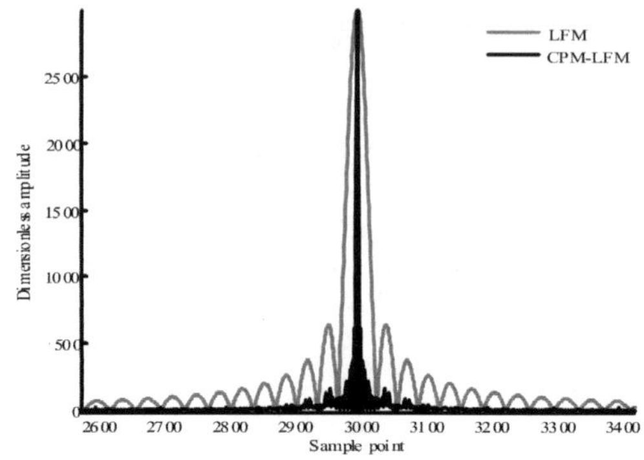

Fig.2, Pulse compression without Hamming window

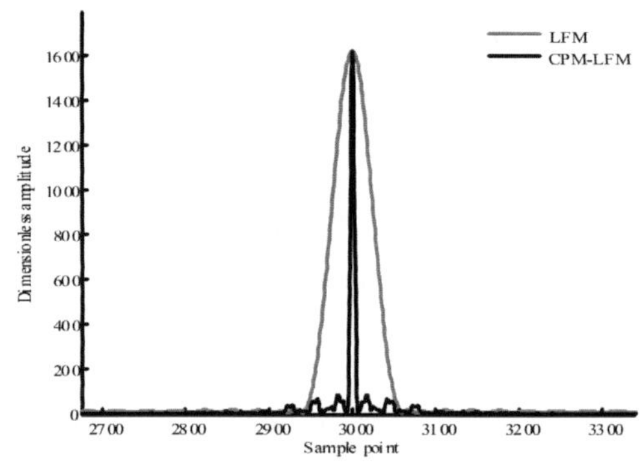

Fig.3, Pulse compression with Hamming window

4 SIMULATION

It can be used that the same objects and simulation conditions, When assessing the signal detection performance, the LFM signal and the intrapulse modulated 20-symbol Continuous Phase Modulation-LFM (CPM-LFM) signal were compared and analyzed in the absence of noise. When assessing the jamming effect, the jamming effects of radio frequency(RF) noise interference and convolution noise interference on the LFM signal under the same jamming-to-signal ratio are evaluated.

4.1 Signal Performance Evaluation

Simulation of LFM signal parameter is set to: Time width , bandwidth , sampling frequency , carrier frequency .Supplementary setting for CPM-LFM are association length , modulation coefficient ,and the random symbols are [1,-1,-1,1,-1,1,1,-1,-1,1,1,-1,-1,1,-1,1,1,-1,-1,1]. Windowing technology is commonly used sidelobe suppression technology in pulse compression technology. For radar signals, windowing is often used to increase the ratio of main and sidelobes and improve signal capability. Therefore, the time-domain pulse compression simulations are performed on the above two signals, and the addition of a Hamming window is considered. Select the PLSR method and K-means evaluation method to evaluate. The results are expressed as and , as follows:

The simulation results without windowing are: $S_{\text{LFM}} = 13.3987$, $S_{\text{CPM-LFM}} = 13.7019$, $P_{\text{LFM}} = 0.8136$, $P_{\text{CPM-LFM}} = 0.8188$; The simulation results of windowing are: $S_{\text{LFM}} = 40.6420$, $S_{\text{CPM-LFM}} = 25.8898$, $P_{\text{LFM}} = 0.9908$, $P_{\text{CPM-LFM}} = 0.9404$ when using Hamming window. It can be seen from the results that the LFM signal has high sidelobes and its windowless recognition is slightly lower than that of the CPM-LFM signal. In other words, the pulse compression effect of the CPM-LFM signal is better than that of the LFM signal, which is consistent with the conclusion obtained by the PSLR method. The algorithm can also determine the performance of the signal pulse pressure results after windowing. Compared with the recognisability without window processing, the recognisability of the two signals after windowing has been significantly improved. It can also be concluded that the result of the two signals plus the Hamming window is that the LFM signal is superior to the CPM-LFM signal, and the conclusion is consistent.

4.2 Assessment of Jamming Effect

Select the LFM signal as the target, taking the two interference technologies of radio frequency noise and convolution noise interference as examples, the proposed algorithm is used to analyze the interference effects of two interference technologies. The parameter is consistent with the parameter setting of the LFM signal in 3.1. Generally speaking, convolution noise interference as a form of smart interference, the radar jamming effect on the pulse compression system is superior to radio frequency noise interference under the same power conditions. Noise has a certain degree of randomness, it can cause fluctuations in the results. Therefore, 800 simulations are performed for each of the different ratios. The result obtained by the Monte Carlo method is used as the final identifiable degree under the condition of the jam to signal ratio. The simulation results are as follows:

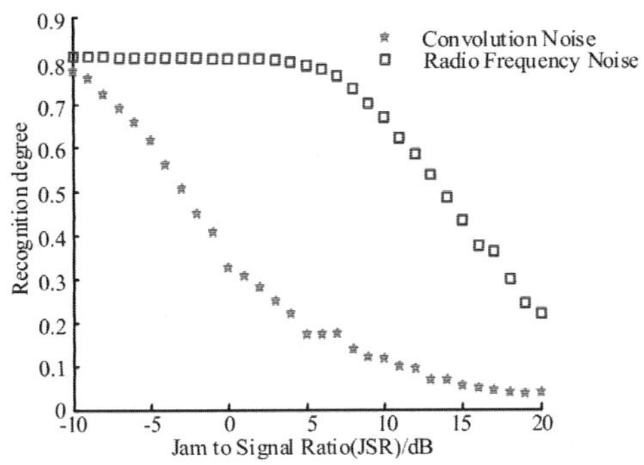

Fig.4, Recognition degree under different interference styles

It can be clearly seen from Figure 4 that the identifiable degree is basically the same under the influence of different interference patterns. The highest value approaches 0.8, which is close to the previously no-noise identifiable degree; Recognition of the target point may be the convolution of the signal noise interference are set in the jam to signal ratio are lower than the range of variation of RF noise, it is superior to RF interference noise, as expected conclusion.

5 CONCLUSIONS

Aimed at the subjectivity existing in the result analysis of pulse compression image, a quantitative method based on clustering analysis is proposed. The simulation shows that the results of the algorithm are consistent with the traditional methods in the evaluation of signal pulse compression performance and jamming effect, and the correctness of the algorithm is demonstrated. The results can be applied to the evaluation system directly. However, the algorithm can not take into account the influence factors besides amplitude, such as the influence of main lobe width on target recognition. This is the place that still needs improving.

References

1. P.L.NIAN, C.H.LU. Jamming suppression of pulse compression radar based on frequency-shifting filter. Telecommunication Engineering, **57**,1152 (2017).
2. Q.TONG. Evaluation of Jamming Effect of Pulse-compression Radar . XIDIAN University,47 (2014)
3. G.Q.SHEN, B.WU, B.HUANG. Research on radar anti-jamming performance based on spectrum sharing. China Radio, **5**,35 (2011)
4. B.Y.WANG, R.B.GAN, J.R.ZHANG, Overview of Electronic Countermeasure Operational Effectiveness Evaluation.Electronic Information Warfare Technology, **32**,54 (2017)
5. Y.C.WU. Research of active jamming to pulse compression radar. University of Electronic Science and Technology of China, 30 (2014)
6. H.LV. Rearch on jamming system of pulse compression radar and jamming effect evaluation , XIDIAN University,51 (2015).
7. S.W.ZHOU, J.YAN, Y.S.ZHOU. Study on square-wave frequency-shifting jamming to linear frequency modulation pulse compression radars.Journal of Telemetry, Tracking and Command,**38**,58 (2017)
8. J.C.HUANG. Improvement and Application of K-means algorithm .Changsha: Central South University, 5 (2013).

Research on Track Deception Technology Based on Jamming of Flexible Lines by Jammers

SHI Zhouyan[1,a], WANG Min[1,a], ZHANG Lu[1,a] , MA Linzhi[1,a]

[1]Air Force Early Warning Academy, Wuhan 430019, China;

Abstract: In order to effectively interfere with radar networks, this paper combines the principle of distance deception jamming and the traditional track deception jamming model, a track deception jamming model based on jamming aircraft flexible route penetration was established. The relevant motion parameter solving method flow is given and simulated. The results show that the model not only can achieve track deception, but also can effectively increase the degree of freedom of the jammers' invasion route, making the penetration route of the jammers more flexible and controllable than the traditional.

1 Introduction

In recent years, radar network technology has achieved rapid development. How to effectively interfere with the radar network and protect its own target has become an urgent problem to be solved. Among various types of interference, track deception and interference technology has the advantages of less resources and high interference utilization. Therefore, this technology has become a research hotspot in the field of electronic interference.

Reference [1] describes the principle of track deception; Reference [2] establishes a multi-aircraft coordinated track deception optimal control model; Reference [3] proposes a radar network track deception technique based on centralized track planning and distributed track coordination; Reference [4] proposed a mathematical model to optimize the interference track; Reference [5] simplifies the model of track deception jamming in drones; Reference [6] proposes a compensation technique. The above studies have achieved good results.

Above the researches, only consider how to generate a false track. Track fraud is mainly achieved through distance deception jamming technology[7]. In the case of false track determination, the movement of the jammers are constrained by false targets. In the study, the jammers' penetration routes are generally made parallel to the false track, which reduces the degree of freedom of the attack route from 3D to 1D[2]. To a great extent, it limits the movement of the jammers. However, in practice, when a multi-penetration radar network based composite interference press and deception[8-9],when the jammer formations are underway, it is sometimes necessary to avoid the radar to detect the exposed area or to adjust the penetration route to suppress the interference. This article presents a jammer flexible penetration of deception track model, the degree of freedom jammer route extended to two-dimensional, and the motion characteristics of the jammers are described by the parameter.

2 Basic Principles

Distance spoofing is the basis of track deception. The jammers intercept the radar pulse signal and forward it after the delay. The main lobe enters the radar receiver, thus producing realistic false targets on the radar. By setting the forwarding delay and controlling the distance between the false target and the radar, a false track can be generated on the radar. In the case of radar network penetration, false trajectories need to be deceived by jamming machines to interfere with all radars, so that false trajectories generated on different radars coincide in position, thereby realizing deception of radar tracks. Track deception diagram is shown in Figure 1.

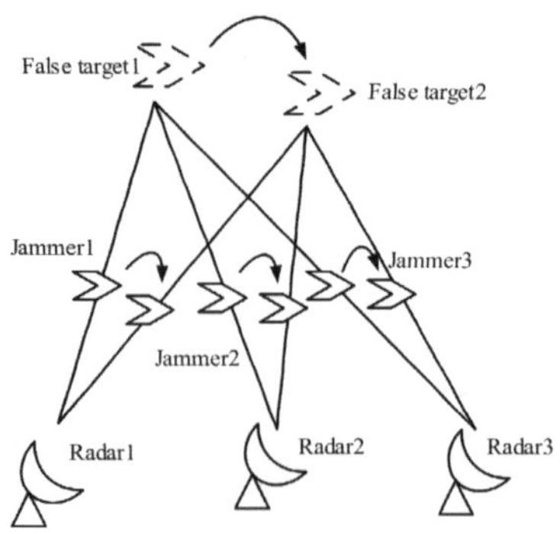

Fig.1. Track deception

Corresponding author: agbgzbz@163.com

From Figure 1, False radar track curves formed with a curved surface, with the premise to the environment and allow the jammers' performance, only these jammers held on the surface. Therefore, this feature can be used to flexibly control the jammers route.

In order to implement the jammers' flexible route penetration, the following conditions must be met:

1) Each jammer flexibility to adjust the velocity of flight, azimuth and elevation, to ensure the radar in connection with false targets.

2) The jammer has Digital RF memory (DRFM), which can receive and delay the radar signal. This technology requires a high delay and therefore requires precise control of the delay time.

3) The location and number of radars are known to ensure that a jammer interferes with a radar.

4) The penetration line setting of the jammer needs to be performed with equipment performance and environment permitting.

3 Flexible Route Defense Mathematical Model

3.1 Sports Model

When there is only one-dimensional degree of freedom, and the jammer course is parallel to the false track, the description of the motion characteristics only needs to calculate the velocity and heading angle. In the process of flexible route penetration, it is necessary to describe its motion characteristics through velocity, velocity azimuth and velocity pitch angle, as shown in Figure 2.

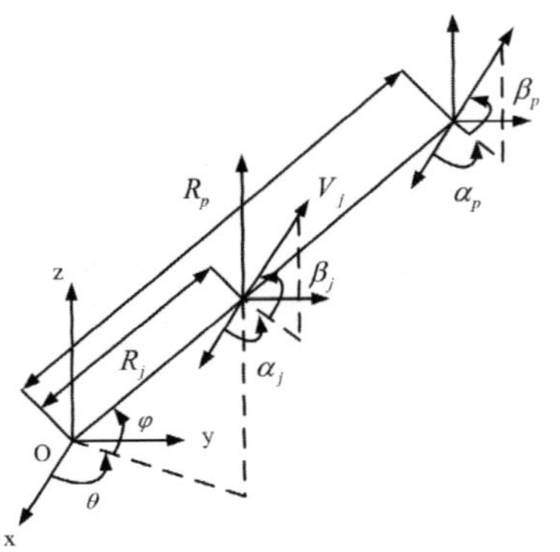

Fig. 2. Motion model

Among them, O, I, P represent radar, jammer and false target; R represents distance; V represents velocity; θ represents position azimuth; φ represents position pitch angle; α represents velocity azimuth; β represents velocity pitch angle. In the rectangular coordinate system, the equation of motion of jammer and false target can be expressed, as shown in formula (1).

$$\begin{cases} \dot{x}_i = V_i \cos\alpha_i \cos\beta_i \\ \dot{y}_i = V_i \sin\alpha_i \cos\beta_i \\ \dot{z}_i = V_i \sin\beta_i \end{cases} \quad (1)$$

Among them, $i = \begin{cases} p, \text{False target} \\ j, j\text{-th jammer} \end{cases}$; $\dot{\otimes}$ means '$\otimes$ derivative of time'. To facilitate the description of the relationship between radar, jammer and false target, the motion model can be converted to a spherical coordinate system with the origin of the radar through the relationship between the spatial Cartesian coordinate system and the spherical coordinate system. In the form of a matrix can be expressed, as shown in formula (2).

$$\begin{bmatrix} \dot{R}_i \\ R_i \dot{\theta} \cos\varphi \\ R_i \dot{\varphi} \end{bmatrix} = \begin{bmatrix} \cos\varphi\cos\theta & \cos\varphi\sin\theta & \sin\varphi \\ -\sin\theta & \cos\theta & 0 \\ -\sin\varphi\cos\theta & -\sin\varphi\sin\theta & \cos\varphi \end{bmatrix} \begin{bmatrix} \dot{x}_i \\ \dot{y}_i \\ \dot{z}_i \end{bmatrix} \quad (2)$$

Simultaneous formula (1) (2):

$$\dot{R}_i = V_i(\cos\varphi\cos\theta\cos\alpha_i\cos\beta_i + \cos\varphi\sin\theta\sin\alpha_i\cos\beta_i + \sin\varphi\sin\beta_i) \quad (3)$$

$$\dot{\theta} = \frac{V_i}{R\cos\varphi}(-\sin\theta\cos\alpha_i\cos\beta_i + \cos\theta\sin\alpha_i\cos\beta_i) \quad (4)$$

$$\dot{\varphi} = \frac{V_i}{R}(-\sin\varphi\cos\theta\cos\alpha_i\cos\beta_i - \sin\varphi\sin\theta\sin\alpha_i\cos\beta_i + \cos\varphi\sin\beta_i) \quad (5)$$

Simultaneous formula (3) (4) (5) can obtain velocity, velocity azimuth and velocity pitch angle, as shown in formula (6)~(8).

$$V_i = ((\dot{R}_i)^2 + (R_i\dot{\theta}\cos\varphi)^2 + (R_i\dot{\varphi})^2)^{1/2} \quad (6)$$

$$\alpha_i = \arctan(P/Q) \quad (7)$$

$$\beta_i = \arcsin(\frac{\dot{R}_i}{V_i} - P\cos\varphi\cos\theta - Q\cos\varphi\sin\theta) \quad (8)$$

In the above formulas,

$$\begin{cases} P = \frac{1}{V_i}(\dot{\theta} R_i \cos\varphi\cos\theta + \dot{R}_i \cos\varphi\sin\theta - \dot{\varphi} R_i \sin\varphi\sin\theta) \\ Q = \frac{1}{V_i}(-\dot{\theta} R_i \cos\varphi\sin\theta + \dot{R}_i \cos\varphi\cos\theta - \dot{\varphi} R_i \sin\varphi\cos\theta) \end{cases}.$$

From the above model, we need to calculate six coupling quantities to calculate equations (6)~(8),coupling quantities are: R 、 θ 、 φ 、 $\dot{R}$ 、 $\dot{\theta}$ and $\dot{\varphi}$ .From the geometric relationship of Figure 2, we can get the formula(9).

$$\begin{cases} R_i = \sqrt{(x_i - x_r)^2 + (y_i - y_r)^2 + (z_i - z_r)^2} \\ \theta = \arctan[(y_i - y_r)/(x_i - x_r)] \\ \varphi = \arcsin[(z_i - z_r)/r_i] \\ \dot{R}_i = [(x_i - x_r)\dot{x}_i + (y_i - y_r)\dot{y}_i + (z_i - z_r)\dot{z}_i]/R_i \\ \dot{\theta} = \dfrac{(x_i - x_r)\dot{y}_i - (y_i - y_r)\dot{x}_i}{\sqrt{(x_i - x_r)^2 + (y_i - y_r)^2}} \\ \dot{\varphi} = \dfrac{\dot{z}_i\sqrt{(x_i - x_r)^2 + (y_i - y_r)^2}}{r_i^2} - \\ \dfrac{(z_i - z_r)}{r_i^2}\dfrac{(x_i - x_r)\dot{x}_i + (y_i - y_r)\dot{y}_i}{\sqrt{(x_i - x_r)^2 + (y_i - y_r)^2}} \end{cases} \tag{9}$$

In summary, Jammer's movement status can be described by the formula (6) to (8).

3.2 Position Model

Interference by the establishment of the position of the model geometric relationships, coordinate jammers can be obtained. The coordinates of radar,jammers and false targets, with the formula (9) a coupling amount can be determined six, additional delay can be obtained from jamming, and then find the jammer to signal the delay amount is obtained.

To perform distance deception jamming on the radar, it is necessary to guarantee the jammer on the connection between the radar and the false target. The line between radar (x_r, y_r, z_r) and false targets (x_p, y_p, z_p) can be expressed, as shown in formula (10).

$$\frac{x - x_p}{x_r - x_p} = \frac{y - y_p}{y_r - y_p} = \frac{z - z_p}{z_r - z_p} \tag{10}$$

Start with the two-dimensional top view of the confrontation scenario, as shown in Figure 3. The route of the jammers can be set in a two-dimensional top view as required. Set the k-th jammer on the two-dimensional plane as $y = f_k(x)$.

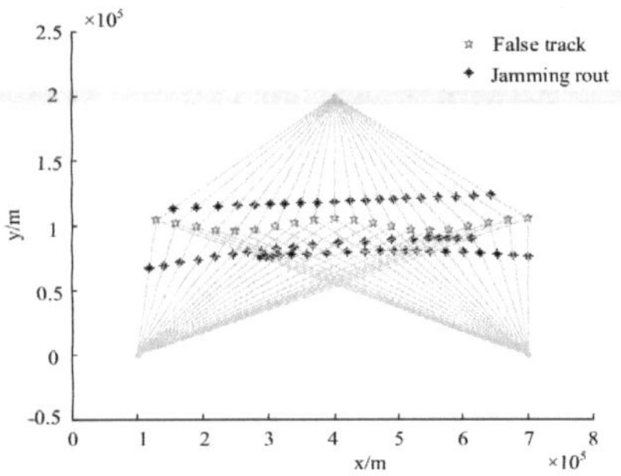

Fig.3. Interference 2D

Extend Figure 3 to three-dimensional space, At this point, $y = f_k(x)$ is represented as a surface perpendicular to the ground. The position of the jammers in the three-dimensional space is the intersection of the straight line and the curved surface $y = f_k(x)$ where the radar false target is located, as shown in Figure 4.

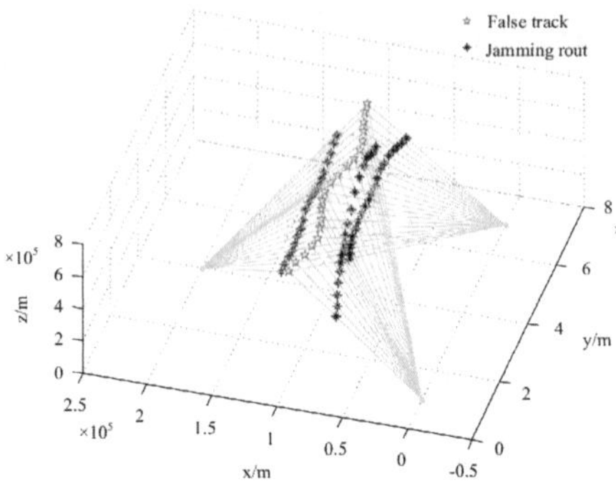

Fig.4. Interference 3D

Bring $y = f_k(x)$ into formula (10), the position of the jammers can be obtained, as shown in formula (11).

$$\begin{cases} x_i = (f_k(x_i) - y_p)(x_r - x_p)/(y_r - y_p) + x_p \\ y_i = f_k(x_i) \\ z_i = (f_k(x_i) - z_p)(z_r - z_p)/(y_r - y_p) + x_p \end{cases} \tag{11}$$

Finally, R_p and R_j are obtained from the coordinates of the radar, the jammers, and the dummy target, and the delay amount of the jammers to the signal can be obtained, as shown in formula (12).

$$\Delta t = \begin{cases} 2(R_p - R_j)/c & R_p < R_j \\ T_r + 2(R_p - R_j)/c & R_p > R_j \end{cases} \tag{12}$$

In summary, with N jammers, the solution steps for the flexible route penetration model as shown in Figure 5.

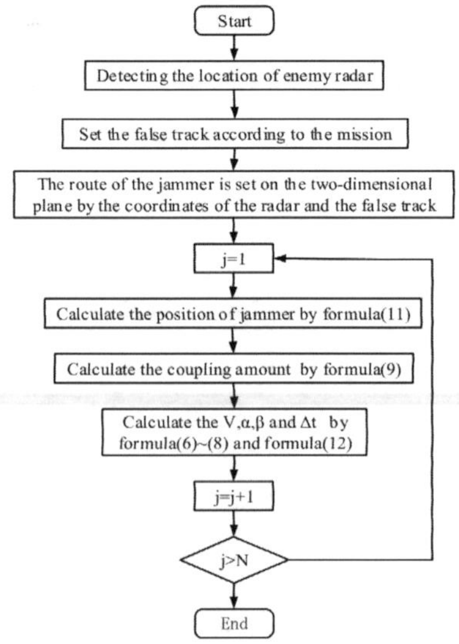

Fig.5. The model solution flowchart

4 Simulation Analysis

First of all, suppose the coordinates of the three radars of the enemy are $(1\times10^5,0,0)$, $(4\times10^5,2\times10^5,0)$, $(7\times10^5,0,0)$ (Unit: m). Track jamming on the radar network by three jammers, the flight time is 2000s. The starting point for planning a false track is $(1\times10^5, 1\times10^5, 0)$. The track expression as shown in formula (13).

$$\begin{cases} x = 1\times10^5 + 300t \\ y = 1\times10^5 + 5000\cos(0.002\pi t) \\ z = 6000 \end{cases} \tag{13}$$

The assumed operational needs, set the surface expression perpendicular to the ground where the jammer is located to be formula (14).

$$\begin{cases} y_1 = -10^{-7}(x - 6\times10^5)^2 + 9\times10^4 \\ y_2 = 0.02x + 1.1\times10^5 \\ y_3 = -10^{-7}(x - 5\times10^5)^2 + 8\times10^4 \end{cases} \tag{14}$$

Substituting formula (13)~(14) into the model of Figure5,three jammers' velocity, velocity azimuth, velocity pitch angle and delay amount can be obtained, as shown in Figure6~Figure9.

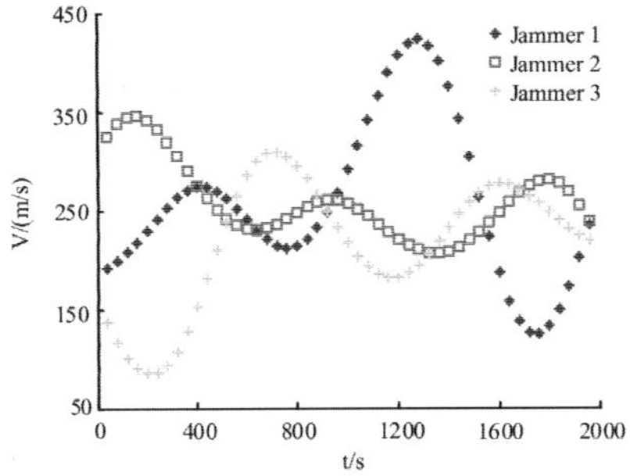

Fig. 6.Jammers' Velocity

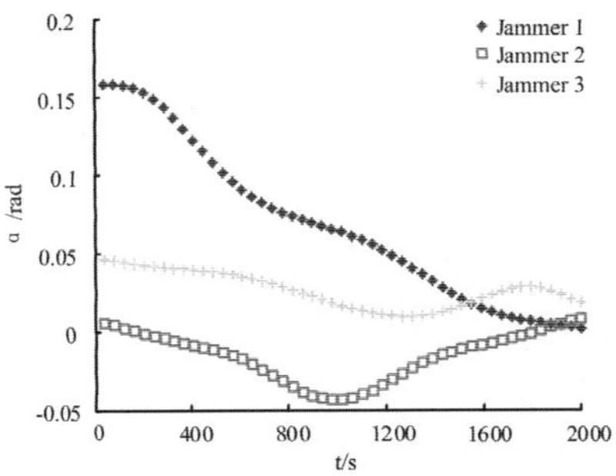

Fig.7.Jammers' Velocity Azimuth

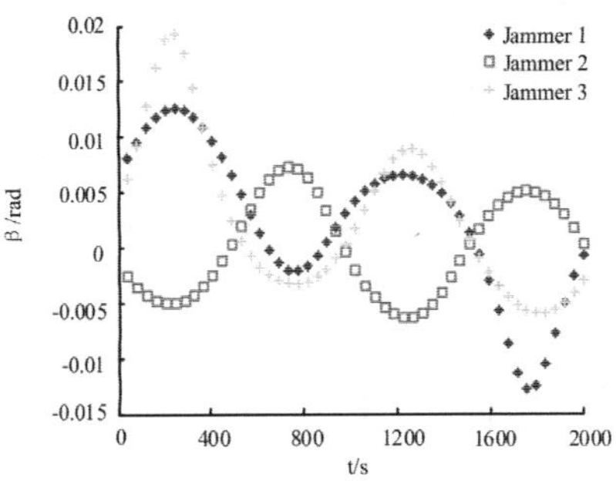

Fig.8.Jammers' Velocity Pitch Angle

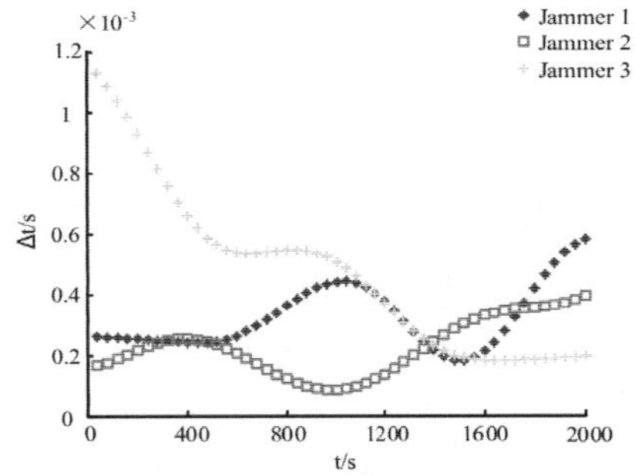

Fig.9.Jammers' Signal Delay Amount

5 Conclusion

This article is based on the traditional track deception jamming technology, considers the situation that the jammers needs to adjust the route, expands the degree of freedom of the jammers' route, and gives the movement model and the solving process of the jammers under the flexible route penetration. Then the parameters of jammers were obtained through simulation. This technology not only can achieve track deception, but also can control the jammer route more flexibly. It can better cooperate with suppressing jamming when it comes to radar network penetration, and provides a reference for deception and suppression of the organic combination of interference.

REFERENCES

1. FAN zhenyu , WANG Lei , SU Jianchun. Technology of track deception for cooperative control of multiple Electronic Combat Air Vehicles [J]. INFORMATION AND ELECTRONIC ENGINEERING,2010,8(3):265-268.
2. LI Fei,ZHOU Zhongliang,GOU Xinyu, et al.Technology for penetrating radar net based on multiple combat air vehicles cooperation track deception. [J].Systems Engineering and Electronics,2013,35(11):2309-2313.
3. YANG Zhong, WANG Guohong, SUN Dianxing. Collborative Programming Technic of Radar Network in Presence of Phantom Track Deception [J]. Command Control & Simulation,2015,37(6):45-49.
4. LI Xiaobo, SUN Lin, ZHOU Qingsong.Strategy for Track Deception Jamming Against Radar Network Using Cooperative Autonomous Vehicle Teams [J]. MODERN DEFENCE TECHNOLOGY,2016,44(6):43-49.
5. GUO Shufen, YU Guowen, XIONG Xin.Research on method of track deception jamming based on cooperative control of UAVs [J]. Journal of Air Force Early Warning Academy,2018,32(1):44-54.
6. LIU Xiang , LI Dongsheng. The deviation compensation for Phantom Tracks Jamming against

https://doi.org/10.1051/matecconf/201817601039

distributed Radar Network [J]. Systems Engineering and Electronics,2018,40.

7. LI Xin,WANG Chunyang. Track deception jamming and its countermeasures Research status and development [J]. Cruise Missile,2013(8):64-67.
8. WU Yuqing. AIMING At the Ntted Radar Electronic Interfrence technology research [D]. School of Electronic Engineering ,2013.60-65.
9. MA Yatao. Research on Deception Jamming against the Network System of Radars [D]. Xi'an University of Electronic Science and Technology,2013.37-45.

Analysis of RDSS Positioning Performance under Elevation Constraints

Yao Fan[1], *Wenxiang* Liu[1,*], *Wei* Xiao[1], and *Guangfu* Sun[1]

[1]Engineering Research Center for Position, Navigation and Time, College of Electronic Science, National University of Defense Technology, Deya Road 109, Changsha, China

Abstract. When using RDSS positioning under elevation constraints, traditional positioning accuracy estimation methods may not reflect the impact of satellite ranging error and elevation error on positioning performance accurately. In order to evaluate RDSS positioning performance more accurately, the RDSS positioning principle is presented, and the weighted position dilution of precision (WPDOP) is used to replace the traditional algorithm. The positioning error calculated by WPDOP is closer to actual results, indicating better prediction capability of positioning performance. Under different elevation error conditions, the position dilution of precision (PDOP) distribution of the service area indicates that the difference between the two precision factors is mainly affected by the elevation error and latitude, while the influence of longitude is small.

1 Introduction

The RDSS positioning and position reporting service is one of the major features of the Beidou global navigation positioning system (BDS-3), and has received more and more attention with the gradual construction of BDS-3. Therefore, the accurate assessment of the positioning performance may facilitate practical use and application development.

After the Beidou-I navigation system completed, the Radio Determination Satellite Service (RDSS) has received intense research.

A detailed summary of various algorithms for Beidou-I navigation and positioning is presented in [1-2]. The traditional precision factor can't be defined because the existence of the elevation error [3]. The actual positioning performance of Beidou-I in the region is obtained by analyzing measured data [4-5]. The position accuracy factor can be defined with reference to the GPS system, but the difference between ranging error and elevation error was ignored [6-7]. The concept of weighted factor is introduced in RNSS [8].

In this paper, the weighted position dilution of precision (WPDOP) algorithm is proposed so that the calculation results of the performance of the RDSS system are closer to reality and the difference between PDOP and WPDOP is analysed.

2 RDSS positioning principle

RDSS is a radio positioning system based on the distance measurement, taking the satellite position as a reference point and three-ball rendezvous as the positioning principle. The RDSS positioning signal flow is shown in Figure 1 [9].

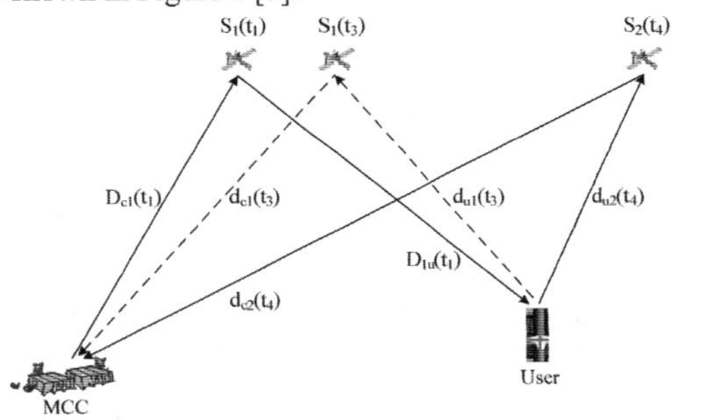

Fig. 1. The RDSS positioning signal flow.

The Master Control Centre (MCC) is the known location on the ground. The satellite S_1 receives the ranging signal transmitted by MCC at time t_1. When the user receives any ranging signal transmitted by S_1 at time t_2, it transmits an answering signal to each visible satellite. Then the MCC will receive the reply signal returned by each satellite. By measuring the time difference accurately, the sum of the MCC-satellite-user roundtrip distance can be obtained. The user's location requires three visible satellites to calculate theoretically. When only two satellites are available, if the user elevation is known, the two-star positioning will be completed, which is dual-satellite navigation system. In order to make the analysis more representative, the analysis and deduction is proposed under the condition that only two satellites are visible in this paper.

The following ranging equation can be derived as

* Corresponding author: liuwenxiang8888@163.com

$$\begin{cases}\rho_1 = D_{c1}(t_1)+c\delta t_{c1O}+c\delta t_{S1}(t_1)+D_{1u}(t_1)+c\delta t_u(t_2) \\ \quad +d_{u1}(t_3)+c\delta t_{S1}(t_3)+d_{c1}(t_3)+c\delta t_{c1I} - \varepsilon_1 \\ \rho_2 = D_{c1}(t_1)+c\delta t_{c1O}+c\delta t_{S1}(t_1)+D_{1u}(t_1)+c\delta t_u(t_2) \\ \quad +d_{u2}(t_4)+c\delta t_{S2}(t_4)+d_{c2}(t_4)+c\delta t_{c2I} - \varepsilon_2\end{cases} \quad (1)$$

where ρ is the MCC-satellite-user round trip distance; t is the arrival time of the signal; Dc1 is the distance between the MCC and the satellite S1; D1u is the distance between the satellite S1 and the user u; dui and dci are respectively the distance between user u and satellite Si and the distance between satellite Si and MCC; δtc is the equipment delay of the inbound and outbound signal of the central station; δtS is the delay of the satellite repeater's inbound and outbound signal equipment; δtu is the delay of the user u forwarding signal; ε is the pseudo-range measurement error; c is the speed of light.

In the ECEF coordinate system, the MCC coordinates (xc, yc, zc), the user u coordinate (x, y, z), and the satellite position (xSi, ySi, zSi) are set. The user position can be expressed as equation (2) on the premise that the user elevation h is known [1].

$$x^2 + y^2 + (z + N_e e^2 sinB)^2 = (N_e + h)^2 \quad (2)$$

where Ne, e, and B respectively represent the radius of curvature of the reference ellipsoid, the eccentricity of the ellipsoid, and the latitude of the user's location.

The distance between the satellite and the monitoring station Dci and dci can be obtained based on the satellite ephemeris and the location of the monitoring and control station. A corrected pseudo-range observation ρ'i is defined by eliminating various ranging errors. Corresponding to the observation ρ'i, the equation becomes

$$D_{1u} + d_{ci} = \rho_i' + \varepsilon_i \quad (3)$$

According to equation (1) (2), considering the three-point intersection method of elevation constraint, the essence of RDSS positioning algorithm will be to solve the following three-dimensional nonlinear equations as

$$\begin{cases} f_1 = \rho_1' + \varepsilon_1 \\ \quad = \sqrt{(x^{(S_1)} - x)^2 + (y^{(S_1)} - y)^2 + (z^{(S_1)} - z)^2} \\ \quad + \sqrt{(x^{(S_1)} - x)^2 + (y^{(S_1)} - y)^2 + (z^{(S_1)} - z)^2} \\ f_2 = \rho_2' + \varepsilon_2 \\ \quad = \sqrt{(x^{(S_1)} - x)^2 + (y^{(S_1)} - y)^2 + (z^{(S_1)} - z)^2} \\ \quad + \sqrt{(x^{(S_2)} - x)^2 + (y^{(S_2)} - y)^2 + (z^{(S_2)} - z)^2} \\ f_h = h + \varepsilon_h \\ \quad = \sqrt{x^2 + y^2 + (z + N_e e^2 sinB)} - N_e \end{cases} \quad (4)$$

Perform the linearization on Equation (4) and use the least-squares method to solve [10]. After completing k-1 iterations, the user position estimate is set to $\boldsymbol{x}_{k-1} = (x_{k-1}, y_{k-1}, z_{k-1})$, then

$$\begin{bmatrix}\Delta x \\ \Delta y \\ \Delta z\end{bmatrix} = (\mathbf{G}^T\mathbf{G})^{-1}\mathbf{G}^T\boldsymbol{b}, \begin{bmatrix}\varepsilon_x \\ \varepsilon_y \\ \varepsilon_z\end{bmatrix} = (\mathbf{G}^T\mathbf{G})^{-1}\mathbf{G}^T\boldsymbol{\varepsilon} \quad (5)$$

where $[\varepsilon_x, \varepsilon_y, \varepsilon_z]^T$ is direction component of the error vector ε, and

$$\mathbf{G} = \begin{bmatrix} f_{1x}' & f_{1y}' & f_{1z}' \\ f_{2x}' & f_{2y}' & f_{2z}' \\ f_{hx}' & f_{hy}' & f_{hz}' \end{bmatrix}, \boldsymbol{b} = \begin{bmatrix}\rho_1' - f_1 \\ \rho_2' - f_2 \\ h - f_h\end{bmatrix}, \boldsymbol{\varepsilon} = \begin{bmatrix}\varepsilon_1 \\ \varepsilon_2 \\ \varepsilon_h\end{bmatrix} \quad (6)$$

After obtaining $[\Delta x, \Delta y, \Delta z]^T$, the user position is updated to $\boldsymbol{x}_k = \boldsymbol{x}_{k-1} + \Delta \boldsymbol{x}$, and Newton iteration operation is continued as the starting point until the solution accuracy is reached.

3 Definition of weighted position dilution of precision

To simplify the analysis, some assumptions are proposed as follows.

The equivalent distance error εi of each satellite is normally distributed. Its mean is 0, and its variance is σpi2 . The measurement error εh of the user's elevation is normally distributed. The mean value is 0, and the variance is σh2. The measurement errors between different satellites, satellites and user elevations are not related to each other.

Based on the above assumptions, the covariance matrix of the positioning error can be deduced as

$$\mathrm{cov}\left(\begin{bmatrix}\varepsilon_x \\ \varepsilon_y \\ \varepsilon_z\end{bmatrix}\right) = (\mathbf{G}^T\mathbf{G})^{-1}\mathbf{G}^T \begin{bmatrix}\sigma_{\rho1}^2 & 0 & 0 \\ 0 & \sigma_{\rho2}^2 & 0 \\ 0 & 0 & \sigma_h^2\end{bmatrix} \mathbf{G}(\mathbf{G}^T\mathbf{G})^{-1} \quad (6)$$

Defining the weight matrix W=diag(w1,w2,wh), where wi, wh is the weighting factor of the i-th satellite from the error variance and elevation error variance, and wi =(σpi/σUERE)2 , wh = (σh/σUERE)2 , (σUERE)2 =σh2+σp12+σp22.

According to this, the weight coefficient matrix H can be defined

$$\mathbf{H} = (\mathbf{G}^T\mathbf{G})^{-1}\mathbf{G}^T\mathbf{W}\mathbf{G}(\mathbf{G}^T\mathbf{G})^{-1} \quad (7)$$

Three-dimensional space positioning error standard deviation

$$\sigma_P = WPDOP \cdot \sigma_{UERE} \quad (8)$$

Corresponding value of WPDOP

$$WPDOP = \sqrt{h_{11} + h_{22} + h_{33}} \quad (9)$$

where hij is the element of the ith row and jth column of matrix H. When $\sigma_{\rho1}^2 = \sigma_{\rho2}^2 = \sigma_h^2$, there is $\mathbf{H} = \frac{1}{3}(\mathbf{G}^T\mathbf{G})^{-1}$. At this time, the WPDOP is consistent with the traditional definition accuracy factor PDOP. Meanwhile, according to the definition, the greater the difference between the satellite ranging error σ_P and the elevation error σ_h, the greater the difference between the WPDOP and the traditional PDOP.

4 Assessment of positioning performance under elevation constraints

4.1 Analysis of PDOP and WPDOP Positioning Performance Assessment Capabilities

The location of the MCC is (116.34°E, 39.98°N, 0m), the user position is (113.00°E, 28.21°N, 30m), and the positions of RDSS satellites are (80.20°E, 0.00°N, 35803000m) and (140.00°E, 0.00°N, 35807000m).

Under the different combination of satellite ranging error σp and elevation error σh, the result σPreal of 10000 simulations is approximated as the true positioning error, and the positioning accuracy estimated by the traditional defined PDOP and the newly defined WPDOP is compared and analysed. The difference between the theoretic error variance and the actual result is shown in Table 1.

Table 1. The comparison of PDOP and WPDOP positioning performance evaluation. (unit: m)

Ranging Error σ_{p1}, σ_{p2}	Elevation Error σ_h	Positioning Error σ_{Preal}	σ_{P1}* (PDOP)	σ_{P2}* (WPDOP)
0	0	0	0	-
	5	9.9086	7.1912	9.0364
	10	17.9395	14.3824	18.0727
	15	27.0176	21.5736	27.1091
5	0	5.4687	10.1699	8.5723
	5	10.5152	12.4555	12.4555
	10	18.8573	17.6147	20.0027
	15	27.5031	23.8505	28.4321

*σ_P= PDOP * σ_{UERE}

As can be seen from Table 1, whenσp1=σp2=σh, the positioning error σPreal is 0, which indicates that the positioning algorithm can accurately solve the user position when the satellite ranging and elevation measurement are accurate. When $\sigma_{p1}=\sigma_{p2}=\sigma_h=5$, σ_{P1} equals to σ_{P2}, the weight coefficient matrix is a unit matrix, degrading the WPDOP into the traditional definition. Both of them have the same theoretical estimation of the positioning error. In the case of $\sigma_p \neq \sigma_h$, compared with PDOP, the estimated positioning error variance σ_{P2} calculated by WPDOP is closer to the actual error. That is to say, WPDOP can reflect the system positioning performance more accurately.

4.2 Differences in PDOP and WPDOP under Different Elevation Error Conditions

In order to reflect the differences between newly and traditional definitions in different regions, this paper calculates the WPDOP and PDOP for different elevation errors within the system service range. In the area (80°E~140°E; 10°N~60°N), the user elevation is set to 0m, and the sampling point spacing is 1°. The ranging error σp is set to 8m, the height error σh is set to 5m, 8m, and 15m (Nan, Su and Zhou, 2013). The positioning accuracy factor at each point is calculated. The result is shown in Figure 2.

It can be seen from Figure2 that along the longitude direction, the change of PDOP is slow, but rapidly declining trend from low latitude to high latitude is presented. It is mainly because that the GEO satellite RDSS system used are distributed in the equatorial plane, resulting in the constellation's geometry constraints to the north and south direction is less than the east and west direction.

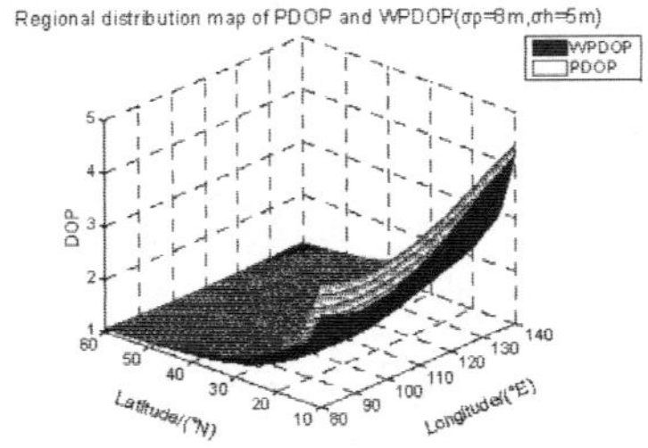

(a) σ_p= 8m, σ_p= 5m

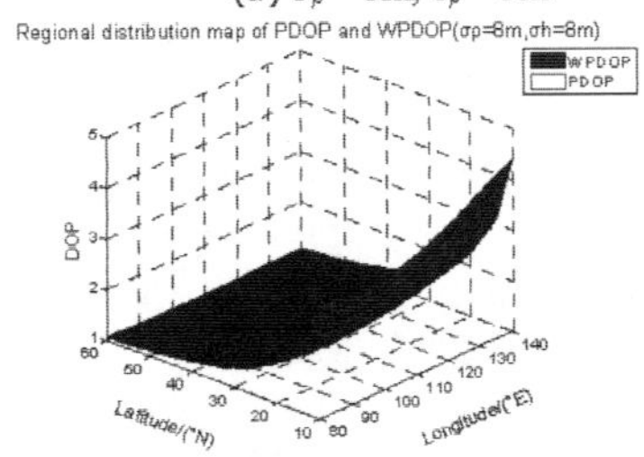

(b)σ_p= 8m, σ_p= 8m

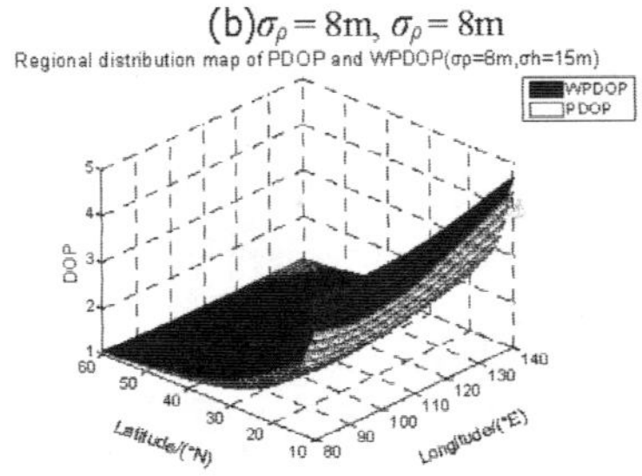

(c)σ_p= 8m, σ_p= 15m

Fig. 2. Regional distribution of PDOP and WPDOP.

The large difference between PDOP and WPDOP in low latitude area, means that the traditional method was used to assess location accuracy will be gravely deviates from the actual performance. Therefore, to assess system service performance accurately, WPDOP should be adopted.

When the elevation error is less than the range error, the elevation has a smaller influence on the positioning performance. But the traditional method will magnifying its influence at this time, leading to the estimation value of the positioning error is higher than the actual situation. When the elevation error is greater than the distance measuring error, elevation impact on positioning performance occupied the main position, which can't be reflected in traditional methods. In this case, traditional

PDOP will cause the positioning error estimate is lower than actual situation.

5 Conclusions

In this paper, the principle of RDSS positioning under the condition of elevation constraint is deduced and the positioning accuracy of RDSS is estimated by WPDOP instead of the traditional PDOP. The simulation results show that the real-time positioning accuracy calculated by WPDOP is more accurate. Moreover, the distribution of PDOP/ WPDOP values in RDSS system service area shows that the value is affected by the latitude significantly instead of the longitude, which is consistent with reality.

This work is supported by the National Science Foundation of China (Nos. 41604016).

References

1. C.L. Peng, Southwest Jiaotong University (2009).
2. W. Huang, Dalian Maritime University (2012).
3. D.X. Zhang, Radio Engineering (2012).
4. X. Nan, R.R. Su, J.H. Zhou, Science China (2013).
5. R. Guo, R.R. Su, L. Liu, *5th Annual Meeting of China Satellite Navigation Academy* (2014).
6. Y.L. Yuan, J. Huang, J. Tao, Computer Applications and Software (2017).
7. Y.L. Yuan, J. Tao, X.Y. Song, *International Conference on Information Engineering* (2017).
8. M.L. Wang, G.F. Sun, F.X. Wang, Chinese Space Science and Technology, **27** (2007).
9. S.S. Tan, National Defense Industry Press, 61 (2011).
10. G. Xie, Electronic Industry Press, 108 (2009).

MATEC Web of Conferences **176**, 01041 (2018) https://doi.org/10.1051/matecconf/201817601041
IFID 2018

An improved method of microscopic image segmentation

Zhang Feng Shou[1],Dong Fang[1],Liu Jian Ting[1] and Meng Xin[1]

[1]Henan university of science and technology,HeNan471023,China.

Abstract: In order to improve the effectiveness and accuracy of image processing in modern medical inspection, a segmentation image optimization algorithm of improved two-dimensional maximum entropy threshold based on genetic algorithm combined with mathematical morphology is proposed, in view of the microscopic cell images characteristic and the shortcomings of the traditional segmentation algorithm. Through theoretical analysis and contrast test, the segmentation method proposed is superior to the traditional threshold segmentation method in microscopic cell images, and the average segmentation time of the improved algorithm is 73% and 44% higher than the traditional two-dimensional maximum entropy threshold and the improved two-dimensional maximum entropy threshold.

1. INTRODUCTION

Image segmentation is the key step of the process from image processing to image analysis[1-3]. The background of high noise microscopic images presents great complexity, therefore,it is difficult to simultaneously extract the object contours possible during filtering image noise by a single image segmentation method[4-5]. In this paper, we would analyze the traditional segmentation algorithm from experiment sand put forward an improved genetic algorithm of threshold segment method by using two-dimensional maximum entropy. Then, the coarse segmentation of microscopic images are presented.Finally,the object contoury extracted after filtering out residual noise and filling small holes in the target by mathematical morphology methods.

2. IMPROVED METHOD

2.1 Improved two-dimensional maximum entropy threshold based on genetic algorithm

The two-dimensional maximum entropy threshold algorithm through the concept of entropy in information theory combines the point gray and the region gray. For low signal-to-noise ratio images,using two-dimensional maximum entropy threshold method can obtain a better image segmentation results[6-8]. The advantage of the traditional two-dimensional maximum entropy threshold algorithm is that it can reduce the digital image sensitivity to noise,but this algorithm is a time-consuming operation and high computational complexity. The gray histogram with an improved two-dimensional maximum entropy threshold algorithm, as shown in Figure 1.

Let the microscopic image be f (x, y) and the gray series be L. Another microscopic image g(x, y) is obtained by adopting neighborhood average to original image, whose gray scale is still L.Image sizeis M×N.Let nij be pixels of f (x, y) in gray value i and g(x, y) in the gray value of j. The probability of the occurrence of (i, j) of the point grey area and the region gray is flowing.

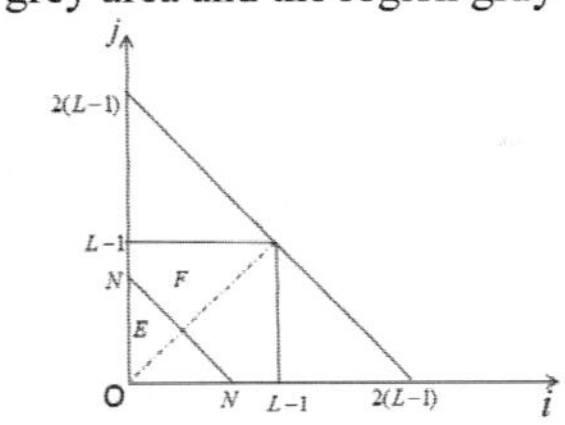

Fig. 1 Improved two-dimensional gray histogram of image

In the method the sum of the pixel gray values and the neighbor average grey values N is the independent variable, pixels smaller than N are divided into one class, and pixels larger than N are divided into another class. The region E and region F respectively represent the target and background in the image,the calculation is reduced from two dimensions to one dimension by finding the best image segmentation pixel value. The processing effect equivalently is first smoothing the image and then segmenting it. The probability of the region E is as follows from the figure 1:

$$P_E = \sum_{i=0}^{N-1} \sum_{j=o}^{N-1} p_{ij}, (i, j \in E) \tag{1}$$

The threshold selection criteria is i+j=N , then the following equations can be obtained

$$P_E(N) = P_E(N-1) + P_{0,N} + P_{1,N-1} + \cdots + P_{N,0} \tag{2}$$

*Corresponding author: {Dong Fang}[a]fantasyericdong@163.com

$$H_E(N) = H_E(N-1) - (P_{0,N} + P_{1,N-1} + \cdots + P_{N,0}) \times \lg(P_{0,N} + P_{1,N-1} + \cdots + P_{N,0}) \quad (3)$$

$$H_E = \ln P_E + \frac{H_E}{P_E}, \quad H_F = \ln(1-P_E) + \frac{H_L - H_E}{1-P_E} \quad (4)$$

The decision function of entropy is defined as

$$\psi(N) = \max\{H_E + H_F\} \quad (5)$$

Genetic algorithm is introduced based on all the above.An improved two-dimensional maximum entropy threshold genetic algorithm is proposed to further reduce computational complexity and shorten the computation time.

In this paper,the improved algorithm is based on the improved two-dimensional entropy threshold algorithm. The sum of the pixel gray values and the neighbor average grey values N is the independent variable, so N is the solution of the problem. Because the range of N is 0~511, the 9-bit binary encoding is adopted when N values are encoded.The N value is encoded into a gene string a={a0,···,a8}, In the formula, a represents the value of N.

The specific process is as follows:

(1)Initial population generation. The solution space is binary encoded and initial population is generated randomly. Population numbers generally take 20 ~ 200.

(2)Determine fitness and fitness function.In this algorithm,equation (4) is fitness function. Its fitness is high when the gene string with a large entropy valuepresents the N value in the equation (4). On the contrary, its fitness is low.

(3)Selection action.The individual ai with the lowest fitness in the current population and the individual aj with the highest fitnessamong generations of populations are found by combining optimal preservation strategy and roulette wheel selection. The code value of aj is instead of ai encoding value,other individuals are selected by probability of roulette wheel selection. Thus, the diversity of the population is maintained while the optimal individual is not destroyed.

(4)Crossover and mutation operation. The crossover and mutation of the biological can make the species evolve rapidly or produce new species, but crossover and mutation operation will speed up the optimization. Crossover rate values generally take 0.4 ~0.99. The original highly fitness gene string will be destructed due to crossover rate is too large, and the crossover rate is too small to keep the search process.Mutation ratevalues generally take 0.0001 ~ 0.1. Genetic algorithm will turn into random search due to the mutation rate is too large, and mutation rate is too small to produce new individuals.

(5)Set criteria of termination calculate on. A practical algorithm must be convergent. In the genetic algorithm, the best gene string is returned when the maximum propagation algebra is achieved, and it is used as two-dimensional segmentation threshold. Then the algorithm is ending, otherwise, returning (2)and proceeding to the next generation.

2.2 Mathematical morphology related operations

After segmenting the microscopic images with animprovedtwo-dimensional maximum entropy threshold based on genetic algorithm, most of the noises are removed, but there is some small holes that goes on in target area and some undesired impurity appeared, so mathematical morphology methods are used to fill the small holes in the target area by multiple close calculation, and remove thin impurity by multiple open calculation. Finally, the object's contour is extracted.

3. EXPERIMENT

In order to verify the effectiveness of segmentation algorithm in this paper,three micrograph were used to experimentalize. The micrographs are BMP format and the resolution is130×130. Experiment platform is Intel(R) Core(TM) CPU 3.4GHz and memory is 4GB, windows 7 operating system, the algorithm is implemented with VS2013+OpenCV3.0 compiler platform.

Microscopic cell original imageis as shown in figure 2.The traditional image segmentation algorithm is difficult to obtain satisfactory results. The first order edge operator Sobel and two order edge operator LoG are used in edge detection.The segmentation effect of microscopic cell images are shown in figure 3.

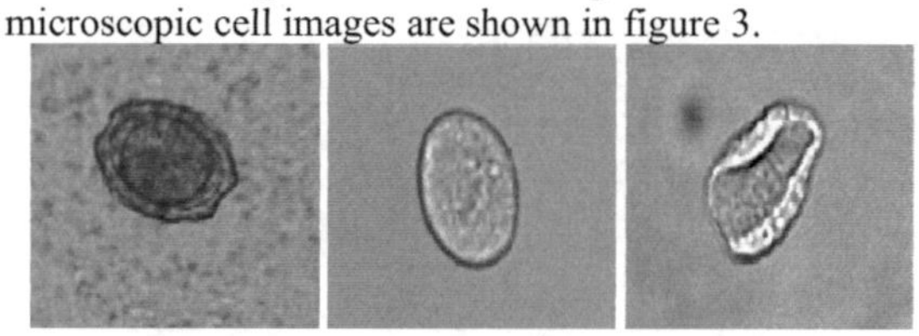

Fig. 2 Microscopic cell original image

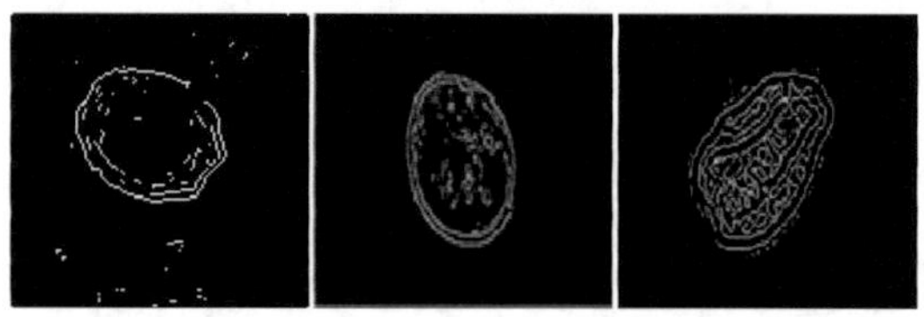

Fig. 3 Image processing of sobel edge detection

As can be seen from the figure 3, sobel edge operator is very sensitive to noise, which makes the target edge and noise benot distinguished.The noise is reduced after dealing with first order edge operators, but double edges and edge breaks are appearing. Therefore, the edge detection can not segment the high noise microscopic image very well.

According to the one-dimensional and two-dimensional gray histogram of microscopic images(Take the case ofmicroscopic image 1, as shown in Figure 4), and Otsu threshold method and two-dimensional maximum entropy threshold method were used to segment the microscopic images, the results are shown in Figure 5.

 https://doi.org/10.1051/matecconf/201817601041

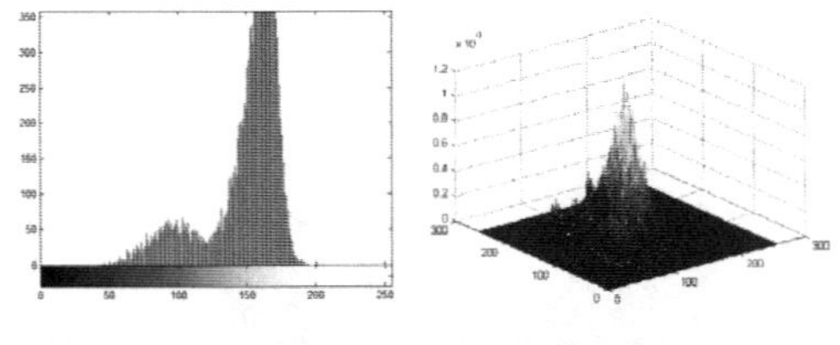

Fig. 4 Grey level histogram

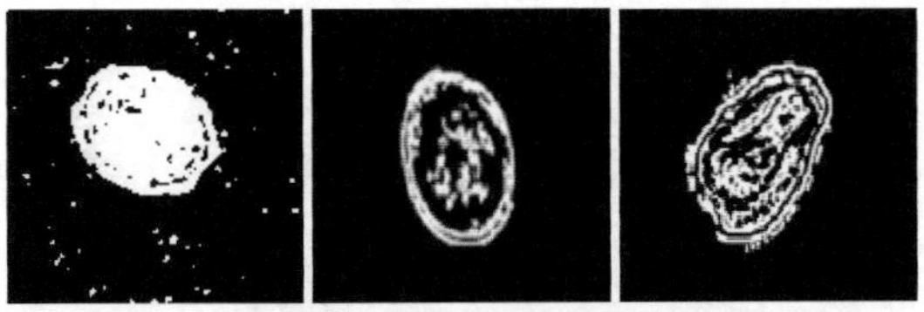

Otsuthreshold segmentation

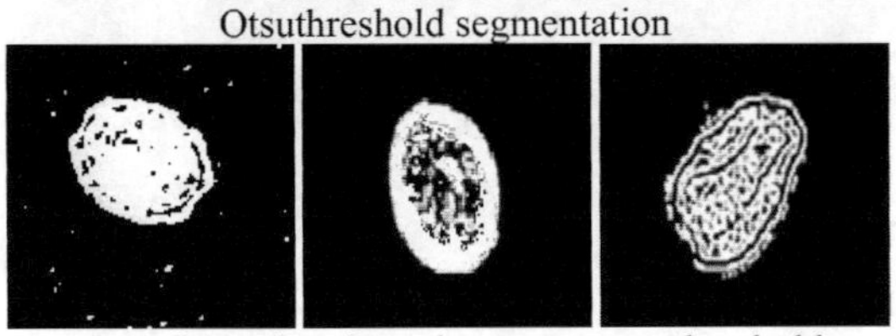

Two-dimensional maximum entropy threshold segmentation

Fig. 5 Threshold segmentation

The figure 5 shown that the traditional threshold segmentation method is poorly segmented the edges of microscopic images. The proposed method is used to segment the microscopic image, and the effect shown in Figure 6.

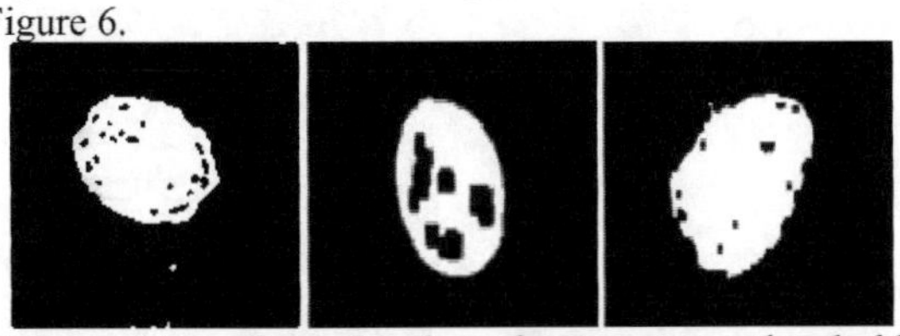

Improved two-dimensional maximum entropy threshold based on genetic algorithm:

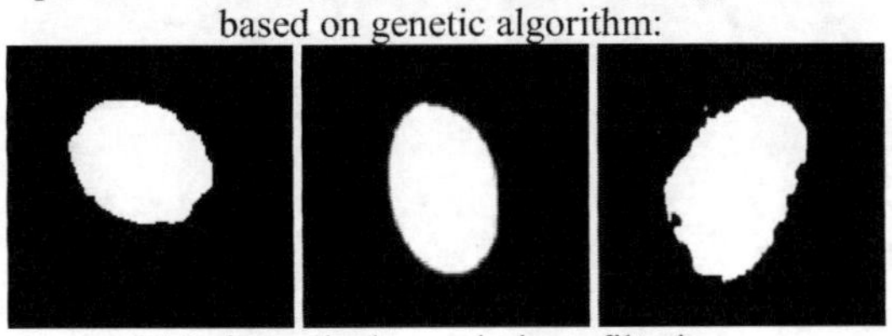

Mathematical morphology filtering

Fig. 6 Segmentation method in this paper

In the improved two-dimensional maximum entropy threshold genetic algorithm, the initial population N is 30, the chromosome has a coding length of 9 bits, the crossover rate is 0.5, the mutation rate is 0.05. After 8 generations, the inheritance converges to the optimum threshold.

Tab.1 The segmentation time comparison (unit:s)

Microscopic cell image	image1	image2	image3
Traditional 2D optimal entropy threshold algorithm	0.704	0.678	0.768
Improved optimal entropy threshold algorithm	0.313	0.389	0.501
The improved algorithm	0.202	0.258	0.241

It can be concluded from Figure 6 and that the object contour is intact, the inner wormhole disappears and the noise in the background is completely removed. Besides, an ideal contour two-value image is obtained. The algorithm operation speed is shown Table 1. From the Table, the average segmentation time of the improved algorithm is 73% higher than the traditional two-dimensional maximum entropy threshold and it is 44% higher than the improved two-dimensional maximum entropy threshold.

4. CONCLUSION

In this paper, an optimization algorithm of improved two-dimensional maximum entropy threshold genetic algorithm based rough segmentation combined with morphology fine segmentation image is proposed. The effect of segmentation microscopic image is very good by the improved optimization algorithm. The result is that the object contour is intact, the inner wormhole disappears and the noise in the background is completely removed.Besides, an ideal microscopic cell contour two-value image was obtained. Through theoretical analysis and contrast test, the segmentation method proposed is superior to the traditional threshold segmentation method in microscopic cell images, and achieve ideal segmentation results, the segmentation accuracy and speed is superior to the traditional threshold segmentation method.

REFERENCES

1. YANG Xiaoqing. Microscopic cell image processing and application based on morphology[J]. Computer Systems & Applications, Vol.2016,(03):p.220-224.
2. Du Peijun. Two dimensional maximum entropy image segmentation based on artificial bee colony optimization[J]. Computer Engineering, 2012,(09):223-225+243.
3. QIAO Lingling, MAO xiaoju. Otsu image segmentation method based on improved genetic algorithm[J]. Journal of Changchun Institute of Technology(Natural Sciences Edition), Vol. 2016,(04):p.105-107.
4. Melkemi K E,MohamedB,Sebti F.A multiagent system approach for image segmentation using genetic algorithms and extremal optimization heuristics[J]. Pattern Recognition Letters, 2016, 27(11):p.1230—1238.

5. TUO Qian. Study of Image thresholding segmentation algorithm on maximum entropy combining genetic algorithm[D]. Kunming University of Science and Technology,2016.
6. Shen Xiaoci. Research of two-dimensional entropy image segmentation method based on genetic algorithm[D]. China University of Geosciences (Beijing) ,2008.
7. Zhao Song, XIA Yanling. Improvement of DNA genetic algorithm two-dimensional maximum entropy image segmentation[J]. Silicon Valley, 2013,(02):250-252+211.
8. PENG Jing, ZHANG Baoge. A two-dimensional maximum entropy segmentation algorithm based on boundary feature[J]. Computer and Digital Engineering, 2008,(07):18-20.

Prediction of Operating Abnormality Rate of Charging Pile Based on Generalized AR(q) Combined Regression

Xu Xin[1], Fu Jun[1], Sun Zhijie[1], Li Xuemei[1], Zhou Guopeng[1]

[1] NCEPRI(Huadian Electric Power Research Institute Co., Ltd.,) Beijing 100045, China

Abstract. The stable operation of charging pile is related to the entire operation efficiency of the charging network of electric vehicles so the prediction of charging pile operation abnormality rate can help the operational department to make operational decisions in advance. This paper uses the electric vehicle charging network operating date in the north of Hebei province, based on the feature of the anomalies records of charging pile, to combine the generalized AR(q) model and the regression model and to predict the abnormality rate of electric vehicle charging network in the north of Hebei province. It is predicted that the average absolute error is 0.0044 and the acceptable prediction effect can be obtained.

1 Introduction

Under the guidance of China's "13th Five-Year Plan" on that the electric vehicle charging infrastructure needs to be constructed in advance and the smart and efficient charging network system with vehicle piles, the coverage area of electric vehicle charging piles is continuously expanding, and the rapidly developing electric vehicle industry needs the stable running charging network. The research and prediction of the charging pile abnormality rate are of great significance on the operation of charging networks and the development of the industry. This article will carry out study on the stability of the charging network system, predict and analyze the abnormality rate of the charging pile operation. At the same time, this paper notices the limit of the time series tools and proposes the abnormality rate prediction model applicable for the charging pile system with the combination of the regression analysis.

2 Charging pile abnormal characteristics

Set the duration of the i-th charging pile has the abnormality on the t-th day as G_{it}, then the abnormality rate g_{it} on the t-th day of this pile will be:

$$g_{it} = \frac{G_{it}}{24}$$

G_{it} includes the sum of fault duration, off-line duration and outage duration for this pile per day. The average abnormality rate g_t of the charging network system is:

$$g_t = \frac{1}{24}\frac{\sum_i G_{it}}{N}$$

In which $\sum_i G_{it}$ is the total duration of failed piles on the tth day, and N is the total number of piles. In the following analysis, we mainly focused on duration of the abnormality G_{it}. The average abnormality duration G_t of one pile per day:

$$G_t = \frac{\sum_i G_{it}}{N}$$

And the average daily abnormality rate of the system:

$$g_t = \frac{G_t}{24}$$

It is easy to calculate.

Charging pile abnormality duration data has its own characteristics. (1) The length of abnormality duration is more significant than whether the abnormality duration is zero.

From the point of view of charging network operation and maintenance, most charging piles are subject to abnormalities due to various failures, offline or outage. Therefore, the problem of abnormality is actually an issue of abnormality duration, and the research focuses on those charging piles that are abnormal. (2) The data platform only responds to abnormal charging piles. If an abnormality occurs in the charging pile, the data platform will automatically display the abnormality start and recovery time; otherwise, the platform will not display any abnormal information. Hence, the data recorded by the platform is the data of the pile where the abnormality has occurred and these data can be observed. (3) The data amount of the abnormal charging piles is relatively less than that of all charging piles so it is relatively easy to handle abnormal charging pile data than all charging pile data. (4) There may be more than one charging pile will have abnormality on the same day, that is, on the t day, it may be observed that $G_{i_1 t}$, $G_{i_2 t}$, ..., $G_{i_S t}$, $S > 1$. Therefore, observations of S times of abnormality duration (S charging piles) can be obtained on day t. (5) The occurrence of abnormalities depends on the history of abnormalities. From the experience of operations, the

* Corresponding author: 676269930@qq.com

abnormality of charging piles is highly correlated with the past abnormalities. So the abnormality duration of the charging pile in the past has great influence on the current abnormality duration length. These characteristics showed that, G_{it} depends on G_{it-1} , G_{it-2}, ... relatively strongly, where G_{it-1}, G_{it-2}, ...are not necessarily corresponding to the abnormality duration on one day or two day before t-th day but ate the duration when the first or first two abnormalities of the i-th pile occurred on t-th day. G_{it-1}, G_{it-2}, ...are the observations of the first or first two abnormalities of the i-th pile and the time intervals for these observations are not necessarily equal.

In addition to the abnormality history, there are other factors that affect the length of the abnormality duration of the charging pile. First of all, the operation and maintenance capabilities of the charging pile operation and maintenance department will have an impact on the abnormality of the charging pile. If the operation and maintenance department has a relatively high level of operation and maintenance business or can deal with the abnormality on site timely (D_{it}) , then the abnormality duration of the charging pile within their scope of jurisdiction should be shorter. Secondly, the operation and maintenance capabilities of the charging pile manufacturers also affect the abnormality of the charging pile. If the hardware quality of the equipment supplied is relatively high or the spare parts can be replaced timely or they can deal with the abnormality on site timely (CW_{it}) then the length of abnormality duration of the charging pile produced by this manufacturer shall be shorter. Third, special hours. In the holidays, the use frequency of the charging piles may be different from that in the usual; During the national important meeting or other special period, the operation and maintenance department will take a major measure of power protection; Sometimes the power grid will also be outage for maintenance in a certain period. Therefore, holidaysSJ_{it}, major days of electricity protectionSZ_{it}n, and duration of power outages WC_{it}will cause changes in the abnormality duration of charging piles. The last factor to consider is the weather. Rainy and snowy, Wind direction and force, temperature (TD_{it}representing the minimum temperature), PM2.5 (represented by PM_{it}), etc. may affect the charging pile hardware and further affect the abnormality duration.

3 Charging pile abnormality prediction models

According to the factors affecting the abnormality of the charging pile, we construct the prediction models as follows.

3.1 Generalized AR(q) Model

According to the characteristics of the charging pile's abnormality data, the duration of the abnormality of i-th pile occurred on t-th day has the unbalanced panel data characteristics in form, but we know from long-term operation knowledge that the abnormality duration mainly depends the length of the abnormality duration of the pile in the past. The spatial effect showed by different piles is not very obvious. We deal with the data of several piles observed in the same day as several observation values but we ignore their spatial effects. Therefore, the model can be considered as:

$$G_{it} = c_0 + c_1 G_{it-1} + \cdots + c_q G_{it-q} + \varepsilon_{it} \qquad (1)$$

Where, c_0 , $c_1, \dots, c_q$ are parameters and ε_{it} is error term. The subscript i corresponds to the i-th pile and can be any one among N piles. But not all the N piles on the same day t can be observed and only the plies with abnormalities can be observed. At the same time, as in fact, it is impossible that all the piles are in normal state so at least one pile per day can be observed. If the spatial effect of i is ignored then only the number of observations will increases. Formula (1)is formally the AR(q) model.

In model (1), t corresponds to day t; but t-1,...,t-q in model (1) represent the days that the previous first....q-th abnormalities of i-th pile. The time interval of day t and t-1 in the model may be more than one day and for simple, it still be represented by that in (1). So the time intervals in the time series in the model (1) are generally unequal and are different from the traditional equal-interval time series. Due to formal similarities and differences in intervals, model (1) is a generalized AR(q) model and the processing needs to consider three points:

1. AR (q) order selection. The size of q in the model (1) is roughly determined, that is, it is to consider which previous abnormality is more appropriate for the charging pile.

2. Coefficient t-test. We use the least square estimation to estimate the model (1) and remove the insignificant coefficient in the model (1).

3. R2 changes. By focusing on changes in R, the goodness of fit of the model is analyzed.

3.2 Operation and weather impact index

Model (1) is similar to AR(q) and has a disadvantage in application. When the data cannot provide the abnormality duration data for the first q times, so it cannot be calculated and cannot be predicted by model (1). In order to be able to predict the abnormality duration of each day, other prediction methods must be introduced to make up for the shortcomings of AR(q).

In addition to the historical abnormality factors of charging piles, there are factors such as the operation and maintenance capabilities of the operating department and manufacturers, special hours, weather, and others affect abnormality duration. Among them, weather factors are natural factors, and other factors are non-natural factors. Therefore, their impact on the abnormality duration of charging piles is divided into two categories which are analyzed with the regression model, respectively.

3.2.1 Operation and maintenance impact index

The operation and maintenance impact index mainly reflects the impact of the operation and maintenance management capabilities of the operation department and the manufacturer on the abnormality duration of the charging pile and is described with the regression model as follows:

$$G_{it} = a_0 + a_1 Y_{it,1} + \cdots + a_k Y_{it,k} + \varepsilon_{it} \quad (2)$$

Among them, $Y_{it,j}$, $j = 1,2,\ldots,k$ represent the j-th operation and maintenance factor affecting the i-th pile on the t-th day. There are k factors in total, including the timeliness ratio of on-site treatment of the operation and maintenance departmentD_{it}, the hardware quality of the equipment CZ_{it} , the timeliness ratio of on-site maintenance CW_{it} , holidays SJ_{it} , major electricity protection daysSZ_{it}, and power outages duration $WC_{it}$and so on. The first half of model (2) is defined as the operation and maintenance impact index$Yindex_{it}$:

$$Yindex_{it} = a_0 + a_1 Y_{it,1} + \cdots + a_k Y_{it,k} \quad (3)$$

$Yindex_{it}$ is not only used for operation department management, quality supervision of manufacturers, but also for abnormality duration prediction.

3.2.2 Weather impact index

The weather impact index mainly reflects the impact of the weather on the abnormality duration of the charging pile and is described with the regression model as follows:

$$G_{it} = b_0 + b_1 T_{it,1} + \cdots + b_p T_{it,p} + \varepsilon_{it} \quad (4)$$

Among them, $T_{it,j}$,$j = 1,2,\ldots,p$ represent j-th weather factor affecting the i-th pile on the t-th day and there are a total of p factors, including rainy and snowy, wind direction and force, temperatureTD_{it}, and PM2.5 and so on. The first half of model (3) is defined as the weather impact index$Tindex_{it}$:

$$Tindex_{it} = b_0 + b_1 T_{it,1} + \cdots + b_p T_{it,p} \quad (5)$$

$Tindex_{it}$can be used for abnormality duration predictions.

3.3 Comprehensive impact index

The operation and maintenance impact index $Yindex_{it}$ combines with the weather impact index $Tindex_{it}$ to form a comprehensive impact index to reflect the total effect of operation and maintenance and weather on the abnormality duration of the charging pile and it is shown as follows with the regression model:

$$G_{it} = d_0 + d_1 Yindex_{it} + d_2 Tindex_{it} + \varepsilon_{it}$$
(6)

The sum of the first three terms of model (6) is called the comprehensive index$Findex_{it}$:

$$Findex_{it} = d_0 + d_1 Yindex_{it} + d_2 Tindex_{it} \quad (7)$$

The operation and maintenance impact index, the weather impact index and the comprehensive impact index will not use the data of the i-th pile before the t-th day, and the operation and maintenance impact index and the weather impact index of each pile every day can be obtained. Therefore, the use of the comprehensive impact index the prediction of the abnormality duration of the charging pile will not be affected by the time delay and at the same time, due to the combination of the two index, it will have better prediction effect than that of the single operation and maintenance index or the weather impact index.

3.4 Generalized AR(q) combined regression prediction model

From the analysis of the generalized AR(q) model, it is known that there will be an abnormality in the charging pile every day. If there are q anomalies of the i-th charging pile before the t-th day, then the generalized AR(q) model (1) can be used to predict its abnormality duration; If the number of abnormality occurred before t days is less than q, then it is unable to use (1) for predictions. However, the comprehensive prediction model (6) or the comprehensive prediction index (7) can be used to predict the abnormality duration. In fields related to energy prediction, the use of combined prediction techniques based on time series prediction is a relatively practical and effective choice. We will use the generalized AR(q) model (1) as the basis and combine the comprehensive prediction index model (6) to predict the abnormality duration. The prediction model is constructed as follows:

$$G_{it} = \begin{cases} c_0 + c_1 G_{it-1} + \cdots + c_q G_{it-q} + \varepsilon_{it} \\ d_0 + d_1 Yindex_{it} + d_2 Tindex_{it} + \varepsilon_{it} \end{cases}$$
(8)

Once the coefficient estimates of (1) and (6) are obtained, the prediction formula can be written as:

$$G_{it} = \begin{cases} c_0 + c_1 G_{it-1} + \cdots + c_q G_{it-q} \\ d_0 + d_1 Yindex_{it} + d_2 Tindex_{it} \end{cases} \quad (9)$$

Based on the prediction model (8) or (9), the predicted value of the abnormality duration of the charging pile per day can be obtained.

4 Estimation and prediction results

In order to obtain the prediction model, we use the operation data of the charging piles from January 2016 to August 2017 in the north of Hebei province to estimate the model (8), and then use the data of September and October of 2017 to carry out predictive analysis.

4.1 Model estimation

The estimation of the model (8) includes the estimation of the generalized AR(q) model (1), and the estimation of the operation and maintenance impact index (2), the weather impact index (4), and the comprehensive impact index (6)

4.1.1 Generalized AR(q) model estimation

Here mainly consider to determine the appropriate order, choose significant historical abnormality variables, and refer to changes in R2. AIC is decreasing and R2 is increasing with the increase of q, as shown in Table 1. But in terms of application, the increase of q will also cause more missing values and more charging piles cannot be predicted. The decreasing speed of AIC and the increasing speed of R2 begin to slow down from q=30, so we choose q=35 as the reference order.

Table 1 Generalized AR(q) Model Order Changes

q	5	10	15	20	25	30	35	40
R^2	0.39	0.417	0.426	0.459	0.494	0.516	0.535	0.546
AIC	129331	92450	65628	46663	33794	24925	18956	15160

In order to ensure the validity of the least squares estimation as much as possible, we remove the insignificant lagged variable in the generalized AR(35) by the t-test, and finally obtain the estimation result AR(28) in Table 2, and R2=0.5126.

Table 2 Generalized AR(q) Estimation Results

Term	Estimate	Std Error	t Ratio	Prob>|t|
Intercept	0.9671	0.2602	3.7171	0.0002
G_{it-1}	0.3818	0.0152	25.0431	0.0000
G_{it-2}	0.1317	0.0164	8.0289	0.0000
G_{it-3}	0.1184	0.0166	7.1461	0.0000
G_{it-4}	0.0797	0.0158	5.0417	0.0000
G_{it-7}	0.0889	0.0147	6.0294	0.0000
G_{it-10}	0.0511	0.0142	3.6028	0.0003
G_{it-28}	0.0364	0.0132	2.7501	0.0060

$AR(28)_{it}$ =0.96+0.38G_{it-1}+0.13G_{it-2}+0.11G_{it-3}+0.07 G_{it-4}+0.08G_{it-7}+0.05G_{it-10}+0.03G_{it-28}

The corresponding estimation formula is

$$G_{it} = AR(28)_{it} \quad (10)$$

4.1.2 Operation and maintenance impact index estimation

The operation and maintenance data of the operation and maintenance departments of five cities and ten charging pile manufacturers in in the north of Hebei province are used to estimate the operation and maintenance impact index results as shown in Table 3 and R2=0.0782.

Table 3 Operation and Maintenance Index Estimation Results

Estimate	Std Error	t Ratio	Prob>|t|
16.5615	0.4424	37.4369	0.0000
-0.2340	0.0286	-8.1904	0.0000
-0.2343	0.0557	-4.2078	0.0000
-2.4181	0.4638	-5.2132	0.0000
0.4174	0.0091	45.9097	0.0000

The corresponding estimation formula is

$$Yindex_{it}=16.56-0.23D_{it}-0.2343SJ_{it}*SZ_{it}-2.41CZ_{it}+0.41WC_{it} \quad (11)$$

4.1.3 Weather impact index estimation

The weather data from five cities in the north of Hebei province is used to estimate the results of the weather impact index as shown in Table 4 and R2 = 0.0973.

Table 4 Weather Impact Index Estimation

Term	Estimate	Std Error	t Ratio	Prob>|t|
Intercept	13.6346	0.0744	183.2001	0.0000
PM_{it}	0.0100	0.0008	12.1189	0.0000
TD_{it}	-0.2012	0.0042	-47.8228	0.0000

The corresponding estimation formula is

$$Tindex_{it}=13.6346+0.0099PM_{it}-0.2012TD_{it} \quad (12)$$

4.1.4 Comprehensive impact index estimate

The estimated operation and maintenance impact index (11) and weather impact index (12) are used for the further estimation of the comprehensive impact index. The results are shown in Table 5, and R2 = 0.1850.

Table 5 Comprehensive Impact Index Estimation

Term	Estimate	Std Error	t Ratio	Prob>|t|
Intercept	14.9623	0.3735	40.0602	0.0000
$Yindex_{it}$	1.0599	0.0199	53.1409	0.0000
$Tindex_{it}$	1.0500	0.0179	58.7176	0.0000

The corresponding estimation formula is

$$Findex_{it}=-14.96+1.05Yindex_{it}+1.04Tindex_{it} \quad (13)$$

The comprehensive impact index corresponds to R2=0.1850 which is greater than the operation and maintenance impact index as R2=0.0782 and the weather impact index as R2=0.0973.

4.1.5 Prediction model estimation

The comprehensive impact index corresponds to R2=0.1850 which is significantly smaller than the R2=0.5126 for the generalized AR(28) model. Therefore, the generalized AR (28) model is used whenever possible in the prediction, and the comprehensive impact index (13) is used as the auxiliary means. Finally we get the following prediction model:

$$G_{it} = \begin{cases} AR(28)_{it} & \text{If can be observed} \\ Findex_{it} & \text{If can not be observ} \end{cases} \quad (14)$$

In which, $AR(28)_{it}$is determined by model (10) and $Findex_{it}$ is given by model (13). Model (14) is a combination of generalized AR(28) model and regression model-generalized AR(28) combined regression.

4.2 Prediction

The abnormalities duration of the charging pile can be predicted with the use of generalized AR(28) combined regression model (14). In order to compare the prediction results, we use the data of the charging piles from the September and October of 2017 in the north of

Hebei province for the analysis. The actual abnormality rate and the predicted abnormality rate are shown as Figure 1 and the predicted abnormality rate is basically consistent with the actual abnormality rate. For the predicted error of abnormality rate, we focus on the absolute error and the predicted absolute error is shown in Figure 2. The average absolute error is 0.0044, and the median is 0.0025, which can meet the needs of the actual prediction of the operation department.

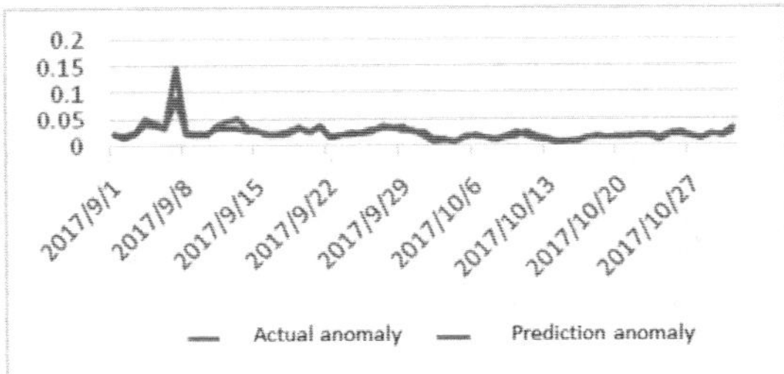

Figure 1 Actual abnormality rate and predicted abnormality rate

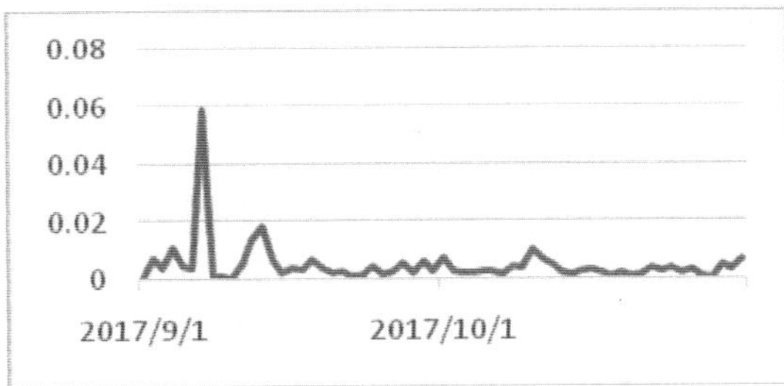

Figure 2 Predicted absolute error

5 Conclusion

Based on the operation data of the charging piles from January 2016 to August 2017 in the north of Hebei province, we used the AR(q) model's relatively accurate advantages in prediction and considered the generalized AR(q) model according to the characteristics of the abnormality duration data of the charging piles, avoiding the defect that the AR(q) model depends on lagged variables and combining the regression models. This generalized AR(q) combined regression prediction model is used for actual prediction and can be basically consistent with the actual abnormality rate. The absolute error effect generated can be accepted by the operation department.

REFERENCES

1. Wang Feilong, Sun Kaihang, Li Yanqing. Demand prediction of electric vehicle charging stations based on user classification [J]. Heilongjiang Electric Power, 2013, 35(2): 132-134.
2. Huang Qixin, Lu Zhuwei, Yang Zhengli. Research on prediction of electric vehicles charging loading [J]. Mechanical and Electrical Information, 2016,27(489):140-141.
3. Chen Lidan, Nie Yongquan, Zhongqing. Prediction model of electric vehicle charging load based on trip chain [J]. Transactions of China Electrotechnical Society, 2015, 30(4): 216-225.
4. Zhang Yuyu, Zhang Yuxin. ARMA time series-based electric vehicle charging station operation state prediction and charging power demand model [J]. Electrotechnical Application, 2016,35(21):52-58.
5. Arias, M.B., Bae, S. Electric vehicle charging demand forecasting model based on big data technologies[J]. Applied Energy, 2016, 183(12):327-339.
6. Majidpour, M., Qiu, C., Chu, P., Pota, HR, Gadh, R. Forecasting the EV charging load based on customer profile or station measurement?[J]. Applied Energy, 2016, 163(2): 134-141.
7. Peng Zhixing, Bao Changjun, Zhao Yang, Yi Honggang, Tang Shaowen, Yu Hao, ChenN Feng. ARIMA product seasonal model and its application in the prediction of infectious diseases[J]. Application of Statistics and Management, 2008,27(2): 362-368.
8. Bin, E. Econometrics of Panel Data Methods and Applications [M]. Oxford University Press, 2017.
9. Box, E.P., Jenkins, G.M., Reinsel, G.C., Ljung, G.M. Time series analysis: forecasting and control[M]. John Wiley & Sons, Inc., 2016.
10. Deb, C., Zhang, F., Yang, J., Lee, SE, Shah, KW A review on time series forecasting techniques for building energy consumption[J]. Renewable and Sustainable Energy Reviews, 2017, 74(7): 902-924.
11. Chen Yan, Shi Zhihui. Mixed financial time series prediction model based on Adaboost and regularized ELM and Its Application [J]. Application of Statistics and Management, 2017, 36(1):113-125.
12. Lu Lin, Xu Wei, Xiangyue, Zhang Yi, Xiong Jun. Research on optimal configuration of multi-regional charging piles based on Markov chain charging load prediction[J]. Engineering Science and Technology, 2017,49(3): 170-178.

Research Progress and Application of Computer Artificial Intelligence Technology

Jin Wei

Northwestern Polytechnical University Ming De College, Xi'an, China 710124

Abstract: With the development of science and technology, artificial intelligence technology has received more and more attention and attention. Under the background of the rapid development of big data and cloud computing, the artificial intelligence industry broke out. There is a huge amount of research on artificial intelligence and the artificial intelligence industry is huge. As far as the artificial intelligence industry in China is concerned, even the start is relatively late, but the industry scale, industrial layout, and technology research are all in a continuous improvement stage. Especially after the deepening of the layout of science and technology and manufacturing industries, the scale of artificial intelligence industry is further developed. More artificial intelligence products will appear at the same time. From the perspective of the concept, development history and new progress of artificial intelligence, this paper combines China's artificial intelligence market and the development of artificial intelligence companies to analyze the current major application areas, and then further explore the future development trend of artificial intelligence.

1 The Concept, Development History and New Progress of Artificial Intelligence

1.1The Concept of Artificial Intelligence

Artificial intelligence technology is an important branch in the field of computers. It refers to the simulation based on computer simulation technology. It simulates human thinking and behavior patterns, so that computer hardware devices can have human-like response capabilities, making computer hardware intelligent on the surface. So as to provide people with corresponding intelligent services. Artificial intelligence technology is not only artificial intelligence robots, but also includes virtual reality, speech recognition, automatic processing, and computer neural networks. In its development, it is not a single development, but a process that interacts with and merges with other disciplines. This technology has high efficiency in processing data, which can effectively solve uncertainties, learn new knowledge, and perform calculations on complex problems and learn the processing features [1].

1.2Artificial Intelligence Development Process

1.2.1The Rise of Artificial Intelligence

The concept of artificial intelligence was first proposed around the 1950s. Afterwards, many researches on artificial intelligence began, and achievements such as proof of machine theorem and processing of LISP table processing languages were achieved. However, due to the rise of artificial intelligence at that time and the fact that the technology involved multiple disciplines and multiple technical fields, artificial intelligence was limited by inference algorithms, machine translations and so on. And in the early development period other technologies also developed slowly.

1.2.2Artificial Intelligence Technology Development Tide

Since then, along with the development of other technologies and further research on artificial intelligence technology, experts and scholars in this field have developed an artificial intelligence expert system until the 1970s. The development of this system has promoted artificial intelligence technology into a new era. At the stage of development, research on artificial intelligence entered a period of high development.

1.2.3 Major Development Period of Artificial Intelligence Technology

With the development of computer technology, after the successful development of the fifth-generation computer, the artificial intelligence technology has also been further developed, and the study of this technology has entered a major period of development. This also shows that the research and development of artificial intelligence technology can not be separated from the development of computer technology, and the two are almost synchronized.

1.3 New Progress in Artificial Intelligence Research

In the information age, people's lives and work have been inseparable from computer networks and often require computers to complete information retrieval and other services. However, the problem that needs to be further solved in the computer field is how to obtain valuable information from complex information data, how to enable computer technology to provide people with real-time and convenient services, and how to make computer interfaces more humanized. These have become hot topics in artificial intelligence research. In addition, with the birth of cloud computing and big data, research on artificial intelligence is also moving toward data mining, knowledge realization, and intelligent interface technology.

2 Artificial Intelligence Market Analysis and China's Artificial Intelligence Enterprise Analysis

2.1 Artificial Intelligence Market Analysis

2016 is the first year of artificial intelligence. Since then, the artificial intelligence industry has broken out with the support of cloud computing and big data. Various researches on artificial intelligence have appeared in people's horizons, and the future market space is also very large. As far as China is concerned, the scale of the artificial intelligence industry reached 10 billion in 2016. The growth rate in 2017 exceeded 50%, and the industrial scale exceeded 15 billion yuan. It is estimated that by 2019, the artificial intelligence market in China will reach 34.4 billion yuan. With the deepening of industrial layout and technological research, as well as the deepening of the layout of technology and manufacturing industries, the market size of artificial intelligence has further expanded, and the emergence of numerous artificial intelligence startup companies will also bring more artificial intelligence products. For the artificial intelligence investment, there were 48 institutions investing in 2015, with an investment of 1.423 billion yuan. It is estimated that by 2021, the market size of artificial intelligence will reach 60 billion yuan [2].

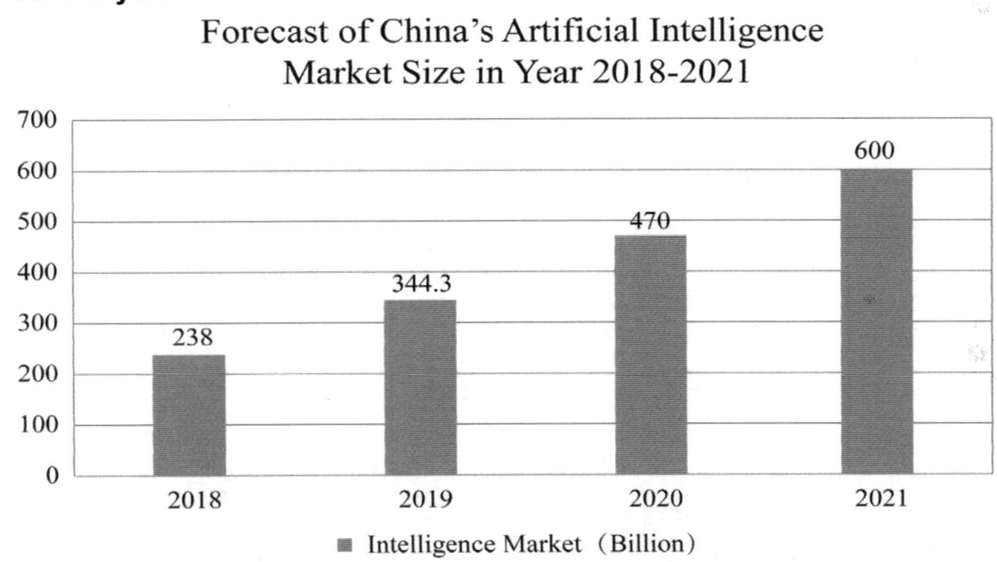

2.2China's Artificial Intelligence Enterprise Analysis

The number of artificial intelligence startup companies in China has risen since 2014, and there has been no decrease in the entrepreneurial enthusiasm for artificial intelligence until 2016, indicating that the artificial intelligence market has great prospects. At the end of 2016, the number of artificial intelligence startup companies reached more than 200. The main two directions of startup companies are voice and vision, and there are also many artificial intelligence dedicated chip companies. Based on an analysis of non-listed companies that use artificial intelligence as their driving technology and business, it was found that most companies were established in 2015, followed by 2014 and 2016. Regarding the startup direction of artificial intelligence startups, the largest number is in the field of computer vision, followed by the field of service robotics and speech, and others include smart medical, machine learning, and smart driving. Among them, computer vision technology is an important core technology of artificial intelligence. It can be applied in fields such as security, finance, hardware, marketing, and driving. The level of technology development is basically close to the international level.

https://doi.org/10.1051/matecconf/201817601043

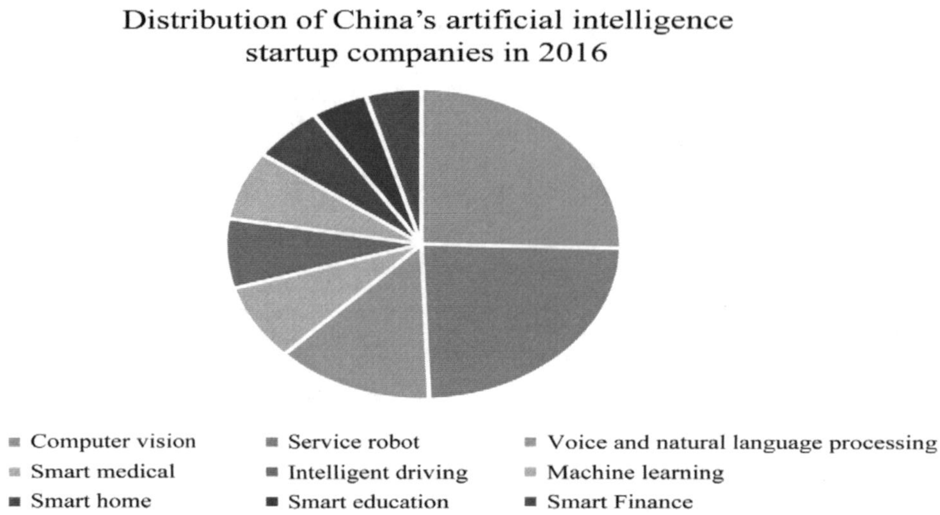

3 Artificial Intelligence Application Area Analysis

3.1 Computer Field

Artificial intelligence technology is developed along with the development of computer technology, so the application in the computer field is also the earliest and the most extensive. Applications included in computer network security, applications in the sharing of computer network resources, applications in speech and natural language processing, etc. One one hand, in terms of computer network security, on the one hand, artificial intelligence can identify useful information from complex data piles through automatic identification technologies and handle them in a timely manner. On the other hand, the intelligent management system can detect the security of network operations in a timely manner. Problems and timely repairs to ensure the normal operation of the computer network. In addition, the sharing of computer network resources not only improves the efficiency of resource sharing but also increases the accuracy of sharing. For example, P2P mode is a way to achieve peer-to-peer resource sharing [3], and the integration of P2P and artificial intelligence will make the resources on the network be used more effectively. As long as the artificial intelligence search software can be used to obtain the desired Resources, channels are open and the actual efficiency is high.

3.2 Remote Autonomous Planning and Control

Remote planning and control refers to the use of artificial intelligence technology to achieve the planning and control of space vehicles in outer space. For example, NASA of the United States uses computer intelligence programs to achieve precise control and planning of spacecrafts. The United States is also the first to use artificial intelligence technology to space outer space. A country that implements autonomous remote planning and control. In the application, it is mainly to link the remote intelligent program with the mission objective in the ground system, and then make autonomous planning for the spacecraft. In addition, dynamic real-time monitoring of spacecraft can be realized, and the actual operation of the spacecraft can be more comprehensively and accurately analyzed. In addition, timely detection of operational problems can be made to promptly issue adjustment commands to control the spacecraft, and ultimately ensure the safety and stability of the spacecraft and provide ground researchers with accurate information data references.

3.3Robotics

The application of the artificial intelligence robot field is the most extensive and the earliest. The robot technology emerged in the 1970s, and has since become a professional discipline applied in many fields. Robotic assistants, for example, are used in the medical field to help surgeons perform surgical procedures. The reason that the scope of artificial intelligence applied in the field of robots is constantly expanding. Apart from technical improvements, it is also related to robot artificial intelligence recognition technology. This technology can greatly reduce costs, and it can also protect internal and external risks. From the perspective of the development trend of China's artificial intelligence entrepreneurial enterprises, the research on service robots has become more in-depth. Service robots have appeared in many stores, restaurants, exhibitions, and other places to provide people with services such as navigation, shopping guides, and explanations. As robots in life are still relatively rare, the technology still needs continuous improvement and improvement.

3.4Expert System and Intelligent Decision System

Artificial intelligence began to replace some of human work with its huge database, even the memory of human beings, so it began to move toward the field of expert systems and intelligent decision systems. In the application, human experience and diagnosis can be analyzed through certain rules and it can made reasonable judgments[4]. The main use is the database of artificial intelligence and then search for something that is related to human memory and form a corresponding pattern. At present, the expert system has been widely used in enterprise management and can quickly formulate corresponding production, scheduling and transportation plans, thereby improving the management level of enterprises, reducing costs and increasing economic benefits.

3.5Applied to Auto Control

Computer vision has always been the main development direction of artificial intelligence entrepreneurial enterprises.With the continuous development of computer vision systems, artificial intelligence technology has also been applied to the automotive field. Through the installation of computer vision systems in automobiles, autonomous control of automobiles can be realized. The car runs steadily on the driveway. At present, the United States has applied this technology to micro-cars to complete autonomous navigation and autonomous driving control through artificial intelligence. However, the application of this field is still only a preliminary stage of exploration. In the future, it is necessary to allow the visual system to accumulate more human application experience, control the direction of the car, and calculate the best driving direction. In the future, driverless cars will become a research hotspot, which is one of the most important applications of artificial intelligence.

4 Artificial Intelligence Future Trends

At present, China is in an important period of economic transformation. The manufacturing industry is facing the problem of industrial upgrading. According to “Made in China 2025”, it is clearly pointed out that intelligent manufacturing and high-end technological innovation should be regarded as key construction projects, and in particular service robots and other artificial intelligence technologies should be We will give priority to the development of technologies in the future to cultivate artificial intelligence core enterprises. From the current research hotspot of artificial intelligence, it mainly focuses on data mining, knowledge realization, and intelligent interface technologies. Therefore, the development of artificial intelligence in the future may be focused on fuzzy processing technology, parallelization, neural networks, and machine emotions. There will be a breakthrough in technology, wider application areas, and more attention to the ethical issues of artificial intelligence.

4.1 Advanced Technology and Wider Application Area

In technology, more attention will be paid to the research of artificial neural networks. Although artificial neural networks can never replace human brains, the processing of information through neuron interactions and the storage of knowledge and information can help humans broaden their knowledge and conduct intelligent control. In the future, the development trend of research on artificial neural networks mainly presents three characteristics: firstly, the artificial neural network model has a fast generation efficiency; secondly, the artificial neural network model is continuously improved and improved; in addition, the artificial neural network is integrated with other calculation methods and applications, such as the combination of neural networks and genetics, and the combination of chaos theory [5].

Although the development of computer technology tends to be gentle at this stage, and integration with other disciplines and fields is also continuing to slow down, artificial intelligence based on computer technology will enter a period of gentle development. However, in the future, artificial intelligence technology will continue to deepen with the development of computer technology, and some relatively low-level artificial intelligence technologies will develop rapidly. However, due to the fact that many fields have not yet reached full integration with other disciplines in applications, there is also great room for development in the future. In addition, in terms of applications, artificial intelligence technology can't really realize the smart life of smart homes under the existing computer technology conditions, and life intelligence is still in an exploratory stage, so in the future, artificial intelligence technology will move towards people’s lives. Closely linked to the development of the direction, the real intelligent robots may approach millions of households in the future, and have a great impact on human daily life. Of course, in the fields of transportation and medical care, the development of artificial intelligence technology will also promote the realization of intelligent transportation and intelligent medical care, and improve the efficiency of work in two areas through fully automated methods.

4.2 More Attention to the Ethical Issues of Artificial Intelligence

Artificial intelligence will increasingly focus on robot emotions in the future development. That is to say, how do intelligent robots “communicate” with each other and get along with humans after they enter human life? Does artificial intelligence have the same thinking as humans, and will human minds be replaced by robots? These issues will be the focus of future research, especially with the continuous progress of artificial intelligence technology, ethical issues will become a hot topic. Regarding the ethical issues of robots, whether robots should have the same emotions and rights as humans will become the focus of every expert, scholars and scientists, and even every member of society.

4.3 Notice Things

With technological breakthroughs in artificial intelligence and thinking about robot emotions, we should pay attention to the following points when we study artificial intelligence technologies in the future: First, we should adhere to the Marxist philosophy of philosophy, that is, we must adhere to the concept of people-oriented, and develop people. The initiative and the role of the main body must not be misplaced in that robots can replace all human activities and even thinking; secondly, they must continuously improve the scientific knowledge and literacy of the public, such as the popularization of scientific and cultural knowledge among the masses, and the promotion of artificial intelligence technology. There is a deep understanding of development so that mistakes can be avoided. In addition, it is necessary to establish the development standards of artificial intelligence and make reasonable plans for the future development and application of artificial intelligence technologies.

5 Conclusion

In summary, artificial intelligence technology has already entered people's life and production, and there are more and more industries related to artificial intelligence. The market scale has gradually expanded, bringing great convenience to people's life and production, and has been obtained in many fields. A wide range of applications. In the future, with the deepening of computer technology, artificial intelligence will achieve a greater breakthrough in technology. Research on neural networks, life intelligence, intelligent robots, intelligent transportation, and intelligent medical care will become a hot topic. However, in its development, people must realize that artificial intelligence is by no means omnipotent and will never replace human beings as a dominant position. Therefore, it is also necessary to study its ethical morality and not to influence correct human values due to the ethical issues of robots. This paper conducts some research and analysis on the application and development of computer artificial intelligence technology. It is concluded that in the future development, we must pay more attention to the development of its technology and application. At the same time, we must pay more attention to the ethical issues and make the development of artificial intelligence technology a human being. Development provides a safe and stable technological environment.

6 References:

1. Luo Yong, Xiang Yixue. Research Progress and Application of Computer Artificial Intelligence Technology[J]. Electronic production2014(18).
2. Wang Jia. Application bottleneck of computer artificial intelligence identification technology [J]. Science and Technology Outlook, 2016 (35).
3. Shi Ruifang. Application of Artificial Intelligence in Computer Network Technology[J]. Communications World, 2016(23).
4. Tan Shiping. Application Analysis of Artificial Intelligence in Computer Network Technology[J]. Silicon Valley, 2013(18): 11+4.
5. Yang Heng. Research progress and application of computer artificial intelligence technology[J]. Information and Communications, 2014(01): 130.

Simple Analysis on the Cause of the Development of Furniture Designer's Brand Industry -- Take MORELESS and OPAL for Example

Liu Xingyin[1], Dong Wenying[1,2,a]

[1]Sichuan Agricultural University, College of Forest, Chengdu 611130, Sichuan, China
[2] Central South University of Forestry and Technology, Changsha 410000, Hunan, China

Abstract: This article analyzes the characteristics of different types of furniture brands based on ordinary brands and designer brands. We also investigates and studies the causes of the development and growth of designer brands, and further combines the successful cases of domestic excellent furniture designer brands to summarize the specific reasons for the formation of the brand of furniture designers, design principles and methods. This paper discusses the development direction, design principles and methods of furniture designer brand, and provides references for the comprehensive exploration of furniture designer's brand development.

1 Definition of Brand Type

In the division of furniture brand, it can be divided into minority brand and popular brand according to the different leading way of product design. In simple terms, the minority brand also called the designer brand, which is dominated by the design style of the designer; and the popular brand is dominated by the market demand. One is the design of subjective consciousness, and the other is the design of the objective requirement, so there are obvious differences between the both in the consumer. The designer brand is guided by the consumer diversification and individualized demand, with the designer's personal design concept as the guidance. The founder of the designer brand furniture is the design director, who controls the design of furniture products, and has independent proposition and attitude of design, and distinctive design language. The designer brand has a deep study on the furniture trend and the ideal life style, and the designer is the strategic core of brand. The popular brand is guided by the consumer market, Keep abreast of consumer preferences and fashion trends, and designs products that meet market demand. The popular brand is usually an enterprise that owns such hardware as manufacturing technology and equipment, and has such software as planning, advertising and marketing capabilities. Therefore, the popular brand has mature and perfect product service system, lower production cost and price advantage. However, compared with the designer brand, its design performance and design level are not enough, and the homogeneity is serious.

2 Case of Designer Brand

2.1 Social Transformation and Development

China is changing from the electrified industrial age to the automated Internet era. The situation of serious information asymmetry in the industrial age has been improved in the Internet age. In the industrial age, manufacturers can not integrate information and they only combine all the needs. From a design point of view, they are design for design, innovation for innovation. In the era of Internet, the market economic system is transformed from producer oriented to consumer oriented. The value of commodities depends more on the psychological needs of consumers, and the product from functional satisfaction to psychological satisfaction.

From the perspective of Internet communication, designer brand furniture which does not possess the financial strength of a popular brand cannot be publicized by TV, newspapers or magazines which needs high cost of advertising. Through the dissemination of the Internet, we can use the brand's official website, WeChat Subscription, Microblog, Douban and Renren which are known to the mainstream media to expand the influence. It can be said that the spread of the Internet has promoted the development of designer brand.

In addition, E-commerce has promoted the development of logistics. The transition from traditional logistics to modern logistics and the formation of information as the core, to strengthen the integration of resources and logistics process optimization, increasingly mature and perfect large logistics companies with the lowest cost of logistics will be this kind of large furniture products delivered to consumers. This is also another reason for the development of the designer brand furniture industry.

*Corresponding author: [a] Doreen0656@126.com

2.2 The Development of Social Economy and the Change of Social Demand

American psychologist Maslow's hierarchy of needs theory points out that human needs are divided into five categories, which are physiological needs, security needs, social needs, esteem needs and self-actualization needs. Five kinds of needs are gradually increasing at the level. Its incentive function will be reduced after the low level needs to be satisfied, and the high level needs will replace the low level need to become the new goal, which will push people towards a higher level. With the development of China's economy after the reform and opening up, some people are getting rich already, and the number is increasing by years. Those who have reached the stage of well-off society are developing to the prosperous stage or have reached the level of prosperity. Popular brand furniture can no longer satisfy the aesthetic needs of such middle and upper class in social strata. In pursuit of actualization needs of higher value, designer brand furniture arises at the historic moment. In addition, with the development of the times, young people seeking personality began to accept the purchase of such brand products.

As the Japanese designer Masayuki Kurokawa's point "Only by starting from a special self can the design truly resonate with others[1]". Designers understand consumers' needs and combine their own design characteristics to create better product experience for consumers. Therefore, the differences of consumers' psychological needs make product development more diversified and personalized.

2.3 Progress in Production Technology

The modern society has close the distance between the designers and the customers, at the same time, it has brought the designer closer to the factory. Designer brands choose to send orders to enterprises with excellent quality and low production cost through the way of OEM (Original Equipment Manufacturing). The processing strength of the factory is combined with the design strength of the designer brand to make the products of the small amount and customized products to avoid waste of resources caused by overcapacity. The designer brand has a good design resource integration ability, which conforms to the development direction of the times.

2.4 National policy

2.4.1 The Development of Urbanization

As the progress of the urbanization process, "The Growth Forecast Report of China ' s Urbanization Rate in 2016-2020 " shows the permanent population of China's urbanization will reach 810 million in 2018, and the urbanization rate of China will reach 63.4% in 2020. This means that the rural population is flooding into cities, buying houses to change their living conditions and Furnish new furniture. Therefore, the market demand for furniture is also increasing, the development prospect of furniture industry is good.

2.4.2 Innovation-driven

Premier Li Keqiang put forward the slogan of "mass entrepreneurship and multitude innovation", and built a new engine for China's economy. Local governments responded to the call and issued various supporting policies for innovation and entrepreneurship, from funding support to the construction of entrepreneurial parks. All these policies are conducive to the development of furniture designer brand. Analysis from the point of view that innovation is the foundation of a nation, the policy support of our country, more professional design background and the higher educational background of designer make the designer brand can be more create a design powerful nation.

2.5 The Change of the Consciousness of Consumption and the Improvement of the Design Level of the Designer

With the improvement of consumers' awareness of health and environmental protection, Economically powerful consumers are more health-conscious and more willing to buy environmentally friendly products. Designer brand furniture has small capacity and short chain of funds, so it is more cautious in design. Designer brand furniture is a "D2C" development model, that means designer to consumer. Designer brands know more about customers who buy their own brands, so the unmarketable rate of the product is lower and the impact on the environment is smaller. According to the survey, most of the designer brand furniture is solid wood furniture, the structure of furniture is mostly connected with tenon joints, the use of adhesives is less, and the wood surface is made of natural wood wax oil. So the furniture almost does not contain three benzene and formaldehyde, which is more safe and healthier to use.As mentioned above, consumer demand has begun to change to the needs of self-realization, and consumers pay more attention to spiritual needs. Therefore, furniture designers are very important in the design, storytelling and culture of the product.

3 Analysis of Designer Brand

The well-known international brands, such as Dior, Chanel, Givenchy, are based on designer brands. At the beginning of the brand, the brand culture and image have been identified. The reason why these designer brands have been standing for a long time is due to the uniqueness of their styles. China's designer brands have come a long way from abroad. But in recent years, with the development of domestic economy, technological progress, improvement of design concept, change of consumption concept and support from various localities, furniture designer brand has mushroomed in the past ten years. Especially in recent years, by participating in the furniture exhibition at home and abroad, the furniture designer brand with creative design strategy has been recognized by the furniture industry.

The consumer group of designer brand furniture is usually a customer with higher income and pursuit personal taste. Such brand positioning is easy to meet the needs of contemporary people in pursuit of individuality, fully embodies their brand characteristics, and expands their market impact in differentiation[2]. Starting from the analysis of influential designer brand furniture can help us further understand the generation, development and future trends of designer brands.

3.1 Designer Zhu Xiaojie and Furniture Designer Brand of OPAL

It has been more than 20 years since zhu xiaojie started the furniture designer brand of OPAL in 1994. Zhu Xiaojie, a Chinese furniture industry leader - led his design team to design and manufacture furniture products has become a banner of industry development, OPAL, the designer brand has become the benchmark of Chinese furniture designer brand and even furniture industry. "Have the collection value of contemporary furniture". This is the market evaluation of the OPAL brand. Because each work is not only unique, but also flowing with the fragrance of the national soil. Zhu Xiaojie paid attention to the texture of wood itself, designed according to the characteristics of wood, and made Chinese design and expressed the Chinese way of life. It has the value of collection which makes the designer brand different from the popular brand. The design idea of OPAL "gives people the art of living". The designer draws inspiration from the traditional Chinese architectural culture, the furniture culture and Taoist thought, combines the natural philosophy of Taoism with the design, and integrates the functional materials emphasized in the Nordic furniture style, and has design a series of furniture works which are popular among the people at home and abroad.

Zhu Xiaojie mentioned in his own furniture "money chair" that is able to express the connotation of the Ming style chair only with some lines . Simple but the cohesion of the power, which is the combination of traditional technology and modern skills and art that means the combination of designer thought and life. The "Money Chair" was designed to express the "The inside is square and the outside is round, each other is slowly sublimation" of the Taoist thought[3]. (Figure1. "Money Chair", designed by Zhu Xiaojie) Not only to inherit the Ming style chair but also emphasizes "design is an idea of imitation".

In Zhu Xiaojie's view, designers should not only get rid of the shackles and find the essence of life, but more important is to know themselves and to guide the design with reality. In addition to the design of furniture, Zhu Xiaojie also using the surplus wood produced in the process of furniture processing to designed a series of functional products with sparrows as a prototype, , such as card case, Wine Opener.(Figure2. Card Case, Wine Opener) As American designer Victor Papanek emphasizes in the book "Design for the real world". The most important part of design is an appropriate element in the process of social change. He stresses that the design should take seriously the use of the limited earth's resources and serve the protection of the earth's ecological environment[4]. A designer should have a sense of social responsibility. Before he starts to design, his social and moral judgement must play a role in balancing the relationship between production and resources, design and materials.

Figure 1. "Money Chair" designed by Zhu Xiaojie

Figure 2. Card Case Wine Opener

3.2 Designer Hou Zhengguang and Furniture Designer Brand of MORELESS

Furniture designer brand of MORELESS was founded by Hou Zhengguang in 2010. It mainly designs, produces and sells original furniture and home furnishings with contemporary Chinese literary and artistic forms. Since listing has been widely liked by the public. "more and less" is a problem, a choice and an attitude. The inevitable return of design is simplicity after paying too much for formalism. "more and less" is both moderate and unique like a nature laws similar to a kind of allelopathy. The connotation of designer brand furniture is "brand", which is the core competitiveness and core values. He pointed out that the future of China's design must be in line with the revival of culture, the reduction of ignorance and what is really suitable for the people of the country. He stressed that as a Chinese designer, we should show the Chinese style in our blood through the design.

The MORELESS of design always stressed the "more" thinking and "less" form, "more" function and "less" material. It's furniture looks simple but actually have plenty of functions. It's natural materials selection, simple design and aesthetic sense of details guide people to feel the unique texture of wood. The MORELESS designs have a simple feeling that takes you away from prosperity and return to tranquility.（Figure3, Figure4）

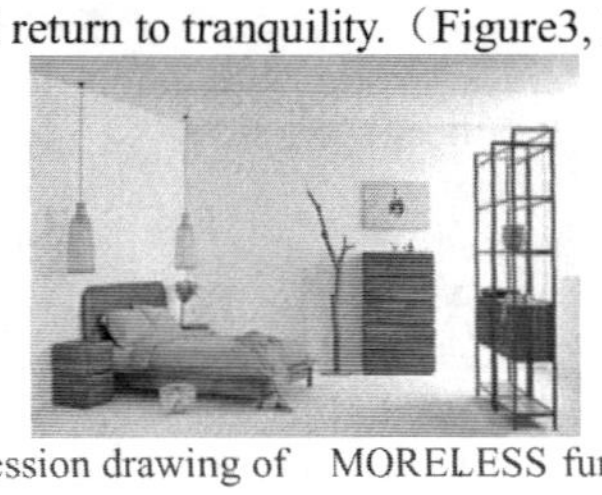

Figure 3. Impression drawing of MORELESS furniture scene

Figure 4. Local details of MORELESS furniture

In the whole operation of MORELESS, the design and marketing are divided. MORELESS is a project invested by Hou Zhengguang's Mooma design company. The role of Mooma just a design investor, responsible for brand packaging, product and space design. All marketing is not involved which is responsible for a completely independent sales company. Because it is the investor, there is a greater voice in the design but the right to speak is also from the sales party and they put forward feedback from the first line market[6]. The whole business operation of MORELESS is successful since its inception in 2010. It has developed into a popular furniture designer brand in just a few years. This is a successful case that emphasizes the design change market and the market guidance design.

4 Conclusions

By analyzing the development process of these designer brands of OPAL and MORELESS which has a leading position in the furniture industry. It can be seen that furniture design with deep thinking rooted in traditional Chinese culture and lifestyle is not only accepted by domestic but also widely praised by foreign countries. As Hegel said, "only the nation is the world". The nationalized language and the emotional language will become a major design trend in the future. Designers are the core of the designer brands, which requires the designers to conform to their own hearts. Only by turning what you want to do into what you can do can you expand your brand influence continuously.

"Creation" is the name of the designer brand, and the designer finds inspiration and the connotation of the product in the traditional culture, art, philosophy and modern life. Through the design technique, the designer transforms this connotation into product characteristics, which satisfies the consumer's psychological needs, that is, the story of the product. Saint Exupéry said "only when the wind of the spirit blows the clay, can we create human beings". Kenya Hara also said, "only when the wind of life philosophy blows people, material and technology, can we create something that transcends the soul of clay". For this reason, "things" are no longer convenient but become elements of life that seem to be able to hear breathing. In the future, the design is to pursue such high-quality creation[7].

Designer brand is a relatively new concept for the whole furniture market. Consumers don't know what type of furniture they want to choose, who only have a general style trend and functional requirement. They need the specific furniture products to be built by designers. Only when the designer's furniture works are placed, can the customers know whether they are in line with their needs. The designer brand is gradually changing the development trend of the whole furniture market, which leads the market trend and affects the consumer's aesthetic. Behind the success of MORELESS, it is also told that furniture designers should learn to understand the market besides designing well, but not blindly cater to the market. The design proposition of designer brand is the framework of the whole brand, and the feedback of the market is the concrete filling of the framework and make the design is more mature.

Acknowledgments

This work was financially supported by the major project of humanities and social sciences of education department of Sichuan province (16SA0006), the "Key Laboratory of Wood Industry and Universities", the project of Undergraduate Scientific Research Interest of Sichuan Agricultural University.

References

1. (Japan) Masayuki Kurokawa. Design and death [M]. He Jinfeng, translation. Electronic Industry Press (2013).
2. Liu Zhong. The rise and development of Chinese independent designer brand [D]. Beijing Institute Of Fashion Technology (2008).
3. Xu Qin. Sit down, Milan,Chinese contemporary chair design exhibition curator Zhu Xiaojie interview [J]. Creative Design Source (2012.3), p. 4-15.
4. (U.S) Victor Papanek. Design for the real world [M]. Zhou Bo, translation. China Citic Press (2013).
5. Wang Shanxiang. Moreless furniture in Shanghai M50 [J]. Interior Design and Decoration (2013.9), p. 122-125.
6. Wang Li. MoreLess? Half of the sea water, half of the flame. Hou Zhengguang interview [J]. Furniture (2011.1), p. 28-33.
7. (Japan) Kenya Hara. dialogue for design [M]. Zhu E translation. Shandong People's Publishing House (2010).

The Research and Development of Quanzhou Cultural and Creative Products Based on "Maritime Silk Road" Culture

Wang Xing-he

Liming Vocational University, Quanzhou 362000, China

Abstract. From the perspective of regional culture, it elaborates the characteristics of Quanzhou "Maritime Silk Road" culture and analyzes the status quo of Quanzhou cultural and creative products. Based on the analysis, it raises the great significance that the regional culture brings to the design and development of cultural and creative products and summarizes its three forms: diverse religious cultures, colorful folk art forms, unique human and architectural landscape, aiming to create economic value and spread Quanzhou "Maritime Silk Road" culture to the world as well.

1 Introduction

Among the domestic and foreign researches on "Cultural and Creative Products", some are about the great significance of developing cultural and creative products by Cultural Relics Departments [1-2], and some are about the creation of cultural and creative brands, which propose the prospect of ceramics and cultural products [3] under the pattern of "Creative Market". There are also some scholars proposing that the traditional utensil culture is the main source of regional culture and the researches of its design is important for developing cultural industries and promoting regional cultural identity. [4] There are lots of researches on "cultural and creative products" in academia and the existing researches on Quanzhou "Maritime Silk Road" culture have also gained numerous achievements, but most of them focus on the inheritance and development of the "Maritime Silk Road" culture, especially the protection and inheritance of "intangible" cultural heritage. In the perspective of protection, some researches put forward the proposals for the protection of Islamic architectural relics in Quanzhou [5] by comparing and analyzing the heritage of the remains of Islamic buildings such as Qingjing Mosque and Tombs of Islamic Saints from the point of view of World Heritage. In terms of cultural exchange, it was pointed out that the Buddhist music and dance in the cultural heritage of Quanzhou is the historical result of the exchange of human civilization in the Middle Ages and it is also a historical necessity for multiple music and dance cultures to collide and blend with each other [7], according to the relationship between the Maritime Silk Road and Nanyin in Quanzhou and the exploration of their origins and introduction ways [6]. However, there are few researches on combining cultural and creative products with the "Maritime Silk Road" culture.

The design of cultural and creative products should be the embodiment of regional cultures, the combination of creativity and culture, and the protection and persistence of "original" culture. Therefore, it is urgent for designers to solve the problem that how to integrate the cultural elements of Quanzhou "Maritime Silk Road" culture into the cultural creative design and create a product with strong regional characteristics of "Maritime Silk Road" culture. Starting with religious cultures, folk art forms, human and architectural landscapes, this article analyzes its basic features, extracts its characteristic elements, and refines its design and development concepts in order to be of some help for the innovation of Quanzhou's "Maritime Silk Road" cultural and creative products.

2 Quanzhou "Maritime Silk Road" Cultural Characteristics

"Geographical culture is a kind of spiritual power that represents the soul of a nation, a regional taste, and the image of a city. [8] "To some extent, the characteristics of urban culture are a manifestation of regional culture.

Quanzhou integrates the essences of the Minyue culture, the Central Plains culture, and the marine culture. It is the starting point of the Maritime Silk Road, the first batch of historical and cultural cities of the State Council, the only city that has three major categories of UN "intangible" projects in the country, and a city with profound historical and cultural background. Quanzhou is a place with a distinctive multicultural view, where Buddhism, Taoism, Islam, Christianity and the like gather, blossom and then leave a large number of precious religious relics. The East and West Towers in Kaiyuan Temple, is China's extant highest stone pavilion tower imitating wooden structure type; Taoist Laojun Statue is listed as national key protected cultural relics;

the Holy Sepulchre is the oldest and most complete Islamic sacred site in our country; Qingjing Temple is the oldest existing Islamic temple built by Arab Muslims in China; Mani Hermitage is the only surviving Mani Buddha and Manichaeism temple in China. Thus, Quanzhou is also known as the "World Religion Museum". At the same time, Quanzhou has a rich and colorful cultural heritage, such as Quanzhou Nanyin known as the living fossil music, Luoyang Bridge being one of the "Four Ancient Famous Bridges" in China, the string puppet of "Chinese Unique", Liyuan Opera known as the living fossil opera of the Southern and Southern Song Dynasty, the traditional Gaojia dramas, "Hui'an Nv" and "Xun'fu Nv" who are famous at home and abroad because of costumes rich in local characteristics. These cultural resources with rich "Maritime Silk Road" characteristics are an important part of Quanzhou's cultural and creative products, and are also the key to expanding Quanzhou's cultural and creative industries' influence

3 Status Quo of Quanzhou "Maritime Silk Road" Culture and Creation Products

State Council's "Several Opinions on Promoting the Integration and Development of Cultural Creation, Design Services, and Relevant Industries" (Guo Fa (2014) No. 10) and Fujian's "Notice on Eight Measures to Promote the Integration and Development of Cultural Creation, Design Services, and Relevant Industries " (Min Zheng (2014) No. 54), both explicitly stated that the cultural and creative industries have an important role in boosting the economic transformation and upgrading, improving the quality of life of the people, and enhancing cultural soft power and the like. Taking Quanzhou as an example, the city's cultural industry added 26.9 billion yuan in 2016, has soared 20 per cent year-on-year growth with last year and nearly 5 per cent points higher than the GDP growth rate over the same period, accounted for 5.4 per cent of the city's GDP and its proposition has continued to increase, therefore it has become the pillar industries for the national economy in Quanzhou. In recent years, the Quanzhou Municipal Party Committee and the Municipal Government have set up a leading group and its office for cultural reform and development work with the mayor being the leader, and have successively introduced a series of important policies to support the development of cultural industries and to escort the research and development of Quanzhou cultural creation products. Quanzhou has 802 cultural relics' protection units at all levels, including 31 at the national level and 83 at the provincial level. There are 601 intangible cultural heritages at all levels, levels and quantities rank among the top three in the country. These abundant cultural resources provide a vast space for the research and development of cultural and creative products. In 2013, Quanzhou was selected as the first "East Asian Cultural Capital" by virtue of its rich cultural history. In 2015, Quanzhou hosted the 14th Asian Art Festival and became the "Eastern Conference Hall" of CCTV 2015 Spring Festival Evening. It fully proves that Quanzhou's geographical and cultural charm is gradually recognized and identified by our people, and solidifies the foundation of research and development of Quanzhou's cultural creation product.

However, few types, serious homogeneity, low technical content and relatively lack of creativity of current cultural and creative products in Quanzhou which can not fully demonstrate the characteristics of Quanzhou's "Maritime Silk Road" and then greatly reduce consumer purchase desire.

4 Application of Regional Culture in Quanzhou's "Maritime Silk Road" Cultural and Creative Products

4.1 Diverse Religious Culture

Quanzhou is known as a religious resort where Buddhism, Taoism, Islam, Catholicism, Christianity and other religions gather and live together harmoniously and leave a large number of valuable religious relics. This is a wonderful spectacle in the history of Chinese and Western cultures, so Quanzhou is also known as the "World Religion Museum" and became the world's first designated unit of UNESCO's "Multicultural Exhibition Center of the World", considering Laojun Statue, Kaiyuan Temple, Qingjing Temple, Mani Hermitage, and the like as the representative. The unique and distinctive diversity of religious culture makes the creativity, form, style and color of cultural and creative products unique and attractive.

Taking Kaiyuan Temple founded in the Tang Dynasty as an example, it is the largest Buddhist temple in Fujian Province, an important cultural relic on the southeast coast of China and it was listed as the second batch of key cultural relic protection units in the country in 1982. The East and West Towers in Kaiyuan Temple built in the Tang Dynasty, the China's extant highest stone pavilion towers imitating wooden structure type, is still standing firm under the severe test of the times, represents the outstanding achievements of Quanzhou stone architecture and carving art, is a gem of Chinese ancient stone buildings and becomes a beautiful business card of Quanzhou. Figure 1 shows a creative bookshelf originating from the East and West Towers. The bookshelf extracts the East-West Towers' silhouette as a design element, and takes the meaning of the mutual protection of the two standing-firm towers. The reddish-brown wooden bookshelf with novel and practical design puts the original boring book-laying behaviour into a strong cultural atmosphere to enhance the interaction between people and products and let the bond of emotions tightly integrate people and products together [9] to leave an indelible impression on consumers, and then deepen their impression of the city of Quanzhou.

https://doi.org/10.1051/matecconf/201817602002

Figure 1 "East and West Towers" Bookshelf Design

Taking Qingjing Temple as an example, it was built on the architectural form of the Islamic Chapel of Damascus in Syria. It is one of the four major Islamic temples in China and is the only temple in the Song Dynasty that has been preserved so far. It was among the first batch of key cultural relic protection units announced by the State Council, is witnesses of friendship and cultural exchanges between China and Arab countries and is one of the important historical sites of overseas exchanges in Quanzhou. Figure 2 shows a creative U disk originating from the "Qingjing Temple". The product is based on the Qingjing Temple gatehouse, injects Islamic sanctity and purity into the U disk design carrier, to brings to consumers a sensation that their ears needs a moment of calmness in the process of eye-catching in the East and West from ancient to modern times. The U disk design is dominated by green and white colour, and its telescopic operation mode not only protects the interface, but also adds aesthetics and great geographical features.

Figure 2 "Qingjing Temple" U Disk Design

4.2 Colorful Folk Art Features

Cultural and artistic forms flourish. Quanzhou Nanyin, with its rich and profound historical and cultural heritage, is one of the country's oldest existing musical species. It has accompanied Quanzhou people's daily life for thousands of years, is a living fossil of musical culture and was listed into the human intangible cultural heritage representative list by UNESCO in 2009. Liyuan Opera known as the living fossil opera of the Southern and Southern Song Dynasty and the traditional Gaojia dramas are still the Quanzhou people's daily entertainment. At the same time, the Quanzhou string puppet of "Chinese Unique", unique palm puppets, chest dancing and other traditional cultural performances, which are amusing and exquisite, let the people dwell upon with great relish. Rich and colourful art culture is an important component of cultural and creative products and has a distinct cultural tension.

Take Nanyin as an example, Quanzhou Nanyin also known as "Chord Tube" which was originated in the Qianqin and formed in the Song Dynasty, is a fusion of the Central Plains music culture and local folk music, and is the oldest Han ancient music in China [10]. It retains the Han people's ancient ethnic singing before the Tang Dynasty and sings with the Southern Fujian Dialect of Quanzhou. It has the cultural expressions of the ancient music of the Central Plains and is very characteristic. In 2006, it was approved by the State Council to be included in the first batch of state-level intangible cultural heritage. In 2009, Nanyin (Quanzhou Chord Tube) was formally listed by UNESCO in the representative list of human intangible cultural heritage. Figure 3 is the "Sweet Voice" cosmetic design. These cosmetics extract the shapes of Nanyin traditional musical instruments as a design element to put the feelings of the town people miss of families and nostalgia into cosmetics. The novel practical design full of stories and implication combine makeup interest and humanistic feelings to expose the consumers to the sound of Nanyin music, and arouse their new emotional experience.

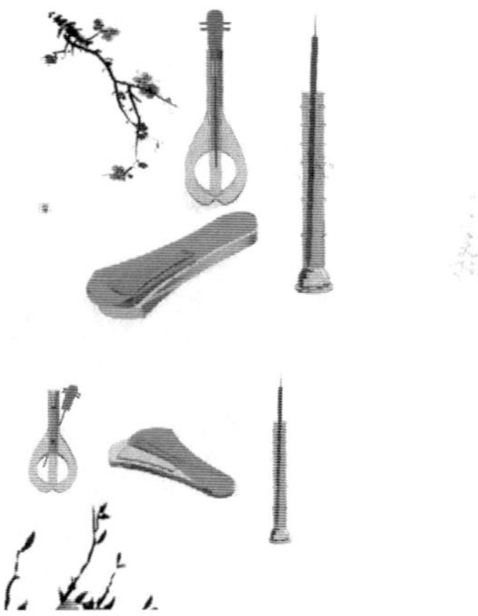

Figure 3 "Sweet Voice" Cosmetic Design

Taking Liyuan Opera, the living fossil of the ancient Southern opera, as an example, which is one kind of old drama originated in Quanzhou during the Song and Yuan Dynasties and has spread widely in Quanzhou, Xiamen, Zhangzhou and other places, being included in the first batch of state-level intangible cultural heritage. Figure 4 is the "Southern Opera" doll alarm clock design. The product is designed with the theme of Liyuan Opera, uses the cute models of the character Liyuan Opera characters and combine the alarm clock, charging, sound together with a memory card for the customers to freely choose their favourite music. These designs preserve the city's memories in cultural and creative gifts, interpret

https://doi.org/10.1051/matecconf/201817602002

urban aesthetics, tell city stories, and highlight the uniqueness of Quanzhou's geographically distinctive products through modern design language.

Figure 4 "Southern Opera" Doll Alarm Clock

4.3 Unique Cultural and Architectural Landscape

Quanzhou is located on the southeastern coast and forms a unique humanistic feature, such as the Hui'an Nv with its distinctive clothing features "feudal head, democratic belly, saving shirt, waste of pants." At the same time, its architecture not only has the characteristics of traditional Chinese architecture, but also has formed its own unique architectural style because of its environment, such as "Da Cuo", "Qi Lou" and the like. All these have become an important carrier of cultural and creative products.

Take Hui'an Nv as an example, they refer to the female of Huidong Peninsula in Hui'an County, Quanzhou. Hui'an County is located in the coastal area, with many people but little land in the area. Because men in the family need to go fishing or go out for a living for a long time under the imperatives of life, Hui'an female bravely shoulder heavy burdens, support their parents in-laws, teach their children, can do all kinds of unskilled work, heavy work and skilled work well. At the same time, their "feudal head, democratic belly, saving shirt, waste of pants" distinctive local characteristics clothing features let them known both at home and abroad. Hui'an Nv spirit is a vivid portrayal of Quanzhou people's spirit of "Love to Fight and Win", and has become a unique cultural feature of Quanzhou. Figure 5 shows the design of the "Hui'an Nv" tumbler alarm clock.

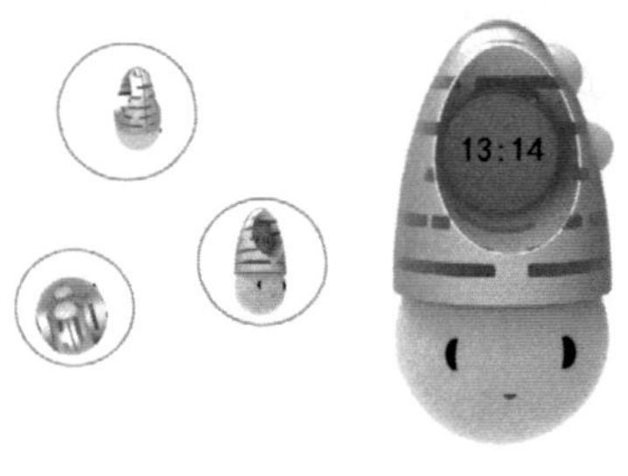

Figure 5 "Hui'an Nv" Tumbler Alarm Clock Design

The "Hui'an Nv" tumbler alarm clock is designed based on Hui'an female image and adopts the image composition method to extract its concise and practical features, and to refine the design elements of the "feudal head and democratic belly" of Hui'an Nv's clothing using the tumbler style to make alarm clocks both practical and geographically attractive and attract more consumers to purchase.

As a carrier of historical culture, architecture not only shows the local folk customs, but also reflects the local artistic achievements and is deeply influenced by local culture. The architecture of Quanzhou not only has the characteristics of a wooden frame roof, a clear symmetry of the central axis and the like of a traditional Chinese building, but also forms a distinctive architectural style due to the southeastern coastal environment and its function of the overseas traffic and trade ports. It has absorbed the essence of Chinese traditional culture, marine culture and the Minyue culture, and has become an important carrier of Maritime Silk Road culture. Different from traditional Chinese architecture using grey bricks as major materials in building walls, Minnan area would like red bricks in building houses, and red brick houses are a major feature of Minnan architecture. They are well-known in the world with beautiful shape and rich local characteristics. Quanzhou red brick building is a typical representative of the "Red Brick District" culture [8]. Take red brick cuo as an example, "Cuo" represents house in the dialect of Minnan. The red brick cuo is the house covered with red brick, which is a typical traditional dwelling and the most representative traditional building in southern Fujian. Its exquisite carvings not only show the mature sculpture art of southern Fujian, but also can exhibit the impact of Islam, Indian Buddhism, Nanyang culture and Western architectural arts. Therefore, it is praised as "Southern Fujian Architecture Grand View Garden". Figure 6 is the "Dovetail Ridge" book and pen holder.

Figure 6 "Dovetail Ridge" Book and Pen Holder Design

The design of the "Dovetail Ridge" book and pen holder is mainly drawn from the dovetail ridge shape of the Quanzhou ancient red brick building and its chief colour is red as the brick. The design contains the bright, open-minded and tough character of the Minnan people and their prayer for good life, and conveys the deep and unique heritage of the red brick culture through the brush and pen holder.

5 Conclusion

Cultural and creative products are unique commodities, which firstly satisfy the functions of products, and should also have rich cultural connotations and distinctive regional characteristics to satisfy consumers' unique emotional experiences and serve as bridges between consumers and local cultural exchanges. Therefore, the research and development of cultural and creative products should be an organic combination of design art and regional culture to make their unique creativity, shape and colour. When consumers use cultural and creative products, they can deepen their understanding of the local cultural traditions and customs to achieve emotional resonance. In the combination process, design art and regional culture complement and promote mutually.

Acknowledgment

[Fund Project] Quanzhou Social Science Planning Project (2017E18); Quanzhou City College Youth Leadership (Professional) Leader Training Plan

References

1. Xu Yaoxin. It is of great significance for cultural relics units to develop cultural and creative products, New Century Library, **11**(2016)
2. Cen Ke. Get rid of "identity imprisonment" and promote the development of cultural and creative products, Cultural Focus, **2** (2017)
3. Liu Qing. Branding: The Outlet of Jingdezhen Ceramics Cultural and Creative Products under the “Creative Market” Model, Journal of Ceramics, **37**(2016)
4. Zhao Decheng, Sha Ying. Regional imagery extraction of ancient artifacts and regional innovative design of products, Packaging Engineering, **38**(2017)
5. Wu Yuxiang, Guan Ruiming. Heritage Values and Protection Planning of Islamic Architecture Remains in Quanzhou. Journal of Huaqiao University(Natural Science), **35** (2014)
6. Wang Yaohua. The Origin of the Foreign Musical Factors in the "Four Famous Musicians" Section of Quanzhou Nanyin and the Examination of Their Incoming Routes. Music Research, **5** (2015)
7. Zhang Yuan. The Study of Buddhism Music and Dance in the Cultural Relics of Quanzhou Maritime Silk Road——Taking “Flying Sky” as an Example. Music Research, **2** (2015):
8. Wang Xinghe. Tourism Creative Product Design Based on Quanzhou Regional Culture. Journal of Liming Vocational University, **2** (2015)
9. LIU Xiaohong. Research on the Development and Design of Fujian Hakka Tulou Culture Products[J]. Packaging Engineering, **5** (2012)
10. Wang Shan. Quanzhou Nanyin. Fuzhou: Fujian People's Publishing House, (2009)

Research on industrial design technology innovation -- a case study of ceramic glaze

Shen Haiyong [a,1] , Dai Yanyan[2] and Li Jun[1]

[1]Shenyang Jianzhu university,college of design and art , 100168, liaoning province shenyang city , China
[2]Shenyang Jianzhu university, center for innovative and entrepreneurship , 100168, liaoning province shenyang , China

Abstract: Taking the technology innovation of ceramic glaze as an example, the innovation of the industrial design technology was analyzed. The way of combining industrial design ideas and design thinking way was put forward. The theoretical connotation of industrial design was broadened. To break with the original industrial design way of thinking, and combined with the practical development of Chinese industrial design, the advanced theory of industrial design was collected, in order to provide constructive suggestions for the theoretical development of industrial design and industrial design education in the future.

1 The development of the industrial design definition

The first use of the concept of industrial design has a very close relationship with the development of modern manufacturing. The industrial design education originated in German, which first appeared in the early 1920s to develop industrial product design and process in the Bauhaus school in Germany. The peak of the practice and development of industrial design happened in the 1930s of the United States with full of commercial atmosphere, the time when the company was faced with many problems about industrial design. The Fortune magazine in United States illustrated this well in February 1934 :

"As a phenomenon, the industrial designer, came into being as mass production raised output to where one after another, industries hitherto without benefit of other engineering design found their products matched by other manufacturers and the market consequently glutted "

In that background, industrial design has successfully created the unprecedented product and new market. Different from ordinary products, industrial design helped manufacturers to create products which were fully functional and full of artistic features, conforming to the aesthetic psychology of customers. In the traditional industrial design theory: The most important contribution for industrial design is to make the product different from others through the design of the color and style, or by enhancing the product details and tiny additional functions. The invention of the new technology innovation is known as radical innovation. The industrial design usually uses less radical innovation to design new product, but adds functions through some mature technology. According to the needs of consumers for the product function, existing inventions and technology are applied to the product, make making consumers get more satisfaction in the use of the product, which is the central task of industrial design.

Traditional cognition for the interpretation of industrial design is hard to meet the requirements of today's market for industrial design, so the new interpretation of the industrial design theory was introduced. For the interpretation of the "design" is developed in the direction of being more profound, it is considered to be a thinking ability of humans naturally formed in the long-term evolution, just as humans use language to express their emotions and communicate with others. The Bureau of Labor Statistics in December 2017 issued the Occupational Outlook Handbook, which made such a definition about industrial design: Industrial design should be applied to mass production of industrial products, such as cars, home appliances, and toys. Through the combination of art, business and engineering, products will be used more convenient. Industrial designers should take the function, aesthetics, production costs, and usability of products into consideration when developing new products. Industrial designers should not only work in offices in a variety of industries, but also travel frequently to testing facilities, design centers, clients' exhibit sites, users' homes or workplaces, and places where the product is manufactured.

Contemporary industrial design as a kind of design services, is committed to create new value growth of the products for enterprise. Before the industrial revolution,

*Corresponding author: [a]shenhaiyong:57113618@qq.com

the cognition of design stayed in craftsman' thinking on handiwork and production process. In the industrial age, we need to be more professional in the division of labor and the accumulation of professional knowledge. At present, the industrial design activities usually take part in the process of the development of new products, including the following characteristics: (1) New products should be created, of which the design styles reach or exceed that of the existing products. (2) The created new products should be the integration and application of new technology. (3) Industrial design activities can improve the sales of products or to create new markets. (4) Design behavior can strengthen and protect the product brand. Innovation has become an integral part of the contemporary industrial design, which includes the following three categories: (1) incremental innovation and improvement of design. (2) all kinds of product style innovation.(3) radical new function of innovation.

At present, the most important skills and qualities of the industrial design are summarized into seven aspects, which can be divided into dominant and hidden qualities. Dominant qualities are more specific skills, while hidden quality is more abstract, which can not be improved through short-term training. For a qualified industrial designer, the following aspects of quality are necessary.

Dominant quality requirements:

(1) Artistic ability: Industrial designers need to quick express their design ideas. Therefore, the designer must express their ideas quickly through the skill of hand drawing.

(2) Computer skills: Industrial designers need to create design and prototype through the aided design tool of computer. In particular, industrial designers need to master the two-dimensional computer-aided drawing software to draw a quick sketch, and three-dimensional modeling software to build a three-dimensional model.

(3) Mechanical skills: Industrial design must understand how to manufacture the new product, at least understand the manufacturing process of his industry.

Hidden quality requirements:

(1) Creativity: This kind of creativity is not an unconstrained style, and industrial designers must have enough creativity to integrate existing technologies and new products .This requires designers to understand the present technology very well.

(2) Analytical skills: Industrial designers need to study the behavior of user through logic and reasoning skills to define the demand for the new product. In particular, industrial designers need to imagine a scene that users use a product, analyze users' behavior, thus provide background support for the design.

(3) Interpersonal skills: Industrial designers need cooperation with customers, as well as the domain expert, so they need to have the ability to cooperate with others. Specifically, industrial designers should discuss the feasibility with researchers, engineers and customers.

(4) Problem - solving skills: Industrial designers decide the product function, size, shape, and even costs. Designers need to consider function, aesthetic, cost, and usability. How to balance art, business and engineering to make the products much easier to be uses is a great test for designers' problem-solving ability.

Industrial design is a typical representative of multidisciplinary cross. Technology determines whether a product idea is feasible, business determines whether a product idea has market potential, while the man-machine factor determines the availability of the product ideas. Industrial designers is an innovative design industry under the background of certain design conditions. Industrial design is a kind of art behavior, which can't be subjectively expressed completely like traditional art. Industrial design contains the science theory and mechanical principle, but it's required to do more to deal with the relationship between people and things. Because industrial design is a multidisciplinary cross, industrial designers are required to have a number of skills and qualities.

2 The innovation research of ceramic glaze

Ceramic glaze decides the physical and chemical properties of ceramic materials, which also affects the result of colour and surface. In China's song dynasty, the five famous kilns have different glaze color. In British the outstanding achievement of Wedgwood series ceramics is about glaze. Taking the innovation of ceramic glaze as an example, research on technological innovation of the industrial design can make us more aware of the importance of the technological innovation in contemporary industrial design.

The classification method of oxide is based on understanding of the chemical composition of ceramic glaze. In this way, we can calculate the high temperature melting temperature of ceramic materials and the relationship among materials in high temperature chemical reaction. First of all, the ceramic glaze is supposed to be completely melted, and only contain the oxide, which is from their raw materials by mixing and melting. This kind of raw material needs to use the oxide classification calculation method to represent the relative amounts of each oxide in the glaze. The kind of raw materials should be decided so that the species and components can be obtained in glaze.

The oxide can be divided into three terms:

RO：$PbO, Na_2O, K_2O, ZnO, CaO, MgO, BaO, Li_2O$

R_2O_3：Al_2O_3, B_2O_3

RO2：SiO_2

In the calculation method, RO oxide is the glaze flux to promote melting in silica glass, which has very strong inhibitory effect on melting. Aluminium oxide, helpless in the oxide melting, has an effect on the reaction with the alkaline action. This kind of oxide classification method gives clear definition on the role of various oxides in molten glaze. All the RO oxides, naturally are not equal in terms of flux activity, but the effect is the same, which can promote the melting through the corrosion of Silicon dioxide.

The characteristics of high temperature liquid metal crystalline glaze: Generally, when the glaze is cooling, it is still a kind of material that is amorphous and non-crystalline However, under special circumstances, the glaze can be crystallized during cooling process, and produce various forms of the crystalline glaze. The ordinary glaze contains alumina, which can not only prevent the glaze from crystallizing, but also increase the consistency to avoid the glaze over flowing. To cooperate with crystalline glaze, the composition of alumina is bound to greatly reduce, usually no more than 0.1 molecular equivalent, of which it is only a third in high temperature glaze. In many kinds of crystalline glaze, there is no alumina. Without Alumina, the glaze often over flows. When manufacturing crystalline glaze ware, flow glaze should be prepared, while at ordinary times the vessels are set on the porcelain clay round cakes. High content zinc oxide is conducive to the development of crystalline glaze. In crystalline glaze, the situation that there is about 0.3 equivalent of zinc is very common, while rutile or titanium oxide also promotes the development of crystallization. As for the basic glaze, lead oxide, alkaline metal or boron can be used as solvent. The alkaline glaze is often used. Because there are a large number of zinc and rutile, the crystalline glaze is a little opaque. Because no or low alumina, the glaze flows and shine. The crystal in the glaze may be very small with a cluster of clusters, or may be large with spectacular appearance. With coloring oxides, such as copper oxide or cobalt oxide, the crystal will appear to be magnificent in the glaze color. The firing process is the decision factor in the production of crystal in glaze. When heating, it can be carried out in accordance with the usual speed, but when cooling, it can not be cooled fast but slowly to a point so that the materials in the glaze can have a tendency to crystallize. The temperature at this point is usually lower than the highest temperature, but higher than the glaze curing temperature. The reaction temperature of the crystalline glaze must be tested to determine. If the composition of glaze is right, at a certain temperature stage, slow cooling can produce a large number of crystal.

The development and application of ceramic glaze has important practical significance for the development of ceramic materials. The characteristics of ceramic crystalline glaze are high strength, moisture proof, fire prevention, acid-proof, alkali resistance, frost resistance, not aging, not metamorphosed, not fade, easy to clean, etc., and it has a rich artistic adornment effect. There is a layer of vitric glaze on the surface of high-temperature glaze of architectural ceramics, which is waterproof, decorative, clean and durable. With metal oxide and natural minerals as colorants, high temperature glaze is decorated on the embryo, which, after high temperature of 1280 degrees' heating, naturally turns out to be colored ceramics, and has high artistic value.

Industrial design technology innovation provides the technical support for the development of industrial design, further widening the idea of design. Up to now, for the development of industrial design, the designer can not be merely content with common-sense understanding of the existing technology, but more deeply understand the technical details of the features and make a breakthrough in the technology. Innovative design thinking is one of the important directions of the future development and application of industrial design. Industrial designers need to know how to use creative design thinking to make technical innovation.

3 The characteristics and essence of design thinking

In many areas, the production and accumulation of theory is through practice. Knowledge is derived from production, in turn, production is used to assess the accuracy of knowledge. Creative people tend to work in two different ways at the same time: as the discoverer of the problem and problem solvers. As discoverer, they have unique curiosity and keen observation power for the unknown. These drives them to find reasonable explanation and the answer to the question. As part of the solvers, they have strong creativity, and they can analyze and synthesize the structure, arrangement, patterns, composition, and concept of the problem based on the existing data. Due to the difference of thinking process, the problem discoverer and solver may be different in thinking and working. In addition, the way of thinking and working may be affected by the difference of majors, research areas, and other factors, but all these will help us to define the essence of innovation design thinking. One of the common features is the practical work.

At present, there is no concrete answers to the essence of creative design thinking, and what makes a person become the creative design thinking, .But we can learn the cognitive way and thinking method of innovative designers according to the characteristics of the known creative design thinking. These features help us to understand the essence of innovation design thinking. In addition to the qualities that innovative designers should have, innovative design itself also has several unique processes.

Characteristics	Description
Human- and environment-centered concern	Designers must continually consider and satisfy what is needed for the development of humans
Ability to visualize	Designers work visually.
Multifunction tendencies	Designers should look at different solutions to a problem and keep the problem in mind.
Systemic vision	Designers should treat problems as system problems with opportunities for systemic solutions involving different procedures and concepts.
Ability to use language as a tool	Designers should be able to verbally explain their creative process and invention, when details and relationships can not be visually expressed.
Affinity for teamwork	Designers need to develop interpersonal skills that allow them to communicate across disciplines and work with other people.
Avoiding the one-sidedness of choice	Designers search competing alternatives before moving to choice making or decision making. They try to find ways to come up with new configurations. This process can help to find an optimum solution, avoiding the one-sidedness of choice.

One characteristic of innovative design thinking is iterations of the design process (iterations: repeat feedback process activities, and its purpose is usually to approximate the required target or result), as well as the exploratory, and sometimes a chaotic process. Innovative design thinking starts from some abstract specifications, and some will develop into a "briefing". These briefings are used to describe a final product, and gradually optimize the product details. In the process of creative design thinking, the conflict between product descriptions and details may happen. Design details of the requirements may change design, or find unexpected problems in the design process. In this case, the design should follow the adjustment cycle between detail requirements and solutions, until the final solution is reached.

References

1. “Industrial Designers” in Fortune magazine 1934
2. Caplan. Ralph, [1982] By Design. St Martins Press; New York.
3. Dumas, Angela, and Mintzberg, Henry, [1989] “Managing Design Designing Management”in Design Management Journal.
4. Dumas, Angela, and Fentem, Andrew, [1998] “Totemics: New Metaphor Techniques tomanage Knowledge from Discovery to Storage and Retrieval. In Technovation.
5. Graham, Pauline, [1996] Mary Parker Follett, Prophet of Management, Harvard Business School.
6. “product design hand-painted techniques”, [Netherlands] Stael China youth press
7. “Chinese fine arts history” Shen Haiyong southwest normal university press
8. “Innovation design thinking” Lu Bainian Tsinghua university press.
9. “Design thinking innovation guide” Wang Keyue etc. Tsinghua university press.
10. “15 seconds illustrations and 30 seconds sketch” Yamada Tian Yafu ,Liaoning cience and technology press
11. “Understanding and innovation: an experience of product design thinking”,Shen Jie, Jiangsu fine arts publishing house
12. “product design and development” magazine, Wang Xuanzheng, Jiangxi fine arts publishing house
13. Paper discussed shallowly product innovation design "huina" enterprise "in 2012 we
14. Thesis "talk about the development trend of art design history studies of literature and art, Chen
15. Shou-zhi wang. "the world modern design history of the China youth press, 2002.

The Design Education of the New Era Urgent Needs to Cultivate Engineering Ethics Consciousness

Liu Wenming[a]

[1]School of Design and Art, Shenyang Jianzhu University, 110168 Shenyang, Liao Ning, China

Abstract: By expounding the inseparable relationship between design and engineering ethics, and comparing the current situation of the development of engineering ethics education at home and abroad, we find that there is a big gap between China's design professional education and western developed countries in the training of engineering ethics awareness. It is proposed that the domestic engineering profession, especially the design profession, is in urgent need of cultivating the designer's engineering ethic awareness, so as to improve the professionalism of the design talents and promote the better development of our country's design education.

1 Introduction

With the rapid development of China's economy, 'Made in China' in the development is gradually undergoing industrial transformation to "Created in China" and "China's Intellectual Creation", resulting in a growing demand for design talents. According to relevant data, in recent years, the design profession has become one of the most popular majors in China's colleges and universities. China has become a big country in higher design education, and the state has increased the training of design and innovation talents. At the same time, accompanied by rapid economic development and intensive construction, a large number of engineering projects and design works that lack ethics and morality have emerged. Based on this status, design education calls for ethical awareness. At present, compared with Western developed countries, there are many aspects such as the lack of teaching resources, backward curriculum design, unreasonable professional construction, and so on. Especially in the training of engineering ethical awareness, there is a big gap, which affects the degree to a certain extent. The overall level of personnel training. In-depth exploration of the designer's ethical awareness in design education in China will play a positive and critical role in the sustainable scientific development of design education.

2 Design and engineering ethics are inseparable

People generally attribute ethical issues to philosophical issues, incorporating the dimension of ethics into the dimension of philosophy. However, the dimensions involved in ethics are exceeded the scope of philosophy. The ethical dimension we talked is the way of people 'do something right', but "do something right" is not just an ethical issue, it is also a practical issue. What is worth noting that ethical issues show certain particularities and that is also closely related to the specific engineering context in the specific engineering practice. We can fully understand the project as a design process.

Xiao Ping's definition of engineering ethics in the book ***Engineering Ethics*** (1999) said: "Engineering ethics is a systemic research and academic construction based on engineering activity as a research object and ethical phenomena." The aim is to help those people who are facing engineering decision-making, engineering design and construction project management to establish clear social responsibility awareness, social value vision and the moral sensitivity to the comprehensive effects of the project, so that they can soberly facing all kinds of conflicts of interests and values in their professional activities, they can make judgments and decisions that is in the common interests of people and long-term development they need, They also can create high-quality products and services for the society with a rigorous scientific attitude and practical professionalism. [1]

Design is a kind of creative behavior, which takes the inspiration of the mind conceived through the conception, formation, refinement, scrutiny, and refinement, then conveyed and represented in a form that people can perceive. The plan and behavior that can translate any idea into a physical object is understood as design. Engineering activities is a process of designing such thoughts and behaviors, so it can be understood that design is the essence of engineering.

Engineering is the art of harnessing the power derived from nature for human use and for the convenience of mankind. The project is produced or manufactured according to the design, so we can say design is the soul of project. The relationship between design and engineering is extended to social relations, that is, the executors of the project must be implemented to specific

*Corresponding author: [a] Liu Wenming, 83373734@qq.com

people. The goals of designers and engineers are the same, and the behaviors are also consistent. The ultimate goal is to turn these thoughts into action. It can also be said that the real engineer is the designer. Because of this, we have to pay due attention to the inevitably problems about design and engineering ethics.

3 The development of engineering ethics education in foreign design education

The development of engineering ethics in Occident and its impact on design education is earlier. In 1852, the American Society of Civil Engineers (ASCE) was founded, then there were many engineering associations in the United States were established one by one and started the gradual professionalization process.

In the early 20th century, the United States began to formulate more formal rules of professional ethics in 1914. ASCE adopted an ethical code in September 1914. During the first 30 years of the 20th century, the engineering ethics code became the most important part of various engineering organizations when carrying out engineering activities. Until affected the related area of the education of engineering and design.

The ethical issues in engineering practice had become a matter of concern after World War II. The impressive building capacity and destructive power of the project caused engineers to rethink profoundly and pay attention to environmental issues and their own ethical responsibilities. The ***Scientist Communications of the United States*** and the Federation of American Scientists special publications had published and some relevant institutes also were established.

The fatal casualties caused by the poor design of the 1972 Ford Pinto vehicle caused public rethinking, this incident prompted engineers to re-examine the law with new mandatory requirements. Directly led to the birth of engineering ethics in North America. The Accreditation Board for Engineering and Technology (ABET) gradually began to take the content of engineering ethics education as one of the contents of engineering degree certification. Until about 2000, the ABET provided a new set of 11 certification standards for college graduates. This prompted engineering ethics, at least nominally, to become an important part of engineering education. At that time, many colleges and universities in the United States began to set up engineering ethics courses and added ethical training to the learning requirements of universities. At this time, students were required to have the ability to understand ethical issues and learn how to solve the ethical dilemmas when they encountered at work. In the late 1970s, engineering ethics was established as a discipline, It was "consisting of the responsibilities and rights of those engaged in engineering, as well as the ideals and personal promises that were expected in the project", the occupational ethics regulations of the engineering communities in the West. Constitutes the main content of engineering ethics. The United States, France, Germany, Japan, Britain and other developed countries have successively carried out engineering ethics education. [2]

After the 1990s, strengthening engineering ethics education and improving the social responsibility of engineers and other engineering practitioners have become an important aspect of engineering education. Since 1994, the American Society of Engineering Education (ASEE) and the National Science Foundation (NSF) published some relevant reports about engineering education reform, respectively, calling for strengthening engineering ethical education in view of the ethical issues faced by engineers. Since 1996, the registered professional engineer examination has incorporated engineering ethics into the "Engineering Foundation" exam. Therefore, engineering ethics education has been incorporated into the system of education certification and project certification.

4 Development and Status of Engineering Ethics Education in Design Education in China

The engineering ethics education which belong to design education started comparatively late in China. At the early stage it was subordinated to ideological and political education. Engineering ethics education is not a simple ideological and political education. They are two totally different kinds of things

The engineering ethics education of the 1990s began to attract the attention of relevant domestic scholars. Some scholars introduced the situation of engineering ethics education in the United States, Germany, Japan, and then published articles to discuss the significance of engineering ethics education, and called for engineering ethics in China's education. Tsinghua University, Dalian University of Technology, Beijing Institute of Technology, Xi'an Jiaotong University and some other science and engineering colleges started to offer courses that relate engineering regulations and case studies.

After entering the 21st century, engineering ethics education aroused considerable interest in government and all circles, especially in higher education, Macro-layout engineering ethics education had become a consensus. At present, there is still a big gap between China's engineering ethics education and foreign advanced countries. Borrowing textbooks from abroad, such as ***Engineering Ethics***, ***Engineering Ethics: Concepts and Cases*** these American books. By contrast, we have few professional textbooks, the foundation of demonstration teaching materials is weak. At the same time, the engineering ethics education curriculum system is weakened. The ethical courses of engineering education are compulsory courses in foreign country, even more important than engineering education itself. The establishment of engineering ethics education courses in colleges and universities is the prerequisite for setting up engineering education courses. But in our country, the vast majority of local engineering colleges neglected engineering ethics education. Some colleges and universities do not even offer related courses. Many schools only set up engineering ethics courses as public elective courses or even public elective courses. The schools which take engineering ethics education as a required course, lack the curriculum system construction, set up only basic elementary courses, and failed to carefully select excellent teaching content. Engineering ethics education is still not paid due attention until now. [3] Especially in China's design education, the cultivation of engineering ethical awareness has not been mentioned yet.

5 As a designer of a new era, it must have a sense of engineering ethics and social responsibility.

As a profession, designers have been given a nobler historical mission in the new era. Not only are they able to design new products with novel styles and complete functions, but also achieve the purpose of stimulating consumption and pursuing profit maximization through sales of these products. They also take on some social responsibility. Now, simple and basic design will no longer be a problem to designers. It is especially important for designers to abide by ethical norms and ethical standards in their work. The opposition, criticism and transcendence of styles indicate that the professional consciousness of designers has been improved and matured. The problems faced by designers are no longer the problems of form or function, and the ethical awareness of engineering as a designer's essential professional qualities should be generally available in the designer community.

Designers should be bold in taking ethical responsibility not just having a sense of engineering ethic. Ethical responsibility includes three parts, A, professional ethical responsibilities which include role responsibilities, duty responsibilities and negligence responsibilities; B, social ethical responsibilities, designers should take more extensive social ethical responsibilities not just responsible for product, company, or loyalty; C, environmental ethical responsibility, designers need to understand the intrinsic value of the environment, rather than the environment as a free product, we must always implement the concept of "sustainable development". The significance of cultivating the designer's engineering ethic awareness lies not only in stimulating the designer's inner sense of responsibility and morality, but also directly putting this kind of engineering ethics consciousness into practice.

6 The cultivation of awareness of engineering ethic contributes to better development of design education

The ultimate goal of design education is to cultivate outstanding design talents. An excellent design talent should not only have comprehensive and complete design capabilities, but also need a sense of engineering ethics and social responsibility. The training of engineering ethics in design education can help to achieve the following development goals:

(1) Helps to form an ethical code for design professions as soon as possible

Design professional ethical standards refer to the code of conduct that designers should be following when they are facing ethical issues, and provide a basis for designers to solve ethical issues. Design professional ethical standards are dynamic. Different social development stages, design ethics norms only reflect the mainstream social values and ethical ideological norms at the time, and therefore have important guiding significance for designers' design practice. Through the cultivation of ethical awareness, it is bound to promote the formation and improvement of design professional ethics.

(2) Helps cultivate designer's engineering ethical awareness and responsibility

Through systematic study and practice, we can gradually cultivate awareness of engineering ethics. Designers who lack a sense of engineering ethics may unconsciously make ethical decisions and actions. Training the designer's awareness of engineering ethic is to increase the designer's sensitivity to engineering ethical issues, increase understanding of ethical issues, and place emphasis on the conscientiousness and initiative of various ethical issues in design practice. This enhances the designer's sense of professional ethics, social moral responsibility and environmental moral responsibility.

(3) Helps enhance designers' ability to make engineering ethics decisions

The decision-making ability of engineering ethics means that in the face of ethical dilemmas, it is difficult to make judgments based only on the ethical guidelines of the project. Designers need to have more sophisticated rational decision-making capabilities. In contemporary design practice, both technical issues and interest relationships are unprecedentedly complicated. Ethical decision-making capabilities have become one of the necessary conditions for dealing with ethical issues.

7 Conclusion

The design education in the new era must shoulder higher historical mission and social responsibility. At present, China's design education has not paid attention to cultivating designers' ethical awareness of engineering. Design education calls for engineering ethic, it is imperative to cultivate designers' awareness of engineering ethic in design education.

References:

1. Wu Jin, Qin Yan. The Core Elements Selection of Engineering Ethics Education Based on AHP and Entropy Method [J]. Value Engineering, 2015,34(14):195-199.
2. He Jing. Moral Philosophy Analysis of the Generation of Engineering Ethics [J]. Morality and Civilization, 2013(01):121-125.
3. Li Changling, Yu Jianjun, Zhang Mengge, Liu Jianxin. Investigation Report on Engineering Ethics Education in Local Engineering Colleges [J]. Industry

and Technology Forum, 2013,12(13): 185-186.

4. Dong Wei. Reflections on the Cultivation of Environmental Art Design Talents in Colleges and Universities from the Perspective of Ethics [J]. Course Education Research, 2012, 9
5. Zhang Fuye. How to Make Ethical Ideas Become the Designer's Consciousness [J]. Art Observation, 2003, 6
6. Zhao Weijun. Ethic Dimension and Designers' Responsibility in Modern Design [J]. Hundred Schools in Arts, 2014, 2
7. Li Zhengfeng, Chong Hangqing, Wang Qian. Engineering ethics. Beijing: Tsinghua University Press, 2016

Analysis on the Key Points of Influential Factors in Product Morphological Design

Juanling Guo[1,a], Kaining Meng [1], Ying Meng [1]

[1]Xihua University, School of Art and Design, Chengdu, China

Abstract. For designing out high-tech products which can attract consumers and satisfy their demands, this paper has analysed the influencial factors of product morphological design. Firstly, the author used the principle of semiotics and man-machine engineering to analyse products systematically, to optimize the complex of "man-machine- environment", and then I studied the product's own factor, man-machine factor and external factor. In addition, this paper explains the influence factors in the product morphological design with examples. Moreover, the function and the form of product are ingeniously combined to improve the quality and connotation of the product. To sum up , this paper based on the theory of influential factors in product morphological design, proposed innovative thought, treat product morphological design from different perspectives, which will provide a reference for the later product design.

1 Product morphological design

Product morphological design is a media to convey information and the carrier for people to explore the world. Design could transform abstract ideas into perception and turn consciousness into cognitive state, which is keep changing and developing. As we all know, the product is designed to serve the society, so if we want to realize the perfect fusion of products and consumers, we cannot ignore the demand of the market. So we have to grasp the market's real needs and social relations. Product design shouldn't only depended on designers' intuition experience, but also links products' multiple functions and form systematically. Both of these include its own factors, man-machine factors and external factors. Designers need to systematically combines design, creation, process, production together, to make ideas integrate into products better. [1] Design is a kind of culture and practice, it emphasis things' supposed states, so as to serve for people, solve problems in people's lives. People can perceive the products and have interaction with them. So as to keep improving people's life quality, make product worth it.

2 Factors affecting product morphological design

The product is complemented by its structure, function, modeling and technology, as a relatively complex symbol system, its visual form is composed of line, color and volume. This kind of visual symbol has been found its value from the beginning of design, and it is designed into form code, then the code is put into practical production. Finally, when consumers use it, they will decode the product and obtain the final impression of it. From the perspective of semiotics, this is product's own modelling factor, but product morphological design dosen't only influent its own factor, but man-machine factor and external factor also will influent product morphological design. Man-machine engineering is an interdiscipline, it doen't only optimize the single element, indeed, it optimize the "human - machine - environment" integration at the same time, to get the best design programme.

*Corresponding author:[a] Juanling Guo: 1130052980@qq.com

2.1 Products own factors

Product design is not as same as art design, so when design product's appearance, we can't take it as a work of art design, which only need consider its aesthetic value and artistic value. However, product's form is the carrier of product's function, they depend on one another. The meaning of product design is to achieve a union of form and function. Designers are supposed to combine product's appearance with its function, in order to satisfy users' function demand and to be innovative and beautiful. What's more, industrial production makes the design and processing of products possible, that is, the so-called "If you can design it, you can produce it."

First of all is to consider products' own factors, like structure, function, size, color, material and processing technology, etc. Surface processing technology can present many different visual effects. And product is not the purpose, but the means to achieve the goal. Qualified product design is not just the design of the exterior renderings, but to choose appropriate materials, reasonable structure, proper colour and finally make out a product that satisfy both of designers and users. Therefore, designers have to consider a lot when making selection. Any product is a system composed of various parts in a certain form. In which there are visible and invisible factors, visible factors like materials, visible structures, shapes; and invisible factors like invisible assembly forms, working principles and product performance.

2.2 Human-computer factors of product

Human sensory organs include the eyes, ears, nose, tongue, skin and limbs, which have different degrees of cognitive ability to the product, therefore, all of them should be considered in the design process. The design should reflect the values of "people-oriented", so it is necessary to fully consider the relationship between man and machine in the modeling, to accord with the cognitive psychology of people.

People's first impression of the product is most from the visual perception, so the designer tend to focuse on the visual effect firstly. Different product forms will give people different visual feelings and convey different meanings. For example, the product of curve modelling, give person round, soft, cosy visual feeling; the product of straight line modelling gives person modern, strong, grand visual feelings. Therefore, in the design process, it is necessary to excavate the visual characteristics of product and the meaning conveyed by the product form.

A good product should lighten the burden of hearing. In design, it is important to reduce the noise and protect people's hearing sense. During the design process, we'd better optimize the structure and study some new materials. For example, replace metal materials by some non-metallic materials, which can not only reduce vibration, but also absorb noise.

Products will be touched by people, so the place to be contacted, the control panel or the switch button must fit human's physiological characteristics. Although tactile sensation is not as sensitive as the visual and auditory senses, different material still give one person with different psychological feelings, such as wood products and wood-like products may have the same visual effect, but the tactile sense is not the same, and person will feel different.

Designers should also notice changes of smell. Take kitchen supplies as example, this kind of products with peculiar smell is easy to bring users rightly bad feeling. Products with bad experience feelings can affect consumers' purchasing desire. So designers are also supposed to be considerate when making choices of materials, had better choose non-polluted and odorless materials.

Using the same action for a long time will cause harm to people. Therefore, in the process of designing products, we should consider the man-machine relationship, movement, balance and body feeling. Design comfortable and appropriate structure to reduce the harm to person. To stand out in a variety of similar products, products must do well in every aspect. As people don't make choices only because of a single feature, every aspect including shape, color, sound, smell or material should be taken into consideration, and combined with people's real demand.

People obtain the impression of products through visual feeling mostly, they only care about products' appearance, color, and have little cognition of their function, material and durability features. Therefore, in the design process, designers also need to furtherly study how to present all the products' features to users.

As shown in the figure 1, a flying fish chair designed by the designer--Montreal, there is a new concept that is to install parallel wood strips on a rotating cylinder, allowing users to rotate the slats at will to get the most comfortable form. It can be a common chair, deck chair, sofa, or a sofa bed. The whole design used the light color series, and a large number of curve shape modeling reflects the product's round, soft and elegant features. Meanwhile, the wood material provided feelings of healthy、green and environmental. The overall form fully considers the human physiology factor, and it's versatile and innovative.

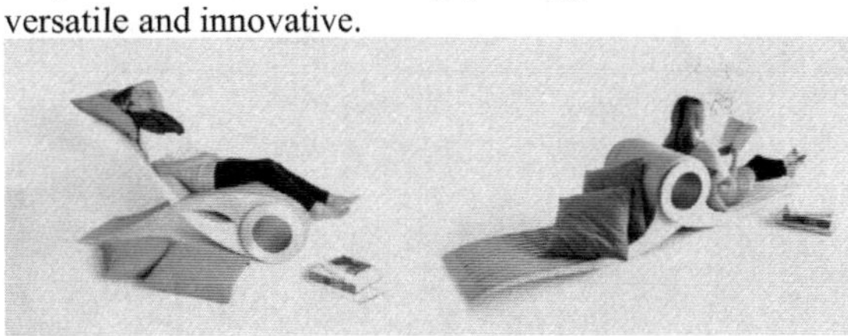

Fig 1. design of flying fish chair.

3 External factors of the product

The external factors of product morphological design doesn't only include relationship between the product and environment, but also national policy factor. Product's influence on the environment is reflected by whether the product will cause pollution and impact on the environment, and whether products will cause noise to the space, etc. Green design is what we're going to follow right now. Multifunctional design, portable design, detachable folding design and other designs can reduce the hazard on the environment.

From the aspect of national policy, we must attach importance to ecological construction and protect ecological environment, which was mentioned by Xi Jinping, the national general secretary, in the 19th people's congress. In the modern society with rapidly developing industrialization, it is everyone's responsibility and obligation to protect the ecological environment. We should base on ecological concept, design high-quality and ecological products. At the same time, the state should have a quality inspection standard for every kind of product, which must be obeyed in the design process. The product should be standardized instead of only pursuing innovation. During the design process, we must ensure that the product can pass the safety test so as to guarantee their safety, otherwise they can easily cause some damages, which violates the original intention of the design, that is to bring convenience to people instead of causing harm.

4 Conclusion

The mainstream of the society is the integration of informatization and industrialization. Industrial design is one of the key links of "Made in China 2025". One of the key problems is to improve the innovative ability of products design

We need to consider product morphological design from many factors we mentioned below, to design out innovative products. In the Internet age, people's demands for healthy, quality life are constantly improving. People's life is closely connected with the development of information technology. Nowadays, a good design should have normal function, and meet futural pepole's demand of life style, product experience and potential taste, etc. The perception that "Design is about making things look good" has gone. In industry 4.0, good design is not just about functional design, it should be the constant innovation of technology, design and users' experience, and consider problems from different angles, provide perfect service, excavate potential demand, design products that conform to the user's psychology, meet the increasing personalized requirements and improve product value.

Acknowledgment

Fund project. Major projects in Sichuan education department. (Item number:W171300); University-level graduate innovation fund project of Xihua University.(Item number:ycjj2017110).

References

1. Lin Liang. Analysis of ergonomic application points in product modeling design, V E,**36**（2015）.
2. Zhang Linghao. Semantics of Products. *Beijing: China Architecture & Building Press*, (2009).
3. Xu Bochu. Industrial Design Procedures and Methods. *Beijing: People's Fine Arts Publishing House*, 2010.
4. Tong Weilin. Analysis of the Three Elements of Product Design. *QunWenDiDi*, **23**(2011).
5. Liu Jingyu. Conceptual Analysis of Product Appearance Design. M D, **02**(2013).
6. Mao Weikang. Discussing industrial design changes under the concept of Industry 4.0. M D, **02**(2016).

https://doi.org/10.1051/matecconf/201817602006

Research on the Reform of the Ability-oriented Innovation and Entrepreneurship Education System for the Design Major

Dong Yan[1,a]

[1]Dalian University Of Science And Technology, Dalian, Liaoning, China

Abstract. The research on the reform of the ability-oriented innovation and entrepreneurship education system is of great significance to promote the quality and entrepreneurship of graduates in product design major of the application-oriented colleges and universities. Aiming to foster students' innovation and entrepreneurship abilities and serve the local economy, the five-in-one education mode integrates with weekly cultivation plan, theoretical teaching, practical teaching, graduation project, and innovation and entrepreneurship program, which is available to deepen the education reform of the product design major, accelerate the application-oriented transformation, and achieve high employment and entrepreneurship rate of graduates.

1 The personnel training system based on innovation and entrepreneurship

Aiming to cultivate innovation and entrepreneurship abilities, the personnel training system is endowed with an vision of making a transformation design for the fostering of the versatile talents with the abilities of practice, innovation and entrepreneurship in a reform way of application practice, discipline, as well as open and communication. The whole training system includes the re-designs of the training objective to reshape the applied talents in terms of the relevant issues, the curriculum system to modularize of the common basic courses, the teaching faculties to establish a mentor system for the interdisciplinary teachers and experts, the teaching platform to shift the module-based teaching to the one combining the studio-based teaching and project teaching, and the practical platform to further the cooperation between school and enterprise by establishing practice bases in the enterprises. Therefore, it can be improved as a five-in-one education system for practice and promotion.

2 Five-in-one education system structure

The five-in-one education system involves five aspects-inter discipline, faculty structure construction, project teaching, further cooperation between school and enterprise, and service for the development of the local economy. The result of the research is of important practical significance for the private application-oriented colleges and universities to boost graduates' high-quality employment and entrepreneurship. With the purposes of training students' innovation and entrepreneurship ability and finally making contributions to the local economy, the five-in-one education mode focuses on a series of teaching researches and practices related to the cultivation plan, theoretical teaching, practical teaching, graduation project, and innovation and entrepreneurship program.(Fig. 1)

.

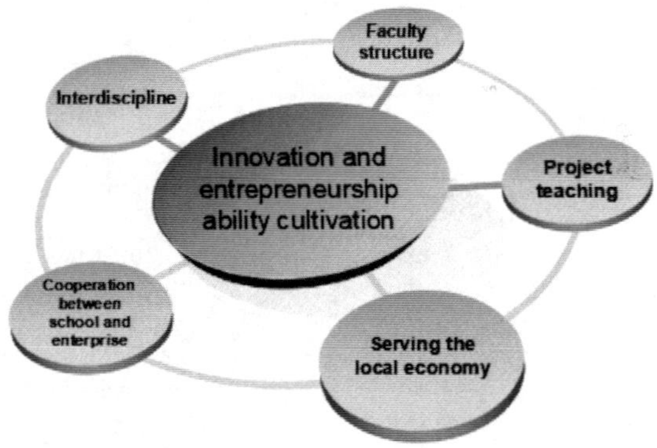

Figure 1. Five-in-one education system

2.1 The all-around and multi-angle integration of disciplines and majors

In order to strengthen students' practical ability and enable them put what they have learned into reality, the school has taken measures relevant to the design studio through all resources such as the establishment of textile design studio, ceramics design studio, and image design studio. When led by teachers to experience the real design project, students have the chance to witness the entire design process, master the whole procedure, and possess the precious work experience, thus making significant effects on the future study and work. In the

*Corresponding author: [a] Dong Yan：274261074@qq.com

other hand, it is also conducive to the profound exchanges and communications between teachers and students, and then promotes students' learning efficiency in the specialized courses of science and engineering. (Fig. 2)

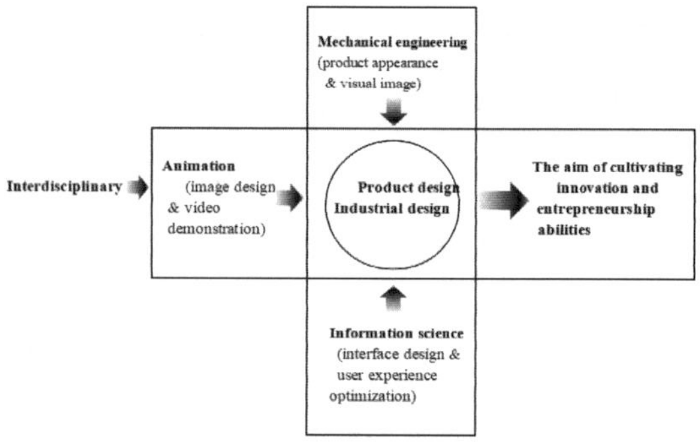

Figure 2. Integration of disciplines and majors

2.2 The construction of faculty structure

The four-year practical teaching requires cooperation of teachers between basic courses and specialized courses. Hence, the school has set up a teaching research team consisting of teachers of the basic courses and the specialized courses, gradually fostered its faculties, and employed experts from enterprises as teachers and instructors to improve students' innovation and entrepreneurship abilities.

2.3 The introduction of project teaching to the curriculum system

Attempts are made to productize the masterpieces shaped in the vocational teaching and research. At present under the influence of the Internet, it is improper to continue the traditional path from product design, lot production, and channel development to marketing. In the other hands, in order to realize design innovation, colleges and universities should construct a interdisciplinary mechanism with collaborative innovation, and transform the technical innovation into students' entrepreneurship; meantime, multiple factors such as the company's management mechanism and capital operation mechanism can be used together for high efficiency.

2.4 The realization of the further cooperation between school and enterprise

The five-in-one education system emphasizes the connections to the related domains in society; both direct employment and self-employment are available. In the last academic year, students are arranged to work in the relevant companies as interns, and their learning conditions will be reported to the school timely, which enables them to put the knowledge they have acquired in the class into practice. In addition, researches on the students' innovation and entrepreneurship projects are conducted. The school cultivate excellent graduates for those enterprises every year and allows priority selection of them. Taking advantage of the enterprises' technologies and equipment to co-share the resources of school and enterprise and combine with the training at class and social practice has not only extended the openness but also promoted the professionalization of the talent cultivation in design major and achieved deeper cooperation between schools and enterprise with mutual benefits.

2.5 The service for the local economy

As the talent training is able to facilitate the development of the local economy, a complete set of long-term and sustaining process must be formed in the marketization of technological achievements. Nowadays, almost no college and university has set up such a mechanism and applied it to the talent cultivation plan. Under such circumstances, enterprises get no information of the schools' projects, and the schools with innovated technologies cannot find the proper enterprises for cooperation either. Hence, barriers between the benefits of the local economy and the teaching and research should be broken in the ways of cultivation plan adjustment, theoretical teaching, practical training, graduation project, and innovation and entrepreneurship program.

3 Five-in-one education system reform measures

3.1 Propelling innovation and entrepreneurship curriculum reform in design major

With various forms such as entrepreneurship class, entrepreneurship training course, entrepreneurship imitation, and practical training of entrepreneurship activities, the students in design majors are taught with enterprise consciousness, entrepreneurship-related knowledge and skills to develop their potentials for entrepreneurship, enhance their abilities to capture, master, make use of, and create opportunities, and make a complete improvement in terms of the quality of the design talents of colleges and universities, thus more qualified entrepreneurs fostered and supplied with enterprising spirits and abilities for society. The practical teaching system with a purpose of developing students' innovation and entrepreneurship abilities should facilitate the new cultivation plan, reduce the credit in the theoretical teaching, and increase the practical credit. Generally, the education reform for the cultivation of innovation and entrepreneurship talents involves the following aspects. (Fig. 3)

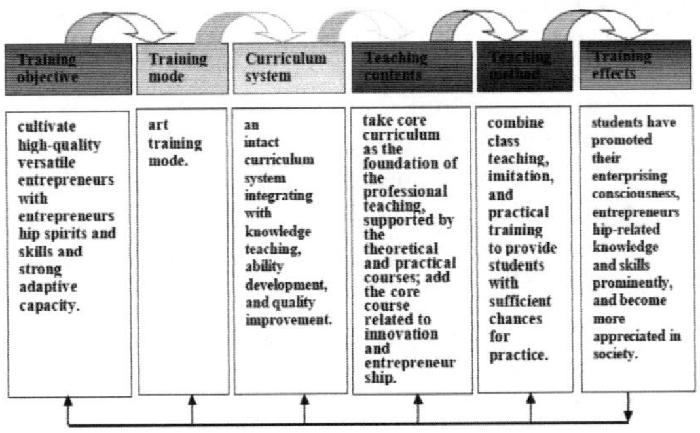

Figure 3. The framework of the education reform plan to train the talents with innovation and entrepreneurship abilities

3.2 Strengthening the professional training course reform to adapt to innovation and entrepreneurship education

In order to intensify innovation and entrepreneurship education, it is important to raise its status to that of the traditional professional training and the academic education. According to the education development trend, the reforms of the professional practical course assessment mode and the graduation project evaluation system are necessary. Four principles concerning the course assessment mode reform are to be followed, including the principle of diverse teaching modes, the principle of complete teaching contents, the principle of multiple evaluation subjects, the principle of instructive assessment results; besides, the reform should concentrate on the exploration of training objective, curriculum system, teaching mode, assessment mode, contents of examination, evaluation process, and information feedback. The practical teaching system based on innovation and entrepreneurship focuses on the cultivation of the five core abilities in design expression, design innovation, information analysis, team cooperation, and design practice.

3.3 Course assessment mode reform

3.3.1 The final oral examination

According to the cultivation plan, teachers make special choice of design and practical courses, and organize the final oral examination in the end of the course. The exam should be checked by the teacher of the course and other relevant professional teachers; they are to give scores and make comments in terms of students' whole oral defense of the homework. They will score rationally and fairly when referring to the evaluation standards and the comments of other teachers.

3.3.2 Scoring collectively

When the course comes to the end, the teaching and research group will organize teachers to score collectively; besides, the teacher of the course will also refer to the certain proportion of the evaluation standards.

3.3.3 Analysis of the test paper

In the beginning of every semester, the teaching and research group will also hold teaching discussions on the results of the test paper analysis, make conclusions on the problems existing in the teaching, analyze to what degrees the students has mastered the knowledge, and then adjust the teaching contents, teaching modes, and teaching methods to ensure the continuous improvement of teaching effect.

3.3.4 summary of the course

Summary is made to conclude the effects and experience of the teaching mode and method reforms on the basis of students' foundations, the aspects of reform with outstanding changes compared with the previous teaching, as well as the reference to the future teaching.

3.4 Graduation project evaluation system reform

To guarantee the quality of the thesis in the graduation project, the real-time management must be achieved in the whole process for the receiving of the latest feedback information. The evaluation and supervision is made from several aspects such as topic selection, sketch design, design scheme confirmation, early check, medium-term inspection, module making, and thesis defense; furthermore, following the graduation project, the work related to the conclusions and assessments of the graduation project also must be conducted to effectively perfect the graduates' design works. For the excellent designs in the graduation projects, teachers can instruct their owners to apply for patents, thus the teaching and research levels available to be promoted.

4 Advantages of five-in-one education system reform

The practical teaching system reform targeting the development of innovation and entrepreneurship abilities belongs to the next special practical link when the basic courses or the theoretical teaching of the specialized courses end. This teaching arrangement is good for students mastering the relevant knowledge and skills taught in the class. What's more, it breaks the traditional teaching mode, and structures a new mode integrating theoretical teaching, practical teaching, and innovation and entrepreneurship training.

First, the reform has established a set of scientific and feasible plan to cultivate talents with innovation and entrepreneurship abilities, thus meeting the current demands of the era when the economy of our country is developed based on the innovation-driven development strategy under the New Normal, comprehensive reforms are made in the higher education, and the high-quality employment is boosted by self-employment.

Second, the reform has formed a complete and appropriate innovation and entrepreneurship curriculum system, broken the traditional personnel training system, and enabled the innovation and entrepreneurship education geared to the needs of all the students in all the majors and every link of the entire study process. It abandons the barriers related to the conservative concepts, resources, and systems, and shaped a teaching vision aiming for education, concentrating on teaching, and relying on service, so that the teaching effects of students and teachers depending on each other and benefiting each other can be made.

Third, the reform has relieved the employment pressure of the graduates from the private colleges and universities, and also promoted their comprehensive competitive forces. Along with the increasing graduates and the decreasing positions offered by the traditional industries, the scientific and technological progress and the rising labor cost have invisibly reduced the employment space. The education and teaching reform is able to develop more talents with innovation and entrepreneurship abilities, so that the employment can be drive by entrepreneurship and the high-quality employment and enterprising are available for those graduates.

Fourth, the reform has built a mature and intact practical teaching platform, and extended the teaching out of the class, thus allowing teachers and students to touch the industry, society, and enterprise through various channels; the active participation in the practical projects enables students to closely link theory with practice and indeed achieve the practical teaching integrating education, practice, and entrepreneurship in the cooperation with the enterprises. The reform is to cultivate the excellent designers who can meet the social demands with high practical abilities, with an ultimate goal of realizing the effective transformation of technological achievements and serving the development and construction of the regional economy with the promoted competitiveness.

5 Conclusion

The ability-oriented innovation and entrepreneurship education system integrates five-in-one education system with teaching to benefit the local economy, and makes comprehensive reforms of the teaching in the design major of the private colleges and universities. Its training objectives of conducting project teaching, realizing further cooperation between school and enterprise, integrating different disciplines, constructing faculty structure, and serving the development of the local economy, is meaningful for the private application-oriented colleges to foster the high-quality talents with innovation and entrepreneurship abilities through reform and practice.

References

1. Chen Jiangning, Innovation and Entrepreneurship Education: the Principal Line of Personnel Training System Construction in Colleges and Universities, Journal of Shangqiu Vocational and Technical College, 2012
2. https://wenku.baidu.com/view/f718fb0590c69ec3d5bb75a0.html?edu_search=true (2010)
3. http://www.lunwentianxia.com/product.free.10073281.1/ (2014)
4. Tian Hongxi & Cao Shangqiu, Characteristics of the Mode Integrating with Art Teaching and Practice, Wenyi Zhengming (2010)
5. Liu Liqun, Establishing a Three-dimensional Practical Teaching System Conducive to the Cultivation of Students' Ability in Innovation and Entrepreneurship, Education and Occupation (2013)
6. Huang Benxiao & Huang Hao, Literature Review on College Students' Innovation and Entrepreneurial Practice Platform Construction, Productivity Research (2014)
7. Chen Zhiwu & Zhang Derong, Improve the Practical Teaching System, Train Applied Innovative Talents, Laboratory Research and Exploration (2012)
8. Hu Tao & Shen Li, Enlightenment of Foreign Innovative and Entrepreneurial Education Models on Chinese Universities, Chinese University Teaching (2013)

Study on Practice Teaching System of Undergraduate Industrial Design in Comprehensive University

Shi Bai[1,2,a], Qiang Sun[1]

[1]School of Art and Design, Bengbu University, 233000 Bengbu, Anhui, China
[2]School of Arts, Southeast University, 210000 Nanjing, Jiangsu, China

Abstract. The Industrial Design of the comprehensive university should actively carry out education and teaching research and reform, where practice teaching plays an increasingly important role in Industrial Design education. Focusing on the training of high-quality professionals, the practice-based Industrial Design teaching system was discussed. The guiding ideology and the formulation of guidelines for establishing a practical teaching system, were proposed as well as a multiple-level innovation and open practice teaching system structure. At the same time, the important features of the practical teaching system of Industrial design are explained, such as proportion of time, teaching module, teaching platform, teaching arrangement, etc. which provide reference theory and method for the practical teaching of Industrial Design.

1 Introduction

With the needs of China's economic and social development, more and more colleges and universities have set up Industrial Design, including a large number of comprehensive and multiple-disciplinary universities. At present, a relatively large number of new Industrial Design talents have been initially formed. Industrial Design as a multiple-disciplinary application-oriented profession, requires comprehensive universities to take advantage of their own strengths and think about how to scientifically arrange relevant teaching systems, to harmonize and rationalize theoretical teaching and practical teaching of courses, and to cultivate talents with design and practical ability and innovative practical ability.

2 Industrial design teaching system

Industrial design aims to guide innovation, promote business success, and provide a better quality of life. It is a design activity that applies a strategic problem-solving process to products, systems, services, and experiences. It is an interdisciplinary profession that closely connects innovation, technology, commerce, research, and consumers, conducts creative activities together, visualizes the problems that need to be solved, proposes solutions, and reconstructs problems. As an opportunity to build better products, systems, services, experiences or business networks, it provides new value and competitive advantage[1]. In recent years, the State Council has successively issued important documents and plans such as *Industrial Transformation and Upgrading Planning 2011-2015, Several Opinions on Promoting the Integration and Development of Cultural and Design Services and Related Industries and Made in China 2025.* In the Industrial design industry, Industrial Design plays a very important role in the development of innovative countries and high-quality economic development. Therefore, the entire design industry urgently needs a large number of highly qualified professionals.

2.1 The goal of talent cultivation

Industrial design has comprehensive, cross-cutting, and systematic disciplinary characteristics. It involves a wide range of content and fields. This requires that university-trained professionals must have a relatively broad knowledge system and a relatively comprehensive practical ability[2]. At present, the industry generally believes that excellent Industrial designers should have the ability to solve problems creatively. Simply put, it is to analyze who you are designing for, what you are designing, why do you design this way, and how your design can solve this problem. Specifically speaking, it is necessary to have the ability to complement logical thinking and visual thinking, good design performance, good model-making ability, data collection and processing ability, good computer-aided design ability, good communication and expression ability, design activity management ability, and the ability to be familiar the product from design and manufacturing to marketing.

2.2 Cultivation emphasis of innovation talent

From a design perspective, innovation starts with problems and comes from practice. Practical teaching emphasizes the individual of students more than

* Corresponding author: [a] artbaishi@163.com

theoretical teaching. Emphasis on practical teaching helps students to fully understand and master theoretical knowledge, and urges students to develop theory and practical style and rigorous and serious work attitude. At the same time, it improves hands-on operational ability and professional competitiveness gradually. In the process of training, students should be guided to actively construct the knowledge system of the subject, in order to cultivate students' exploration spirit, innovation consciousness, and comprehensive quality to generate the combined effects of knowledge, emotion, intention, and energy, so as to help students obtain innovative design results and obtain their own comprehensive development. Industrial design as a comprehensive, cross-cutting, and systematic edge discipline, whose essence is innovation, must enable students to build a sound professional knowledge and skills and reserve the knowledge structure and literacy that can adapt to social development by strengthening the practical teaching process in the limited time of on-campus learning. Making practicality plays a huge role in the training of design talents' comprehensive capabilities is also one of the important features of modern industrial design education in the world.

3 Establish a practical teaching system for innovative applications

3.1 Guiding principles and guidelines

The teaching model of Industrial design practice in integrated universities is different from that of art schools. It is difficult to adopt a mature design studio system. The formulation of the entire practical teaching system must be based on the orientation of personnel training and personnel training programs in the school. In order to establish a practical teaching system that meets the needs of Industrial design professionals in the school's general education requirements, there must be clear principles and guidelines.

(1) Conduct systematic organic teaching of all aspects of practice teaching, adhere to the tandem nature of the practice teaching system, and establish a goal system for talent practice ability training.

(2) Make full use of the school's shared resources and elements, make effective use of the practice centers and laboratories inside and outside schools, and strive to create interdisciplinary and integrated collaborative teaching conditions so that organic quality education and professional skills training are organically combined.

(3) The practical teaching system should highlight certain professional features. The teaching content and module structure should clearly reflect the complete knowledge chain and skill sequence of the Industrial design profession

(4) Adhere to the open teaching thinking, adopt corresponding practical teaching modes and means for different practical teaching links, and focus on the optimization of teaching effects.

3.2 Reasonable practice teaching architecture

Establish the goal of fostering applied Industrial design talents with "thick foundation, strong ability, high compounding, and heavy features", scientifically adjust the proportion of theoretical teaching and practical teaching, reform the original curriculum experimental design, and set up a link to increase innovation and entrepreneurship practice teaching. Finally, an open Industrial design practice teaching architecture is established with multiple-level innovation and application based on design performance and skill operation, based on design thinking and design and practical ability, and supported by design research and off-campus practice.

4 Important features of industrial design practice teaching system

4.1 Improve the proportion of class hours in practical teaching

Practical teaching and theoretical teaching are both important links in the teaching system. Both are complementary and have equal status. In view of the characteristics of the discipline of Industrial design, it is necessary to begin by formulating and revising the training plan for talents, and to make full use of the existing teaching conditions to establish a scientific and rational curriculum system and a practical teaching system that conforms to the development law of professionals. The content of theoretical teaching and practical teaching should be optimized and integrated, and efforts should be made to harmonize and coordinate system design, to communicate with each other, to be relatively independent, and to gradually improve. In order to cultivate students' comprehensive professional knowledge and skills and their ability to innovate and start-up, the specific requirements of each teaching session are refined. Inviting peer experts to fully demonstrate and improve the proportion of hours of practical teaching, so that the ratio of theoretical teaching and practical teaching of the professional 6:4. The common time ratio of comprehensive universities should be broken to make the practice teaching system safe.

4.2 Multiple-level progressive practice teaching module

The innovative application of Industrial design practice teaching system adopts multiple-level progressive practice teaching modules, which are divided into four levels: general basic knowledge practice, professional foundation practice, professional comprehensive practice, and innovative design practice. Among them, based on the design performance and skill operation, the main line of various product design topics, relying on design training, design research, and extracurricular activities as an aid to the orderly implementation of various aspects of practical teaching.

(1) The level of general basic knowledge is set for junior students, focusing on students' acceptance of systematic design concepts, providing academic background and basic skills for follow-up related courses, inspiring students' interest of study and desires to explore in Industrial Design. Practical teaching at this stage is mainly performed in the computer room, professional laboratory, design practice center, and off-campus practice base of the school. Practice teaching links and methods are mainly cognitive practice, materials practice, metalworking practice, sketching practice, professional basic courses and experiments.

(2) The level of professional foundation practice is set for students of grades 2-3. Through the practical training of professional basic courses in this subject, students can master the normative design flow, good design habits, scientific design methods, reasonable design experience, and develop good hands-on skills and innovation. Practical teaching at this stage is mainly conducted in professional laboratories, design practice centers, and off-campus practice bases. Practice teaching links and methods are mainly model-making, molding techniques, computer-aided design, practice of course exercises, professional investigations and professional internships.

(3) The level of professional comprehensive practice is set for students in grades 3-4 to train students to apply their own knowledge and skills to thematic design research and practice through the comprehensive practice of professional curriculum practice, design special research practice, graduation practice, graduation design, etc. , focusing on cultivating students' ability to find problems, analyze problems, and solve problems. Practical teaching at this stage is mainly conducted in professional laboratories, design practice centers, and off-campus practice bases or enterprises.

(4) The level of innovation design practice mainly refers to the expansion of the practice beyond the prescribed teaching plan, including discipline competitions, professional design competitions, innovative entrepreneurship training programs for university students, and production, research and development projects[3]. This type of practical activity has rich levels, diverse forms, and high flexibility. It can give full play to the students' autonomy and enterprising spirit, and ultimately train professionals with innovative ideas and abilities.

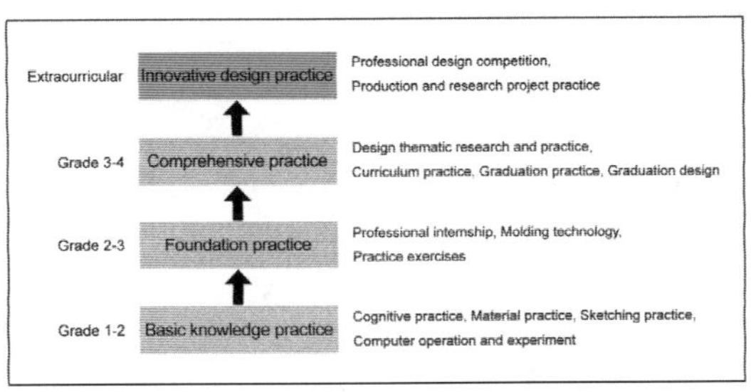

Figure 1. Practice teaching system of industrial design

4.3 Internal and external combined innovative practice teaching platform

The Industrial design practice teaching system needs to be implemented through two kinds of teaching platforms: on-campus and off-campus. The on-campus teaching platform includes a studio, a computer training center, a model production room, a professional laboratory, a design practice center, etc. It mainly conducts various types of professional skills training, curriculum experimental training, computer aided design training, material processing technology training, metalworking practice, design research and other practical courses outside the teaching plan and independent practice links. The off-campus teaching platform includes an off-campus practice base, practical training bases for school-industry cooperation, and a production-learning-research cooperation practice center. It mainly carries out teaching and research activities such as production and research projects, professional investigations, professional internships, graduation practice, and graduation design. In recent years, most universities in China are actively exploring and attempting to establish a practical teaching base with different functions outside the school. Through cooperation with related companies, we have gradually created a professional practice model of "real issues, true design, and real environment"[4]. This will greatly promote the training of professionals.

The off-campus teaching platform is an effective supplement to the practical teaching system. Through out-of-school practice training, students learn about society and enterprises, are familiar with the implementation process of design projects, enhance professional knowledge and skills, and establish a spirit of communication and cooperation. Of course, we must note that although the practice outside the school is an important part of talent cultivation, the university itself needs to continue to evolve. Because university education undertakes the important task of research and innovation, it is necessary to establish students' forward-looking awareness, innovative spirit, and exploration skills in personnel training. Therefore, courses on "Designing Special Topics in Research and Practice" should be set up in the practical teaching in schools. Design teachers and corporate designers from well-known colleges and universities should hold short-term "Workshops" so that students can continuously learn rich design concepts, design methods, humanities and literacy, strive to achieve energy and energy, both strong practical ability, but also a strong ability to design thinking and development potential.

4.4 Combination of work and study practice teaching arrangements

Reference is made to the combination of learning and teaching patterns that have been used by foreign tertiary institutions for learning semesters and work semesters alternately, and to give full play to the two different teaching platform resources inside and outside the school. On the one hand, the classroom teaching in the school education must be closely followed. On the other hand, the internship work should also be taken into consideration. The two should be organically combined[5]. It is better to arrange two internships during the undergraduate years. The first summer vacation between the second and third grades can be arranged at the internship practice base, learning by "problem-oriented". After studying certain professional courses, students are promptly involved in the production, study and research projects and corporate design projects so that students can test their abilities in practice and discover shortages. Afterwards, they will start targeted learning with questions, which can effectively improve students' initiative and interest in learning. They can also help students to further understand what they have studied and what they will do in the future so that they can make reasonable plans for their career development as soon as possible.

Another internship is scheduled for the fourth grade winter vacation. Students choose suitable internship units for a three-month graduation internship with the help of tutors according to their professional aspirations and professional expertise. Students have completed the study of the professional courses before this time. Through the participation of the "quasi-professional designer" in the work of the company, students can receive comprehensive training to improve their ability and attainment from all angles.

5 Practical teaching needs support of hardware and software

The development of Industrial Design practice teaching requires a complete teaching system structure and perfect software and hardware support. The hardware mainly refers to the campus computer room, professional laboratory, design practice center, design workshop and off-campus internship practice base. The software mainly refers to the practical teaching staff, practice teaching mode, practical teaching content, practical teaching security system, and evaluation mechanism. When the level of software and hardware construction matches the structure of the practical teaching system, the effectiveness of practical teaching can be maximized. In recent years, many colleges and universities have achieved certain results in practical teaching software and hardware construction, such as the establishment of computer-aided design laboratories, product processing technology laboratories, interaction design laboratories, three-dimensional printing laboratories, design practice centers, design and research centers, etc. In addition, a school-enterprise cooperation practice base and a production-learning-research project cooperation base have also been established outside the school; Many colleges and universities also employ "dual-energy" teachers, select professional teachers to participate in corporate training, formulate curriculum syllabus, curriculum design practices, professional practice management methods, graduation design specifications, and assessment standards.

Through the analysis of the exploration and implementation of Industrial design practice teaching, hardware is the necessary foundation and the precondition for all practical teaching activities. The software plays a key role in the level of practical teaching, the quality of practical teaching and the effect of practical teaching. In the meanwhile, the degree of emphasis on practical teaching and the allocation of teaching funds by school management departments are also indispensable factors that affect the construction of practical teaching systems.

Acknowledgment

Funding: Supported by Social Science Key Project of Bengbu University (No.2017SK04zd), Experimental Teaching and Experimental Technology Research Project of Bengbu University (No. 2016syxm17), Quality Engineering Project of Bengbu University (No. 2016JYXM25).

References

1. Guo.H.J,Wang.H.B, On the Difficulty and Strategy of Improving the Employment Competitiveness of Industrial Design Graduates, Design Research, 04(2017); 20-25
2. Xu.J,The Study of Product Design“Progressive Project-Based Learning”Teaching Model,(Doctor Thesis) Jiangnan University, Wuxi, Jiangsu, China, 2017
3. Xi.X.Y,Meng.L.L, Research on the Training Mode of College Students' Innovation and Entrepreneurship Based on Discipline Competition, Modern Vocational Education, 28(2017); 60-62
4. Hou.Y,Analysis of Purpose and Content in Practice Education of Universities Industrial Design, Design, 02(2015); 142-143
5. Fan.X.X,Work Integrated Learning Mode in Austral ia and Its Enlightenment, Journal of Teacher Education, 03(2017); 102-108

MATEC Web of Conferences **176**, 02008 (2018) https://doi.org/10.1051/matecconf/201817602008
IFID 2018

MINIMIZED Design for the Packaging of Shenyang Specialties Against the Internet-Based Background

YANG Meng[1,a], ZHANG Xiaohui[1]

[1]Shenyang Aerospace University School of Design & Art, 110136 Shenyang, China

Abstract. The focus herein is innovative design ideas for the packaging of Shenyang specialties under the concept of minimization. Through analyzing the current status of the packaging of Shenyang specialties, the relevance between minimized design and specialty package is discussed, while based on actual cases, studies are carried out to find solutions for problems including waste of resources resulted from excessive packaging, homogenization of package images, blurring of audience identification, and unitary sales channel. By redesigning the packaging of Shenyang specialties against the internet-based background and increasing visibility of specialty products, new ideas and methods for the package design of Shenyang specialties are provided taking minimized concept as the entry point, thus to realize value guidance and culture communication under the concept of minimization.

1 Introduction

The focus herein is innovative design ideas for the packaging of Shenyang specialties under the concept of minimization. Through analyzing the current status of the packaging of Shenyang specialties, the relevance between minimized design and specialty package is discussed, while based on actual cases, studies are carried out to find solutions for problems including waste of resources resulted from excessive packaging, homogenization of package images, blurring of audience identification, and unitary sales channel. By redesigning the packaging of Shenyang specialties against the internet-based background and increasing visibility of specialty products, new ideas and methods for the package design of Shenyang specialties are provided taking minimized concept as the entry point, thus to realize value guidance and culture communication under the concept of minimization.

2 The current situation and problems of the packaging of Shenyang specialties

Shenyang is a city with distinct regional features. Since specialties are an important driving force for the development of tourism economy, it's an important task of package design to endow specialties with vitality. To make full use of e-commerce platforms to expand the market and achieve trans-regional and sales, the packaging of specialties must be adjusted and modified to build the brand image of Shenyang specialties and improve the cultural connotation and artistic quality of package design, and thus to satisfy requirements on packaging brought by e-commerce platforms. Main problems existing in the packaging of Shenyang specialties:

2.1 Problems during the process of purchasing

Research shows that, there are mainly two problems existing in the packaging of Shenyang specialties during the process of purchasing: the first is that the awareness of brand promotion is poor. With respect to extraction and use of local elements, the commonly applied method is to pile up some simple visual elements of products, which is not sufficient to demonstrate the relationship between elements and the package, nor the unique regional and ethnical appeals. Such brand images are not beneficial for communication and promotion. The second is that the styles are highly homogenized. Style designs mainly use regular rectangular boxes, which lacks creativity and won't arouse consumers' interests in buying or desire to consume.

2.2 Problems after purchasing

After purchasing behavior is completed, the other identity of commodity package emerges, namely, it should be environmental friendly, without excessive packaging or waste producing. Results of excessive packaging: the first is increasing pressure on logistics and transportation. This is reflected in aspects including excessively bulky and heavy packaging, and poorly arranged internal structure, and too many materials used, all of which are the results of exquisite packaging. Consequently, the packaging is beyond general requirements for commodity packing in terms of size, space and volume, and brings heavy burden to logistics. The second is lacking of considerations for the

* Corresponding author: [a] yangm1978@163.com

sustainable use of materials. Selection of packaging materials lacks environmental considerations, thus materials that are difficult to recycle including plastics and paper are used most commonly, which will cause environmental pollution and waste of resources.

3 Analysis on demands for minimized packaging design for Shenyang specialties against the internet-based background

3.1 Analysis on merchants' demand for minimized packaging of specialties

Compared to the business model of physical stores, online sales can save large quantities of promotional costs and store-related costs, as all the promotions can be finished through online platforms. Under this new selling model, commodities can be identified through code scanning, and information about them will be clear at a glance, hence, the target of this event will be achieved as long as the exclusive express packaging can communicate information[1]. To continuously expand the market share, merchants must increase the visibility of commodities, and enable the packaging to win a place in fierce market competition and draw people's attention, thus to bring consumers with visual enjoyment and spiritual relax. While designing the packaging of Shenyang specialties, more attention should be paid on the visual image creation for the packaging, to allow consumers to see the appeal of Shenyang specialties and stimulate their design to buy.

3.2 Analysis on consumers' demand for minimized packaging of specialties

As participants of the shopping process, consumers' demand for packaging usually determines the development trend of packaging. Consumers wish to receive commodities with express packaging that is flawless, easy to open and humanized, and at the same time, has certain regional characters to highlight unique historical and cultural information of the place of origin. Therefore, the selection of packaging materials is very important. Research shows that, people prefer environmental friendly materials with resources from the nature, which bring people natural senses of intimacy, reality and plainness, and satisfy their emotional demands.

Using natural materials with regional characters can not only demonstrate the unique cultural appeal, but also realize the environmental friendly design concept. While handling materials, the original mechanism of natural materials should be made good use of, in order to minimize machining and retain the beauty of the materials themselves. Consumers who buy specialties prefer the primitive feeling brought by natural materials. For example, using straws to create plain packaging for Shenyang specialties and using natural materials to make packaging containers will touch the souls of consumers, without losing regional characters of Shenyang.

3.3 Analysis on demand of logistics for minimized packaging of specialties

As a means of goods transportation, logistics is the bridge for merchants to deliver goods to consumers, and plays an important role in the process of online shopping[2]. For commodities bought online, the packaging structure should be optimized not only to satisfy functions including protecting commodities, facilitating transportation and being durable, but also to lower the production cost and protect the environment by using least possible materials, without reducing functions of commodity packaging. The minimized design concept should be promoted, by reasonably saving materials used in packaging and giving full play to recycling of resources.

Compared to static conditions, commodities are more likely to be damaged during the process of transportation because they are vulnerable to impact of external forces and tossing resulted from road transportation. With respect to this problem, the most common solution is to add a larger external package filled with corrugated paper, white foam filler and dunnage bags as buffer materials. Therefore, appropriate structures should be selected based on the characteristics of commodities and materials, to provide effective protection and optimize the packaging design to be suitable for logistics handling and transportation. Internal structure of specialty packaging can be optimized based on ergonomic principles, to reduce the size and volume of packaging, use of materials, and pressure on logistics[3].

For example: Figure 1 is the combined dried fruit package design of Taiwan good fruit that packs cantaloupe, pineapple, apple and orange separately and then together into an external package, which reduces the overall volume and further makes the packaging suitable for logistics transportation.

Figure 1. Combined dried fruit package of Taiwan good fruit.

https://doi.org/10.1051/matecconf/201817602008

4 Solutions to minimized design for the packaging of Shenyang specialties against the internet-based background

4.1 Highlighting the reasonability of packaging structure

Packaging structure indicates the mutual constructive relationship among the shapes of different parts or units[4]. As specialties against the internet-based background, the first thing to think about should be innovative and pioneering design of the packaging structure. Design of packaging structure should take in to account various factors including the shape characters of commodities, features of packing materials, spatial requirements of transportation and storage, and ergonomic performance when carried and used by consumers.

Commodity categories, size requirements and classification provided by e-commerce platforms are rather unitary. Therefore, to divide sizes reasonably utilizing limited space, studies and classifications of the commodity attributes should be carried out. Packaging structure and materials should be designed based on different commodity attributes, to make commodity packaging more suitable for sales on e-commerce platforms without reducing the life span of the packaging. As shown in Figure 2, the packaging of Charlie Bohea Tea boasts a design concept different from ordinary ones, which uses an interesting hexagon box that looks like a honeycomb, to distinguish itself from the general concept of demonstrating the profound history and culture of tea. Trying to break out of tradition and demonstrate the modern characteristics of tea, Charlie Bohea Tea tells consumers that this is a both traditional and modern tea through the structure and color system of the packaging.

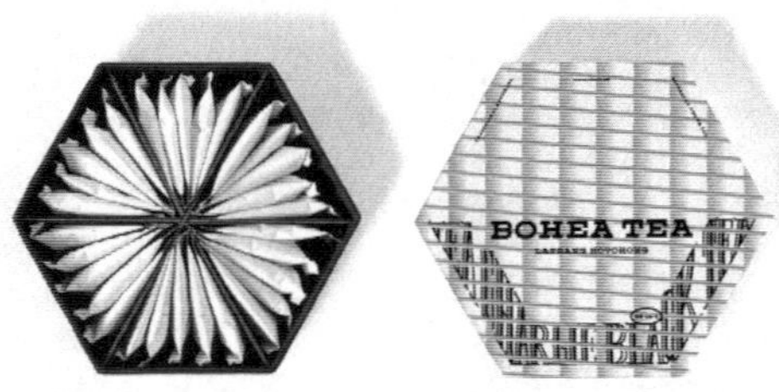

Figure 2. The packaging of Charlie Bohea Tea.

4.2 Emphasizing standardization of packing sizes

Confronted with the uncertainty of shopping environment against the internet based background, the packaging design should take full account of the unification and standardization of packing sizes. This will not only protect commodities from broken during transportation, but also lower the transportation costs, thus to gain consumers' recognition of the quality and awareness and favorability of the brand.

From the perspective of functions, the packaging structure involves commodity protection, and being convenient for storage, transportation, use and sales. Convenience is an important factor for the design of packaging structure[5], which is mainly reflected in aspects including transportation, carrying and use. During material selection and production of the packaging, attributes of specialties should be analysed , to enable the packaging to improve its protection of safety while being environmental friendly. As shown in Figure 3, TAKECO 1982 is a Japanese mixed seasoning brand, which, inspired by cargo transportation and sail elements, designed the packaging into triangles with patterns on them representing the fusion of seasoning cultures, while the size of the box is suitable for holding with two hands, and giving out as a gift. The triangle shape and appreciate size have made it more convenient for transportation of online sales.

Figure 3. The packaging of Takeco Yoshiyama seasonings.

4.3 Modularizing the configuration of packaging space

Modularized design and configuration space inside the packaging box will not only facilitate classification, but also utilize the limited space reasonable and reduce the pressure on logistics[6]. If the space is not configured reasonably, use of fillings will be increased imperceptibly, and accidental damages to commodities are likely to happen. This will bring heavy burden to logistics and increase merchants' transportation costs. Small-sized merchants operating on e-commerce platforms often attract consumers to buy the commodities by covering the postage, hence how to save money for e-commerce buyers and sellers becomes our focus. Therefore, during this process, the packing sizes of commodities are the priority of design. For example, in Figure 4, the packaging of Shenyang agricultural specialties targeted at e-commerce platforms is designed by the author with patterns based on the perspective of Northeast folk customs, while the graphic and cultural renderings are finished with "Eight Weird of the Northeast" as the regional cultural symbol. Different from ordinary plastic vacuum packaging, it is designed with aluminum can as packing material to distinguish it from common rice products in bulk and in bags. This packaging not only satisfies the demand for shelf life of rice products, but also conforms to consumers' psychological expectation for the preservation effect of the product.

Figure 4. Author design the packaging of "Eight Weird of the Northeast" rice.

5 Conclusion

As the first step for consumers to learn about commodities and generate the willingness to buy, packaging is an invisible bridge between commodities and consumers. With the development of technology, packaging design of commodities is also moving towards a deeper level. Against the internet-based background, the involvement of e-commerce channels provides commodity sales with more alternatives. Based on current consuming model of e-commerce, the concept of minimized design for the packaging of specialties is put forward herein, to come up with and formulate packaging design planning that fits different ideas from the perspectives including regional culture of brand, target consumer group, sales characters and demand of times, and further to realize demand of Shenyang specialties for minimized packaging design through demonstration of localized values, recycling of materials and standardization of sizes. The packaging structure is to be optimized based on researches on consumers' psychology and ergonomics, to design packages that are suitable for the internet-based environment and satisfy consumers demands by optimizing.

References:

1. K. Bian, Y. Yang, Packaging Engineering, **33**, 56 (2012)
2. H. Tian, Y. Qiu, Modern Decoration, **1**, 15 (2014)
3. W. Wang, Z. Wu, Packaging Engineering, **24**, 8 (2015)
4. Z. Wei, J. Wei, J. Lin, Packaging Engineering, **24**, 88 (2014)
5. F. Zeng, W. Wang, F. Wang, Design, (2014)
6. H. Yang, Art Panorama, **07**, 141 (2016)

The Application of Traditional Culture in Industrial Design in New Epoch

Wu Shuang

Ningxia Institute of Science and Technology, 753000 NingXia,China

Abstract. This paper is based on industrial design, collation and analysis the Chinese traditional culture to expound the essentiality in design. From the perspective of design aesthetics to discuss the Chinese traditional cultural characteristics express under the background of the new era with artistic language, to provide new design ideas for industrial design with Chinese characteristics in the new era.

1 Introduction

Industrial design takes engineering, aesthetics, and economics as the basic elements. The rational design of the product's shape, structure, colour, and function is an organic combination of aesthetics and industrial technology. The rapid development of modern science and technology has provided new exhibition space for industrial design. Technical, scientific and functional features have all increased the sensory experience of design works for the public, but they have overlooked the aesthetic and cultural value.

As an ancient civilization with a long cultural history, China has a long history of culture. Traditional culture is rich in connotation, broad in subject matter, and possesses unique oriental cultural aesthetic interests. Fully understanding the role of traditional Chinese culture, extracting the aesthetic elements and essential characteristics of traditional culture, and organically integrating modern technology, and applying creative methods to industrial design is an important issue faced by modern designers. It is also an important link need to be reflection. A reasonable combination of these two aspects will not only increase the aesthetic value of the products, but also increase the cultural self-confidence and cultural soft power.

2 The basic connotation of traditional culture

Chinese traditional culture is a spiritual cultural heritage accumulated by the Chinese nation in long-term practice activities, and it is also a concrete manifestation of the unique way of thinking of the Chinese nation. The intersection of economic production methods, political systems, and patriarchal relations has formed the basic features of traditional Chinese culture.

The "Imagery" and "Symbolize" are the essence in Chinese traditional aesthetics and the concrete expression of the thinking mode of the Chinese nation. The mode of economic production, patriarchal relations combine with national characteristics formed the basic cultural features.

"Imagery" refers to the subjective emotion of the aesthetic subject. "Symbolize" refers to the objective aesthetic imagery." Imagery" and "Symbolize" both embody the subjective consciousness of the aesthetic subject and the object characteristics of the aesthetic object. The utility function of the aesthetic object is directly back during the use of utensils, and its shape shows the spiritual sensory experience brought about by the material production culture level, highlighting the aesthetic characteristics under the characteristics of the times. The organic combination of these aspects constitutes a complete aesthetic activity. As a perceptual existence, people and objects are attracted to each other and the material form is more aesthetically implied.

2.1 The "Artistic Conception" of Chinese Traditional Culture

From the perspective of creativity, the artistic conception about Chinese traditional culture is a recreation activities, it let the aesthetical products combine with designer's subjective emotion.

2.1.1 Natural symbolic

Chinese civilization has been accumulated for thousands of years, made Chinese people have a unique understanding of nature, and the attachments to natural worship and attachment directly affected the external appearance of the product. This design concept has been embodied in ancient people's designs. For example, applying the simple natural concept of hemispherical dome cosmology in coins directly displays the natural symbolic features, symbolizes the natural concept, and applies its “shape”. In ancient times, the “Borrowing Scenery” function of doors and windows also displayed the aesthetic charm with Chinese characteristics. A large

[a] Corresponding author: Wu Shuang, 296767898@qq.com

number of decorative patterns on the door were rich in cultural features, which not only added the formal beauty of the doors and windows, but also highlighted its cultural heritage, and shaped the “form” and “object”. The combination shows the design ideas of Chinese traditional culture.

2.1.2 Allegorical symbolic

Chinese traditional aesthetics advocates the expression of "idea" and "image", which is different from typical figurative art in the West. The image conveys more of the cultural and philosophical value of aesthetic objects. "Book of Changes" remarked: "The apparatus is still like", and the design of utensils needs to be made on the basis of observing the images of natural things. It has a simple natural value and deep cultural connotation, and is similar to the modern western bionics, but its content the dialectical thought of Yin and Yang. Harmony of Man and Nature..

The understanding of the image by the ancients came from natural things, heaven and earth, water and fire, wind and thunder, and the natural laws of human beings. These aspects have profoundly affected China's unique aesthetic ideas. I Ching sixty-four hexagrams use "-" and "- -"simplifying all things in the world, not only embody a form of beauty, but also shows the unique thinking of the ancients on the relationship between heaven and earth. Yin-Yang thought, heaven and man thought, primal chaos thought are the important category in traditional Chinese aesthetics.

2.1.3 Cultural aesthetic value

Industrial design has a long history. Its origins derive from the basic needs of mankind for life. Its original purpose is to serve mankind and is the crystallization of the use of human creative thinking. Modern industrial design reflects the progress of modern science and technology, and its artistic conception expression is based on this material foundation. It also combined with traditional culture and modern design concepts. Reasonable design can make its functional elements, economic elements and cultural values unique, not only emphasizing the function of objects, but also satisfying the relationship between objects and people.

Aesthetic activities originate from social practice and are constantly changing with the development of history. Traditional culture has continuity and integrity, which deeply affects Chinese people's aesthetic sense. The beauty of artistic conception in traditional art thought is expressed through "Imagery" and "Symbolize". In popular language, "Imagery" represented creativity, cultural connotation and aesthetic value of an artwork. " Symbolize "conveyed the inner feelings of an aesthetic subject represented by utensils. The organic combination of images can form a complete aesthetic practice activity, which is also a concrete demonstration of the artistic conception in traditional culture.

Artistic beauty is unique in traditional culture, and it also provides a new way of thinking for modern design. Designers should proceed from reality, refinement and integration the quintessence in design. Embody Chinese cultural characteristics to improve the ornamental value and spiritual enjoyment.

2.2 The essential characteristics of traditional culture

The essence of traditional culture belongs to the category of aesthetics. It involves the subjective cognition of Chinese people's laws of nature and the aesthetic rules of artistic creation, and reflects the rich aesthetic psychology of the Chinese nation. On the whole, traditional Chinese culture pays attention to the spiritual experience that people bring in life, aesthetics, and implication.

2.2.1 Eastern life philosophy

Chinese culture has been polished for a long period of time to form a unique Chinese civilization. The Oriental view of life believes that all things in the entire universe and the universe have an active inner life. The eternal continuation and movement that determines this life is a kind of invisible sound, but it is everywhere in human life and nature.

"Dao" literal interpretation in Chinese means road, is orderly and regular. However, the specific trajectory and specific role of the change cannot be seen, so the “Dao” also possesses abstract features. This “nothingness” is not absent, but cannot be exhausted by the language and cannot be limited to a specific range.

"Dao" represents the basic laws of the universe and the deep understanding of life in traditional culture. “Tube Guan Zhong” said: “It’s shape, don’t smell its voice, and it's the order, it's the road”, Song-dynasty philosophers said: "The Dao is the heart," and the Zen saying: "The heart is the Buddha." It shows that "Dao" is the core of oriental life philosophy, embodies the unique cognition of Chinese philosophy to the objective world, and presents its unique recognition of life.

Therefore, the essence of "Dao" in Chinese traditional culture is not limited to the regular changes in the material category. What it contains is more about understanding and comprehending the life of the universe. This view of life takes Dao as the basic body in the universe, and builds a humanistic universal life outlook with Chinese characteristics, which is also the essence of Chinese art.

2.2.2 Oriental aesthetic imagery

In Chinese traditional culture, aesthetic image not only constitute by specific form, but also combine with related artistic symbols. What it conveys more is the sum of the artistic aesthetic sentiment conveyed by such visual images, pictures, and symbols, and the rich artistic fantasies and artistic associations that may trigger. In Chinese traditional art activities, the unique aesthetic mentality also created special aesthetic images. The artist's character, style, and accomplishment are all important requirements to achieve the aesthetic level of the works of art. .

In the works of art, the awareness of beauty can be extended to the resonance of the spiritual field through the expression of rationality, and the effect of beauty can be conveyed to become a unique eastern style aesthetic image.

3 The necessity of introducing traditional culture into contemporary design

3.1 Industrial design plays an important role in society

Industrial design combines science and technology with products to form products. It is a display of the achievements of science and technology and innovative thinking. It is also a comprehensive expression of artistic practice activities. In 1980, the International Federation of Industrial Design Associations defined the industrial design as follows: "For mass-produced products, with training, technical knowledge, experience, and visual experience, the material, structure, form, colour, surface finish, and decoration of the product are given. With new quality and specifications, and solving issues related to display, market development, etc., it is called industrial design."

Industrial design based on aesthetics, engineering, and economics, designs products and plays an important role in the socio-economic structure. In the design process, functional elements, human-computer interaction elements, shape elements, and aesthetic elements are all important links for ensuring product quality and improving product market competitiveness. Only designing products with aesthetic height and satisfying the public's psychological needs is a good design work. At the same time, industrial design also focuses on the design of product usage, safety, humanization, etc. It can be said that excellent design can greatly enhance the competitiveness and added value of products, promote the development of enterprises, and revitalize regional and national economies. Promote the sound development of productivity.

In the context of the new era, industrial design is not only the designer's self-expression art, but also a necessary means to enhance the user experience and create a brand effect. With the continuous improvement of people's living standards, the importance of industrial design is increasingly demonstrated. It can be said that industrial design, on the one hand, converts technology into market demand products, on the other hand, reflects market information to enterprises, and then promotes the development of enterprises and increases the vitality of enterprises. This is the driving force of social and economic development and the country's soft power.

3.2 The Need for Industrial Design to Integrate with Traditional Culture

The relationship between culture and design can reveal the purpose and motivation of design activities. The cultural connotation of design enables us to understand industrial design from a cultural perspective, thus enabling us to understand industrial design more comprehensively and deeply.

Industrial design is not a mere artistic creation, nor is it a science and technology design. It is a cultural re-creation of a product. Therefore, the essence of industrial design is the cultural design of objects. Product competition is the main body of market competition. Its specific performance is the competition of design and technology. In the competition of design, after swift development of science and technology, China ignores the concern for the nature of design, and separates the product from the culture, and cannot satisfy people's spiritual pursuit. This is not only an obstacle to the development of the industrial design field, but also affects the design concept of modern products by Chinese enterprises and lacks market competitiveness.

Under this background, the industrial design of the new era should be a complex of art and technology. As a carrier of culture, it must have cultural and artistic content to satisfy people's enjoyment in the spiritual realm. This is also the culture and technology in modern society.

3.3 The Specific Performance of Traditional Culture in Modern Furniture Design

Furniture is closely related in our lives. It is an artistic carrier of traditional culture and can profoundly reflect human social civilization. This material existence and creation activity reflect social politics, economy, art, science and technology and other elements.

In modern times, people's consumption of furniture gradually shifts from purely functional demands to the satisfaction of spiritual emotions. From the perspective of furniture design, the elements of human emotion constitute the driving force of furniture consumption activities, making furniture consumption activities have more emotional colour and aesthetic imagery. Designers need to understand the new design concepts, feel the life interest, make furniture inspire the user's spiritual resonance and more aesthetic value of art

The Rose Chair is one of the traditional Chinese furniture that prevailed in the Ming Dynasty and was also loved by many people in modern times. Figure 1 shows the modern rose chair designed by Zhu Xiaojie. It respects the original shape and image of the rose chair and adopts the principle of concrete. The reinforcement is strung in a very thin column of logs and stabilized by the way of building metal structure. The cowhide cushion is manually secured to the dark wooden frame by a bright line. The overall work is very classical Chinese traditional style. The application of metal feet and steel wire extensions reveals a harmonious and comfortable modern design sense. Figure 2 is the design of the money chair, the use of concise lines to express the charm of the Ming-style chair, but it condenses the typical characteristics of traditional culture. Combined of metal and wood is a combination of modern technology and traditional culture. The multi-material mashup highlights the beauty of the work, and its design essence is rooted in Chinese traditional culture. It inherits Chinese aesthetic philosophy, combined with designer's concepts, shows more humanistic concern.

Figure 1. The rose chair

Figure 2. The money chair

4 Creating Industrial Design with Chinese Characteristics in a New Era

4.1 Use traditional "object"

To create industrial designs with Chinese characteristics in a new era, we can learn from the shapes, functions, colours, and materials of traditional beauty.

Appearance is the visual direct expression of objects, and the rational application of traditional utensils appearance features can effectively enhance the visual sensibility, thus creating a design work with Chinese cultural temperament; at the same time, the rational use of traditional decorative elements can also enhance the work from the side. The artistic aesthetic symbolism, such as traditional patterns, colours, and surface treatment methods, these elements are used as decorative means, and their own emphasis is more on the symbol of the aesthetic spirit. Therefore, appropriate reference to traditional decorative methods can also highlight Chinese characteristics in design works.

4.2 Use traditional "meaning"

China's traditional culture is partly disseminated with materials as its carrier, such as Ming-style armchairs, chopsticks, and various forms of artistic expression; the other part is inherited in an ideological manner, which deeply affects people's practical activities and aesthetic values.

"As a matter of metaphysics, it is shaped as a device." Artistic conception is the high-level realm pursued by traditional cultural creation ideas. Modern industrial design should draw on excellent cultural traditions, trace the beauty of artistic conception under the material elements of traditional culture, and tap its rich spiritual connotation. Fully understand the "meaning" of traditional culture, refine its cultural essence, conduct analysis, design, and re-creation, apply these cultural elements ingeniously, display traditional cultural and aesthetic images, and reflect the spirit of the times.

5 Conclusion

Under the background of the rapid development of science and technology, Chinese design should not be limited by imitating and following western design. Ignoring the country's outstanding traditional culture will make China's industrial design work in a passive and lost position under the wave of modernization and technology. Modern industrial design needs to extract elements from traditional culture, shape ethnic features, and form an independent and excellent design style so that it can stand out in the international competition.

At the same time, in the context of global development, the use of modern industrial design works and the transmission of traditional Chinese culture cannot be accompanied only by appearance and appearance, but also capture its internal aesthetic values and spiritual outlook; Industrial design not only to absorb the essence of Chinese traditional culture, but also accord with modern design concept. Not only to inherit and learn from traditional culture, but also to innovate and develop from traditional culture. Only by grasping the pulse of the times and grasping the core values can we achieve the industrial design with Chinese characteristics and give it new vitality, so that the traditional Chinese culture will regenerate in the new era and demonstrate the cultural confidence with Chinese characteristics.

References

1. Liu Guanzhong. Thinking on the structure mechanism of industrial design industry in China [J]. Design,2013(10):158-163
2. Wang Zhenfu.The beauty of great ease[M]. Peking University Press,2006 :123-125
3. Li Zehou.Chinese Aesthetics[M]. Guangxi Normal University press, 2002 :57-58
4. Zong Baihua.Aesthetics and artistic conception[M]. Chinese People's Publishing House,1987 : 156-171
5. Wang Shouzhi.History of world industrial design[M].China Youth Publishing House,2002 :30-35

Probe into the Long-term Mechanism of "Studio Model" Teaching Internal Quality Guarantee

Yong Zhang[1,a], Yingying Shao[1] and Hongjie Yu[1]

[1] Liaoning Shihua University, School of Art and Design, 113001 Fushun, China

Abstract. Under the background of mass entrepreneurship and innovation, improving the quality of the teaching results and accomplishing the conversion of teaching achievements are the changes for the reform and development of colleges and universities. The reform of "Studio Model" teaching is more conducive to the improvement of undergraduate teaching quality, converse to results orientation. The effective quality guarantee mechanism is the important guarantee for forming undergraduate teaching method reform. Through the discussion of the concept and method of Carnegie Mellon University and the colleges of China. This paper puts forward the teaching reformation and exploration of the "Studio Model", Based on the idea of implementing the "effective teaching", this paper constructs the results-oriented curriculum in a pragmatic and innovative way, designs the teaching with the design competition and the practice project as the motivation.

1 Introduction

In classes of design, the "Studio Model" teaching is more conducive to have further study of complex problems and improve the knowledge, ability and quality of college students. At present, it has become an important direction of the teaching reformation of college design. The Studio Model is different from the traditional teaching mode, and the form is more conductive to have free and open. Whether traditional system management or the reformation of advanced innovation model, the aim is to guarantee the quality of teaching. Therefore, how to guarantee internal quality of reformation of teaching mode, and establish a long term mechanism for innovation of teaching model has become the most important reformation of studio teaching model.

2 Practice the concept of "Effective Teaching" in school

"Effective Teaching" is a teaching concept which was developed in the 1960s. The main figure is Benjamin Bloom, an American educational psychologist who believes that "Effective Teaching begins by knowing exactly what you want to achieve" [1]. The core of effective teaching concept is to pay attention to the needs, growth and development of students. The University of Carnegie Mellon has always used effective teaching as an important aspect of undergraduate education. In 1982, it established the, Aiboli Centre for Excellence in Teaching and Educational Innovation, to provide necessary guidance and support for effective "Teaching" and "Learning" [2]. The "Effective Teaching" has significant meaning of guiding in school, more conveniently and effectively. The rapid development of information technology and media makes the access to information more convenient and effective, the traditional classroom model can not meet the needs of the students. The unilateral acquisition of knowledge is so boring that the information received by teachers and students is often duplicated. he students sleep in class, play with their mobile phones in class, and even questions the usefulness and significance of what they are learning. Schools installs indoor cameras, block cell phone signals, and ask teachers to strengthen classroom management. The Office of academic Affairs-Teachers-students change the phenomenon from top to bottom in the way of pressure conduction rather than solve the problem.This phenomenon has filled the whole semester. "Credit hours" should be the time for students to study, and the ways to acquire knowledge, it should be diverse. Therefore, the classroom should not become exclusive stage of teachers. Teachers should have good professional teaching skills, The teachers also need to set an example for students, They should as well can fully develop interest and motivation, and promote independent and effective learning for students [2]. Taking Liaoning Shihua University (LSHU for short) as an example, since the establishment of the College of Art and Design in 2015, taking students as the center, training people as the core, combined with the characteristics of regional industry and service local cultural characteristics to determine the "effective teaching" of the orientation and characteristics of the school.Establishing the orientation and characteristics of "effective teaching" to train students,combining regional industry characteristics and Service local culture.

*Corresponding author: [a] 176978002@qq.com

Professional orientation: to serve the local cultural industry and the development of petrochemical industry as the orientation, the application of undergraduate education is the lead. Combined with the old industrial base in northeast China, the cultural characteristics of the Fushun Manchu and the before Qing Dynasty and non-material cultural heritage of amber and agate, the design of products, environmental art design and visual communication design as the direction of social needs are taught in the professional knowledge of design. Students have the ability to think and solve problems systematically by using the thought of design, focus on harmony and unity from human to product to environment, so as to provide senior personnel for revitalizing the old industrial base, serving the petroleum equipment manufacturing industry and promoting the development of local cultural industry.

Specialty characteristics: Building a "studio model" teaching model for schools and enterprises as a carrier, the using real subjects, with the main direction of petrochemical, equipment manufacturing, transportation equipment, local cultural creative products, agate and amber carving creativity, furniture design, environmental art and visual transmission. We will set up a multi-level team structure of experts and external professionals with advanced academic titles at the core of the workshop, conduct seminars, experiential, practical and exploratory classroom teaching, and initiate collaborative innovation in cooperation cross specialty union, school to school union, school to enterprise union and… through variety ways to train the students to be professionals. Cooperating and innovating inter school, inter school, school to enterprise and international facilities is great to build a new mode of training personnel who can be taught through studying and taught through creation.

3 Pragmatism and Innovation in Results-based Curriculum Construction

3.1 Definition of impact of goals on the results

"Purpose is that sense that we are part of something bigger than ourselves, that we are needed, that we have something better ahead to work for. Purpose is what creates true happiness." Facebook founder Mark Elliot Zuckerberg said in a 2017 Harvard University speech. Goals have the function of guiding, challenging oneself and strengthening self-confidence, use the result to motivate oneself, better results will be achieved. Enforcement is the ability to transform goals into results. LSHU is in the process of the practical teaching reformation. The principal focuses on teaching management, the dean of School of Art and Design directly manages teaching and organizes all teachers to participate in the revision of the teaching plan, and systematizes the system of subject and the logical relationship between courses. The teachers discuss and revise the teaching syllabus. They also study the content of the curriculum to achieve anticipated results of teaching. The teachers carry out the discussion session of "pre-course presentation and after-school summary", so that teachers can set standards and norms for the design of the class, process control and evaluation of each part of the curriculum. Teachers must be able to understand and control the whole system of professional courses, rather than taking a separate course in the traditional way. Every course is an important of the training plan of the students. creating a cause-and-effect logic that links up and connects. Every course is a causal connection. Only in this way can teachers think, improve and effectively implement their of instruction, focusing on issues that students are willing to learn and teach themselves.

3.2 Outcome orientation to break the logic of linear thinking

In the teaching mode of product design, it is emphasized that the program and method of product design are the center of design activities. Linear thinking product design model is suitable for companies and enterprises to manage. Through,design and assign design tasks through the design process, even new employees can successfully complete the task.As for teaching, linear thinking, which is guided by design program, will constraint the cognition of design, and Linear thinking makes students focus on finishing the whole design on schedule [3]. In linear thinking, "brainstorming" is often used in order to improve efficiency to force oneself to find new problems. In the end, it will quickly transform the "problem representation" into "conceptual design", ignoring the "origin" of the design, lacking in-depth study of people's way of life, and failing to solve the problem from a pragmatic and demand perspectively.

I studied School of Design of Dalian Minzu University with my thinking and questions. Their School of Design is one of the most successful departments with "Studio Model". The aim of the course is to move the course forward by providing students with a great deal of time to consult materials and to solve complex problems in practice, such as technology and materials, while teachers and students spend more time in the course than the total number of hours. Finally, through the annual Design Festival, students presented, compared, exchanged and presented with results. The work is surprising.

In the course of the studio education, it is found that because each student has a different professional foundation, according to the same linear thinking product design model, the design results did not break through, even at the end of successive semesters did not change the student's performance, some students' credits have been very high but some students' have been very low. This is a situation that we should think about thoroughly. If the ways and means of solving problems are not the only ones, then how can we break the logic of linear thinking? After thinking thoroughly, we try to design a new task to test the appeal question, which requires solving the problem. The result of the design can not be shown in a virtual way (hand-drawn or computer rendering). It must be an object. When the subject was announced, everyone was in a different situation. The quiet students are thinking of drawing a plan. Some active students go to the market for materials. One week later, 17 students submit 17 physical programmes. It is difficult to tell who designed them from the perspective of the programme alone. The task breaks our teachers' former impression of the students. A lot underachievers may impress the teacher. Everyone is confident when they finally show and explain their results, because everyone is doing what they do best.

3.3 Demand-oriented role shift

Under the influence of Carnegie Mellon's research university culture, the Aiboli Center for Excellence in Teaching and Educational Innovation focuses on applying the relevant research of "learning science" to teaching practice and advocates "research-oriented" and "data-driven" teaching practice. To encourage teachers to carry out relevant teaching research around the "needs of teaching and learning", so we can improve the quality of teaching and learning [4]. In the research of professional teaching direction studio, we follow the teaching research of "teaching" and "learning". Teaching is led by students and the role of teachers is transformed into guides and managers. As a guide, students demand more of teachers' teaching ability and subject knowledge structure. Teachers must keep pace with times and they also need to have the attitude of continuous learning. set an example for students from the professional perspective, so that teachers can form in front of students with awe, mutual trust and hope. Instead of the traditional way to intensify the conflict, the teaching model of the School of Art Design of LSHU will be detailed. Small classes are formed which contain 15 students. Teachers of studio are responsible for the study and employment of students. Undergraduate education uses tutorial system, which is a way that teachers to teach their students. After students enter the studio to study, we will cancel the old form of class. The new class is the studio. The teacher in charge of the studio is the head teacher. The advantage of dual identity in "Studio Model" is that it can meet the needs of the students in all aspects. From daily life to professional study, this is more conducive to cultivating their personality. School teachers are required to have a talk with each student at least once a month heart-to-heart. From the perspective of studio teaching to team building, teachers have been difficult to separate the dual roles. The activity of heart-to-heart talk has changed into "periodic information feedback". At first students do their own summary first. And then the teachers will give feedback according to the current condition of the students. In the process of communication, students can raise some claim and help the teachers. And teachers and students can plan further for their study through exchange of information. Working indoor advocacy is a part of life, and students should learn to do more meaningful things in limited time. Teachers are in such roles to set an example, encourage each other, competing, form a strong learning atmosphere.

4 Teaching of Design affected by design competitions and practical projects

Project design I, project design II and project design III are the three stages in which students learn in a studio. The stages are guided by the overall goal of the program. Professional subjects are designed as carriers to make students' ability to study by themselves, use knowledge to solve practical problems and the ability of communication. Project Design I, Project Design II and Project Design III span fifth, sixth and seventh semesters. It is a continuous process of continuous progression and progressive improvement. Through the classical design reproduction, Project Design I enhance the ability of the students' basic form, improve their aesthetic and modeling ability with line extraction and feature expression, and finally express the design theme accurately. Project Design II is to design competition to be a standard. It can broaden their minds. It can limit the subject. It makes the students to concentrate better. It makes students innovate and gives them the courage to challenge. To make students master the main parts of knowledge, the students learn in practice. Train them have better ability of thinking analysis. So that students form a model of scientific design thinking. Car Design Awards of China is the most important car design event in China. The design mission is written by world-renowned automotive OEM. The competition judges are composed of design directors from famous auto companies. It creates great opportunity for student designers to win an authoritative award and embark on a career in automotive design [5]. Transportation and Large Equipment studio in 2017 were nominated in Car Design Awards of China(CDN for short). Liaoning Shihua University was at the tenth place along with Beijing Institute of Technology, Hubei Institute of Fine Arts and Jiangsu University. In 2018, in the ninth Car Design Awards of China, five pieces of work were nominated and it was one of the most nominated universities. Our course does not participate the competition blindly or the it has utilitarian purpose. But to grasp the design of evaluation standard through international design platform. It's also for keeping the education ideas and methods of advanced and authority.

The main goal of Project Design III is to train students to study comprehensive subjects from the design standardization operation ability. On the basis of the theory of product innovation and design people focus on the social hot spots, pain points, interests, and the focus of the government concerned, the relationship between human and things, in comprehensive and systematic way to solve more complex problems. Through the social problem investigation, further study of creative solutions to complex problems and put forward comprehensive, design for the graduation and employment.

Case 1: ocean ball cleaning machine design project. Ocean ball is indoor amusement park covers an area of the larger a way of amusement, its numerous manual cleaning is difficult. It is a good way of getting ready for Graduation Thesis. Through the development of ocean ball cleaning equipment at home and abroad the analysis of the current situation and market demand, product research and development mode of "original design" has begun. Research as the theoretical basis, ensure Marine ball cleaning effect and the efficiency is the premise, developing the ocean ball cleaning machine design and prototype experimental study, at present it has already completed three prototype design iteration.

Case 2: Parent-Child Chair design project. The traditional children's dining chair is specially designed for children, which is limited by the size of the structure and the rapid growth of children. Traditional children dining chair function is single, easy to eliminate. In order to solve the above problem, we designed a dual-purpose chair, aimed at children eat chair design into the double purpose of chairs, two functions are implemented by reverse positive and opposite, one end is children eat chair, chair at the other end is adult. Parent-Child Chair won the 2017A' Design Award silver Award and 2017 China Red Star Original Design Award, which has achieved the transformation and production of the product, and the whole teaching process is to advocate" to work with creativity and to start a business with achievements ".

5 Conclusion

Studio pattern breaks the traditional mode of classroom teaching. The classroom teaching of "Studio Model" has cultivated the students subjective consciousness. Carrying out classroom teaching raises the students subjective consciousness. The mode of classroom teaching is discussion, experiential, practical, exploratory and open. Today, under the background of mass entrepreneurship and innovation, it is of great importance to cultivate the subject consciousness of designers [6]. The School of Art and Design of LSHU has carried out the "Studio Model" for three years, which is now beginning to take shape, but also ushered in the bottleneck period of reformation and innovation promotion. Only to the "studio" mode teaching continuously explore, the mechanism of internal quality assurance and research, we can promote the curriculum reform and improving the quality of student learning. In the whole process of implement and carry out only when the teacher is willing and active participation truly meaningful. Give full play to teachers' professional practice of the concept of "effective teaching", students' learning results of design, evaluation and application of enthusiasm, promoting undergraduate teaching quality has a long way to go [2].

References

1. M.X. Shan, Investigation and analysis of effective instruction in American Higher Educational Institution: Taking The University of Florida As an Example, Higher Education Exploration, **9**, 56 (2015)
2. L.L. Jia, Analysis on the Long-term Mechanism of Internal Quality Assurance of First-class Undergraduate Teaching, Modern Education Management, **8**, 77 (2017)
3. J. Zhang, Production of Concept and Innovative Design Methods:Promoting Design Teaching with International Design Competition, ZHUANGSHI, **10**, 108 (2017)
4. http//www.cmu.edu (webpage checked 20/08/2016)
5. http://www.cardesignevents.com (webpage checked 20/01/2018)
6. B.Y. Chen, Q. Liu, Studio Startup Education Mode:Connotation, Superiority and Prospect, University Education Science, **1**, 98 (2017)

Reinterpreting Form Bionic Design and its Application in Design Innovation with Multiple Methods

Qiao Yang[1,a]

[1]Design Art and Media School, Nanjing University of Science and Technology, 21009, Nanjing, China

Abstract. This paper expounds the background and market demands of the application of Form Bionic Design (FBD) in design innovation. Then it analyses the advantages of FBD and existing misunderstandings on its definition and application, leading to the topic on how to correctly understand the classification of Bionic Design. Also it clarifies the significance of the integration of Bionic Design, proposing that FBD should follow the requirements of users and Design Hardpoints (DHPs). Then through a series of design cases it introduces the application of FBD compromised with several special methods, which includes User-experiencing in simulation, Modular Design for system optimization and Keywords on style positioning. Meanwhile it respectively discusses the purpose, the function and particular application of each method, providing practical reference for its particular combination with FBD.

1 Background

The Internet has accelerated the modern economy, spawning an increasing number of new economic enterprises, such as Alibaba, Amazon, and eBay.

Driven by this trend, consumption desire has been greatly satisfied. Therefore the passion for novelty has extremely inflated, while the expectation for new design has risen dramatically. In order to meet booming market and changing consumption companies have constantly tried to apply extraordinary elements into design to ensure profits rising. Meanwhile, as the product cycle continues to shorten, designers have to create new design as soon as possible.

With the rapid development of science and technology, enterprises try to apply new technologies and new materials in innovation design. However, it normally takes longer than companies hope. Because, no matter how much value can be achieved from new application, it has to take a series of experimental tests and make certain improvements before it accesses to the market. Therefore, companies have to abandon the idea of applying new technologies or materials which cannot help cater the rapid growth of the market and the diversification of the consumption in such short term.

In order to address time-consuming problem of new applications, enterprises adopt many innovative design methods in the stage of product design and development, seeking to reduce costs and ensure effective profits while meeting the growing needs for innovation. NOKIA, SIEMENS and other major international companies have put forward the concept of "Design Library". Through this method they hope that enterprise designers and design teams can carry out forward-looking design exploration, and reserve concepts for future, so as to ensure them sufficient innovation to take the lead in the industry.

However, this method is extremely costly. It is unknown whether storage designs can really meet the future needs of enterprises and its practical effect cannot be seen until tomorrow. So for many small and medium-sized enterprises (SMEs) with limited cost, this method is not suitable. In contrast, Form Bionic Design (FBD) with natural advantages becomes one appropriate option, which can benefit the rapid and effective innovation with minimum expendure.

2 Advantages of FBD

The advantages of FBD are presented in the following aspects.

Firstly, the reference of FBD has a perfect natural model which organically integrates the structure and appearance to ensure good operation. Therefore it provides a quick-effective master for designers, who can quickly capture innovative ideas from natural ecosystems. Meanwhile it contributes to accurate positioning of appropriate referenced FBD model and highly reduces creative exploration.

Secondly, with numerous ecological prototypes in nature, FBD provides designers a rich bionic database with sufficient creative resources.

Thirdly, FBD reduces damages caused by less experimental time in quick application of new technologies and materials, which must be tested in a great number of regulation experiments before real application in products. So that is a long-term preparation which is also influenced by cost, production mode and many other factors. When these products enter into the market, it is more likely to see that new designs

*Corresponding author: [a] Qiao Yang: mikejoe88@126.com

may not satify customers nees which have already been changed. Fortunately, this problem can be solved by FBD, which can produce experimental prototypes extremely fast and provide sufficent resources and references for later design modification and development. In addtion, FBD can controls the cost effectively to enhance innovation under limitions of production and time.

3 Reinterpret FBD and its application

However, there are many misunderstandings on the definition and the application of FBD. Two of the most prominent ones are "separating form innovation from integrated design" and "lacking considerations for user needs and Design Hardpoints ".

3.1. FBD and Integrated Design

In some cases FBD has been completely seen as a pure form-simulation method, which not only separates exterior shape from functional requirements but also shields available inner structure in reference objects. In this way, new form will lack the support of the intrinsic functional-structure. Then it results in the loss of usability while designers must spend more time on building up matching functional structure according to the new appearance. Therefore, it not only loses initial time advantage of FBD, but also requires extra time to verify the rationality of new functional-structure influenced by the appearance change.

Thus, FBD is not just simple form mimicry. In FBD any form in nature can be used as if it can effectively unify form and functional structure. In fact, the reference prototype selected in FBD can provide rapid and intuitive application template, which is helpful for designers to quickly produce a suitable innovative model, effectively integrated with form, structure, and function.

Most misunderstandings are caused by a false understanding of bionic classification. It is well known that Bionic Design has many categories and the most commonly mentioned are functional bionics, structural bionics and form bionics.

However, since function, structure and form are unified in design and cannot be totally separated from each other, so why this classification has such independent name nominally? The truth is that one bionic concept is initially proposed from one angle belonging to one of these three aspects. For example, the Sea Harrier fighter typically belongs to functional bionics design. Its original intention is to realize the function of vertical take-off and landing, so that the carrier aircraft can take off and land quickly on a small aircraft carrier. Coincidentally, the function principle of sea piper flight just met this requirement. Another case is the gull-wing doors on sports car which is a typical example of form bionics. The original design purpose is to provide users' unusual visual experience. Through seagull-like doors, it satisfies the desire of hunting for novelty.

To sum up, function, structure and form in FBD have no strict boundaries in design. First of all, the function can be realized through the internal structure, while it builds up the carrier of appearance with external design to connect users. Secondly, the structure is not only the skeleton of the shape but also the benchmark for the smooth realization of target function. Finally, the form is the ultimate carrier of product design. Functionally, it is an external load module to protect internal structure and realize function. Visually, it is an external platform to guide usage and meet aesthetic needs.

3.2 User requirements and Design Hardpoints

In other cases user requirements and Design Hardpoints (DHPs) have been ignored in FBD.

Undoubtedly, the terminal object of design is to satisfy users. Therefore it is necessary to consider physical and psychological needs of users in FBD. Such user-centred considerations will help position appropriate reference of bionic form. Meanwhile, testing standards can be pre-set for later optimization and modification to promote design more reasonable.

DHPs in automotive design can be applied in other categories of product design. It is significant to define DHPs, including standards and requirements for function, size, material, human-factors, cost, process, installation and etc. In this way, the accuracy of design orientation can be guaranteed in the initial stage. Moreover, it can meet current production technical conditions and cost requirements [1]. In addition, it can set the applicable range and test standards for the later stage of FBD, reducing errors and saving costs.

Design Hardpoints is the general name of the control point (or coordinate), control line, control surface and control structure which are determined in the process of general layout design. It ensures the coordination and assembly of parts and meets styling requirements. This is the most important principle in design and selection of parts, accessories and body. It can make the components organized without mess. Also it is an important method of concurrent design, once determined then not easy to adjust. The DHPs is the soul of all design. [2]

According to the discussion above, it is obvious that FBD is not equal to pure form duplication. On the one hand, FBD can be applied effectively and reasonably as if the design satisfies DHPs. Otherwise its application will be totally failed. On the other hand, it is very crucial to develop adequate user-centred thinking and satisfy users' needs in FBD.

4 FBD applied with multiple methods

In order to meet the market demand for quick innovation and erase misunderstandings of FBD, it has integrated many methods with unique advantages to enhance the practical efficacy of FBD. Moreover this method helps increase the innovative value of design by meeting the changing needs of users timely.

The basic frame of FBD will still adopt traditional design process because it is beneficial for easy

https://doi.org/10.1051/matecconf/201817602011

application of FBD in SMEs. In addition, the introduction of special methods in different stages of FBD can help update design and launch innovation step by step, according to actual conditions such as cost and producing level.

In the following part three different available methods applied in FBD are illustrated in details.

4.1. User-experiencing in Simulation

Simulation is the imitation of the operation of a real-world process or system. [3]

User-experiencing in simulation is used to discover useful and creative ideas by studying the adaptation and rationality of human-machine interaction in the simulation scenario. Meanwhile, by observing users' habits in usage and operating, designers can explore new functional models so as to provide reliable creative originals for FBD. Furthermore, it provides the testing criteria of user satisfaction for later optimization and final determination.

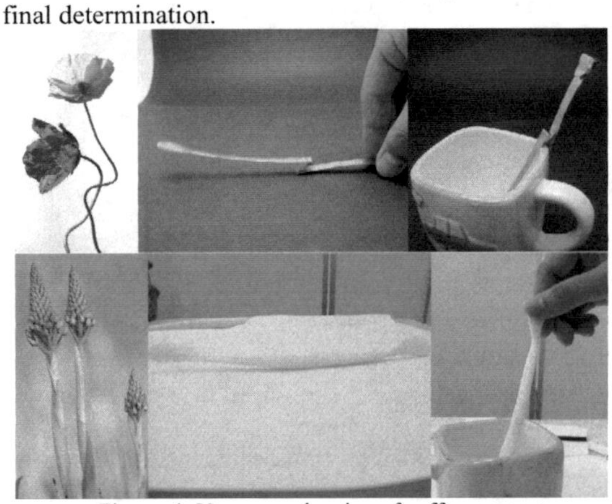

Figure 1. User-experiencing of coffee spoon

This method also helps to deduce reasonable and accurate aesthetic trends. According to the clear style positions, it can quickly promote a large number of styling designs, in which customers can really achieve enjoyment in vision. In Figure 1 the design of coffee spoon successfully combines User-experience in simulation with FBD to develop new concepts, which can meet demands of both usage and aesthetics.

4.2. Modular Design

Modular design, or "modularity in design", is a design approach that subdivides a system into smaller parts called modules or skids that can be independently created and then used in different systems. [4]

Modular design integrates the advantages of standardization and customization. This is usually due to the cost of putting up interfaces between modules. Under most circumstances a standard component is less expensive than a component designed and built for use in only one product. This lower cost is possible primarily because the standard component will be produced in higher volume, allowing greater economies of scale and more learning. [5]

Figure 2. Modular design of Hair-Cleaner

First of all, the simplification of modular design helps quickly improve product innovation. By component optimization, novel appearance models can be obtained through minimal morphological changes. After that, suitable models can be found by comparing different new combinations. In this way, it is so quick to define DHPs accurately, which include motion space of functional units, mounting position of components, structure pattern and etc. All these DHPs provide a set of criterion for testing the reasonableness of subsequent designs.

Secondly, the serialization of modular design enables products to upgrade at different innovation levels through modular replacement. In order to accurately evaluating the rationality and feasibility of design, designers should pay more attention to technical parameters, such as original structure, material characteristics and parts' setting positions.

Thirdly, new technology implanted into a module can also stimulate new innovation opportunities.

In general, modular design is usually divided into three stages: functional module differentiation, module reorganization and model comparison. The details of each step are as follows:

Step 1. By analysing function and structure modules are differentiated functionally to establish the original model.

Step 2. Each functional group (or components groups which are needed to complete one function) is set up as a separate unit and then they are reorganized in different ways for creating new models.

Step 3. New models will be evaluated in a series of tests of the feasibility in many aspects, which includes engineering, man-machine, cost, material and processing difficulties. Then these models will be compared through functional experiments, man-machine analysis, cost analysis and etc. Finally, the most suitable module design can be found.

4.3. Keywords on style position

In FBD, how to ensure the selected reference to be applicable for design, especially for new form-styling?

How to ensure the shape meets the aesthetic needs? This method, called as Keywords on style position, gives a valid answer which is presented in details as follows.

First of all, main function structure and HPs are determined according to the previous positioning. Next, a series of styling keywords that fit the user's preferences are listed one by one. Referring to the selected keywords, the related morphological reference objects are selected from the form-biomimetic point of view. Then, shapes of selected objects are refined and applied to FBD, which will continuously be optimized according to the pre-determined standards of users' needs and HPs.

As figures shown in below, the motorboat design, a typical example of FBD, describes the specific application of Keywords on styling position.

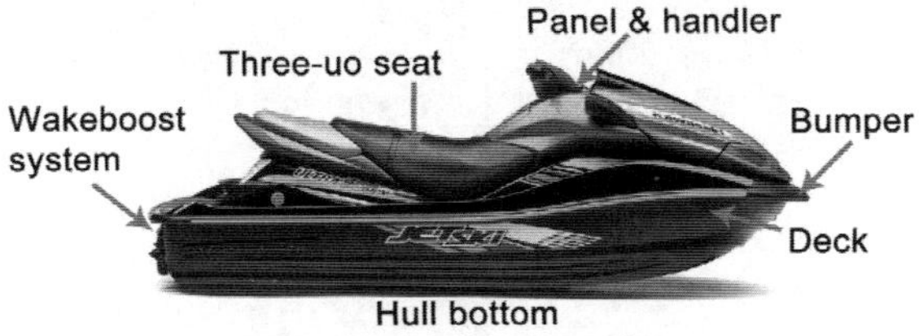

Figure 3. Modular of motorboat

Figure 4. Keywords of users' favourite style

Figure 5. Relevant references

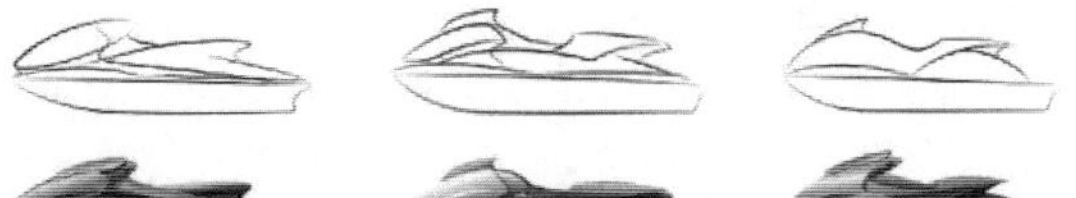

Figure 6. Shape refining and optimization

5 Results

FBD effectively promotes rapid design innovation and provides SMEs more opportunities to win the market while saving costs. FBD is not a simple form reproduction. In application it needs to consider more about users' requirements and HPs. Timely integration of other methods in different stages of FBD can effectively combine various advantages of multiple sides to improve the accuracy of innovation positioning and the practical value of new design.

References

1. X.Y. He, Y.F. Xie, *Humanization Design* (Jiangsu Fine Arts Publishing House, 2001)
2. C.Z. Sun, Y.C. Lei, Shanghai Auto **3**, 33(2007）
3. J. Banks, J. Carson, B. Nelson, D. Nicol, *Discrete-Event System Simulation*, (Prentice Hall, 2001)
4. F. Salimi, F. Salimi, *A Systems Approach to Managing the Complexities of Process Industries*, 234(Elsevier, 2017)
5. Ulrich.K, Res Policy **24(3)**, 431(1995)

Research on the Role of Design Aesthetics in Modern Design

Yehua Qu[1], Xuanbo Mao[2] Dian Li[3]

[1, 3]Shenyang University of Chemical Technology, Department of Industry & Art Design, Shenyang, China
[2]Dalian University, School of Art, Dalian, China

Abstract. The essence of design is "to create things according to the laws of beauty". The factor of beauty is one of the most important criteria to evaluate the quality of design, and consumers will recognize those products with perfect combination of technology and form. With the expansion of the consumer society and the spread of the aesthetics of everyday life, the social status of design is increasingly prominent. Whether or not the design can be accepted or recognized by consumers in the end, aesthetics is one of the most important factors.

1 Design aesthetics

Design aesthetics, as the name suggests, should be about the aesthetics of design, or the discipline of exploring the beauty of design. Design aesthetics is a window to know design and understand it from the perspective of aesthetics.

"The research object of design aesthetics includes all fields of art design. From product to design process and design method; from the use and consumption of things to obtaining a variety of value, especially the acquisition of aesthetic value; from design plan, conception to design technology and manufacturing; from the practical function of things to the design of cultural taste, artistic form and style; from the form of creation to the thought and ideal of the creation; from the existence of design objects to the history of design art style and the research of art history, it involves many aspects". [2] [3]

"Design and Aes-thetics" may be more accurate than "Design Aesthetics" to accurately convey the "intersecting" characteristics of the combination of "design" and "aesthetics". Design aesthetics is the product of interdisciplinary integration. The study of it has been complicated since the theory of design itself remains to be perfected and the complexity of the aesthetics itself. [6]

In this cross field, we can not only study the design from the aesthetic point of view, but also develop the aesthetic research with the design as the object. Therefore, the design aesthetics can be an integral part of the theory of "design" and a branch of applied aesthetics.

2 The design phenomena

All the design phenomena in the field of traditional, modern and even the contemporary art include many aspects.

2.1 The form system of the design

This includes the connotation and extension of the design, the form features, the aesthetic law and the trend of development, etc.

2.2 The designer

This includes designer's knowledge structure, life experience, ideology, aesthetic pursuit and social ethics, etc.

2.3 The impact and constrains

This means the impact and constraints of scientific and technological level, material selection, market information and other factors on the design results during the design and production process.

2.4 Local culture

Local culture includes the cultural background, national tradition, popular trends and information feedback in the process of consumption of the designed product.

2.5 The intersecting and connection

The intersecting and connection between design and other related disciplines, such as culture, philosophy, art, sociology and psychology. In short, the common goal is to build a harmonious relationship between man and nature and society.

*Corresponding author: quyehua@126.com

3 The characteristics of design aesthetics

Design is a frontier subject that is based on technology and art and it combines the two in its application. Its research object, scope and application are different from the traditional art discipline. As a theoretical branch of design discipline, the theory of design aesthetics is also different from traditional aesthetic art research. Design aesthetics is an attempt to apply basic design principles to art design; it is applied not only in art design, but also in industrial design. As applied aesthetics, design aesthetics focuses on the specific aesthetic problems of basic necessities of life, which are closely related to day-to-day life. Its wide application not only beautifies the living environment, but also improves the quality of life. [6]

3.1 Practicality

Practicality is one of the most basic characteristics and it determines its wide application in life. Some ornaments in life can reflect more aesthetic feeling through the help of design aesthetics.

3.2 Technology

It is mainly manifested in the fact that design aesthetics has certain technical standards. Only when it reaches a certain level can it be recognized and then be accepted and show its value. Especially in enriching the value of aesthetic needs, it has gained better development opportunities.

3.3 Aesthetic

As a member of the aesthetic system, aesthetics is also the foundation for its continuous development. Because of aesthetics, design aesthetics has become more popular

3.4 Innovation

Design aesthetics is not stagnant, but developing in continuous innovation. Through the integration of innovative ideas and elements, it can show better aesthetic experience and proper value.

3.5 Times

Any aesthetics cannot escape the category of the times. The design aesthetics also changes with the development of the times. It adapts to the demand of the design aesthetics in the new era through the changes. If we throw away the times and then talk about design aesthetics, we will lose the most basic premise and become a rootless wood.

4 Difficulties of design aesthetics

Talking about difficulties of design aesthetics, there are four pairs of contradictions that should be dealt with first.

4.1 People and products

Traditional aesthetics attaches great importance to the subjective position of people in aesthetic activities. It emphasizes the design principle of "people oriented" in product design. Modern design cannot make this subjectivity absolute. The highest realm of design aesthetics is the harmony, perfect combination and unity between man and thing, man and environment, man and nature.

4.2 Technology and art

Design is directly constrained by the development level of modern science and technology. Factors related to technology development, such as materials, technology and information, would affect the artistic performance of design. Therefore, we must be good at utilizing the advantages and characteristics of modern technology and the aesthetic features of modern materials. Although the artistic expression of the design is metaphysical and super technical, it is necessary to pay attention to the change of the realistic aesthetic concept and take the initiative to accept the influence of the social fashion and aesthetic taste caused by the change of technology.

4.3 Function and form

Function refers to the basic functions, technologies, ideas and other material factors related to products. Unlike pure art, design first pays attention to practical utilitarianism, which is also a constituent element of design beauty. At the same time, we should also emphasize the aesthetic factors such as modelling, colour and decoration, which is the spiritual requirement of modern products and products related needs. The practical utilitarian and aesthetic forms are equally important, the material connotation of design will be greatly affected if function is ignored. Similarly, ignoring form equals to ignoring people's spiritual need for design.

4.4 Subjective and objective

Pure art creation is free; it belongs to subjective activity and it is the individual emotional expression behaviour of an artist. Although design also needs freedom of creation and subjective performance, they are limited. It must conform to objective requirements. Design must regard the acceptance of consumers and the public as the first priority. Design is a more objective activity that combines the designers with the public. [1] [5]

5 Research scopes of design aesthetics

5.1 The fundamental problems of design aesthetics

5.1.1 Design aesthetics

Design aesthetics mainly includes the connotation, nature and composition of the beauty of design; the form and style of the beauty of design; the cultural connotation of the beauty of design; the form beauty of the design, the creation and realm of the beauty of design, etc.

5.1.2 The history of the development of design aesthetics

The history of the development of design aesthetics mainly includes the development history of design style, the history of design aesthetics, the design department (such as product design, process design, architectural design, etc.), and the history of aesthetics.

5.1.3 Design department aesthetics

Design department aesthetics mainly includes visual communication design aesthetics, product design aesthetics, architectural design aesthetics, environmental design aesthetics, process design aesthetics, etc.

5.2 The aesthetic problems in the process of design activities

5.2.1 The aesthetic of the designer

The aesthetic of the designer mainly includes the designer's aesthetic accomplishment, aesthetic ideal, artistic individuality, design thinking, etc.

5.2.2 The law of aesthetic design

The law of aesthetic design mainly includes the beauty of design and technology, the beauty of design and market, the beauty of design and production, the beauty of design and form rule, etc.

5.2.3 Design aesthetic concepts

Design aesthetic concepts includes the historical formation, evolution, modern form and future development trend of design aesthetics.

5.2.4 Design aesthetic taste

Design aesthetic taste mainly includes the social aesthetic interest, the individual aesthetic interest, the individuality and common characteristics of the beauty of design.

5.3 Designing consumption aesthetics issue

This mainly includes the connotation, ways, methods and implementation of aesthetic education.

5.4 The educational problem of design aesthetic

It mainly includes the connotation, ways, methods and implementation of aesthetic education. [1]

6 Modern design aesthetics

6.1 Aesthetics and modern aesthetics

Aesthetics is a branch of philosophy. Design aesthetics is a branch of aesthetics, it is a discipline about the idea of beauty. Design aesthetics is also a kind of applied aesthetics. It is a discipline that combines design practice and human life. It is the thinking of human about beauty of design in life and design practice. In fact, design aesthetics is quite different from general aesthetics. It has many unique characteristics and some of them have surpassed the category of traditional aesthetics. Design aesthetics has a unique feature.

Design aesthetics is a practical aesthetics and applied aesthetics, with its own aesthetic theories (functional design aesthetics, formal design aesthetics, psychological design aesthetics, evolutionism design aesthetics, and semiotics design aesthetics, etc.) Even though it shares the common aesthetic theory with art aesthetics, (for example, psychological aesthetics), the content and emphasis of design aesthetics are different. Design aesthetics must study the design practice combined with market economy, focusing more on the beauty of human sense, people's aesthetic experience in social life practice and the interaction between designer and people.

The beauty of modern design is a new and unique beauty created by the development of modern society and the practice of modern design. Some characteristics of the beauty of modern design are determined by the combination of science and art, rationality and intuition, material and spirit, the comprehensiveness and uniqueness of philosophy and life. These characteristics include artificiality, practical nature, technology, innovativeness, functionality, life, sensory and mental integration, humanism and humanity beauty, etc. The aesthetic sense of the spirit and culture of the design is also an important part of the beauty of the design. The beauty of the design can be only the pleasure of the shape, the texture and the colour to the senses. It can also be a metaphor, the symbol of the identity of the cultural symbol and the confirmation of the self. [4]

6.2 Features of the beauty of modern design

The birth of modern design is to beautify people's lives by beautifying the industrial products produced in batches. It can be said that the core of modern design concept is to beautify life and pursue beauty. However, due to the technology and practicality of design, the aesthetics of design product is inseparable from innovation, convenience and practicality. Through these innovations and practicality, design is to transform and beautify people's lives, satisfy people's emotional needs and needs for comfortableness and convenience. That is to say the beauty of design is the beauty of practice, the beauty of life and the beauty of human nature.

6.3 Problems to be solved in modern design aesthetics

6.3.1 The difference between design and art, the beauty of design and the beauty of art

We should be clear about the difference between design and art and technology. Art is pure spiritual enjoyment or pure emotional experience. It is not utilitarian. Creation is personalized and cannot be duplicated. Design is closely combined with the needs and satisfaction of people's spiritual enjoyment, emotional experience and function. It is utilitarian, practical and it is mass production, standardized and replicable. Handicraft is between art and design. It can be used, but its production is personalized, manual, non-industrialized and standardized. Therefore, the beauty of design is different from the beauty of art.

6.3.2 The practical problem of the beauty of design

One of the fundamental characteristics of traditional artistic beauty or natural beauty is non-utilitarian and non-practical. In design, the experience of beauty of all design products is based on the good functions of products, it must be closely integrated with practicality. This is the fundamental difference between designing products and works of art. [4]

7 The relationship between design aesthetics and modern design

The relationship between design aesthetics and modern design is dialectical. There has been a lot of discussion in the academic world. In a simple way, design aesthetics and the formation and development of design are synchronous and interacted. For one thing, technology led industrial civilization gave birth to modern design after the industrial revolution, which resulted in the emerging discipline of design aesthetics and the basic theoretical structure of it. For another thing, the research of design aesthetics in the field of aesthetics and theory also guides the development of modern design. It also analyses the problems arising from the development of modern design, and puts forward reasonable solutions and ways. As an inevitable product of the design of art theory and aesthetic development in modern society, the position of design aesthetics has not been questioned in the design and art world.

In today's era, technology is everywhere. Design is indispensable to life; technology and design are inseparable. Whether it is the beauty of the handicraft design or the rational beauty of modern industrial technology, it shows the indispensable position of design aesthetics in the design and industrial production.

8 Conclusions

Design comes from life. To conform the design aesthetics to the times is to give the design "positive energy" of this era. This is the responsibility that given by this era to the designers, it is also the proper meaning of design aesthetics. Design should be based on life. Life is changing and developing, design should also be developing and innovating, so that it can be compatible with the future development of our era. This is the meaning of existence of design aesthetics. The mission of modern design aesthetics is to explore the essence of modern design, create new forms and promote the development of modern design movement using the law of aesthetic.

References

1. JX. Yao, Decoration. J. **141** (2005)
2. BQ. Huang, Journal of Hunan University of Science and Technology, Social Science Edition. J. **5** (2012)
3. LG. Zhang, *Aesthetics of art design* (Shandong Education Press, Ji'nan, 2002)
4. JY. Qiu, Beauty and Times. J. **12** (2010)
5. CP. Wang, GL. Zhang, Hundred Schools in Arts. J. **105** (2008)
6. XL. Wang, QX. Zhao, Design Theory. J. (2012)

Research on innovative application of silver material in modern jewelry design

Qinqin Yu[1,a], Kaining Meng[1] and Juanling Guo[1]

[1]Xihua University, School of Art and Design, Chengdu, China

Abstract. Based on the understanding of are used, the jewelry material, the method of modeling semantics is applied to know more about the application of traditional materials and modern materials in the jewelry design. The related design principle of the innovative combination of the silver material, traditional material and modern material in the jewelry design was analyzed, and the status quo of the modern silver jewelry design was solved, which is monotonous in the combination materials, old-fashioned in pattern and conservative in the creation style. Hence, the innovative application of materials, innovative expression of patterns, and the creation style that integrates culture and art was realized. The development trend of silver jewelry design was explored, which can provide more direction for the development of silver jewelry in the future.

1 Introduction

Jewelry can not only decorate our clothes, bring out our temperament, at the same time, it convey the feelings and attitudes of contemporary people. Silver material is deeply loved by people because of its own unique properties. The history of wearing silver ornaments goes back to ancient times, "Silver culture" is almost accompanied by the material civilization of mankind. However, more creations of silver jewellery mostly remain in a few ethnic minorities such as the Miao silver ornaments, the Dai silver ornaments, etc. as well as some handwork workshops.Most of the silver ornaments still dare not to break the traditional style of creation, the combination of a single material, pattern tradition, so that the silver jewelry in the creation is difficult to have a new breakthrough. For the contemporary jewellery design, the contemporary characteristics and cultural connotations must be given on a traditional basis. The traditional patterns need to be redesigned, the traditional crafts need to be innovated again, and the new jewelry design and processing materials also need to be excavated. If we can combine silver materials with different materials and seek inspiration from our lives and emotions, we will push silverware to a diverse, ecological and creative jewelry design field.

2 Understanding of silver material

2.1 The Origin of Silver ornaments

The history of love of silver jewelry goes back to ancient times. In ancient times, silver jewelry not only demonstrated its identity and status, but also preserved its value and was a legacy that could be left to future generations. Not only that, in many ethnic minority areas in our country, the silver jewelry of Miao, Yi and other regions also entrusted them with their admiration and awe of good things, silver also can pray for the protection of the gods. In modern times, people are also aware of the health benefits of silver jewelry. "Silver as ornaments" which is a common cultural phenomenon in the world, along with the material civilization of mankind from beginning to end.

2.2 Characteristics of silver material

Silver has stable chemical properties, high thermal conductivity and good electrical conductivity. It is difficult to be corroded by chemicals. It is soft and ductile. Its reflectivity is extremely high, reaching more than 99%. Silver material is not only good and cheap, and silver ornaments can also play a certain health effect. The toxic and bactericidal effects have also made silver jewelry very popular. Make silver decoration always with its unique quaint, elegant amorous feelings, Show a unique status in today's respected personal, and stylish society!

3 Jewelry material

3.1 Traditional jewelry material

Traditional jewelry materials, such as gold, silver, copper, jade, precious stones. Tt is determined by the value of traditional jewelry.Since ancient times, people have been fond of gold and silver jewelry. Gold and silver jewelry can not only show identity and status, but

*Corresponding author: [a] Qinqin Yu: 475084594@qq.com

also preserve the value of the family can be left to future generations.

3.2 Modern jewelry material

As the younger generation of consumers needs to express their individuality and unique appearance. The change of jewelry design based on aesthetics and innovation has caused a fresh vitality. Do not pursue luxury, do not seek permanent preservation of value has become a leading consumer power. With different ideas, this makes jewelry concept and material innovation over and over again. For example, plastic, paper rubber, wood, ceramic acrylic, leather and other daily materials have great plasticity and potential power, and are loved and recognized by the younger generation.

4 Innovative application of silver ornaments based on styling semantics

Styling semantics is a study of the meaning of product language. By studying the symbolic characteristics of the form of artificial objects in the use situation, which make the design of the product have a specific connotation. When designing silver with traditional materials and modern materials, we should give full consideration to the influence of modeling semantics on patterns, materials and creative styles.

4.1 Innovative design of silver materials with traditional materials

Compared with the weight of precious metal and precious stones in traditional jewelry design, the contemporary jewelry design is superior to the complexity of structure, the balance of weight and body, and the concept contained. The famous jewelry designer Hanna Hedman's works are inspired by human weaknesses, the dark side of the human world, death, nature and stories.She believes that good , serious, and disturbing things can make a strong contrast, reflecting a special sense of beauty.This series of jewelry uses copper and silver oxide as the main materials, and trying to inject these materials into their own souls. At the same time, she also prefers the traditional jewelry making process, it is clearly visible that the traditional techniques of cutting or drilling in jewelry production. Making a piece of jewelry is like creating a story, each part is made independently, and gradually evolved into a whole.In the works of Hannah Herdman, there are various elements of rich artistic atmosphere, cathartic display characteristics, colorful dreams, and functional requirements.

Figure 1. Artistic Jewelry by Hanna Hedman.

Karl Fritsch also loves making jewelry from traditional materials, most of his works are made of traditional materials such as silver, iron and emerald and so on. He pursued the state of natural When he was creating, didn't expect the result of the production to be.Instead, it captures the most aesthetically pleasing state of the moment in the production process. His work is often abstract which he thinks this is the perfect work.This will be the best performance of jewelry art.

4.2 Innovative design of silver materials with modern materials

Breaking the shackles of traditional jewelry design materials, the use of materials becomes more active. Making modern jewelry appear more tactile, interesting and personality. The variety of new materials also means an endless space of possibilities and imagination. When making jewelry selections, Iris Bodemer pays special attention to material must be able to express ideas. She boldly uses a combination of new materials such as meteorites, pyrites, horns, wool, corals, beech wood and silver materials. She believes that these common materials from around can better reflect the cognition and love of life.

Maria Cristina Bellucci often uses silver when she makes jewelry. She like to look at things differently in daily life. Here is a series of works that she uses silver, colored pencils, and black sandalwood as the main materials, separation of objects with special emotions from the environment in daily life. Colored pencils are rich in color. Combining, cutting, and chamfering jewelry will show unique patterns. Patterns created by this method not only convey lively emotions, but also give unique and rich patterns to jewelry. Create a completely new perspective by reshaping or reinventing it. At this time, a magnificent jewelry will be presented to everyone.

Figure 2. Artistic Jewelry by Maria Cristina Bellucci.

5 Innovative Application of Silver material in Modern Jewelry Design

The beauty in the depths of the "Natural Dialogue" is the time for solidification. This series of jewelry is mainly made of 999 silver, phosphorite, and natural malachite natural turquoise. The most traditional jewelry manufacturing techniques are used, such as casting, inlaying, and engraving and so on. This series of jewelry escaped the traditional complex patterns, by applying a reasonable combination of natural stones of different depths, to show the unique texture of this series of jewelry . At the same time, it does not lose its unique elegance and simplicity. This series of jewelry is inspired by the hard and natural shape of the original ore which is linking beauty to heaven, and it is like a gift from nature. With the characteristics of a natural form of nature, jewelry is infused with the beauty of the inspiration of all things in nature to maintain the crudest original form of ore, in order to express the beauty of nature and paying tribute to life. Through this series of jewelry as if into the exploration of nature, feeling its texture, touching its temperature, listening to its feelinfs which can make a busy person come to a conversation with nature. "Natural Dialogue" This series of jewelry innovations in materials and performance techniques which is a good interpretation of the integration of jewelry culture and art in jewelry design.

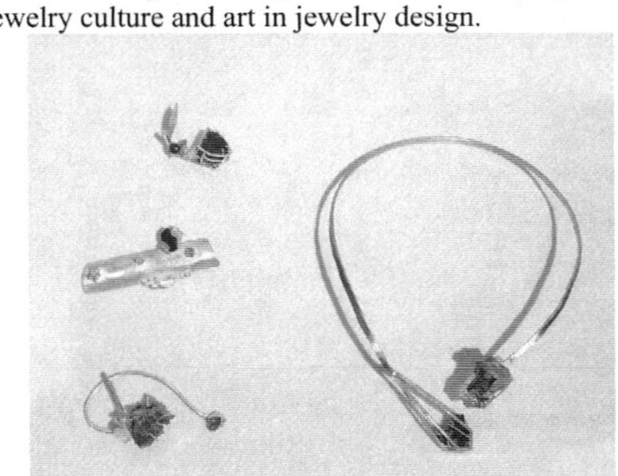

Figure 3. "Natural Dialogue"picture from Chu independent design studio.

6 Conclusion

Jewelry has become the carrier of people's personal life attitude in daily life. Rejuvenation of creative designers, increasing attention to environmental protection, and the pursuit of freedom of life has caused the demand for jewelry has shifted from purely material to spiritual. The history of love of silver jewelry is even more ancient. Not only is the unique property of the silver material itself, but also is that silverware is already a representative of jewelry culture. Traditional silver ornaments have been difficult to meet people's consumption needs. Dare to break the traditional creative style of silverware, the innovative application of materials and the innovative expression of patterns, can better meet the market demand of consumers. The design of any product is not merely the design of a piece of useful instrument or machinery; instead, it must show various beautiful ideals and interests in the life activities of humankind.The method of styling semantics provides more directions for the development of silver ornaments and makes the related design of silver ornaments becomes a real design field which combines culture and art.

Acknowledgment

Fund project. Major projects in Sichuan education department. (Item number: W171300) ; University-level graduate innovation fund project of Xihua University. (Item number: ycjj2017110).

References

1. Jiao Chen; Qin Yang. Exploration on the development of jewelry design of synthetic materials. HSNU, **33**(2016)
2. Kaijie Huo.The aesthetic consciousness of the dragon symbol of miao nationality and its application in jewelry design. China university of geosciences .Beijing, (2016)
3. Hua Yang. Cultural inheritance and innovation of jewelry art. LISAT, **33**(2017)
4. Xiaolin Gao. Application of acrylic material in modern jewelry design. SAAC, (2015)
5. Yu Yan . Cultural heritage keyword: silver. NA, (2017)
6. Binfei Luo; Jing Huang; Yuping Zhang. On the bottle design of sichuan wine from the perspective of styling semantics. A, **37**(2016)
7. Ming Zhang. The construction of contemporary jewelry design. O, (2018)
8. Na Zhang. Application of traditional Miao silver pattern in modern jewelry design. AE, (2017)
9. Edited by Design-Ma-Ma Design Studio. *Contemporary jewelry art The Innovation of Materials and Aesthetics* .China Youth Publishing, Beijing, (2011)

https://doi.org/10.1051/matecconf/201817602013

10. Luigi T.De Luca, *Propulsion physics* (EDP Sciences, Les Ulis, 2009)
11. F. De Lillo, F. Cecconi, G. Lacorata, A. Vulpiani, EPL, **84** (2008)

Research on the Strategy of Product Ecological Structure Design under Global Ocean Pollution

Chun Li [1,a] , Kaining Meng [2] and Qinqin Yu[3]

[1]Xihua University, School of Art and Design, Chengdu, China

Abstract. Serious pollution problems in the global offshore area are caused by a large number of municipal wastes from land. The reason is that there are many unenvironmental structure designs in the product design, which brings a lot of waste of resources and environmental pollution and other problems. Based on the principle of 3R, this article integrates the thought of ecological structure design into the "human-machine-environment" ecosystems ; establishes the ideological system of product ecological structure design; confirms the feasibility of product's ecological structure design with analysis of relevant design cases. Then to establish the assessment system of the economical system to evaluate the ecology of the product structure design.

1 Introduction

In the continuously developing society, there are a lot of material wealth, but there are also more and more household garbage. Because the ocean locates at the low-lying area of the whole biosphere, it becomes the destination of global garbage.[1] Victor Papanek, the American critic, proposed the ethic ideas of design in his book *Design for the real world* which was published in 1971, he holds that designers should have sense of social responsibility, and design products with the consideration of ecology and environment protection. [2] So we are supposed to have ecological structure design thinking, reduce waste of resources and garbage pollution in design.

2 Marine pollution and product ecological structure design

2.1 the problem of global marine waste pollution

Achim Steiner, the executive director of the United Nations Environment Programme, has publicly stated that 80% of marine pollution is derived from land. In 2015, scientists from University of Georgia published research in the Journal of science, which further presented the problem of marine garbage pollution. This report was the first global data assessment after 1970. It shows that, at present, in the top 20 countries with the most serious marine waste pollution, there are 19 developing countries, and the main elements of the coastal waste are daily waste.

2.2 Product ecological structure design

Product ecological design could consider from the aspects of environment and commerce. From environment aspect, designers should try to minimize the resource consume in the using process, reduce the cost and make product become more competitive. From commerce aspect, according to product's function, site and space, product structure can be divided into external structure, core structure, space structure and system structure. Through different design methods to reach the highest utilization rate of resources, so as to realize the sustainable application of products.

3 Product ecological structure design strategy

3.1 Ensure the ecological structure of the external structure of products

Product external structure refers to some additional structures to products, for instance, the packaging structure of products is one kind of external structure. As ecological structure design, product packaging should firstly reduce the volume, material and simplify the structure, to decrease unnecessary material waste in the packaging process. It ensures that the packaging function remains unchanged and realizes the recyclability of products. For example, figure 1.

*Corresponding author: [a] Chun Li: 939112581@qq.com

https://doi.org/10.1051/matecconf/201817602014

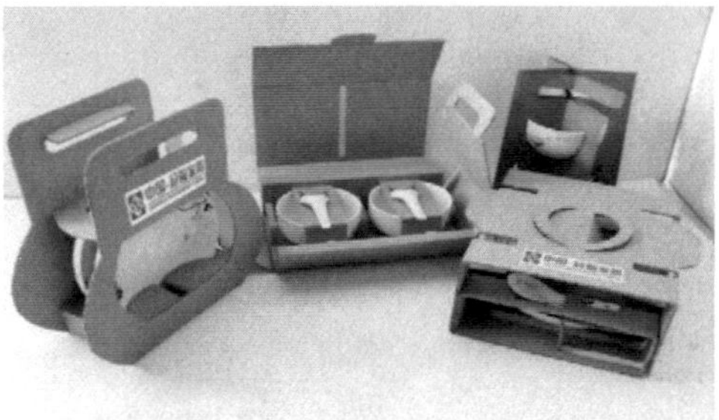

Figure 1. Packaging design of porcelain. (web)

Secondly, choose the materials that can be recycled many times rather than disposable material. The small parts of product external structure should emphasize the replaceable design, minimize the type and quantity of parts and ensure the unity of structure. For example, figure 2.

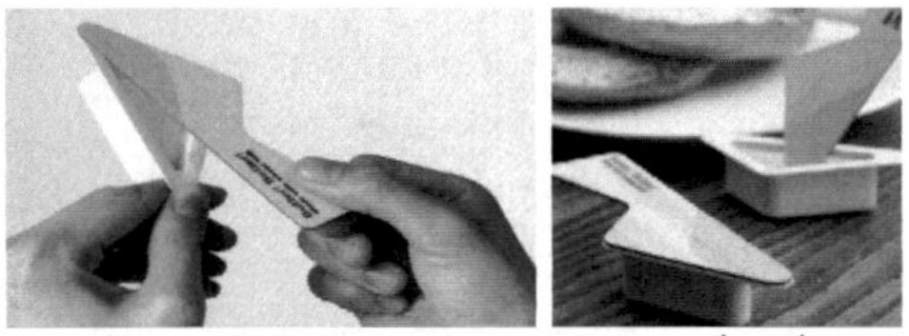

Figure 2. Butter packaging design. (web)

Finally, product's packaging structure should have additional function, [3] to simplify products' using steps, make products more convenient and humanized. Additional functions of product packaging structure can be divided into three categories: auxiliary function, circulating function and collection function. Besides, designers should also make a guiding structural design, guiding users to use them and play products' additional function better. For example, figure 3.

Figure3. Packaging design of the cans. (web)

3.2 Ensure the core structure of the product is ecological.

Product's core structure refers to product's own core function structure. Kenya Hara, a Japanese designer put forward that product design should focus on quality, not quantity. Therefore, design of product's core structure should firstly guarantee the basic structure and avoid unnecessary complicated structures to reduce material waste. For example, figure 4.

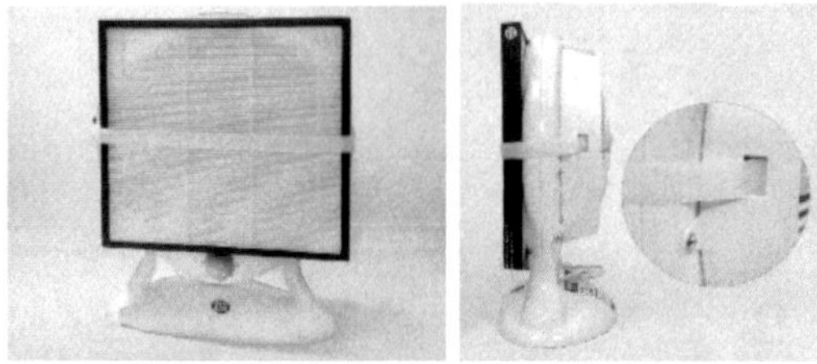

Figure 4. Air cleaner design. (web)

What's more, we should consider the application of collapsible structure in product structure design .at present, products with Single function can't satisfy people's daily needs. designers begin to explore and design "multifunctional" products.[4] Product's folding structure can not only make product more functional, satisfy daily needs, but also reduce the cost of transportation and storage, and then reduce the waste of resources. For example, figure 5.

Figure 5. Design of folding paper cup. (web)

Finally, we should pay more attention to the design of product's circular structure. Through redesigning the waste products, give them using function, so as to reduce the garbage amount, and reduce the threat of waste products to the ecosystem. For example, figure 6.

Figure 6. Small sprayer design. (web)

3.3 Ensure the ecology of products spatial structure.

The spatial structure means how to use appropriate product structure design to solve the problems of products' space placement. Through structural design adjustment, maximize the use of space and save products' materials. Because there are many corners in the indoor space can't replace ordinary products, it wastes lots of space and makes the action space narrower. Therefore, the design of space structure is mostly made of custom-made structure. After observing the whole space, the designer will rationally plan every corner, reduce the product parts, achieve the purpose of saving materials and space resources. For example, figure 7.

https://doi.org/10.1051/matecconf/201817602014

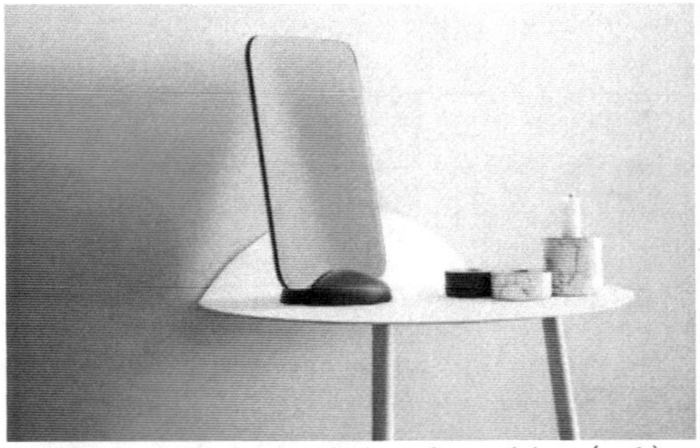

Figure 7. Packaging design of porcelain. (web)

3.4 Guarantee the ecology of product system structure.

Ecological design can be divided into broad sense and narrow sense. Narrow sense of ecology refers to design itself, while broad sense of ecological design refers to human-product-environment. Therefore, design should consider ecology and environment system. By design methods to realize the harmonious development of human-machine-environment (both of natural environment and social environment). [5] So, product structure design should depends on users' behavior, specific environment and usage scenario to define the specific design. In other words, designers are supposed to not only consider users' daily situation, but also the special situation they may encounter.

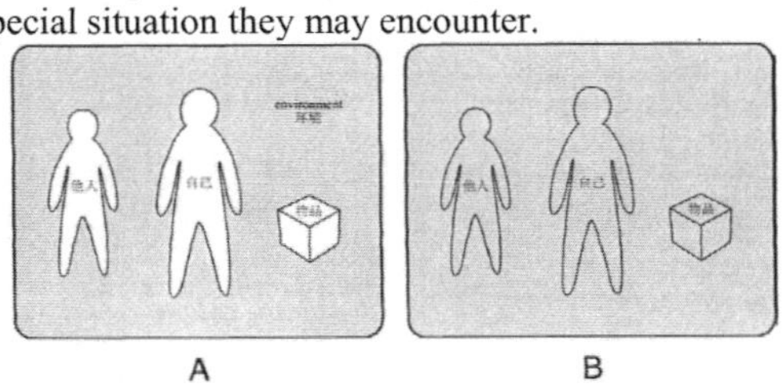

Figure 8. human-machine–environment schematic diagram *(The ecology of design)*

The "oneself" in figure A is looking out, and the 'oneself' in B can be viewed from outside of the picture. So, it can also be defined as the environment. It's not only looking at the surrounding environment, but to look at the part that we didn't see. Figure B has integrated oneself into the environment and become a part of it. In figure B, environment and people are integrated into a whole, [5] which is system structure.

Design of the system structure can start with ecological psychology, the core of it is affordance, which points out the possibility that the environment can be provided to biological behavior. The similarity between design and affordance is that it's impossible if we want to design by ourselves. We must find out an appropriate boundary, like the outline between two objects to achieve the ecological system of human-product-environment. [6]

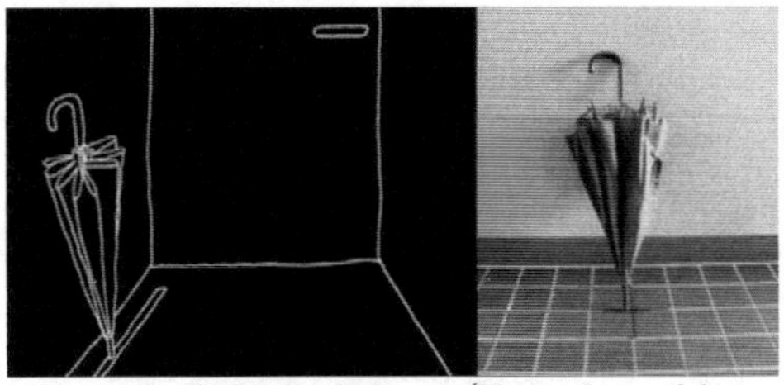

Figure 8. Umbrella design. *(The ecology of design)*

As shown in the left of Figure 9, the designer made an unusual structure, he dug a crack on the flat ground. When the guest come, they will subconsciously place their umbrellas in this crack. The water will go out along the crack, which achieves designer's original intention. Water will not affect the tidiness of the whole floor, everything is in order. In this system, the most critical structure is this special crack on the ground.

4 The implementation of the product ecological structure strategy

4.1 Cultivate the ecological consciousness of the designer

Training designers' awareness of ecological design can be considered from colleges and society aspects. Colleges and universities should set up relevant courses about ecological design, cultivates students' consciousness of ecological design and sense of social responsibility. In addition, lectures should also be organized to enable students to know the frontier knowledge of ecological design. The society mainly target at in-service designers, and design companies should set up special ecology design teams. When design companies communicate with Party A companies, designers are supposed to pass on the concept of ecological structure design to attract the attention of the whole industry and related industries, and then promotes the people's awareness of ecological structure design.

4.2 establish the evaluation system of product ecological structure design

Enterprises should set up professional departments to conduct ecological assessment of product structure, and use 3R principle to evaluate from two angles: environment and commerce:

(1) By comparing with the traditional related product structure, we can see whether the environmental and economic benefits of new products are better than traditional design.

(2) Whether the product meet the company's pre-defined ecological structural design objectives and whether it can bring benefit to the company and society.

The ability and cooperation of project members and their communication with other relevant parties, as well as whether project members completely understand the product's ecological structure.

In view of these above problems, we can sum up a report on the evaluation of the product ecological structure project, and invite relevant users, environmental protection experts, professional designers, and government environmental protection personnel to evaluate the ecology of the product structure again, to guarantee the ecology of product structure.

5 Conclusion

The ocean covers 2/3 of the earth's area. Global marine pollution will definitely affect the whole environment and the quality of people's lives. We must protect environment, reduce current environmental pollution, so that people can live in a healthy space. Therefore, ecological design is an important trend in contemporary design. The concept of environmental protection should be designer's basic quality. Designers should use different ecological structure design strategies for different product structures, to save resources, reduce waste pollution. In that way, designers can be called be responsible for every product and be responsible for the homes we live on.

Acknowledgment

Fund project. Major projects in Sichuan education department. (Item number: W171300); University-level graduate innovation fund project of Xihua University. (Item number: ycjj2017110).

Reference

1. Zhang Yuan, Liu Shan. Pollution of plastic waste: marine disaster.EE, 2-5(2015)
2. Papanek Victor. *Design for the Real World* .M. CITIC,5(2012)
3. WenYa Qian. The follow-up function design of product packaging. HUT, (2015)
4. XiuPu Hua. Application and research of folding structure in product design . D, 44-45(2017)
5. Xue Bai. On the design methods and development trend of contemporary China's conservation oriented society . TAI , 29-33 (2015)
6. Hou tengwu、Sasaki Tadashi 、Naoto Fukasawa. *The ecology of design : New design textbook.* M.GNUP,(2016)

The Challenges and Transformation of Design Education in Contemporary China

Dr. Peipei Yu[1] and Prof. Bob Jerrard[2]

[1]Researcher, Faculty of Art, Design and Media, Birmingham City University, Birmingham, United Kingdom B4 7RJ
[2]Emeritus Professor of Design Studies, Faculty of Art, Design and Media, Birmingham City University, Birmingham, United Kingdom B4 7RJ

Abstract. This paper explores, through comprehensive perspectives, the challenges of the current design education system in China under the contemporary context. The influences that have transformed design in China from both historical and contemporary context are described mainly from literature. Interview data from professors from various design institutions and senior designers in companies in China were analysed to provide differing perspectives. The research findings show the inter-relationship between the various cultural and historical influences on Chinese design education. The authors conclude on how education might benefit from concentrating on this inter-relationship.

1 Introduction

The opening-up policy of China from its closed-doors brought in a new and exciting world of culture, including design predominantly from the West. China has changed dramatically in recent decades, from the conservative communism that restricted markets, to the open-door policy in 1980s which saw an aggressive adoption of capitalism within the communist ideology [1]. China is currently the most populous country in the world and the world's second largest economy after the United States [2]. The 'opening-up' policy introduced in the 1980's saw an acceleration in the Chinese economy, with vast job creation and high levels of migration to major cities. In the past 30 years, 300 million people have been urbanised, while, it is estimated that by 2026, a total of 500 million people will be classed as the middle class – creating a rapid growth in demand for consumer goods [3]. According to the research of Woetzel and Towson [4], professors at Peking University's Guanghua School of Management, China's strong consumer market will continue to surprise the world with its market growth, which is the fastest compared with any other countries in the world [5], along with the greatest potential amongst emerging economies to be the next economic superpower.

However, despite the presence of a flourishing economy, design education in China has not followed through in its development in comparison to the country's economy. In an increasingly globalised economy, the financial, cultural and consumer ideals of the West have become widespread. China, alongside most of the developing world, has since been consuming and adapting to the culture-specific products that consist mainly of what [6] named "English language centric products". With increasing Western influence in a growing Chinese economy, various imitation products have created a new trend - a shanzhai (imitation) phenomenon in product designing which has flourished amongst an upcoming society; individuals have a growing income alongside an increasing demand for products associated with a certain economic status. However, such aspiration is not only present in industry, but also in design education – which traces back to the philosophy and socio-economic situation of imperial China. This paper will address the origins of product design through its historical contexts in China. It also constructs a justification for the transformation of product design in China by linking such contexts with more recent mechanised and informational periods. The existing educational perspective in design is described from interviews with designers and professors from design institutions in China. Cultural originality with regards to the Western influence on product design development in China is also described.

2 Desig4n Origin and Transformation in China

According to Pevsner [7] the concept of design originated from the thinking of William Morris (1834-1896), the leader of Arts and Crafts Movement, and John Ruskin (1819-1900), a leading English art critic of the Victorian era. Both men advocated the concept of artisan craftsmanship, and placed an importance on aesthetics in response to the mechanical production of goods during the Industrial Revolution, which produced items that lacked design creativity and principles [8] More recently, China has also seen the growth of industrialisation and the significant growth of mass-produced goods. The development of Chinese industries from a product design history can be seen in the four periods addressed [9]: a)

https://doi.org/10.1051/matecconf/201817602015

the emergence of heavy industry through the Westernisation Movement from 1860 to 1911; b) the DEVELOPMENT and formation of modern industrial structures post-revolution from 1911 to 1927; c) the rise of the Kuomintang Government, which gave way to increased development of industries from 1927 to 1937; and d), the formation of the People's Republic of China, which then saw a rapid increase in domestic industries within China from 1937 to 1949. The industrial periods from 1860 to 1937, which are now seen as the beginnings of industrialisation in China, were greatly influenced by Western technology with a similar emphasis on the mechanical production of the Industrial Revolution. In the wake of the revival of Chinese industries, there were nationalistic sentiments to resist the 'invasion' of Western influences, which encouraged the Chinese to learn advanced Western science and technology, as well as social management systems for appropriated use [10] which at that time was deemed more effective and developed. The nationalistic sentiment also led to the boycotting of foreign goods in the early 1900s, including those from Japan and Germany. This allowed local manufacturers to promote domestic products and revive Chinese manufacturing through patriotic motivation [11]. However, due to China's boycotting of foreign influence, the development of technologies in product design and manufacturing lagged severely behind the West, its severity highlighted especially during the Cultural Revolution in the 1970s. As described by Chen and Tang [12], China was losing out not only through its industrial immaturity and lack of technical know-how, but also through the development and understanding of modern design ideology linked to cultural awareness during the period of industrialisation. Henceforth, it is to be deduced that the backwardness of Chinese industrialisation in the period of rapid global industrialisation has resulted in the deficiency in maturity and originality of Chinese contemporary product design. As evidenced by Ling [13], the Chinese business communities, which started manufacturing products through varying degrees of acquired Western technology and knowledge, struggled with the appropriate technical capacity and know-how to produced quality Chinese goods.

The conceptualisation of 'design' is not of Chinese descent, product design has a Western origin, which, through cultural influence, made its way to the East. Also, the on-going 'idea' of design was largely attributed as a Western ideology [14], which saw its embryonic beginnings in the Industrial Revolution and underwent a century of maturing through the post-industrial age of mass production [15]. Morris and Kwok [16] provide a context for researching Chinese product design originality suggesting that product design was brought into China mainly through trade, following the Chinese open-door policy of the 1980s [17]. Indeed, understanding product design as an industry in China has a history of only 30 years, and the similarity and obvious lack or originality of Chinese product design over the last three decades, can be explained by these early Western influences. The pioneer educators of product design in Chinese universities were also influenced by Western design methodology, introduced by academic colleagues with a Western design education.

3 The Challenges of Design Education in China

The teaching of product design ideas and philosophy was introduced by Western countries to China [18]. Such education played a significant role in transferring the concept and idea of design to a younger Chinese generation, in order to produce designers for contemporary society in China. In order to bring Chinese cultural brands to a global audience, it is essential that the educators share but also adapt the same concept and idea in order to guide students. At the beginning of the 1980s, many universities – such as the Academy of Art and Design, at Tsinghua University (1984), and the School of Design, Hunan University (1982) – pioneered the industrial design education in China. All of the course founders studied design in various Western countries for many years in order to observe the Western teaching system [19]. Over the next four decades, the Chinese design education system continued to develop, based upon the Western teaching structure[14]. Given the high demand, Chinese design education has grown significantly in recent years and the number of universities which have design courses has exceeded 1,000. When interviewed, [20] stated that there are around 700 universities which offer industrial design and 100 or more students graduate from different universities each year. However, [20] also indicated that most courses operate at a basic level of industrial design understanding, and because of limited faculty resources and the education system of some universities, the capability to conduct high quality design projects cannot currently be achieved.

At present, the design education systems in various Chinese universities have similar features, in that they have a large student numbers; some course structures and teaching outcomes are indistinct; most of institutions focus is on design skills rather than research and creative ability [21]. To some degree, those issues limit the comprehensive development of the students. Such discrepancies could be attributed to the universities literally following other countries' design progress, whilst ignoring the indigenous design quality and cultural values of Chinese products. [19] concluded that the teaching of product design in China typically falls into a three-phase teaching form: a) modelling foundation, b) specialty foundation and c), professional design. The challenges for the design educators in China are the internal connection between these phases; a systematic teaching model could be formed and achieved, although the provision of comprehensive training skills also falls short. The long term goal must be to expand the education foundation and cultivate inter-disciplinary talents applicable to the requirements of the time [22].

4 Research Findings

Based on the interviews conducted with educators of product design in a number of Chinese universities as part of this paper, findings have suggested that education is an important factor in the design development in China. Evidence from literature also suggests that educators brought the teaching ethos on design from the West [14] back to China in the 1980's [18], when the country was facing a healthy economy with high demand for production from both within and outside China. Due to the Westernised approach in design education, highlighted in the aspects of concept cultivation, education model and teaching methodology – students in China graduating from these institutions would naturally be equipped with a Western design inclination rather than one of Chinese origins.

Based on the authors' literature review of the design industry, it is suggested that design companies have also contributed to the lack of originality in contemporary Chinese product design. Design companies in China have rushed to produce imitated goods to capitalise on the Chinese consumers' appetite for branded products [23] [24]. From the authors interviews of Chinese design professionals, design companies seek quick and instant profits, focusing their efforts on marketing, rapid production chain expansion and technical replication accuracy. Instead of investing in original design, they have often focussed on the imitation of branded goods to satisfy the growing domestic demand for cheaper alternatives to Western products that are overly expensive compared to the average income of a Chinese consumer [25]. The Westernisation of designing in design companies is also interlinked with the education of graduates, as design companies employ young graduates with little or no fieldwork experience [26] but who have been Westernised in their design inclination and preference, leading to a further lack of Chinese cultural originality in Chinese contemporary product design.

5 Discussion

Combining the findings from literature on Chinese contemporary product design with the interview findings conducted with scholars and practitioners from the product design education and industry, this study proposed an inter-relationship between the various factors influncing the cultural originality in Chinese contemporary design, as illustrated in Figure 1.

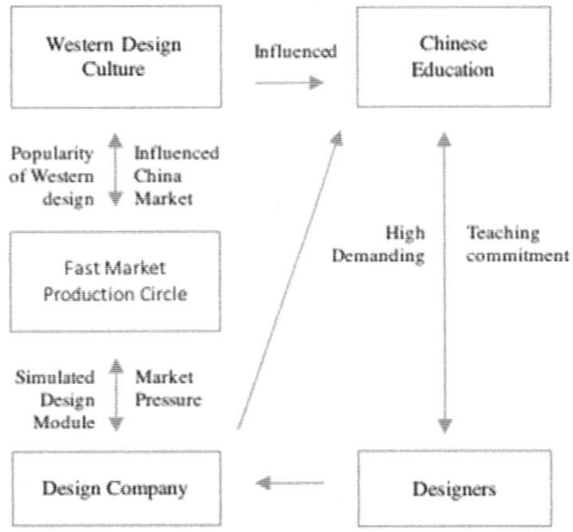

Figure 1. The inter-relationship in China influenced by Western culture

There are strong connections between each section. Western design culture has been influencing Chinese design since the industrial age, leading to the importing of Western technological and design educational learning into China. This leads to a Westernised approach in teaching and, hence, the professional development of Chinese designers with a lack of originality in their design thinking. These graduating designers either formed their own company or worked for other Chinese companies that fed into the growing Chinese market. A market which, in it's current state of rapid growth, demands globally popular and mature Western products. The inter-relationships between all these factors have caused the lack of cultural originality in contemporary Chinese products. The outcomes of the complex inter-relationships point to several new factors influencing Chinese design creativity and originality. The combined imitation phenomenon could be acknowledged as the inevitable outcome during the design development of a growing economy such as China.

6 Conclusions

A fusion of Chinese and Western elements might be the new way to innovate in the use of ancient Chinese elements, and may improve the creative skills as a soft power, assisting the national brand in the eyes of the world and rebuilding national confidence in contemporary design. Economic globalisation inevitably cause great friction with different cultures. Whether it is the eastward transmission of Western sciences, or the dissemination of Oriental learning, different cultures still retain their respective characteristics while seeking mutual recognition [27]. Design thinking is able to uniquely bring together differing cultural knowledge and experiences, hence from a educaiton perspective, the institutions should adopt the attitude of respect towards cultural depths and differences in their designing process. Manifesting Chinese traditional elements in contemporary design appears initially successful. Students should have a profound confidence coupled with a good understanding of Chinese traditional culture in order to incorporate Chineseness in various ways. In the globalisation context, it is necessary to seek plenty of methods to properly integrate into modern product design.

Design education is one of the most signification factors in design development of contemporary China and it is the main method of imparting the importance of important cultural values in design, given that university education is the primary way to inspire potential designers. Therefore, the teaching of design in China and the methodology of training needs to be rethink if the aim is to cultivate more culturally original designers.

References

1. J. Diamond, J. Liu. China's environment in a globalizing world. Nature. **435.7046**. (2005)
2. D. Barboza, China passes Japan as second-largest economy. The New York Times. 15. (2010)
3. X. Liu, Y. Li and F. Feng. Thirty Years of Legal Theory China's Reform and Opening up: 1978-2008 Law and Social Development. **5**. 003. (2008)
4. J. Woetzel, J. Towson. *The One Hour China Book: Two Peking University Professors Cayman Islands*, Towson Group (2008)
5. Z. Ma, M. Yu, C. Gao, J. Zhou, Z. Yang. Institutional constraints of product innovation in China: Evidence from international joint ventures. Journal of Business Research. **68**. (2015)
6. P. M. Sathikh, S. Kumar. *Culture in Transition - How 'global products' are changing user behavior. Faculty of Engineering* National University of Singapore. (2009)
7. N. Pevsner, *Pioneers of Modern Design: From William Morris to Walter Gropius.*Yale University Press. (2005)
8. J. Auerbach, The Great Exhbition of 1851: A Nation on Display (1999)
9. D. Zhang, An analysis of the thought of human is an integral part of nature in Chinese Philosophy. Journal of Peking University . **1**. (1985)
10. J. P. Heap, The Management of Innovation and Design. London, Cassell, (1989).
11. M. Chen, The Art of Zen in Japanese MUJI Packaging Design. Packaging Engineering. **4**. 36. (2010)
12. Y. Chen, J. Tang, An Discussion of Globalization and Chinese Culture with Art & Design. Architecture & Culture **10**. (2010)
13. A.Y. Ling, A Question of "Chineseness": The Chinese Diaspora in Singapore 1819-1950s. Degree of Doctor of Philosophy, University of Stirling. (2001).
14. Y. Yan, Chinese design is a pseudo proposition (2011)
15. D. Raizman, History of modern design: Graphics and products since the industrial revolution. Laurence King Publishing. (2003)
16. M. W. Morris, and L. Kwok, Creativity east and west: Perspectives and parallels. Management and Organization Review. **6**. 3. (2010)
17. G. S. Insch, M. J. Brad. The impact of country-of-origin cues on consumer perceptions of product quality: A binational test of the decomposed country-of-origin construct. Journal of Business Research. **57**. 3. (2004)
18. X. Liu, Y. Li, F. Feng. Thirty Years of Legal Theory in China's Reform and Opening up: 1978-2008 Law and Social Development. **5**. 003. (2008)
19. S. Wang, Critical Study on Chinese Design Education. (2007)
20. C. Zhao, Academy of Arts & Design, Tsinghua University, research filed trip interview (2015)
21. L. Justice, Product Design Education in China (2011)
22. R. Cox, The Zen arts: An anthropological study of the culture of aesthetic form in Japan, Routledge. (2013)
23. X. Leng, M. Zhang, Shanzhai as a Weak Brand in Contemporary China Marketing. International Journal of China Marketing. **1**. 2. (2011)
24. Z. Sheng, Y. Shi, Shanzhai manufacturing – an alternative innovation phenomenon in China. Journal of Science and Technology Policy in China. **1**. 1. (2010)
25. R. Tan, Market ecology breeds Chinese cottage culture. (2012)
26. W. Lu, L. Heng, L. Shen,T. Huang, Strengths, weaknesses, opportunities, and threats analysis of Chinese construction companies in the global market. Journal of Management in Engineering. **25**. 4. (2009)
27. T. Fernandes, A guide to designing international user interfaces. (1995)

MATEC Web of Conferences 176, 02016 (2018) https://doi.org/10.1051/matecconf/201817602016
IFID 2018

Design Factors Extraction and Application of Five Dynasties Yaozhou Porcelain Decoration

Qin Song[1,a], Wang Yi[1]

[1] Xi'an University of Technology, School of Art and Design, 710054, Xi'an, China

Abstract. For the better development of Yaozhou Kiln, the article is proposed a research method about cultural and creative products based on the example of extracting the lotus patterns on the Yanzhou Kiln in the Five Dynasties. By collecting data and extracting forms, through the combination of qualitative and quantitative, it mines the obscure information of the Yaozhou porcelain ornamentation in the Five Dynasties. The article analyzes the form evaluations of the 18 representative lotus patterns in the Five Dynasties by semantic difference method, extracts their stylized inheritance and recessive genes and makes the conclusion to guide the cultural and creative products design of the Yaozhou Kiln, which not only supplies a fresh design perspective for the innovation development of the famous domestic traditional kilns as a reference, but also a useful supplements for the research of the design art methodology.

1 Introduction

The core area of Yaozhou Kiln is located in Tongchuan City, Shaanxi Province. Yaozhou Porcelain is a representative of the northern celadon with dignified and elegant styling, bright colors, distinctive patterns, beautiful and orderly structure, novel and unique decoration techniques. The ceramic decorative pattern is an important part of the Yaozhou Kiln ceramics. It not only records and expresses the unique lifestyle and aesthetic concepts of the people at that time, but also reflects the intelligence and wisdom of the Yaozhou people in the creation of the ornament based on the specific cultural environment. Due to various factors such as geographical environment and commercial information, Yaozhou Kiln Ceramics gradually lost its glory in its period of great prosperity. Its inheritance, development and branding are also facing much difficulties. Therefore, it is proposed that a research method about extracting the design factors of the emblazonry on Yaozhou Kiln ceramics in the Five Dynasties.

At present, domestic methods and applications for the refining research of cultural products are still at an initial stage. Most of the existing researches include the refining of architectural culture factors, cultural relics form factors, and dress pattern factors. Yan Bingyi et al. [1] took painted pottery culture of Banpo relics as the research object, introduced the design process based on genetic engineering, and constructed the style cultural gene pool; Wang Weiwei et al. [2] adopted Salt culture and the costume culture of Han Dynasty as the research object, and he took eye movement experiments and spectrogram analysis methods to extract cultural factors and apply them to product design; Zhou Xiaozhou et al. [3] used FSA method and Delphi method to statistically summarize dominant DNA genetic factors of product family from the microscopic perspective, and applied the SD method to find recessive DNA genetic factors from a macro perspective, which provides feasibility guidance for product family design; Jay PM [4] proposed a design language extraction and evolution algorithm based on cultural algorithms, using Buick as an example for application verification; Raphaelle[5] et al. studied the recognition method that integrates customer requirements into the semantics of product initial design, and studied the relationship between design and semantics through regression analysis.

The above research used different methods to extract cultural product factors for different subjects and provided effective solutions to the problem. However, the research on the use of the ceramic design factors of a specific period of time has rarely been carried out. In this paper, the design method combines qualitative and quantitative analysis, and based on an in-depth analysis of the existing methods of researching design factors, a set of method models based on correlation analysis and in line with the design language extraction and derivation design are proposed to enable traditional culture and products design practices are better integrated with each other.

2 Construction of research process

Yaozhou porcelains in different time have its unique cultural connotations and artistic expressions in different periods. As a special art form that integrates practicality and art, the cultural and artistic information it contains is rich and varied. Yaozhou Porcelain is also the convergence product of multiculturalism and contains many cultural connotations. Therefore, this article mainly selects Five Dynasties of Yaozhou Porcelain

* Corresponding author: [a] qinbinbin@126.com

ornamentation as the research object. Based on a deep understanding of the typical art features and craftsmanship culture of Yaozhou Kiln celadon of the Five Dynasties, a large number of sample data were collected and selected through shooting and scanning, and the selected sample pictures were processed and simplified to form the sample curve using flat software. After samples is collected and processed, the perceptual vocabulary is screened by methods such as clustering and fuzzy comprehensive evaluation. The key perceptive adjectives are selected through questionnaire survey, and the representative lotus patterns of the Yaozhou porcelains of the Five Dynasties are selected as Samples of patterns are analyzed based on the semantic difference method to analyze statistical representative samples, then reference thresholds and other design criteria are obtained. Finally, computer-aided design is used to verify whether the scheme of resulting diagram meets design demands.

3 Factor extraction

3.1 Method introduction

This study is divided into two steps. Firstly, the clustering method is used to cluster the samples, the most suitable group is divided, and the eigenvalues of each group are identified. And then, the semantic difference method is applied to analyze and evaluate a representative sample with the semantic difference components table. The design-related evaluation data was obtained [6].

The advantage of clustering method is that it does not add too much judgment basis, but identifies the hidden objective laws among the data, and then recognizes and clusters them, so that the clustering result is more objective and reliable[7]. The specific process is as follows: (1) Describe the characteristics of objective traits visible in the ceramic decoration of Yaozhou Kiln, including the composition of a picture, main body, structure, lines, arrangement ways etc. (2) Correspond one by one with the characteristics of ceramic decoration in Yaozhou Kiln.

3.2 Participants selection

There is a total of 42 participants, of whom 5 are experts, 3 are artisans, 3 are workers working in Yaozhou Kiln, 2 are sales staff of Yaozhou Kiln Ceramics, 4 are product designers, 12 are design students at school, and 13 people are Yaozhou Kiln Ceramic users. Participants including 23 females and 19 males, who aged 20 to 45 years old. All of them have a certain understanding of Yaozhou Kiln.

3.3 Building Sensitive Vocabulary Database

First, a perceptual vocabulary database was established based on the experimental object design. According to the previous study, the factors affecting the decorative features were divided into composition, theme, structure, and lines in a sequence according to the proportion of importance. Through consulting and discussing with relevant experts and analyzing and researching a large amount of ceramic decoration materials of the Yaozhou Kiln during the period of the Five Dynasties, 40 style inheritance features affecting ornamentation were listed [8]. Select relevant vocabulary from them and remove adjectives that are not related to the experimental goal or have similar meanings. According to Osgood's research results, we selected 12 pairs of adjective pairs from emotional factors, mode factors and structural factors. Each of these factors had 4 groups, as shown in the Table1.

Table.1 Image adjective pairs.

Types	Emotional factors	Mode factors	Structural factors
1	Untrammeled - Exquisite	Plump - Thin	Delicate - Vigorous
2	Intensity - Preciseness	Elegance - Austere	Concise - Complex
3	Swank - Connotative	Gorgeous - Fresh	Vivid - Natural
4	Lively - Sober	Robust - Flexible	Smooth - Rigid

3.4 Data collection, statistics and analysis

The emblazonry is a part of the body of the ceramics, which has aesthetic and ornamental decorative features. For future generations, it is also an important historical research material that studies the customs, aesthetics, culture, and major historical events at that time. In the history of Yaozhou Kiln, it has extensively absorbed multicultural factors, including religious subjects, making its pattern rich and varied, and its expressiveness is gorgeous. The Yaozhou Kiln in the contains a large number of animal and plant patterns of Buddhist cultural factors. The lotus pattern is the most representative because ancient people often use the cover and the lotus petals to decorate artifacts. The lotus pattern is also an early pattern used by Yaozhou Kiln. In the Five Dynasties, the Tang and early Song dynasties, porcelains and tricolors of various glazes were adorned with plastic and engraved upward and covered lotus petals [9].

The lotus pattern is one of the most typical patterns of the Yaozhou Kiln celadon of the Five Dynasties. Five, six, and seven petals are the most common patterns. There are 12 or more patterns, and the lotus petals are fat and mellow, and the patterns are regular. It continued to be used in the early Song Dynasty, but its shape became thinner and less visible later. This article first collected the pattern of lotus patterns in the Five Dynasties period. The lotus patterns were divided into 18 patterns numbered P1-P18. The analysis of artistic features and intentional symbology was conducted separately. The samples were analyzed using the semantic difference method. Then the inheritance relationship of the pattern elements was extracted and the pattern gene was extracted to prepare for the next design study. As shown in Figure 1.

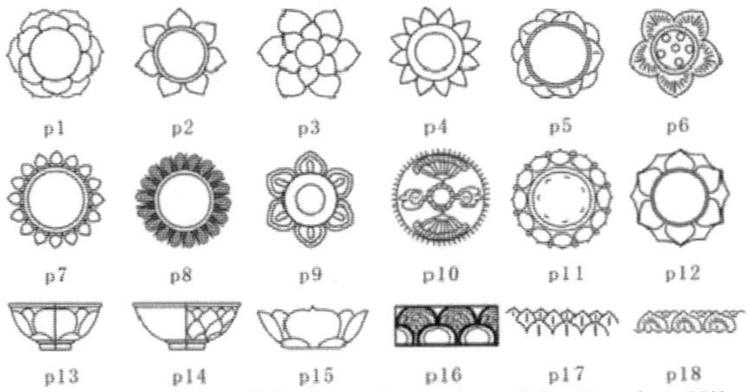

Figure 1. Samples of the lotus decoration of the Yaozhou Kiln in the Five Dynasty.

P1. Huangbao Kiln Site P2. Huangbao Kiln Site P3. Huangbao Kiln Site P4. Pingquan Xiaojigou Liao Mausoleum P5. Dingzhou Jingzhi Temple Taji P6. Faku Museum Ye Maotai M22 P7. Yaozhou Kiln Museum Tibet P8. Shaanxi History Museum P9. Yaozhou Kiln Museum Museum P10. Shaanxi History Museum Collection P11. Lotus petals (bed golden groove M5 lotus care) P12. Huangbao Kiln site P13. Huangbao Kiln Site A type IV type lotus P14. Faku Ye Maotai M7 P15. Lotus petal pattern (Yao Maotai M7 bowl) P16. Lotus petal pattern (Ye-Mai Taiwan M7 bowl) P17. Huangbao Kiln Site seal lotus petals P18. Huangbao Kiln Site paste model

A questionnaire survey was conducted based on the semantic difference method to understand the target group's emotional evaluation of the product. The target group can score at the corresponding position in each perceptual adjective based on its perception of each product. Finally, statistical analysis of the questionnaire survey data provides the basis for subsequent development. In this round, the expert scoring method was used. A total of 12 industry experts and designers were selected to conduct the questionnaire survey. Figure 3 shows an example of a sample questionnaire.

	-3	-2	-1	0	1	2	3	
Untrammeled								Exquisite
Plump								Thin
Delicate								Vigorous
Intensity								Preciseness
Elegance								Austere
Concise								Complex
Swank								Connotative
Gorgeous								Fresh
Vivid								Natural
Lively								Sober
Robust								Flexible
Smooth								Rigid

Figure 3. Example of a Five Dynasties Yaozhou porcelain ornament questionnaire.

The weighted average method is used to count the expert scores of different adjectives in each sample, and the calculation formula according to the weighted average value is formula (1):

$$x = \frac{1}{n}\sum_{k=1}^{n} x_k f_k \qquad (1)$$

x - the score given by the expert;

f - the number of occurrences of each score;

n - the number of experts.

From formula (1), The weighted average number of adjectives in each sample was calculated by $\sum_{k=1}^{n} f_k = n$, and the results are shown in Figure 2.

	Untrammeled	Plump	Delicate	Intensit	Elegance	Concise	Swank	Gorgeous	Vivid	Lively	Robust	Smooth
P1	0.583	0.083	-0.167	0.25	0.167	0.083	-0.167	0	0	-0.25	0.583	-0.25
P2	-0.5	-0.083	-0.75	0.083	0.583	-1.417	0.5	0.833	0.916	0.167	0.75	-0.583
P3	0.083	-0.416	-0.5	0	-0.5	0.583	0	-0.5	-1.417	-0.167	1.667	-1.25
P4	-0.25	0.666	-0.25	0	0.333	-0.416	-0.25	0.5	0.25	0.083	-1	0.25
P5	0.333	-1.25	-0.333	0.5	-0.916	-0.166	0.583	-0.416	0.083	-0.167	0.167	-0.417
P6	0.667	-1.333	0.5	0.5	-0.833	1.833	-0.083	-1.25	-0.666	0	0.083	-0.083
P7	-0.25	-1.416	-0.75	0.167	-1.167	0.083	0.667	-0.083	-0.083	-0.167	0.25	-1
P8	-0.833	-1.417	0.667	-1.833	-1	2.25	-0.917	-2.083	-0.667	0.583	0.167	-0.167
P9	0.333	-1.583	0.083	0.333	0	-0.333	0.5	0.25	0.167	-0.167	1.083	-0.667
P10	0	-0.417	0.5	-1.083	0.667	2	0.25	2.083	-1.25	0.083	-0.083	-0.333
P11	1.167	-1.583	-0.333	-1.333	-1.417	0.833	0.053	-0.583	0.083	0.167	1.5	-1.333
P12	-1.083	-1.667	-0.333	0.833	-0.833	-1.25	0.5	0.5	0.75	-0.333	-0.667	-1
P13	1.083	-1.083	-0.25	0.833	-1.167	0.083	1.083	0	0.667	-0.083	1.083	0.167
P14	1.083	0.833	1.083	0.167	1.25	0.5	0.667	0.917	0.417	0.083	0.083	0.083
P15	1.417	-1	-0.667	0.5	1.5	-0.917	0.75	-0.5	0.167	-0.5	1.083	-1.667
P16	0.167	-1	1.083	-0.5	0	0.333	-0.33	-1.583	-0.5	0.333	0.25	0.5
P17	0.083	-0.917	0.083	0.667	-0.333	0.333	0.5	0.417	0.083	-0.667	1.417	-0.533
P18	1.417	0.083	0.667	0.5	0.417	1.583	0.25	0.667	1	0.583	1.417	1.167

Figure 2. Expert scoring weighted average value table.

Weighted average value of expert's score is input into SPSS software for factor analysis. The main objective of the factor analysis method is to reduce the number of variables and use the factor analysis to obtain contribution values of the eigenvalues and variance, which can explain the product's intentional vocabulary with the least factors [10]. From Table 3, it can be seen that the decoration of Yaozhou Kiln of the Five Dynasties was greatly influenced by two principal components, which were from components 1 to component 5, and their initial eigenvalues were all bigger than 1, and the variance contribution values were 34.226%, 15.415%, 13.441%, and 10.262%, 9.597%, respectively, which can get the variance of 82.941% of the original variable. The two mainly components can represent the information of all variables. So, SPSS selects the five principal components to extract the sum of squares and replaces all the original variables with these 5 principal components. As shown in the Table 3.

The concept of gravel chart comes from geology. There are often many small gravels below the rock slope [11]. The gravel chart has feature values as the vertical axis and components on the horizontal axis. The steep part of the chart has a large feature value, which contains much information. And has the flat part has a small feature value and contains little information. From Table 4, it can be seen intuitively that component 1 contains most of the information. It starts at component 6 to changing to be flatter. From the gravel chart shown in Figure 4, there are 5 principal components with eigenvalues ≥1. Before the fifth inflection point, the eigenvalues are generally higher and are connected into a steep polyline. From the fifth inflection point, the linear gradient becomes gentle. The gravel chart shows that this data is suitable for applying factor analysis to reduce the dimension. It is appropriate to analyze these five factors.

Table.3 Characteristic Root and Variance Contribution.

No	contribution values of the eigenvalues	contribution values of the variance %	accumulation%
1	4.107	34.226	34.226
2	1.850	15.415	49.641
3	1.613	13.441	63.082
4	1.231	10.262	73.343
5	1.152	9.597	82.940
6	0.717	5.972	88.912
7	0.623	5.193	94.105
8	0.362	3.015	97.121
9	0.223	1.855	98.976
10	0.070	0.584	99.560
11	0.042	0.353	99.913
12	0.010	0.087	100.000

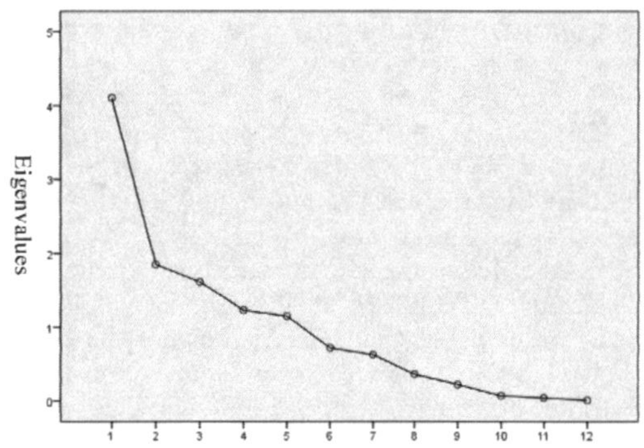

Figure 4. Gravel char.

The composition matrix is derived from the mainly component extraction method. From the Table 4, it can be seen that emotional adjectives are most affected by component 1, and component 1 plays an important role in the overall data. Therefore, the data of component 1 is mainly referenced. And according to the relevant values of component 1 we can draw a conclusion that concise, lively and delicate are the 3 most important factors of expert statistics. Among them, the most consummate and valued factor elected by the consumers are the concise, then the liveliness ranks second, and the last is fresh. The experts pay less attention to delicate and vividness. According to the statistical analysis results, finally, we chosen the concise, then the liveliness ranks second, and the last is fresh as a Five Dynasties Yaozhou Kiln utensils decoration design factor. the concise, then the liveliness ranks second, and the last is fresh.

Table 3. Component Matrix.

Types	1	2	3	4	5
Untrammeled	0.031	0.572	0.680	-0.196	-0.114
Plump	0.125	-0.556	0.696	-0.152	-0.361
Delicate	0.672	0.073	-0.019	0.316	0.605
Intensity	-0.667	0.086	0.337	-0.320	0.387
Elegance	-0.264	-0.344	0.432	0.617	0.043
Concise	0.848	0.262	0.031	0.200	-0.004
Swank	-0.772	0.312	0.097	0.135	0.408
Gorgeous	-0.542	-0.390	0.178	0.477	0.112
Vivid	-0.713	-0.182	-0.220	-0.356	0.202
Lively	0.801	-0.125	0.007	-0.079	0.173
Robust	-0.107	0.797	0.293	0.201	-0.110
Smooth	0.594	-0.282	0.434	-0.358	0.479

3.5 Creation design of the Five-Dynasties Yaozhou porcelain lotus flower ornament

During the period of the Five Dynasties, porcelain in Yaozhou Kiln was mainly celadon firing, and utensil types were tableware, wine sets, and tea sets. And it is often made on a piece of artifact in the form of a sculpture, which pays great attention to the artistic effect of three-dimensional space and plays a prominent role in the vividness of the modeling of objects. The tea and water separation cup are used as the main body of the Yaozhou Kiln furniture design. As shown in Figure 5, there is a pot consisting of a cup, a lid and three parts, which can satisfy the use of brewing tea and tea alone, and it is easy to store and use. The design is functionally portable and beautiful, simplifies the traditional tea drinking process, which is concise, lively, and become the main key factor of design factors. The cup mouth adopts the lotus flower mouth design and pays tribute to the beauty of the traditional Yaozhou Kiln culture. Lotus flower design extraction factor of the Five-Dynasties Yaozhou Kiln are used on the body of the cup. So, the body's simple lotus style segmentation is both elegance and delicate. The lid with a lively design factor use a rotating design makes this product suitable for movement, changing the unfit situation of traditional tea set and modern home or office environment.

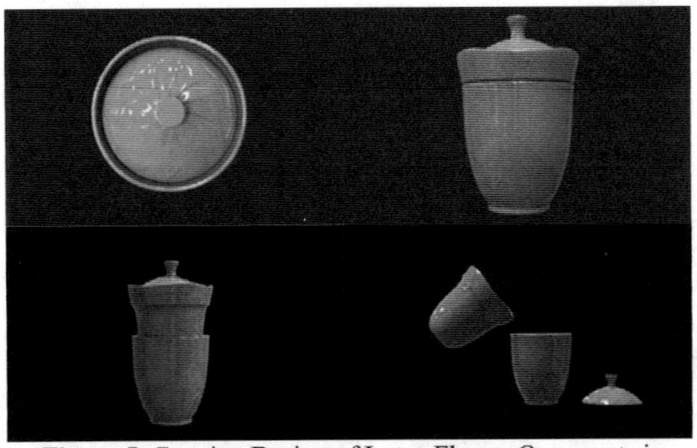

Figure 5. Creation Design of Lotus Flower Ornaments in Yaozhou Kiln in the Five Dynasties.

4 Conclusion

Yaozhou Kiln has rich cultural connotations and different levels of research in various fields. At present, the research of Yaozhou Kiln arts tends that were lied more stress on the past than on the present, making its product system tend to be conservative and self-styled. Tradition and modernity are not binary oppositions, but interconnected, expressed, and advanced. The idealized Yaozhou Kiln cultural and creative product not only needs the characteristics of inheriting the traditional forms, but also demands the artistic appeal of the current culture. They need to inherit the semantics of the traditional Yaozhou Kiln and break through the traditional design logic and shaping of the Yaozhou Kiln. Seeking the symbolic significance and new aesthetic value of ceramic art in the new era is to find a new opportunity for the development of Yaozhou Kiln. Therefore, effective design production is needed to penetrate into the people's current life. This article extracts the design elements of the important lotus ornament in the development of the Yaozhou Kiln culture by using the semantic difference method as a new design method, which can more efficiently and conveniently protect and disseminate precious Yao porcelain ornamentation. Through the analysis of the typical characteristics of the ceramic decoration of the Yaozhou Kiln in the Five Dynasties and the influence factors of the composition of the adjectives, the linear and recessive features were extracted, which proved that the semantic difference method is an effective method for extracting traditional cultural elements.

Acknowledgements

This study was supported by General project of Shanxi Art Humanities and Social Science Foundation (Grant Number sy2016048); General project of the humanities and social sciences fund of the Shanxi Provincial Education Department（Grant Number 17JK0524）; Xi'an science and technology university science research project humanities general project（Grant Number 106-256091703）.

References

1. Gou Bingchen,Yu Hui,Li Zhenfang,et al.Application of culture gene extraction and design in Banpo painted pottery[J].Journal of Northwestern Polytechnical University(Social Sciences),2011, 31(4): 66-69, 104.
2. Wang Weiwei,Liu Yin,Wang Yi. Extraction of Design Factors of Saline Soil Culture Based on Visual Correlation Analysis[J].Journal of Graphics.2016.37(1):60-65
3. Zhou Xiaozhou,Xue Chengqi,et al. Extraction of heritable factors of product family design DNA [J]. Journal of Southeast University(Natural Science Edition), 2016.46（6）:1192-1196
4. JAY P M. Speaking the Buick Language: Capturing, Under-standing and Exploring Brand Identity with Shape Gram-mars[J]. Design Studies,2004.25(1): 1-9.
5. RAPHAELLE D, JEROME P, XAVIER F, et al. Identi-fication of Sensory Variables Towards the Integration of User Requirements into Preliminary Design[J]. In-ternational Journal of Industrial Ergonomics, 2007(37): 1-1.
6. Dou Jinhua. Design of walking aids for disabled persons based on semantic differential method [J]. Journal of Machine Design, 2014.31(6):118-121
7. Xu Jiang,Wang Haixian,Sun Shouqian.Method of product generative design based on style evolution model [J]. Journal of Southeast University(Natural Science Edition),.2012.42(4):654-657
8. Liu Zijian,Liang Jinfeng. Yaozhou Kiln Ceramic Decoration Based on Product Design DNA [J]. Packaging Engineering.2016.37(4):45-51
9. Zhao Chunyan. Folk Customs Artistic Style of Ornament's Veins on Yao Zhou Kiln Pottery Art [D]. Xi'an:Xi'an Academy of Fine Arts,2008.
10. Xu Zhanmin,Li Yang. Application of Extraction Model of Product Design Factors of Floral Culture [J]. Journal of Graphics.2017.38(1):45-51
11. Lu Zhaolin,Li Shengbo,Zhang Yue, et al.Product design oriented to industrial design.DNA Research status and progress [J]. Journal of Machine Design,2014.31(12):432-436.

MATEC Web of Conferences **176**, 02017 (2018) https://doi.org/10.1051/matecconf/201817602017
IFID 2018

The Color Application of the Representative Pop Art in Modern Design —— Illustrated by the Case of MAOS Design [i]

JI Qian [1], ZHENG Jiayu [1,a]

[1]Huazhong University of Science and Technology,430074 Wuhan

Abstract. This study uses Kuler tools to extract color from representative traditional Pop Art works. A total of 25 color samples have been extracted and put into the HSB model for position distribution analysis, while 70 color samples have been extracted from the Pop style modern design works. Through analyzing and contrasting the color samples of traditional pop art and modern pop art design work, the author has summarized the similarities and differences in order to provide new ideas for color research and application.

1 Overview of Pop Art style

Pop Art was born in the British art form in the mid-1950s, and Pop Art is also called neo-realism [1]. Pop is often regarded as a "popular, fashionable" acronym, so it represents a popular culture.

The characteristics of Pop style are mainly in the following three aspects [2]:

(1) Pursuing popularity and popular interest, emphasizing novelty and uniqueness in design, and adopting strong color processing.

(2) Pop style is not a simple and consistent style, but a mixture of various styles from the perspective of design.

(3) The pursuit of unique and rarity, it's constantly changing.

2 Color characteristics of Andy Warhol and Roy Lichtenstein's Pop Art works

Andy Warhol is the initiator and main advocator of the American Pop Art Movement and has made a unique contribution to the development of Pop Art [3]. (Figure 1).

Figure 1. The representative work of Andy Warhol. left: Marilyn Diptych, middle: Queen Elizabeth, Right: Cattle

As a superstar of Pop Art, Roy Lichtenstein has promoted a new era in the artistic expression of American painting. His works represent his humorous life [4]. (Figure 2).

Figure 2. The representative work of Roy Lichtenstein. In the Car (1963 painting)

Photoshop and Kuler is the main color extraction tools of the research. Andy Warhol's representative work Marilyn Monroe has been used as a trial exploration for color extraction. One of the method is to import the image into Photoshop and save it in web format to get the main colors. Photoshop extracts the colors, but also black strokes and gray shadows, however they are not the target research object in this paper, so Photoshop tools is not convenient for the study of the color. While through method 2, the image will be imported into Kuler, select the color scene button for extraction, there are 6 modes of color scene, including colorful, light, soft, deep, dark and customization, so method 2 is more suitable for the research. Figure 3 shows the Photoshop extraction color interface, and Figure 4 is the Kuler extraction color interface.

* Corresponding author: [a] 1104508815@qq.com

Figure 3. Photoshop extraction color interface

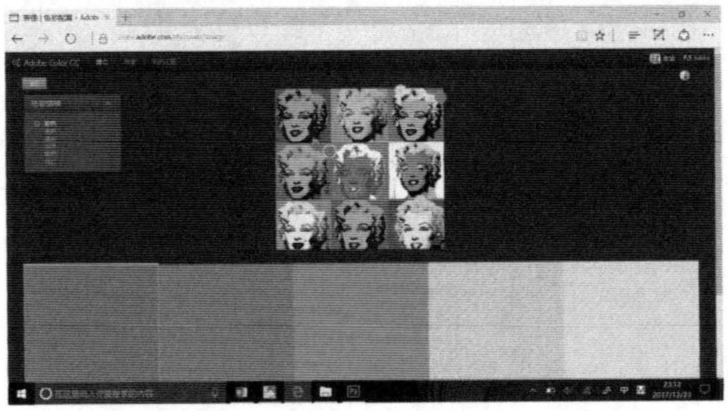

Figure 4. Kuler extraction color interface.

Kuler has been used to select the "colorful" mode for color extraction, and the color extraction analysis of the representative works of the two Pop Art leader figures can objectively summarize the color characteristics of Pop Art. Figure 5 is the color extraction by using Kuler.

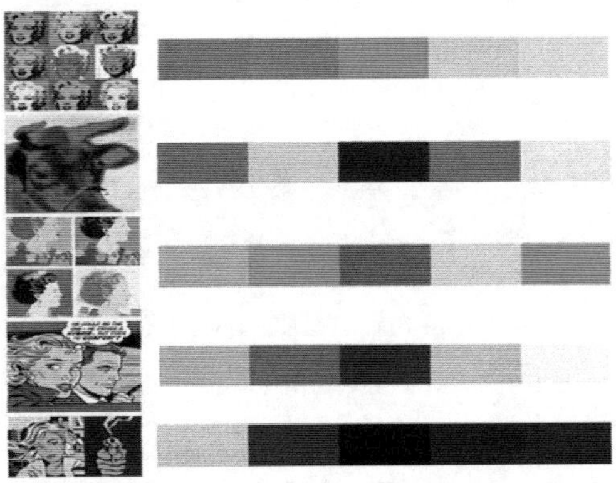

Figure 5. Color extraction by using Kuler

The color samples are extracted from the HSB value using a Photoshop color-sucking tool. The HSB is a color mode based on the human eye, where H represents the hue, S represents the saturation, and B represents the brightness [5]. Figure 6 is the HSB color model.

(1) Hue: In the standard color ring of 0 ~ 360 °, according to the angle value identification. For example, red is 0° and orange is 30° [6].

(2) Saturation: refers to the intensity or purity of the color. Saturation represents the proportion of color components in hue, measured as a percentage from 0% (gray) to 100% (fully saturated). Saturation on the colored facade gradually increases from inside to outside [7].

(3) Brightness: It is the degree of lightness and darkness of the color. It is usually measured from the percentage of 0 (black) to 100% (white). It gradually decreases from the top to the bottom in the color facade. The upper edge is 100%, the bottom line is 0% [8].

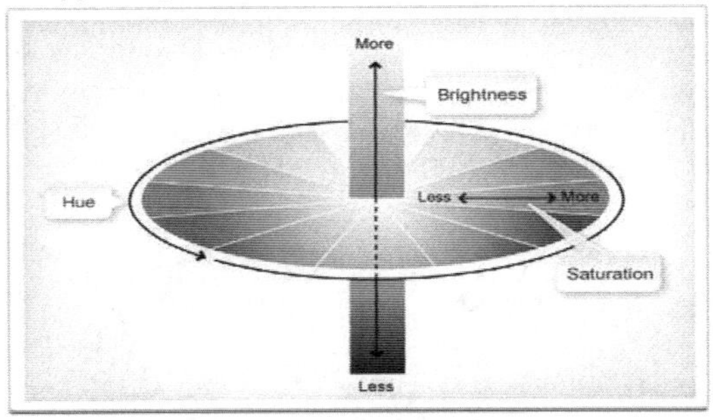

Figure 6. HSB color model

The extraction and analysis of the HSB values will provide the clues to obtain the main potential color rules of the representative Pop Art works. Figure 7 shows the HSB colors of pop art works.

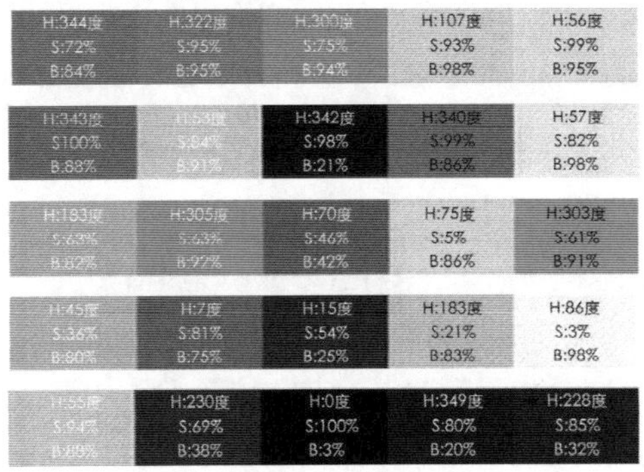

Figure 7. HSB colors of pop art works

Put the extracted color samples into the HSB model to get the color distribution of representative Pop Art works. Figure 8 shows the HSB color distribution map of them. According to the above analysis, there are 25 color samples extracted from the Pop Art representative works. The B is on the left side of the map and the H and S are on the right side of the map.

In the left B distribution chart, there are 17 out of the 25 sample points being located between 80% and 100%, accounting for 0.68; 7 out of the 25 sample points between 20% and 80%, accounting for 0.28; only 1 sample point between 0% and 20%, accounting for 0.04. Therefore, the brightness is higher in the above representative works of Pop art, the brightness is mainly above 80 %.

In the right H distribution chart, there are 9 samples between 0 to 90°, accounting for 0.36; 3 samples between 90 to 180°, accounting for 0.12; 3 samples between 180 to 270°, accounting for 0.12; 10 samples between 270 ~ 360 °, accounting for 0.4. Therefor in the above representative works of pop art design in the distribution of red, orange and purple more.

 https://doi.org/10.1051/matecconf/201817602017

In the right S distribution chart, there are 2 samples between 0%~20%, accounting for 0.08; 2 samples between 20%~40%, accounting for 0.08; 3 samples between 40%~60%, accounting for 0.12; 8 samples between 60%~80%, accounting for 0.32; 10 samples between 80%~100%, accounting for 0.4. Therefore, in the above pop art representative design samples, the saturation ratio is the mainly among 80% to 100%, and 72% of the samples are distributed between 60% and 100% of saturation; The saturation of the representative design works of pop art is high, and the saturation of most samples is above 60%.

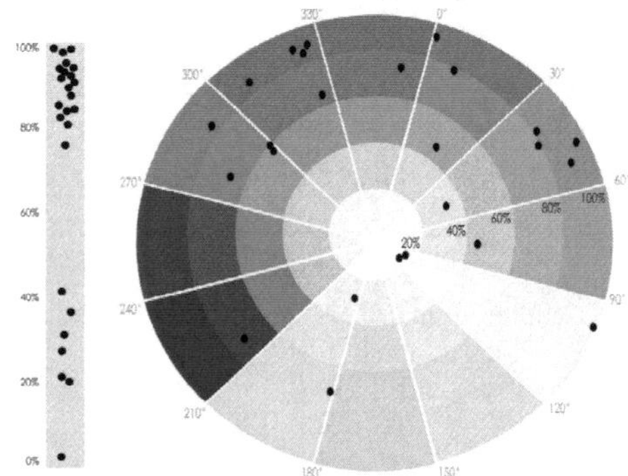

Figure 8. Pop Art representative works HSB color distribution. The left represents the sample brightness (B), the right represents the sample hue (H) and saturation (S)

3 The color application of representive Pop Art works in modern design

The style of Pop Art applications in modern design is numerous and extensive. The use of Pop Art style in graphic design can make people feel relaxed and pleased and have strong infectivity, can disseminate information while bringing people and art closer together [9]. MAOS is chosen to analyse the color of representative popular culture communication as an example in order to find the features of the modern pop style.

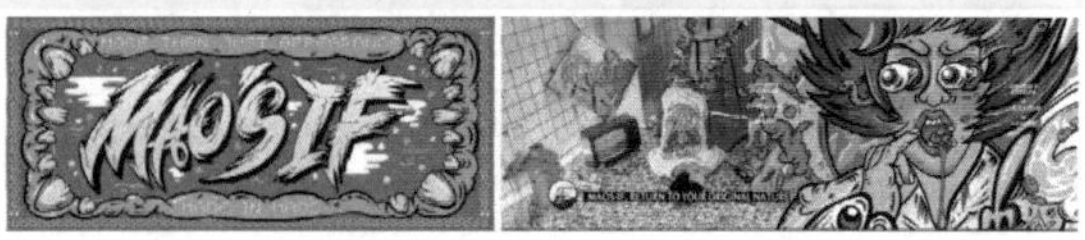

Figure 9. Works of MAOS

It is a cultural media company founded in Beijing by independent designer Mao Ting in 2015. The company's main production projects are brand image packaging, stage vision and visual image packaging of concert, party, TV, video platforms and online programs, such as "Sweet Talk", "Summer Sweetheart", "College students are here.", "Big vs. Trump", "The Temptation of Dinner" and "1.3 Billion Decibels". The influence of the program is very extensive. The main audiences of these programs are young people, they prefer the bold visual style. In the spread of popular culture, their works have subverted the entertainment industry's perception of visual packaging of variety shows; they are diverse in style and easy to attract attention. Figure 9 is a work of a seemingly cultural studio. In this section, color has been extracted and analysed of the two series of works designed by MAOS through the same methods.

The program with the most attention is the "Qipa Shuo" which is the first Chinese speech talent show created by Iqiyi in 2014. Its total hits have broken 100 million, and the amount of microblog topic readings also easily breaks the 1 billion marks. Attracted a large number of fans after 80s and 90s, figure 10 shows the color design of QiPaShuo. The designer said "pink is a candy color, on behalf of fun, cute and young; purple represents romantic, dreamy and authoritative; ice green is a symbol of fresh and clean sunlight. [10]" Those are 3 main colors that are commonly used in the show.

Seven graphic visual designs based on different scenes and themes for the posters of QiPaShuo have been analyzed to explore the color of the visual design, Figure 10 shows the color extraction of visual design.

Figure 10. Color extraction of QiPaShuo

In addition to the visual communication for the show, it also involves the product packaging design. Figure 11 shows that the color of packaging design for KFC, which reflects the youth's passion and trend is very bold.

Figure 11. KFC packaging design

Figure 12 shows the visual color extraction of KFC packaging.

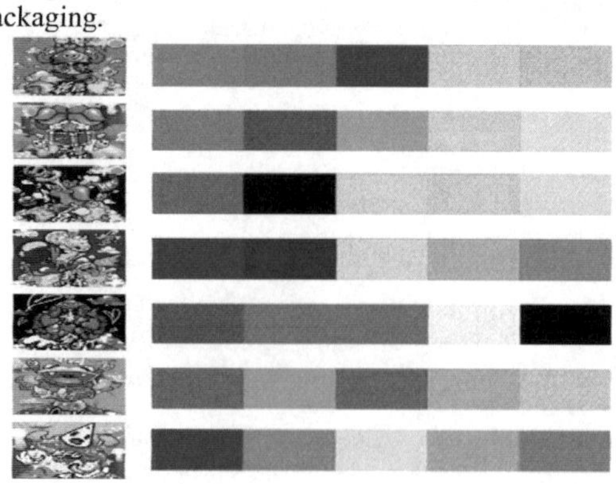

Figure 12. Color extraction of KFC

Using Photoshop to demonstrate the HSB values of the colors in QiPaShuo and KFC, Figure 13 shows the distribution of extracted colors in the HSB model, figure 14 is the HSB color distribution map. The series of works extracted above have a total of 70 color samples.

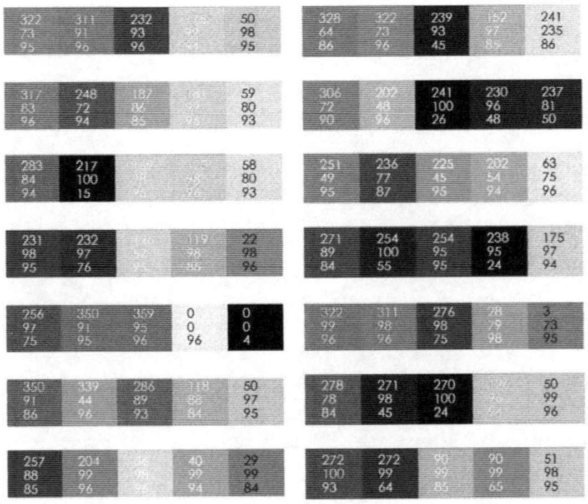

Figure 13. HSB value of QiPaShuo and KFC

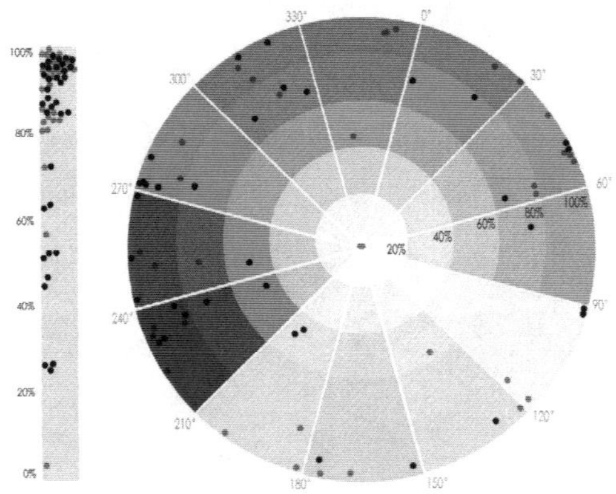

Figure 14. Color distribution in HSB of MAOS works. The left represents the sample brightness (B), the right represents the sample hue (H) and saturation (S)

It shows that the color samples are mainly distributed among 80%~100% in the saturation distribution chart, and mainly concentrated in the range of 70%~100% in brightness ratio distribution chart. Hue is larger in blue, purple and red, and other color samples are evenly distributed in hue.

4 Conclusion and outlook

The color brightness and saturation of Pop Art works are very high. The modern Pop Art works are more colorful than the initial Pop Art works, and the collocations are more diverse (Figure 15).

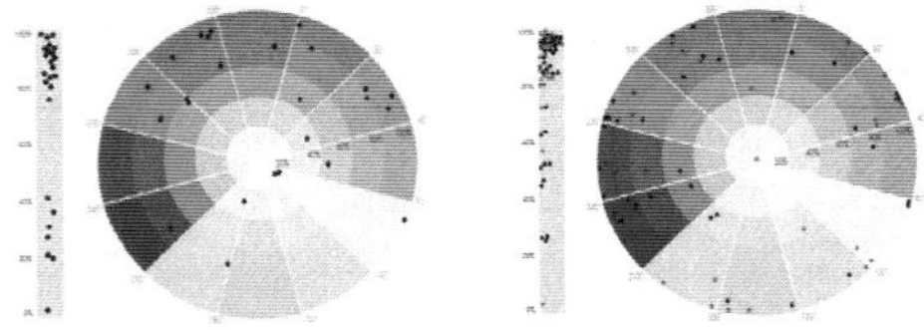

Figure 15. Color Distribution of Pop Art and modern works

This paper mainly discusses the distribution of color usage of Pop Art and modern design, Kuler is used to extract the colors in the works, and then analyzes the color samples through HSB to obtain the HSB color distribution map. However, this paper does not match the color of pop art and the analysis of the proportion of color in the screen is analyzed. How high saturation of the color will make the picture more harmonious and unified is the content of the follow-up discussion of the research, so as to deeply understand the color matching of Pop Art and get the principle of gorgeous matching instead of tacky collocation.

Acknowledgment

Supported by National Natural Science Foundation of China (Grant No: 51708236)
Supported by Fundamental Research Funds for the Central Universities (Grant No: 2016YXMS273)

References

1. L.Y. Li. Pop Art. M. People's Fine Arts Publishing House (2008)
2. X.L. Yin. Links between Fine Arts and Design from the Viewpoint Pop Art. J. Decoration, 2003(1):105-105.
3. M.T. Jiang. Pop Art Research by Andy Warhol. D. Anhui University of Finance and Economics, 2015.
4. Y.Liu, H. Liu. Behind the Image: Roy Lichtenstein Pop Art and Influence. J. Fine Arts, 2014(2).
5. G.S. Huang. Color Design. M. China Textile Press, 2001.
6. X.M. He, D.Q. Lu, J.L. Lu, et al. Research on the Color HSB Images of Women's Shoes. J. Packaging Engineering, 2017(14): 174-178.
7. L. Qu, N. Wang, G.Y. Wu, et al. Vehicle License Plate Location Based on Color Saturation and Character Features. J. Computer Technology and Development, 2003, 13(9):6-7.
8. H.Y. Wang, J. Shao, Y. Gao, et al. Color Design of Helmet Aiming Interface. J. Electro-optics & Control, 2016(6):64-67.
9. M.J. Hu. The Application of Pop Art in Modern Decorative Art: Taking Graphic Design as an Example. J. Art Education Research, 2017(13).

https://doi.org/10.1051/matecconf/201817602017

10. Y.Y. Chen. "QiPaShuo"—Rational Carnival under the Background of Visual Culture Communication. J . Journal Research Guide, 2015(11).

MATEC Web of Conferences **176**, 02018 (2018) https://doi.org/10.1051/matecconf/201817602018
IFID 2018

Outdoor Lighting Design Teaching Exploration with Creative Thinking as Its Core

Liu Xiaoxi[1,a,b], Chen Yansong[2] and Zhang Xinyue[1]

[1] Faculty of Arts, Communication University of China, 100024, Beijing, China
[2] Neuroscience and Intelligent Media Institute, Communication University of China, 100024,Beijing, China

Abstract. Creative thinking is the ability to think creatively. It is of great guidance for the development of lighting design major to combine the spirit of innovation and the advantage of creativity when designing. Based on intention extraction, space reconstruction, environmental narrative and system construction, this paper, integrating creative thinking construction into the task of the "Four Orders of Design" in outdoor lighting design, aims to help lighting design majors to form creative thinking and make an organic whole of technology and art in lighting design projects.

1 The significance of creative thinking in lighting design teaching

In modern society, lighting design, being a rising branch of professional design, corelates with several other fields and practice of this industry including architectural design, environmental art design, public art design. While integrating culture, art, environment, and technique, lighting design needs not only to satisfy public functional requirement of nighttime activities but also people's yearning for a better life. By sorting out the tendency and demand of lighting design market, one can easily find the strengthening epochal feature and increasing influence of lighting design. Light elements start to appear at urban space by means of interactive installation and media architecture. Therefore, it has become top priorities in lighting design teaching to incorporate concerning design concept and creative thinking into design of lighting environment and foster professionals with solid theoretical foundation and innovative design abilities.

Generally speaking, creative thinking is one of the primary drivers of design improvement and technological change [1]. For one thing, creative thinking of lighting design includes thinking through imagination, spatial thinking, logical thinking and systematic thinking. For another, it also absorbs the essence of art philosophy, artistic aesthetics, and art psychology. This paper holds that the process of lighting design shows a strong link of technique and art, which turns the production-centered design activity into solution-centered design activity. As a result, lighting design provides solution to complicated connection, which embodies in a variety of aspects such as innovation of design concept, regeneration development of nightscape, development of night economy, promotion of public participation and cultural communication. In David Kelley's opinion, the core aim of design education is to bring out the full creative potential in every student and make them feel delightful in creation through constant design training. Gradually their creativities will be strengthened and finally they themselves will gain creative confidence [2]. Therefore, the focal point and difficulty of this course is to foster creative thinking. We chose to explore practice design projects with openness, to guide students to incorporate creative thinking in the "Four Orders of Design" of lighting design. In this way we expect to systematically integrate technique and art, and finally solve the problem of complexity in designing.

* Corresponding author: [a] lxxcici@163.com

2 Exploration of curriculum design

The main theoretical knowledge of this course focused on the principle and method of outdoor lighting design along with its aesthetic presentation and art performance. On the practice part, taking the internal balance and coordination of the course into consideration, students were divided into several groups to fulfil the design task. The practice phase of this course adopted open proposition. With the design task being outdoor lighting design of "Baitasi Remade (the revival of the White Pagoda Temple)", students could choose any area of Baitasi (the White Pagoda Temple) historical and cultural preservation zone to perform their design. It is significant to impart the basic theoretical knowledge of outdoor lighting design to students. After that, this course endeavoured to foster students' creative thinking into each step of outdoor lighting design and lead them to apply multiple lighting elements and lighting medium in their practical project. Thus, the ultimate evaluation criteria of this course were not confined to the presentation of the design but the manifestation of creative thinking. It is required students to actively develop their thinking during the whole process, to take comprehensive consideration of environmental benefits, economic benefits and social benefit, and finally to reflect the kind of creative thinking with culture uniqueness and communication feature in their design task.

During the practice teaching part, the author also tried to organize the curriculum in the form of cooperative education with Folk Games, an undergraduate course from School of Animation and Digital Arts. Cooperative education holds the advantage to broaden the designing horizon and foster creative thinking for students from both courses. That especially helped lighting design majors to improve their abilities on the level of design "Activities" and "System". During the process of collaborative teaching, students from different professional background were grouped together and work collaboratively, in which way students from folk games course could also design their games creatively in different environment of urban space.

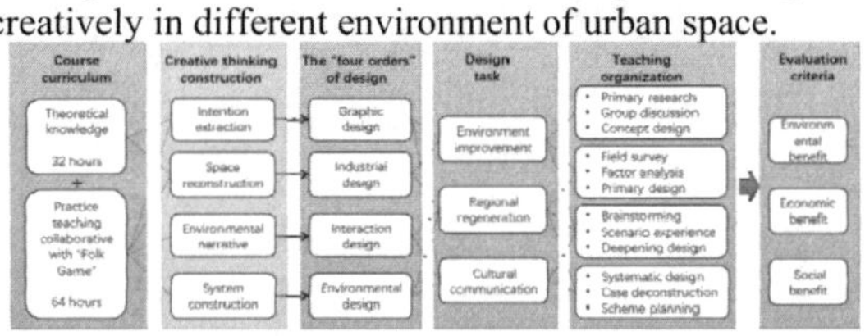

Figure 1. The curriculum design of outdoor lighting design with creative thinking as its core (created by the author)

3 The teaching practice with frame of creative thinking as its core

Lighting design has appeared and developed with people's constant pursuit of a better life. While cross-integrating with other fields of art, the connotation of lighting design is also enriched by its utility function and creative thinking. The main task of outdoor lighting design involves a whole process which unifies lighting elements application on physical level, concept efficient expression on presenting level, ensuring service experience on phycological level, combining public participation and smart technique on interacting level, as well as social culture and economy development on communication level.

"Four Orders of Design" means to categorize design projects into four layers: graphic design by using symbols and characters; industrial design by studying a physical object; interaction design by focusing on how human beings relate to other human beings through the mediating influence of products; and environmental design by organizing a system or environment [3]. "Four Orders of Design" begins to guide outdoor lighting design moving forward to a more mature direction when the practice task of the collaborative course develops from "tangible artifact" design activity to the balance of more complicated relations. However, to introduce creative thinking into the whole teaching process of this course, it needs to connect "Four Orders of Design" with creative thinking, and help students gradually transform from "primary design" to "secondary design".

3.1. Intention extraction based on imaginary thinking

After receiving the design task in the practice teaching part, students were asked to make background analysis, primary research and data integration to determine design area in accordance with the design task. During this process, creative thinking required students to, extending from thinking through imagination, create a new image through synthetic representation, analogy association, graphic externalization and symbols extension.

To be specific, students need analyze the spatial type of the selected area under the training of "intention extraction", extending the fundamental theories of outdoor lighting design to constructing different object spaces according to place, path and area, the three properties of the space [4], exploring comprehensively the expressions of different spaces, and finally abstracting the internal association. For instance, the design objects of figure 2, the street space, which belongs to path property, required students to focus more on small-scale scenes and linear symbols in extracting and analyzing intentions.

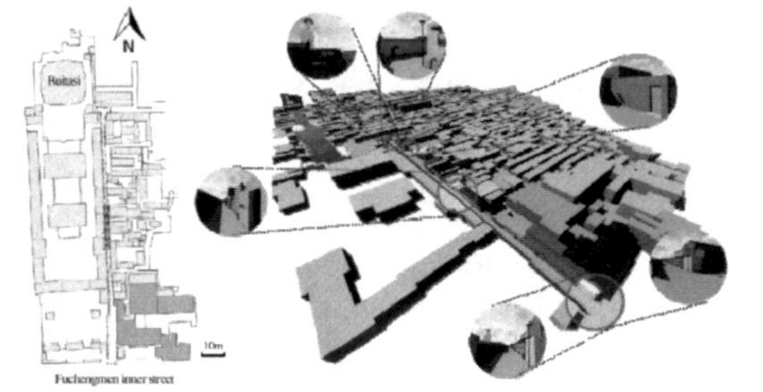

Figure 2. Analysis of design scheme of street space in selected topics (students' assignment)

"Intention extraction" is on the premise of taking prerequisite theoretical course. Initiating from the "origin" of design, it enables creative thinking to function on the dimension of performance by means of thinking through imagination and to explore the symbolic expressions using light as medium based on different space properties. This process is part of the initial design in teaching practice, therefore the overt and covert design factors are mixed, which is likely to lead to the vagueness of intention extraction and leaves much more creating space for the next step of design.

3.2. Spatial restructure based on spatial thinking

After establishing the design intention of outdoor lighting environment, students are needed to study the background information and material of the design objects elaborately and conduct in-depth researches on field survey. In this process, on the one hand, spatial thinking of creative thinking demanded students to systematically master the modification of space and the insertion and transfixion of dimensional interface. On the other hand, it required students to think comprehensively of the relations between object, human and space in design.

To put it in a more elaborate way, students needed to study the "tangible artifact" with its subjective elements (including the characteristics, visual aesthetics, physiology and psychology, main behavior patterns and relevant culture) and objective elements (including the geographical, climate, time and space environment features of site, relevant norms of the design, the latest technological innovations, era and economic background, sustainable development of design and communication of information etc.) in the design object, under the premise of constantly demonstrating and adjusting the physical dimension and performance dimension of the design.

The process of "spatial reconstruction" centers on human experience of the psychological dimension of lighting design, gradually representing the design intention in the reconstructed space by means of light elements. As shown in Figure 3, the quantitative design of light was expressed from the macro perspective through the research on spatial planning, analysis of the characteristics of visual horizon, investigation of the trend of crowd flow, contemplating lighting environment between object and space, human and space, space and space.

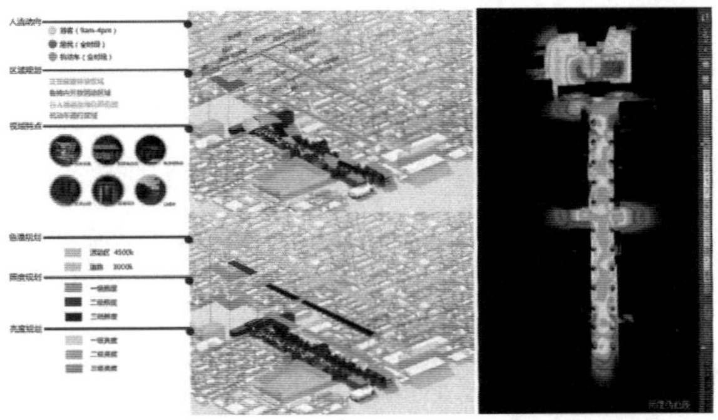

Figure 3. Space lighting design determined by analyzing subjective and objective elements (students' assignment)

3.3. Environmental narrative based on divergent thinking

After exploring the preliminary expression of "tangible artifact" in the design project, students have to think about the design of environmental narrative by divergent thinking. Environmental narrative asks students to master the basic regulations and rules of narrative, and moreover, to take objective realities into consideration. The existing theoretical knowledge and technologies of interactive design should be integrated into the artistic expression of outdoor lighting design by divergent thinking training. It could help students organize activities and events which can enhance experience, intensify emotion and build space narrative logic in their design projects.

This design process, driven by public participation on interaction level in lighting design, has creative thinking, in its divergent form, function on interaction design and focuses on interaction strategy and interaction means from the perspective of space narrative. Combing with the collaborative teaching of Folk Games, the lack of interactive technique could be compensated by the lighting design majors, and more lighting-centered artistic expression on visual presentation could be complemented by game design majors in the meantime. When creating activities and incidents of environmental narrative in divergent thinking, all types of "dynamic lighting" design, be it media architecture design on urban scale or dynamic lighting scene on street and space scale, as influential factors for visual cognition, should be analyzed thoroughly to be able to establish safe and friendly interacting experience in different environment [5]. This process significantly affects the quality and sensation of outdoor lighting environment. As can be seen in figure 4, by divergent thinking, students, taking the differences of subjects' age and gender into consideration, simulated specific "activities and incidents" in this chosen area. To establish safe and friendly interacting experience, the visual cognition effects should be analysed. And finally, the specific "object" and lighting elements for environmental narrative are designed.

Figure 4. Activities and incidents of lighting design caused by divergent thinking (students' assignment)

3.4. System construction based on systematic thinking

During teaching practice of outdoor lighting design, besides the graphic design of intention extraction, industrial design of tangible artifact, interaction design of environmental narrative, the fourth layers of "four orders of design", environmental design by organizing a system should also be paid more attention. Moreover, creative thinking, in the form of systematic thinking, guides us to ponder over communication elements including senders, receivers, channels, information, cultural codes and theme in a comprehensive way. Also, it leads us to apply innovative idea and communication theory in outdoor lighting design from environmental level, by which design strategy will be upgraded to a systematic level. And by means of integration and deduction, creative thinking and design will permeate itself with corresponding cultural background and spirit of time.

In the process of collaborative teaching, creative thinking, guided by "system construction", not only connected the artistry and technology beyond human being's production, life, work and entertainment, but also integrated several technological theories including multimedia technology, interaction technology and game technology into lighting design methodologies. In that way, Baitasi historical and cultural preservation zone was redesigned and the traditional culture was revitalized. Specifically speaking, after deeply delving the traditional regional culture of Baitasi area, students analyzed the connection between the environmental feature and interrelationship among human (substance) and environment. Given all those, to systematic perform creative outdoor lighting design from the communication perspective, the most environmental-suitable and communication-free design scheme was finally generated with traditional culture and folk games as the core of creative thinking.

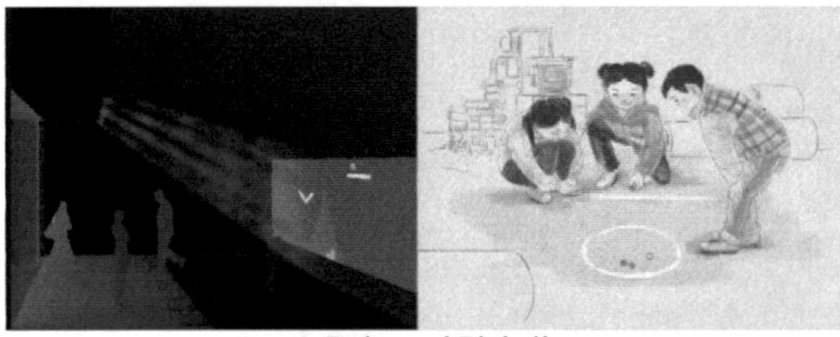

a. Baita and Pinball

b. Passing Luxun and Baita

Figure 5. Outdoor lighting design based on the creative strategy of traditional folk games (students' assignment)

Professor Amos Rapoport stated that environment holds meaning as part of a cultural system of symbols and influences our actions and our determinations of social order [6]. Environment is a non-verbal system and channel that allows designer and receiver to communicate between human and environment. The design of outdoor lighting environment in this layer aimed at realizing culture continuity, enables creative thinking function as systematic thinking on the dissemination of design. By deeply delving the connection between human(substance) and environment, human(substance) and local culture, this process enhances the interaction and entertainment of spatial experience, and to some extent, promote traditional folk culture to the modern world. As shown in fig.5a, traditional pinball game is the prototype of this creative design. Students used the red wall of Baitasi as the medium of motion-sensing game, borrowing the rules and strategy of playing traditional pinball game to invent a game named "Baita and Pinball". Fig.5b was a creative design, the game of Passing Luxun and Baita, prototyped on traditional hopscotch, using weight-sensing lighting tiles and interactive projection as medium and borrowing the form of hopscotch, bringing more folk elements and traditional culture for this historical and cultural preservation zone, meanwhile systematically associating the Luxun Museum with Baitasi.

4 Conclusion

Creative thinking construction in outdoor lighting environment is a process that starts from the "primary design" and continually develops towards the "secondary design". Besides, this teaching exploration with creative thinking construction as its core also complements the awkward situation of design education that "what we neglect, the value of exploration, experiment, insolubility and possibility, is exactly what may improve education quality and foster creativity" in China [7]. This course has injected traditional curriculum gene of Communication University of China into outdoor lighting design course. Students were encouraged to break the limit of their own major in practice, and they also integrated creative design thinking into each layer of the "Four Orders" of outdoor lighting design. By deconstructing and reconstructing, students performed lighting design on Baitasi historical and cultural preservation zone in an artistic, comfortable, and interactive way, which represented the cross-disciplinary and cross-medium feature of lighting design and its epochal influence.

Acknowledgment

This paper was funded by the project (51508301) of Natural Science Foundation of China, and was funded by Science and Technology Plans of Ministry of Housing and Urban-Rural Development of the People's Republic of China, and Opening Projects of Beijing Advanced Innovation Center for Future Urban Design, Beijing University of Civil Engineering and Architecture (UDC2017020312)

References

1. E. B. N. Sanders, P. J. Stappers, Co-design, **4(1)**, 5-18 (2008)
2. Q. Dai, W. Yang, B. Zhang, New Architecture, **2**, 112-115 (2012)
3. R. Buchanan, Design issues, **17(4)**, 3-23 (2001)
4. W. Zhu, *Space, Symbol, City: A Design Theory of City* (China Architecture & Building Press, Beijing, 1993)
5. X. Liu, Zhuangshi Journal, **3**, 101-103 (2016).
6. R. Amos, *The Meaning of the Built Environment: A Nonverbal Communication Approach* (University of Arizona Press, 1990)
7. L. Wu, Journal of Nanjing Arts Institute (Fine Arts & Design),**2**, 5-9(2014)

Teaching Research on the manual Model of Product Design

Liu Ying[1], Liu Xiaojing[1] and Chen Yi[2, a]

[1]Cnetral South University, Industrial Design Department, 410083 Changsha Hunan, China
[2]Guzhi Science and Technology Co., Ltd. 410083 Changsha Hunan, China

Abstract. This paper discribes the spatial thinking ability ,materials processing ,design easthetics application and technical implementation are four aspects that very important to cultivate students' professional quality when building a manual model. It stresses the handwork l model course has played positive significance in the aspect of design basic teaching under the background of High-Tech.

1 Introduction

In current teaching of Industrial Design major, the technical methods of model production has become abundant. The computer auxiliary manufacture and 3D printing technology can present the design effects in a rapid and accurate manner[1]. There numbers of softwares that can produce 3D spatial effect. However, its virtual effect has the 2D plane display feature, and the computer has certain limitations when shaped displaying (perspective view, chromatic aberration of layers, depth of field of camera etc.). In addition, the rapid processing technology directly generates the substantial results, and the teaching process can skip the process of design implementation[2]. It can be seen from the essence of experience-typed teaching, and the convenient technical methods cannot replace the process of direct experience accumulation completely. However, the process of handmade model can display or represent the design content through creating the actual space scene or repeating experience[3].Students can understand and construct knowledge, develop practical ability and generate design significance in the course of experiencing the deduction process.

2 Cultivation of professional ability

The handmade model is a form of 3D direct visual expression, which is the effective method of understanding the virtual space indention of product in the course of shaped design derivation[4]. The production process includes several steps,for example ,interpret drawings, identify drawings, spatial thinking, shape production, design elaboration, surface treatment. Each production step has different focus on the professional training of students. As a whole, manual model making is a practical training to cultivate students' spatial imagination ability, and to exercise students' ability to solve design problems according to the actual situation.

2 .1 Imagination thinking methods

Designing drawings is the basis for model production and it is the special "Visual Language" of designers[5]. Model production firstly requires the students to learn how to interpret drawings and identify drawing, recognize the marks, labels and rules of graphical representation, understand various graphic symbols as the designing language, as well as master the meaning of various designing elements. The purpose of interpreting drawings and identifying drawing is to construct the 2D-typed graphical description as the virtual 3D spatial in mind. The process is the result of mutual penetration operation and mutual deepened complementation of two kinds of imagination thinking methods.

The handmade model is a converting process of designing concept from 2D graphic representations to 3D substantial space. It enables students to present designing thinking from 3D visual field and sense the stereoscopic space relationship. It reflect the complex spatial problems which cannot be understood in the plane drawings. Beginners are not good at space analysis and shaping they usually be constrained to the 2D plane concepts on the draft designing step of graphical analysis and shape treatment with short thinking on the structure, organization and composition in space. Decompose the spatial structure by modeling, make use of internal and external consistency of space as well as the penetration of space to generate the medium for participating space and experiencing designing elements.

Through the visual observation and sensation to the handmade model, Students can understand the relationship between structure and surface, part and whole, as well as unit and environment. The whole process enables students to directly feel the physical dimension and the sense of space[6]. Comparing the spatial conditions with the graphical conditions, and the various emerging problems on substantial shapes can

* Corresponding author: a 48316365@qq.com

strengthen the controlling ability of students to the spatial shape and ratio scale from 3D visual field.

2.2 Knowledge of materials

Through the handmade model, Students can directly learn some relevant knowledge on the structural properties and shaping process of model materials etc[7]. Understanding the properties of materials is the basis of designing, Otherness of products' function and shapes determines their diversity, process involved in the model production. Teachers have to help students to improve basic cognition on materials technology through theory lectures and demonstrations,so，students can gradually accumulate knowledge about properties of materials and experiences of processing technology.

Except physical properties, product design also emphasize the sensation of materials. The texture property of materials and expression of beauty sense are realized in the materials selection and visual configuration. Many sorts of textures that formed by architectual difference of material show characteristics of diferrent texture . The perceptual system of human beings obtain the perceptual information from the surface texture properties of model so as to generate the experienced psychological comprehensive senses: soft and hard, light and weight, cold and warm, dry and wet, thick and thin etc. The material, texture and physical properties etc. for the materials of model are all the conditions that need to be considered by the students when selecting the materials of model[8].

2.3 Aesthetic experience

The manual model is the miniature reflection of the design content. It represents the design concept with the elements of the entity shape, the structure line, the volume relation and so on, and needs to conform to the law of the design form beauty. The basis of formal beauty is a sense of balance between vision and psychology, which comes from the balance of form, colour and space. Students must abide by the rules of proportion and scale, rhythm and rhythm, contrast and unity in the process of manual model making. The structure lines, the outline lines and the parting lines need to be strengthened in different degrees. The functional view plane, transition surface and subtraction surface also require the variation of space rhythm. In addition, the training of colour in manual model making has higher requirements than graphic design. The colour processing of the model is not only the generalization of the design effect, but also the colour change factor under the condition of space light. The intensity, angle, distance and environment of the light source will have a direct impact on the colour performance of the model, even with the original design effect diagram to produce the colour difference.

From the visual performance point of view, the manual model should not only reflect the design content intuitively and objectively, The application of aesthetics and the treatment of art can enrich the students aesthetic experience and enhance the theoretical learning effect of design aesthetics. This kind of aesthetics is very important for the design works to have artistic appeal

2.4 Craft skills

Skilled process is the guarantee of model making implementation. Students need to be trained in the relevant knowledge and be able to master various process and tool operation skills. Manual model making process can intuitively show the process of processing operation. Students can experience the characteristics of various tools by hand operation and understand the specific use method. In view of some exploratory design, the performance of some products, such as strength, rigidity, vibration and noise, needs to be proved repeatedly. Students need to analyze and calculate the manual model to get the relevant data of product structure and performance, and then apply the results of theoretical analysis and size structure to the improvement of the model. The students can verify the rationality of theoretical analysis by handwork model making, and provide the feasibility basis for the model to the actual production transformation of the product.

Based on the technical implementation of each process, students can express the design ideas more freely, consolidate the professional theory knowledge, and solidify the basis for the design practice work in the future.

As for the technical implementation of each production step, the students are able to freely express their own designing concepts, strengthen the professional theoretic knowledge, as well as reinforce the foundation for the practical design work in the future.

3 Conclusion

Basing on the above analysis,by handwork model making, students can understand the form connection of each interface in the space in an all-round way, and train the students to look at the design content in a systematic way, so as to avoid forming one-sided and isolated design thinking formula. From the abstract form to the two-dimensional scheme presupposition to the three-dimensional entity model, with the three-dimensional deepening of the graphic thinking, Manual model making provides an experience-intuitive experience process for students to design ideas, and an effective teaching method for college design education to break through the teaching cycle of from picture to picture.

Acknowledgment

The paper is the final supporting material for Hunan philosophy and social science foundation project "Industrial design value and performance evaluation research", Item No.: 16yba369

References

1. Gong Wenfei, Yu Huilan, Improve Practical Ability Starts from Model Production-Research on Teaching of Model Production for Students in Industrial Design Major [J]. Changchun University of Science and Technology Academic Journal (High-education), 04 (2007)
2. Bao Lei. Analysis on Substatial Model Design and Production of Industrial Design. Nanjing University of the Arts Academic Journal (Arts and Design), 02 (2008)
3. Liander• Caney. Spirit of Apple Design: Johnny•Ive. Times Press, 09 (2014)
4. Liu Ming. Research on Practical Teaching of Product Design Major. Teaching Practice and Exploration, 06 (2016).
5. Liu Guanzhong, Design is an indestructible "The Third Wisdom"of Human Beings in Future [J] Design, 12 (2013).
6. Lin Jiaxin, Wang Huabing etc. Current Status and Exploration of Industrial Design ABS Model Production Teaching Experience.Tu Xue Academic Journal, 07 (2013)
7. Zhao Jianghong. Meaning of Design Arts.Hunan University Press, 04 (2005).
8. Yao Limin, Duan Wenyu. Analysis on Teaching Method Reform in High Education.China University Teaching, 08 (2013)
9. Wu Qiong. Materials and Process Analysis on Product Handmade Model. Package Engineering, 29 (2008.)
10. Wu Qiong. Draft Model and Product Design.Mechanical Design, 23 (2006).

Discuss the application of innovative service thinking in the design of qualia goods---Take the case of The One South Garden as an example

Wei Bi[1,2], Ju Wu[2] and Rungtai Lin [2]

[1]School of Jewellery, West Yunnan University of Applied Sciences,
[2]Graduate School of Creative Industry Design,National Taiwan University of Arts

Abstract: In recent years, aesthetics is rising rapidly accompanied by the knowledge economy, and the government has also begun to put forth effort to carry out the concept of designing service industry chain, and its emphasis is on how to add value of design creativity in culture, achieve design industry, and form an aesthetic economy. The creative life industry refers to the "core knowledge" that integrates the life industry with creativity, providing life industry of "deep experience" and "high-quality aesthetic feeling". It emphasizes that because of adapting to the trend of cultural economy and experience economy, it shall take customer experience as the core, through "products", "services", "activities" and "fields" to satisfy the consumer's life proposition, create a unique taste of life, and form a life style recognized by the consumer and through innovative service thinking to attract consumers' attention and maintain consumers' deep moving. The creative life industry has the characteristics of cultural life and industrial culture. Facing the trend of experience economy, it is an important issue to be discussed in depth how the creative life industry uses "experience" to develop customer experience values, thereby create economic benefits and deeply cultivate cultural values. Therefore, this study discusses how to use "perceptual fields" and "qualia products" through the case of The One South Park to strengthen and deeply cultivate the moving of consumers, to simulate how to transform from an invisible qualia experience into a tangible creative product, and to provide a reference for enterprises that want to enhance their industrial competitiveness with a qualia experience.

1 Preface

In recent years, the decline of traditional industries has made it necessary for us to change our thinking and discuss out a new mode of industrial thinking. If the traditional industry wants to have a certain status in the future, it must have its own cultural brand. In addition to the promotion of technology, it must also have both creative design and humanistic care. How to transform "culture" into "creativity" and add value of products "design", that is, how does "cultural creativity" "add value of design". It will be the primary topic for Taiwan to develop a cultural and creative industry and enhance the competitiveness of the design industry in the future. The economic development of Taiwan has gradually evolved from "manufacturing economy" to "knowledge economy" and "creative economy", and it has begun to think about how to go from "professional subcontractor" to "brand" or "design" which has higher value.

At present, many industries are in the transitional period and their focus of the economy has gradually shifted from the traditional manufacturing industry to the service industry. And the goods purchased by consumers are no longer just the entities of commodities themselves, furthermore, it is further extended to the intangible meaning and identity behind the goods. Therefore, a product that is only material and meaningless will no longer attract the attention of consumers. Only goods with "style" and "aesthetics" can outshine others; that is, generally so-called "taste" goods. It is also because design and aesthetics have gradually become an important element of the commodity itself, and matched with its own "quality" and the "brand" element that can enhance the added value, and then the "Qualia" is gradually focused and constructed. Through the combination of three aspects of the "taste" of design, aesthetics perspectives, the "quality" of manufacturing perspectives, and "branding" of marketing perspectives, it can create "Qualia" goods that make consumers feel happy, unique, and happy, which is the direction of service innovation design and development in the future.

In recent years, aesthetics is rising rapidly accompanied by the knowledge economy. The government has actively designed the concept of industrial chain to set up a plan for the development of a cultural and creative industry. The emphasis of the entire cultural and creative industry plan is on how cultures add value to "design creativity" to become profitable "cultural businesses", and then to form an "esthetic economy". Today, enterprises face the impact of "economic globalization". How to combine culture to develop their design creativity and face the challenge of the wave of "market globalization" with "design in geochemistry" to create product features. On the other hand, the concept of "consumer-centric" service innovation design plays a key role in aesthetics economy and experience design. It is also the primary topic for Taiwan to develop its creative life industry and enhance the competitiveness of the design industry in the future.

The creative life industry has the characteristics of cultural life and industrial culture. Facing the trend of experience economy, it is an important issue worth discussing deeply how the creative life industry uses "experience" to develop customer experience values, thereby creating economic benefits and deeply cultivating cultural values. This study combines experience-related theories and models and proposes the "qualia experience model". And it discusses how to use "sensitive fields", "moving experience" and "qualia products" through the case of The One South Garden to strengthen and deeply cultivate the moving of consumers. Under the thinking of service innovation design, it provides a reference for the enterprise to move toward the qualia experience economy, and serves as an aim to fully enhance the competitiveness of small and medium-sized enterprises.

2 Discussion of literature

Lin Rongtai proposes the "integration of cultural, aesthetic economy contributed to the aesthetic design of new industries" and hopes that through the introduction of culture, technology, and aesthetics, the cultural and creative industries are transformed into a creative life industry based on "service innovation". According to the various industries defined by the Cultural and Creative Industries Promotion Group in Economic Ministry, the definition of the creative life industry refers to "integrating the core knowledge of the life industry with creativity to provide an industry with deep experience and high quality aesthetic feeling". The main contents include three major elements of "core knowledge", "deep experience" and "high quality beauty". The characteristics of the life creative industries are based on existing industries and framed on the use of life culture, aesthetics, and creativity. Through the design of creative life and providing quality living experiences, the business model of integrated service innovation and design has been developed. The relevant literature of experiences, perceptual field and qualia goods we have discussed are as follows:

2.1 Experience economy

Pine II and Gilmore put forward the theory of "experience economy" and regard "experience" as the output of economic type from the value produced by economic activity. It is also an added value of tradable money and goods or commodity. Pine II and Gilmore have further divided the value of economic activity output into four types of goods: commodities, goods, services, and experience from the consumption experience. Li Renfang has the following instructions in the preface to the Chinese version of the book, for the enterprise managers: "If you charge for raw materials, you are a primary product company. If you charge for tangible product, you are a commodity company. If you charge for your activity, you are the service company. If you charge for the time you spend with your customers, you are experience company."

With the rise of experience economy and the transformation of consumption patterns, the symbolic meaning of consumption has evolved from satisfying the basic usage needs to becoming a reflection of consumers' pursuit of self-style identity and life value. Therefore, the core value of future products has changed from the past "use" satisfaction to the "user" pleasure, which is the so-called "From Use to User", and from the manifestation of "function" in the past to the "feeling" experience of users, which is the so-called "From Function to Feeling". Finally, the value of the product has also changed from the pursuit of "hi-tech" quality to the appeal the taste of "hi-touch", which is the called "From Hi-tech to Hi-touch". Therefore, the intangible perceptual value behind the product gradually exceeds the use value of the goods and becomes a key factor influencing consumers' purchase behavior (Lin Rongtai, Lin Boxian, 2009).

2.2 Perceptual field

Space is a situation and a way of telling stories. From the display design of showcases to the design of large-scale playgrounds, that is a field that creates atmosphere through situational design. In the life style of new life ideas and experiencing new values, a type of leisure life through the field has already quietly entered the lives of Taiwan consumers. From the IKEA of the Metropolis Shopping Centre to the lavender forests in the outskirts of the country, or The One South Garden, where all show the experience charm created by the field. Imagine that a couple, who hold their hands with each other, walk in the field created by IKEA and sit on the IKEA sofa in the living room to feel the warmth of the home. Then they copy the product number with the imagination created by the field to the downstairs warehouse to find boxes of products. This is the situational experience that IKEA creates for the customer to build a home.

Many researchers have mentioned that through the creation of a physical environment, many clues can be provided to consumers. These suggestions have a big impact on customers' impressions. Bitner (1992) first defined the service field as "do effective service behavior in specific physical environment". Lin (2004) used the concept of gestalt psychology to discuss and explain how individuals obtain impressions from the service field, and produce emotional reactions. Therefore, whether it is a trendy or open display design, and consumers or visitors may want to bring home the IKEA consumer field setting situation, because its situation display has evoked the consumer's past experience, or some emotional factors. Therefore, how does the spatial field create to satisfy the customer's psychology and what kind of experience or image does the spatial field bring to the customer? From a perceptual engineering point of view, a successful emotional field includes three levels:

(1) Can the customer see (situational perception)?

(2) Can the customer understand (situational awareness)?

(3) Can the customer be moved (to change behavior)? In short, a successful emotional fields must attract customers through the design of the field, and then allow customers to feel the function of creating a situation, and finally, to achieve the purpose of moving the soul of the consumer. This is the main purpose of this study.

2.3 Qualia goods

The so-called "Qualia" is a kind of life meaning and emotional satisfaction, and it touches the deepest feelings in consumer's heart with a touching romance. Qualiagoodsor services extend on the basis of quality, constructuniqueness and increasethe added value of goods and services through the presentation of five qualias of perceptual value, namely, Attractiveness, Beauty, Creativity, Delicacy and Engineering, and then arousecustomer's spiritual joy and moving.What is the difference between qualiagoods and general industrial products? The design of general industrial products in the past focuses on "function" (use), but the design of qualiagoods in the future focuses on "people" (user). Qualiagoods pursue the aesthetic features of "art", and general industrial products pursue "standard" technical specifications, so the difference is that aesthetic features of "art" are the requirements for "people", while "standard" technical specificationsare the quality control of "objects".Qualia goods are the expression of "human nature",and general industrial products are the pursuit of "propertyof objects"; qualiagoods are the pursuit of sensibility, and general industrial products are the demand of "reason"; and qualiagoods focus on "story", and general industrial products pursue "rationality". We need some stories to embellish our lives, and good qualiagoods usually have a moving story, that's why qualiagoods touch people. The concept of qualiagoods is generally arranged as follows: science and technology is the basis of qualia goods, so pursue "perceptual science and technology"; human nature is the beginning of qualia products, so focuson "humanistic design"; and culture is the source of design thinking,so pursue "qualia creativity". Therefore, modern designers must integrate "perceptual science and technology" and "humanistic design" to create a humanized product and service environment with "qualia creativity".

3 Research methodand framework

This study is basically based on the research framework of "Integrate culture and aesthetic economy to promoteemerging industries of aesthetic design" proposed by Lin Rongtai.In terms of creative life industry, design can be divided into four assessment dimensions: core knowledge, deep experience, high-quality aesthetic feeling, and life advocacy.In terms of the design of creative living goods, Lin Rongtai (2008) divides the added value of the design of creative living goodsinto four stages, namely, added value of science and technology, cultural creativity, aesthetic experience and economic benefits in the middle of the upper half of Figure 1. In terms of service innovation design, each sub-plan is based on this framework, and then cooperates with the goals ofoverall plan to achieve the service innovation design of life creativity, life style, life taste and lifepattern, formingthe results both studied separately and integratedunder common framework, such as the integration of three levels and different stagesin Figure 1.

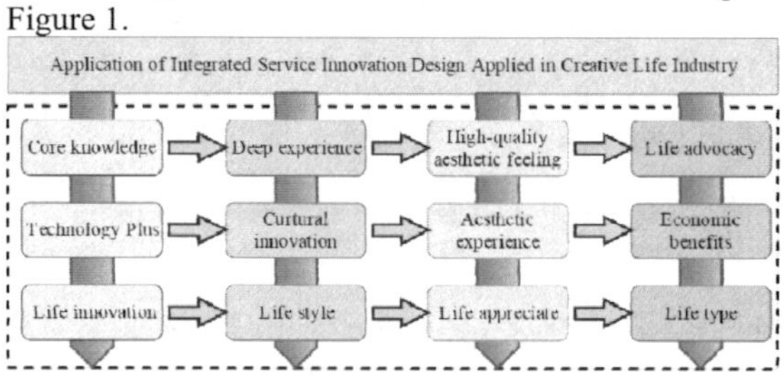

Figure 1. Research framework for integrating creative life industry (Lin Rongtai, 2008)

In order to achieve the purpose of applying service innovation design to creative life industry, this study plans to integrate four assessment dimensions, namely, core knowledge, deep experience, high-quality aesthetic feeling and life advocacy, and discusses the industrial chain of service innovation design through experience design and aesthetic experience. And then according to the concept of design chain, this study introduces the concept of service innovation design into the sustainable management model of creative life industry, that is, combine the creative model of cultural products and the management model of enterprises, as shown in Figure 1. From Figure 1, we can clearly see the vertical integration of the depth of upper, middle and lower reaches of the research plan and the combination of horizontal breadth, which can achieve the goal of sustainable development of creative life industry through transforming the creativity of service innovation into the design ofscientific and technological goods. And then through the horizontal connectionin the research process, each sub-plan has its own research goal, and through the integration of research procedures, the relationship between each other can be formed and the goal of integrated research can be achieved.

According to the above analysis, the creative life industry is based on the integration of culture and aesthetic economy, and it promotes the integration of cultural art and science and technology through the development of life industry, and its actual practice for promotion is to useaesthetic economy to stimulate cross-field industry innovation and achieve the goal of promoting the development of emerging industries.Its overall goal is as follows: integrate culture and science and technology and shape Taiwan style; create aesthetic economy and rebuild Taiwanmiracle. And then according to the above framework of aesthetic economy, from the four aspects of culture, science and technology, aesthetics and economy, the four goals of this integrated research plan are as follows:

(1) culture is the life style, and it needs promotion strategy with endless creativity;

(2) science and technology is the life creativity, and it needs pragmatic approach supported by design;

(3) aesthetics is the life taste, and it needs the promotion activities involving the participation of the whole people;

(4) economyis the life pattern, and it needs life concept of the overall construction.

These goals can be two levels: innovation opportunity and entrepreneurial opportunity. In the first level, innovation opportunity formulates and implements specific and effective strategies and measures by aiming at specific key issues in traditional industry, technology industry and design service industry, and enhances the innovative competitiveness of various design industries through life pattern and life creativity by means of culture and technology.In the second level, entrepreneurial opportunity creates life taste and life style in an all-round way by means of aesthetics and economy, and comprehensively promotesand strengthens the design research, design talent training and cross-industry or horizontal alliances to form the creative life industry through the promotion of the aesthetics of the whole people, thus enhancing the overall energy and image of Taiwan's creative life industry.

4 Case study

In 1980s, architect Han Baode and the owner of South GardenWang Tiwumet each other, and then a unique garden that combines the characteristics of Jiangnan garden, traditional China and Fujian style building was created, with 27 hectares of boundless green area and valleys hiding in, it is like the pavilion in wonderland, as shown in Figure 2. The original idea of founder Wang is to build a farm as the place for the aged to share family happiness and enjoy nature withtheir relatives and friends.Mr. Han Baodeproposes to build a Jiangnan style garden in accordance with the features of the terrain, because only by creating an independent Paradise can truly wash away the uproar and relax the mind and body.Historical reasonscreate the perceptual field of South Garden, just as the architect of South Garden Han Baode said: "It's hard to imagine the realization of this dream, how fortunate I am to finish it in such a short time,maybe it's a chance that Ji Cheng and Li Yu expect but fail to grasp". (Lin Rongtai, 2010) "The One" is a life style brand established by The One. With the pursuitof "harmonious and happy" life as the goal, a humanistic insistence, a creative viewpoint, and an original thinking, through concrete deduction of design value, are integrated into the objects and fields in life, and play therole of the bridge forfive senses and six feelings of beautiful life. The One believes that design starts from life, and every aspect of life begins with "one", build a day's time, a space, an attitude, and a life.What The One provides is every simple "one", and we can see the obvious life style of The One in every day, every point and every detail of life. The One takes the transfer of oriental aesthetics as its duty, and it is different from the traditional creation concept of totem thinking in the east, and we interpret the new oriental humanistic feelings with simple and gorgeous design style.Simpleness is a choice for extreme simple materials, and also a humanistic persistence with warm meaning; and gorgeousness is a true color inadvertently revealed, and also a spirit of craft carving.We experience the initial and final movement of life between the constringency of simpleness and the luxury of gorgeousness. We show the connotations of qualia goods and pass the life style of The One with the use of extreme simple materials, a humanistic persistence with warm meaning, an oriental freehand aesthetic view, and a spirit of craft carving.

In the early spring of 2007, The One reconstructed the "perceptual field" of South Garden with the spirit of "restoring the old as the old", adhered to the "simple and gorgeous" design aesthetics, selected a lot of materials from South Garden as design elements, and designed the "qualia goods with" life aesthetics; and combined the qualia goodsadvocating simple life and the "perceptual field" with rich cultural deposits to achieve the model of creative life industry. In the mid autumn of 2008, The one Humanistic Leisure Inn of South Garden was opened again to provide five senses and six feelings of new experience for modern gentlemen and beauties.Based on the four functions in Figure 4, this paper studies how The One South Garden buildsthequalia goods into the model of creative life industry through perceptual field.A brief description is as follows:

(1) Field experience (feast eyes): when first come to South Garden, the "ancientry recalling emotion" of Jiangnan garden arouses, after savoring and slow travel, the style combined with the local characteristicsappears indistinctly. When enter wing room, the "simple and gorgeous"design style of The One is shown in the elegance and tranquility, and the simple and low-key designis the best interpretation of "modern fashion".The graceful"modern fashion" is shown in the "ancientry recalling emotion" of Jiangnan garden; the service area of South Garden has made the best use of the virtues of"ancientry recalling emotion" and "modern fashion".

(2) Experience activity (far from uproar): when first come to South Garden, the experience of green bamboo and traildeclares the "far from uproar". The subsequent "green hill, green valley, colorful butterfly, blue magpie and white egret, chirping of cicadas, crowing of birds, croaking of frogs, goose's song and water's sound, after rain, when fog, and under the first sun, the day curtain and the moonlight", are the in-depth experience activities. With the guidance of the artist in the village and the striking charm on the red brick, customers immerse themselves in a zither music situation before dinner, and will have the new experience of human leisure, feel 27 hectares of boundless green area, experience the quiet of

South Garden, but not see the graceful charm of South Garden, thus the goal of "far from uproar" is achieved.

(3)Cultural connotation (self study): cultural connotation includes formand ritual. The architectural design of South Garden shows the elements of Chinese garden building: pavilion, platform, building, attic, hall, shed, porch, bridge, etc, which are the main forms of garden building, andalso shows the inner symbolic meaning through the ingenious forms. For example, the vaseshaped gate with the shape of vase (form) contains the symbolic meaning of safe come-in and go-out (ritual). The building of South Garden integrates Taiwan's local characteristics such as red brick, red tile, cypress wood, and so on, thus creating a unique garden building and forming another architectural ceremony.The rich cultural deposits of South Garden allow customers to learn various forms and rituals from the experience inthe building of South Garden and understand cultural connotation, thus the effect of "self study" is achieved.

(4) Five-sense experience (entertain oneself as well as others): through the aforementioned qualia goods and customers' experience of five senses and six feelings, The One strengthens the customers'impression on the experience. Taking bambooknown as oriental gentlemanas the design concept, scholars describe bamboo as "sage and gentleman", and the designer turns the image of "bamboo joint" into the dining utensils on the table to praise bamboo's solid root, straight personality, empty heart, chastity, and other characters and sentiments and further present bamboo's simple but elegant, and quiet beauty. Through this kind of qualia goodsfull of senses and feelings, customers are easy to immerse themselves in and re-tell the story of their experience, thus the purpose of "entertaining oneself as well as others" is achieved.

5 Conclusion

"Culture" is a kind of life style, "design" is a kind of life taste, "creativity" is a kind of recognition by moving, and "industry' is the medium, means or method to realize cultural design creativity.Therefore, on the cultural level, through cultural creativity, design achieves a kind of design taste and forms a life style through industry.The creative life industry displays the charm of qualia goods through perceptual field, that is, "form products and apply to life". Therefore, the essence of qualia goods is"practical", the result is "pragmatic", and the value is "life oriented".

In terms of perceptual field, design is a cultural creative activity, and its ultimate goal is to form life culture and create perceptual living environment.On the other hand, design is a comprehensive shaping activity with purposes, conditions, rationalization and creativity, and it focuses on the "sociality" of the interaction between "man and objects"; reasonable shaping combining "physical function" and "psychological function" pays attention to "man machine system"and consider "human factor engineering"; finally, the design is integrated into "economic activities" to create "life style", form "life culture", and achieve "perceptual" living environment.

Through the case The One South Garden, this paper discusses how to strengthen and deeply touch consumers through "perceptual field" and "qualia goods", and it just shows the tip of the iceberg of creative life industry, serves as a trigger and provides relevant research reference. The related issues about how to use the cultural deposits of "perceptual field" and "qualia goods" to cultivate cultural value and create economic benefits in the futureshould be further discussed.

References

1. Baer, D., Wolf, M., & Risley, R. (1968). *Some current dimensions of applied behavior analysis. Journal of Applied Behavior Analysis*, 1, 91 - 97.
2. Jackson, R. and Halle, M. (1956). *The Fundamentals of Language, The Hague: Mouton.*
3. Norman, D. A. (1988). The Psychology of Everyday Things. New York: Basic Boks.
4. Read, H. (1967). Education Through Art. London: Faber and Faber.
5. Read, H. (1967). Education Through Art. London: Faber and Faber.
6. Rubin, J.A. (1984). Child art therapy. New York: Van Nostrand Reinhold.
7. .Lin Rongtai, Sun Mingxian, Tu Liangjin (2008).Exploring Autistic Children's Inner World with Mental Models. The 13th Annual Conference and Symposium of the Design Society of the Republic of China, May 17th, 2008, Chang Gung University. Human Factors Engineering and Cognition, P162.
8. Lin Rongtai, Tu Liangjin, Sun Mingxian, Xie Yicheng, Huang Yuanqing, and Zhang Yaping (2009). The Model of Communication Beyond Language: A Case Study of Autistic Children's Image Communication. International Symposium and Collection of Papers on Special Education and Art psychotherapies, May 30, 2009, National Taizhong University of Education(NTZUE). Children's Art Psychotherapies for Children with Difficulties in Health Care and Emotion, P55.

Emerging Roles in Design Expansion: 'The Third Group' Involved in Design

Chen Xiang[1] and Wei Liu[1,a]

[1]College of Design and Innovation, Tongji University, Shanghai, China, 200092

Abstract. Design, regarded as the key factor of innovation, has evidently developed diversified designer-user relationships in order to release productivity. However, to further leverage design capabilities, 'the third group' of people who are neither design experts nor users will collaborate with designers through their expertise and fill the skill gap between designers and users. This study therefore aims to explore how 'the third group' form integral roles in the design expansion terrain. To address the research question, this study adopts semi-structured interview as the research method, through which 17 informants experienced in design practices without design background are investigated. Subsequently, the results are classified into five roles 'the third group' can play in the design collaboration with detail clarifications, which include 'vision practitioner' 'business model designer', 'organization facilitator', 'language manipulator' and 'scenario composer'. Finally, the conclusion is set to contribute to identification of the design expansion terrain and the adaptive roles, which could be beneficial for non-design professionals to gain a position in design collaboration and also for designers to broaden abilities to collaborate across disciplines.

1 Introduction

The production mode in China and even the world has been going through an important transition. In the past, design department was regarded as the additional part of product development to serve client's need [1]. However, things have changed since China expects to turn the volume production to higher quality production, which suggests that innovation could be a strong stimulating factor and rely very much on design [2].

Considering limited design research community, there has to be a third group of people to join in the expanding design practices, to bring about product innovation and to lead design to success. Although some global market leaders have the foresight to merge business, technology and design for building innovation and exploring future possibilities, in fact, cross-discipline practice and project based learning still lack experience in China [3]. The adaptive principle, role, language and structure in this new terrain of design expansion remain little to be understood.

Based on the literature of cross-functional collaboration, participatory design and design leadership characterization, the research adopts interview as the research method. People who have already actively involved in design practice without design background are selected as the informants in this study. This research has explored the following three perspectives. What are the potential roles needed in the design expansion? How can non-design professionals adapt to the design practice and align their capability, task division and background? How can cross-discipline collaboration and project-based learning team come into being?

2 Theoretical Foundation

2.1 New terrain of design expansion

It is started with Kotler and Rath stating that: "design is a strategic tool that companies can use to gain a sustainable competitive advantage" [4]. The overall design awareness in management and organization studies is arising [5]. Design is welcomed to a broader range since it emerges as an approach meant to "harness the creativity of the designer within the context of business" [6], "orient innovation" [7], put into practices rather than just business strategy talking [8], serve as "strategy visualizers" and "core competency prospectors" [9].

Norman has specified "a third discipline" inserted in the middle of business and design to translate between the abstractions of research and the realities of practice [10]. This third discipline is more clarified in new product development. For avoiding time, human and financial resource loss, to bring new product to the market faster and cheaper [11], the collaboration between design and other functions is encouraged to add a new level of interactions [12] and to carry out a broad array of tasks [13]. It is also supported that design group should be product development process leader [14], which is specified as integrator, interpreter, coordinator and facilitator [15].

*Corresponding author: [a] wei.liu@tongji.edu.cn

Although the new terrain of design expansion is emerging, the nature of the functional integration and the roles of various functional groups are still under investigation.

2.2 Human resource gap for 'the third group'

The traditional design mode is very direct that designers make products while the target users adopt. As the problems are getting more and more complicated [16], user-centred design methodology comes up. While designers act as users, users can also act as designers to form participatory design, increasing users' power and adding productivity into the product [17, 18]. In addition, the user group are also linked with the direct and indirect stakeholders through the system thinking [19]. Moreover, the evolution to co-designing is changing the landscape of design practice, creating new domains of collective creativity [20]. Based on various designer- user relationships [21], it could be speculated that to empower human resource to join design will become a trend to fulfil a good design.

Sanders defines co-design in a broader sense to refer to the creativity of designers and people not trained in design, which will change how, what to design and who design and also affect the tools and methods that the new teams of co-designers will use [20].

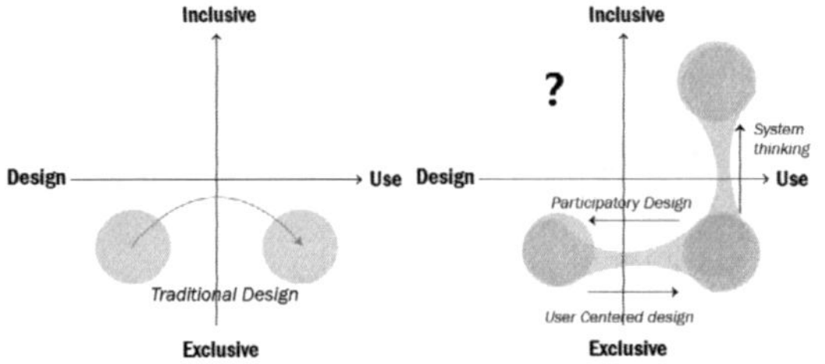

Figure 1. The transition of designer-user relationship with design quadrant still keeps exclusive.

However, there is still a quadrant which very few has studied. With the need to engage diversified expertise into the design procedure, there are not only 'user designers' in the crossroads of users and designers but also 'the third group' who are actually neither users nor design professionals and involve actively in design to leverage design capacities. To meet the future challenges in economic, technological and social areas, 'the third group' has a great potential.

2.3 Emerging roles characterizations

To feed the terrain of design expansion, various discussions are conducted on new standard of human resource and functional role clarifications.

With the departure as designers, Sanders conclude designer will go beyond designing products to design for people's purposes [20]. Valtone traces back from 1950s to depict the changing role of industrial designer, from sole creator, part of multi-disciplinary team, end-user expert, coordinator, creating experiences and pushing national innovation [22]. Similar classifications regard designer as strategist to coordinate with strategy, storyteller to build experience, co-creator to empower users and facilitator to guide design process [23].

Beyond designers, roles in general cross-discipline collaboration are studied. IDEO characterises 10 personas to form a creative firm along the innovation developing stages which are to learn creative principles, to move idea forward and to make innovation into reality [24]. Similarly, a cross-discipline study identifies 8 roles as facilitator to manage process, informer to bring in specific knowledge, user contextualizer and storyteller to speak for users, and evaluator, idea generator, interpreter and questioner to work in the design process [25]. It is noteworthy that role studies on a broader range of people are usually conducted on the process timeline and the background of participants are merely taken into consideration.

Design leaders are the forerunners in the new terrain of design expansion. Their general characteristic is intermediate. Based on Norman's proposition of "transitional developers" bridging design and business [10], a role of advocacy is assumed as "design interpreter" to influence and synthesize opportunities from both strategic and operational views [26]. As to education background, Miller and Moultrie find formal design training and extensive industry experience are necessary based on fashion industry studies [27]. However, on a broader scale of business, studies also show that design training is not a prerequisite for leading design projects [28]. Topalian has mapped major tasks to lead design in a rich and demanding spectrum with business and society, while confirming executives from every discipline to play a full part[29].Furthermore, their common qualities can be concluded as envisioning future and nurturing environment for innovations [30]. In the skill domain, Miller and Moutrie identify 5 interdependent skillsets -- cognitive skills, interpersonal skills, business skills, strategic skills and design skills [27].

Successful practices on the terrain of design expansion are emerging and the human resource needs are transformative. It is hereby prospective for individuals from non-design background to enter design field, bring about innovations and even become design leaders.

2.4 Research gap

This study proposes the research gaps as follows: Firstly, the broadened roles for designers are still limited to the design research community, which can't bridge the gap in the new terrain of design towards business and society. Secondly, roles allocated by innovation process view are still disconnected with participants' expertise. Thirdly, inductive skills or quality requirements are too fragmentary to form into role portfolios in order to guide 'the third group'. Finally, the general characteristics are not specified into specific functions as well. Although design leaders can be used as reference for 'the third group', being a leader is not the only possibility.

The purpose of this study is to align the background, capabilities, working responsibilities into concrete roles in a design process, so as to provide an integral guide for 'the third group' to approach the new terrain of design expansion.

3 Research Method

As the aim of the research is to study how 'the third group' form integral roles in the expanded design practices, the nature of which is inherently exploratory and inductive, semi-structured interview is adopted to generate qualitative insights to form an integrated understanding of the roles in design practices. Themes of the interview questionnaire include the following: education background, personal characteristics, project experiences, behaviour and work division in a design process overall and also in each stage, influence and explanations for actions, related skills and capabilities, differentiations from designers and future plan. Informants are asked to narrate a typical design process which represents their common approach to get engaged in design activities. Then they are guided to go deeper into describing their actions, reasons and impact. Data of their common skills similar to designers as well as their unique skills to facilitate particular actions are both collected. How they form their skill sets and how they plan to develop further are asked as part of the questions to collect data for role paths. Moreover, they are encouraged to generate understanding of their own role with evidence of their project experiences.

Since the cross-discipline collaboration and project based learning oriented by design discipline are rare, cross-discipline master students whose bachelor studies are not related to design in the College of Design and Innovation in Tongji University are selected as the key informants. These interviewees experienced in design teamwork comprise a representative sample with different education background, grade, age and design project experience.

Table 1. Participant composition

No.	Education Background	Gender	Design Projects Participated
1	Business Management	Male	18 Projects
2	Political science	Female	15 Projects
3	Economics	Female	7 Projects
4	Accounting	Female	15 Projects
5	Communication Media	Female	14 Projects
6	Advertising	Male	15 Projects
7	Chemistry	Female	7 Projects
8	Physics	Female	6 Projects
9	Materials science	Male	6 Projects
10	English	Female	8 Projects
11	French	Male	18 Projects
12	Information Management	Female	10 Projects
13	Computer science	Male	19 Projects
14	Civil engineering	Male	7 Projects
15	Environmental engineering	Female	8 Projects
16	Electronic engineering	Male	18 Projects
17	Mechanical engineering	Female	17 Projects

In total, 17 interviews are conducted. Each of them ranges from 30 minutes to 60 minutes. The interviews are audio recorded and transcribed to generate around 58000 words of text-based data. Through ground analysis, the interview transcript is generalized into categories with sufficient meaning by coordinating background, capabilities, work content and work importance. Then the clusters emerge around distinct roles which correlate with themes addressed in literature review. The outcome of this research is robust characterizations of roles for 'the third group' and how they illuminate the practices in the new terrain of design expansion.

4 Research findings

Five key roles are synthesized from research data, which include vision practitioner, scenario composer, language manipulator, business model designer and organization facilitator. All the roles are interrelated in the design collaboration.

Figure 2. The 5 key roles 'the third group' can play in design collaboration.

4.1 Vision practitioner

Currently, the mainstream of designers are treating existing problems as the design space. However, more opportunities lie in the new design space which is open source and question-oriented [31]. The design space should be expanded from only examining the current situations to asking questions behind the situation and towards the future [32].

Through interview, there are insights guiding to characterise vision practitioner:

- When there are no authorities, students with strong self-efficacy always lead the team.

- Some students get anxious easily in facing enormous possibilities and new directions, which shows their dislike of ambiguity.

Common ways to empower students to build vision are to allow them to select the problem they take excitement in or to find them a real client.

The role fighting for a shared value and posing thought-provoking questions to the society is identified as vision practitioner. It is proved that committed enthusiasts can build idea visionaries to "persevere against frustration and ambiguity" [33]. Vision practitioners might not be design experts, while they are visionary and responsible to endow products with new or added value. People possessing large amount of user experience often come up with identified vision, perceive unrecognized ideas, turn ideas into feasible framework and persuade people the value of ideas.

4.2 Business model designer

A business model describes the rationale of how an organization creates, delivers, and captures value [36]. Since business model generation is based on exploring all opportunities and options, analytical and synthesizing abilities of politics, economy, society and technology are rather significant.

In the business aspect, the customer-product tie is strengthened by examining customer segmentation, product mix, brand strength, customer loyalty and distribution channels. As to the industry environment, the industry market growth and industrial environment factors like new technologies are primarily to be investigated for developing strategies. Moreover, the competitive strategy, partner strategy and the business canvass need to be developed through contemplating the major players, their market shares and product differentiation.

In addition, money is not the only trade-off. Business models not only organize "the way they make money" but also "the way they convey meanings, beliefs, values and organizational culture" through operational and strategic circles [34]. To form a feasible and sustainable operation model for product and service, the physical and emotional gain of user as well stakeholders are usually carefully analysed. Business experts should take value considerations and identify value conflicts based on psychological propositions. The whole model needs to be evidence based and to be tested and modified.

To achieve that, people who study business management, public relations or who are employed in management consultancies are great candidates. The most obstacle for them is getting familiar with design practice.

4.3 Organization facilitator

Facilitator who aims at assisting design project by managing the internal and external human source is of great significance. This role takes effect in many circumstances.

Firstly, to contact direct users as well as exterior consultants and stakeholders, facilitators are good at identifying and engaging targeted people through diversified ways, such us social network and low-cost online tools. Interpersonal skills are needed to inform users of their roles in the design process, to motivate users in different stages and to ensure users a delightful experience.

Secondly, since the schemes of workshop need to align with the goal and stimulate productivity, facilitator always thinks of diversified organizational forms by setting human contacts, number of groups, amount of time, tools as well as the physical environment. In that way, facilitators could also be able to bring inspirations to designers and to facilitate teamwork.

Finally, facilitator should also appear as the representative of the company to business partner in the industry chain. Facilitator acts as negotiator to understand the value of potential partners and maintain relationships with partners.

As facilitators, they come up with lots of organization innovations by activity planning and public relationship management. So the targeted expertise mainly comes from marketing professionals and human resource managers.

4.4 Language manipulator

Language, which locates in the deep root of nation and culture, is very general and stable. Language has been essential to enable common ground and synthesis via mixing disciplinary language, use of analogies and metaphors, sketches, imprecision and hedging words around project goals, gestures to communicate issue and generating new languages [25]. Language takes effect mainly in two process of design, the fuzzy front end of adding possibilities and the final stage to convey the design outcome to users.

In the first process of exploration, communicating and synthesizing the right message of ideas to the team is the top priority. A hypothesis of design thinking is to use visualization as much as possible. The assumption is challenged due to that efficient communication is based on participants, encoding, transmitting, decoding and the environmental noise. Visualization requires the expertise of encoding, otherwise it will slow down the decoding or cause misunderstanding instead. Therefore, concise verbal language expressions as well as other languages must be combined with visualizations, while the proportion of languages should depend on the features of participants.

In the second process to convey design value to users, language skills are necessary for converting vison into compacted and essential words which can be understood by everyone. Analogies and metaphors are treated as effective social interaction role of as language tools for elaborate mental representations and for reducing uncertainty [36].

Therefore, except for new languages like programming, verbalization, dialogue, copywriting and naming are all great expertise for 'the third group' to get competitive, which add great value to the whole process.

4.5 Scenario composer

Scenario composer means to envision users' roles, motivations, behaviours, reactions, obstacles as well as satisfaction, based on a set of integrated assumptions in deep root of culture. Unlike the language, stories provide a narrative that unfolds over time, which allows for a more complicated set of relationships to develop [37]. Informants also emphasize frequently the importance of building visual stories with reasonable imagination.

There are many similarities between design and screen writing. They both stand on qualitative research which emphasizes empathy, insights and vivid characters. Moreover, neither composers nor designers will stop upon that point, since both of their final aims are to propose questions, to inspire people, to get social responsible and to construct a whole new world view, which can arouse trust, feelings, opinions and behaviour changes from the audience. Although screen writers tend to be more imaginative and artistic, which makes them look unrealistic and unfocused, the core spirit of composing is increasingly needed in the innovation-driven and future-oriented era.

Composing scenarios is an appropriate field for 'the third group' to make breakthroughs and build expertise upon, since innovation need composers to add flesh and blood to the blueprint, to evoke sympathy as well as to convince audience. People who study advertisement, marketing, writing, theatre and drama are all candidates ready for this work.

5 Conclusion

This study synthesizes 5 key roles for 'the third group' to play in the design expansion terrain, which include vision practitioner to question assumptions and motivate people, business model designer to formulate feasible operation strategy, organization facilitator to coordinate human resource, language manipulator to manage communication and scenario composer to create story plots. Each role aligns definition, features, capability together with work responsibilities, which not only portray the new terrain of design expansion, but also provide appropriate entries for people to build their paths into design collaboration.

As 'the third group' from different disciplines gradually enter the vacant area and work inclusively into design process, they can grasp the design skills and thinking, form strong ties with designers and bring about synergistic effect to improve the design process and outcome.

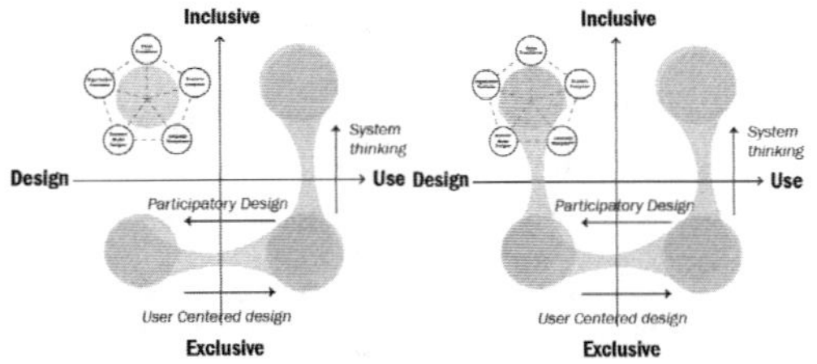

Figure 3. 'The third group' enter the landscape, complete functions and connect closely with designers.

This study has important implications for career as well as education. Guides of roles not only help people who are interested in design to gain a right position and to explore new opportunities, but also help them capture a leading position in the current market vacancy of design collaboration. In addition, they can also choose to gain experience in design, grow competitive and go back to their original field. Moreover, it also provides guidance for professional designers to extend abilities to collaborate across disciplines. In addition, students who participate in design-led collaboration programs can ease their pressure and adapt the active learning as soon as possible according to the role paths explanations. They may use the guide as measurement dimensions of their performances.

With the demanding spectrum of design awareness toward business and society, this study is expected to help clarify the ambiguity and facilitate the efficacy of design collaboration. Meanwhile, through the role paths clarifications, we believe that more people from non-design background would be encouraged and engaged in design practices to push innovations into a new level.

References

1. L. Yongxiang, Mechanical Engineer **1**,4 (2005)
2. L. Yongxiang, China Mechanical Engineering **21**, 379 (2010)
3. H. Shufang, *Research on relationship between team heterogeneity and original innovation performance on interdisciplinary cooperation* (Zhejiang University, 2016)
4. P. Kotler, G. Alexander Rath, Journal of business strategy **5**, 16 (1984)
5. R. Turner, *Design leadership: securing the strategic value of design* (Routledge, London, 2016)
6. H. Collins, Design Management Review 24, 35(2013)
7. A. Rylander, Design Management Journal **4**, 7 (2009)
8. J. Liedtka, Design Management Review **21**, 6 (2010)
9. V. Seidel, Design Management Review **11**, 35 (2000)
10. D. A. Norman, Interactions **17**, 9 (2010)
11. A. R. Jassawalla, H. C. Sashittal,. the Academy of Management Executive **13,** 50 (1999)

12. K. Bo Young, International Journal of Design **2**, 43 (2008)
13. B. Von Stamm, *Managing innovation, design and creativity* (Wiley & Sons, Chichester, 2003)
14. H. Perks, R. Cooper, C. Jones, Journal of Product Innovation Management **22**, 111 (2005).
15. R. Turner, Design Management Review **11**, 42 (2000)
16. R. Buchanan, Design issues **8**, 5 (1992)
17. M. Steen, Science and engineering ethics **19**, 945 (2013)
18. W. Liu, J. Moultrie, (2013). *Exploring innovative ways for companies to engage with customers through the internet in developing new products.* (Design Management Symposium, 2013)
19. G. Melles, I. de Vere, V. Misic, CoDesign **7**, 143- (2011)
20. E. N. B. Sanders, P. J. Stappers, Co-design, **4**, 5 (2008)
21. T. Keinonen, *Designers, users and justice* (Bloomsbury Publishing, London, 2017)
22. A. Valtonen, *Six decades and six different roles for the industrial designer* (Nordes Conference, Copenhagen, 2005)
23. J. Yee, L. Tan, P. Meredith, *The emergent roles of a designer in the development of an e learning service* (Nordic Service Design Conference, 2009)
24. T. Kelley, *The ten faces of innovation: IDEO's strategies for beating the devil's advocate & driving creativity throughout your organization* (Broadway Business, 2005)
25. R. S. Adams, L. Mann, S. Jordan, S. Daly, *About: designing. analysing design meetings*, (CRC Press/Balkema, Leiden, 2009)
26. S. Bucolo, C. Wrigley, J. Matthews, Design Management Journal **7**, 18 (2012).,
27. K. Miller, J. Moultrie, Design Management Journal **8**, 35 (2013)
28. A. Topalian, *The handbook of design management* (A&C Black, Edinburgh, 2011)
29. A. Topalian, Design Management Journal **7**, 29 (2012)
30. R. Turner, A. Topalian, *Core responsibilities of design leaders in commercially demanding environments* (Inaugural Session Design Leadership Forum, 2002)
31. E. N. B. Sanders, She Ji: The Journal of Design, Economics, and Innovation **3**: 3 (2017)
32. U. Dandavate, E. B. N. Sanders, S. Stuart, *The human factors and ergonomics society annual meeting* (CA: SAGE Publications, Los Angeles, 1996)
33. H. Florén, J. Frishammar, California Management Review **54**, 20 (2012)
34. C. Battistella, G. Biotto, A. F. De Toni, Management Decision **50**, 718 (2012)
35. A. Osterwalder, Y. Pigneur, *Business model generation: a handbook for visionaries, game changers, and challengers* (John Wiley & Sons, New Jersey, 2010)
36. L. J. Ball, B. T. Christensen, Design Studies **30**, 169 (2009)
37. V. P. Seidel, S. O'Mahony, Organization Science **25**, 691 (2014)

MATEC Web of Conferences **176**, 02022 (2018)
IFID 2018
https://doi.org/10.1051/matecconf/201817602022

Analysis and Apocalypse of Japanese Style Creation Aesthetics

Peng Xin-qin [1,a]

[1]Visual dean, Art&Design Department, Bengbu university, Anhui, China

Abstract. Japanese style design has a good reputation in the world design community. Its elegant details, metaphorical techniques, quiet and tranquil aesthetic style, and the simplest form of the natural true design concept are praised by the world. The analysis of its aesthetic characteristics can be of great inspiration to the reference and modern construction of Chinese product aesthetics.

1 Introduction

The modern design of Japan was established after World War II. It has been mature since 1953, and has taken a place in the contemporary world design. Analyzing its aesthetic characteristics can play a role in product design in modern China. At the same time, with the "jump frog strategy [1]", combined with China's rich social and a long traditional culture, it can effectively promote the integration of Chinese design resources and economic takeoff.

2 Aesthetic is the Experience Construction of the Subject and Object

Aesthetics are a construction activity[2], and it is the process of the aesthetic object being constructed by the imagination of the aesthetic subject. In this process, the main body constructs psychological facts and inner images. The two sides through the "isomorphism", as the object of the beauty of the form of the body through the psychological structure of the body, when the two "homomorphism", beauty can be displayed on the object. This kind of aesthetic is relative and dynamic. With the increasingly rich nature of human strength and psychological structure, the relationship between human and reality is expanding. This aesthetic activity is the interaction and construction process of the interaction between subject and object. This construction is a two-way process. It also constructs the object world while constructing the main body's aesthetic psychological structure[3].

Aesthetics comes from a need, a fifth level need, that is, the need for order, harmony and beauty.

According to the latest Maslow needs theory, the needs is divided into six levels: one for biological needs (Physiological needs), that is to meet the biological needs of human beings; the second is the security needs (Safety needs), including safety, life stability, and freedom from suffering, threat or disease; and third, love and belonging. The needs (Love and belonging), such as: friendship, love and affiliation needs. Fourth is the need for respect (Esteem), and the need for respect can be divided into three categories: self-esteem, respect for others and power desires, including self respect, self evaluation and respect for others; the fifth is the need for experience and cognition (Experience purpose, meaning and realizing), that is, the cognition and sense of intrinsic potential. The sixth is self actualization need. that is, to develop its potential to achieve its own development needs [4]. As shown in Figure 1. As far as design aesthetics is concerned, the theory of needs is actually aimed at the aesthetic subject, and it is actually a construction process completed by means of aesthetic objects.

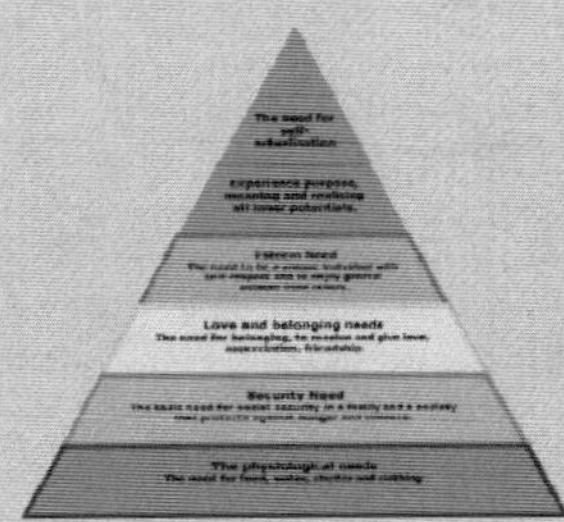

Figure 1. The six level of needs theory.

3 Analysis of Japanese Creation Aesthetics

Japanese contemporary aesthetics of creation are mainly embodied in the works of some excellent design products and designers. Japanese style creation, aesthetics are mainly embodied in two aspects in the field of product design. First, its traditional Zen aesthetics embody the design and modern design of Japanese traditional utensils. Second, its contemporary simplicity and light and short wind are embodied in the design of modern products, especially in the design of electronic products and transportation tools. Among

*Corresponding author: [a] 46098831@qq.com

them, the most representative is Japanese industrial design, such as WUJI design and main designer, such as the original design practice of Kenya Hara. The following two aspects are analyzed.

3.1. An analysis of the aesthetic characteristics of traditional Japanese utensils

Japan is a regional nation with a long history. The design of traditional utensils has experienced hundreds of years of history, and it has continued to survive and develop in Contemporary Japanese society. It is mainly embodied in the design of daily products, such as traditional furniture, porcelain, iron, tableware, lacquer ware and other living products. The traditional implement in Japan are mostly produced by traditional techniques, and are famous for their simple modeling and quiet aesthetic characteristics. For example, the lacquer of Wajima in Ishikawa County, as shown in Figure 2, Japanese lacquer is not only used to eat, but it inherits a long culture. In Japanese tradition, lacquer ware is the spirit of ceremonies and ceremonies.

At the same time, the atmosphere of festivals is brought into daily life. The design model of this dish is simple, highlighting the natural texture of the wood itself, without any superfluous ornaments, only the change and contrast of the size arc, the unifying of the lonely bowl, the color of the monochromatic class color paint, and the wood material used in the lacquer is made of the whole natural Rohan cypress or beech. And then planned by the plank division, the craft is exquisite. The wood embryo is thin enough to penetrate the wood embryo to see the other side. Finally, the lacquer made from the paint of the lacquer tree has been given the bright and beautiful luster. Therefore, in the use of material, this product is loyal to the nature of material and keeps the beauty of simplicity; in the use of color, the name of the local animals and plants is named, and the aesthetic feeling of Japanese naturalism is embodied; in the artistic expression, the logs are used to reduce the traces of the cave to be carved naturally. To hold the true position of life.

Figure 2. Lacquerware in Wajima, Ishikawa County.

Different from the cultural characteristics of the Chinese Confucianism and Taoism, Japan is the influence of the Buddhist culture of the single nation. The Buddhist Zen thought has formed a unique Japanese Zen thought since the introduction of India through China. It began in the Tang and Song dynasties in China, especially by the hands of the Kamakura Shogunate, the Chinese Zen. The aesthetics were introduced into Japan, and combined with the faith of the local deity quickly, which produced the greatest change and maturity of the Japanese ontological philosophy, the birth of the Zen Aesthetics of Japan, the influence of the various fields of Japanese society, especially the traditional cultural form, and the combination of two with the long spirit of Bushido in Japan. The death is like a life and death view, and at the same time, it affects the Japanese martial arts people's attention to repair their minds and abandon their miscellaneous thoughts.

People usually refer to the Zen spirit of Japan by Wabi, Sabi and Shibui. Here, these three positions are used to describe their design aesthetics. "Wabi" means to be far away from the world and to live in a Zen forest. As far as the aesthetic of the utensils is concerned, it can refer to the simplicity and simplicity of the retreats, the unsatisfactory and irregular beauty of nature; the Sabi refers to the impermanence of Buddhism, and the things in the world are transient and vicissitudes, which are reflected in the utensils, mainly utensils. The beauty of some of the traces left over and the gloss of the "pulp" of the years, and the meaning of the beauty of incomplete; Shibu "astringent" means convergent, Unostentatious, or simple and elegant [5].

3.2 The beauty of modern Japanese product creation

The modern Japanese product design is mainly characterized by miniaturization, convenience, versatility and detail oriented process. Due to the limited territory of Japan, to develop a developed economy in a limited territory, what we need is pioneering and wisdom. Therefore, the Japanese design, which shows obvious modernity characteristics, is mainly embodied in the full consideration of the relationship between high technology and environment, ecology and products, such as the concept of Kansei Engineering, electronic robot, automobile product and architectural design, which is famous for the sustainable design concept of technology and environmental protection. Therefore, we can also see the embodiment of Japanese design aesthetics in modern product design, focusing on the original ecology of the natural environment, the simple beauty of the human living environment and the beauty of morals that pay attention to the social environment.

For example, the design of MUJI is simple, simple and environmentally friendly. With the last element to restore the natural truth, with no consideration, the inner structure and the subtle features are implied in the external image, symbol, and the words have the best meaning, and the profound connotation is embodied in the extrinsic products.

This CD music player, see Figure 3, looks like an old-fashioned fan. When you pull down a rope, with a clack,

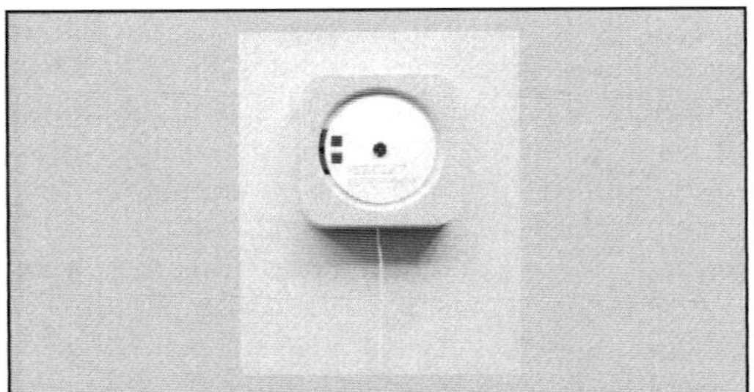

Figure 3. MUJI hanging wall CD machine.

the CD player begins to play music, which seems to allow users to recall the happy hours of their childhood. Naoto Fukasawa, the designer of MUJI, expressed the most clean design interacts with the most concise abstract forms and simple colors. It expressed the essence of his intuition, design by undesigned technique, at the same time, the design details were also very thorough, and the limited few design elements were properly balanced. With the image of Zen Buddhism and aesthetic qualities.

There are many similar products, such as Japanese cars, compared with American cars, economic, oil saving, small space, simple materials, small pollution to the environment, and some famous Japanese design companies, such as TOYOTA, SONY, Panasonic, Canon, MITSUBISHI, Nikon, SANYO developed. FANUC is the most powerful enterprise in the production, design, manufacture and sales of professional CNC systems, accounting for 70% of the global market share. Under the premise of satisfying technology, we should consider people's aesthetic habits and aesthetic psychology. From the view of the world layout, Japan is a small island country. Under the boundless sea, it is easy to produce the psychological feelings of the people. It is a important geographical factor and the Humanistic Psychological factor in the Japanese philosophy. The Japanese industry is developed, the society is long in technology, and the Japanese are not ignored. The perceptual factor of human emotion is embodied in the aesthetic of product design, which is a kind of beauty, of silence, simplicity, irregularity and asymmetry, and the harmony between yin and Yang of the utensils. The design of MUJI embodies the philosophical and aesthetic features of "no plan" and "Yin Yang transformation". MUJI is "NO BRAND", and no brand is a big brand.

4 Conclusion

Japanese industrial design is realized by combining the excellent cultural traditions of our nation and western modern design ideas with the help of advanced scientific and technological research. In the development of modern economic and industrial design, we do not forget the excellent cultural heritage of the nation, and combine the spirit of God, the view of geographical resources and the design of modernity in the nation, thus forming a double track parallel product and aesthetic style of modern Japanese design. First, in the traditional utensils, the Japanese to the environment protection and cherish the achievement of their small and exquisite, simple and silent design of the wind. Second, in the modern product design, the Japanese Shibu design aesthetics emphasize the grim, order and elegance, Wabi claims the original, plain, both and the West. It is a combination of rationalism and design aesthetics, symbiotic with exquisite details, simple form metaphor and modular design beauty.

As far as the aesthetic subject is concerned, the designer, in shaping the product, has been well versed in the idiosyncratic characteristics of the Zen Aesthetics of Japan, and integrates it in the expression of product form, color, material and metaphor, thus constructing the aesthetic object. When the user is watching and using the product, the aesthetic object which is merged into the product can be used. The psychological structure of users' history and culture resonates, and beauty comes into being.

Compared with the single race and cultural tradition in Japan, China is rich in nature and rich in natural resources. This sense of superiority has caused the young generation of today's use of articles and the waste of living habits. In the field of product design, the design of sustainable system is not too much for the design of sustainable system. Social integration service design is currently on the agenda. We should carry forward the fine tradition of the Chinese Mohist's thrift and frugality rather than the decadent lifestyle of the poor and extravagant pursuit of Western hedonism, which is the trampling of the main personality and the great destruction of the self-agreement of the aesthetic subject. In the field of product design, the loss of respect for things, goods and design, although temporarily can be changed to a brilliant visual aesthetic effect, but this effect belongs to the privileged class and aristocracy, divorced from the people, is not long. In the long run, it makes the people lose respect for the utensils, ignore the natural essence of the objects, and eventually lose the aesthetic self-discipline of the aesthetic subject leading to the aesthetic deviation and the loss of human nature. The method is also a philosophical aesthetic thought contrary to the return of Chinese Taoism to nature. We should have the least respect for utensils, which is the first revelation of Japanese artifact aesthetics to contemporary Chinese product aesthetics.

On the second level, from the Japanese style Wabi and Shibu contemporary creation aesthetic style, Japanese aesthetics is based on the austere, detailed and modularized, and elegant aesthetic qualities, and the beauty of order and irregularity, the beauty of nature and the incompleteness of the imperfection.

The opposing factors are finally unified in the design of the noumenon. China's contemporary product design should also seek its own aesthetic design in the rush and unification. One is to take advantage of the advanced foreign technology and design experience to consider the rich and rich social resources and leap frog strategy to realize the leap forward development of industrial design and product aesthetics; the two, respect the excellent tradition of our nation, integrate the national aesthetics with the excellent design aesthetics of foreign countries, treat them equally and harmonization. And the method of feedback to achieve harmony and unity in "hedging", that is, the above impulse and unification.

In short, compared with Japanese contemporary aesthetics of creation and Chinese product design aesthetics, "harmony soul and talent [6]" can be seen in the differences between China and Japan. This difference is the difference in economic development, the difference in design level and level, the difference of design method and manufacturing process, cultural difference, and the difference of design thinking and mode of operation. At the moment, China needs to adjust several directions to make the design business fly, and through the design of the aesthetic style of Chinese design and the erect position of the world design and national forest.

Firstly, we should quickly integrate the natural and social resources of China, adjust the design and manufacture mode, give order rectification to the design enterprises that destroy the natural environment; secondly, protect the traditional natural resources and develop biological and industrial technology, rather than simply promote the development of the design through the sale of goods and the virtual economy of the network. Thirdly, to improve the cultural connotation and aesthetic interest, to build a symbiotic environment between the aesthetic subject and the aesthetic object, to refine and develop the excellent heritage of the Confucianism, Taoism, and to reshape the unique aesthetic style of China's product design. Finally, the construction of excellent design education and the design of talent reserve mechanism requires the government, the society and the university education. The mechanism of cooperation and the vigorous reform of the teaching team are not overnight. At present, this reform can only be promoted by improving the excellent design talents and encouraging the creation of folk outstanding designers. For example, in the reform of design education in Colleges and universities, we can improve the situation by creating an atmosphere of respecting the excellent cultural heritage and refining the essence of Chinese cultural tradition in practice. We take the opportunity of improving traditional Chinese literature and art aesthetics and symbols. We take the opportunity of improving the main philosophy and aesthetics in history. The bad design education situation and the declining moral and ethical trend can be changed through the above efforts. Through the call of the design ethics and the design of the logical order, these two measures have buried the aesthetic style of the fine product design with Chinese characteristics in the future. As Xu Hengchun said in the book of design aesthetics, the creation of aesthetic value is on the one hand, on the other hand, on the basis of the molding of the human senses and psychology, only in the correspondence and Isomorphism of the two can people perceive the beauty of things [7]. From the analysis of aesthetic subject and guest relations, the aesthetic of product design is to build aesthetic objects through the first aesthetic subject (product stylist) with a certain medium, and then the aesthetic object is reacting on the second aesthetic subject (i.e. the user), if the second aesthetic subject is produced by some elements in the aesthetic object when watching or using the product. With aesthetic sympathy, beauty is presented. Therefore, this is an aesthetic process and an aesthetic context, mainly through the aesthetic subject to be fully highlighted, the aesthetic subject of wisdom, consciousness, cultural, psychological structure and aesthetic levels are particularly important, he is the key to determine whether the above four can be realized. Therefore, in this regard, it is the fundamental to cultivate excellent design talents with high comprehensive quality. The case of Japanese attention to the design of education and aesthetic education has also given us a correct inspiration.

ACKNOWLEDGMENT

Funded projects: Humanities and Social Sciences key projects in Anhui Province (No. SK2017A0635)

References

1. Ezio Manzini, Joon Sang Baek, Zhong Fang translation. For social innovation and sustainable design: the hypothesis about China's "frog jumping strategy". J. Creativity and design. **22**, 4 (2010)
2. Liu Xian Jie, *Modern architecture theory* (China Construction Industry Press, Beijing, 2008) p 167
3. Liu Xian Jie, *Modern architecture theory* (China Construction Industry Press, Beijing, 2008) p 212
4. Ling Jiyao, Xu heng alcohol. *Art design* (people's publishing house, Shanghai, 2000) p 267.
5. Gao Dan. poetic dwelling-On the beauty of Japanese Zen culture and MUJI design. J. Popular literature. **120**, 13 (2014).
6. Li Liang Zhi. *World history of industrial design* (China Light Industry Press, Beijing, 2006) p 196
7. Xu Heng alcohol. *Design aesthetics* (Tsinghua University press, Beijing, 2006) p 70.

The Concept Transformation of Design Education Based on Internationalized Teaching Exchange

Xu Jiao[1],XU Ming[1a]

[1]Cnetral South University, Visual Communication and Digital Media Design Department, 410083 Changsha Hunan, China

Abstract: In the **perspective** of globalization, the internationalization of education has become an inevitable trend in the development of current design education. The original intention of internationalization of education is to promote the reform of design education by absorbing and learning from international advanced educational resources. This paper combines many years of practical experience of international design education exchanges in Central South University, and has conducted beneficial discussions in teaching concepts, teaching methods, teaching modes, etc., and proposes new ideas for value education, process control, and modeless teaching, which are powerful promoting the reform of design education and achieving a close connection with international advanced design education.

1 Introduction

In the process of transition from traditional arts and crafts to modern design, artistic and perceptual thinking still occupy the leading position of design education. As a result, the scientific and social design of the design is obviously insufficient, and the teaching concept, teaching purpose and teaching form are also too conservative, and the educational framework of design has not been rearranged from the ideological understanding level. For this reason, Central South University has launched a nine-year international design education exchange practice and exploration, established annual design teaching exchange mechanism with many universities in the United States and the United Kingdom, and strived to absorb and learn from the western advanced design education concept, adjust and improve the teaching concept, teaching methods and teaching mode of design education, and actively promote the teaching reform of design education.

2 Transformation of teaching concept: from Functionalism to Value Education

Traditional design teaching is often based on the "functionalist" teaching concept. In the design it is often reflected that it tends to focus too much on the specific material form and its commodity nature. This type of teaching model allows students to develop a linear way of thinking, which focuses only on the ontology of design, and ignores the spiritual value of design. To address this issue, we have introduced the value education concept, which is advocated by western developed countries, into international design teaching. The essence of value education is to oppose the concept of functionalism education and to counteract the tendency of scientism. Its theoretical basis is a practical attempt to promote the meaning of life and the pursuit of value.

The value education concept is first reflected in the setting of the theme of internationalized design and teaching exchange, focusing on the expansion from the creation of material forms to non-material forms, aiming to cultivate students' sense of social responsibility, public moral awareness and cultural understanding. Among them, according to the social hot issues, "social issues research" was set up, the theme of "green design" was put forward according to environmental issues, and the "Chinese and English culture impression" was set according to the cultural value identification problem, and the theme of "vaccination" was set according to health problems. Secondly, value education encourages students to proceed from their social responsibilities to observe subtle observations of life, to discover differences in historical cultures, values, ways of behavior and existing social problems in different countries, and to propose solutions to problems and correct attitudes to life through design. Therefore, value education can abandon man's natural life, individual life, realize the transcendence towards cultural life and historical life. [1] Thematic teaching exchange based on the concept of value education transcends the limitation of professional ontology, expands the space and field of design, effectively stimulates the students' thinking limit, and makes the education itself more actively pays attention to social issues and cultural traditions, and take the design as a way to reflect social and cultural issues.

3 Turning of Teaching Methods: From Results to Process Control

Traditional design education tends to focus only on the final design results while neglecting the process. Of course, designing the final effect is important, but the most important thing for teaching is learning methods in the process. For this reason, we propose the process control method, which is to control every step in the teaching process through the design method. The abstract concepts, logical relationships and structural levels in the class knowledge points are visualized. And the teaching process and the design methods are organically combined. [2] As for the controlling of teaching process, it can be summarized as three important steps: analytical design, creative expression, and critical discussion.

3.1 Analytical Design

Analytical design is the process of concept proof, which is also an application method. It guides students to use design as a tool to "research" objects. Through the investigation of a large number of text and data information using pie charts, histograms, mind maps and other forms of visual processing. Data analysis, structural analysis and comparative analysis was conduct to find out the logical relationship and internal structure relationships between the information. The thinking models, paths and laws are presented and analyzed in a multidimensional visual way. The analysis session effectively solved the problem of students applying their knowledge and cultivated students' logical thinking ability and comprehensive design ability.

3.2 Creative Expression

The creative expression can be said as a process of conceptual visualization, which is also the conversion process of from rational thinking to affective thinking, and from a logical language to a visual language. In this process, we emphasize the importance of visual thinking. Students are required to visualize the key words obtained from logical thinking during brainstorming, reconstruct visual language, and conduct visual semantics transformation training. And basis on their ideas, students are required to analysis the mode of expression, the mode of realization media and the investigation of realize technology, which not only can be expressed in a static form, but also can be creatively expressed ideas dynamically.

3.3 Critical Discussion

The critical discussion is a substantive method of communication and interaction. Michael Bierut pointed out that although criticism is essentially in opposition to the object of criticism, the conclusion may not be pessimistic, and the process of criticism may bring a new opportunity for critics. [3] Criticism is not a process that runs through the entire process of designing teaching but is a process of teaching that happening after the creative expression. This allows students to fully develop the design's creativity and expression. A mature design work needs continuous polishing and repeated improvement. Through multi-angle, multi-faceted criticism and self-examination of the work, the author's design theme, creative intention, expression style, and design means are demonstrated and analyzed from the perspective of critical thinking. Defects and deficiencies in the design are constantly discovered, which makes the problems in the works become apparent, and inspire everyone to jointly explore ways to solve them, which allows students to get a lot of knowledge through a few examples.

4 The Transformation of Teaching Methods: From Paradigmatic Teaching to Paradigm Teaching

The traditional exemplary teaching uses a single teacher as the main body of the curriculum indoctrination teaching. There is a disconnect between the curriculums and the disconnect between theory and practice, which results in the problem that students cannot effectively connect the knowledge points of various courses. That is difficult to meet the needs of social development and students' knowledge. In this context, we need to break through the previous system and seek out a teaching method that can stimulate students' creative thinking—Non-Exemplary teaching. Non-Exemplary teaching is a possible teaching method proposed in relation to paradigmatic teaching. It is a unity of the attitude of seeking truth from facts, the position of anti-systematization, and the method of integrating creation.

4.1 Take project topics as aggregation points

The non-exemplary teaching is based on the theme of the international teaching project, and formulates relevant international exchange courses, lectures and cultural inspections. The curriculum is flexible, no professional boundaries and classifications. And even students can be allowed to participate in the specific settings of the curriculum. There is no fixed model for the curriculum, and it is a constant adjustment process according to specific projects and progress. For example, in the "Chinese-British Culture" theme exchange, teachers at Coventry University in the United Kingdom have suggested that many students in China cannot apply the essence of professional theories to their own design practice. For this purpose, we set up a special lecture on “Design Style and Genre Analysis” and proposed the concept of “Anti-Design”. Through the analysis of typical ideas, typical forms, and typical styles of Chinese and Western art history, we will conduct an analysis of “Study the principles and gain knowledge”. Find out its laws and principles and present them in your own design work through redesign.

4.2 Take on-site teaching as driving force

In the traditional design teaching of the past, although teachers expect to use the "Theory to Guide Practice" method to take control of the teaching, and thus extract the so-called systematic, logical, standardized teaching knowledge. However, through classroom teaching, students can feel certain problems in a clarifying specific situation, but it is still not clear where exactly the problems are. Dewey emphasized that personal subjective experience is a crucial beginning of the inquiry process, which makes the current situation questionable, and that expressing and sharing this experience is also crucial. "Exploration is not a purely logical process, and feeling is a useful, directional existed and throughout each stage."[4] In the process of formulating the internationalized design and teaching exchange plan, we reasonably set up on-site teaching links according to the theme requirement. First of all, through the on-site feelings, the design direction is initially chosen. In the process of investigation or exploration, relevant experts and scholars are arranged to teach so that teachers and students can deepen their understanding of the topics of exchange. Second, make a live statement, which can inspire design thinking, capture in-situ clues, and refine creative points. On-site teaching makes it easier for students to acquire a material carrier that expresses their design ideas more profoundly on the basis of perceptual knowledge. Through practical experience and scene reproduction, students can consolidate classroom teaching content, expand the time and space of classroom instruction, and enrich the cultural connotation of international exchanges.

5 Conclusion

Through the international design of teaching exchange projects, we have focused on integrating high-quality teaching resources and advanced educational concepts from abroad into the teaching reforms of design. We have conducted beneficial explorations in teaching concepts, teaching methods and teaching methods. We will also have an in-depth discussion in specific aspects of these ideas shift in the future.

Acknowledgment

The paper is the final supporting material for Central South University Education and Teaching Reform project "Visualization Teaching Exploration and Practice Research of Designing Professional Process", Item No.: 2017jy56

References

1. Wang Lu. The Ontology Foundation of Value Education[J]. Educational Research, 03(2014).
2. Xu Jiao, Sun Xiangming. Process Visualization Teaching Based on International Teaching Exchange [J]. Decoration,05(2017).
3. Lu Ying.Critical Enlightenment for Chinese Design[J]. Decoration, 01(2012).
4. Bruce Brown.Design Issues[M],Beijing: Tsinghua University Press,05(2016)

Research on the Present Condition and Product Design of Suiling Black Pottery in Heilongjiang Province

Li Xiaoqi[1] , Zhao Aili[1 a] ,Jia Mengshi[1] ,Yan Zhenxing[1],Yang Liangliang[1]andWang Weijie[1]

[1]Heilongjiang Bayi Agricultural University, Industrial Design, China

Abstract: The paper surveys and analyzes the basic present condition of Suiling black pottery in Heilongjiang Province, and innovates and designs black pottery products. This paper combines traditional technologies with modern design methods to enrich the categories of black pottery products, expands the industry chain, and promotes the economic development of Suiling. The rapid development of modern industry led to the decline of handicraft, and the development of Suiling black pottery has stagnated. Handicrafts should be designed and transformed to ensure the inheritance of traditional culture and skills.

1 Introduction

As the birthplace of modern black pottery, Heilongjiang Suiling black pottery has special differences from black pottery in other areas: pure hand-made, natural black by firing, no artificial coloring, matt finished products, good air permeability, good adsorption, black with blue. Suiling black pottery is the artistic treasure of Heilongjiang. In order to carry forward this kind of folk traditional art, black pottery is brought into people's daily life through innovative design, and the black pottery culture of Suiling was appreciated by more people.

2 Development history of Suiling black pottery

Black pottery began its development from the Neolithic period. As an important art category in arts and crafts, it has a rich cultural heritage. The foundation and history of black pottery can be traced back to the most primitive stage of human life production. Pottery initially did not exist as arts and crafts; it was first used as a daily use of functional appliances, convenience for people's life, and then had the need to meet the conditions of human aesthetic demand [1].

In the early days, the color of the Suiling black pottery is red, and there were always gray products in the finished product after kiln firing, and the founder of Suiling black pottery, Kou Hualin, solved the black pottery smoking and carburizing technology. The black color of black pottery is formed in the late period of kiln sealing, resulting in insufficient combustion of fireweed and smoky carburization. The formed pottery surface is matt, there is no obvious reflective gloss, and there are a lot of carbon micro particles on the bottle body, showing point crystal clear. Most of the early experiments were grey and a few were black. People tried and innovated to obtain the best temperature and time, and they produced black pottery with pure color.

In 1957, the products produced by the Suiling pottery factory were mainly used for pottery and water pots in people's daily lives, and some simple patterns were painted on the outer surface. In this stage, black pottery products were still in practical pottery. The artistry of the ornamentation needed to be improved, but it bore the artistic spirit of the Suiling people, and reflected the human's pursuit of nature and beauty.

Beginning in 1961, Suiling black pottery received the attention of the famous Mr. Liu Jiadi, and he then organized a number of professional designers to make art direction and creation in Suiling clay pottery factory. [2] This is an important change to the artistic development of Suiling black pottery. By drawing on books, teaching experience and professional pattern design, black pottery has achieved great improvement in artistic value and cultural connotation. Later, the classic double hollowed-out flowerpot was designed and produced by Kou Hualin. The "multi-layer hollowed-out carving" technique in the classic double-layer hollowed-out flowerpot is one of the characteristics of the Suiling black pottery.

So far, the black pottery companies in Suiling still maintain a pure hand-made method. Based on the traditional craftsmanship of Suiling, it has been improved and the type of ware is multiple. The black pottery is black and matte by using the secondary carburizing method.

From the development point of view, Suiling black pottery changed from the completely practical product to the artistic product. In this process, the artistic attainments of black pottery reached a certain height but weakened the practicality of the product. Form follows function, the modelling form of product is indispensable, but practicality is the most basic requirement, artistic

[a] Corresponding author: aili_ailie@hotmail.com

performance should be based around functional utility. Japan's Liu Zongyue once put forward the view: "The beauty of craftsmanship is the practical beauty. All the beauty comes from the heart of service. When artifacts lose their practical value, they also lose the beauty." [3] The beauty of craftsmanship lies in its practicality, the closer to life, and the more able to embody the beauty of the craftsmanship of the product.

3 Present condition of Suiling black pottery

Nowadays, traditional black pottery products in Heilongjiang Province have formed unique aesthetic features and cultural connotations under specific social and natural backgrounds, which are of great research value. Because black pottery has a wide range of raw materials, black pottery develops rapidly. At present, the traditional black pottery market has matured, but there are problems such as the imperfect cultural market mechanism, a single level of product structure, and weak awareness of cultural innovation, which has led to a dilemma of low overall economic efficiency and difficulty in inheriting traditional skills. After a long period of development, Suiling black pottery is still dominated by handicrafts, its characteristics have led to the inability to mass-produce products, high production costs and restriction on consumer groups. At the same time, due to the long production cycle, transportation difficulties and other reasons, the market cannot be opened. Although the art value of Suiling black pottery and Jingdezhen porcelain, Yixing purple sands pottery and other pottery and porcelain are all equal, the popularity of Suiling black pottery is far lower than that of the latter two.

Therefore, it is imperative to adopt transformation design, integrate business models and design processes, transform traditional design thinking into innovative service thinking, and enable research results to exhibit black pottery's artistic features and practicality at the same time, and eventually form black pottery's innovative product design and promotion ideas, to achieve serialization, continuous, personalized development purposes.

4 Research content

4.1 Comparative analysis of black pottery of same kind

There are many excavation sites of black pottery including: Rizhao, Xingjing, Longshan, and Suiling. The black pottery culture of Suiling is different from the black pottery culture of other regions, and has not been affected by other cultures. Suiling black pottery is completely independent without reference to any other black pottery products. In this paper, the typical Rizhao pottery, Xingjing black sand and Suiling black pottery were selected for comparative analysis, as shown in table 1.

Table 1. Comparison of Rizhao black pottery, Xinjing black sand and Suiling black pottery.

	Rizhao black pottery	Yinjing black sand	Suiling black pottery
Type of ware	Bottle, brick, tile, cylinder	Pan, pot, kettle	Bottle, pot, basin, ball, tube.
Pattern	String, row, carving.	Dragon and phoenix lion fish, orchid bamboo	Folk paper cutting, ancient auspicious animals and graphic symbols, eight diagram.
Materials	Rizhao two city mud	Black sand mixed with Xingjing Baishan mud and cinder	Suiling yellow clay
Craft	Nine - layer mud extraction method, water embellish smolder process, traditional swallow - nest clay.	Shaped moule with windlass	Hand billet, hollow carving.

Rizhao black pottery: the production process used by Rizhao black pottery is nine - layer mud extraction, water embellish smolder process, traditional swallow - nest clay. Rizhao black pottery adopts the two city mud with the unique characteristics of fine color and purity. Rizhao black pottery is fired from the original earth kiln, and the ceramic ware is fine and polished with a dark and shiny surface. Rizhao black pottery is mostly vases, plane reliefs, sculptures, and various crafts. Rizhao black pottery is less decorative, mostly plain polished. The patterns are only bow string pattern, dermographic and hollow decoration.

Xingjing black sand: the shape of Xingjing sander is round and thick and full of shape. It is made of black sand mixed with Xingjing Baishan mud and cinder. The texture of this kind of black sand is coarse, the grain feel is more obvious. Xingjing black sand mainly consists of two types, one is traditional modeling, the other is modern modeling. The traditional modelling is mainly casserole, modern modelling is tea set, sculpture handicraft and so on. Xingjing black sand production is made by using the mould and windlass. The decorative patterns on the surface are generally the folk styles of dragon, phoenix, lion, fish, orchid, bamboo and chrysanthemum.

Suiling black pottery: Suiling black pottery has different varieties according to different classification standards, which can be divided into more than twenty kinds of bottle, pot, basin, ball, tube. The inspiration of the decoration is mainly from the folk paper-cut and the carved patterns on the box, mainly for the ancient auspicious animals, auspicious symbols and the eight diagrams. The yellow clay unique to Suiling makes the black pottery black and matt with blue. One of the characteristics of the Suiling black pottery is exquisite hollow carving technique, openwork carving pattern.

4.2 User and market analysis

We did a survey which was conducted on black pottery products and other pottery products. The survey covered products cognition, promotion channels, purchase channels, and consumer demand of black pottery. The analysis contents are shown in Table 2.

Table 2. User survey and analysis

	Collector	**Middle-class**	**General consumer**
Feature	Value the artistic value of the product	Value the cultural connotation of products	Value the practicality of the product and appearance
Purchasing power	High	Medium	Low
Economic capability	Strong	Medium	General

After investigation, it was found that more than 50% of the population had no knowledge of the black pottery, and most of the people who had heard of the Suiling black pottery were Suiling locals. This result fully shows that the government of the black pottery origin and the black pottery producers and sales staff has paid insufficient attention to black pottery propaganda. They did not publicize and promote the traditional black pottery products through effective propaganda methods, which greatly limited the development and inheritance of black pottery.

In terms of purchasing, most consumers will choose to buy in the mall or through the Internet. The price of the specialty stores is generally higher and fewer people choose to buy through it. This also shows the importance of online advertising. The analysis shows that most of the black pottery products purchased by consumers are used for daily life. The existing black pottery products are mostly handicrafts, which are used for decoration or collection. The black pottery manufacturers need to increase the existing product categories for the market demand, and improve the practicality of the products. The statistics show that the consumer demand of black pottery products is small and the purchasing power is low. The main reason for this problem is that the product positioning of Suiling black pottery is too high, and the black pottery industry needs to increase the middle and low-end products and expand the consumer group.

In terms of product style, the styles that modern people generally appreciate are simple and fresh, and the existing styles are complicated, and the carvings are hollow and delicate, which are more suitable as art collections and should be adjusted to meet the needs of consumers. Through data analysis, we can find that consumers in today's society pay more attention to their own inner and spiritual needs. In addition to the value of appearance, the cultural connotation of products has become more and more important.

Surveys show that, although consumers know little about black pottery and related products, they have more understanding of other pottery or ceramic products and can analyze black pottery and related products by drawing on consumers' attitudes and opinions on similar products. Consumers are in expectation of black pottery products with both artistic value and practicality.

4.3 Field investigation

During the study, two black pottery production companies were visited in Suiling County, Heilongjiang Province. The sales channels of Suiling black pottery in Heilongjiang Province are very single, mainly by offline entity store, followed by sales agents. Since the production of black pottery is all made by hand, the production cycle is long, the temperature and humidity are strict, and the accidental burst in the process of boiling makes black pottery a rare and undemanding product. In a total cost-to-profit ratio of finished black pottery products, handcrafting accounted for 46%, electricity bills, transportation, preservation, etc. accounted for 30%, so the profit of black pottery was very small. Such conditions make the price of black pottery remain high.

In the process of on-the-spot investigation, we found that the presence of counterfeiting manufacturer, in order to reduce cost, shorten production cycle, they moved black pottery to the batch production line, used rough and inferior molds to make fake black pottery, using paint color dark shiny effect. The defective products that have been fired are masked by artificially colored cracks with rough technique. Black pottery is difficult to identify, without its own standards. Compared with other art value less than the black pottery products, the market is not standardized and orderly.

The production cycle of Suiling black pottery is long and the production process is complex. The selection and preparation of materials will take three to four months. First, the yellow clay will be added to the water to be crushed and stirred, filtered and precipitated, and then the clay bar will be drawn. This process will screen the small stones in the clay completely, preventing them from cracking and breaking the surrounding pottery in the process of firing. Then, the throwing is drawn; the throwing is dried to the point where it can be hand-carved. During this process, there will be at least two times of polishing, so that the ceramic body will become smooth and perfect. After the hand carving is finished, the drying stage is carried out. The drying stage is divided into three parts: dry, medium and warm drying, high temperature dries, it takes three weeks. After the drying is completed, firing is performed. The firing takes 12-15 hours and the temperature is between 700-1000°C.

In this condition, every black pottery product that is fired is a blend of utensils and ingenuity. Exquisite hollow carving reveals the sentiments of artisans. The artifacts produced on the industrial assembly line can achieve the same level of refinement, but the product is soulless, and artistic value and cultural connotation are not as good as traditional handmade products.

5 Innovation path analysis

In order to solve the problem of small scale, single product variety and low practicability, it is necessary to change the product positioning problem in the industry. The products of black pottery are located in high-end art collections, high-end souvenirs and high-end gifts, which limited the market [3]. We should enrich the production line of black pottery and expand the coverage rate of consumers.

In the past, the black pottery product positioning is a work of art, the practicality of art is low, and the collection is high. Consumers are different from art collectors. Consumers are more concerned with the practicality, quality and cost performance of products, while collectors value the artistic value of products. With economic development, commodities are no longer simply easy to use and have more added value, such as brand value and cultural connotation. More and more consumers are willing to purchase products with cultural added value to enhance their aesthetic and taste. Consumers want commodities to bring more meaning to manifest their value.

The surface of the black pottery is matte, the bottle is black and elegant, and there will be streamers in the light. Chosen materials and unique firing technology makes the black pottery itself is able to adjust the humidity of the indoor environment. Such features can be applied to the office products to provide clean air and comfortable environment for users. The color of black pottery is a quiet, simple but elegant, the appearance model is decorated with rich and varied and cultural ornamentation, which can reflect the cultural connotation of black pottery and fully integrate into the office environment. In addition, the black pottery hollow carving technology is mature, it is used in the design of candlesticks, fragrance lamps and other home products, the traditional handicrafts are given a second meaning. At the same time because of the influence of firing techniques, black pottery has activated carbon adsorption. In this severe environment of air pollution, everyone pays more attention to physical health and environmental conditions. Black pottery products with green features will regulate the relationship between people and the environment, improve the quality of human life, and promote the harmonious development of people and the environment. This kind of product with both practicality and strong cultural connotation can enable people to come into contact with the traditional art of the Chinese nation, bring more artistic influence to people, and make the national culture more widely spread.

Therefore, based on the production process of black pottery, the characteristics of the materials and the characteristics of the finished product, the product target population of Suiling black pottery and the current market supply and demand relationship are analyzed, the existing black pottery products are improved, black pottery is matched with other materials, and the external decoration is simplified. Designing the same product that is mainly based on decorative features, removing the original complex decorative carvings, the appearance is simple and elegant, easy to match with the modern living room, in line with modern aesthetic needs. The quality of the black pottery products is an improvement for the home environment. More practicable and artistically balanced products can change the condition of Suiling black pottery, increase product variety, increase awareness, and bring more economic benefits.

6 Innovative product designs

According to the previous research, the innovative product design was carried out. In view of the material characteristics of black pottery, black pottery materials are used as part of the product for the characteristics of products. At the same time, black pottery has the same adsorption as activated carbon. This kind of green and environmental protection features, under the severe environment of the current air pollution problem, everyone pays more attention to physical health and environmental conditions, and black pottery products will undoubtedly receive customers' appreciation. This kind of product with both practicality and strong cultural background will attract more consumer groups, change the present situation, increase product variety, increase popularity, and bring more economic benefits. The black pottery product category is positioned as fragrance lamps, table lamps, vases, etc. The following are design examples.

6.1 Fragrance candlestick of black pottery

Fragrance candlestick is used more commonly in people's life; it is a kind of common household goods. The market share of fragrance candles added essential oil with different functions is growing. According to 2016 report, the retail market for American household fragrances is about $6.4 billion. A kind of candlestick designed with black pottery is used in combination with fragrance candle. A candle is placed on the upper part, and an electronic watch that can display the time is on the lower part. There are two functions of storing the candle and serving as a watch. The shape is a cylinder with rounded edges. There is no ornamentation on the device, the appearance is simple, and the material characteristics of the black pottery are fully displayed, as shown in Figure 1.

Figure 1. Fragrance candlestick of black pottery

6.2 Pottery charm—black pottery decoration

"Pottery charm" black pottery decoration is a fine work combining traditional Suiling black pottery and modern design ideas. The main materials are black clay, pine and glass. The decoration material is simple and unsophisticated, and the structure is simple and bright. It is suitable for home furnishing, flower arrangement and other usage. The production process of the product is very exquisite from the materials selection. Each processing step is to express the beauty of the essence of black pottery. The unique design idea makes the decoration possess the traditional wisdom and the modern beauty, and it also has a touch of Zen thought in use. The traditional black pottery material makes it full of Zen, such as the trees in the tranquil temple, which is always silent and full of wisdom. See Figure 2.

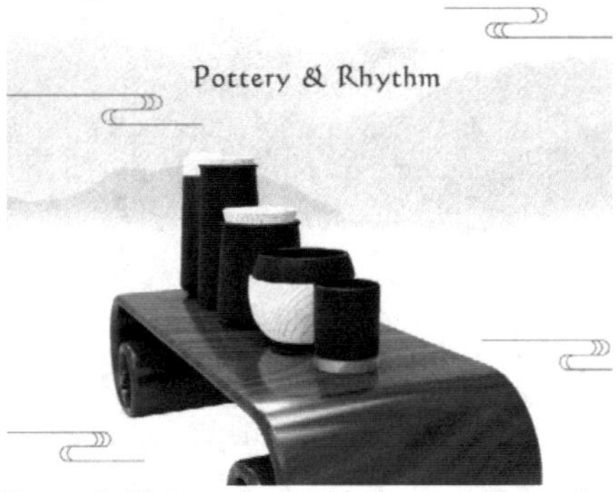

Figure 2. "Pottery charm" black pottery decoration

7 Conclusions

The ingenious spirit and cultural value represented by the Suiling black pottery are incomparable with other similar products. Suiling black pottery still maintains the pure hand craft, which is particularly valuable in the modern mechanized production atmosphere. A Japanese said, "the fundamental difference between a hand and a machine is that the hand is connected to the heart, and the machine has no heart." Each of the Suiling black pottery is integrated into the emotions of the workers, and the cultural value experience cannot be replaced by the mechanized production. The innovative design of black pottery products enables the process characteristics to be reflected, which is more practical. It transforms traditional handicrafts and returns to people's daily lives, deepens people's understanding of traditional crafts, and makes the hand-made spirit and traditional national culture better inherited.

Acknowledgment

This thesis is from Heilongjiang Bayi Agricultural University's national undergraduate innovation training program. (Project number：201710223021)

References

1. Kaihong Wang. On the Development of Modern Black Pottery Culture Ecology under the Perspective of "Non-heritage" **[d]**. Northeast Normal University (2016).
2. Jiali Liu. A Review of the Suiling Black Pottery **[J]** Decoration, 1998 (06) :52-54.
3. Zongyue Liu. The Way of Craft **[M]** Guilin: Guangxi Normal University Press, (2011)
4. Xiao He. Rizhao Black Pottery Craft and Artistic Survival [J] Art and Design (Theory), 2017, 2(05): 124-126.

Toys Featured in Tools and Tools Featured in Toys

Zhang Tian-cheng[1], Zhang Chun-yan [2]

[1]CNC Engineering Department, Anhui Technical College of Mechanical and Electrical Engineering, Anhui Wuhu, China
[2]School of Mechanical and Vehicle Engineering, Bengbu College , , Anhui Bengbu, China

Abstract. Experience design and crossover development become one of the future directions. The trend of more convenient life highlights the need for the integrated design of tools and toys, and the rapid development of productivity, as a main driving force, makes the project possible. The emotionalization of tools and the practicality of toys shift during the evolution of the integrated design, which will enhance the user's sensory experience. More attention should be paid to the interaction of rational and affective thinking and crossover products, to promote the all-round development and more experience design, meanwhile, the industrial design should conform to the popular aesthetics.

1 Introduction

People's ultimate aim, in general, is to create a happy, healthy and peaceful life for each individual in various ways, such as the progress of human civilization, the development of science and technology as well as a lifetime's effort. [1] The human design civilization experiences a series of changes, from the unconscious tools design to the conscious service scheme, from the original society's "design for survival" to the experience design of the concept era, which are the outcomes of the rapid development in the industry; However, the development of product design has never denied the belief that individuals and groups should all satisfy the integration of practical and spiritual function.

The concept of toys featured in tools and tools featured in toys innovates the ideas. The syncretism of the function of tools and the easiness of toys is undoubtedly a perfect ending. Tools and toys mentioned in this article are different from the concept of *dictionaries* and other authoritative books. Tools are defined as the products that meet the practical needs of human beings, which provide practicability. Meanwhile, toys are products that can satisfy peoples' spirit and emotional needs, which focus on the spiritual function. The evolution of the reciprocal transformation of toys and tools is an epitome of the peoples' desires to pursue both good material life and spiritual life.

2 Sensory and experiential design as needed

The primitive meaning of the sensory and experiential design that adapts to the all-round development of human beings and to promote felicity, harmony and happiness, instead of luxury and isolation. The concept of toys featured in tools and tools featured in toys implies the deep integration of rational and emotional information, practica lity and emotionality, which reflects the ultimate value of human psychological needs and real goal around a series of people's psychology, behavior, emotional appeal.

2.1About needs

(1) Definition of needs

Needs, in this article, is supposed to help people's production activities, to provide convenience in all aspects or to meet human's desire for better material and spiritual enjoyment. [2] From a psychological point of view, the concept of "needs" implies some form of "scarcity", "problem to solve" and "urgent desire". [3] Material enjoyment and spiritual enjoyment are the universal interests and pursuits of human existence.

(2) Real needs

The development of information technology not only isolates us from the real life, but also ignores the most basic human needs from the spiritual level. T. S. Eliot, a famous poet, once said, "Although television makes many people laugh at the same joke at the same time, it still makes people feel lonely." "We need to push forward the development of intelligence, and we want a balance between high technology and high emotion," John Naisbitt said in his book " Mind Set! ". [4] Hayao Miyazaki, a world animation master, said in his interview of "Spirited Away": We live in a "recreational" society. Adults are constantly seeking entertainment to fill the emptiness of the mind, and the phenomenon also embodies in the child. Excessive entertainment makes their perception passivated, and their creativity is diminished. [5] Adults use excessive or even low-level entertainment to fill gaps in the mind. In the child's world, the inflow of entertainment, the narrow

*Corresponding author: [1] skgcztc@163.com, [2]53849182@qq.com

living space, the passivation of perception and the lack of companionship, have reduced their talent for creativity. Therefore, we need to advocate the "true", "good" and "beauty" of the products and eliminate "false" "evil" and "ugly" at the same time. We need to restore the numbness of consciousness, wake up the sleeping creativity, and explore the more meaningful values in the human subconscious, in order to balance the material needs and spiritual needs of human beings. If we do so, it will be easier for us to discover people's healthy and harmonious life style, rather than stimulating the most primitive and foolish desires.

2.2 Designs adapted to senses and experience

(1) Sensory design

The so-called sense organs, generally refer to eye, ear, tongue, nose, body and so on, which have special physiological structures and functions, and are able to accept the different stimuli from the outside world and produce the senses of vision, hearing, taste, smell and touch, thus achieving psychological comfort and satisfaction of the needs for self-actualization.[6] Generally speaking, the functions of vision, hearing and touch account for 65%, 25% and 10% respectively[7]. Accordingly, human beings have attached so much pleasure for eyes, that they always make intentional or unintentional efforts to decorations when designing a product. So, in China, whether it is in the field of high-end patented products or in the popular wholesale market, there is a superb collection of products claiming exterior attractiveness, which also shows the lack of innovation in product designs and technology, as well as the reality that the industrial designs are too exclusive but uncompetitive.

(2) Experiential design

In the field of biology, vision, hearing, taste, smell and touch constitute the main ways for human beings to understand and perceive the world. Through the indefinable combination of various senses, human beings experience the products, and they can even use synaesthesia, such as seeing the sound, smelling the shapes, touching the colors, hearing the tastes, etc., to guide their external and internal activities. At the same time, according to the actual needs of some special groups, such as women, children, the aged and the disabled, industrial designers should get breakthroughs from different sensory experiences, including the appearance, the functions, the modes of use, the positioning of products, the operational environment, the innovation of science and technology and so on, which will surely challenge the patience consciousness and habitual thinking of human beings. A large number of studies have shown that cross experience can actually bring a better and more unique feelings to human beings, so as to get the humanistic concern besides the actual use experience. For example, the zippers specially designed for the blind, has solved the problem that the normal persons can not get well-dressed quickly under the dim light; and another product for the blind, the voiced traffic lights, also make it safer for smartphone addicts to cross over the intersections.

As an analytical means of human psychological needs, sense and experience make us realize the common mode behind the toys featured in tools and tools featured in toys ---- sensory and experiential design based on practicality and emotionality: the tool-like toys, the toy-like tools, as well as the dual identity of tools and toys, which provides possibilities for promoting the overall development of human mental health and expanding the space for industrial design.

3 Toys featured in tools

As one of the basic categories of products, the tool has been serving as the extension of human brains and physical limbs, and enhances their ability to adapt to the outside world. It is an important means and result of human practice. [8] Based on Maslow's theory of hierarchy of needs, Patrick Jordan, the director of the PHILPS Design Aesthetics Research Association, proposes three hierarchies of human needs for products: functionality, usability and happiness. Although this theory treats the various purposes of product designs in isolation, it interprets the purposes that humans impose to the products by verifying the functional beauty of modernism and beauty in form of postmodernism and digital era, and provides theoretical support for the concept of toys featured in tools.

3.1 Essence of toys featured in tools

The toys featured in tools means that, on the basis of the practicality, more emotional connotations should be given to the products, making the product not only rational and perceptual, but also practical and emotional. Such toys featured in tools can transmit their practical functions appropriately, and convey emotional resonance to humans, such as health, well-being, happiness, etc.. Li Zhengdao, a winner of Nobel Prize in Physics, once holds that, without emotions, can our wisdom create a new path? Without intelligence, can emotions achieve perfect results? They are likely to be non separable. If so, art and science are actually two sides of a coin, which originate from the noblest part of human activities and pursue profundity, universality and meaningfulness. Thus, being beneficial, interesting and meaningful has become the lifeblood of toys featured in tools.

3.2 Status quo of the researches on toys featured in tools

(1) Application status of toys featured in tools

Nowadays, the society has been stepping into the era of right brain, and the abundant tools have strengthened people's pursuit of spiritual life, such as appearance, sound, taste, smell, touch, character and so on, which is the reason for the elimination of traditional product designs. For example, the game functions, comprehensive functions and fashionable styles of mobile phones are emerging one after another; as long as conditions permit, private cars that are usually used as travel tools can be modified into luxury toys at will; the horse riding, boating, spinning wheel, even gliding parachute, hot air balloon and sailing ship, that are not often seen in ordinary people's lives, have gradually evolved into toys for experiential games. Interactivity, including multiplicity of connotations, diversification, convenience of use, miniaturization of sizes and sensory experience, is the future development trend of toys featured in tools, who bear the responsibility of making people feel healthy and happy.

(2) Manifestation patterns of toys featured in tools

The purposes of toys featured in tools can be summarized as making people feel a sense of health, well-being and happiness, however, there are many ways to realize it. The sensory and experiential design as needed provides a set of useful manifestation patterns for the toys featured in tools. Therefore, the appearance, sound, taste, smell, touch and character of the products constitute the main means to realize it, which also promotes the diversification of product designs. Among them, the inspection of interest is the most successful example of toys featured in tools. Due to the indifference of interpersonal relationship, life is often in danger of losing control, and worries and anxieties devour people's hearts. As a result, DIY products, which are randomly shaped according to consumers' preferences, satisfy people's psychological needs to a certain extent. The portable chopsticks, as shown in Figure 1, are made of soft metal, thus they may be turned into pipes, chopsticks, or even a ring that can be worn on the wrist like a bracelet. As it can be used whenever and wherever possible, the goals of significant decrease of the use of disposable chopsticks and protection of valuable natural resources can be achieved. Taking chopsticks as a prop, the environment as a scene, to perceive its connotation by firsthand experience will be propitious to change people's ways of living and behaving, thus inspiring more creative thoughts.

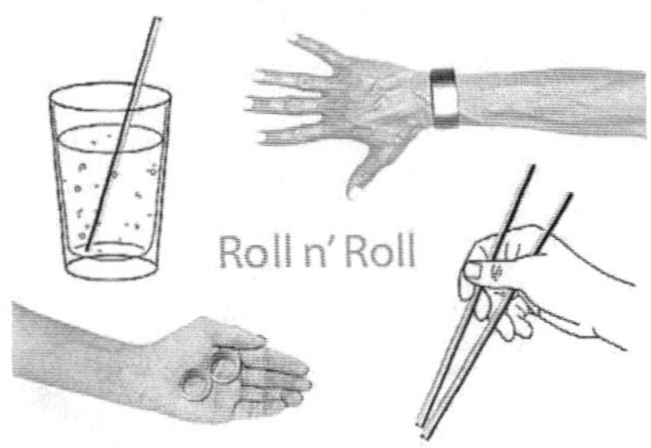

Fig.1 Portable chopsticks

4 Toys featured in tools

As far as traditional thinking is concerned, Chinese people generally believe that excessive attention to trivialities saps the will, and toys are exclusive to children. In Japan, the sales of adult toys accounts for about 65% of the annual market turnover of 900 billion yen. Most (84%) adults between the age of 18 and 69 admit having toys, and nearly half of the persons investigated claim that they have more than 20 peripheral products of comics and animations. In the United States, more than 40% toys are designed for adults every year. In China, the young ones' demands for adult toys has already reached 50 billion yuan.[9] Toy design has long been an important category of industrial design traditionally. Now, featuring multiple identities, it has entered our daily life as both a popular cultural phenomenon and even a tool with educational function.

4.1 Essence of tools featured in toys

The concept of tools featured in toys requires to treat toys for the purpose of satisfying people's multiple demands in essence, endowing practicality to the toys that only please people in the spiritual level. In the process of meeting human spiritual and emotional needs, toys gradually integrate the appropriate practical value, and achieve the combination of emotionality and practicability. It can be said that, such toys serve as educational tools for children, and has the the effect of healing and pleasure for adults. Such toys will surely become an indispensable part to all stages of life. The essential characteristics of tools featured in toys are the interactivity that is intertwined with happiness, education, health, functionalization, security, science and technology, globalization, the all-aged design and integration.

4.2 Application status and manifestation of tools featured in toys

The development of instrumentalized toys has been a time-honored trend. According to the Encyclopedia, early toys are developed from self-defense and instincts. In many cultures, the first thing to teach children is how to use weapons, many physical games and athletic sports come from competitions and wars.[10] On the one hand, the development of science and technology, the abundance of materials and the complexity of consumption mentality, make traditional toys no longer win the hearts of all. On the other hand, the application of new materials and technologies has injected new vitality into the tools featured in toys. The rapid growth of everyday toys and animated peripheral products has prompted the instrumentalization of toys as the epoch features of product consumption and design.

(1) Everyday toys

Adding ordinary daily attributes to toys will greatly enrich the connotations of toys and broaden the designers' minds. For example, the robot girl serving in a dining room, the robot called Baymax greeting people at a bank, and the child watch with a positioning function, are all possess multiple functions of entertainment and education, as well as a great potential value. The design of building blocks of calendar, see Figure 2, is inspired by the spirit of building blocks and made of resin, an environmentally friendly material, and it tells people the date of any month in any year after random placement of numbers. This design not only makes people feel the joy of hands-on and restores the feelings of young people, but also reminds people of date. One object with multifunction is convenient, practical and environmental friendly.

Fig.2 Building blocks of calendar

(2) Animated peripheral products

The emergence of animated peripheral products is inseparable from toys.[11] The so-called animated peripheral products, also known as animation derivatives, are collectively referred to as Hobby, which include all physical manifestations that are related to the animated images, and are divided into hard and soft peripheral products.[12] Although animated images only exist in the virtual world, they are in fact the Utopia in our subconscious mind, and are often able to transmit positive energy. As is shown in Figure 3, the Disguise Transformers watch is designed for children only. Featuring a built-in drive structure, it looks like a normal watch, however, in particular cases, especially under the call of self-defense, the watch can be turned into a Transformers. In a nutshell, it is not only a watch, but also a toy.

Fig.3 Disguise transformers watches

It is worth noting that the specific animated peripheral products have obvious characteristics of the regions and the times. With various external factors, such as the increasing age, the value orientation, etc., it is easy for them to be obsolete, especially in today's society that puts particular emphasis on personalized design and fast pace. A large number of eliminated animated peripheral products have become garbage. As long as there is an Andy, who will grow up, there will be abandoned toys. Nothing will keep unchanged forever. And time does not only lead toys to the tragic fate of being neglected, but also takes away too much of our childhood feelings.[13] This brings about another principle of product design, that the life cycle and the commodity circulation must be taken into account, for the purpose of cherishing resources and protecting environment; concerning about the green design of animated peripheral products is a major issue in the future.

5 Conclusions

As is known to all, what the industrial designers should do is not to make simple additions merely, in other words, they should try their best to achieve greater added value through industrial design. From the consumers' point of view, products must meet the multiple needs of human beings, so as to express the endless spiritual and material pursuit of human beings. Therefore, the toys featured in tools and the tools featured in toys should be regarded as an indispensable direction for human's pursuit of health, happiness and harmonious lives. The integration of tools and toys will become one of the important topics of future design. Holding the courage and consciousness to break through the exterior attractiveness, and bearing the responsibility of for the good of next generation, great importance must be attached to the cultural connotation of products, while giving them gorgeous appearances; when pursuing the value expression of the true, the good and the beautiful, the value guidance method of the false, the evil and the ugly have to be removed to the utmost of our power, and the practical function and emotional appeal must be integrated into one. This is a major issue for future designers.

References

1. Li Geng,The Aesthetic Turn of Mass Culture,Beauty & Times[J],2007.10(321)
2. Kepu Wenzhai,2007(11)
3. Gao Nan,Methods and Cases of Industrial Design Innovation[M], Chemical Industry Press, 2006.1(1)
4. The Era of Right Brain Highlights the Management of Human Senses, Human Resources,2007.11(264)
5. Xu Jing& Wang Yang, Reading -- World Classic Animation[M], Blossom Press, 2005.8(1)
6. Ren Lisheng, Design Psychology[M], Chemical Industry Press, 2005.8(1)
7. Zhang Ying,Visual Sense-False Sense-Toy[J], Art & Design,2005.10(150)
8. Chen Hanqing,Product Design[M], Huazhong University of Science and Technology Press, 2005.11(1)
9. Choice, 2008(1)
10. Zhang Pei& Wang Hongge, Toys and Innovative Design[M], Chemical Industry Press, 2006.2(1)
11. Zhou Lanping , History of Comic and Animation[M], Chongqing Publishing Group & Chongqing Publishing House, 2007.4(1)
12. Zhao Juntao &Tan Beilin, CorelDRAW & Flash 8 Animation Art Design[M], Tsinghua University Press, 2007.1(1)
13. Sun Taotao, An Analysis of the Narrative Mode of Toy Story III[J], Art Science and Technology, 2015(5)

Online Learning Space and Wisdom Teaching

Yanxia Wu[1]

[1]Institute of humanities, Jiangxi University of Traditional Chinese Medicine, Nan chang, China

Abstract: Online Learning Space is a virtual learning environment which has evolved with the development of information technology and the continuous deepening of educational concepts. The wisdom teaching is a teaching by using teaching methods and teaching strategies rationally based on the Online Learning Space,to complete the transition from knowledge to wisdom,so that students can become intelligent talents. The wisdom teaching has two goals: to promote the individual growth and to foster innovative talents. Online Learning Space in different stages provides different support for Wisdom teaching activities, and realizes the goal of Wisdom teaching in different degrees.

1 INTRODUCTION

The study mainly studied two questions: What is the goal of Wisdom Teaching? What kind of support can the Online Learning Space provide for Wisdom Teaching activities?

2 RESEARCH STATUS AT HOME AND ABROAD

2.1 Research Status At Abroad

The research on Learning Space started in 2003 at abroad, mainly exploring how to reform school environment to meet the learning needs of the "Digital Generation". At present, the research of Learning Space includes all aspects of the learning ranging from the planning, design, implementation to evaluation of learning ,and the developed countries such as the United States, Britain and Australia have all done useful attempts.

American scholar Brown (Brown, 2005), based on the characteristics of new learners, has made clear the design principles, technology configuration and related learning styles of Learning Space. The book " Learning Space" published by EDUCAUSE, a research institute of higher education in the United States, is the first monograph to introduce Learning Space systematically in 2006. It expounds the trend of Learning Space design from three aspects: the change of students, the development of technology and the understanding of learning. Subsequently, Australian Professor David (Radcliffe, 2008) proposed a "pedagogies-learning-space-technology (PST)" framework for Learning Space design and evaluation. He regards information technology, teaching method and Learning Space as the three elements of learning space design. He thinks that the three interact with each other. Teachers should pay full attention to the role of the interaction among the three in classroom teaching. Proper combination of a variety of factors can promote efficient learning. In 2010, the British Learning Technology Association released the Research Report on "Design Guidelines for Learning Space in the 21st Century,"which pointed out that Learning Space is a priority for future research. The Learning Space can be summarized by four key words: motivation, collaboration, personalization and flexibility; learning space should stimulate students' learning motivation, support students' collaborative learning, provide students with a personalized environment, and make a flexible change about space layouts to meet the needs. With the publication of "Learning Space Journal " at the University of North Carolina in 2011, the learning space research, as an important aspect of learning environment research,has drawn increasing attention from researchers, practitioners and policymakers in the world. The research and practice on Learning Space from the United States, Britain and Australia shows that Online Learning Space refers to the entire school space, including not only classrooms, libraries, outdoor learning area and other physical space, but also the school virtual space, we can say that Learning Space is the integration of an educational institution of physical space and virtual space.

The concept of Learning Space is gradually evolving from the original formal and physical environment to the informal, virtual digital learning environment, and then to the current Online Learning Space. Research on Online Learning Space abroad mainly focuses on the concept and description, design concepts and ideas, platform development and design, teaching applications, etc., emphasizing "learner-centered ", "learners take the

*Corresponding author:wuyanxia2000@sina.com

initiative to create content ", and "learners make an interactive conversation with other learners ". For this learner-center Online Learning Space, Stephen Downes defines it as a combination of a tool, a service, a person, and a resource etc.

2.2 Research status in China

The literature number of domestic Online Learning Space is relatively small. with "Online Learning Space " as the title for searching on CNKI, there are 161 articles retrieved.

Table 1. Number of papers published over the years

Year	2010	2011	2012	2013	2014	2015	2016	2017
Number of papers	1	1	2	18	24	30	62	22

As can be seen from Table I, the study of Online Learning Space in China has only received academic attention in recent eight years. The document first appeared in 2010. At this time, Liu Haitao and Yu Jiao, a modern education technology center of Central South University, pioneered the construction of an Online Learning Space suitable for students' individual learning. From 2010 to 2012, there were only 4 relevant literatures. It is clear that Online Learning Space of this stage has not aroused much attention from the academic community.As can be seen from the table I, since 2013, the number of literatures has increased rapidly, and Online Learning Space has drawn more and more attention. Driven by the "three links and two platforms" policy, the Online Learning Space has become increasingly active, and a great deal of relevant research has emerged. By analyzing the research content of the literature, it can be seen that at present, there is not a unified understanding of Online Learning Space in the field of domestic research and practice.The main reasons are: (1) there is no consensus on the connotation of Online Learning Space; (2) the definition of the components of Online Learning Space is unclear. This leads to a certain confusion of understanding. The connotation and elements of Online Learning Space guide practice. The clearer the connotation and constituent elements of Online Learning Space are, the more targeted the construction is, the more effective the implementation will be. In the "13th Five-Year Plan" period, under the background of "Online Learning Space for all", it is particularly necessary to make a comprehensive discussion about these problems.

3 THE CONNOTATION OF ONLINE LEARNING SPACE

Online Learning Space is a virtual learning environment which has gradually evolved with the development of information technology and the continuous deepening of educational concepts.When it comes to the connotation of the Online Learning Space, basically two views are presented.The broad Online Learning Space refers to a virtual space that runs on any platform carrier to supports online teaching activities.The narrow sense of Online Learning Space refers to the special educational service platform, which supports online teaching activities. It provides an online platform for various space services such as student space, teacher space, parental space,manager space, and institutional space. The object of this study is a broad Online Learning Space. Information technology refers to a system of means and methods for collecting, processing, storing, communicating, and applying information. With the continuous development of information technology,the representing methods of online learning resource,learning services methods,and human-computer interaction methods are continuously evolving, and the form of Online Learning Space is constantly changing and its functions are constantly improving accordingly. Therefore, in the different stages of information technology development, the connotation of Online Learning Space is different. This article will discuss the connotation of Online Learning Space from the three stages of information technology development: Web1.0, Web2.0, and Web3.0.

Table 2: The connotation of online learning space

Information Technology Development	The connotation of online learning space		
	representing methods of resource	learning services methods	human-computer interaction
Web1.0	multi-media resources	A large number of knowledge database	Digital education resources are one-way process .
Web2.0	Multi-media resources are becoming open and generative.	The ubiquitous, mobile, and instant learning platform	Various interactive environment
Web3.0	Digital education resources are more personalized and adaptable.	multi-synergy , virtual integrated, and accurate learning platform	high-immersion and contextual learning experience environment

4 THE TECHNICAL SUPPORTS FOR WISDOM TEACHING PROVIDED BY THE ONLINE LEARNING SPACE

The wisdom teaching is a teaching by using teaching methods and teaching strategies rationally based on the Online Learning Space,to complete the transition from knowledge to wisdom,so that students can become intelligent talents. The wisdom teaching has two goals: to promote the individual growth and to foster innovative talents. Online Learning Space in different stages provides different support for Wisdom Teaching activities, and realizes the goal of Wisdom Teaching in different degrees.

To study the support for wisdom teaching activities provided by the Online Learning Space , it is critical to analyze the support services that the online learning space provides for the core elements of teaching activities. The Online Learning Space is a virtual learning environment that has gradually evolved with the development of information technology. The Online Learning Space is a space that supports teaching and learning innovation. With the support of the Online Learning Space, the teaching goal is constantly changing from mastering knowledge to developing wisdom.The teaching resources are no longer limited to traditional textbooks and become an online learning platform built by experts, teachers, and students. Teachers will become the leader in acquiring resources, counselors in self-learning , guides in deconstructing and reconstructing , and promoters in communicating . Students will become the subject of learning. With the support of the Online Learning Space, the development direction of Wisdom Teaching is as follows:

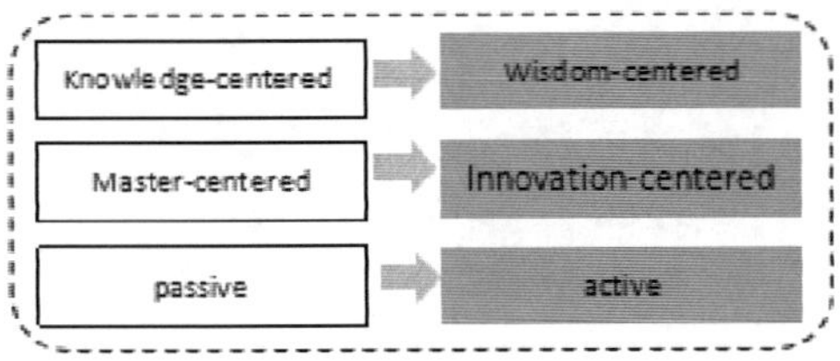

Traditional teaching value knowledge and leave out wisdom. With regard to the relationship between knowledge and wisdom,Dewey, an American educationalist, holds that knowledge is the learning that has been acquired and stored, while wisdom is the ability to use knowledge to guide life and improve life. With the support of an increasingly sophisticated Online Learning Space,the narrow goals of acquiring knowledge has been transferred to the innovative goals of wisdom development; classroom teaching based on imparting, comprehending and memorizing knowledge is changing to develop students' ability of innovation and creativity.All the time, Students have always been passive recipients in the classroom. With the development of Online Learning Space, students have more opportunities for independent learning, more convenient access to resources and learning tools, and greater power to organize and develop individual learning plans.

5 CONCLUSIONS

At present, the development of Online Learning Space is in full swing, but its application is still relatively primary and fragmented, which fails to integrate effectively with teaching practice and lacks a feasible normal application model. The full realization of wisdom teaching will still take time.

REFERENCES

1. Wang Shizeng.Research on the construction of teachers' personal space based on network teaching and research platform [J]. China Electrochemical Education, 2012, (11): 140-142.
2. Huang Lihua, Zhou Yifa, Chen Xuejun. The construction of class network learning space under the background of Banban Tong [J]. China Electrical education, 2014, (3): 86-90.
3. Wu Zhongliang, Zhao Lei. A preliminary study of the overturned classroom teaching model based on the network learning space [J]. China Electric education, 2014, (4): 121-126.
4. Bi Jiajuan, Yang Xianmin. Construction of personal learning space from the perspective of communicationism [J]. China Electrochemical Education, 2014, (8): 48-54.
5. Zhang Shiming, Xu Hexiang, Qian Dongming, et al. Analysis of "Network Learning Space All-Access" System in Cloud Architecture Mode [J]. Journal of East China Normal University (Natural Science Edition), 2014, (2): 30-39.
6. Zhu Zhiting, Guan Jueqi . "The construction framework ofOnline Learning Space for all" [J]. China Electrochemical Education, 2013, (10): 1-7.
7. Zhu Zhiting, Guan Jueqi, Liu Jun. Personal learning space: new focus of digital learning environment design [J]. China Electrochemical Education, 2013, (3): 1-6.
8. Whiteside, A., Brooks, D.C., & Walker, J.D.. Making the case for space: three years of empirical research on formal and informal learning environments [J/OL]. EDUCAUSE Quarterly, 2010, 33(3).
9. Radcliffe, D. A Pedagogy-Space-Technology (PST) Framework for Designing and Evaluating Learning Places [A].Proceedings of the Next Generation Learning Spaces Colloquium [C].Brisbane:The University of Queensland,2008. 9–16.
10. Astrid M. Sølvberg and Marit Rismark. Learning spaces in mobile learning Environments[J].Active Learning in Higher Education, 2012,13(1) :23-33.

Empirical Research on Industrial Design Contribution Rate under Statistical Frame

Xiaojing Liu[1], Ying Liu[1 a] and Xinyuan Xue[1]

[1]Central South University, School of architecture and art, 410083 Changsha City, Hunan, China

Abstract. This paper studies the evaluation method of industrial design contribution rate from the statistical frame, strives to realize the extension of research results and the replication of research method. This paper firstly identifies the connecting points with the statistics of national scientific activities through streamlining the relationship between industrial design and R&D; and then it selects the appropriate calculating model and variants according to the characteristics of industrial design, as well as established the accumulating effects regression model as per the development rules of product; finally it applies the statistical data of random sampling to calculate the industrial rate of ShunDe District in 2012 and analyzes the research results

1 Introduction

Currently the trend of industrial design leading the innovation and upgrading of enterprise is blooming. However, when discussing how much value the industrial design can bring, people always mention the research results of the United States, UK and Japan, and there is little empirical research data involved with the value contribution rate of industrial design in China [2-3]. In 2011, Beijing Industrial Design Promotion Center has calculated the industrial contribution rate in Beijing through the questionnaire and the survey data was 1:12.99[1]. This significant research attempt has been attracting a broad attention. However, the research method of questionnaire is consuming time and stamina, which is inconvenient to duplicate and promote. In addition, the objective aspects in the course of collecting data and samples need to be further improved. Such current situation has demonstrated that the research on the field of industrial design value evaluation still needs to be deepened, so as to enable the management level of industrial design to follow up the step of industry development.

2 Why making research on the industrial design contribution rate

2.1 Industrial design contribution rate

The contribution rate is one of the indexes for analyzing the economic benefit. It refers to the rate between the number of effective or useful results and the resources consumption and occupation volume, and that is, the rate between output volume and input volume. The contribution rate is usually used for analyzing the degree of effects ofeach factor in the economic increase. This index represents the driving force of industrial design to economy, and it can be used to evaluate the health degree of industrial design development.

Industrial design is a creative activity with multiple input and multiple output. Its input includes capital, manpower, equipment, modelling etc. And its output includes economic benefit, social benefit, environmental benefit etc. When performing the evaluation of industrial design contribution rate, the output of economic benefit shall be taken as the main data.

2.2 Significance of researching contribution rate

It is well known that the industrial design plays an important strategically role in the transformation and upgrading of national manufacturing industry. However, what is exactly the value of industrial design? How to calculate it? What the differences between different industries and environments? Such series of problems have directly reflected the management level of industrial design for one country. The industrial contribution rate is an important evaluation index to reflect the value of industrial design, which can directly evaluate the entire status of industrial design development. The scientific evaluation method of industrial design contribution rate can realize the long-term monitoring to the development status of targeted object industrial design, as well as carry out the horizontal comparison with the other objects to discover the characteristics and advantages of their own development.

We can analyze the significance of industrial design contribution rate from four levels. From the government level, it is able to help the governments to understand the entire development status of industrial design, differences in regions and industries to facilitate the

*Corresponding author: [a] 81413450@qq.com

issuance of relevant targeted polities. From the industry level, it is help to comprehensively understand the degree of correlation between industrial design and industry development, as well as draft the industry development strategies from their own characteristics and advantages. From the enterprise level, it can help us pragmatically understand the economic benefit of enterprises brought by the industrial design so as to help the enterprises transform and upgrade, as well as stimulate the limited resources to distribute reasonably. From the designing company level, it follows the contribution rate of industrial design project to reflect the designing capacity of company, so as to directly reflect the competition strength during the tendering and quotation of project.

3 How to calculate the industrial design contribution rate

3.1 Industrial design under the statistical frame

In order to recognize and analyze the industrial design contribution rate in a scientific way, it is necessary to find the indexes and data that can reflect the characteristics of industrial design and ensure its objectivity, availability and consistency. However, in order to ensure that the indexes and data are consistent on the multiple levels of governments, industry and enterprises, currently the most available way is to connect with the statistical frame. First of all, understand the quantitative means and analyze methods of the current statistical frame in China to the statistical indexes of industrial design and relevant activities, and then identify the specific indexes representing the industry characteristics of industrial design, as well as clarify the relationship between these indexes and current statistical indexes.

Streamline the concept and scope of industrial design from the national statistical frame, identify that the industrial design belongs to the statistics of enterprise science and technology activities included in the scope of R&D (Research & Development). R&D covers most of the basic research, application research and test development. However, the research activities of industrial design are included in the application research. The prototype creativity and modeling creativity of industrial design are included in its test development. The specific relationship can be indicated by the following figure 1: [4]

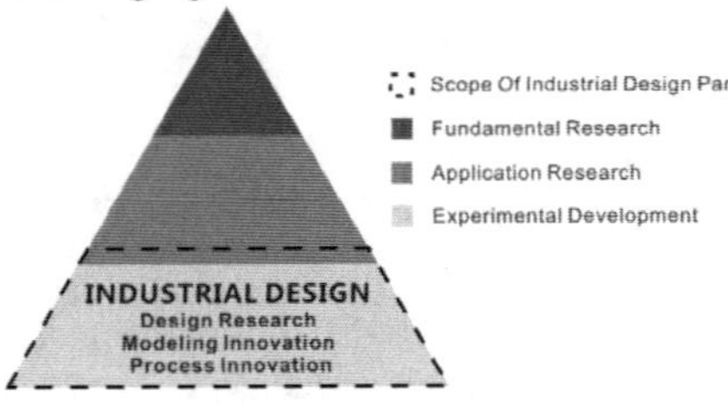

Figure 1 The relationship between R&D and industrial design in the statistical category of scientific and technological activities of enterprises

R&D is a very important index in the scientific activity statistics. The government perform routine statistics every year, and carry out the special general survey every ten years, and the rules for statistics have become mature. We can streamline the relevant indexes of industrial design from the statistical frame of R&D according to the relationship structure between industrial design and R&D, as well as abstract the statistical data to carry out the research on the industrial design contribution rate.

3.2 Selection of model and variable

Through comparing and analyzing hundreds of relevant literature on the research methods of contribution rate at home and abroad, this paper mainly focuses on the contribution rate calculation of R&D or scientific resources, and applies the regression analysis method, index method and ratio method. We finally apply the multiple linear regression models to calculate the contribution rate of industrial design through weighting the strength of various research methods, combining the industry properties of industrial design and considering the adaptability to the statistical frame. [5-6]

The key point of applying the regression model to calculate the contribution rate is the selection of independent variant, dependent variable and control variable.

The capital investment of product development is selected as the independent variable. It includes the input indexes of industrial design e.g. operational capital, human resource, equipment and facilities, conceptual creativity etc. It is able to transform each input index into the fund amount to unify the quantitative indexes during specifically selecting the independent variables. The sites for equipment and facilities are finally converted into the currency funds to reckon in the product cost, manpower input can be converted into the remuneration to reckon in the input cost. Therefore, from the perspective of cost accounting, the capital input of industrial design can cover the input of various resources, which can also comprehensively weight the R&D input cost of enterprises. In the annual scientific statistics, it is able to conclude the development expense for new product from the total amount of scientific activities expenses, that is, the expenses of enterprises used for the research, design, research and fabrication of models, as well as test and experiment etc. We can regard the expenses for the development of new product (exclude the expenses of technical improvement that don't belong to the industrial design activities) as the capital input of industrial design for the product development of enterprises.

The sales income of the new product is selected as the dependent variable. The value of industrial design can be reflected by the product financial indexes of enterprises e.g. sale income of new product and production cost reduction etc. The purpose of one enterprise to carry out the industrial design is to increase the sales income of new product, which is the reflection of economic value of industrial design. Therefore, the index of sales income for new product can be taken as the output index, which is in line with the properties of industrial design. The sales income of new product in the scientific activities of enterprises is the routine index, and it can collect data directly.

The sales capacity of enterprises is selected as the control variable. The sales capacity of enterprises refers to the capacity of enterprises to enable the customers to accept new product within the shortest time, which is particularly important for new product to obtain the final economic benefit, and it will affect the relationship between the input of industrial design and output of enterprises performance. By referring to the practice of Bouwen Lin, Yikuan Lee etc. in "R&D intensity and Commercialization orientation effects on financial performance" [7], it utilizes the sales cost to reflect the level of sales capacity. Generally speaking, only the large-scaled enterprises are able to possess the sufficient funds to construct the complete sales channels and sales methods, in which the sale cost is usually high, and it is difficult for the middle-and-small-scaled enterprises to input the capital investment in the sales of new product. We can directly collect the statistical data from the sales cost of a new product, and utilize its natural logarithm to indicate the sales capacity of the new product.

3.3 Construction of accumulated effect and models

New product requires several steps from designing R&D to realizing the commercialization, as well as from just entering into the market to being recognized by market. However, the sharp increase of sales also needs a long process. Therefore, the input of industrial design has a certain hysteretic effect on the output benefit of enterprises, and that is indicated as the product development of industrial design is the continuous accumulation process of multiple-year input and multiple-year output. The input of industrial design is the year-by-year accumulated stock instead of the current-year throughput. The research survey has shown that the average sales period for new product is 3-5 years, and the effective period of new product recognized by China is 3 years. Therefore, it could be considered that the average period of cumulative effect of industrial design is 3 years. By referring to the book named 《Knowledge based Economy》 (1996) on the basic concepts of stock measurement, we can utilize the perpetual inventory(stock) system of physical stock to calculate the accumulated stock of industrial design input within 3 years. [8-10]

Drawing on the basic idea of DECD on stock measure, we can build the cumulative effect regression model of industrial design contribution rate [5]:

$$\mathrm{NPS}_t = \beta_1 \ln \mathrm{ME}_{t-1} + \beta_2 \mathrm{ID}_{t-1} + \varepsilon$$

In which NPS_t represents the sales income of new product in the year t, ME_{t-1}represents the sales capacity in the t-1 year (natural logarithm of sales expense), $\mathrm{ID}_{t-1}$is the cumulative industrial design input in the t-1 year, ε is the random interference end item. If the cumulative development expense of new product is 0, the sales income of new product will not exist, thus there will be no regular number.

4 Empirical analysis of industrial design contribution rate

4.1 Source of data and data handling

In order to empirically analyze the industrial design contribution rate, we strive to connect with the national statistical frame, as well as collect the relatively objective, fair true data of enterprises to generate the continuous and stable data base for the relevant units, enterprises and scholars to analyze. According to the regulations of Statistics Laws of the People's Republic of China and the requirements of scientific statistical annual report policy of National Statistics Bureau, the enterprises declare the performance of scientific activities of enterprises every year to the Statistics Bureau through the Performance Sheet of Scientific Project for the Scaled and Above Industrial Enterprises and Performance Sheet of Scientific Activities for the Scaled and Above Industrial Enterprises. We will take Shunde District as the research object, through research and visit to the statistical departments of enterprises and governments, and randomly collect the data of survey sheets of scientific activities for 60 scaled and above manufacturing enterprises from 2010 to 2012 as the research samples.

In order to eliminate the influences of inflation, we select the consumption index of residents in Foshan City from 2010 to 2012, carry out the deflation to the output and control variables to conclude the invariable price by taking 2010 as the base period. Substitute the total capital of industrial design input of selected samples from 2010 to 2012 into the perpetual inventory system model to conclude the accumulate stock of industrial design input in 2012.

4.2 Calculate data and results analysis

We input the successive 3-year cumulative stock of industrial design input capital, the sales income of enterprises in 2012 and the statistical data of sales expenses for the new product in the software Eviews6 to calculate the industrial design contribution rate in 2012. The results obtained are shown in table 1:

Table1 Empirical Study on correlation of sales income of new products in industrial design area

Variable	Coefficien	Std.Error	t-Statistic	Prob.
ME	590.6990	293.7710	2.010747	0.0490
ID	101.0295	5.418471	18.64539	0.0000
R-squared	0.929123		D.W	1.742936

Substitute the results into the above sheet into the regression model to conclude the relationship between the cumulative expense input of industrial design and the sales income for the new product of enterprises as below:

$$\widehat{NPS} = 590.70ME + 101.03ID$$

It can be seen from the above Table that R^2=0929, which is approaching to 1, so the fitting degree of model is high. Under the 5% significance level, these two independent variables can be tested via t statistics, which indicates that the independent variable can explain the dependent variable to a great extent. D.W testing value is approaching 2, and the auto-correlation between independent variables is low, which indicates that the modelling is reasonable. The empirical results have shown that the industrial design input has the significant positive correlation with the sales income of a new product. The increase of 1 unit industrial design input can bring 101.03 units of sales income of a new product. The empirical results have shown that the industrial design contribution rate of Shunde District in 2012 is 1:101.03. It needs to stress that this value is the overall average level of Shunde District in 2012. If we extend this evaluation method for year-by-year tracking, we can directly understand the actual status of industrial design development of Shunde District.

5 Conclusions

Exploring the evaluation method of scientific industrial design contribution rate from the statistical frame, and striving to realize the extension of research results and the re-producibility of research method is a work of great significance. Currently, the research is relying on the domestic exiting statistical regulations and data, the research results can basically reflect the industrial design contribution level of regions and industries. If the management levels of design in enterprises are keeping improving, as well as each index and data have realized to take the enterprises as the subject and segment to each new product development project, it is able to display the industrial design contribution rate of manufacturing enterprises and designing companies by utilizing this calculation method. Thus it is undoubted? to form the four-level integrated consistent evaluation system for governments, industries, manufacturing enterprises and designing companies, which is better advantageous to the technical operation and comparison analysis in the practical work.

But still, there are certainly some problems existing in the research on industrial design contribution rate. Firstly the calculation method only considers the 3-year cumulative input of industrial design for the ordinal product development project, however, the development time for some innovative product projects with breakthrough property usually exceeds 3 years, and the benefit generated by them can be greatly reflected in the products of second-generation and third-generation. Currently it is still unable to identify the method to directly calculate the industrial design cumulative stock for the innovative product with breakthrough property. Secondly, when making research on the industrial design contribution rate in Shunde District, it was able to collect the successive 3-year data samples for only 60 manufacturing enterprises due to the limited objective conditions. If it's during the actual calculation work, the number of samples collected shall be as per the total number of manufacturing enterprises within the area to ensure that the research results have strong representativeness.

Acknowledgment

The project of the Hunan Province philosophy and Social Science Fund "Research on value and performance evaluation of industrial design"， Number:16yba369

Reference

1. Dongliang Chen, The value of industrial design， *Oriental Enterprise Culture*,2(2011)
2. Xiaojing Liu, Research on value evaluation of industrial design ， An empirical research report based on the development status of Shunde District ， *Tianjin People's Fine Arts Publishing House* ， (2014)
3. Crawford, M., and A. Di Benedetto. *New products management (9th ed.).* New York: McGraw-Hill/Irwin, (2008)
4. Statistical report system of enterprise (unit) scientific and technological activities, National Bureau of Statistics of the People's Republic of China，12(2013)
5. OECD, Knowledeg-Based Economy ， *Beijing Machinery Industry Press*,(1996)
6. Haoxiang Wang, The correlation between R&D cost input and enterprise value- Based on the data of high and new technology enterprises listed in China, Capital University of Economics and Business, PHD， Capital University of Economics and Business ， Beijing (2012)
7. BW Lin， Y Lee， SC Hung, R&D intensity and commercialization orientation effects on financial performance, *Journal of Business Research* , 59 ,**6**, (2006)
8. Bouwen Lin, Yikuan Lee and Shichang Hung, *R&D intensity and Commercialization orientation effects on financial performance, Journal of Business Research* ,(2006)
9. Gemser, Gerda Leenders, and Mark A.A. How Integrating Industrial Design in the Product Development Process Impacts on Company Performance, Journal of Product Innovation, **18**(2001)
10. Maohua Jie,Yuanyuan Wang, R&D investment and enterprise value of resource-based enterprises, Journal of Industrial technology,**8**(2011)

On the Reconstruction of Advertising Ethics in the New Media Era

XU Ming[1], Xu Jiao[1a]

[1]Cnetral South University, Visual Communication and Digital Media Design Department, 410083 Changsha Hunan, China

Abstract. The advent of the "new media era" has greatly promoted the reform and development of the advertising industry, while it has also made the entire advertising industry field face some new difficulties. Among them, the loss of advertising ethics is one of the core issues to be solved urgently. In the process of the development of new media advertising, there are endless ethical anomie phenomena. Therefore, how to propose countermeasures against problems and propose strategies for reconstructing advertising ethics from the above aspects in the new media era is a theoretical category that this article focuses on.

1. Introduction

From time immemorial, China has been regarded as an ethical society. "Ethics" has also been forged to maintain the basic principles of group social survival and healthy development in the long smelting of culture. "Advertising ethics is about the survival and healthy development of advertising communication activities, and the basic principles and values of maintaining the harmonious operation of the integrated social system ecological environment brought by advertising communication activities." [1] With the revitalization of digital and internet communication technologies, the inherent structure and distribution of rights in the traditional advertising industry have also been dissolved to some extent, even if the traditional positions of TV, radio, newspapers, and other traditional advertising seem unbreakable.

However, the fact is that new media advertising are also increasingly demonstrating the advancement of their commercial leadership and social influence. Instead, we must note that the new media era has also provided a breeding ground for the spread of decadent cultures and negative thoughts. The complex new situation has forced us to rethink the ethical anomalies behind the seemingly flashy nature of the advertising industry under the support of new media technology. Therefore, in this context, it seems that the advertising discourse has caused severe challenges to the traditional ethical framework.

2. The enhancement of quality education for advertising practitioners

The so-called "enhancement of the quality education for advertising professionals" is mainly to seek a balance strategy between profits and ethics. It is not possible to adopt a "one size fits all" approach. Ultimately, as a commercial activity, the primary purpose of advertising is to make profits especially in the context of the new media era, where competition is fiercer and business survival becomes more urgent. As for how to put this measure into practice, it can be considered from the following aspects.

First of all, the National Advertising Association or the State Administration of Radio and TV regularly hold public lectures or competitions to conduct ethical and moral education for the advertising practitioners. Secondly, publicity and awards are given to the leading enterprises that have a better relationship between righteousness and benefit so that they can establish a good industry benchmark as soon as possible, which provides the right external motivation mechanism for those advertising practitioners who are at the two ends of morality and interests. Finally, it is adept at drawing on domestic and foreign classic marketing cases or advertising models. In this regard, the autonomy and principle highlighted by New York Times newspaper are very worthy of attention. For a long time, the newspaper of New York Times adhered to strict standards of adequacy for advertising, even if the hard threshold caused the company to lose tens of millions of dollars in advertising each year. However, it has won praise from the entire industry and society over time. At present, the newspaper of New York Times daily turnover has been as high as millions of dollars.

From this example, it is concluded that the so-called righteousness and benefit are not absolute opposites. As long as the right choice is taken and the vision is long-term, unexpected spiritual and material dual wealth will be obtained. Of course, all this is based on the good ethical quality, social responsibility, and wise business mindset of the advertising industry.

*Corresponding author: [a] 24376543@qq.com

3. Basic principles for building cross-cultural advertising ethics

The arrival of the "new media era" means that the exchanges between different cultures are more frequent. In this process, the ethical dilemmas of cross-cultural communication are gradually exposed, such as the imbalance of information dissemination, cultural misreading and transitional interpretation, and ethics conflict of ethics ideas and cultural hegemonism, which constitutes disharmony in heterogeneous cultural exchanges. In the ethical reflection of cross-cultural advertising, the author attempts to put forward general ethical principles for these ethical issues. The core elements of the ethical issues probably include the following aspects.

The first principle is tolerance and mutual trust. American scholar Fang Long once pointed out, "Tolerance allows others to have freedom of action and judgment, and tolerance of patience and justice different from their own views." [2] In this regard, due to the multi-source generation of different cultures, it is no longer necessary to coercively demand the same. In addition, holding a tolerant heart and seeking unity in diversity can further promote world cultural prosperity, which just as a Chinese proverb says "Gentlemen seek harmony but not uniformity".

The second principle is freedom and equality. For cross-cultural communication, "freedom" here is not absolute freedom. In fact, absolute freedom may not be possible. This article only refers to the elimination of situations in which certain cultural barriers are intentionally set or an elastic cultural circle between the local and the outside world is sealed. In other words, the development of cross-cultural advertising communication can be promoted only by mutual exchange and cooperation in an equal manner on the basis of freedom.

The third principle is self-respect and self-discipline. It should be said that this principle is a supplement to the second principle. Whether it is positive freedom or negative freedom, neither can it be "arbitrary" or "indulgent" in the spread of culture, especially in social context of "new media era", thereby the third principle of self-respect and self-discipline are even more important.

4. The ethical principles of advocating "balance of righteousness and benefit"

The disputes and choices between righteousness and benefit have always been a major problem that has plagued human life. As mentioned above, the chaotic images presented by the advertising ethics of the "new media era" can track its origins on the issue of justice and benefit. Therefore, it is necessary to seek the idea of coordinating the contradiction between righteousness and benefit in traditional culture, so as to stipulate the current phenomenon of anomie in advertising ethics.

Judging from the history of ethical thought in ancient China, the "defense of righteousness and benefit" is not only a lush peak in Chinese language, but also a main thread that runs through traditional Chinese ethics. For example, the Analects of Confucius says, "The mind of the superior man is conversant with righteousness; the mind of the mean man is conversant with gain." Meanwhile, the diametrical opposition between the superior man and the mean man is used to show the different values of justice and profit. In fact, it also highlights the concept of raising moral values and denigrating private interests.

Mencius's argument on righteousness and benefit inherited the view of Confucius and inspired Xun Qing's viewpoint. Mencius. Kao Tzu (part one) says, "I like life, and I also like righteousness. If I cannot keep the two together, I will let life go, and choose righteousness." This is a more systematic inheritance and exertion of Confucius' thoughts because it puts death's meaning above the benefits of life. Also, it emphasizes the pre-existence of righteousness in the height of the ontology of life and morality.

Xunzi, on the premise of a thorough investigation of human nature, confessed that everyone had a "desire heart". On the other hand, he believed that the ruler's cultivation through valued moralization and education could enable the people to insist on "moral righteousness" while observing material desire. In short, the righteousness and benefit view of Xunzi can be summed up as "The man, who in sight of gain remembers righteousness".

New media advertising was developed under the background of reform and opening up and global awareness. Thus, it has a specific era connotation. However, we also gradually realized that the fast-paced life created by the "new media" has broken the accumulated long-standing balance of righteousness and benefit. Therefore, we cast our reflection horizon into traditional ideas of the harmony between righteousness and benefit in this dilemma, which is quite new in the era. Besides, this reflection not only enriches the ethical connotation of modern advertising, but also promotes the orderly development of new media advertising.

5. The perfection of new media advertising social norms system and operation mechanism of the industry

The new media advertising social norm system should consist of the following aspects. First, it is proposed to establish an ethical review system for new media advertising. For example, many hospitals have begun to establish medical ethics committees to deal with the ethical issues encountered in the medical process. New media advertising can also follow the example, and many Western countries have such precedents. For example, Australia has a national commercial television association, which includes advertising approval and advertising review committees; the United Kingdom also has independent television committee, whose main duty is to supervise television advertising and examine the ethical implications of television advertising. Therefore, the institutions such as the Internet Advertising Ethics

Research on Publishing CIM Model Change Events through OPC UA

Zewu Peng[1], Churan Deng[1,*], Bojian Wen[1], and Qingping Xu[2]

[1]Information Centre of Guangdong Power Grid Corporation, 510600 Guangzhou, China.
[2]Weihai CIMSTech Co., Ltd, 264200 Weihai, China

Abstract. This paper studies how to publish the change events of CIM model using OPC UA, and proposes a method to publish CIM model change events using OPC UA based on mapping CIM model to OPC UA address space. By comparing with the CIS GDA model change notification service function in the legacy CIS interface, it is confirmed that the OPC UA service completely covers the original CIS GDA model change notification service function. Base-Model-Change-Event-Type and the more detailed General-Model-Change-Event-Type, Semantic-Change-Event-Type are used to provide appropriate model change information for clients through OPC UA Event service. CIM model change events in data platform of distribution grid and utilization system are published using OPC UA, the research results have been verified.

1 Introduction

The IEC61970, IEC61968 and IEC62541 series standards developed by the International Electrotechnical Commission (IEC) have been widely used in the power industry. The domestic and foreign power companies are now using these standards in a large number of practical application system of power dispatching, electric power production and marketing. The data platform of distribution grid and utilization system of Guangdong Power Grid (referred to as DUSYS) is built entirely on international standards, mainly including two aspects: 1) information model, the Unified Information Model of Distribution and Utilization system (DUUM), is based on IEC TC57 Common Information Model (CIM); 2) data is provide through OPC Unified Architecture (OPC UA), the new version of Component Interface Specification [1]. The data platform models and collects the primary and secondary data of distribution grid and utilization system together to achieve full integration of distribution network production and operation data.

Through continuously aggregating data from multiple application systems in the field of distribution grid and distribution system, the DUSYS becomes a centralized data access point of grid model. To ensure that platform-based applications can quickly track model changes as platform-managed grid models change, the platform needs to issue model change notifications whenever grid model data changes. So that each application can start the corresponding model data synchronization process, tracking grid model changes in a timely manner, and ensure that the grid model data used is complete and correct.

In this paper, we research how to use OPC UA to publish the CIM model change data. Firstly, the CIM and OPC UA specifications are analysed to determine the management mode of CIM model in the OPC UA address space. Then a standardized publishing method of CIM model change events is determined, and a software implementation scheme is given.

2 OPC UA address space management for CIM model

The Common Information Model (CIM) is an abstract model that describes all the major objects of an electric utility, especially those related to electric operations [2]. The Common Information Model of Power System - TC57 CIM, provided by the International Electrotechnical Commission's 57th Technical Committee (TC57) has been most widely used. IEC TC57 CIM integrates the logical composition of the power grid, the physical entities of the equipment with the locations, document, records and measurement data required for power management. It uses information technology such as object-oriented modelling and XML to refine the information model, covers all dimensions of power information. This good information model has played an important role in the establishment of the standardized data centre for distribution and utilization power network management.

The data access services come with the Power CIM model were originally due to the EPRI's Energy Management System Application Programming Interface (EMS-API) project and were eventually defined as Component Interface Specification (CIS). The first edition of CIS service includes series of standards such as IEC 61970 402/403/404/405/407, which are based on

* Corresponding author: dengchuran@gdxx.csg.cn

Review Committee can be established in the social norm system of new media advertising in China.

Secondly, the ethical laws and regulations for new media advertising have been further improved, that is, and the reconstruction of advertising ethics has been incorporated into the scope of the legal system, thereby making advertising ethics legal. It is worth mentioning that the 14th meeting of the Standing Committee of the 12th (China) NPC Standing Committee passed the revised Advertising Law. The new Internet advertising regulation is a major highlight. "The Internet is a brand-new thing. There are no existing chapters on Internet advertising law. This time, Internet advertising is stipulated. For example, Internet advertising should be closed with a single key and e-mails cannot be sent without consent." [3]In any case, if there were no laws and regulations in the standardization of advertising ethics, the standardization of advertising ethics would become unfounded. As a new media, its features of hidden and anonymity bring more variables. Since the law is a state-enforced social security system, it is even more necessary for the government to participate in this situation. The current ethical reconstruction of new media advertising should focus on the existing Advertising Law and formulate more perfect laws and regulations. Finally, effective social supervision systems and industry self-regulatory mechanisms should be established.

Social supervision is another supervision system besides administrative management. The ethical regulation of new media advertising must involve the participation of the entire society to make great achievement. At this point, many online advertising companies and consumer associations can be combined to establish supervision methods such as toll-free hotlines and public emails; In addition, organizations or individuals who actively report the phenomena of advertising ethics anomie should be rewarded or punished. In contrast, those who involved in the protection of bad phenomena should be punished, and serious cases are subject to legal sanctions. Through the above-mentioned measures, it is believed that we would make changes to the current the phenomena of the new media advertising ethics anomie in China to some extent.

6. Conclusion

Nowadays, no matter if it is TV commercials, outdoor advertising or online advertising; it is full of illusory images, rhetorical words, and the ideological connotations of various corrupt and extravagant endorsements. Even if the revolutionary tide of the new media era brings unprecedented opportunities to the advertising industry, we must admit that the impact of moral disorientation on the advertising industry will eventually become stronger with the passage of time while it is not so obvious. Therefore, the alternative of "integration" or "dispersion" should be the primary issue for us to face the rationality and inevitability of advertising ethics.

Acknowledgment

The paper is the final supporting material for Hunan philosophy and social science foundation project "Research on Advertising Design
Ethics ", Item No.: 12ZD85

References

1. Robert K•Logan. Understanding New Media: Extend ing Marshall Mcluhan[M], Fudan University Press(2 012).
2. Hendrik Willem Van Loon .Tolerant[M],SDX Joint Publishing Company(1985).
3. Livelihood concerns,New <Advertising law>Septem ber Highlights Ten Highlights[J], Fujian Quality Tec hnical Supervision,07(2015).

Research on Basic Database for Real Property Unified Registration

Guang Yang[1], Zhihan Yang[2], and Zhijie Han[1]

[1]College of Surveying and Geo-Informatics, Tongji University, Shanghai, China
[2]School of Economics and Management, Tongji University, Shanghai, China

Abstract. This paper researches Shanghai's real property registration, studying the data integration of the information database of real property unified registration in Shanghai and the establishment of information systems of real property unified registration. The means of data cleaning and data integration are used to consolidate all kinds of basic data for real property which are in complex structure and different formats, building a basic information database for real property and providing a strong support for the establishment of information platform.

1 Introduction

In November 2013, the 31st executive meeting of the State Council declared that the Ministry of Land and Resources was responsible for the guidance and supervision of the unified registration for real property throughout the country, including land, houses, grassland, woodland, sea area and so on, in order to achieve the "Four Unification" of registration organizations， registration books， registration basis and information platform. Subsequently, the SCOPSR (State Commission Office of Public Sectors Reform) issued "The Notice on the Duties of Integrating the Real Property Registration" to define its specific requirements. [1]

The Ministry of Land and Resources believes that the informatization level of Shanghai is high and its practical experience is rich, as it is the first to implement the registration of houses together with land in the country. It hopes that Shanghai will set an example and take the lead on the informatization of the real property unified registration, so that it authorizes the Information Center of the Resource of House and Land of Shanghai to undertake this nationwide work of "The Standard of Information Database for Real Property Registration" and "The Framework Plan for Real Property Unified Registration". Heilongjiang Province and other districts also decide to study and copy the informatization mode of Shanghai's real property unified registration. To build the basic platform of information management of real property registration is a significant support for both the implementation of the requirement from The State Council about the "Four Unification" of registration organizations，registration books，registration basis and information platform, and the promotion of accelerating the implementation of the real property unified registration regulation.

Information platform is the key component of the "Four Unification", and it is also an important technological support for its implementation. With the realistic requirements of easing the masses' burden, ensuring transaction safety and sounding social credit system, information platform mainly aims at providing the legal and convenient service of information sharing and enquiry, on the premise of ensuring the information of real property is registered completely, accurately and timely. As a result, it is necessary to build up a unified database for real property registration to ensure that the information is complete, accurate as well as timely, through updating the data related to the registration on the receptionist in real time.

The beginning to build the unified database of real property registration is that there is a great deal of registration data of land, houses, woodland, grassland and sea areas in each department of each level in government institutions over the years under the decentralized registration system. Due to the differences among the databases of houses, woodland and grassland and the distinction of their data quality, it is tough to integrate and consolidate those data. In the course of setting up the information database, the data at the municipal level is the real origin of the data, which is the emphasis for the consolidation, coding and variation mechanism of the registration data of real property.

Against the backdrop mentioned above, it is of great practical significance to study how to use proper techniques and methods to build the information database of real property unified registration, so as to develop the information platform for real property unified registration, ensuring that the relevant departments implement the unified registration accurately and efficiently.

2 The Current Situation of Real Property Unified Registration and the Overview of Basic Data

2.1 The Current Situation of Real Property Unified Registration

At present, as the real property registration is decentralized in different departments, there are a number of problems, such as the business rules is not unified or the data construct is not unified, etc. The status of domestic real property registration has following characteristics.

2.1.1 The Registration is not Unified

Currently, the work of real property registration is dispersed at different departments. The usage rights of the construction land and collective land ownership are registered in the land department, while the house ownership and other rights of houses are registered in the house and rural-urban building departments. In terms of the rural land contractual management right, grassland ownership or usage rights, they are registered in agriculture sector, while the ownership and right to use forest land are registered by the forestry department. In addition, the registration of the use of surface and intertidal zone are in the fishery sector, and the right to use sea is in the maritime sector. [2] These problems are mainly because the registration organizations and relevant laws are not unified.

2.1.2 The Business Rules is not Unified

The ministry of land and resources, the ministry of housing and urban-rural development, the forestry administration, ministry of agriculture and other departments have their respective laws as basis. [3] The forestry administration has the *Forestry Law* as a support for forest land registration. Grassland registration is carried out by the ministry of agriculture, which is based on the *Grassland Law*. While there is the *Contracting of Rural Land Law* for the registration of the rural land contract, with respect to house registration, there is the *Urban Real Estate Administration Law* for the ministry of housing and urban-rural development to carry out. Similarly, the fisheries sector has the *Fisheries Law* for the registration of the use right of surface and intertidal zone for aquaculture, and maritime department has the *Management Law for the Usage of Sea Area* for the registration of the intertidal zone of the sea area. Besides, the industry and commerce department implement the *Guaranty Law* for the mortgage of real property. As for the ministry of land and resources, the *Law of Land Administration* is undertook for the registration for land, in the Article 11th Section 3rd of which it is also clearly defined that certifications of ownership or the usage rights of the woodland and grassland, as well as the usage right of the surface and intertidal zone for aquaculture should be respectively in accordance with the relevant provisions of the *Forest Law of the People's Republic of China*, the *Grassland Law of the People's Republic of China* and the *Fishery Law of the People's Republic of China*, which shows the status quo of dispersed registration of land. [4]

2.1.3 The Data Model is not Unified

In the business about the registration of real property in each department, most of them have the concept on registration books or record cards. However, the meaning of this concept has so many differences in details that the interrelation of these elements cannot be described in a unified manner, especially in the deal with real property, rights, oblige and the registration process. Namely, they do not have the unified model of the data.

2.2 The Overview of Basic Data

The registration of the real property, involving the current land, houses, grassland, woodland, sea area and contractual right of rural land, etc., are in the charge of different sectors. [5] Therefore, the standard of the data and the business process are different, administrated on the basis of respectively independent system. Accordingly, to set up a unified basic platform of the information management for real property registration requires the design to be based on data consolidation, business process, and information system. With land as the core of the unified registration system of real property, its central idea is that the registrations of various use rights must rely on the corresponding registrations of land ownership, and the registration of the attached objects on the land shall depend on the registration of land use rights, while the subsequent registration should correspond to the early registration. [6]

The basic database of the registration information of real property is integrated and built by teasing and standardizing the current registration information of the real property that is in scattered storage with different format and different medium, according to the Database Standard of the Registration Information of Real Property, which lays a solid foundation for supporting the operation of the unified registration platform of real property. The principal sources of basic data are shown as follows.

Firstly, daily registration business. All of the implementation and its results as well as the process information of the real property registration will be brought into the database as the new source for the data. Secondly, deposit data of the real property registration. A large quantity of deposit data from previous registration under the dispersed-registration system, which is about the registration of land, houses, woodland, grassland and sea area, would be integrated to set up the interrelation on the basis of the unified database standard. In other words, apartments must be attached with the ownership information and buildings with the land information, all of which should be put into the database of real property registration. Thirdly, data of the results of cadastral rights survey. The results of boundary survey and ownership survey would be incorporated into the database as the basis of real property registration, through sorting out the integrated and consolidated data.

3 Data Consolidation Roadmap

3.1 Data Consolidation Objects

The scope of the consolidation of information about real property registration includes the registration books and the historical registration files as well as the space information, including the information of land ownership, the usage right of construction land, the usage right of homestead, real estate rights, contractual rights of land, the use right of farmland, forestry rights, the use right of sea area and non-resident island, as well as the building ownership and water entitlement. The objects of data consolidation are stored through three kinds of medium. Firstly, it is electronic registration information. The original information of the real property registration has been completed by means of informatization. The existent and more intact data has set up electronic registration information database, which has formed the electronic registration books and electronic examination and approval archives. Secondly, it is electronic record. The registration archives database has been built for the original registration process and registration results, according to the relevant requirements of records management, and the file index has been established. Thirdly, it is the paper files. The process and results of registration are still stored in traditional paper-based way.

3.2 Data Consolidation Process

3.2.1 Preparation

First of all, do the status quo survey about current registration information of real property well, collect the data standard of original registration, compare and analyze them with the Database Standard of the Registration Information of Real Property. After extracting a certain amount of data for the plot test, draw up the mapping relation chart of data and thus to formulate the detailed execution plans and technical instructions. [7]

3.2.2 Data Standardization

Then, according to the implementation plans and technical instructions, the original registration information would be standardized based on the data description of the Real Property Registration Information Database. This step mainly contains the following aspects. First of all, it is the specification for semantic consistency, which is designed to solve problems about the same name with heterogeneous medium and the same medium with different names. Then, it is the data type matching, dealing with problems about non-uniform data types, decimal numerical digit and quantity units. Further, it is unified coordinate system, settling the problem that coordinate reference is inconsistent in a specific geographical area. Finally, it should be the information complement. The incomplete core registration information needs to be replenished in order to ensure the data completeness.

3.2.3 Reconstruction of Data Logical Relationship

Moreover, basing on the requirements of information correlation of real property register, standardized registration information ought to be used to establish electronic registration information book respectively about the land ownership, use right of construction land, use right of homestead land, real estate right, contractual right of land, use right of farmland, forestry right, use right of the sea area and non-resident island, ownership of construction and water-drawing right and so on. Besides, the related information of unified registration objects should be linked together, associated with the registration process and registration file.

3.2.4 Locating Registration Information in Relevant Land

In addition, it is necessary to locate the registration information with complete logical relationship in relevant land, including the land ownership, use right of construction land, use right of homestead land, real estate right, contractual right of land, use right of farmland, forestry right, use right of the sea area and non-resident island, ownership of construction and water-drawing right and so on, so as to code each plot of land and record it, and code the real property unit according to the code rules of real property units.

3.2.5 Data Storage

The final step is to store the data that has been settled according to the above steps, in accordance with the Database Standard of the Registration Information of Real Property. Both spatial information and non-spatial information should achieve their data collection as required.

3.3 Data Consolidation Flow Path

Database consolidation preparation: The flow chart of preparation is shown in the Figure 1.

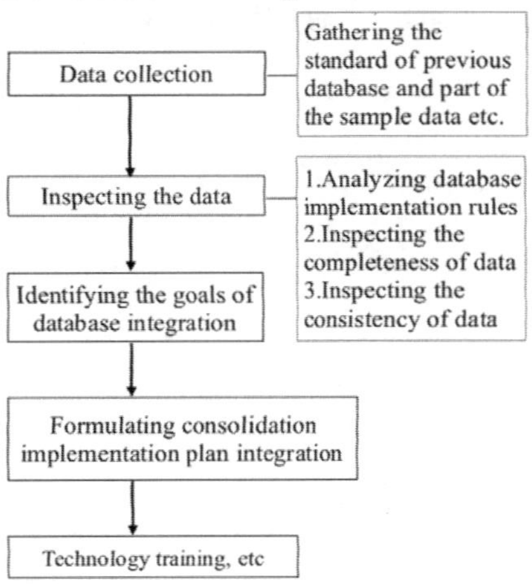

Fig.1. The flow chart of database consolidation preparation

Data standardization: (the land ownership, use right of construction land, use right of homestead land, real estate right, contractual right of land, use right of farmland, forestry right, use right of the sea area and non-resident island, ownership of construction and water-drawing right, etc.) (1) Semantic consistency standardization, (2) Data type standardization, (3) Coordinate reference consistency, (4) Information complement.

Reconstruction of logical relationship: The registration information about the land ownership, use right of construction land, use right of homestead land, real estate right, contractual right of land, use right of farmland, forestry right, use right of the sea area and non-resident island, ownership of construction and water-drawing right ought to build up the logical relationship, taking the registration object as unit, in order to form the relevant electronic register.

Locating the registration information to the relevant land: The electronic register of the land ownership, use right of construction land, use right of homestead land, real estate right, contractual right of land, use right of farmland, forestry right, use right of the sea area and non-resident island, ownership of construction and water-drawing right should be located to the land in the form of real property registers. They are coded according to the coding regulation of land and real property units, so as to form real property registers. [8]

Storing data: In accordance with the Database Standard of the Registration Information of Real Property, store the data that contains the information of the land ownership, use right of construction land, use right of homestead land, real estate right, contractual right of land, use right of farmland, forestry right, use right of the sea area and non-resident island, ownership of construction and water-drawing right.

4 Conclusions

All in all, real property unified registration involves several aspects including institutional policies, institutional personnel, laws and regulations, technical standard and so on, with limited time, tough tasks, widespread influence and wide-covered range. Certainly, data is the blood of the system and is the premise condition for all tasks. Setting up the basic database of real property unified registration is the preliminary work for real property unified registration, to which the preparation of basic data is especially significant. There is no doubt that the basic database of unified registration information of real property provides the data support for the whole real property unified registration, and is also the key to support the information platform. Meanwhile it is the backbone for carrying out the registration business of real property, and is essential in the whole real property unified registration.

References

1. L H. Wang, Z H. Sun, Y. Peng, et al., The Study of Building the Basic Platform of the Data Consolidation and Management of Real Property Registration Information, *Geomatics World*, **4**, 76-82, (2014)
2. C H. Yan, The Research on the Current Situation on the Purpose of Building the Real Property Registration System, *Legal system and economy*, **9**, (2014)
3. Z Y. Tong, The Research on the Registration System for Real Property, Shandong University, (2013)
4. Z C. Li, The Study of Real Property Unification Registration, East China University of Political Science and Law, (2011)
5. National People's Congress, *Property Law of the People's Republic of China*, People's Publishing House, (2007)
6. M Z. Wang, The Research on the Building of the Registration System of Real Property In China, *Truth Seeking*, **S1**, 95-96, (2012)
7. Z M. Zhang, H Y. Xu, Research on Key Technologies of Data Integration Construction for the Land Registration of Real Property and Real Estate Data, Modern Mapping, **39(4)**, 56-58, (2016)
8. X. Cheng, The Research on the Unit of Real Property Registration, *Real estate in China*, **3**, 27-28, (2011)

the relevant standards of OPC and OMG and have been widely applied. With the introduction of the concept of smart grid, the demand for power system management and information exchange has been further improved. The CIM model interface system needs to be adapted to the needs of Internet access. The first version of the CIS service, which is mainly targeted at applications running on the LAN or intranet, has also been upgraded to use the OPC Unified Architecture(OPC UA) adopted directly by IEC 62541.

Compared with the first version of CIS service that data is difficult to be integrated by client applications due to model, real time, event and history data are separately described, the OPC UA specification of the new generation of CIS integrates the classic OPC data access specification into a single service-oriented architecture. OPC UA uses a consistent and complete address space, security model and service model to unify the metadata (information model), data, history and events into one address space for collaborative management, providing a series of secure and reliable services for data accessing, alarming, historical data accessing [3].

OPC UA uses reliable communication mechanisms, configurable timeouts, automated error checking and automatic recovery mechanisms to ensure efficient communications and data transfer across firewalls. And it also enhances the robustness of the architecture with technical advantages of unified model control, data security exchange, high reliability and platform independence, and can be adapted to many fields such as device data management and communication, enterprise modelling and information exchange.

The objects and related information provided by the OPC UA server to the client is referred to as the server's address space. In OPC UA, the rules and basic components of information model building are the OPC UA address space model. The UA Information Model uses notions to define its own, domain-specific types and constraints, as well as well-defined instances.

Although OPC UA has been adopted as a new generation of CIS service standards, it is not specifically formulated for power automation applications but rather as a common inter-industry standard for industrial control automation applications. Unlike the CIM model explicitly adopted as the power information model, the address space model defined by the OPC UA specification is an OPC UA proprietary information model description. Therefore, to apply OPC UA specification in power system, we must first solve the coordination and integration of power CIM model and OPC UA address space model, that is, managing CIM Model in OPC UA address space.

Table 1 shows the basic mapping schemes from CIM model to UA address space model [4].

Table 1. Rules of Mapping CIM Model to OPC UA Address Space Model.

CIM Model		UA address space model
package(Schema)		UA Object Node
data	Primitive	UA built-in basic types
type	Enumeration	UA Enum Node
	DataType	UA VariableType Node
	Compound	UA VariableType Node
object type		UA ObjectType Node
object Instance		UA Object Node
attribute of object		UA Variable Node (MeasurementValue.Value or StateVariable.Value)
		UA Property Node
type of association between objects		UA Reference Type
instance of association between objects		UA Reference

These mappings define how the CIM model is organized in the OPC UA address space and are also the basis for publishing CIM model change events via OPC UA.

3 Standardized publishing of CIM model change events

3.1 Event service of CIS GDA

In the first version of discarded CIS services, the GDA Event Service defined in IEC 61970 403 Generic Data Access (GDA) gives a standard way of publishing CIM model change events. GDA Event Services provide methods to inform clients that specific data changes have taken place and ensure consistent data access.

The GDA event module allows the client to receive a model data change event callback from the server. The structure of the model data change event is *ResourceChangeEvent*, in the structure, *version* is a unique integer that the GDA server assigns to each data change, the value of *version* in an event equals to the value returned from the GDA's *current_version*() method at the time of the event. *Affected* is a sequence of resource identifiers, *verbs* is a sequence of numbers to indicate how data changed. For each member of the affected sequence, there must be a member of the verbs sequence. The verb value defined by the GDA standard is a set of enumerations that represent the type of data change (Table 2).

Table 2. Enumeration of GDA data change types.

Verb	Meaning
VERB_CREATED	object created
VERB_DELETED	object deleted
VERB_CHANGED	attribute changed
VERB_CANCELED	operation cancelled
VERB_CLOSED	operation closed

Among them, VERB_CANCELED, VERB_CLOSED corresponding to the business process-related actions, such as closing the work order or cancelling the control request, are less practical used; VERB_CREATED, VERB_DELETED and VERB_CHANGED corresponding to the model creation, deletion, and attribute value changes, respectively, by setting the corresponding *affected* value to identifier of class or object, can describe model changes at schema or object level. If the *affected* sequence length is zero, the client MUST assume that any or all of the data provided by the data provider may have changed.

Applications that concerns about changes in the CIM model typically use GDA Query service to get the required CIM model data during the initialization phase, then register GDA event listener to listen for changes. Upon receipt of the change notification, the GDA query service is used to obtain the up-to-date status of the change data so as to keep track of the CIM model data continuously to ensure the integrity and consistency of the CIM model data used.

3.2 Event service of OPC UA

3.2.1 Event model

The OPC UA event model defines a common event system that can be used in different areas to report the occurrence of an event through an event notification. The event is not directly accessible in the address space. Clients can subscribe to the corresponding events via objects and views. The node's *EventNotifier* attribute determines whether events can be subscribed to from the node.

OPC UA defines a hierarchy of extensible basic event types, with different fields for different event types. Clients can retrieve this information through the event type hierarchy that the server exposes in its address space. Using the event type hierarchy information, the client can create a filter based on the fields of interest and the type of event. OPC UA defines a series of standard event types that are represented in the address space as ObjectType node and directly or indirectly based on *BaseEventType*. *BaseEventType* uses UA properties to expose fields listed in Table 3.

Table 3. Property Set of BaseEventType.

UA Property	Value type	Meaning
EventId	ByteString	unique identifier generated by the server
EventType	NodeId	node ID of the event type
SourceNode	NodeId	node ID of event source
SourceName	String	description of event source
Time	UtcTime	event time
ReceiveTime	UtcTime	time when event receivedby UA Server
LocalTime	TimeZoneDataType	timezone
Message	LocalizedText	localized text description of the event
Severity	UInt16	indicating the severity of the event

Each concrete event type that is a descendant type of *BaseEventType* can extends specific fields according to its own characteristics.

In the OPC UA address space, the standard reference type *HasEventSource* associates event sources in a non-looping hierarchy whose child reference type, *HasNotifier*, is used to associate different node nodes of the *EventNotifier* to establish the hierarchy of event notification objects organization. When an event notifier references another event notifier, all events in the referenced event notifier are exposed by the reference.

The Server object, which is a standard object in the OPC UA Address Space, acts as the server's root notifier. It always provides server-wide events as if *HasNotifier* was declared for all event sources in the server. Clients can subscribe to the Server object to get all the events on the server.

3.2.2 Event service

OPC UA provides complete service support for subscribing, filtering and releasing events, including *View* services set, *Attribute* services set, *MonitoredItem* services set, and *Subscription* services set. The UA view is a publicly defined subset of address spaces created by the server. The view defaults to the full address space. The *view* service set allows the client to browse through the nodes in the view. *Attribute* service set are used for reading and writing node attribute values. The *MonitoredItem* services set defines services that allow clients to create, modify, and delete *MonitoredItems* used to monitor attributes for value changes and objects for events [5]. *MonitoredItem* monitors variable, attribute and event notifier. When it detectes an event that meets one of the criteria, a corresponding notification is generated. The *Subscription* service set is used by the client to create and maintain subscriptions. Subscriptions are entities that issue notification messages periodically for the monitoring items assigned to them. The notification message contains a common message header, followed by a series of notifications. The format of the notification depends on the type of item being monitored (i.e. variables, properties and event notifiers).

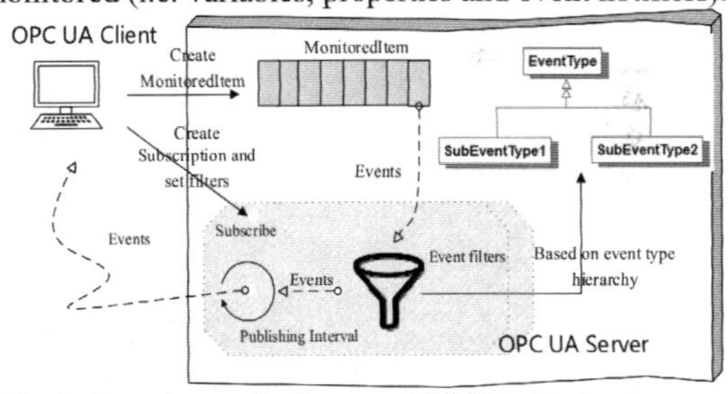

Fig. 1. Event interaction between OPC UA client and server.

Event interaction between OPC UA client and server starts with client's object nodes browsing in the in the address space through *View* service. By using the *Attribute* service to read the value of the *EventNotifier* property of a node, the client can determine which nodes generate events and create an event monitor entry for a specific node.

As shown in Figure 1, the client can create a filter based on the field of interest and the type of event by using the *View* service to retrieve the event type hierarchy information that the server exposed in the address space when creating the *MonitoredItem*. Finally, the client creates and maintains a subscription that contains a particular *MonitoredItem*, which can be notified by the server when a monitored item detects an event or alarm and sent to the client by subscription.

In the CIS GDA event service, the server sends events to the client through callbacks. Unlike CIS GDA, OPC UA uses polling for message exchange via one-way connections. This approach is firewall-friendly, and can reduce the development difficulty of the client. To ensure secure and reliable delivery of messages between clients and server, OPC UA has developed a fully-fledged subscription-publishing model that provides clear handling rules for subscription life-cycle maintenance, detection and retransmission of lost messages, message queue size management, etc. The relative services are *Publish* and *Republish*.

3.2.3 Model change event

In the OPC UA standard event system, an event of model change is used to indicate a change in the address space structure. Changes may be caused by adding, deleting nodes or references. Changes to the *DataType* attirbute of a variable or variable type are also counted as model changes.

As shown in Figure 2, *BaseModelChangeEventType* is the basic type of OPC UA model change event. *BaseModelChangeEventType* does not contain detail information of the change, only tells a change have occurred, so the client needs to perform process as if all nodes have changed or each node maybe have changed. This is the same semantic representation of a GDA model change event when the *affected* member length is zero. *GeneralModelChangeEventType*, as a subclass of *BaseModelChangeEventType*, provides more detailed update details, contains information about the node being changed and the operation that generated the *ModelChangeEvent* (for example, adding a node, deleting a node, etc.).

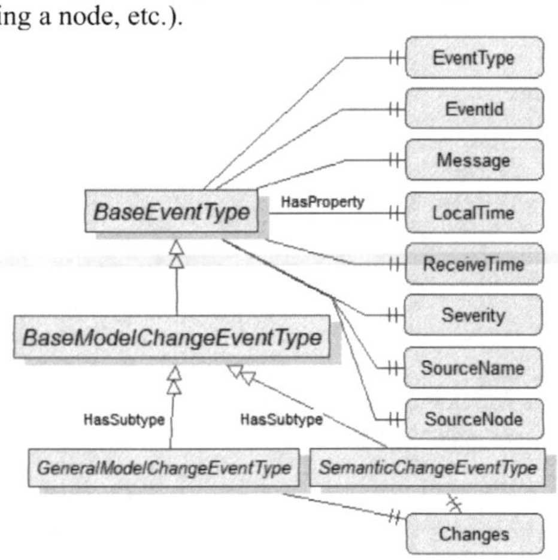

Fig. 2. Model change event types and properties.

An OPC UA server can publish model change notifications using types of model change events as appropriate, the specific granularity used is determined by the server based on performance requirements and update type. The server can also define subclasses to add additional information.

BaseModelChangeEventType does not extend any UA properties, *GeneralModelChangeEventType* adds a 'Change' property. The value type of 'Change' is *ModelChangeStructureDataType* . This datatype has such members: 1)*verb*, which describes the type of change that has taken place on the affected node; 2)*affected*, the node ID of the node that has changed. According to value of *verb* property, the client should assume that the affected node has been created or deleted, a reference has been added or deleted, or the data type has changed; 3)*affectedType*, if the affected node is an object or variable, *affectedType* contains the *NodeId* of the *TypeDefinitionNode* of the affected node, otherwise it is null.

The value of the *verb* member is a set of enumerations used to represent the type of data change, as shown in Table 4.

Table 4. Enumeration of OPC UA data change types.

Verb	Meaning
NodeAdded	"*affected*" node added
NodeDeleted	"*affected*" node deleted
ReferenceAdded	a reference to "*affected*" node added
ReferenceDeleted	a reference to "*affected*" node deleted
DataTypeChanged	When "*affected*" node is a *Variable* or *VariableType*, indicating the data type of Variable or *VariableType* has changed

As can be seen from the above table, comparing to data structure defined in CIS GDA Events(Table 2), the information provided by the OPC UA for model change event directly covers the change of the node reference (that is, the association between objects), which facilitates clients' processing.

3.2.4 Value change event

Different from CIS GDA event model, which publishes event with VERB_CHANGED when attribute changes, the change of value of variable in OPC UA address space does not cause model change event. In OPC UA, a change of value notification publication uses a different mechanism depending on the mode of value modelling.

The OPC UA Information Model defines two types of variables: data variable and property.

OPC UA data variable is used to represent the object's data, such as the temperature of the temperature sensor. According to the mapping rules in Table 1, the *MeasurementValue.Value* and *StateVariable.Value* attributes of the CIM model are mapped to data variables. OPC UA standard defines that changes in the value of data variables are published as data change notification which can be subscribed to by clients.

The OPC UA property is used to represent the characteristics of a node, such as temperature engineering units. According to the mapping rules in Table 1, attributes other than *MeasurementValue. Value* and *StateVariable.Value* are mapped as properties. OPC UA standard defines that property value change triggers semantic change event (*SemanticChangeEventType*, Figure 2).

3.3 Client processing

The client can listen directly to the root notifications of the OPC UA server to get the model change events in the entire address space. This can be achieved by creating an event monitor on the standard *Server* object node in the address space.

If only the field of the model change event itself is focused on, the filter may be set to limit the event type to the *GeneralModelChangeEventType* event type, and the field concerned is '*Changes*'.

4 Implementation of OPC UA publishing for CIM model change events

In the DUSYS, OPC UA Publishing for CIM model change events is implemented as a module of OPC UA server. The implementation scheme is shown in Figure 3. The server adopts the standard OPC UA hierarchical application architecture, realizes the mapping from CIM model data to OPC UA address space. Based on this mapping, CIM model changes are monitored, model change events are generated in time and posted to clients.

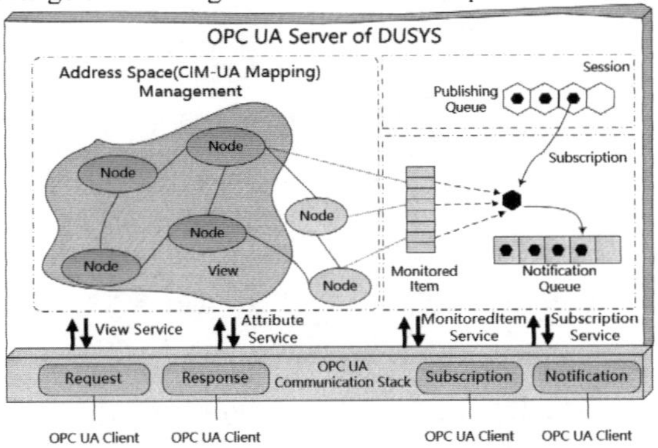

Fig. 3. Publishing OPC UA model change events.

The CIM model change events in the OPC UA server are generated according to the client using the node management service (*NodeManagement* service set) to add, modify, and delete nodes and references in the CIM model in the address space. The implementation of *NodeManagement* service set generates events when node management operation completed: *AddNodes* service creates events of *NodeAdded* type; *DeleteNodes* service create events of *NodeDeleted* type; *AddReferences* service creates events of *ReferenceAdded* type; *DeleteReferences* service creates events of *ReferenceDeleted* type.

When clients using the *Write* service of the *Attribute* services set to modify the "DataType" attribute of *Variable* or *VariableType* node, data change type of the event is *DataTypeChanged.*

When clients using the *Write* service of *Attribute* services set to modify properties of UA Variable node, event with *SemanticChangeEventType* type is generated if variable node not mapped from CIM attribute *MeasurementValue.Value* or *StateVariable.Value.*

To facilitate client-side processing, when the creation or deletion of property nodes mapped from CIM objects are caused by creation or deletion of CIM objects, the UA server does not generate CIM model change events for these property nodes, and only generated model change events for object nodes. Because the deletion of a CIM object node will result in relative reference to be deleted automatically, in that case, *ReferenceDeleted* events are not generated.

The OPC UA server of DUSYS enables full subscription feature of OPC UA subscriptions for all UA event types including model change events by creating message queues of *MonitoredItem*, data changes, and event notification for clients' subscription.

In publishing CIM model change events, notification message queues are configured as "queuing and buffering all notifications" or "only queuing and buffering recent notifications to be transmitted for the subscription", so the situation that events may occur at a faster rate than publishing rate (which is actually the frequency of client-side polls)can be handled. Each message in the notification message queue is assigned a sequence number that allows the client to detect the missing message, thus the standard mechanism of loss message detection and retransmission is supported.

5 Conclusion

Publishing CIM model change events through OPC UA is an important problem that must be solved when applying OPC UA to provide data accessing service for grid model data. Through analysis and comparison, it is confirmed that the OPC UA, as a new generation of CIS, has the ability to publish CIM model change events, and completely covers the original CIS GDA model change notification service function. The types and contents of events corresponding to different model changes are clearly given. The standardized publishing method and software implementation of CIM model change events are discussed in detail. Based on the mapping of the CIM model to the OPC UA address space, the OPC UA server generates corresponding events for the CIM model update operations and sends them to clients through the OPC UA services. Adopt event compression strategy is adopted to improve client processing efficiency.

The Scheme of publishing CIM model change events through OPC UA has been successfully applied to the data platform of distribution grid and utilization system of Guangdong Power Grid. It provides standardized CIM model change tracking method for platform-based power grid applications and satisfies data consistent requirements of distribution and utilization application, makes the management and exchange of power system data easier and more secure.

References

1. Y. Cao, J.G. Yao, S.Ch. Yang. Automation of Electric Power Systems. **35(17)**,1-4 (2011)
2. IEC. EMS-API part 301. (2009)
3. R. Hua. China Instrumentation. **2**,54-56 (2013)
4. S.Y. Xie, Q. Yang, Q.P. Xu. Automation of Electric Power Systems. **40(14)**, 115-121(2016)

5. IEC. OPC UA Part 4. (2011)

Web-based Agricultural Technology Evaluation Information System: Design, Application and Evaluation

Yanzhao Ren[1], Minjuan Wang[1], Wanlin Gao 1*, Hui Hu1, Xuerui Chen1

[1] College of Information and Electrical Engineering, China Agricultural University, 100083, Beijing, China;

Abstract: This study describes the web-based agricultural technology evaluation information system, which has been shown to provide a flexible interface with which to arrange various assessment and information management function procedures. Secondly, this study examines the effects of the application of the academic misconduct detection mechanism and abnormally scoring mechanism. In an evaluative study with the two evaluation business cycle of the system, it has been found that this system is more efficient, more accurate and more rigorous than the traditional offline evaluation model. It has also been shown that cheating behaviour in agricultural technological achievements information declaration and evaluation link can be detected accurately and promptly.

1 INTRODUCTION

Agricultural science and technology achievements transformation is the only way to improve technological productivity and promote agriculture. In this process, the protection of the achievements' intellectual property rights is very important (Li xian, 2006). In the past few years, our government has set up special funds and awards at all levels to support these types of transformation projects, which achieved good results. However, some important questions arise (Li HaiYan, 2000). Is it possible to keep fair and open in the process of agricultural science and technology achievements evaluation? How should the reviews of these achievements be standardized? How should the achievements be managed and promoted? These are the problems we need to study in the process of agricultural scientific and technological achievements evaluation (M. Radwan, Senousy, & M. Riad, 2017) (Jin ZhenHui, 2006).

Some people have done some works on the management of evaluation of scientific and technological achievements. Yemao and others designed the Dayu Water Conservancy Science Information System, which is the basis of the Dayu prize award (Yang SiBo, 2002) (Ye Ma, 2007). Feng Li designed the Textile Science Appraisal System, which is divided into two parts, the back and the front. The background management functions include code, importing recommendation, and summary tables. The front include export and import of the recommendation, print recommendation, adding projects, submitting the recommendation online, etc. (Feng Li, 2012) (Wang ChenYe, 2012). Hua lei designed a model household agricultural science and technology application system, which can satisfy the declaration on the function, evaluation, examination and approval, and model household information management's needs (Hua Lei, 2013). The management system of scientific achievements main functions are to management the scientific research in colleges and universities, so as to help teachers report their scientific research and the staff in technology department to create statistics for everyone's scientific research, and provide the most direct basis for the bonuses(Huang Wei,2013)(Jiang LiHua,2014). However, there is no correlative literature for instituting a system for scientific and technological achievements reward system which can complete the entire workflow of Achievements evaluation on-line (Chen, 2017).

Based on the above analysis, we designed an agricultural science and technology achievements system based on the MVC (Model View Controller)(yurong,2013), using Spring MVC + Spring + Hibernate framework, which can managed organically and applied to evaluate the achievements(Vabo, Slettebø, & Fossum,2016). The goal of this system is to monitor the achievements online, in order to review and unify management of the business process and effectively improve and manage personnel's work efficiency.

*Corresponding author: xiaozhaochina@cau.edu.cn

2 ANALYSIS OF TECHNOLOGICAL ACHIEVEMENTS EVALUATION PROCESS

Agricultural science and technology achievements assessing work process mainly includes achievement collection and review, expert estimation and results announcement. In the collection process, the information related to technique collection scope, time axis and sponsor is publicized at first. The qualified units apply and obtain the production application quota after they got the .notice. And then those units distribute the application places to the achievements owners according to the rules of each unit. The holders who get the position prepare relative technical information and sent them to the qualified units. The units concentrate all the achievements files and sent them to sponsor. The sponsor and the qualified units all have rights to investigate and return the application documents. In the expert estimation link, technological subjects and reviewers are grouped according to professional field, and the judges participate in review meeting to grade fruitions after received an invitation. During this process, the organizer is responsible for supervising the reviewing and critiquing. After the estimation work, the results are checked and publicized. In traditional way, the management of activities associate with agricultural scientific and technological achievements was carried out with non-informatization (Theo S.Eicher, 2017) (Yuan Xiaoqing, 2015). The information of the achievements are transported in the form of paper material and accessory disk. As a result, the processing procedure is relatively cumbersome and the management sites are scattered, which makes mistakes and the loss of the applying materials a common occurrence (Lingxian Zhang2013). Decentralized management creates information synchronization, delayed feedback of consequences, low efficiency of management, low management quality, and unorganized data. Much more resources are spent on unifying progress of each link, organizing on-the-spot meeting for evaluation and so on.

In this paper, the way to complete the whole process steps in the evaluation online, beginning with the quota distribution and ending with review completed, is researched (Xue Dong,2007). And the technic of academic misconduct detection and monitoring of abnormally scoring. This chain of processing steps are two of the most important and complicated process segments in the review workflow (Hou Xin, 2015).

3 DEIGN OF KEY TECHNOLOGY ROADMAP

As mentioned above, the functions that detect the academic misconduct and monitor the abnormally scoring are foundation for ensuring the fairness during system running process.

3.1 Academic misconduct detection mechanism

The academic immoral behaviours in this activity mainly include the following three cases: the award-winning scientific and technological achievements participate in the evaluation again, the core technology of the achievement is similar to other people, and the same scientific and technological achievements occupies more than one quota. If one achievement fit into one of these scenarios, the contents of the accomplishment introduction and technical innovation of it will have one corresponding version which has a high repetition rate at least.

Aiming at the above problems, this paper presents two kinds of content comparison models: whole database comparison and specify results comparison. And the two ways mentioned above have the same content comparison logic.

In this algorithm, the segmentation of the literatures being compared will be finished at first. Before the next step, an important parameter which limits the conditions for repetitive content should be determined. If the number of continuous character which are continuous character with others is equal or more than the figure be set before, these character segment are firmly believed to be consistent with repeated conditions. The matrix can be used to explain this process.

$$S_i = \begin{bmatrix} i \\ detectsentencetxt \\ simsentencetxtname \\ simsentencetxt \\ simsentencestate \\ beginindexes[0] \\ beginindexes[1] \\ endindexes[0] \\ endindexes[1] \end{bmatrix}^T \quad (1)$$

The elements of this matrix record the comparison results between single sentences. In this matrix, ‘i’ means the sentence label of the reference articles, and other parameters have the following mapping relationships: ‘detectsentencetxt’, the content of detected sentence; ‘simsentencetxtname’, reference name; ‘simsentencetxt’, the content of referenced sentence; ‘simsentencestate’, marking of test results; ‘beginindexes[0]’, the starting location of repeated section in detected sentence; ‘endindexes[0]’, the ending location of repeated section in detected sentence; ‘beginindexes[1]’, the starting location of repeated section in referenced sentence; ‘endindexes[1]’, the ending location of repeated section in referenced sentence.

$$P = \left[detectsentencetxt \middle| \; S_1 \; \cdots \; S_i \right] \quad (2)$$

The data about the result that one sentence compared with all sentences of one achievement's content is included in P. The meaning of parameter i is the number of sentences of the whole reference article.

$$L=\left[detectsentencetxt \middle| \; P_1 \; \cdots \; P_m \right] \quad (3)$$

In this way, the L can include the results of the comparison between the sentences with the achievements which are pre-set. The index m means the number of articles which are specified contrast samples.

$$R=\begin{bmatrix} 1| & L_1 \\ \cdots| & \cdots \\ n| & L_n \end{bmatrix} \quad (4)$$

The index i is the number of the sentences of the detected achievement's contents. And the label of sentence is put in R with the result matrix L which is mapped with it. By this mode, we encapsulate the multidimensional test results into a matrix and it can be reversed to the bottom.

3.2 Abnormally scoring mechanism

The organizational form of the assessing activity is many experts to many projects. The judges and achievements are grouped on the basis of their profession. In assessment, the scoring mechanism will maintain fairness with two modes: weighting method and re-examining method. And the precondition of monitoring core algorithm of them is that the scoring of experts is in accord with the independent and identically distributed. This rule can be obtained by analyzing historical data (João Carneiro, Diogo Martinho, Goreti Marreiros, 2016). After the first round of evaluation, we can get the expectation (μ_p) and the standard deviation (σ_p) of the scores of every projects. So if the score given by the judges is in the range of $\mu_p \pm \sigma_p$, the review behaviour of them is concealed normal and the weight (w) of score will be set to 1. If the score is in the range of $\mu_p \pm \sigma_p$ to $\mu p \pm 2\sigma p$, the weight should be set to 0.5 for it is believed lower than the norms. The weight is 0 for the residual condition. The algorithm of the final score (s_p) is as follows:

$$s_p = \frac{\sum_{j=1}^{m} s_j * w_j}{\sum_{i=1}^{m} w_i} \quad (5)$$

In the above formula, m is the number of experts who evaluate the project. The factor S_j is the score of one project from an expert and S_j is the corresponding weight. If the most of the weight indexes of the scores which are given by one expert is unreasonably low, the result will be investigated. As corresponding measures, new judges will be attended to re-examine the relative projects.

May be parts of members of one group will give a low label grade to an achievement, and this will lead to a low s. It should be also be paid attention to. Solving this problem, the scores (s_p) of the entire group are taken as sample and the μ_g and σ_g are gotten. So if the s_p is not in the range of $\mu g \pm 2\sigma g$, the evaluation behaviour point at it will be assessed and whether it should be re-rated would be decided according to the assessment result.

4 SYSTEM DEVELOPMENT

4.1 System service

The system in general needs to implement the following functions:

(1) Reward for users to declare an index, the results of the review and distribution, and the distribution of the unified management of achievements.

(2) Online users declare a function of agricultural sci-tech achievements.

(3) Recommendation units to the agricultural scientific and technological achievements for the management function.

(4) Evaluator review the user allocation of agricultural science and technology achievements score function.

Therefore, the system function modules are divided into different user login modules including, declared units, recommended unit for function module, review function module, and reward function module five parts. This module is shown in Figure 1.

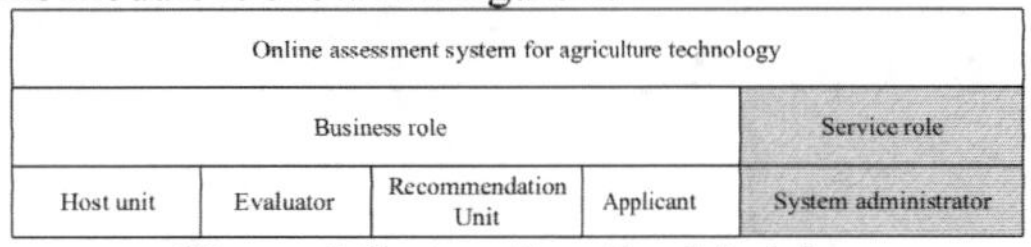

Figure 1 System Function Modules

Agricultural science and technology achievements of online return and review work process mainly includes initialization, confirmation, material declaration, opinion and order form review, distribution, Evaluator, expert ratings, and reviews.

This process is shown in figure2.

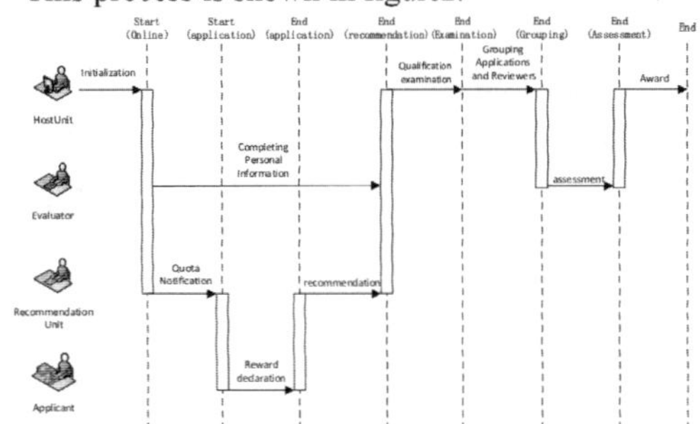

Figure 2 declare and review of flow diagram

According to the working process of the awards, the overall business process of the system is shown in figure 3(Saif Ur Rehman Khan, 2016).

(1) Reward for users to recommend unit assigned to declare index.

(2) Recommended unit in offline notification to declare indexes corresponding to user accounts about informing declare units.

(3) Declare units begin after landing system online declaration, after the declaration is submitted to the archive.

(4) Recommended unit declares an initial review of scientific and technological achievements, if it is qualified to confirm recommend. If not qualified, then it is returned to the declare unit for further modification.

(5) Demand rewards have been recommended to the management of the group of the agricultural scientific and technological achievements. They are mainly a recommended form of rechecking during the course of agricultural scientific and technological achievements and review. The review form is done by the group for the work assigned, corresponding to review and Evaluator and if it is unqualified, they can choose to return for modification or have it directly eliminated. Directly eliminated results will not be sent back to participate in additional review.

(6) Evaluator can be assigned to their results in accordance with the scores and submit those results to be reviewed against the rules.

(7) It is expected for all the experts all items to make a review after comparison and appraisal, according to the rules, in order to select the corresponding project award.

(8) The results can be managed after the end of the link of prizes.

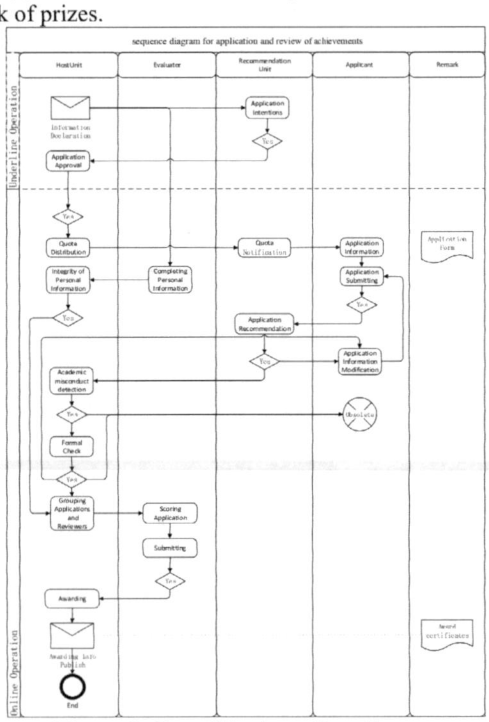

Figure 3. Overall business flow diagram

4.2 System structure

The platform is based on B/S architecture, which both takes advantage of the network and the function of the system at the same time (Re Zhongfang, 2004). It adds the business logic layer and separates the user from the data layer, which reduces the load of the Web Server and avoids any negative influence caused by the overall performance of the whole system (Shi Xingjian, 2004). The System architecture (MVC) is shown in Figure4.

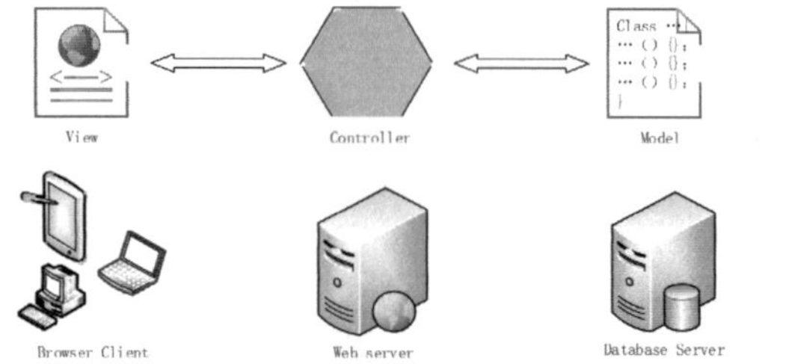

Figure 4 System architecture

The MVC model, with the characteristics of clear design, easy to use and extend distribution, separate the program performance, control and data, which has the advantage in a web application and in adaptation into the systems that are multiuser, extensible, maintainable, and have a high level of interactivity (J. C. Chang, S. R. Hanna,2004).

The presentation layer: The user interface section, used for the dialogue between the user and the system function. Mainly used to check the user keyboard input and the output of the operation result. To complete this, the languages JavaScript, jQuery were used (Xiaochang Liu, 2016).

The business logic layer: The business logic algorithm processes the input, called the database layer, and then returns the data results. The layer mainly includes the business functions and the data function, business function layer can be resolved within the function, but data function must rely on interactions with the data layer can be completed. And the subsystem in this part was developed the java language (Jie Shen, 2015).

The database layer: The centralized management of the database, including business entities and the data operation (Ximing Li, Jihong Ouyang, You Lu, 2015).

5 SYSTEM APPLICATION

The system is deployed on a server connected to Internet, so it can be tested by the users in different regions with different ways of surfing the Internet. The server's main configuration parameters are as follows: operating system: windows server 2008; web server: Tomcat 6.0; CPU: Xeon E3-1220; Memory type: 8G DDR3 ECC.

During the trial operation of the system, about 20 recommended units and 60 application unit or applicants were invited to load this system to complete the simulated reporting procedures. The system implements the reservation functions. In formal application, about 132 recommended units and 574 application units have use the system to participate in the information of their technological achievements.

5.1 Duplicate checking function

This function is evaluated with one case by comparing the detected achievement information with that of the previous award winning results. There are about 800 samples and everyone has about 4000-5000 characters. The function is mainly directed against individual unethical behaviour. The similarity of every achievement can be queried by formulating factors. And the interface of the detailed information of repetition rate detection results is also be provided for every projects. It will lead to the similarity details page. In this page, if one or more sentences repeat with the sample, it will be shown in red. The related sentences, topic and award information of sample are also displayed.

5.2 Abnormally scoring function

To guarantee fairness of evaluation and validate the consistency of the evaluating result and Technical level of achievement, we prepare two algorithms described above. The scenario represents different angle of the measurement with group sample synthesis model.

In the details information analysis, we present scoring record for every projects. It is defined to a sufficient level of detail for investigating for the score of every metric given by experts. The same rule applies when the scoring behaviour of one expert.

6 RESULTS AND DISCUSSION

Compared with the traditional evaluation model and method, this system has the following features:

(1) The System Work Flow is clear.

For the characters of science achievements include systematic structure, correlation of discipline, the complexity of the content and species diversity, the achievements of agricultural science and technology of online reporting and review process has carried on the detailed analysis, fully reflecting the project application and review process, in order to declare the project appraisal status has carried on the detailed classification of users at a glance and is easy to operate. It can be found that the average expenditure of web-based system is considerably lower than that of traditional way for peer assessment cycle. And it also show that the average expenditure of second online cycle is less than the first one for the reason that part of the workload is spent on real time consulting services for system usage during the first on-line operation. The related time data are shown in table 1

Table1 workload comparison chart

	traditional			online	
	2008-2009	2010-2011	2012-2013	2014-2015	2016-2017
total (term)	355	367	373	587	769
working hours (h)	2900	3110	3350	1140	970
Average expenditure (h/term)	8.17	8.47	8.98	1.94	1.39

(2) Monitoring of academic wrongdoing

During the application submitting link, after the application units upload their application documents, the main technical content is extracted and stored in the database and it will be compared with the data in the historical database which includes the filing of scientific and technological achievements over the years. The result will generate a report contains repeat rate and duplicate content. These functions will prevent repeated declaration and plagiarism. During the first review cycle, there were 28 technical achievements were returned for content reasons. It is accounting for 5.6% of the total number of declarations. In the second cycle, it dropped to 0.1% with the same standard, it means there were only 1 of 769 were return.

(3) Supervising appraisal activity anomalies

To determine whether judges performed more objectively in their assessments of agriculture achievements? This system analysis review activity from two viewpoints, one is counting the total score and individual score of each project, then screening of abnormal data depend on the rating distribution. The other aspect is doing statistical analysis on judges' scoring data, emphasizing the unusual discrete case of per expert marking moths. After the first system cycle was end, we compared the assessment data from two aspects mentioned above. The lower the technological innovation was, the smaller the deviation was between the experts scoring, and therefore the more objective the score was. By using the system algorithm to detect the distribution of points can make the discrete fraction distribution is found in time. This function has played a good role, making the appeal rate drop year by year as shown in table 2.

Table2 Appeal rate

	traditional			online	
	2008-2009	2010-2011	2012-2013	2014-2015	2016-2017
appeal rate	12	10	13	1	0.3

7. CONCLUSION

Peer-assessments are methods of evaluation highly recommended by researchers, but the traditional pen-and-paper-based peer-assessment method has many restrictions. This study contributes to the field by designing the web-based assessment information system, and provides the procedures for online information management, online review and academic wrongdoing monitoring expecting that it can help minimize the difficulties in agriculture technology information management and evaluation. With the network application review and most of the information becomes electronic, there will be a reduced volume of materials submitted. We expect that the web-based system will stimulate more in-depth thinking as well as further development on ways to integrate web technology with the agricultural technology assessment models.

ACKNOWLEDGEMENT

This work was supported by National Spark Program Key Project (Grant #: 2015GA600002).

Authors' Instructions

Yanzhao Ren, PhD Student, Box 105, China Agricultural University, No 17, QingHua East Road Haidian District, Beijing, P.R. China. Yanzhao Ren obtained his Master of Engineering in Agricultural Machine Engineering from Shandong University of Technology, Zibo, China in 2012.He is currently pursuing his PhD in Agricultural Electrification and Automation at China Agricultural University, Beijing. His research direction is computer application technology and intelligent information processing. His research subjects includes automatic control technology of greenhouse environment, automatic operating equipment, agricultural informatization, Agricultural IoT.

References

1. Chen, R. Y. (2017). An intelligent value stream-based approach to collaboration of food traceability cyber physical system by fog computing. Food Control, 71, 124-136
2. M. Radwan, N., Senousy, M. B., & M. Riad, A. E. D. (2017). A new expert system for learning management systems evaluation based on neutrosophic sets. Expert Systems
3. Vabo, G., Slettebø, Å. & Fossum, M. (2016). An Evaluation of an Action Research Nursing Documentation Project. Journal of Clinical Nursing
4. Li Xian. (2006)Life Cycle Assessment Theory and System Analysis of Agricultural Science and Technology Achievements. Jilin University
5. Li HaiYan. (2000). Establishment of Index System for Medical Achievements and Development of Comprehensive Evaluation System. First Military Medical University
6. Yang SiBo. (2002). the evaluation method research and software system implementation of scientific and technical achievements [D]. Tianjin Polytechnic University.
7. Wang ChenYe. (2012). A Study on the Operation Mode and Performance Evaluation of Scientific and Technological Achievements in Universities of Our Country. Harbin Engineering University
8. Huang Wei. (2013). the Study on Performance Evaluation of China Scientific and Technological Achievement Transformation and its Influence Factors and Countermeasures. Jilin University,
9. Jiang LiHua. (2014). Study on Theory and Method of Science and Technology Innovation for Agriculture Institutes, Chinese Academy of Agricultural Sciences.
10. Ye Ma, Zhao Hui, Wang Lei, Li Jianghua. (2007). the design and implementation of Dayu water conservancy science information system. TECHNICAL SUPERVISION IN WATER RESOURCES, 15(5):49-51.
11. Hua Lei. (2013). the design and implementation of Agricultural science and technology system.
12. João Carneiro, Diogo Martinho, Goreti Marreiros, Paulo Novais. (2016). Intelligent negotiation model for ubiquitous group decision scenarios. Frontiers of Information Technology & Electronic Engineering, 17(4): 296-308. http://dx.doi.org/10.1631/FITEE.1500344
13. Xue Dong-Liang. (2007). scientific research management system, AGRICULTURE NETWORK INFORMATION, (10):210-212.
14. Shi Xingjian, Xu Liangxian. (2004). Research and Application of Hibernate in Struts, COMPUTER ENGINEERING, 30(zl):165-167,190.
15. Feng Li. (2012). The development and application of textile science appraisal system.
16. Yuan Xiaoqing. (2015). Study on Model and Method of Agricultural Informatization Level and Benefit Evaluation. China Agricultural University.
17. Hou Xin. (2015). the Research on Quality Assurance and Quality Evaluation Mode of Postgraduate Education. Shanxi University of Finance and Economics.
18. Theo S.Eicher, OliyerRoehn. (2007). Sources of the German Productivity Demise: Tracing the Effects of Industry-Level Information and Communication Technology Investment. German Economic Review. (2)
19. Re Zhongfang, ZHANG Hua, YAN Ming-song, Chen Shifu. (2004). Overview of the Research in Model-View-Controller Pattern, APPLICATION RESEARCH OF COMPUTERS. 21(10).
20. Lingxian Zhang,Xue Liu,Daoliang Li,Zetian Fu.(2013).Evaluation of the rural informatization level in four Chinese regions: A methodology based on catastrophe theory . Mathematical and Computer Modelling. (3-4).
21. Jin ZhenHui. (2006). Research on the Method at Science and Technology Protect Evalution, Kunming University of Science and Technology.
22. J. C. Chang,S. R. Hanna.(2004).Air quality model performance evaluation . Meteorology and Atmospheric Physics, (1-3)
23. Xi-ming Li, Ji-hong Ouyang, You Lu. (2015). Topic modeling for large-scale text data. Frontiers of Information Technology & Electronic Engineering, 16(6): 457-465. http://dx.doi.org/10.1631/FITEE.1400352
24. Saif Ur Rehman Khan, Sai Peck Lee, Mohammad Dabbagh, Muhammad Tahir, Muzafar Khan, Muhammad Arif. RePizer. (2016).a framework for prioritization of software requirements. Frontiers of Information Technology & Electronic Engineering, 17(8): 750-765. http://dx.doi.org/10.1631/FITEE.1500162

An Empirical Study on Financing Preference of Listed Military Industry Enterprises in China

Li-Na Chen*, Ying Lei

31008 Unit, PLA, 100091, BeiJing, China

Abstract. Financing is an important part in the development of military enterprises, and it plays an important role in the development of military enterprises. By using empirical analysis method, 22 companies are selected as samples. The factor analysis and multivariate linear regression method are used to quantitatively analyze the internal factors of the company. These internal factors affect the financing preference of listed companies in China's military industry. Then conclusions are drawn and relevant suggestions are put forward.

1 INTRODUCTION

The defense industry as an important industry of China's economic development and a pillar industry to safeguard national security, especially China is facing the external environment of the general peace and local wars in the international situation, and its role is increasingly prominent in the development of the national economy. However, with the development of China's market economy, the development of military industry is lagging behind the development of other industries. It is mainly reflected in the low profit margin, the single source of funds and the lack of funds. There are many reasons for the above problems, but the financing problem is more prominent. And financing, as the key link of the enterprise development, plays an important role in the development of the enterprise. However, the financing mode of military industrial enterprises in China is still dominated by traditional bank loans. To some extent, this limits the fact that enterprises can not make extensive use of capital market to promote the development of enterprises, resulting in a series of problems, such as high cost of financing and low efficiency of fund utilization. Therefore, it is necessary for us to study the financing problems of our military enterprises systematically, so as to improve the financing efficiency and broaden the financing channels for military enterprises.

Some scholars have studied the above problems. For example, Rui Ma used the data of 2006-2008 of China's military industrial enterprises to make an empirical study on the relationship between the military enterprises and the government and the banks. Shusheng Li used comparative method to study the financing ways of Chinese military enterprises and the US military industry enterprises, and put forward suggestions for the problems of the financing of our military enterprises. Jianchang Liu and other problems in the financing of military enterprises in China are analyzed, and measures to improve the problems are put forward. Xu Zhang and other methods used fuzzy evaluation method to evaluate the financing mode of China's military industry. According to the conclusion of evaluation, we put forward some suggestions for the financing problems of China's military industry. By analyzing the current situation of investment and financing in China's military industry, Shuxia Ren put forward the problems in the financing of China's military industry, and put forward corresponding strategies according to the actual situation.

The above scholars have analyzed the problems in our military industry financing from different levels, and put forward the corresponding measures and suggestions. But most of them are studied from a statistical or descriptive point of view or one aspect of the financing. This paper will study the problems of military industry financing in China from the perspective of empirical analysis, and put forward some relevant suggestions.

2 VARIABLE SELECTION

(1) Dependent Variable

In the selection of the dependent variables, this paper chooses the average shareholder equity ratio of the listed companies in the military industry for 2012-2015 years, which can be more intuitively responsive to the equity financing preference.

(2) Independent Variable

At present, most scholars consider all the listed companies when they choose relevant indicators, while the analysis for a specific industry is relatively few, especially for the military industry, the empirical research of financing preference is basically blank. This paper combines the characteristics of China's military industry and the availability of relevant data.9 factors, such as profitability, debt paying ability, growth ability, operating capacity, dividend payment level, tax shield

* Corresponding author: Li-Na Chen: 9309806@qq.com

value, enterprise scale, CVOA and HERF, are selected as the object of empirical analysis of the influencing factors of financing preference of military industry listed companies. 23 indicators, such as earnings per share, Roe, are used as concrete indicators to carry out empirical research.

Table 1. Empirical Analysis Index Selection of Listed Companies in Military Industry.

Index classification	Index name	Index definition
Profitability	Earnings per share	Net margin/ Total equity
	Roe	Net margin / Net assets
	Return on assets	Net margin / Average asset total
	Net profit margin	Net margin/ Operating income
Debt paying ability	Current ratio	Circulating assets / Cash liabilities
	Quick ratio	Quick assets / Cash liabilities
	Interest coverage ratio	(Total profit + Capital charges) / Interest cost
Growth ability	EPSG	(Final - Beginning) / Beginning
	Increase rate of business revenue	(Final - Beginning) / Beginning
	Net profit growth rate	(Final - Beginning) / Beginning
	Total Assets Growth Rate	(Final - Beginning) / Beginning
operating capacity	inventory turnover ratio	Sales income/average inventory
	average accounts receivable turnover ratio	Sales income/Average accounts receivable
	Equity Turnover	Sales income / Average shareholders' equity
	Turnover of total capital	Sales income / Average total assets
Dividend payment level	Dividend per share	Total dividend / Total stock
	Dividend payout ratio	Dividend per share / Earnings per share
Tax shield value	Effective tax rates	Income tax / Total profit
Enterprise scale	LN total assets	The logarithm of the total assets
	LN income	The logarithm of business income
Collateral Value of Assets	Hypothecary value	(Inventory + Fixed assets) / Total assets
HERF	The proportion of the top five shareholders	Total share of the top five shareholders / Total equity
	First largest shareholder ratio	Number of first largest shareholder / Total share capital
Capital composition	Asset-liability ratio	Gross liabilities/ Total assets
	Equity Ratio	Shareholders' equity / Total assets

3 EMPIRICAL ANALYSIS

(1) Data and Sample Selection

The sample size, 2013, 2014, 2015, and three years' data of the listed military companies are analyzed in this paper to analyze the main factors that affect the capital structure of military listed companies. In order to ensure the effectiveness of the sample data, the enterprises that issue A shares listed on the main board market are selected. In order to ensure the true reliability of the data, the sample of ST military listed companies is eliminated, and 22 effective samples are finally obtained.

The data used in this paper are derived from the Wind financial advisory terminal database. The full text data processing and analysis mainly uses the Excel2007 and SPSS20.0 statistical analysis software.

(2) Factor Construction

The eigenvalue and variance contribution rate of the extracted principal component factors are shown in Table 2. It can be seen from the table that the eigenvalue of the first factor is 6.668, accounting for 29.484% of the variance; The eigenvalues of the second factors are 3.523, accounting for 15.529% of the variance; The cumulative contribution rate of the variance of the first 7 factors is 83.62%, It can be seen that the variance explained by the other 16 factors is only 16.38%, which indicates that the 7 factors extracted in this paper well preserve the information of the original variable, so the extracted common factor has good representativeness.

Table 2. Factor eigenvalue and cumulative variance contribution rate.

Ingre dients	Initial Eigenvalues			Extracting square sum and loading		
	Total	Variance %	accumulate %	Total	Variance %	accumulate %
1	6.668	29.484	29.484	6.668	29.484	29.484
2	3.523	15.529	45.013	3.523	15.529	45.013
3	2.699	11.478	56.491	2.699	11.478	56.491
4	1.979	8.624	65.115	1.979	8.624	65.115
5	1.680	7.743	72.858	1.680	7.743	72.858
6	1.211	5.569	78.427	1.211	5.569	78.427
7	1.136	5.194	83.621	1.136	5.194	83.621
8	0.888	3.942	87.563			
9	0.794	3.255	90.818			
10	0.535	2.474	93.292			
11	0.460	2.023	95.315			
12	0.331	1.853	97.168			
13	0.235	1.052	98.22			
14	0.151	0.671	98.891			
15	0.112	0.465	99.356			
16	0.065	0.299	99.655			
17	0.040	0.181	99.836			
18	0.026	0.113	99.949			
19	0.009	0.048	99.997			
20	0.001	0.002	99.999			
21	0.000	0.001	100			
22	3.68E-17	1.63E-16	100			
	-6E-16	-2.64E-15	100			

$F_i\left(i=1,2...7\right)$ is defined as a common factor. Through the observation of the factor load matrix, it is found that： F_1 has an absolute value of load on earnings per share, Roe, return on assets and net profit margin. So we think the main reflection of the company's profitability, what we call "profitability" factor. The $F_2 \sim F_7$ can be found in the current ratio and quick ratio, EPSG and net profit growth rate, the growth ability of the company, average accounts receivable turnover ratio and inventory turnover ratio, The proportion of the top five shareholders and First largest shareholder ratio, hypothecary value, dividend payout ratio has absolute value greater load coefficient.

$F_2 \sim F_7$ are called "debt paying ability" factor, "Growth ability" factor, "operating capability" factor, "equity structure" factor, "Collateral Value of Assets" factor and "Dividend payment level" factor respectively.

(3) Model Building

The shareholder equity ratio (Y) is the ratio of the owner's equity to the total assets. The average shareholder equity ratio of Listed Companies in the military industry for nearly three years can be more intuitively responsive to equity financing preference. In this paper, the principal component analysis method is selected to extract 7 principal component factors as independent variables. Because of the factor analysis, the correlation between variables and multiple collinearity are eliminated, and the seven principal component factors are calculated by the factor score matrix.

$$Y = b_0 + \sum_{i=1}^{7} b_i F_i + \varepsilon$$

b_0 is a constant term, ε is a random variable

(4) Test Results and Analysis

Table 3. Test Results

Model		Sum of squares	df	Mean square	F	Sig.
1	Regression	15.148	7	2.361	8.940	.001[a]
	Residual error	4.661	14	0.348		
	Total	21.000	21			

a. Predictive Variable: (Constant), Common factor 7, Common factor2, Common factor5, Common factor6, Common factor3, Common factor1, Common factor4
b. Dependent variable: Equity Ratio

Table 4. Model Coefficient Table

Model		Unstandardized Coefficients		Standardized beta coefficients	t	Sig.
		B	Standard error	Trial version		
1	(constant)	-1.532E-6	.124		.000	1.000
	common factor 1	.240	.127	0.248	1.950	0.068
	common factor2	-.766	.127	-0.768	-6.043	0
	common factor3	-.201	.127	0.198	1.559	0.136
	common factor4	-.092	.127	-0.090	-0.709	0.481
	common factor5	.142	.127	0.139	1.090	0.286
	common factor6	-.213	.127	0.201	1.584	0.131
	common factor7	-2.065E-5	.127	.000	.000	1.000

a. Dependent Variable： Equity Ratio

The results of the multivariate linear regression model are as follows:

$$Y = -1.558E^{-6} + 0.240F_1 - 0.776F_2 - 0.201F_3$$
$$-0.092F_4 + 0.142F_5 - 0.213F_6 - 2.065E^{-5}F_7 + \varepsilon$$

Through the empirical analysis of the financing preference of the listed companies in the military industry, we can see that： The profitability of an enterprise is positively related to the equity ratio, with a coefficient of 0.240. Because the stronger the profitability of an enterprise, the more profits can be retained for the redevelopment of the enterprise. The short term solvency of an enterprise is anti-related to the equity ratio, and its coefficient is -0.766. The stronger the solvency of the enterprise is, the stronger the liquidity is, the easier it is for the business to merge from the bank loan or the issue bond to the debt fund, and the relative level of debt increases, resulting in a relative reduction of the stockholders' equity ratio. The growth ability of the enterprise is positively related to the equity ratio, and its coefficient is -0.201. The better the growth ability of enterprises is, the better prospects for enterprises to be compared with other enterprises or the whole market. Therefore, enterprises are reluctant to issue shares to the capital market, and on the other hand, most Chinese military enterprises rely on bank loans for financing. The operating capacity of an enterprise is anti-related to the equity ratio, and its coefficient is -0.091. In theory, The better the operating capacity of an enterprise shows, the better the enterprise's capacity for capital turnover. The smaller the demand for debt, the relatively low level of debt and the relative increase in the equity ratio. That is, the operating capacity is proportional to the equity ratio. But the empirical results of this paper are opposite. It shows that China's military enterprises are not willing to finance the market. The ratio of equity structure and equity ratio has a positive correlation to a certain extent, with a coefficient of 0.140. The more centralized the ownership of the enterprises, the greater the influence of the shareholders to the financing preference of the listed companies. To make the financing needs of the listed companies more satisfied through equity financing. The Collateral Value of Assets and the equity ratio are in a positive correlation to a certain extent, with a coefficient of -0.203. Most of our military listed companies belong to large and medium-sized state-owned enterprises, representing the relative position and the right to speak in the military industry. In theory, the larger the scale, the greater the proportion of tangible assets (fixed assets and inventory). The greater the asset guarantee value is, the higher the credit of the enterprise is, the easier it is to get the debt financing such as bank loans, and the ratio of stockholders' equity is also lower. There is a positive correlation between the dividend payment level and the equity ratio to a certain extent, the coefficient of which is -2.065E-5. When the profitability of a company is constant, the higher the dividend payout level, the less the retained earnings and the lower the stockholder's equity ratio. This shows that the listed companies of the military industry prefer bank loans.

4 CONCLUSIONS

Through the analysis of the above results, we find that profitability, short-term debt paying ability, growth ability, equity structure and Collateral Value of Assets have different effects on the financing preference of China's military industry listed companies. Therefore, for military industry listed companies, when financing is carried out, we should combine the unique characteristics of military enterprises and adhere to the basic principles of total financing revenue and total cost of financing to determine the optimal capital structure of enterprises. In terms of specific measures, we should consider the main factors that influence the financing preference of military industry listed companies, so as to consider improving the structure of related factors, so as to achieve the best corporate capital structure, so that the value of enterprises can be maximized.

(1) Optimizing the Equity Structure of Enterprises

At present, the state-owned shares of China's military listed companies account for a large proportion. Therefore, the decision-making level should consider reducing the state-owned shares and encouraging the transfering of the legal person shareholders, so that the legal investors can be more concerned about the long-term interests of the company and the development of the company's business. Moreover, whether state-owned shares or corporate shares are common stocks, they should gradually circulate state-owned shares and public shares, which is conducive to the optimal allocation of resources.

(2) The Government Promotes Financial Innovation

The government should actively promote the financial market, financial product innovation, the establishment of a multi-level and diversified capital market system, to diversify the financing instruments and financing mode, promote the development of private equity and bond market, reducing the financing cost of listed companies, to meet the needs of listed companies and investor diversification, improve the efficiency of resource allocation.

REFERENCES

1. Ma Rui, Fu construction. An Empirical Study on the convenience of debt financing for listed military enterprises [J]. Heilongjiang foreign trade and economic economic and trade, 2010,(**06**):117-119.
2. Li Shusheng. Research on stock financing preference of listed military enterprises in China [D]. Henan University,2011.
3. Liu Jianchang, Shi Xiu, Zhang Xiaoqian, Xie Wen Qiang. Research on the financing model of military industrial enterprises in China [J]. Industrial Economic Forum,2015,(**04**):118-126.
4. Zhang Xu, Liu Jianchang, Hou Guangxi. Comprehensive evaluation of multiple financing methods in military enterprises -- Based on the [J]. Technology and economy of fuzzy network analysis, 2013, (**11**):81-87+118.
5. Ren Shuxia. Research on the investment and financing model of military industry enterprises in China based on the development of military and civilian integration, [J].Modern economic information,2016,(**11**):300.

Knowledge Evolution of Complex Agent Networks

Zhao Yeqing *

School of Computer and Information Engineering, Anyang Normal University, 455000 He Nan, China

Abstract. In order to study the interaction between structure change of social network and knowledge propagation, this paper proposes a complex agent network model to discover the inner rule and restraining factors of the knowledge diffusion in the network system. The agents take advantage of different social radius to form acquaintance networks based on the theory of social circles in the knowledge propagation network model, and the dynamic evolution process of knowledge network is realized according the defined rules of knowledge communication. Simulation results show that this model based on social circle theory can better realize the characteristics of the actual social network than the traditional network model established before, at the same time the social radius of knowledge agent for knowledge dissemination in knowledge network has the obvious effect. It can narrow the knowledge gap for the knowledge agents in social network and good social relation network can be developed.

1 Introduction

The study on the dynamic mechanism of knowledge communication based on complex networks has become the potential development direction of further research on knowledge dissemination. However, due to the complexity of knowledge dissemination in the social networks, the current research on knowledge communication is in a preliminary state, and the dynamics of knowledge networks system is just starting. In the real world, mutual influence exists between the dynamic interaction of knowledge dissemination and dynamic evolution of social networks structure, on the one hand, the social networks structure affects the performance and mode of knowledge dissemination, on the other hand, the social activities of knowledge propagation will in turn affect the dynamic characteristics of corresponding social networks. Cowan and Jonard[1]models knowledge diffusion as a barter process in which agents exchange different types of knowledge, and find that the performance of the system exhibits clear 'small world' properties, in that the steady-state level of average knowledge is maximal when the structure is a small world. On the basis of Cowan and Jonard models, Morone and Taylor[2] study the dynamics of knowledge propagation and the evolution of formation network in the process of interactive learning by considering the impact network structure on individual behavior. R Cowan, N Jonard, JB Zimmermann[3]model the formation of innovation networks as they emerge from bilateral decisions, they focus attention on the effects of the knowledge and information regime on network formation to study the co-evolution mechanism of knowledge communication in bilateral cooperation networks. Zhang Hao [4] studied the dissemination and diffusion of knowledge in universities by using the theory of small world network [5], and adjusted the relevant parameters to promote the virtuous circle of knowledge network by putting forward the concept of knowledge diffusion frequency and agglomeration degree of knowledge diffusion. The networks theory agent-based social circle [6] is used to construct the actual social networks model with a variety of statistical features of social networks. The social networks are generated through micro individual behaviors. The generation and evolution of the networks are managed by agents, and the evolution process of the networks is closer to the operation mechanism of the real society. So, the social circle networks model can flexibly describe the large-scale space-time coupling social networks.

2 Social circle network

For the sake of building social network model [7-9] with various statistical features of the social network, HAMILL L put forward the Agent-based social circles network theory. Firstly, each agent has different social communication radius and the space coordinates. Secondly, each agent generate the social networks with statistical properties of actual social network by their space position based on the social circles network theory, such as the differences in the radius of the individual networks lead to the differences in the network sizes, the network scale evolves over time, the network has a positive correlation, the evolution of the network can form a community structure ,the social networks have a relatively short average path, and the population density of the network community is low.

The social circles network model is based on the ideas of social space and distance, which abstracted as a

* Corresponding author: zhaoyq0603@163.com

larger social map to show the distribution and connection of the crowd in the society. The social circle of each individual represents the social scope of the individual, that is, the individual knows other individuals in his social circle, and the size of the social circle is described by the social radius. In the social circle network, the scale of the agent social networks varies with the size of the social radius, and the scale changes with time. At the same time, the social circle networks model has the characteristics of low population density, degree positive correlation, community structure with a short path and Poisson distribution with a fat tail. The micro knowledge communication network is a typical social network. The social circle network can reflect the characteristics of knowledge dissemination in the real society. So, the social circle network can be used to build the microscopic knowledge propagation network model.

3 Knowledge network models

Definition 1 Knowledge network model based on social circle is $SCs = (V(s), E(s), \varphi(s), R(s))$,where:

$V(s) = \{Agent_{ij} \mid i, j \in N^+\}$ is a non-empty finite set, which represents the type and the number of agent in the system.

$E(s) = \{e_k \mid k \in N\}$ is a finite set that doesn't intersect with a $V(s)$,which represents the number of edges associated with agent in the system.

$\psi_s = \{r_{xy}, x, y \in V(s); x \neq y\}$ is the mapping function of the correlation relation between different agents in the system. $r_{xy} = 1$, it means that there is a direct connection between x and y , $r_{xy} = 0$, it indicates that there is no edge between x and y .

$R(s) = \{rule_i \mid i \in N\}$ is the rules set in the system.

Definition 2 Agent is a 4-tuple $Ag = (m, v, k, a)$,where:

m is the identity of agent, which is unique and consists of digital strings.

v is the category of agent, which is used to distinguish types of agents in the system.

k is the local knowledge library of agent, which represents the basic cognitive level of each agent .

a is the personality of agent, which represents the individual performance of the agent in the process of knowledge dissemination, it is defined as follows:

$a = (p, sr, r, lk)$, where:

p represents the location in the two-dimensional space where agent is located.

sr represents the size of social radius for agent.

r is the strength of the relationship, which is a measure of the degree of relationships between the agent and the neighboring agents.

lk is the knowledge level, which means that the amount of agent knowledge.

4 Simulation and results

To achieve the simulation of the model, the simulation platform adopted in this paper is an agent-based development tool, Net- logo 5.1, which is especially suitable for modeling complex systems with time series. The user can establish the interaction of macro models and micro-behavior, and the dynamic knowledge network system can emerge by the interaction between independent agents. Netlogo uses a simple logo language structure, which inherits the related concepts of the logo language. The main body is represented by turtles, while the environment of turtles is represented by patches and the system network was built by the linking (directed edge and undirected edge).

4.1 Social network evolution

The self-centered social networks (personal network) show the relationship between individuals and others. The social network is the aggregation of the individual networks, and the size of the individual network depends on the type of relationship in the network. Based on relationship strength, Boissevain[10]divided the relationship into strongest relation (the closest person or friends, closest to the strongest connection total is about 5), strong relation (often contact person or good friends, the number of 5 to 10), medium relation(contact friends or not often contact friends, the number of 20 to 30), weak relation (the daily economic activities related to the people, about 100 to 500), the weakest link (that may know, the number can be more than 500). At the same time, Boissevain believes that a few individuals have a large number of connections, while most individuals have fewer connections. Gilbert [11] research shows that the maintenance of social networks requires cost, so the size of a personal network is limited. The social relations network model shown in Figure 1 is generated by randomly distributing 1000 agent in 100000 unit area in two-dimensional space, where (a)(Sr=15) and (b)(Sr=45) denote the initial social relationship network generated by the social radius (SR) of 15 and 45, respectively. Besides,(c)(Sr1=15,Sr2=30) and (d)(Sr1=25,Sr2=45) means that the social radius(Sr1) of 80%agents is set to 15 (or 25) (the most agents in a social network have less knowledge, because their vision range is small, and only a small range of other agents are connected to form a small circle), and the social radius (Sr2) of 20% agents is set to 35 (or 45) (such as the key figures, who act as knowledge disseminator in the knowledge network, whose social circles should be large, and also plays the role of connecting the different small circle). Figures 2, 3 show the network degree distribution and cluster coefficient distribution of the initial social relations network shown by Figure 1 (d).

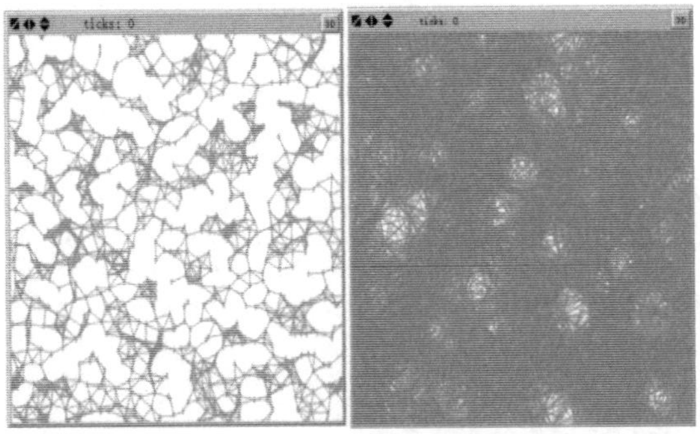

(a) (b)

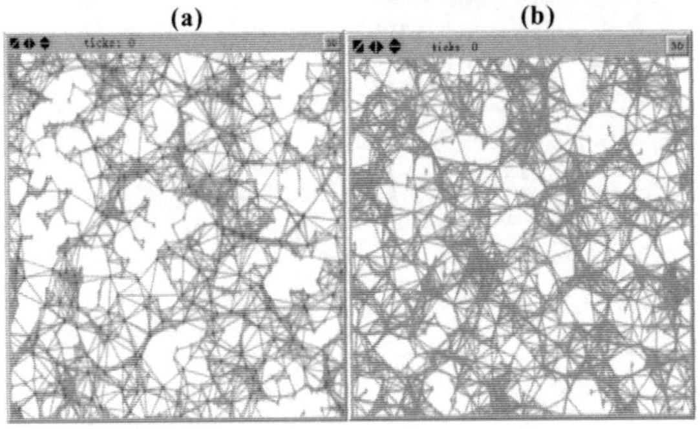

(c) (d)

Fig. 1. Social network of different radius

The social network model constructed by the social circle theory can realize most of the characteristics of the social network. In terms of individual networks, firstly, to limit the network scale and match the generated network with the actual social network through the social circle. Secondly, the size of the social circle can be adjusted by the social radius to find the parameter values of two suitable social circle sizes that form a continuous long tail distribution. Thirdly, there is a higher clustering coefficient in the social network. Fourthly, the individual network can move with time. For the whole network, social network has low density, exists significant positive correlation between degree and degree, and community structure and short path length. So, it can be seen that the social network model embodies the social network structure characteristics of the knowledge communication network.

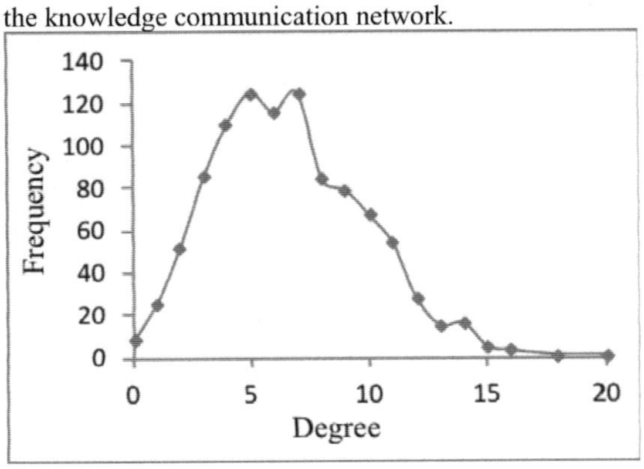

Fig. 2. Degree distribution

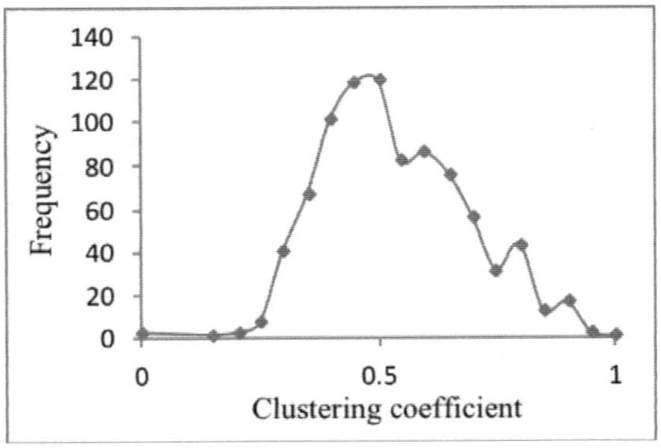

Fig. 3. Clustering coefficient

4.2 Knowledge network evolution

In the actual complex relationships of social network, due to the heterogeneity of knowledge agents, the social radius of each knowledge agent in the society is different based on the influence of many factors such as social status and social environment. For simplicity, we assume that the social radius of knowledge agent in the knowledge network is divided into two categories: Sr1 and Sr2 (Sr1 stands for smaller social radius, and Sr2 represents the larger social radius), p is the ratio of the number of knowledge disseminators to the total number of people.

In order to study the influence of the social radius of knowledge disseminators and the ratio of the people on knowledge dissemination in actual knowledge network, as shown in Figure 4, we simulate the different social radius Sr1 and Sr2 and the ratio of knowledge propagator P. The simulation results shown in Figure 4 show that when determining the value of Sr1 and Sr2 in knowledge network, we can change the efficiency of knowledge dissemination in knowledge network by changing the ratio of the total number of knowledge agents in the knowledge network system (the mean radius of the social network is 40). When the P value is large, the mean of knowledge increases in the knowledge network system, due to its larger social radius, faster speed for the dissemination of knowledge in the knowledge network, so the whole knowledge network system can reach a higher knowledge level in a relatively short period of time. When the number of knowledge disseminators reaches a certain proportion in the network, as shown in Figure 5, such as the value of Sr1 is 10, the value of P is 30%, it is the knowledge propagation process under different social network structure (Sr2 different values). From Figure 5, it can be found that when the radius of knowledge network becomes larger and larger, that is to say, the circle of acquaintances become larger. At the same time, with the increase of knowledge receivers, the knowledge transmission efficiency of the knowledge network system is higher; the time will be significantly shorter for knowledge network system achieving a higher level of knowledge.

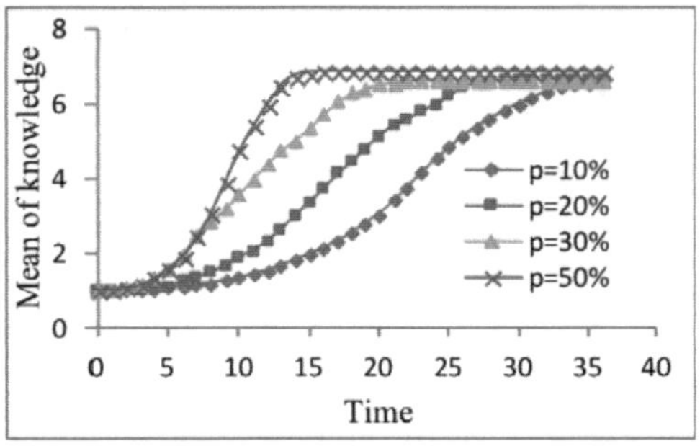

Fig. 4. when Sr_1=20 and Sr_2=40, knowledge network evolution graph for different p value

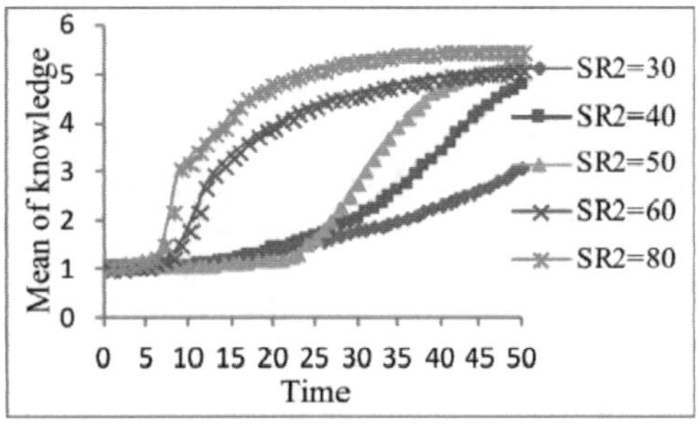

Fig. 5. when P=30%, knowledge network evolution graph for different social radius

5 Conclusion

A complex agent dynamic network model is proposed in this paper. Based on the theory of social circle network, the relationship between the network structure and the knowledge transmission of knowledge network system is simulated. In this model, knowledge agent generates social network of acquaintances through social radius and realizes the dynamic propagation process of knowledge network under the constraint of the rule of knowledge propagation and rule of knowledge evolution. The simulation results show that the social radius of knowledge disseminator and their proportion in the whole knowledge network all play a positive role for optimizing the network system structure and knowledge evolution efficiency.

Acknowledgements

This work is supported by the key scientific and technological project of Henan province under Grant nos. 172102210168 and 16A520001.

References

1. Cowan R, Jonard N. Journal of Economic Dynamics & Control. **28**,8,1557-1575 (2004).
2. Morone P, Taylor R. Journal of Evolutionary Economics.**14**, 3,327-351(2004).
3. Cowan R, Jonard N, Zimmermann J B. Management Science. **53**,7,1051-1067(2007).
4. Zhang Hao. Information science.**29**,9,1294-1297(2011).
5. Watts D J, Strogatz S H. Nature.**393**, 6684, 440-442(1998).
6. Hamill L, Gilbert N. Journal of Artificial Societies & Social Simulation.**12**, 2, 3-25(2009).
7. Zhang Shouming,Yu Qunxiu,Bi Guihong. Journal of System Simulation. **29**,3, 463-478 (2017).
8. Yu Qunxiu,Bi Guihong,Zhang Shouming. Computer Engineering. **42**,7,277-286(2016).
9. Bi Guihong,He Xiaoli,Wang Hairui. Journal of Systems & Management.**25**, 2,353-363(2016).
10. Boissevain J. Friends of Friends. American Economic Review. **25**,7,666-667(1974).
11. Hamill L, Gilbert N. Emergence Complexity & Organization. **12**,4,78-94(2010).

Community Mining Algorithm Based on Structural Similarity

Yaqiong Liu[1], Lu Wang*, Guoqing Chen[2]

[1]College of Information Science and Engineering, Shandong Agricultural University, Tai'an, China
[2]College of Agricultural, Shandong Agricultural University, Tai'an, China

Abstract. In order to improve the efficiency of community mining algorithm and the accuracy of community classification, a community mining algorithm based on structural similarity is proposed in this paper. The algorithm uses the structural similarity as an edge weight to perform the operation of the loop deletion, and implements community merging for isolated nodes, thus improving the precision of community division. The algorithm is compared with GN and SSNCA algorithm in classic data sets such as Zachary network, football data and dolphin social network. The experimental results show that the algorithm can effectively detect the community structure in complex networks, and the accuracy of classification and operation speed are obviously improved.

1 Introduction

In the real world, many systems can be described as networks, such as social networks, biological networks. These networks have high complexity and are therefore called "complex networks" ([1]). Complex networks have become one of the most important interdisciplinary fields of interdisciplinary research. The nodes in the network and the edges represent some kind of connection. In these networks, there are characteristics of the community structure that "the same group of nodes with close connection and sparse connection between different groups" ([2]). The purpose of complex network community mining is to detect and reveal the community structure inherent in heterogeneous complex networks.

At present, domestic and foreign scholars have proposed a variety of community mining algorithms from different perspectives on the issue of community mining. Girvan and others first proposed the GN algorithm ([3]) for community mining. Liu Dayou used structural similarity to replace the edge number in GN algorithm to realize community mining ([4]).Li Zhaonan proposed a community mining algorithm based on the similarity degree of node distance ([5]).For sparse networks, the precision of community division of the above algorithm is not high and the time complexity of the algorithm is high. Based on the above problems, this paper starts with improving the accuracy and operational efficiency of community division presents a community mining algorithm based on structural similarity.

2 Network representation method and formula construction

2.1 Complex Network Diagram Structure

We use a graph G=(V, E)to abstract the complex network. The node V={V_i}set represents the individual in the complex network, and the set of edges $E = \{(i,j)|i,j \in V\}$is the relation between individuals.

2.2 Community structure

In complex networks the nodes of the same group are closely linked, and the node links between different groups are sparse and the community characteristics shown are called community structures. In a complex network G, a community is defined as C_i , and the collection of communities is represented as P={C_1,C_2,C_3...C_k}

2.3 Modularity function Q

In 2004 Newman proposed a quantitative standard for characterizing the strengths and weaknesses of the network community structure, which is called the modular function Q ([6]). The community structure P of high module value indicates that the nodes in the community are closely connected and the nodes in the community are sparse. The formal definition of module degree is defined as:

$$Q = \frac{1}{2m}\sum_{ij}((A_{ij} - \frac{d_i d_j}{2m}) \times \partial(v(i), v(j))) \quad (1)$$

$A = (A_{ij})_{n\times n}$ represents the adjacency matrix of the network, If there is an edge connection between node iand node j, then $A_{ij} = 1$,Unbounded connected with

Corresponding author: liuyaq@sdau.edu.cn wangl@sdau.edu.cn

$A_{ij} = 0$. For the function $\partial(u,r)$, if u = r is 1, otherwise, it is 0. The symbol of d_i represents the degree of node i, defined as $d_i = \sum_j A_{ij}$.The symbol of $m = \frac{1}{2}\sum_{ij} A_{ij}$ represents the total number of edges in network G.

3 Data clustering algorithm SSNCA based on K neighbor network

3.1 Introduction of SSNCA algorithm

SSNCA algorithm is a network clustering algorithm based on structured similarity ([7]).The specific steps are as follows:

Step1：Calculate the structural similarity values of all edges in the network.

Step2: Remove the edge with the lowest structural similarity value from the network.

Step3: Recalculate the structured similarity values of all edges affected by step 2.

Step4: Repeat the above steps until there is no edge deletion.

Step5: Select the clustering result that maximizes the value of the Q function as the best community for the network.

3.2 Structure similarity formula construction

Definition 1: The node neighborhood set $\Gamma(i)$ is expressed as the neighbor node of the node i plus its own set.

$$\Gamma(i) = \{j \in V|(i,j) \in E\} \cup \{i\} \quad (2)$$

Definition 2: Let $i, j \in V$, Structural similarity $\sigma(i,j)$ is represented as

$$\sigma(i,j) = \frac{|\Gamma(i)|\cap|\Gamma(j)|}{\sqrt{|\Gamma(i)|\Gamma(j)|}|} \quad (3)$$

The structural similarity is used to judge the similarity between two points. The larger the value is, the closer the two nodes are, the more likely it is to belong to a community. The SSNCA algorithm uses structural similarity to replace the number of edge in the GN algorithm and improves the calculation speed. However, because only one edge with the smallest structural similarity is deleted at the same time, the computation efficiency is slow, and the problem of isolated points after community division is not considered. Therefore, the effect of community division is not accurate enough, and the calculation efficiency needs to be improved.

4 Community Mining Algorithm SSMCA Based on Structural Similarity

4.1 Introduction of SSMCA algorithm

In order to solve the problem of isolated points in community division, a community mining algorithm SSMCA (the SSNCA based on Merge, SSMCA) based on structured similarity is proposed to improve community accuracy.

Based on the SSNCA algorithm, the algorithm starts from how to accurately divide communities, and adopts circular edge deletion operation to reduce the number of iterations, and then merges the isolated points after dividing the community, so as to achieve the purpose of better division of community structure.

Therefore, this paper introduces the critical value parameter a , used to delete the similarity degree is less than a , in order to avoid blindly selecting the a value and reduce the community classification accuracy, this paper gives the optimal selection strategy: community setting step length in Δa , calculating the module function Q corresponding to the discrete critical value within the critical value interval, find out the critical value corresponding to the maximum Q value and divide the community as the best community division.

4.2 Community similarity formula construction

Definition 3(Community structure similarity) Let $i, j \in V$, community structure similarity C_{ij} expressed as:

$$C_{ij} = \frac{\textit{The number of links between } C_i \textit{ and } C_j}{\sqrt{d_{ci}d_{cj}}} \quad (4)$$

$$d_{ci} = \sum_{j=1}^{|C_i|} degree(V_j) \quad (5)$$

The degree (V_i) indicates the degree of nodes in the graph G, that is, the number of adjacent nodes of V_i.

4.3 SSMCA algorithm steps

Step1：Given the critical interval [x, y], (0<x<y<1), and the step length Δa, the number of cycles in the critical value interval is i, i = 1 , and a1 = x + Δa

Step2：The edge is used to calculate the structural similarity between the two nodes connected by the edge, and then the structure similarity is given as the weight to the edge.

Step3：According to the set critical value value a, perform the loop delete edge operation; repeat the steps 2 until no edge is deleted, take the breadth first traversal to obtain the community division under the critical value, then use formula 1 to calculate modularity function Q.

Step4：If $i + 1 < \frac{y-x}{\Delta a}$, then let $a_{i+1} = a_i + \Delta a$, continue to step 3, otherwise stop the loop.Find the community partition of the above maximum Q value as the result of optimal community segmentation.

Step5：The isolated point is considered as an independent community, calculating the similarity of the community structures between them (formula 4, 5) and sorting and merging.

Figure 1 shows a variation curve of the modularity function Q with the critical value a (Δa = 0.02) obtained by the SSMCA algorithm in the Zachary network. Where the X-axis represents the different critical value a, and the Y-axis represents the Q value obtained at the selected critical value a. From the figure, we can see that when a ∈ [0.3,0.34], the maximum Q value is 0.235, which corresponds to the best community division. In the critical value interval [0.3,0.34] the Q value remains unchanged, indicating that deleting a certain part of the network does not affect the overall community structure.

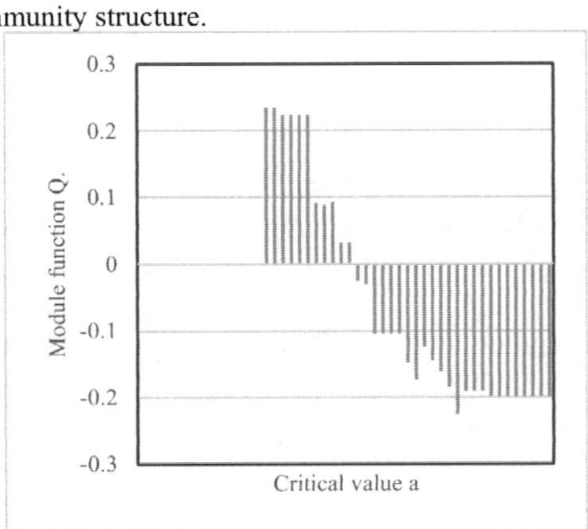

Fig. 1. Zachary network modularity function Q change diagram with critical value a

5 Experimental results and analysis of SSMCA algorithm

This paper uses SSMCA algorithm to perform simulation experiments on classical data sets. The results are compared with GN algorithm and SSNCA algorithm. Experiments show that the SSMCA algorithm can effectively detect the community structure effectively, and the calculation speed and community division accuracy are significantly improved.

The experimental environment of this algorithm is: Intel(R) Core(TM) i5-6600 CPU@3.30GHZ, memory 4GB, operating system Windows 7 Ultimate Edition, and programming software MATLAB 2014b.

5.1 Comparison of SSMCA algorithm and classical algorithm results

5.1.1 Zachary network

Figure 2 shows the Zachary network ([8]) nodes 1 and 33 in the figure represent the club managers and the coaches. The nodes of different shapes and colors represent members of each group after splitting.

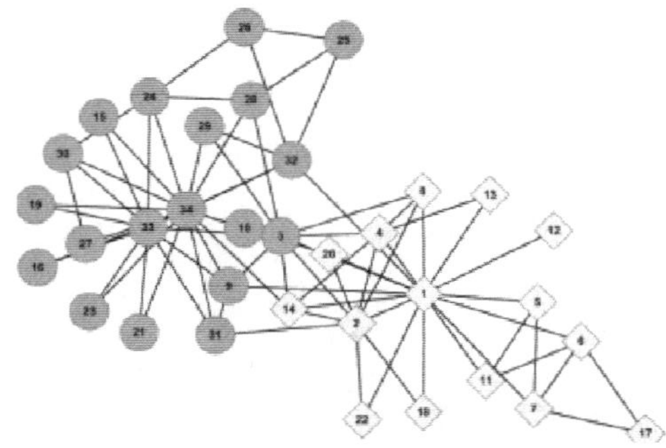

Fig. 2. Original network

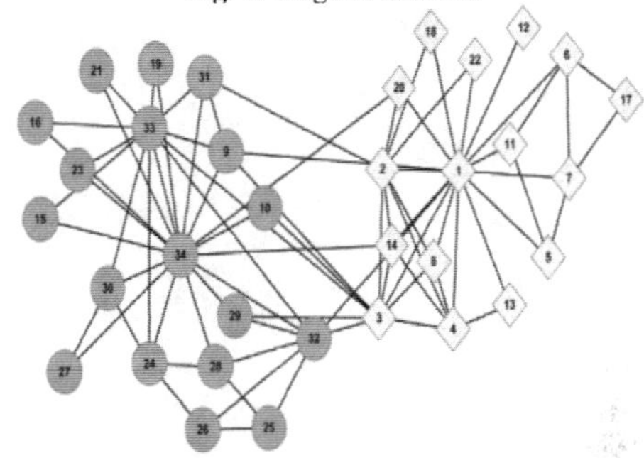

Fig. 3. GN algorithm detection network

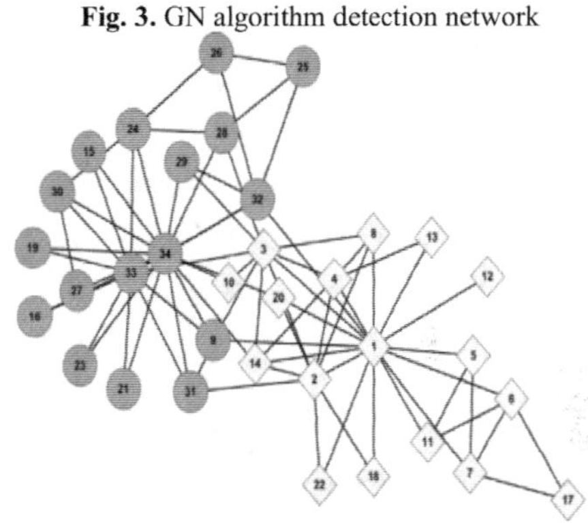

Fig. 4. SSNCA algorithm detection network

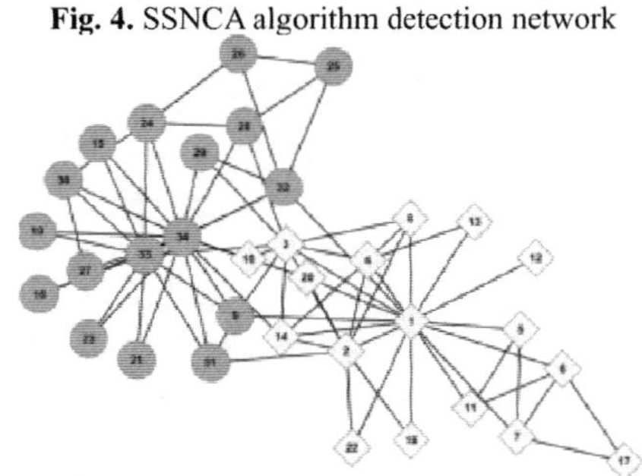

Fig. 5. SSMCA algorithm detection network

Using the GN algorithm, the SSNCA algorithm obtains Figure 3 and Figure 4. The result of the community division using the SSMCA algorithm is shown in Figure 5. In the figure, the yellow diamond node set and the red circular node set represent two

https://doi.org/10.1051/matecconf/201817603008

divided communities respectively. SSMCA algorithm and SSNCA algorithm are almost identical (see Figure 4 for details). After investigation and comparison, the new algorithm is consistent with the real situation.

5.1.2 Dolphin social network data set

The dolphin data set was obtained by D. Lussean includes 62 nodes and 159 edges ([9]). As shown in Figure 6, the circle in the figure represents the node set that successfully belongs to the community, and the different colors represent different communities. Unfortunately, there are isolated points 37, 40, and 56 (shown as triangles) after the community was divided into communities.

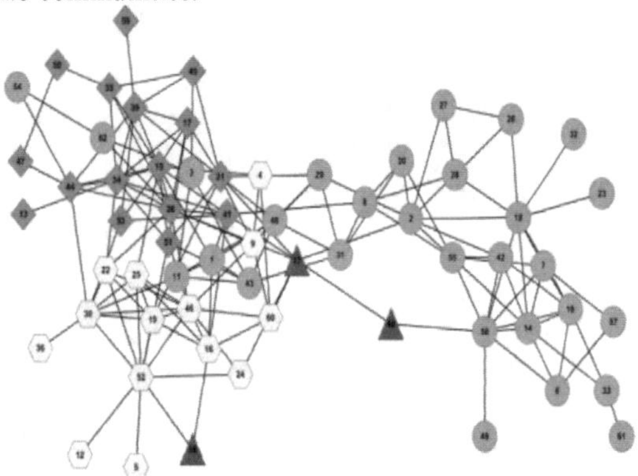

Fig. 6. SSNCA algorithm detection network

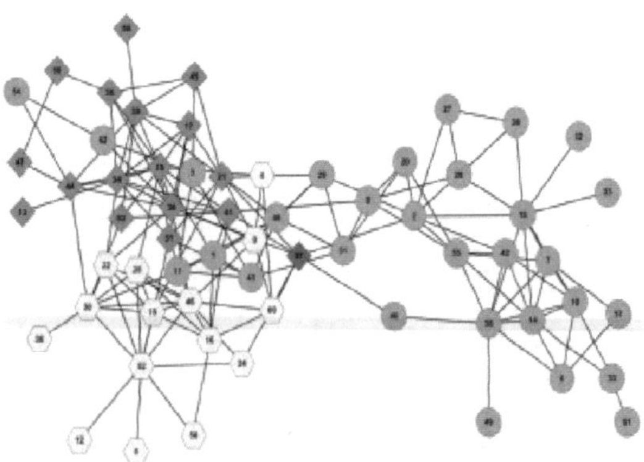

Fig. 7. SSMCA algorithm detection network

Using our new algorithm, SSMCA, the community division was mapped to figure 7, and the new algorithm also divided the network into three communities, with three different shapes of points representing different three communities. Unlike SSNCA algorithm in this paper, the algorithm of the isolated points in 37, 40, 56 in the community, to achieve the purpose of the new algorithm is better than SSNCA algorithm, and the experimental results are basically consistent with the actual network community.

5.1.3 American university football data set

The U.S. college football data set contains a total of 115 nodes and there are 613 connected edges. ([10]).The SSMCA algorithm was used to divide the community. The results are shown in Figure 8. The algorithm divides the network into 12 communities, and Figure 9 gives a statistical graph of the number of teams in each community, which is basically between 7 and 11 branches, which is consistent with the actual situation Therefore, the algorithm can find the community structure effectively.

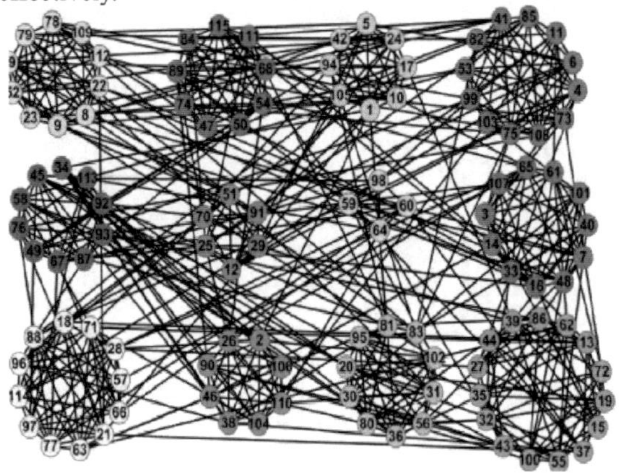

Fig. 8. Football Community Divisio

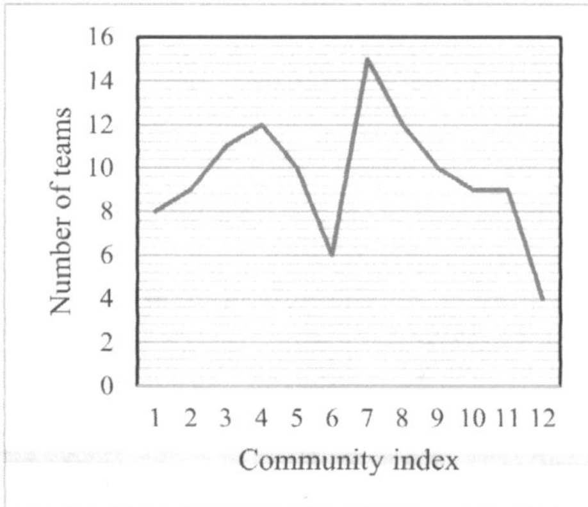

Fig. 9. Community Team Statistics

5.2 Comprehensive comparison of data sets

Experiments show that the SSMCA algorithm has significantly improved the accuracy of community division, and effective community consolidation has been implemented for the isolated points that existed after the community was divided, and the operation efficiency of the algorithm has been greatly improved.

Table 1 shows the statistical data of the experimental network. Table 2 shows the time consuming and accuracy standard comparison of GN algorithm, SSNCA algorithm and SSMCA algorithm for community partition of Zachary data set, the dolphin social network, and the football data set. We use the metric system based on Information theory NMI as the accuracy measure standard of the algorithm ([11]) The values in the table are the average values obtained 100 times.

For different data sets of the same algorithm, the larger the network size, the longer the operation time. For the same data sets of different algorithms, our algorithm can reasonably divide the network in terms of accuracy standards, and the running time is the fastest when the length is set to 0.02, followed by SSNCA, and the GN algorithm is the slowest. In terms of accuracy, the SSNCA algorithm in the dolphin social network has three isolated points. The SSMCA algorithm successfully classifies outliers into the community, which solves the problem well. In the football data set, the GN algorithm only divides 11 communities. SSMCA algorithm is well divided into 12 communities that match the actual results. In conclusion, the experimental results show that the proposed algorithm can effectively find the community structure effectively and significantly improve the computational efficiency and community classification accuracy of the SSNCA algorithm.

Table 1. Data Set Statistics

Data set	Node	edge	The network diameter
Zachary Network	34	78	5
Dolphin social network	62	159	8
Football data set	115	613	4

Table 2. Comparison of SSMCA and other algorithms on real networks known for three cluster structures

	Zachary Network		Dolphin social network		Football data set	
algorithm	time	NMI	time	NMI	time	NMI
GN	0.28	57.98 %	1.20	44.17 %	14.84	87.89 %
SSNCA	0.21	68.37 %	1.06	52.95 %	11.04	88.49 %
SSMCA	0.19	89.54 %	0.57	87.66 %	1.796	92.68 %

6 Conclusion

This paper aims at improving the SSNCA algorithm, using the community similarity formula to merge the isolated points that exist after the community division, and on this basis, a community similarity mining algorithm SSMCA based on structural similarity is proposed. The algorithm can solve the problem of isolated points left after community division, and it can improve the accuracy of community division, and greatly shorten the running time of algorithm greatly. The algorithm is applied to real data set Zachary data set, dolphin social network, football data set, and compared with GN and SSNCA algorithms. Experiments show that the algorithm has obvious advantages in community division accuracy and running time. The next step will be to improve the accuracy of the algorithm for community segmentation of large networks.

Acknowledgment

National Natural Science Foundation of China (91746104) The Optimum Allocation of Annual Light and Temperature Resources and Group Regulation Techniques for Wheat and Maize (005-35432)

References

1. Newman M E J, Detecting community structure in networks[J].European Physical Journal B,**38**（2）: 321-330(2004).
2. Berger-Wolf T Y, Saia J. A framework for analysis of dynamic social networks[C]// Twelfth ACM SIGKDD International Conference on Knowledge Discovery and Data Mining, Philadelphia, Pa, Usa, August. DBLP:523-528,(2006).
3. Girvan M, Newman M E J, Community structure in social and biological networks [J]. Proceedings of the National Academy of Sciences of the United States of America, **99**(12):7821-6(2002).
4. Bo Y, Liu D Y, Liu J, et al. Complex Network Clustering Algorithms[J]. Journal of Software, **20**(1) (2009).
5. Zhaonan L I, Yang B, Liu D. Distance Similarity Algorithm for Mining Communities from Complex Networks[J]. Journal of Frontiers of Computer Science & Technology, **5**(4):336-346(2011).
6. Newman M E J, Girvan M. Finding and evaluating community structure in networks [J]. Phys. Rev. E, **69**(2):026113(2004).
7. Kim brother, Liu Jie, Jia Zhengxue, Liu Dayou, Data clustering algorithm of k nearest neighbor network based on [J].Pattern recognition and artificial intelligence, **23** (4): 546-551(2010).
8. Zachary W W. An Information Flow Model for Conflict and Fission in Small Groups[J]. Journal of Anthropological Research, **33**(4):452-473(1977).
9. Lusseau D. The emergent properties of a dolphin social network.[J]. Proceedings Biological Sciences, **270** Suppl 2(supplement 2):S186(2003).
10. Girvan M, Newman M E J. Community structure in social and biological networks[J]. Proceedings of National Academy of Science, **9**(12): 7821-7826(2002).

11. Danon L, Duch J, Diaz-Guilera A, et al. Comparing community structure identification. J Stat Mech: P09008[J]. Journal of Statistical Mechanics Theory & Experiment, 2005(9) (2005).

Saliency Detection with Sparse Prototypes: An Approach Based on Multi-Dictionary Sparse Encoding

Jun Wang*, Zemin Wu, Chang Tian and Lei Hu

College of Communications Engineering, Army Engineering University of PLA, Nanjing, China.

Abstract. This paper proposes a bottom-up saliency detection algorithm based on multi-dictionary sparse recovery. Firstly, the SLIC algorithm is used to segment the image into superpixels in multilevel and atoms with a high background possibility are selected from the boundary superpixels to construct the multi-dictionary. Secondly, sparse recovery of the entire image is achieved using multi-dictionary to get sub-saliency maps from the perspective of sparse recovery errors. The final saliency map is generated in a weighted fusion manner. Experimental results on three public datasets demonstrate the effectiveness of our model.

1 Introduction

Visual saliency detection aims to identify the most distinctive regions in an image that draw human attention. This topic has received increasing interest in recent years because of its wide range of applications such as image segmentation, image retrieval, target recognition, image classification, and video compression. Although much significant progress has been made, salient object detection remains a challenging problem.

Sparse representation has been widely used in computer vision task in recent years. The typical sparse representation based saliency detection models have the following two types. The first type is the centre-surround model. Li et al. [1] and Han et al. [2] reconstruct a central image patches using its nearby local regions (i.e., using the nearby local regions as dictionary to recovery the centre patch) and then defined its saliency degree using sparse reconstruction error. However, a given patch is usually very similar to those nearby. As a result, the internal region of a large object cannot be detected well. The second method is based on the hypothesis that image boundaries belong to the background in most cases. Li et al. [3] and Jia et al. [4] propose to construct a background dictionary using superpixels at image boundary and perform sparse recovery to get the saliency map, as shown in Figure 2(a). Recovery error is used to determine saliency degree. In general, their performance is better than that of centre-surround model. However, they are imprecise for using the entire boundary superpixels as dictionary atoms if the object appears on the boundary.

Different from pervious works, in this paper, we propose a bottom-up saliency detection algorithm with sparse prototypes. First, the SLIC algorithm [5] is used to segment the image into superpixels in multi-level and reliable atoms is selected from boundary super-pixels to construct multi-dictionary. Second, sparse encoding of the entire image is achieved based on these dictionaries. The initial sub-saliency maps are generated according to the sparse recovery errors. The final saliency map is obtained through sub-saliency maps' fusion. Our algorithm flow is shown in Fig. 1 and we name it 'MDSR' in the following.

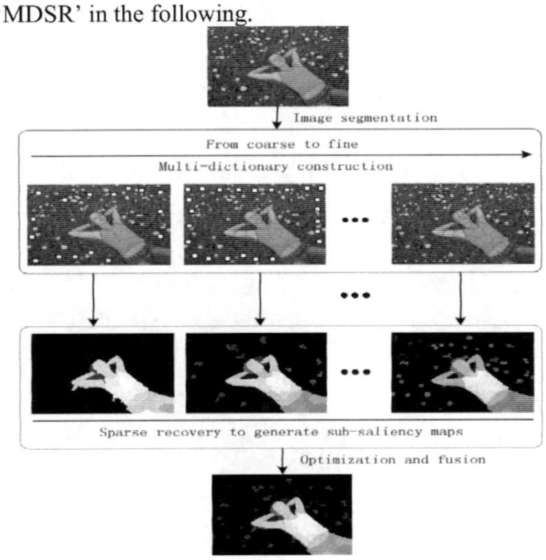

Fig. 1. The overall flow of our algorithm

2 Dictionary construction

To better capture intrinsic structural information and improve computational efficiency, an input image I is segmented into N super-pixels $\{p_i\}_{i=1}^{N}$ by the simple linear iterative clustering (SLIC) algorithm. The mean colour features $\mathbf{c}_i$ in CIE-Lab colour space and mean

* Corresponding author: wangjun_ice@126.com

normalized coordinates $\mathbf{x}_i$ of pixels are used to describe each superpixel p_i .

$$p_i = [\mathbf{c}_i ; \mathbf{x}_i] \quad (1)$$

Therefore, the entire image can be represented as:

$$I = [p_i, p_2, ..., p_N] \quad (2)$$

It has been shown that image boundaries are good visual cues for background models which can be exploited for saliency detection [3, 4]. On the other hand, salient object are likely to appear at the centre of a scene. But these assumptions may not always hold. So instead of directly extracted all the image boundary superpixels to construct dictionary, we firstly compute the background possibility of each boundary superpixel:

$$P_{bg}(p_i) = 1 - \exp\left(-\frac{BC^2(p_i)}{2\delta^2}\right) \quad (3)$$

$BC(p_i)$ stands for the boundary connectivity of superpixel p_i, which was proposed by Zhu et al. [6] to estimate the probability that an image patch belongs to background. It is defined by:

$$BC(p_i) = \frac{L(p_i)}{\sqrt{A(p_i)}} \quad (4)$$

$$L(p_i) = \sum_{j=1}^{N} \exp\left(-\frac{d_{geo}^2(p_i, p_j)}{2\delta_L^2}\right) \times \delta(p_j \in I^{bd}) \quad (5)$$

$$A(p_i) = \sum_{j=1}^{N} \exp\left(-\frac{d_{geo}^2(p_i, p_j)}{2\delta_L^2}\right) \quad (6)$$

Where $L(p_i)$ is the length along the image boundary I^{bd} . $\delta(\cdot)$ is 1 for superpixels on the image boundary and 0 otherwise. $A(p_i)$ represents the spanning area of p_i , and $d_{geo}^2(p_i, p_j)$ indicates the geodesic distance between the superpixel p_i and p_j in the CIE-Lab colour space.

Then we select the boundary superpixels with its background possibility value bigger than ξ as the atoms. ξ is defined as bellow:

$$\xi = \frac{1}{2K} \sum_{j=1}^{K} P_{bg}(p_j) \quad (7)$$

K denotes the number of all boundary superpixels. The dictionary $\mathbf{D}$ is constructed based on the selected atoms, as shown in Fig. 2(b).

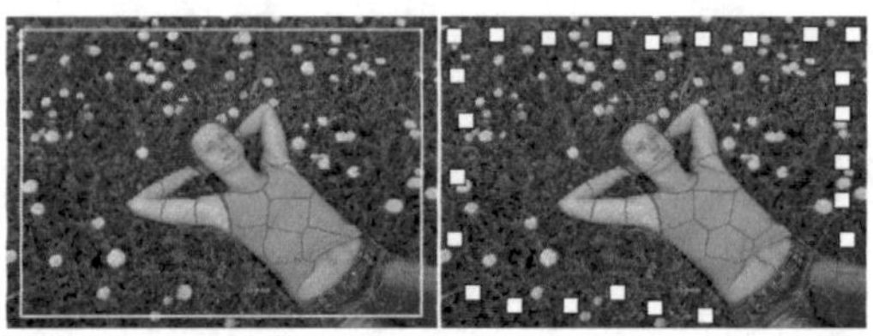

Fig. 2. Comparison of dictionary construction: (a) traditional methods which directly use the entire boundary superpixels as the atoms of dictionary. (b) Our method that select the superpixels with high background possibility as the atoms (the superpixels marked with small white square).

3 Saliency computing

3.1 Sparse encoding

We use the set of dictionary $\mathbf{D}$ as the bases for sparse representation, and encoded the superpixel p_i by:

$$\mathbf{a}_i = \arg\min_{\mathbf{a}_i} \|p_i - \mathbf{D}\cdot\mathbf{a}_i\|_2^2 + \lambda\|\mathbf{a}\|_1 \quad (8)$$

The sparse recovery error is:

$$\varepsilon_i = \|p_i - \mathbf{D}\cdot\mathbf{a}_i\|_2^2 \quad (9)$$

Therefore, the reconstruction error matrix $\mathbf{D}$ of the entire image based dictionary is:

$$\mathbf{E} = [\varepsilon_1, \varepsilon_2, ..., \varepsilon_N] \quad (10)$$

According to theory of sparse representation, for the superpixels belonging to salient region (e.g., the person in Fig. 2), their features are quite different from the atoms in the dictionary, so the sparse recovery error is larger than that of superpixels belonging to the background (e.g., the lawn in Fig. 2). So, we could calculate the saliency value of every superpixel via sparse recovery error. To reduce the impact of some noise, we use a sigmoid function to optimize it.

$$\mathbf{S} = [s_1, s_2, ..., s_N] \quad (11)$$

$$s_i = \frac{1}{1 + \exp\left(-b(\varepsilon_i - \bar{\varepsilon})/\bar{\varepsilon}\right)} \quad (12)$$

s_i is the saliency value of superpixel p_i . $\bar{\varepsilon}$ is the mean of ε . b control the magnitude of stretch and is set to 10 empirically.

3.2 Saliency fusion

The scale of salient object is different, and the degree of its contact with the image boundary also varies under different circumstance. To handle this problem, we segment the image at M different scales. At every segment scale, we construct the dictionary respectively as shown in Fig. 1. We perform sparse recovery and optimize tasks based on every dictionary to get M sub-saliency maps. The final saliency map is calculated in a weighted fusion manner:

$$\mathbf{S}_{final} = \frac{1}{M} \sum_{i=1}^{M} \mathbf{S}_i \quad (13)$$

4 Experiment result

4.1 Experiment setting

We test each algorithm on three public datasets ASD [7], MSRA5000 [8], and SED2 [9]. ASD consists of 1,000 images. It is simple and widely used in practice. MSRA5000 consists of 5,000 challenging images characterized by complex backgrounds and objects at the boundary. SED2 has 100 images, where each image has two objects. Most objects in SED2 are located at the boundary.

For each image, we obtained 10 saliency maps using the proposed model and other 9 state-of-the-art methods: GB [10], SR [11], PCA [12], DSR [3], LR [13], RPCA [14], BFS [15], RBD [6], and BSCA [16]. We use AUC value and MAE value to evaluate all algorithms. For each method, a binary map is obtained by segmenting each saliency map with a given threshold $T \in [0,255]$ and then compared with the ground truth mask G to compute the true positive and false positive rates to plot the ROC curve and compute the area under ROC curve to get the AUC value. The MAE metric calculates the average absolute error between the saliency map and ground truth mask of test image ($W \times H$ resolution) in pixel:

$$MAE = \frac{1}{W \times H} \sum_{i=1}^{W} \sum_{j=1}^{H} \left| S(i,j) - G(i,j) \right| \qquad (14)$$

When in experiment, we segment every test image at three scale (i.e., we set $M = 3$) for accuracy and efficiency. The segment parameters are [100 10], [200 20] and [300 30]. The parameter δ in equation (3) is set to 1. The sparse reconstruction parameter λ in equation (8) is set to 0.01.

4.2 Experiment results

As in shown in Table 1, our proposed algorithm outperforms other 9 methods lower MAE and higher AUC scores, which indicates the predicted saliency map is more similar to ground truth. Note that, the advantage of our algorithm is more obvious than others in SED2 datasets, demonstrating the effectiveness of MDSR in addressing the boundary saliency problems. A visual comparison of several saliency maps is give in Fig. 3. For the first example, the image background is complicated and there is an interference object at the boundary. For the other test images, the salient object all contacts the image boundaries. As can be seen clearly, compared with the saliency maps generated by other algorithms, our results can highlight the salient object more clearly and completely under different scenes, which demonstrates the robustness of our model.

Table 1: Comparison of AUC and MAE value on three public datasets. (The best performance are marked with red color)

	ASD		MSRA5000		SED2	
	AUC	MAE	AUC	MAE	AUC	MAE
GB	.8858	.2289	.8711	.2411	.8441	.2436
SR	.7651	.2299	.7553	.2422	.8193	.2250
RPCA	.8994	.2090	.8724	.2265	.8536	.2284
PCA	.9702	.1552	.9481	.1889	.9157	.2015
LR	.9584	.1885	.9238	.2215	.8869	.2374
BFS	.9702	.1285	.9481	.1666	.9157	.1669
DSR	.9792	.0809	.9530	.1204	.9172	.1388
BSCA	.9783	.0855	.9533	.1312	.8965	.1632
RBD	.9702	.0659	.9481	.1106	.9157	.1301
Ours	.9810	.0558	.9527	.1101	.9441	.1289

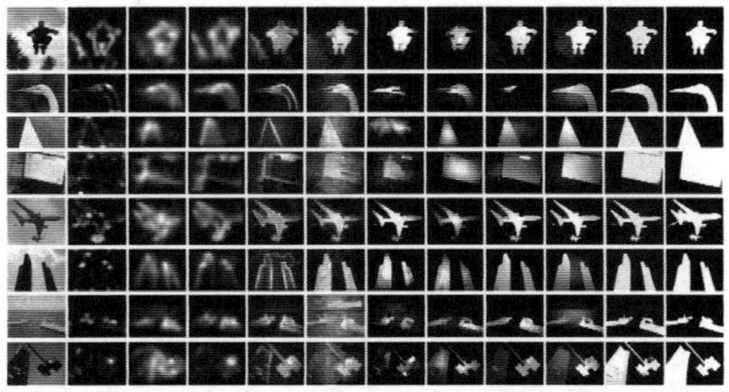

Fig. 3. Visual comparison between our results and others. (a) Input. (b) SR. (c) GB. (d) RPCA. (e) PCA. (f) LR. (g) DSR. (h) BFS. (i) RBD. (j) BSCA. (k) Ours. (l) Ground truth mask.

5. Conclusion

In this paper, we propose a bottom-up saliency detection algorithm via multi-dictionary sparse encoding. To handle the misjudgment problem when salient objects appear at the image boundary, we segment the image in multilevel. In each segment level, we compute the background possibility of superpixels located at image boundaries and then select the reliable ones as the atoms of dictionary. Based on the multi-dictionary, sparse encoding of the whole image is achieved and the saliency map s are generated according to the sparse recovery errors. Experimental results demonstrate the effectiveness of our algorithm.

It is necessary to explain that our method also has good expansibility. If we have a strict requirement for the accuracy of the result in practice, we can set a larger M. However, if we emphasis on the speediness, we can set a smaller M. In the further research, we will focus on the relationship between the speediness and accuracy of our algorithm.

References

1. Li Y, Zhou Y, Xu L, et al. Incremental sparse saliency detection. *IEEE International Conference on Image Processing*. IEEE Press, 2009: 3057-3060.
2. B. Han, H. Zhu, and Y.D. Ding, 2011. Bottom-up Saliency based on weighted sparse coding residual. In *Proceeding of ACM International conference on multimedia*, 2011: 1117-1120.
3. X. Li, H. Lu, Zhang, X. Ruan et al, 2013. Saliency detection via dense and sparse reconstruction. In *IEEE International Conference on Computer Vision*.
4. Jia. C, J. Qi, X. Li et al. (2016), "Saliency detection via a unified generative and discriminative model". *Neurocomputing*, Vol. 173 No.P2, pp. 406-417.
5. Achanta R, Shaji A, Smith K, et al. (2012), "Slic superpixels compared to state-of-the-art superpixel methods". *IEEE Transactions on Pattern Analysis and Machine Intelligence*, Vol. 34 No.12, pp. 2274–2281.
6. Zhu W, Liang S, Wei Y, et al, 2014. Saliency optimization from robust background detection. In

IEEE Conference on Computer Vision and Pattern Recognition (CVPR). Columbus, USA.

7. Achanta R, Hemani S, Estrada F, et al, 2009. Frequency-tuned salient region detection. In *IEEE Conference on Computer Vision and Pattern Recognition (CVPR),* Miami, USA.
8. Liu T, Sun J, Zheng N, et al. "Learning to detect a salient object". *IEEE Transactions on Pattern Analysis and Machine Intelligence*. 2011, 33(2): 353-367.
9. Alpert S, Galun M, Brandt A, et al. "Image segmentation by probabilistic bottom-up aggregation and cue integration". *IEEE Transactions on Pattern Analysis and Machine Intelligence*, 2012, 34(2): 315-327.
10. Harel J, Koch C, and Perona P, 2006. Graph-based visual saliency. In *Proceedings of Neural Information Processing Systems.*
11. Hou X, Zhang L., 2007. Saliency detection: a spectral residual approach. In *IEEE Conference on Computer Vision and Pattern Recognition (CVPR)*, Portland, USA.
12. Margolin R, Tal A, and Zelnik-Manor L, 2013. What makes a patch distinct? In *IEEE Conference on Computer Vision and Pattern Recognition (CVPR)*, Portland, USA.
13. X. Shen, Y. Wu, 2012. "A Unified Approach to Salient Object Detection via Low Rank Matrix Recovery". *Computer Vision and Pattern Recognition*, Vol. 23 No. 10, pp. 853-860.
14. J. Yan, M Zhu, H Liu, et al. (2010), "Visual Saliency Detection via Sparse Pursuit". *IEEE Signal Processing Letters*, Vol. 17 No. 8, pp. 739-742.
15. J Wang, H Lu, N Tong, et al. (2016), "Saliency Detection via Background and Foreground Seed Selection". *Neurocomputing*, Vol. 152 No. C, pp. 359-268.
16. Qin Y, Lu H, Xu Y, et al, 2015. Saliency detection via cellular automata. In *IEEE Conference on Computer Vision and Pattern Recognition (CVPR)*, Boston, USA, pp. 111-119.

Adaptive Target Birth Intensity for ET-PHD Filter

Lu Miao, Xin-xi Feng and Luo-jia Chi

School of Information and Navigation, Air Force Engineering University, Xi'an, China

Abstract. An adaptive tracking algorithm based on Extended target Probability Hypothesis Density (ET-PHD) filter is proposed for extended target tracking problem with priori unknown target birth intensity.The algorithm is implemented by gaussian mixture, where the target birth intensity is generated by measurement-driven, and the persistent and the newborn targets intensity are respectively predicted and updated. The simulation results show that the proposed algorithm improves the performance of the probability hypothesis density filter in the extended target tracking.

1 INTRODUCTION

Multiple target tracking technology is widely used in sensor networks, machine recognition and positioning, and other fields. Its aim is to continuously predict and update the state of the dynamic target of the number of time varying according to the sensor observation in the clutter environment. Due to the continuous improvement of sensor resolution, more and more attention and research are paid to the extended target tracking problem, and the extended target occupies multiple sensor resolution units at each observation moment.

Traditional multi-target tracking is based on data Association technology, which exists combinatorial explosion and associated uncertainty problem, and is not suitable for multiple extended target tracking. Mahler first uses the Random finite set theory to solve the multi-target tracking problem and proposes the extended target Probability Hypothesis Density (ET-PHD) filter[1]. The existing PHD implementation methods include Gaussian mixture method[2] and particle method[3], and their improved algorithm[4-7].

For the traditional ET-PHD filter, it is assumed that the target birth intensity is a priori known, but in situations where the targets may appear anywhere in the surveillance volume. For this problem, the literature [8] proposed a measurement-driven PHD filter. However, this algorithm only used the measurement location information and ignored the likelihood information. The literature [9] improves on this, and puts forward an adaptive particle PHD filtering algorithm based on measurement-driven. The algorithm is based on the measurement-driven to obtain the target birth intensity, and simultaneously predicts and updates the persistent and the newborn targets. The filtering performance is improved by making full use of the measurement likelihood information.

In this paper, an adaptive extended target tracking algorithm based on ET-PHD filter is proposed to solve the extended target tracking problem with priori unknown target birth intensity. The target birth intensity was obtained by adaptive updating of the measured information obtained by each scan, so as to solve the dependence on the priori hypothesis. In the process of filtering, the persistent and the newborn targets are predicted and updated simultaneously. The simulation results show that the proposed algorithm improves the stability of the extended target number estimation and has better state estimation accuracy.

2 ADAPTIVE ET-PHD FILTERING ALGORITHM AND GAUSSIAN MIXTURE IMPLEMENTATION

2.1. Adaptive ET-PHD filtering algorithm

In time k, the extended target is divided into two categories: persistent target and newborn target, and differentiated by label β.

$$\beta = \begin{cases} 0, & persistent\ target \\ 1, & newborn\ \ target \end{cases} \tag{1}$$

Make the following assumptions:

Assumption 1: The extended target measurements obeys Poisson distribution and is independent of the target state, i.e., $\gamma(\cdot) = \gamma$;

Assumption 2: The target survival and detection probability are independent with target state , i.e., $P_{S,k}(\cdot) = P_S$ and $P_{D,k}(\cdot) = P_D$;

Assumption 3: The clutter intensity obeys the Poisson distribution and is uniformly distributed in the observed region.

In time k, the prediction of ET-PHD filter with unknown new target intensity is as follows:

*Corresponding author: 1766584727@qq.com, fengxinxi2005@aliyun.com, 592255820@qq.com

$$D_{k|k-1}(x_k,\beta)=\begin{cases}\int p_S f_{k|k-1}(x_k|x_{k-1})\cdot \\ (D_{k-1}(x_{k-1},1)+D_{k-1}(x_{k-1},0))dx_{k-1} & \beta=0 \\ D_k^b(x_k,1) & \beta=1\end{cases} \quad (2)$$

In time k, the posterior PHD is multiplied by predictive PHD and measurement pseudo likelihood function, i.e., $D_k(x_k)=L_{Z_k}(x_k)D_{k|k-1}(x_k)$.

The persistent target is updated to:

$$D_k(x_k,0)=L_{Z_k}(x_k,0)D_{k|k-1}(x_k,0) \quad (3)$$

$$L_{z_k}(x_k)=1-\left(1-e^{-\gamma(x_k)}\right)P_D(x_k)+e^{-\gamma(x_k)}P_D(x)\cdot \sum_{p\angle Z_k}\omega_p\sum_{W\in p}\frac{\gamma(x_k)^{|W|}}{d_w}\prod_{z_k\in W}\frac{g_k(z_k|x_k)}{\lambda_k c_k(z_k)} \quad (4)$$

The newborn target is updated to:

$$D_k(x_k,1)=L_{Z_k}(x_k,1)D_{k|k-1}(x_k,1) \quad (5)$$

Since the newborn target is obtained from the measurement set, it is always detected, that is, $P_D=1$. Its pseudo likelihood function is:

$$L_{z_k}(x_k,1)=\sum_{p\angle Z_k}e^{-\gamma(x)}\cdot\omega_p\sum_{W\in p}\frac{\gamma(x)^{|W|}}{d_w}\prod_{z_k\in W}\frac{g_k(z_k|x_k)}{\lambda_k c_k(z_k)} \quad (6)$$

The weight in the formula (4) and (6) are calculated by:

$$d_W=\delta_{|W|,1}+D_{k|k-1}(x_k,0)\left[e^{-\gamma}P_D\gamma^{|W|}\prod_{z_k\in W}\frac{g_k(z_k^x|x_k)}{\lambda_k c_k(z_k)}\right] + D_{k|k-1}(x_k,1)\left[e^{-\gamma}\gamma^{|W|}\prod_{z_k\in W}\frac{g_k(z_k^x|x_k)}{\lambda_k c_k(z_k)}\right] \quad (7)$$

In the formula, $\delta_{|W|,1}$ is the Kronecker function; $p\angle Z_k$ represents the partition of the measurement set Z_k; W is non-empty cell in P; $|W|$ represents the observed number in the dividing unit; ω_p and d_w are the weights of P and W respectively; λ_k is the clutter observation expectation number; and $c_k(z_k)$ is the clutter distribution in the monitoring area.

2.2 Gaussian mixture implementation

Compared with the particle implementation of the PHD filter algorithm, gaussian mixture is more advantageous in computational efficiency and state extraction because it avoids particle sampling and clustering operations.

Step1. Predict

Suppose the posterior PHD intensity in time k-1 is gaussian mixture, namely:

$$D_{k-1}(x_{k-1},0)=\sum_{j=1}^{J_{k-1}^p}w_{p,k-1}^{(j)}\mathrm{N}\left(x;m_{p,k-1}^{(j)},P_{p,k-1}^{(j)}\right) \quad (8)$$

$$D_{k-1}(x_{k-1},1)=\sum_{j=1}^{J_{k-1}^b}w_{b,k-1}^{(j)}\mathrm{N}\left(x;m_{b,k-1}^{(j)},P_{b,k-1}^{(j)}\right) \quad (9)$$

In the equation, J_{k-1} indicates the number of gaussian component, and w_{k-1}^j, m_{k-1}^j and P_{k-1}^j respectively indicate weight value, mean value and covariance of jth gaussian component.

The Gauss term used to predict the persistent target in time k consists of the Gauss term of the persistent target and the newborn target in time k-1, namely:

$$\left\{w_{k-1}^{(j)},m_{k-1}^{(j)},P_{k-1}^{(j)}\right\}_{j=1}^{J_{k-1}}=\left\{w_{p,k-1}^{(j)},m_{p,k-1}^{(j)},P_{p,k-1}^{(j)}\right\}_{j=1}^{J_{k-1}^p} \cup\left\{w_{b,k-1}^{(j)},m_{b,k-1}^{(j)},P_{b,k-1}^{(j)}\right\}_{j=1}^{J_{k-1}^b} \quad (10)$$

In time k, persistent target prediction intensity is expressed as Gaussian mixed form, namely:

$$D_{k|k-1}(x_k,0)=\sum_{j=1}^{J_{k-1}}w_{p,k|k-1}^{(j)}\mathrm{N}\left(x;m_{p,k|k-1}^{(j)},P_{p,k|k-1}^{(j)}\right) \quad (11)$$

$$w_{p,k|k-1}^{(j)}=p_S w_{k-1}^{(j)} \quad (12)$$

$$m_{p,k|k-1}^{(j)}=f\left(m_{k-1}^{j}\right) \quad (13)$$

$$P_{p,k|k-1}^{(j)}=Q+FP_{k-1}^{(j)}F^T \quad (14)$$

In the formula, $f(\cdot)$ is the state transfer function; F is its Jacobian matrix; Q is the process noise variance.

The target birth intensity is obtained by the measurement drive, which is the inversion of the measurement partition unit. In time k, the predictive intensity of the newborn target is expressed as:

$$D_{k|k-1}(x_k,1)=\sum_{j=1}^{J_{k|k-1}^b}w_{b,k|k-1}^{(j)}\mathrm{N}\left(x;m_{b,k|k-1}^{(j)},P_{b,k|k-1}^{(j)}\right) \quad (15)$$

$$J_{k|k-1}^b=\sum_{p\angle Z_k}|p| \quad (16)$$

$$w_{b,k|k-1}^{(j)}=\frac{v_{b,k|k-1}}{J_{b,k|k-1}^b} \quad (17)$$

$$m_{b,k|k-1}=h^{-1}\left(z_{k,j}\right) \quad (18)$$

$$P_{b,k|k-1}=HRH^T \quad (19)$$

In the equation, $h(\cdot)$ is the measurement equation; H is its Jacobian matrix; R is the measurement noise variance; $|p|$ represents the number of units W of pth measurement division; and $v_{b,k|k-1}$ is the expected number of the newborn target.

Step2. Update

In time k, the persistent target intensity update is expressed as:

$$D_{k|k}(x_k)=\sum_{m=1}^{J_{k-1}}w_{p,k}^{(m)}N\left(x;m_{p,k}^{(m)},P_{p,k}^{(m)}\right)+ \sum_{p\angle Z_k}\sum_{W\in p}\sum_{j=1}^{J_{k-1}}w_{p,k}^{(j)}N\left(x;m_{p,k}^{(j)},P_{p,k}^{(j)}\right) \quad (20)$$

The Gauss term of the part not detected in the formula is:

$$w_{p,k}^{(m)}=\left(1-\left(1-e^{-\gamma}\right)P_D\right)w_{p,k|k-1}^{(m)} \quad (21)$$

$$m_{p,k}^{(m)}=m_{k|k-1}^{(m)} \quad (22)$$

$$P_{p,k}^{(m)}=P_{k|k-1}^{(m)} \quad (23)$$

The Gauss term of the part detected is:

$$w_k^j = \omega_p \frac{e^{-\gamma} p_D \gamma^{|W|}}{d_W} \times \prod_{z_k \in W} \frac{N\left(z_k^W; H_k^W m_{k|k-1}^{(j)}, S_{k|k-1}^{(j)}\right)}{\lambda_k c_k(z_k)} w_{k|k-1}^{(j)} \tag{24}$$

$$m_k^j = m_{k|k-1}^j + K_k^j\left(z_k^W - H_k^W m_{k|k-1}^j\right) \tag{25}$$

$$P_k^j = \left(I - K_k^j H_k^W\right) P_{k|k-1}^j \tag{26}$$

$$S_{k|k-1}^j = H_k^W P_{k|k-1}^j \left(H_k^W\right)^T + R_k^W \tag{27}$$

$$K_k^j = P_{k|k-1}^j \left(H_k^W\right)^T \left(S_{k|k-1}^j\right)^{-1} \tag{28}$$

In time k, the newborn target intensity update is expressed as:

$$D_{k|k}(x_k, 1) = \sum_{j=1}^{J_k^b} w_{b,k|k}^{(j)} \mathrm{N}\left(x; m_{b,k|k}^{(j)}, P_{b,k|k}^{(j)}\right) \tag{29}$$

In contrast to the persistent target, the update of the Gauss term of the newborn target intensity function contains only the detection part. The Gauss term formula is:

$$w_k^j = \omega_p \frac{e^{-\gamma} \gamma^{|W|}}{d_W} \times \prod_{Z_k \in W} \frac{w_{b,k|k-1}^{(j)}}{\lambda_k c_k(z_k)} \tag{30}$$

$$m_{b,k}^{(j)} = m_{b,k|k-1}^{(j)} \tag{31}$$

$$P_{b,k}^{(j)} = P_{b,k|k-1}^{(j)} \tag{32}$$

The weight in the formula (24) and (30) are calculated by:

$$d_W = \delta_{|W|,1} + \sum_{j=1}^{J_{k-1}} e^{-\gamma} p_D \gamma^{|W|} \times \prod_{Z_k \in W} \frac{N\left(z_k^W; H_k^W m_{k|k-1}^{(j)}, S_{k|k-1}^{(j)}\right)}{\lambda_k c_k(z_k)} w_{k|k-1}^{(j)} + \sum_{i=1}^{J_{k|k-1}^b} e^{-\gamma} \gamma^{|W|} \times \prod_{Z_k \in W} \frac{w_{b,k|k-1}^{(i)}}{\lambda_k c_k(z_k)} \tag{33}$$

Step3. Pruning and Merging

The Gauss term of Gaussian mixture algorithm is increasing with time, so it is necessary to prun and merge Gauss terms in order to make calculation feasible. The basic idea is: to keep the Gaussian term with large weight, and to merge the Gaussian term with similar distance.

Step4.Target extraction

Extract the state of the extended target:

$$\hat{X}_k = \left\{m_k^j \middle| w_k^j > 0.5\right\}_{j=1}^{\hat{N}(k)} \tag{34}$$

3 Simulation Result and Analysis

It is assumed that sensor tracks four extended targets in two-dimension plane. The surveillance area is [-1000,1000]m×[-1000,1000]m and sampling time T=1s, and observation duration is 100s. Equations of motion and observation of targets all satisfy linear Gaussian model. The extended target motion and the observational equations are:

$$X_k = \begin{bmatrix} 1 & 0 & T & 0 \\ 0 & 1 & 0 & T \\ 0 & 0 & 1 & 0 \\ 0 & 0 & 0 & 1 \end{bmatrix} X_{k-1} + \begin{bmatrix} T^2/2 & 0 \\ 0 & T^2/2 \\ T & 0 \\ 0 & T \end{bmatrix} \begin{bmatrix} w_{1,k} \\ w_{2,k} \end{bmatrix} \tag{35}$$

$$Z_k = \begin{bmatrix} 1 & 0 & 0 & 0 \\ 0 & 1 & 0 & 0 \end{bmatrix} X_k + \begin{bmatrix} R_{1,k} \\ R_{2,k} \end{bmatrix} \tag{36}$$

The process noise $[w_{1,k}, w_{2,k}]^T$ and observation noise $[R_{1,k}, R_{2,k}]^T$ are zero-mean Gaussian white noises, in which the standard difference of the process noise component $\sigma_{w_1} = \sigma_{w_2} = 2m/s^2$, and the observed noise component standard difference $\sigma_{R_1} = \sigma_{R_2} = 10m$. The probability of survival is set to $P_{s,k}$=0.99, and the probability of detection is $P_{D,k}$=0.99. The extended target measurements and the clutter all obey the Poisson distribution with the mean value of 10, the Gaussian term pruning threshold $T_p=10^{-4}$, the fusion threshold U=4, and the maximum Gaussian term J_{max}=100.

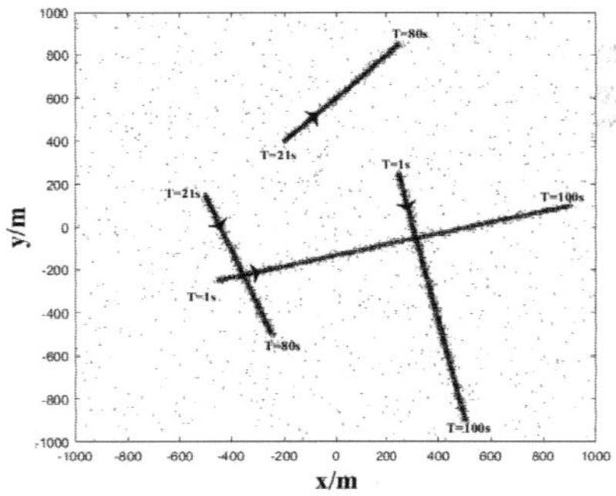

Figure 1: Motion trail of targets in clutter environment.

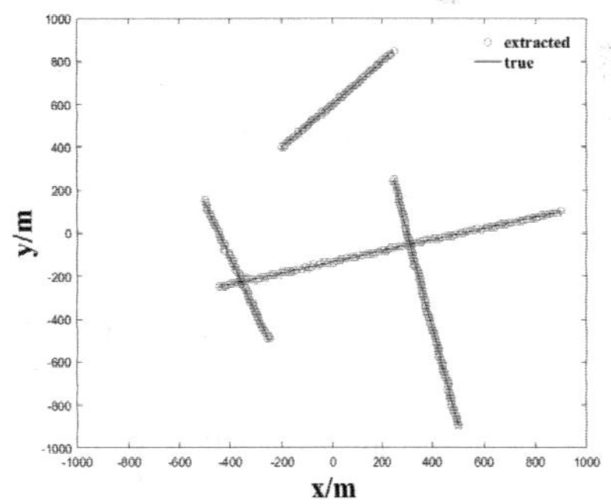

Figure 2: Result of filtering.

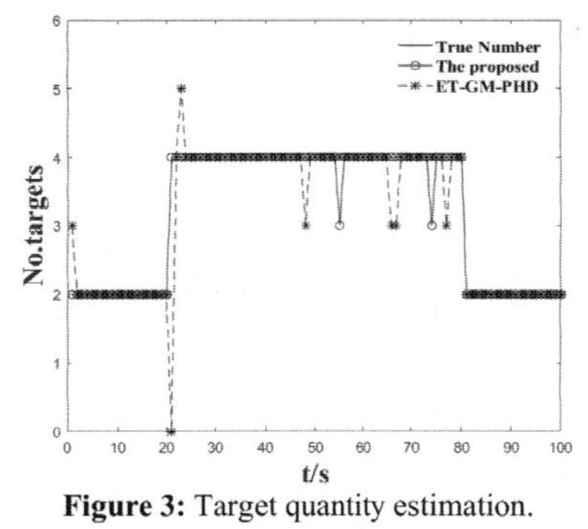

Figure 3: Target quantity estimation.

Motion trail of extended targets in clutter environment and result of filtering are shown in Fig. 1 and Fig. 2, and target quantity estimation is shown in Fig. 3. It is shown that the proposed algorithm can be used to adaptively design the target birth intensity and realize the effective tracking of the extended targets.

50 times of Monte-Carlo simulation can be conducted to compare the improved algorithm and the original algorithm. We evaluate the performance of the algorithm through the target number estimation, OSPA distance[10] (p=2,c=80) and the average computation time. It is shown from table 1 that the improved algorithm can improve the accuracy of target number estimation and has better state estimation result than the original ET-GM-PHD filtering algorithm, because the persistent and the newborn targets intensity are respectively predicted and updated, which allows it sufficiently take full advantage of the measurement likelihood information.

Table 1 Filter Performance Comparison

Filtering algorithm	**Target number estimate accuracy rate**	**Average ospa/m**	**Average calculated time/s**
Improved algorithm	97.3%	11.3	1.10
Original algorithm	94.1%	15.8	1.05

4 Conclusions

In this paper, an adaptive extended target PHD filter based on measurement-driven birth intensity is proposed. The algorithm uses the measurements to drive target birth intensity function so as to relax the previously imposed limitation that target birth intensity is a priori known, and the persistent and the newborn targets intensity are respectively predicted and updated to make full use of measurement-likelihood information. The simulation results show that the proposed algorithm improves the estimation accuracy of both the number of targets and target status.

References

1. R. Mahler. PHD Filters for Nonstandard Targets, I: Extended Targets[C]. In: Proceedings of the 12th International Conference on Information Fusion. USA:IEEE, 2009: 915-921.
2. K. Granstrom, C. Lundquist, U. Orguner. Extended Target Tracking Using a Gaussian-Mixture PHD Filter[J]. IEEE Trans. Aerosp. Electron. Syst., 2012, 48(4): 3268-3286.
3. Y. Li, H. Xiao, Z Song, et al. A new Multiple Extended Target Tracking Algorithm Using PHD Filter[J]. Signal Process, 2013, 93(12): 3578-3588.
4. C. Lundquist, K. Granstrom, U. Orguner. An extended target CPHD Filter and a Gamma Gaussian Inverse Wishart Implementation[J]. Journal of Selected Topics in Signal Processing, 2013, 7(3): 472-483.
5. M. Baum, U. D. Hanebeck. Random Hypersurface Models for Extended Object Tracking[C]. IEEE International Symposium on Signal Processing and Information Technology. IEEE, 2010: 178-183.
6. K. Granstrom, U. Orguner. On spawning and combination of extended/group targets modeled with random matrices[J]. IEEE Transactions on Signal Processing, 2013,61(3): 678-692.
7. N. Wahlström, E. Ozkan. Extended Target Tracking Using Gaussian Processes[J]. IEEE Transactions on Signal Processing, 2015, 63(16): 4165-4178.
8. M. Tobias, A. Lanterman. Techniques for birth-particle placement in the probability hypothesis density particle filter applied to passive radar[J]. IET Radar, Sonar & Navigation, 2008,2(5): 351-365.
9. B. Ristic, D. Clark, B. N. Vo, et al. Adaptive target birth intensity for PHD and CPHD filters[J]. IEEE Transactions on Aerospace and Electronic Systems. 2012, 48(2): 1656-1668.
10. B. Ristic, B. N. Vo, D. Clark, et al. A Metric for Performance Evaluation of Multi-target Tracking Algorithms[J]. IEEE Trans. Signal Process., 2011, 59(7): 3452-3457.

MATEC Web of Conferences **176**, 03011 (2018) https://doi.org/10.1051/matecconf/201817603011
IFID 2018

Statistical analysis of city and the villages Internet users based on user logs

ZHANG Yi-wen,BAI Yan-qi,YANG An-ju

College of Information Engineering, An Hui Xin Hua University, Hefei 230088

Abstract. In recent years, with the rapid increase of users active on the Internet, Internet users access log is also increasing rapidly. According to the user's Internet access log analysis of the characteristics of user behavior on the Internet. In this paper, we classify the statistical analysis of the behavior of Internet users by collecting information and data on urban and rural Internet user behavior. This result may provide a basis for guiding the behavior of Internet software manufacturers or government.

1 INTRODUCTION

When the users visit the Internet, the website will regard log as the carrier and record the interactive information which users use on internet.Statistical analysis [1] is an important method of discovering the law and undertanding the essence from the large amount of logs data. The analysis of users' logs[2] and studing in-depth characteristic behaviors of users can explore rules which the users search, reveal the intention which users search,and provide reference for improving the quality of search engine. Thorouth thinking and discussions based on Web mining technology show that Web logs file contains a large number of information that users have access.Analysis of these data will help reserchers know retrieval law and understand users' search behaviors much better.

The author firstly divides the users into three types of users:urban,suburban and rural.Besides,the author also analyzes differences of three types of users in income,age and education through statistical analysis of users attribute information and internet users behaviors data .According to the SPSS statistical software,analyze the differences of internet behaviors,what is said above is helpful to provide the government, software developers and e-commerce with guidance for understanding of the behaviors' characteristics of each users more accurately.

2 BEHAVOIRS OF INTERNET USER

2.1 web logs of internet users

Users Logs [3], known as Web Logs which generally record the interaction between Web users and websites, are important data source for Web log mining.

A corresponding log file will be formed when a user switchs on each time, such as the following log examples "0ab6bbbedff24ec8baac905f45ae314c_2012-05-07_21-22-38.txt",recorded the sample of ID 0ab6bbbedff24ec8baac905f45ae314c during the 2012-05-07 day,since 21:22:38,the operator can further access to the sample of the population attribute information whose ID is "0ab6bbbedff24ec8baac905f45ae314c" by demographic.CSV.

2.2 behavoirs of internet user

Extract the fields,the name of programs used by the users. Are represented by N in the behavior logs of the above Internet users[4.]Extract the name of programs used by each users and act it as behavior of Internet users.

3 BEHAVOIR ANALYSIS OF INTERNET USER

3.1 dada collection and pretreatment

Data of this Paper is derived from a contest held by Didital hall,this study randomly selects 1000 samples of users in log behavior in the following four weeks:from 2012-05-07 to 2012-05-13, 2012-06-04 to 2012-06-04,from 2012-05-13 to 2012-07-08,2012-08-06 to 2012-08-06,and the corresponding attribute information of sample population.

Demographic information includes the users' birth year, gender, educational background,educational degree, region, category and so on. The logs of behaviors include users' boot time and the corresponding process after startup.

(1)Extract all online processes of each users within 4 weeks .

(2)Calculate the frequency used by each process from all processes of each users within 4 weeks .

(3)The Internet behaviors can be divided into [5]different software about video , chat tools, browser, games, entertainment , music, office, security, antivirus, download tools, office, input method, graphic images, mobile phones, digital, program ming development, news and information, reading, transl ation and network applications, systems, tools and other s oftware which hold a total of 17 classes, and calculate the frequency of indivi dual net citizen' behaviors within 4 weeks.

3.2 analysis of internet user' basic information

According to the gender, educational background, occupation, income, region and other attributes of Internet users[6], analysis in sequence is shown:most of the respondents were male (77.6%), the oldest was 75 years old, the youngest was 8 years old, the average was 33.02 years old, and the standard deviation was 9.270. The highest degree was (39.2%), followed by junior college (29.0%), primary school and below(0.3%) is least among those surveies. The kind of people who were surveyed was varoius and dispersive. There are a large number of employees, students and professional technicians, accounting for 21.1%, 17.5% and 14.4% respectively. The income of the respondents is also uneven, with the largest number of people with incomes of 3001-5000 yuan, accounting for 22.6%, the minimum of 500 yuan and below,accounting for 3.4%, and the non-income accounting for 14.8%. The citizens account for 64.0%.

According to difference of users' location [7], the users are divided into three categories: urban users, suburban users and rural users.

The proportion of these users are shown in table 1:

Table 1 User Distribution table

	num	percentage (%)
city	640	64.0
suburban	73	7.3
rural	127	12.7
unknown	160	16.0
total	100	100.0

Table 2 shows that there are 640 users(64%) in the city, 73 (7.3%) in the suburbs, 127 (12.7%) in rural areas, and 160 (16%) not knowing the geographical location. The users related mainly focus on urban users.

table 2 the diversty of user basics

	Category	City	Suburban	Rural	Chi-Square value	p P Value
Gender	Male	510	61	102	0.621	0.733
	Female	130	12	25		
Income		86	14	28	45.611	<0.0001
	<=500Yuan	13	2	7		
	501 ~ 1000 Yuan	21	4	8		
	1001 ~ 1500 Yuan	34	4	17		
	1501 ~ 2000 Yuan	64	11	11		
	2001 ~ 3000 Yuan	156	14	25		
	3001 ~ 5000 Yuan	147	18	22		
	5001 ~ 8000 Yuan	76	4	5		
	8001 ~ 12000 Yuan	30	0	1		
	>=12000	13	2.0	3		
Degree	Primary and below	1	6	2	158.246	<0.0001
	Junior	22	21	18		
	Senior/secondary/technical School	101	14	33		
	College	200	31	35		
	University degree	275	1	35		
	Master and above	41	0	4		

Table2 shows that:

(1) There are 510 males and 130 females in the city, 61 males and 12 females in the suburbs, 102 females and 25 males in rural areas, and the largest gender gap lies in urban users. The chi-square test was conducted on the constitute of urban male and female , suburban and rural areas,with the value of 0.621, p=0.733>0.05, which indicates that the differences between the male and female in urban, suburban and rural areas were not statistically significant.

(2) Income mainly concentrates on the range of 2001 yuan to 5000 yuan in urban, suburban and rural users , however ,there is a very big part of rural users has no income,.No matter what kind of income level which people is at, the number of urban users is the largest ,followed by country users and the number of

suburb users .The chi-square test was conducted on the constitute of suburban and rural users with different income levels ,with the value of 45.611, p = 45.611 < 0.05, indicates that the differences of subur and rural are statistically significant,the level of urban uses' income is higher than that of suburban and rural users.

(3) Eeducation of urban users is primarily university undergraduate and college, eeducation of suburban users is mainly college and middle school,education of rural users mainly high school,secondary technical school, college and university undergraduate course. In general, Internet users mainly focus on the completion of nine-year compulsory education and above, few people among the primary school and below use internet . The chi-square test was conducted on the constitute of suburban and rural users with different educational level , with value of 158.246, p = 158.246 < 0.05,which indicates that urban, suburban and rural educational level was statistically significant. Urban users have higher educational levels than suburban and rural users.

Table 3 year of birth of urban, suburban and rural users

	NP	Min	MAX	Mean	Sd	Chi-S	p
City	640	1939	2004	1980.21	9.394		
Suburban	73	1963	1998	1982.77	7.455	34.93	<0.0001
Rural	127	1963	2001	1985.1	6.660		

NP: Number of people;MIN: Minimum; MAX: Maximum Value ;Mean: Mean value; Sd: Standard deviation; Chi-S:Chi-Square value.

Table 3 shows that the biggest year of birth of urban users is 1939 , the biggest year of birth of suburban and rural users is 1963 on average, the smallest year of birth of urban users is 2004, the smallest year of birth of suburban users is 1998, the smallest year of birth of rural users is 2001. The chi-square test was conducted on non-parametric test of the birth year of urban, suburban and rural users with value of 34.93, p=0.0001<0.05,which indicates the difference of birth year in urban, suburban and rural areas is statistically significant. The average age of urban users is greater than suburban and rural users.

4 CONCLUSION AND FUTURE WORK

The quality of statistical analysis based on users logs [8] mainly depends on the quality of users attribute data and behavior data. The more accurate data of users leads to the more accurate result of statistical analysis.

The author statistically analyzes behavior logs of 1000 users in four weeks .Because sample sizes is small , there are three types- the urban, suburban and rural users who need to be analyzed , and the number of each type users is not very big, three types of result can't accuratelly representative the attributes and behaviors of urban,suburban and rural Internet users. The results have some bias and still need to continue to expand the sample size to do corresponding research. The next step is to expand the analysis scale, increase the recommendation of other information, expand the data scale, and build a higher level of users statistical analysis. Aiming at the scale of users, it is better to use a more refined method to improve the efficiency of users behavior statistical analysis.

Acknowledgments

This work was Supported by Foundation for The Excellent Youth Scholars of anhui province program under Grant Nos.gxyqZD2018087.

References

1. Duricki D A, Soleman S, Moon L D. Analysis of longitudinal data from animals with missing values using SPSS[J]. Nature Protocols, 2016, 11(6):1112.
2. Starkings S. IBM SPSS statistics 19 made simple by Colin D. Gray and Paul R. Kinnear[J]. International Statistical Review,2012,80(2):333-334.
3. Son H, Friedmann E, Thomas S A. Application of pattern mixture models to address missing data in longitudinal data analysis using SPSS.[J]. Nursing Research, 2012, 61(3):págs. 195-203..
4. Jiliang, TANG, Xufei, et al. Enriching short text representation in microblog for clustering[J]. Frontiers of Computer Science, 2012, 6(1):88-101.
5. Wang Xuefeng W, Jie R, Youguo W. Co-inventor Analysis on China's international technology collaboration in US patent activities: 1976-2010[J]. Procedia Engineering,2012(37):314-322.
6. Secar M. Statistic analysis of international tourism on romanian seaside [J].Annals of the University of Petrosani,Economics,2010,10(1):327-334.
7. Yeung P. SPSS survival manual. A step by step guide to data analysis using IBM SPSS (5th ed) [Book Review][J]. Aotearoa New Zealand Social Work, 2014, 26(4).
8. Dunn P. SPSS survival manual: a step by step guide to data analysis using IBM SPSS[J]. Australian & New Zealand Journal of Public Health, 2013, 37(6):597-598.

Optimization Acceleration Integral Method Based on Power Spectrum Estimation

Ruijie Guo[1 2,*], Shengbo Ye1 and Yicai Ji [1,2]

[1] Key Laboratory of Electromagnetic Radiation and Sensing Technology, Chinese Academy of Sciences, Beijing 100190, China
[2] University of Chinese Academy of Sciences, Beijing 100049, China

Abstract. Due to the excellent performance of the frequency domain integration method, it is widely used for acceleration integral calculations. However, the frequency-domain integration needs to select the effective integration frequency band to achieve its optimal integration performance. This paper proposes the method with power spectrum density (PSD) estimation to realize the optimization integral of the acceleration signal. By analysing the power spectrum density of the acceleration signal, the optimal low frequency cut-off frequency is obtained. Combined with frequency domain integration algorithm, it can effectively remove low-frequency noise and improve integral accuracy. Then, the novel algorithm tested by an experiment platform with a vibration bench. Experiment results show that this algorithm can adaptively select the low-frequency cut-off frequency and realize frequency domain integration optimization and the integration error is controlled within ±0.2mm.

1 INTRODUCTION

Time domain integration and frequency domain integration are two commonly used integration methods for acceleration integration. However, the presence of DC components in the acquisition signal, temperature drift, unstable sensor low-frequency performance, and ambient environment interference will all can generate trending items in the signal[1-3]. The trend items become more obvious when integrating to speed and displacement, which causes the signal to have a baseline drift, more than this, the displacement signal obtained by the integral will be seriously distorted. Therefore, the effective removal of low-frequency noise in the acceleration signal and correction of the signal baseline after integration has become an important subject for researchers to study.

The article[4] proposed to control the integral trend term error by high-pass filtering the signal before and after integration, however, when the frequency of the main component of the signal is low, the filtering is not sufficient, and the phase of each frequency component is easily distorted[5]. Wang Jianfeng proposed a method that performing an integration in the time domain first and then performing an integration in the frequency domain in 2010[6]. This method both can reduce the cumulative error of the time domain integration and reduce the low-frequency truncation error of the frequency domain integration, however, it also has the dis-advantages of both methods. By establishing the trend term control equation, the article[7-8] solved the inverse problem to obtain system characteristics, derived the frequency response function of the acceleration input and displacement output, and then put forward a new filter .The algorithm comprehensively considered the effective control of the integral error while avoiding the loss of low-frequency information as much as possible, and has a wide range of application .However, the calculation process of the new filter is more complicated. When the target frequency is low, the filter transition band becomes shorter, which causes oscillation in the frequency domain[9].

In this paper, we proposed the algorithm with power spectrum density (PSD) estimation to select the cut-off frequency of the frequency integration. Then, the method can obtain the optimization integration results of the acceleration signal.

2 PRINCIPLE OF FREQUENCY DOMAIN INTEGRATION

The trapezoidal formula and the Simpson formula are usually used to integrate the measurement signal in the time domain to obtain the displacement signal. Trend terms are usually eliminated by least-square fitting. However, the trend items generated during the integration process cannot be completely removed, and residual small errors will be cumulatively amplified, which will have a great impact on the accuracy of the integration.

The frequency-domain integration method is simple in principle and usually provides good integration results. This method not only can effectively avoid the cumulative amplification effect of time-domain integration on tiny error signals, but also can easily select the cut-off frequency, which will realize the

* Corresponding author: guoruijie15@mails.ucas.edu.cn

function of the band-pass filter. Due to its high stability and accuracy, it has become the most widely used method. Firstly, convert the acceleration signal from the time domain to the frequency domain, then use the nature of the forward and inverse Fourier transform:

$$F[\int_{-\infty}^{t} f(t)dt] = \frac{1}{jk} F[f(t)] \quad (1)$$

Then calculate directly in the frequency domain with the sine and cosine integral interchange relationship. After suppress or remove low-frequency components from the signal, then convert the signal to the time domain, so as to achieve the purpose of correcting the baseline. Assuming that the acceleration signal is *a(n)*, its signal in the frequency domain is:

$$A(k) = \sum_{k=0}^{N-1} a(n) e^{-j2\pi k \frac{n}{N}} \quad (2)$$

Velocity *v(n)* is obtained by one integral of acceleration, and displacement *s(n)* can be obtained by quadratic integral. They can be respectively expressed as:

$$v(n) = \frac{A}{jk} = \sum_{k=0}^{N-1} \frac{1}{j2\pi k \Delta f} H(k) a_n e^{-j2\pi k \frac{n}{N}} \quad (3)$$

$$s(n) = -\frac{A}{k^2} = \sum_{k=0}^{N-1} \frac{1}{-(2\pi k \Delta f)^2} H(k) a_n e^{-j2\pi k \frac{n}{N}}$$

Among them,

$$H(k) = \begin{cases} 1 & f_d \le kf \le f_u \\ 0 & others \end{cases} \quad (4)$$

where Δf is frequency resolution, fd and fu are the lower limit and the upper limit of cut-off frequency respectively, N is the number of data points, k is the frequency corresponding to the Fourier component. It can be seen from equation (3), frequency domain integration has amplifying effect on low-frequency frequencies, if the low-frequency cut-off frequency is not selected correctly, low frequency noise will be present in the signal, which will directly affect the accuracy of the integration.

The commonly used low-frequency cut-off frequency selection method is based on empirical selection or comparison through a large number of attempts. So there is some obvious defects:

(1) Artificially select of the low-frequency cut-off frequency is needed, which cannot completely eliminate the problem of the trend item, or eliminate the useful signal, so that the integral result will have a large error.

(2) It is not possible to determine which low-frequency cut-off frequency can minimize the error in the actual signal processing and achieve the best processing effect.

In order to improve the frequency domain integration performance, this paper proposes an acceleration integral method based on PSD estimation. According to the characteristics of the acceleration power spectrum, this method adaptively selects the cut-off frequency and removes trend items as much as possible.

3 INTEGRATION METHOD BASED ON PSD

3.1 Power Spectrum Estimation

The PSD estimation can obtain the power spectral density of the signal, which is used to estimate the frequency components of the signal. Common PSD estimation methods can be divided into non-parametric PSD estimation and parameter PSD estimation. Different methods have different effects for different types of signals. This paper uses Welch power spectrum estimation to process acceleration signal.

The Welch method belongs to the non-parametric spectral estimation method, which is characterized by two aspects: (1). It allows subsequences $a_i(n)$ to overlap each other;(2) It can be windowed for each subsequence, which can generate average correction period graph.

Assuming that adjacent subsequences are offset by d points, each subsequence length is L, then the ith sequence can be represented as:

$$a_i(n) = a(n+id), n = 0,1,\cdots,L-1 \quad (5)$$

Among them, the overlapping number of subsequence $a_i(n)$ and $a_{i+1}(n)$ is (L-d), if the entire sample point is covered by K subsequences, the relationship between the sample point lengths N and K can be expressed as:

$$N = L + d(K-1) \quad (6)$$

When using Welch PSD estimation, it's always need to window the subsequence signals. The window function is $w(n)$, the Welch spectral estimate of the signal $a(n)$ can be expressed as:

$$\hat{P}_{aa}(e^{j\omega}) = \frac{1}{KL} \sum_{i=0}^{K-1} \left| \sum_{n=0}^{L-1} w(n) a(n+id) e^{-jn\omega} \right|^2 \quad (7)$$

Welch spectral estimation is an asymptotic unbiased estimate of the PSD.

The optimal low-frequency cut-off frequency can be effectively obtained through PSD estimation in acceleration integrals, combined with the frequency domain integration algorithm to obtain the optimal displacement result. By constructing a vibration test stand and designing the actual test of the road surface, the PSD estimation method is used to achieve the estimation of the optimal low-frequency cut-off frequency, and the integration of the acceleration and the integral quality evaluation are realized.

3.2 Integration Algorithm

The high-frequency noise of the acceleration signal can be effectively removed by preprocessing such as DC removal and filtering. However, for low-frequency noise, careful consideration is needed. The selection of the cut-off frequency determines the size of the truncation error and will affect the accuracy of the integration. When the vehicle stops moving, the power spectrum intensity of the acceleration signal decreases as the frequency increases. When the vehicle is moving, peaks will appear in the power spectrum, and the frequency band where the spikes are located is the frequency band where the acceleration signal is located. Therefore, the most frequent cutoff frequency can be obtained by analyzing the power spectrum of the acceleration signal. The processing flow chart is shown in Fig.1.

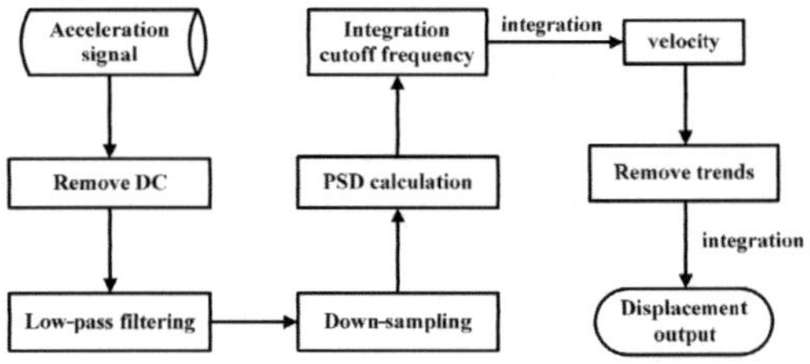

Fig.1. Acceleration processing method flow chart.

The operating steps of acceleration processing method is: (1) Input the dynamic acceleration signal $a_0(t)$, Then after removing the DC component, low-pass filtering, de-noising, down-sampling and other preprocessing, it can get the preconditioned acceleration signal *a(t)*;

(2)By analyzing the PSD sequence $X(k), k = 1,2,3,\cdots$ of the pre-processed acceleration signal, record sequence maximum extreme point *k*, commend $kk = k - i + 1$, $m = X(kk-1) - X(kk)$; if $m>0$, then $F_{opt} = kk * df$ is the low frequency cutoff frequency that we needed, otherwise, continue to iterate until m<0, then the low frequency cutoff frequency F_{opt} is obtained by the proposed method. The Algorithm processing flow chart is shown in Fig.2. Where $df = fs / nfft$, fs is the sampling frequency, and nfft is the number of points in the Fourier transform.

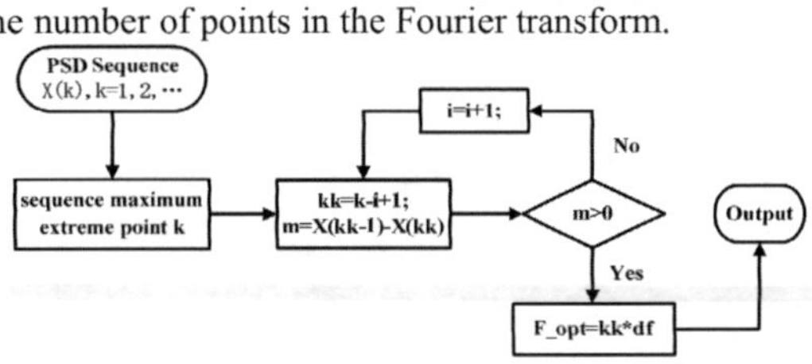

Fig.2. Algorithm flow chart.

(3) The extracted low frequency cutoff frequency is applied to the integral process of the acceleration frequency domain, and the speed signal is obtained by once integration and the displacement signal is obtained by double integration. And use inverse Fourier transform to change them into time domain signals.

(4) Output the displacement signal after the baseline offset correction.

4 EXPERIMENT AND RESULTS

In order to verify the effectiveness of the integration algorithm based on PSD estimation, the displacement-time signal and acceleration signal were obtained using a vibration experiment device. Using this method to integrate the acceleration signal, the displacement-time curve obtained by the integration is compared with the displacement-time signal measured by the laser range finder. Because the transient signal is more complex, so the vibration algorithm can be used to evaluate the integral algorithm.

4.1 Platform And Experiment

The vibration test bench is shown in Fig.3. The laser displacement sensor and acceleration sensor are installed in the middle of the beam. A detection platform is placed below the beam and its flatness is 0.05mm/150mm.

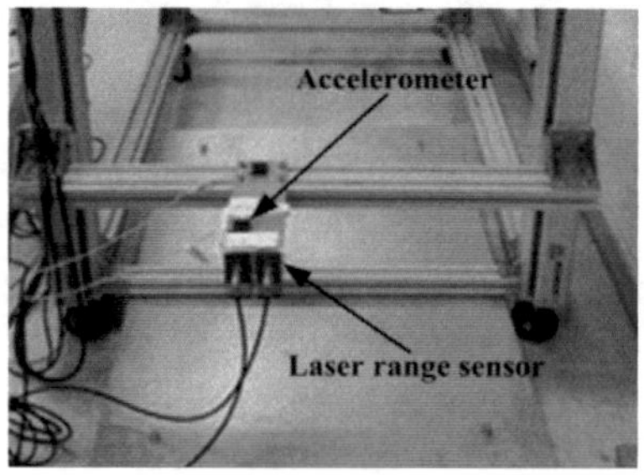

Fig.3. Vibration test bench.

The test bench controls the cross beam by stepping motor to perform vertical reciprocating motion, where the motion amplitude is 6mm and the motion speed is about 4mm/s. The displacement of the OMS-8198 laser ranging sensor was used in the experiment with sample rate of 50kHz and ranging accuracy of 0.05mm. And SDI 2220-002 uniaxial acceleration sensor was used in the experiment, with response frequency of 400Hz.

The pre-processed acceleration signal is shown in Fig.4(a). The PSD analysis of the pre-processed acceleration signal is shown in Fig.4(b). From the Fig.4(b), it can be concluded that the extracted low frequency cutoff frequency(LFCF) is 0.2975Hz.The velocity signal obtained by integrating acceleration once without baseline offset correction and the displacement signal obtained by the second integral are shown in Fig.5(a), (b).It can be seen that there are obvious trend items .The velocity signal obtained by integrating acceleration once with baseline offset correction and the displacement signal obtained by the second integral are shown in Fig.6(a), (b). The schematic diagram of the comparison of the displacement obtained by this method and the measured displacement is shown in Fig.e7(a). The difference between them is shown in Fig.7(b). As can be seen from the Fig.7, the difference between the integral and measured displacement after the PSD processing is ±0.2mm, which is less than 1mm required by the national road test specification.

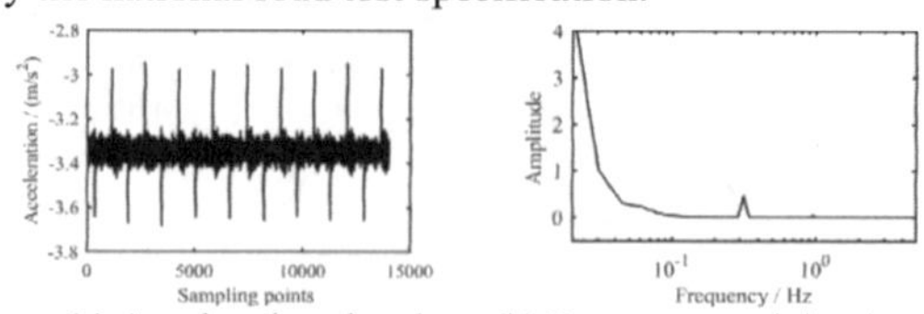

(a) Acceleration signal (b) Power spectral density

Fig.4. Acceleration signal and power spectral density.

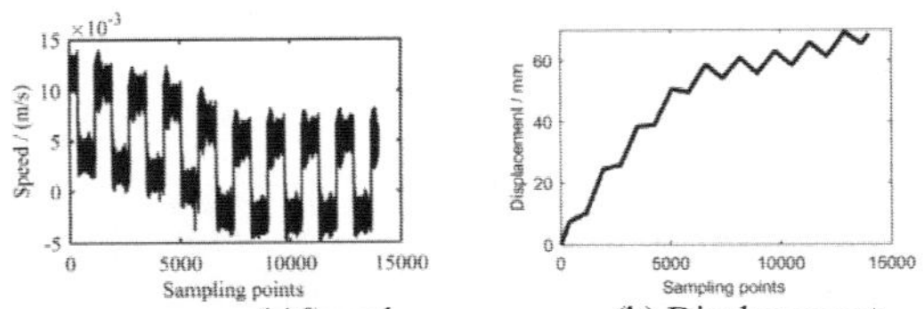

(a)Speed (b) Displacement

Fig.5. Speed and displacement without baseline offset correction.

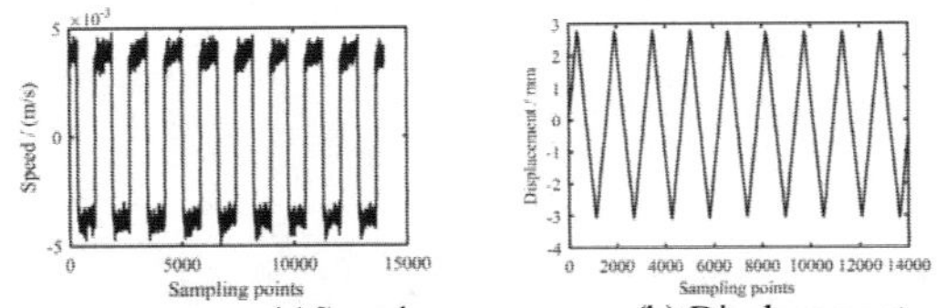

(a)Speed (b) Displacement

Fig.6. Speed and displacement with baseline offset correction.

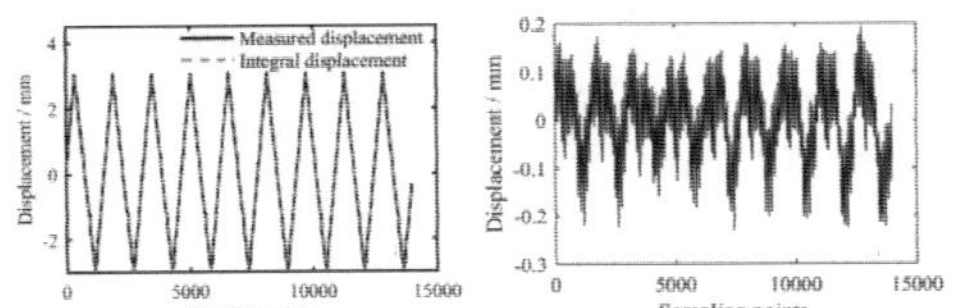

(a) Integral displacement (b) Error curve

Fig.7. Comparion of integral displacement and measured displacement.

4.2 Displacement Integration Results of Different Cutoff Frequency

Different low frequency cutoff frequencies (LFCF) will affect the accuracy of the acceleration integral displacement. The optimal low-frequency cut-off frequency (F_opt) is obtained by estimating the power spectrum of the acceleration signal, and the reference low-frequency cut-off frequencies of 0.1 Hz and 0.32 Hz are selected at the same time. The results of the integral displacement at different cut-off frequencies are shown in Fig.8(a). The integral displacement error curve is shown in Fig.8(b).

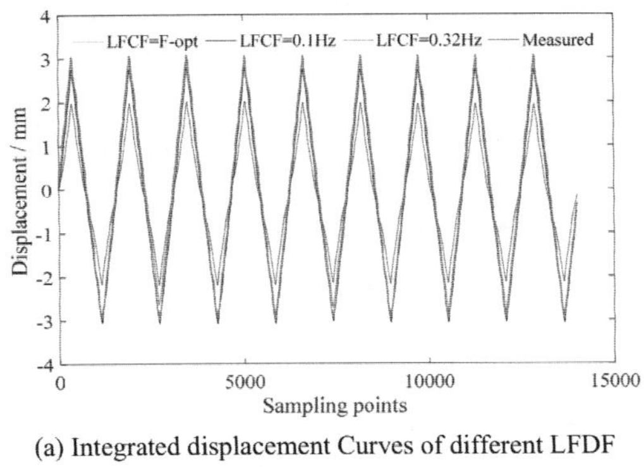

(a) Integrated displacement Curves of different LFDF

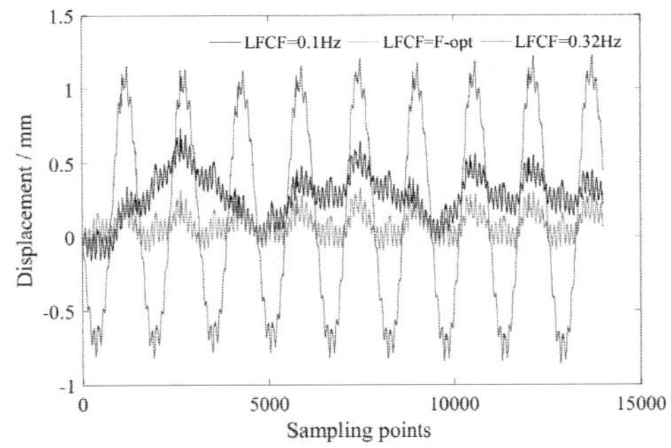

(b) Error curves of different LFCF

Fig.8. Comparison of different low frequency cut-off frequency.

As can be seen from Figure8, when the integrated low-frequency cut-off frequency LFCF = 0.1Hz, the integral error is about 0.6mm. When the integral cut-off frequency LFCF = 0.32 Hz, the integration error reaches 1.3 mm. It can be seen in the figure that the integration error increases when the selected low frequency cut-off frequency is higher or lower than the optimal cutoff frequency (F_opt). The test shows that the effectiveness of the proposed algorithm is verified.

5 CONCLUSIONS

Acquiring the displacement by integrating the acceleration signal twice is widely used in the aspects of carrier vibration testing and displacement detection. It is of great significance to improve the integral accuracy of acceleration. Based on the traditional frequency-domain integration, this paper proposed a novel method to obtain the best integration cut-off frequency by estimating the power spectrum of the acceleration, thereby improving the integration accuracy. Through the detection of the vibration test platform, it is proved that the algorithm can effectively intercept the integration frequency band and achieve the optimization of the integration result, so that the integration error is controlled within ±0.2mm. The next step will further optimize the algorithm and complete the actual road surface application test to achieve the purpose of engineering application.

REFERENCES

1. Q Xu. Journal of Vibration Measurement & Diagnosis, (1997).
2. N Li, DS Li, HN Li. Scientia Sinica, (2016).
3. F Cai. Chinese Journal of Scientific Instrument, (2006).
4. A Smyth, ML Wu. Mechanical Systems and Signal Processing,21: 706-723(2007) .
5. MK Gu, ZH Lv. Mechanical Science & Technology for Aerospace Engineering, (2011).
6. JF Wang.computer science, 37 :201-202, 237(2010).
7. YH Hong , HK Kim ,HS Lee .Journal of Sound &

Vibration, 329(23):4980-5003(2010).

8. HS Lee ,YH Hong ,HW Park . International Journal for Numerical Methods in Engineering, 82(4):403-434(2010).
9. B Lotfi ,L Huang .Measurement, 90:242-249(2016).

MATEC Web of Conferences **176**, 03013 (2018) https://doi.org/10.1051/matecconf/201817603013
IFID 2018

Design and Implementation of Service and Management System of Agricultural Technicians

Yang Lu[1,2], Furong Wang[1,2*], Changshou Luo[1,2], Weishui Yu[1,2], Jun Yu [1,2]

[1] Institute of Agricultural Information and Economics,Beijing Academy of Agriculture and Forestry Sciences, No.9, Shuguang Huayuan Road,Beijing,China
[2]Rural Distance Information Service Engineering Technology Research Center of Beijing, No.9, Shuguang Huayuan Road,Beijing,China

Abstract. This paper proposes a design idea of service and management system of agricultural technicians, which includes the design of management system, logical structure, service flow and management module. It introduced "DiDi Agrotechnique" product which developed based on this design idea. The "DiDi Agrotechnique" product includes two parts: One is mobile phone APP which realized one-button Q&A operation on agricultural technical consultation, the other is back-end management system, which realized management of agricultural service process and automatic statistics of service data. This product has great significance for integrating agricultural technicians, providing O2O agricultural technical services, and improving management efficiency, which has the practical value for extensive use.

1 Introduction

At present, with the rapid development of computer science and network technology, the PC and mobile devices have been applied widely, which creates conditions for the establishment and application of a unified management system. The agricultural technology need an integrated management system to grasp the dynamics of agricultural technology promotion in time, accelerate the innovation of the agricultural technology and achieve systematic and standardized agricultural technology promotion. In recent years, government departments, scientific research institutions, and enterprises have successively established the network system of agricultural technology, which facilitated the solution of technical problems encountered by farmers in the agricultural production process and meanwhile integrated the relevant agricultural technical resources.

However, through field investigation, it has been found several problems, such as the cost of agricultural expert services is high, experts general are far away from farmers and cannot quickly reach the scene to solve the problem. Then we also found that the operation of agricultural technology consulting services product in the market is complicated and the implementation scope is not widely. The basic-level agricultural technicians have the characteristics of being familiar with their local agricultural environment and technology needs, and sloving problems quickly, they can provide convenient door-to-door service. However, the rate of integration and utilization of the agricultural technician resources is not high, and the superior departments are unable to grasp their specific service conditions during the management process. So corresponding service products and management systems should be designed to integrate and manage agricultural technology resources, which will achieve O2O services of agricultural technology and monitor the whole service process. These products and systems are beneficial to quantify and assess the service of agricultural technique, and promote the service quality of basic-level agricultural technicians.

* Corresponding author: Furong Wang wfr828@126.com

2 System design

2.1 Integrated design idea

2.1.1 Management System design

Combined with the agricultural administrative management system, and the specific requirements of managers and users, the management system involves four layers as shown in Figure 1. The provincial (municipal) level administrators have the authority to audit and check the data which submitted by the subordinate districts and counties, they can also manage the background system. The county (district) level administrator has the authority of account checking, account allocation and background system management. Basic-level agricultural technicians are the ties that connect farmers and superior management departments, in order to promote the management and the service , they are necessary to log in with a superior account number and fill in real-name information. Farmers are users of this system, need to register and fill the basic information before they use it.

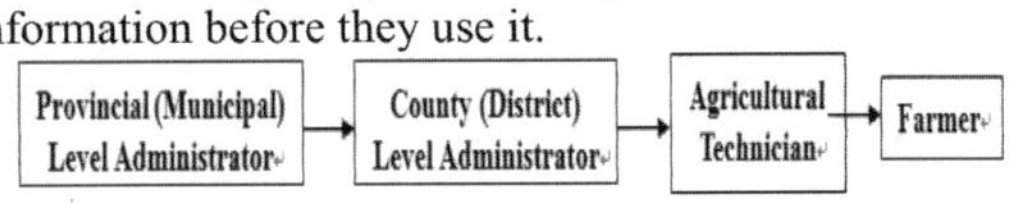

Figure.1. Management system design.

2.1.2 Logical structure design and developme-nt technology

According to the logical layering principle and object oriented principle, the whole system can be divided into three layers: the client layer, the application layer, and the data layer. The client layer is designed based on the PC and the mobile device, its specific form can be webpage or APP. Operator can use defined services or functions to realize human-computer interaction. The client layer displays the system output data; The application layer analyzes and processes the customer's application request, calculates the data and then returns to the client layer; The data layer is a database management system, the main function is data storage and management.

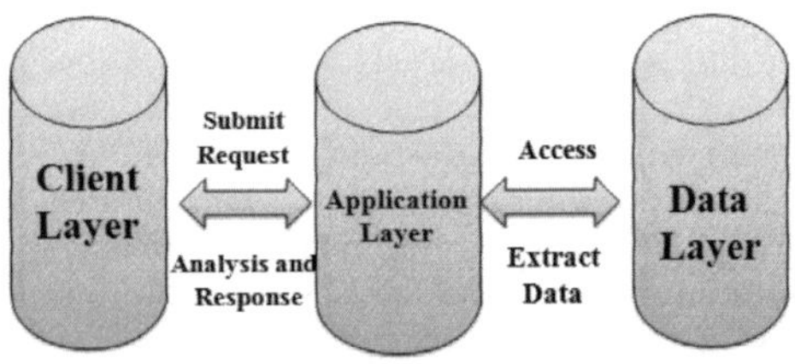

Figure.2. System logic structure diagram.

The front-end service software and back-end management platform of the system can be written in C# and JAVA languages, developed and designed with Visual Studio, SQL Sever, SQLite, Webservice, and GIS components.

2.2 Service flow design

To get through the channels of farmers, agricultural technicians and experts, and establish Q&A database, the service system design is divided into two parts .When user asks a question with device, the question will be sent in the form of voice, text, pictures, etc. On one hand, if the agricultural technician can solve it, they will provide telephone or on-site service. But if the agricultural technician cannot answer it, the system will sent the question to the back-end expert, who contact the user to resolve it through remote device. Finally, the user evaluate the service and the entire process ended. On the other hand, in order to realize online self-service inquiry, the system will establish Q&A database and background manager will record and classify the user's questions.The questions of voice can be converted into text by using TTS, then using natural language processing technology to achieve precise intelligent Q&A service (Specific process shown in Figure 3).

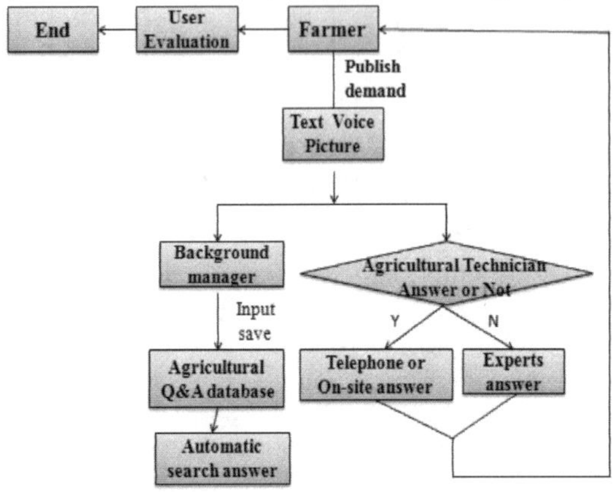

Figure.3. The diagram of service flow.

2.3. Management module design

The agricultural technology management system platform mainly includes five modules: (1) Personnel information management module, managers can use this module to manage and audit the information of farmers, agricultural technicians and experts; (2) Announcement management module, the system regularly push policy and technical news, system notifications. (3) Question database management module, through this module, background manager can check , edit and answer the questions which collected by the front-end device. (4) Statistical analysis module, managers can check the status of registration, demand, and service at any time. This module provides the function of automatic statistics and analysis of data, then it can form and export chart. (5) Dictionary management module, this module can be used to construct fields of proprietary information, such as domain classification, demand classification, administrative classification, etc.

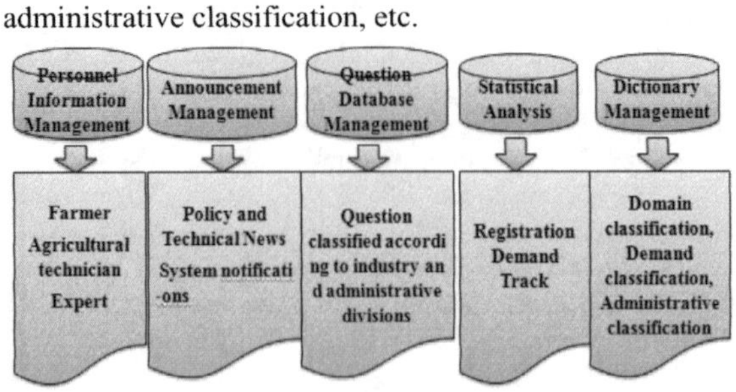

Figure.4. The diagram of agricultural technology management system platform.

3. System implementation and application

By combining the design concept of agricultural technician service and management system, using "3S" Technologies, Webservice technology, storage and management technology, we develope “DiDi Agrotechnique” APP and back-end management system.The product can provide users with convenient and “O2O” agricultural technology services,it could integrate basic-level agricultural technology resources, and connect farmers and agricultural experts of college and research institutes. In addition, the system can provide a management platform for the superior management department to timely acquire and analyze the data such as the service of agricultural technicians and the needs of farmers.

3.1. Implementation of “DiDi Agrotech-nique” APP

In order to make the user easy to use, the product adopts one-button Q&A service form, UI interface uses visual map positioning technology. Farmers can register and use the APP after filling in a few simple information. Click the "Demand" button below to enter the "Publication Requirements" page. Farmers can make an appointment to solve, and then simply describe the questions they need to consult in the form of voice or text, and upload live photos. After the agricultural technician answers the question, the farmer can evaluate the service of the agricultural technician and give marks to the agricultural technician. If the question is not answered, the system will transfer the question to the back-end expert of the 12396 Agricultural Technology Service Hotline to solve it.

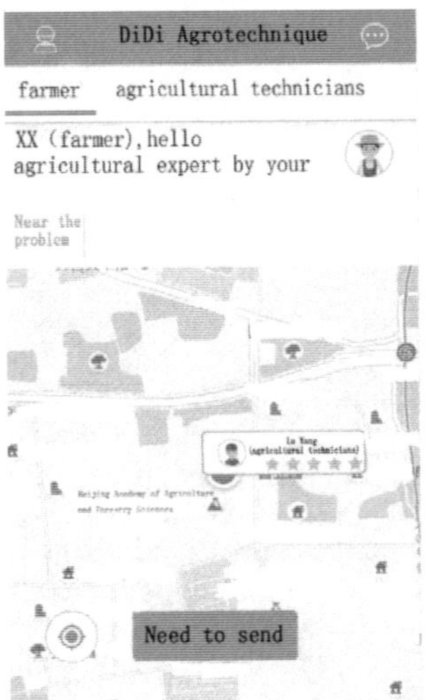

Figure.5. “DiDi Agrotechnique”APP page.

The agricultural technician operates with the grab task mode. When a farmer sends out a demand, the agricultural technician will receive a system notification (As shown in Figure6).The agricultural technician can judge whether to grab the task by checking the details of the demand. After accepting the task successfully, it can be solved by calling or going to the scene. If the agricultural technician chooses to go to the site, the system will enter the map interface to navigate, and the service track will be also recorded by the backend system. If the agricultural technician who has grabbed the task can not solve this problem, he can cancel the order or query the answer by consulting the expert and then answer it. After the task is completed, the agricultural technician needs to record and submit the solution.

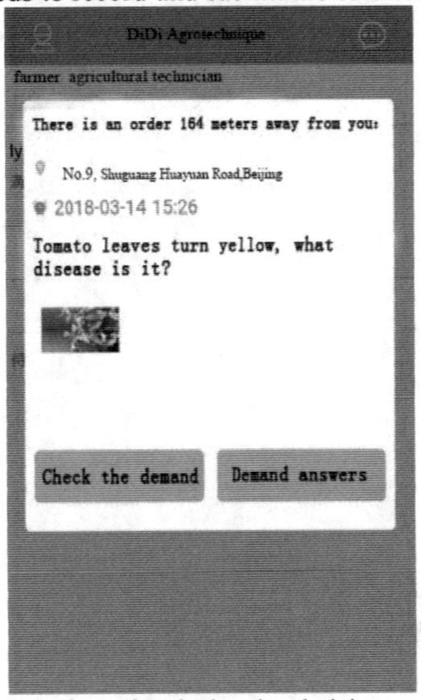

Figure .6. Interface of agricultural technician receive notification.

3.2. Implementation of “DiDi Agrotech-nique” Back-end Management Syst-em

The “DiDi Agrotechnique” Back-end Management System is the platform for superior agricultural department to manage basic-level agricultural technicians .It has the characteristics of clear hierarchy, comprehensive and automatic statistics. The system is divided into 8 modules: Demand Management, User Management, Subsidy Management, Statistical Analysis, 12396, System Notification, Question Feedback, and Dictionary Management. Each module is set up submodules, administrators can easily access, manage, and analyze data through them.

First, the administrator log in the account, by the Demand Management module, he can check requirement list according to the key word, service method, order time, and other categories, and then he can also check the service track of the agricultural technician, as shown in Figure8.In the User Management module, administrator can manage the information of the agricultural technicians and farmers, and audit the account of the agricultural technicians. At the same time, the geographical distribution of the users and the check-in status can be viewed. Subsidy Management detailed record on the examines and rewards of the agricultural technicians, and it can export the corresponding data sheet. Statistical Analysis module realizes automatic data analysis result. The user registration status, demand status, service status, etc. are displayed by means of charts which is shown in the right interface of Figure 7. 12396 module realizes the connection of "DiDi Agrotechnique" Back-end Management System and 12396 Agricultural Technology Service Hotline. It links 12396 expert resources and agriculture Q&A database together. 8.System Notification module manages system messages display of APP. 9.Question Feedback module can real-time control the user's reaction during use. 10.Dictionary management module includes management of domain list and requirement type list, administrators can set service time of agricultural technicians in this module.

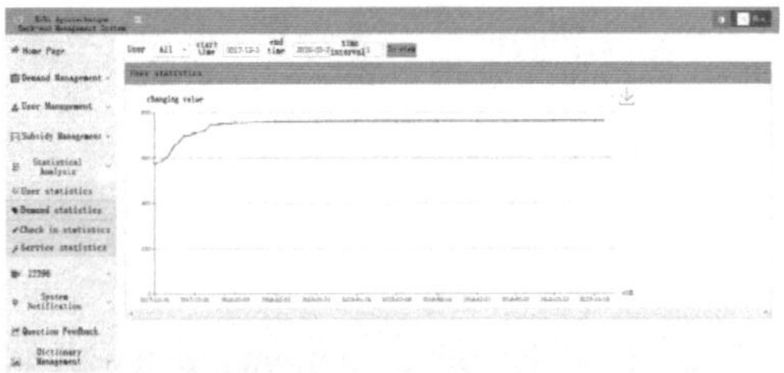

Figure.7. Interface of"DiDi Agrotechnique" Back-end Management System.

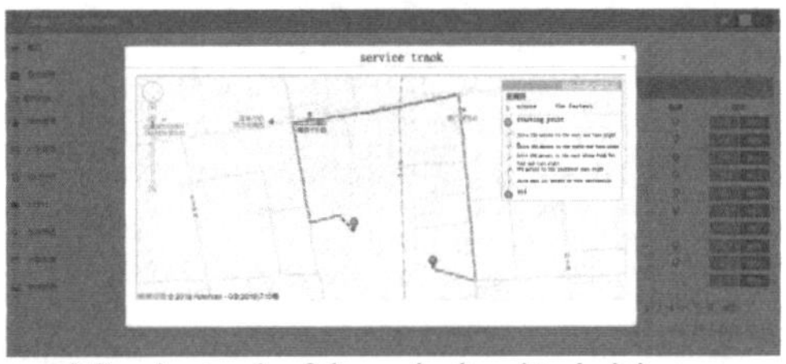

Figure .8. Service track of the agricultural technician.

4. Conclusion

Agricultural technicians are an important part of the agricultural technology promotion and service system. The Service and Management System of Agricultural technicians designed in this paper can make basic-level agricultural technology resources efficiently used and promote the optimum allocation of agricultural technician. At the same time, this system can provide an efficient information platform for agricultural technician services, provide convenient O2O services for farmers, and provide accurate management and decision-making data support for government management departments.

"DiDi Agrotechnique"APP is developed based on above system design concept, it is a mobile phone product for service and management of agricultural technology promotion .The product reformed agricultural technology services means and functional design of system, established a bridge of agricultural technicians and farmers through mobile. It can improve the precision of agricultural technology promotion work, provide more convenient and efficient O2O agricultural technology services for famers, and broaden the service scope and service methods of the basic-level agricultural technicians. "DiDi Agrotechnique" Back-end Management System can record and track the service information of each agricultural technician in detail, and realize the detailed assessment of individual performance and work ability of agricultural technicians. At present, the product has been applied in demonstration areas, which has obtained great effects. After continuous improving and upgrading, it will have the practical value for extensive use.

ACKNOWLEDGEMENTS

The research work was supported by the Beijing excellent talent project: Research on key technology of m anmachine conversation in agricultural science and techn ology consultation and application of Be- ijing, Tianjin and Hebei, the international cooperation fun d of BAAFS: A comparative study on the agricultural sci ence and technology information service- e system in China, the United States and Canada, th- e \2018 Beijing financing agricultural funds: Appli- cation and demonstration of "Nongkexiaozhi" cons- lting service robot and WebAPP in agricultural productio n, the young scientist fund of BAAFS: Analysis of omnipotent agricultural technicians' training effect and relevant affecting factors in Beijing (NO.QNJJ201803)

REFERENCES

1. CHEN Xin-zhong, LI Fang-fang. Retrospect and Prospect of Research on Our Agricultural Technology Extension [J]. Journal of Huazhong Agricultural University(Social Sciences Edition, 2014, 33(5):24-33.
2. Junhui Shao. The Design and Implementation of Primary Agricultural Technology Extension System for Bazhou[D]. Shandong University, 2015.
3. 3 .MENG Meng. Model Design of Closed-loop Supply Chain for Tropical Agricultural Products in Hainan Province [J]. Chinese Journal of Tropical Agriculture, 2016, 36(10):87-92.
4. Yu W, Luo C, Zheng Y, et al. Research on the development and preliminary application of Beijing agricultural sci-tech service hotline WebApp in agricultural consulting services[J]. 2017, 231(1):012030.
5. Wei Chen, Shupu Guo. Studies on Progress and Trend of Agricultural and Rural Informatization in China, [J]. Hubei Agricultural Sciences, 2013,52(22) 5625-5629

MATEC Web of Conferences **176**, 03014 (2018) https://doi.org/10.1051/matecconf/201817603014
IFID 2018

Research and Design of Cross-Language Vertical Search Engine for Special Agricultural E-commerce Platform

Yaru Cao[1], Ning Ma[2], Fucheng Wan[3] and Xiangzhen He[4]

[1,2,3,4]Northwest Minzu University, Lanzhou city, Gansu province, China

Abstract. Based on the research of vertical search engine and cross-language information retrieval, a cross-language vertical search engine design for e-commerce platform is proposed. It aims to solve the problem that it is difficult for Internet users to quickly, efficiently, and comprehensively search for valuable products, especially ethnic minority netizens. Cross-language in this article mainly refers to the conversion of Chinese, English, and Tibetan. Using dictionary-based query translation method to translate query words to achieve cross-language function. Improved Heritrix designed a web crawler information collection method. Using HtmlParser to achieve structured information extraction, and using Lucene to build an index and achieve retrieval.

1 INTRODUCTION

With the rapid development of science and technology, the Internet quickly enters every area of social life and plays a role that cannot be underestimated. According to statistics from CNNIC, as of December 2017, online shopping users reached 533 million, and the search engine penetration rate was 82.8%. But most of the vertical search engines are now based on Chinese. For ethnic minority peoples in ethnic areas, they do not have very perfect Chinese reading ability. When he was faced with a huge Chinese webpage in e-commerce, they couldn't retrieve the Chinese products they wanted. This type of user naturally generates a strong demand for cross-language search information.

2 SYSTEM INTRODUCTION

2.1 Cross-Language Vertical Search Engine Concept

The vertical search engine is a new search model developed to reduce the general search engine's search results in terms of accuracy, accuracy, and professionalism. The vertical search engine is a deep search that serves a specific field, a specific group of people, or a specific demand, and has a distinctive industry color. The cross-language vertical search engine refers to the addition of cross-language functions on the basis of vertical search engines. In this article, when the user belongs to Tibetan language query words, the Chinese description information can be retrieved.

2.2 System Function Requirements Analysis

The cross-language vertical search engine of the e-commerce platform for featured agricultural products is an extension of the vertical search engine. In addition to having "professional, refined, and deep" industry characteristics, it also has a variety of language conversion functions. In addition, it also has the basic functions of a vertical search engine system, including information acquisition, structured information extraction, construction index, information search, user interface. In summary, the system includes six functional modules as shown in Figure 1.

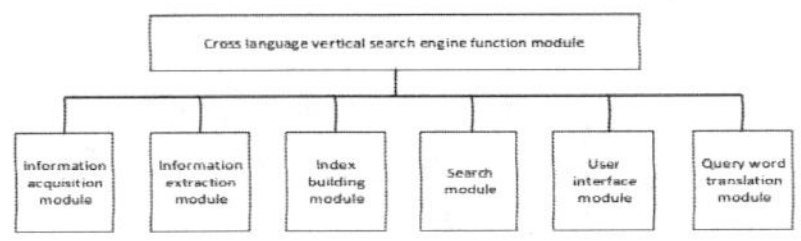

Fig. 1. Functional Module

3 SYSTEM DESIGN

3.1 System Architecture

The system is mainly divided into six modules: information acquisition module, information extraction module, index construction module, search module, query word translation module, and user interface module. The information acquisition module is to extend the specific Web pages of the "Belt and Road Special Product Network" through the extension of Herritrix Extractor and Frontier Scheduler, and download it to a locally created mirrored

Corresponding author:11195825322@qq.com, 26105112@qq.com, 3306261663@qq.com, 45967148@qq.com

folder. The information extraction module uses HTML Parser to extract the product metadata from the downloaded product page information to form structured data. This system has extracted the picture address, title, content, original URL address and other data in the web page. This system has extracted the picture address, title, content, original URL address and other data in the web page. At the same time, insert this information into the MySQL database. The index module builds an index library by building a full-text search of the metadata information of the commodity by extending Lucene's functionality. The search module uses Lucene to match the query terms entered by the user with the index library, and feeds the search results back to the user. The query word translation module translates into multiple language-written query words through a single-language query word in a multi-language dictionary database, and is collectively handed over to the system for retrieval. The system architecture is shown in Figure 2.

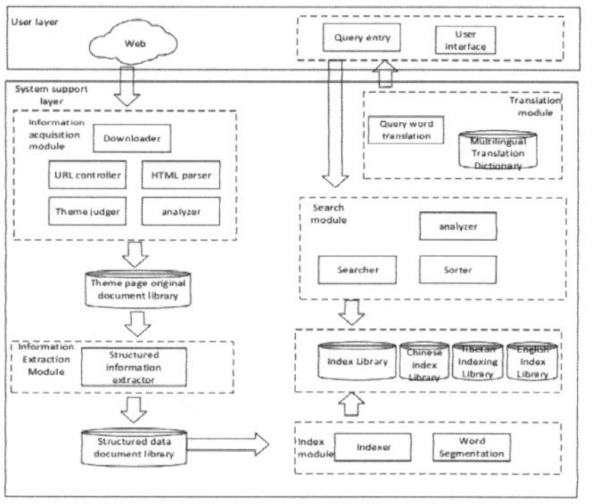

Fig. 2. Cross-Language Vertical Search Engine System Architecture

3.2 Information Acquisition Module Design

This system uses Heritrix as a tool for automatically collecting information. Heritrix does not have a directional capture function. It only captures all web page information and does not meet the requirements of this system. Therefore, in this design, the Extractor is customized according to the characteristics of the URL of the desired web page to replace the originally embedded class. Second, it further expands the Frontier Scheduler implementation to crawl specific types of content. This class is a Post Professor. Its role is to add the link from the previous Extractor analysis to Frontier for further processing. By limiting Heritrix's crawling behavior, download the required web page information.

3.3 Design of Structured Information Extraction Module

The source code of the web pages that Heritrix has crawled contains a lot of useless semi-structured data such as HTML tags. You need to extract the required information from it and save it for use when creating an index. This article chooses the structured information extraction tool HtmlParser, which extracts different content data according to the meaning and attributes of the web page tag. Although the contents of the HTML files may not be exactly the same, they have the same basic framework:

<html> <head> <title> </title> <meta> </meta> </head> <body> </body> </html>

The information to be extracted in this section is the subject part between <body></body>.

3.4 Design of Index Module

The role of the index is similar to the role of the book catalog. According to the page number in the catalog, the required detailed information can be quickly found and the retrieval speed can be greatly improved. The index is to index the structured data extracted from the previous link and stored in the index database. Such as product name, product brand, product price and other data, the schematic diagram of the establishment of the index shown in Figure 3.

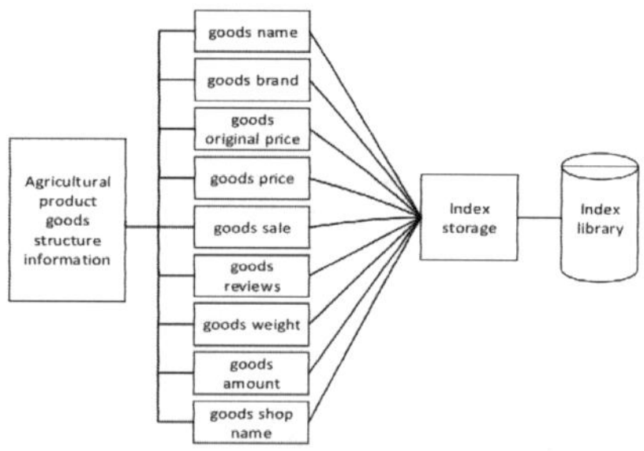

Fig. 3. Index establishment

3.5 Query Word Translation Module Design

Cross-language information retrieval is essentially a match between single-language query words and multi-lingual retrieved resources. The system uses a dictionary-based query translation method, which is based on a single language information retrieval system and adds a language converter on top of it. After the user enters the query word, the query word written in other languages supported by the system is translated by the language converter, and then the single language information search can be performed. Obviously, this language converter is the core of the technology that is the most important for the translation of query terms. The multilingual dictionary in this design is this language converter. The multilingual dictionary used by this system is the research team of the National Institute of Information Technology of Northwest China University for Nationalities through the excavation and organization of ethnic agricultural resources. A handmade multi lingual national dictionary library of agricultural products (abbreviated as a multi-language dictionary) Based on the analysis and design of the translation of query terms, the model is set up in the three languages of English, Chinese, and English as an example. As shown in Figure 4.

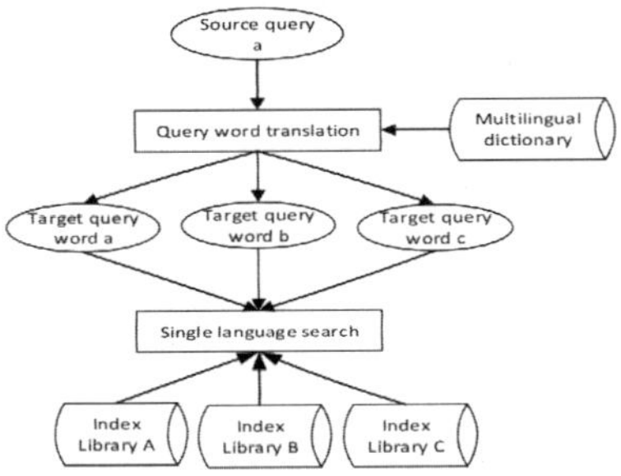

Fig. 4. query word translation model

This module is based on a multilingual dictionary of human translation. It guarantees the correct correspondence between words and words. Compared to machine translation, it solves the problem of "word polysemy" and greatly increases the accuracy rate.

3.6 Search Module Design

The search module searches for all document records according to a certain search strategy in the index file to be generated, and feeds the result set back to the user in a certain order. The system uses Lucene to achieve retrieval. The process is actually connected to the user while the other side is connected to the index library and the search module client. The input query type matches a source language to other languages through a query word translation module, and then is delivered to the user terminal of the search module. The end of the index database is to take the user's query words to the index database to match the index entries. Finding the document record through the pointer of the index item generates a plurality of inverted document lists. Finally, all the document records are merged and classified and returned to the user in a certain order. As shown in Figure 5.

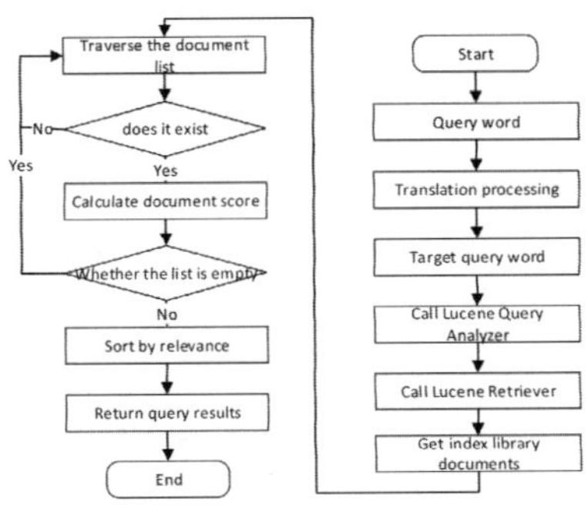

Fig. 5. Search Module Workflow

3.7 User Interface Design

The user interface module adds two pages to the system. One is the search engine homepage index .html, and the other is the search results page search .jsp. Design related pages based on the principles of natural harmony. As shown in Figure 6.

Fig. 6. User Interface

4 Conclusions

This paper first analyzes the universality of search engines through data analysis and the difficulties of ethnic minority netizens in searching for valuable information. This leads to the importance and urgency of the research and design of the cross-language vertical search engine for the e-commerce platform for featured agricultural products. Secondly, the six major functional modules of the system are identified by analyzing the needs of cross-language vertical search engines. Finally, analyze and design the overall framework of the system and each functional module.

At present, China's study of Tibetan, Mongolian and Uyghur language processing is not mature enough. Combining cross-language and vertical search engines in an e-commerce environment is rare. Mature use is a goal in the future. In the future research work, we need to improve and optimize cross-language.

Acknowledgement

This research was supported by the National Science-technology Support Plan Projects (Grant NO. 2015BAD29B01) and the Fundamental Research Funds for the Central Universities (31920170155).

References

1. China Internet Network Information Center, The 31th China Internet Development Statistics Report, http://www.cnnic.cn/, 2017.12.
2. Pu Hong, 2016. Research and Implementation of Lucene-Based Search Engine. Dalian University of Technology.
3. Mingqing Wang, 2010. Research and Implementation of Web Vertical Search Engine Technology Based on JAVA+Lucene+Heritrix. Hebei University of Technology,
4. Zhou, Yachao Li, TaoJiang, Hongzhi Yu, Yangji Jia, 2011. Dictionary-based Cross-Language Retrieval System in Tibetan and ChineseJournal of Northwest University for Nationalities(Natural Science), vol. 32, pp. 40-43. (in Chinese)
5. Heng Wang, Shaoshan Wang, 2013. Research and Implementation of Subject-Oriented Intra-domain Vertical Search Engine System Journal of Ningxia University (Natural Science Edition), vol. 34, pp. 54-57 (in Chinese).
6. Story R.E, 1996. An Explanation of the Effectiveness of Latent Semantic Index by Means of a Bayesian Regression Model. Information Processing and Management, vol. 32, pp. 329-344.

7. Chuanming Jin, 2011. Research and Implementation of Vertical Search Engine. Yunnan University (in Chinese).
8. Zhe Qiu, Taotao Fu. Lucene, 2017. 2.0+Heriteix develops its own search engine. Posts & Telecom Press (in Chinese).
9. Fucheng Wan, Dongchen Li, Xiangzhen He, 2014. Tao Xu. Research on Tibetan Text Indexing Strategy for Information Retrieval. Computer Engineering and Applications, vol. 50, pp 208-211 (in Chinese).
10. YunQiang Liu, 2010. Research and Design of Vertical Search Engine. Computer Applications and Software, vol.27, pp 130-133 (in China).

Research on Crowdsourcing Camera Mode System based on Block Chain Technology

Dou Hu [1], Chuang Ma [1], Yuanlong Gao [1] and Wenlong Liu [1]

[1]School of Information and Communication Engineering, Dalian University of Technology, Dalian, China

Abstract. As a new business model, the crowdsourcing camera mode has been paid close attention in recent years. However, traditional crowdsourcing operations rely too much on centralized institutions, which have many drawbacks. It is precisely because of this that the superiority of block chain technology is reflected. With the flourishing development of the Internet and the ever-changing block chain technology, this paper provides the research on crowdsourcing camera mode based on block chain technology from four aspects including the analysis of decentralization, the strengthen of security precautions, the establishment of appropriate systems and the gradually transition of token system.

1 INTRODUCTION

In recent years, the rise of the Internet has led to the development of a large number of emerging industries, among which the 'photographing and making money' is a self-service crowdsourcing service model under the mobile Internet that is also known as the crowdsourcing camera mode. The users first download the applications (APPs) of the crowdsourcing camera mode, then register as a member of the APP, and then receive the tasks of taking a picture, and earn a reward for accomplishing the tasks. The crowdsourcing service model provides enterprises with various business inspections and information collection. Compared with traditional market survey methods, it can greatly reduce survey costs, and effectively guarantee the authenticity of survey data and shorten the survey period.

However, the trust between people, operating costs, and redundant central institutions are all obstacles to this approach. If the crowdsourcing service model is operated in a traditional commercial manner, there is bound to be a central agency [1]. Hence, the photographing tasks will be transferred through the central agency. Moreover, the establishment of a large-scale trading platform not only increases the operating cost of crowdsourcing services and the response time to events, but also presents a great security risk. Considering the characteristics of the block chain technology, including decentralization, high security, strong scalability, and low transaction costs, this paper researches a new operating plan based on block chain technology for crowdsourcing camera mode.

The rest of the paper is organized as follows. In section II, we introduce the traditional crowdsourcing camera mode. The research of crowdsourcing service system model based on the block chain technology is given in section III. Finally, section IV ends the paper with the conclusion.

2THE TRADITIONAL CROWDSOURCING CAMERA SERVICE

The architecture of traditional the crowdsourcing camera mode can be summarized as shown in Fig 1.

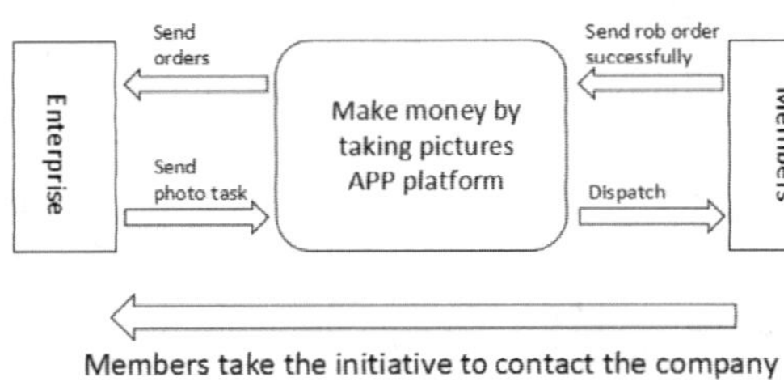

Fig 1: The architecture of traditional the crowdsourcing camera mode

From Fig 1, the app serves as a third-party trading platform, which is the hub of the transaction. However, there are many security risks in traditional crowdsourcing. The first is the issue of trust. For this mode, tasks are distributed through the APP, so the

*Corresponding author: Wenlong Liu: liuwl@dlut.edu.cn

number of people receiving the tasks is large, and the large number of people will lead to uneven quality of professionalism, such as identity fraud, perfunctory tasks, once the platform is unable to identify true or false, it will create a crisis of confidence. What is more, due to the different amount of tasks and the degree of difficulty in photographing, it is easy for people to lose trust in the platform. Second is the security issue. Because the platform collects a large amount of information about the transaction and even includes private information, once the information is leaked, the platform system will be compromised. The third problem is miscellaneous issues. The redundancy of platform information is mixed, and the recipient cannot distinguish authenticity from others. This can lead to inefficiencies in the operation process. In other words, the participation of third-party platforms will lead to low levels of effectiveness.

In order to address the above issues, the crowdsourcing service system model based on the block chain technology are proposed which is introduced in next section.

3 CROWDSOURCING CAMERA SYSTEM BASED ON BLOCK CHAIN TECHNOLOGY

3.1 More reasonable decentralization

Considering the issues of the trust, security, and miscellaneous in the traditional centralized operation model, which is combined with information security, which inevitably represents its existence risk. For this regard, the block chain technology can be an available solution, due to the characteristic of decentralization. The "centralization" in the block chain is a distributed data storage structure for the purpose of protecting the security of information. Firstly, due to the open and transparent distributed storage characteristics of block chains, it can adopt distributed storage based on Peer to Peer (P2P) networks where each node saves one data backup. Hence, the trust degree is greatly improved. Then the block chain has features that cannot be modified and can be traced, and security is fully guaranteed. Finally, block chain technology is decentralized, decentralizing information to both sides of the transaction, making information communications more efficient, reducing operating costs, providing faster response time, and greatly improving efficiency.

In the case of cross-border payments and exchange systems as an example [2], we illustrate the cost saving effect of centralization and the improvement of system security. Traditional cross-border payment and exchange systems rely on centralized intermediary credit to connect different entities in the financial market. This scheme requires the reduction of information asymmetry and the trust mechanisms established by the authority to achieve the value transfer and all participants unanimously recognized the central authority with absolute credibility. This will lead to high costs, increase the time of payment exchange process, weaken the liquidity of funds, and there are also payment and system risks in terms of security.

However, the situation will change when the centralization is abandoned and adopt the logic of decentralization in block chain technology. On the one hand, decentralization avoids the breakdown of the entire system caused by the attack that central organization suffered. Benefit by the existence of distributed ledgers, each node has a complete copy of the ledger, and the failure of some nodes is insufficient to affect the entire network. On the other hand, it reduces the cost of establishing a third-party central hub. It has become an efficient and low-cost global block chain network financial transmission protocol. According to McKinsey's calculations, this solution will reduce the cost of each transaction from US$26 to US$15 and save about 42.3% of the cost. According to China's 2015 cross-border payment and settlement of approximately 800 billion Yuan, we will save 336 billion Yuan every year.

3.2 Strengthen safety precautions

The system of block chain cannot be deleted and cannot be changed. Each node in the chain is central. The block chain has its unique features in terms of security.

Through P2P download, P-CDN distributed storage and distributed computing. A large amount of data has been distributed to countless computers to achieve packaging, disperse the danger in centre and increase efficiency.

JAVA can be used to achieve a simple block chain design [3]. Specifically, the 'crypto-js' library can be used to create a block and the block chain class can connect the block, and define the last block of the hash. In this way, a simple block chain is generated. Of course, it can be optimized using Proof of Work (POW) or P2P networks. POW can be used to prevent misuse and defence against attacks through a simple amount of calculations. The incentive measure is to generate a mining mechanism that can be generated using the function known as 'minePendingTransactions' in JAVA.

In this case, information is difficult to modify. It is highly distributed and it reduces external risks. So block chain technology is very good at controlling information security.

In summary, two proposals are proposed for the crowdsourcing service mode secure encryption method as follow:

1.Using the Tech Target and session key consultation mechanisms based on block chain [4]. The identity-based encryption algorithm IBE can use the user's identity as a public key for encryption or signature verification. To avoid the loss of public keys and result in security issues and to prevent replay attacks, the public key needs to be updated regularly.

2.Similar to food traceability technology, we provide customers with tracking services system. The tracking services system includes physical, communications, database and interface layers. Among them, block chain technology is applied to the database layer and communication layer. The physical layer mainly includes smart sensors and actuators for data acquisition and forwarding to the upper layer protocol, which is substantially similar to the physical layer in the structure of the Internet of Things. The communication layer of the traceability system uses Ethernet platform based on block chain technology and hash information transfer protocol to prevent the attacked node from destroying the system through the network. In the e-commerce environment, the frequency of transactions, the area involved, and the number of commodities have increased substantially [5]-[6]. Incomplete and asymmetric information among various entities has increased the risk of monetary payment links.

In 2016, the third-party Internet payment transaction in China reached 19.2 trillion Yuan, a year-on-year increase of 62%. In the face of the increasing number of Internet transactions, the security construction of the payment link has become the key. In the block chain technology, transaction data cannot be tampered with the characteristics of transaction traceability. It can be used as a simple and effective tracking tool to jointly maintain a reliable database. To the utmost extent it guarantees the security of the transaction process.

3.3 Establish the appropriate systems

In addition to Bitcoin and Ethernet, a number of systems related to block chain have emerged in recent years which can be used for the crowdsourcing model. Hyperledger is an open source project launched by the Linux Foundation in 2015 that promotes block chain digital technology and transaction verification [7]-[8]. Because of the characteristics of the peer-to-peer network in hyperledger, distributed ledger technology is completely shared, transparent, and decentralized, and is well-suited for node-network-based business model applications. hyperledger has identity and auditability, private transactions and confidentiality contracts, users can choose their own consensus algorithms and write chain code (also known as: smart contracts) performance, and scalability through mainstream programming languages.

In the research and development of block chain application projects for the photo-financing and crowd-sourcing project, the research and improvement of consensus algorithms is very important. Therefore, the development environment based on the hyperledger can be used not only for programming development of enterprise-level application projects, but also for performance analysis tests of related consensus algorithms, smart contracts, and the like. Taking the Hyperledger development environment as an example, we have integrated the following system building steps:

Step 1: Build a test environment on a Linux system. According to the network environment construction plan of the four verification nodes given on the official website, the Docker installation test environment is used in the virtual machine.

Step 2: Build a test network. Multiple dockers are installed on one PC to carry multiple authentication nodes; multiple dockers are installed on multiple PCs to achieve communication between dockers so as to expand the network scale.

Step 3: View the consensus module, analyze the source code. Understand the writing specification format of the consensus code and find the relevant event interface.

Step 4: Determine the boot interface and consensus event flow of the consensus module. Find the boot consensus algorithm interface function to find all the parameters and related parameters for the consensus algorithm in the system.

Step 5: Change the original PBFT consensus code, replace and test the validity of the consensus algorithm.

In summary, by properly constructing a suitable system such as hyperledger, a crowdsourcing camera model can be better operated.

3.4 Gradual transition to the token system

The crowdsourcing service model of the 'photographs and making money' is still an emerging niche industry. Therefore, in the current stage, efforts should be made to strengthen the publicity of such crowd-sourcing models and enhance the crowd-sourcing model's influence and popularity.

After the crowdsourcing operation model is more popular, it should be gradually transformed from the original common currency system to the token system. Using tokens such as Bitcoin [9] as a reward for rewards, there is no application at the beginning of the application of the token system, but only the currency equal to the exchange of labour for the replacement of the currency. The currency then shows its value elsewhere and is used as a currency of circulation. In the second phase, new applications emerged on this platform and new smart contracts emerged. At this time, there is a new possibility. Tokens can gain access to applications that come from their own platform, and then they will turn around in this sector. Then they must reward those who provide value for their uses. This forms a closed loop.

4 CONCLUSIONS

The generation of crowdsourcing camera models such as photo-taking and making money will further promote the development of the Internet and block chain. Through analysis, it can be seen that block chain technology has some obvious advantages for crowdsourcing operations, but at the same time, there are also many challenges. For the problems that may be foreseen, we have given the above suggestions for improvement.

REFERENCES

1. Axelrod, R., Cohen, M. Harnessing Complexity [J]. The Free Press, New York, 1999.
2. Halder, P., Das, S. H. JaSTA-2: Second version of the Java Superposition T-matrix Application [J]. Computer Physics Communications, 2017.
3. Agrawal, A., Catalini, C. and Goldfarb, A. The Geography of Crowd funding [J]. Social Science Electronic Publishing, 2011.
4. Armstrong, M., Wright, J. Two-Sided Markets, The New Palgrave Dictionary of Economics [M]. Basingstoke: Palgrave Macmillan, 2008
5. Nakamoto, S. Bitcoin: A peer to peer Electronic Cash System [EB/OL], 2016.
6. Nakamoto, S. Bitcoin: A peer-to-peer electronic cash system [OL]. https://bitcoin.org/bitcoin.pdf, 2008.
7. Aiello, D, Luca, D.D., Gionfriddo, E., Naccarato, A., Napoli, A., Romano, E., Russo, A., Sindona, G. and Tagarelli, A. Review: Multistage mass spectrometry in quality, safety and origin of foods [J]. European Journal of Mass Spectrometry, 2011, 17(1):2-3.
8. Satoshi N. Bitcoin: A peer-to-peer electronic cash system, 2008. https://bitco.in/pdf/bitcoin.pdf
9. Hyperledger [EB/OL], 2017. https: //www.hyperledger. org/

Upgrading Development and Application of Agricultural Information Service System Based on WeChat Public Platform——A Case of WeChat Public Platform of 12396 Beijing new rural sci-tech service hotline

WeiShui Yu[1,2], Qiang Guo[1,2]*, ChangShou Luo[1,2], YaMing Zheng[1,2],Lu Yang[1,2],FuRong Wang[1,2]

[1] Institute of Agricultural Information and Economics, Beijing Academy of Agriculture and Forestry Sciences, Beijing, 100097, China
[2] Rural Distance Information Service Engineering Technology Research Center of Beijing, Beijing, 100097, China

Abstract. The WeChat public platform is a new service platform based on WeChat applications that provides business services and user management for individuals, businesses and organizations. It provides a new solution to the lag of agricultural information dissem-ination in the traditional media. However, services based on Tencent's backend can only meet the basic needs of users and reduce the user's experience in agricultural science and technology consulting process. In order to provide efficient and convenient service to users and solve existing problems in consultation process, the platform-related API were used to upgrade the 12396 hotline WeChat public platform to an integrated agricultural information interactive service system. It mainly carries out the following three aspects to upgrade development. Firstly, 12396 hotline WeChat public platform added two sub-menu items, "use ask" and "expert answer" to push the user's question to expert directly, reducing the backend customer service's works and improving the efficiency of problem solving. Secondly, 12396 WeChat public platform upgraded and developed an integrated "one-stop" micro-site to allow users know the agriculture market timely, releasing supply and demand information, etc. Thirdly, the 12396 WeChat public platform combined initiative push information with the user's automatic acquisition of information by sending keywords which increased user selectivity. The upgraded platform has obtained a good preliminary application achievement and recognized and welcomed by users. Finally, we concluded and looked forward to the future development direction of agricultural mobile consulting.

1 Introduction

Under the background of the rapid development of modern information technology, new models of information services are emerging and strengthening agricultural information services will be one of the effective measures to solve the "three rural issues" [1]. According to "The 41st China statistical report on internet development" [2] released by the China Internet Network Information Center, by December 2017, the number of Internet users in China reached 772 million, among them 735 million people used the mobile phone to access the internet, accounting for 97.5%. With the continuous development of smart phones and the improvement of mobile phones application experience, the trend of mobile phones as the main Internet terminals for users has become more apparent. WeChat, an intelligent communication APP based on smart phones, is favored by users as it peer-to-peer information reception and transmission methods. According to the 2017 WeChat application report, there are 902 million people visit WeChat every day on average, with an increase rate of 17% year-on-year, meanwhile, the number of voice messages and video calls via WeChat increased significantly. With the development of mobile Internet, WeChat APP will become a cost-effective approach offering agriculture information for more and more farmers who use it.

1.1 The application status of WeChat public platform

The WeChat public platform is a new service platform based on WeChat applications that provides business services and user management for individuals, businesses and organizations. With its huge user base and rich API interface, the WeChat public platform is favored by many developers. Until now, the number of WeChat public platform has exceeded 20 million since it launched in August 2012, among which the agriculture related accounts were 5688, increased 10 times compared with that during 2012 to 2016 [3]. Under such a development trend, exploring an integrated agricultural service platform

* Correspondence author: guoq@agri.ac.cn

based on the WeChat public platform can increase the efficiency of agricultural science and technology information dissemination and improve the service accuracy to farmers.

1.2 The necessity of upgrading 12396 WeChat public platform

"12396 Beijing new rural sci-tech service hotline (abbreviation: 12396 hotline) " was established by the Rural Development Center of Beijing Municipal Science and Technology Commission and Beijing Academy of Agriculture and Forestry Sciences. It is a science and technology information service integrated platform for agriculture and provides agricultural technology information consulting services free with more than one hundred experts. The 12396 hotline WeChat public platform was opened in 2014 and accumulated a certain amount of users and reputation in the early stage. However, the services based on Tencent's backend system can only meet the basic needs of users. The following questions need to be addressed: Firstly, the backend of the WeChat public platform is mainly based on the PC side. If the expert wants to answer the question directly, he will go through all the consulting questions or through the secondary processing by the service personnel. As a result, the response efficiency is relatively low. What's more, the Tencent stipulates the replying time within 48 hours, reducing the flexibility of user consultation. Secondly, the number of front menu in the WeChat public platform is limited, so it is impossible to fully display all the service function. Thirdly, WeChat service messages can only be pushed 4 times per month with up to 8 messages each time, which relatively limits the interaction between WeChat public platform and users. In order to solve the above problems, 12396 hotline WeChat public platform was upgraded, combined with previous survey results and the experience in building process, operation and maintenance of the excellent agricultural WeChat public platform. After the platform upgraded, it will further improve service efficiency, optimize user experience, reduce service costs, accelerate publicity and promotion, and enhance brand image.

2 Upgrading development of WeChat public platform

2.1 Integration of user consultation and expert solutions to WeChat public platform

In order to improve the efficiency of the platform and reduce the difficulty of sorting out the agricultural technical problems, two external links, "user ask" and "expert answer", have been developed based on the 12396 hotline WeChat public platform, so that the users' questions can directly reach the expert without server's help. User can upload questions via "voice or text message" according to the agricultural field through "user ask" menu. The question was pushed to the expert who specialized in the corresponding fields. The expert can view the users' questions through the "expert answer" menu and can reply to the user's questions through mobile phone directly. Interfaces of the two menus are shown in Fig.1. Through these two external menus, users and experts can be connected directly, reducing unnecessary work in the middle and improving the efficiency of answering questions. In this way, it also avoids the problem that the WeChat public platform cannot directly interact with users after 48 hours.

Fig. 1. Interfaces of the "user ask" (left) and "expert answer" (right)

2.2 Development of micro-websites for comprehensive service on agricultural science and technology information

The WeChat public platform provides a framework for the user personalized interface settings. Each public platform can only set three first-level menus and each first-level menu can only have five sub-menus. To some extent, it limits the public platform function relatively, if not add external links. In order to facilitate users to understand the development of the agricultural industry quickly, 12396 WeChat public platform develops an integrated service platform, the micro site. Interface of 12396 WeChat micro website is shown in Fig.2, There are mainly six functions of micro websites, i.e., "expert introduction" "online consultation" "information to get rich" "Varieties information" "supply-demand center" "market information". Through the micro website, users can learn about the information on latest crop variety and agricultural products market development, release supply and demand information and browse all the users' questions, so as to fully understand the dynamics of the agricultural industry.

2.3 Combine user self-acquisition messages with platform-proactive push messages

The Tencent also stipulates the number of messages to be sent in WeChat service account with four times a month, eight messages each time. To a certain extent, this kind of regulation regulates the WeChat public platform and prevents information flooding. However, it also relatively limits the interaction between the WeChat public platform and users. Combined with the characteristics of Beijing-Tianjin-Hebei agricultural development, 12396 WeChat public platform developed the "vegetable artifact" for better user serving. By sending keyword or resource number, people can obtain relevant information about the varieties and technologies according to the platform prompt messages. This self-service information acquisition method has effectively enhanced the interaction between the WeChat public platform and users and optimized the user's consultation experience.

Fig. 2. Interface of 12396 WeChat micro-website

3 Promotion and application status

Compared with the APP, the WeChat public platform only needs to scan the QR code with WeChat instead of installing, therefore, the promotion cost is relatively low [4].In order to obtain target users accurately, the 12396 WeChat public platform mainly uses a combination method of "online + offline" to enhance its influence and serve more people continuously. Online promotion: mainly through the 12396 Beijing new rural sci-tech service consultation channels, including WeChat, websites, Weibo, QQ group and other channels, to introduce functions of the upgraded WeChat public platform and available services, etc. Offline promotion: the online users were increased through offline promotion ways such as the 12396 countryside training, 12396 community service and special presentations, science and technology weeks.

After the 12396 WeChat public platform was upgraded, the initial promotion effect is good. At present, there are more than 6,000 registered users, including individual farmers, associations or cooperative members, agricultural technicians, ordinary citizens, enterprises, institutions, and researchers. Among all registered users, Beijing has the most, accounting for 43%, Beijing-Tianjin-Hebei account for 50%, followed by Shandong province. User distribution area is shown in Figure 3. The upgraded function of "micro-sites and vegetable artifact" have also been favored and praised by users, with clicks and visits continuously increased. Consultation questions include agricultural technology, policy, information about achieving prosperity, and market information. Categories of users' consulting questions are shown in Figure 4.

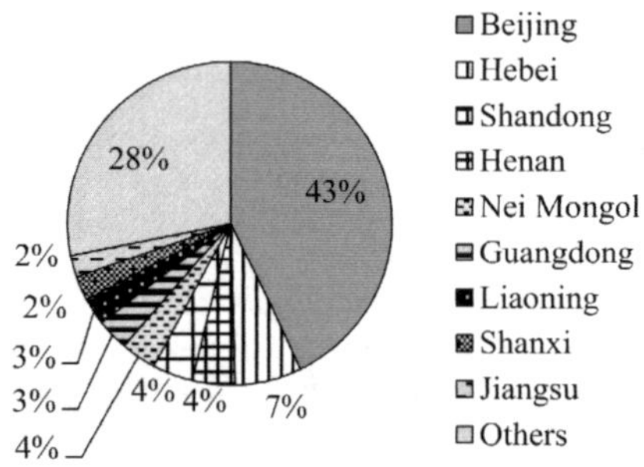

Fig. 3. User distribution area

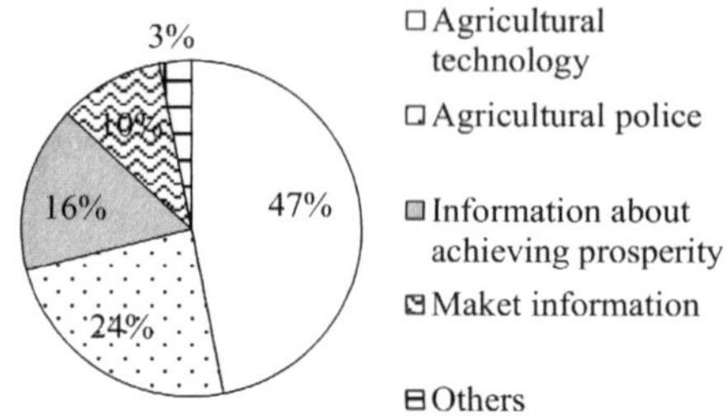

Fig. 4. Categories of users' consulting questions

4 Conclusion and outlook

The 12396 hotline WeChat public platform has upgraded as an integrated agricultural service platform by optimizing resource allocation, adding external links, to provide users with a better experience. In conclusion, we developed an agricultural information service mode based on WeChat public platform, constructed a kind of agricultural information service model for mobile applications, and provided an effective way for farmers to solve practical problems in agricultural production and management whenever and wherever.

With the continuous development of the WeChat public platform, new changes will also take place in WeChat-based agricultural science and technology information consulting services. First and foremost, agricultural science and technology consulting services will become increasingly intelligent [5].With the rapid development of science and technology, the trend of intelligent and automated mobile consulting services is becoming more and more obvious. Technologies such as intelligent voice and image recognition will be applied to agricultural science and technology consulting services. And we believe that the era of "AI+ agricultural technology consulting" will certainly be realized in the near future. Secondly, agricultural science and technology information consulting services will become more comprehensive [6]. The agricultural consulting service will be upgraded and developed into various aspects such as "buying, selling, asking, managing, and learning". It will not only provide agricultural technology information, but also show and sell new products and new technologies, to promote agricultural scientific research achievements to practical applications. Last but not least, the agricultural consulting service will integrate the advantages of new media, such as live broadcast, which characterized by good performance, rich content, strong interaction, and unlimited geographical areas. It can display the products, online survey, dialogue interview, and online training simultaneously, providing more convenient and efficient scientific and technological information services [7].

Acknowledgment

The research work was supported by the Beijing excellent talent project: Research on key technology of man-machine conversation in agricultural science and technology consultation and application of Beijing, Tianjin and Hebei, the international cooperation fund of BAAFS: A comparative study on the agricultural science and technology information service system in China, the United States and Canada, the 2018 Beijing financing agricultural funds: Application and demonstration of "Nongkexiaozhi" consulting service robot and WebAPP in agricultural production, the young scientist fund of BAAFS: Analysis of omnipotent agricultural technicians' training effect and relevant affecting factors in Beijing (NO.QNJJ201803)

References

1. Zheng, H. G., & Hai-Yan, H. U. (2005). On agricultural information service models and their role in "agriculture, rural area, and farmer". Journal of Library & Information Sciences in Agriculture. **17**, 2, 137 – 140 (2005).
2. CNNIC, The 41st China statistical report on internet development, (2017), http://cnnic.cn/gywm/xwzx/rdxw/201801/t20180131_70188.htm.
3. Deng, C. M., Liu, Y. Q., & Yu-Ping, L. I.. Agricultural information service research based on wechat——a case of wechat public platform of tropical agricultural science and technology service. Journal of Anhui Agricultural Sciences. **44**, 28, 237-240, (2016).
4. Tan Baibing. We Chat service analysis and Application inagricultural extension information dissemination [D]. Chongqing Normal University, (2016).
5. Shewei, X. U., Wang, D., Denghua, L. I., & Gao, L. Progress and outlook of china's "internet+" modern agriculture. Agriculture Network Information. **1**. (2017)
6. Zhang, H. F. (2014). Prospect of application of agricultural information service platform based on android intelligent mobile phone. Heilongjiang Agricultural Sciences. **8**, 126-128, (2014).

7. Bai, Y.. Application of traditional media to new media integration on agricultural information service. Agriculture Network Information, **11**, 55-57 (2014).

MATEC Web of Conferences **176**, 03017 (2018) https://doi.org/10.1051/matecconf/201817603017
IFID 2018

Big Data in Medical Research and Application

Teng Yilin [1], *Cao* Gaofang[1], and *Wang* Rui[1,*]

[1] Binzhou Medical University Binhai Road 346#, Laishan District, Yantai City, Shandong Province

Abstract. With the advanced instruments and information technology integrated in biomedical science more and more extensively, the advent of the big data era has had a significant impact on biomedical research, making human awareness of themselves and diseases more profound. The future medicine tends to combine data and medicine, to master gene database and medical human disease data, then to apply data statistics and analysis and application in healthcare. New techniques of big data in medicine are bound to make medical research and application more predictable. This paper introduces the main sources and characteristics of medical big data, points out the necessity of big data research in medical field, summarizes the current research in medical big data and its application in disease prediction, clinical assistance and pharmaceutical research and development. In other aspects, it analyses the problems of medical big data in applied research.

1 Introduction

With the development of information technology, the era of big data came since the rapid growth of data volume. At the beginning, big data refers to a set of data that are too large and complex for traditional data processing methods to deal with [1]. Later, big data tends to be the use of predictive analytics, user behaviour analytics, or certain other advanced data analytics methods that extract value from data, while seldom to a particular size of data set [2]. Nowadays, data resources become the same important strategic resources as natural resources, and it became the source of new inventions and new technologies as well. Although the data is priceless, but its value is like to extract the essential from a large mass of material. It means data fusion will produce far greater value than value of the single data [3].

The significance of big data is to provide "big insights ": collect information from different sources, and then analyse the information to reveal trends that cannot be found by traditional methods. Among all the industries which discover value from big data, medicine industry is likely to achieve the greatest return so that it is an important field about big data application. With big data, healthcare providers can not only know how to improve profitability and operational efficiency, but also find a way to promote human health level directly. How to develop and utilize the medical big data has become the focus of attention.

2 Medical Big Data

According to the International Data Companies (IDC), the big data market in China will increase five times in 2012 - 2016, where the largest portion of it will be concentrated in the four major industries of government, banking, medicine and telecommunications [4]. Groves P, Kayyali B et al. [5] put forward that big data will have an important influence on the American medical industry, and many potential values are gradually revealed. Eric [6] pointed out that big data would lead "creative destruction" to the entire medical system, including management and diagnostic. This kind of destruction may take place in medical clinical diagnosis data, such as medical images, records, examination, diagnosis and treatment expenses, etc.; it may also take place in drug research and development, epidemiological investigation, pathogenesis, physiological and pathological changes, etc. Thus big data in medicine tends to be direction of future medical development.

2.1 The concept of medical big data

In a 2001 research report and related lectures, META group [7] used "3Vs" model for describing big data, i.e. increasing volume (amount of data), velocity (speed of data in and out), and variety (range of data types and sources). Then De Mauro [8] added that "Big Data represents the Information assets characterized by

* Corresponding author: oucwangrui@163.com

such a High Volume, Velocity and Variety to require specific Technology and Analytical Methods for its transformation into Value". IBM cooperation expanded the 3Vs of big to more other complementary characteristics of:

Volume: big data doesn't sample; it just observes and tracks what happens

Velocity: big data is often available in real-time

Variety: big data draws from text, images, audio, video; plus it completes missing pieces through data fusion

Value: the value of the data is low relative. It means huge amounts of information, but low density value.

Veracity: data needs to be accuracy and trustable, that is, the quality of data.

On the premise of satisfying these basic characteristics of big data, data related to the medical and health service process and results can be called the medical big data.

2.2 The source of medical big data

The source of medical big data can be divided into medical data and health data. Medical data includes hospital clinical data, research data of institutions, etc.; health data includes public health monitoring data, personal health behaviour data, etc. **Table 1** shows the specific types of data sources

Table 1. source of medical big data.

	source	types
Medical data	Clinical medicine	Electronic medical records, medical images, inspection and detection reports, medical equipment testing, etc
	Pharmaceutical r&d	Clinical trials, drug research and development, medical equipment r & d
	Biomedical Science	Genomics, metabolomics, proteomics, etc
Health data	Public health	Population basic information, life death record, disease detection, nutrition health survey, health risk factors investigation, etc
	Personal health	Wearable equipment, household testing instruments, fitness sports records, drug purchase records and so on
	Health network	Health website or app behavior record, search engine, wechat micro blog, instant messaging, etc

3 Application of medical big data

3.1 Disease prediction

The trend of big data development is to overcome the shortcomings of traditional sampling survey which is unable to fully and accurately predict the results. Therefore, medical big data can be well applied to real-time biological monitoring and public health monitoring, public health monitoring includes infectious disease surveillance, chronic non-communicable diseases and related risk factors monitoring. In addition, the epidemic situation monitoring can be carried out through the large data of electronic medical records, and the epidemic of infectious diseases can be predicted through the network information.

In 2009, Google used to predict the spread of winter flu, and a wave of big data changes in public health. Recently, Google announced that Google X hatched a medical health project called "baseline", using big data to prevent cancer. The project is thought to be Google's most ambitious and most difficult project ever. "Baseline" uses the massive storage and computing power to bombard a very large amount of the gene and molecular information in the human body. According to the data statistics, the human body structure data of healthy people are obtained, and then the abnormality of the molecular level of the individual is found.

It can be noticed that multiple data fusion will lead to a variety of diseases prediction. In molecular biology, "Omics" mainly includes Genomics, Proteinomics, Metabolomics, transcriptomics, lipidomics, Immunomics, glycomics, RNAomics and so on. The root "-ome" translation is a collection of individual systems, such as genomics, which is a combination of all the genes in an organism. the subject is to study the genes and the relationships between these genes.

From public health and personal health data to the level of individual cell biology "omics".The use of big data mining, data fusion and data analysis methods can provide a comprehensive, new understanding of the occurrence and prevention of disease, also conduct to the prevention of individual diseases in addition.

The 2011 e. coli O104 incident in Germany caused worldwide concern. In the field of bacterial infectious diseases, new and emergent bacterial infections are particularly arrested. Genomics provides a new powerful technology in Screening and identification of infectious diseases, tracing of the source of infectious diseases, and variation of pathogenic factors. Data analysis for infectious disease shows that big data played a good performance.

Another case is Human Connectome project, which is a comprehensive map of neural connections in the brain. More broadly, a connectome would include the mapping of all neural connections within an organism's nervous system.

With the help of artificial intelligence, neuroscientists using machine learning system abroad, draw a map of the outermost equivalent unprecedented human brain, the subdivision of the cerebral cortex, identified the lines on each hemisphere of the brain, and split it into 180 cortex region, of which 97 area has not been described before, but now clarify the architecture, function, and the different between them.

The new map of the human brain by Glasser, M. F. et al. [9] using magnetic resonance imaging (MRI) scan of 210 healthy adults, using a variety of image data, combined with machine learning system. Figure 1 shows the human brain divided into discrete areas based on structure and function.

Research of "Human Connectome" could investigate the association between brain network and cognitive change caused by dementia, schizophrenia or related genetic characteristics and clinical symptoms. It enhances the understanding of the pathogenesis of neuropsychiatric diseases, the characteristics of brain damage and the mechanism of brain reorganization, and provides a scientific basis for the prevention, diagnosis and early treatment of these diseases by utilizing the big data of MRI and other materials.

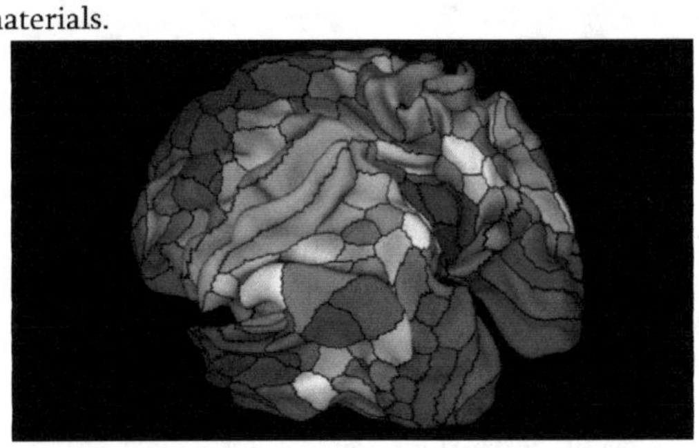

Figure 1: Map of human brain

3.2 Clinical assistance

Medical big data can assist clinical decision, it can improve diagnosis efficiency and treatment quality. The most advanced application of medical big data assistance is "precision medicine"[10]. Precise medical treatment, also called personalized medical treatment, refers to a customized medical model, which is based on personal genomic information, combining with relevant environmental information such as proteomics and metabonomics, and designing the most proper treatment scheme for patients, so as to achieve the maximum therapeutic effect and minimize side effects. Figure 2 shows that medical big data of Genomics can predict the treatment effect. It can be found that when there are two "G"s in the gene, the treatment would be effective, and only one "G" would lead to the non-effectiveness. What's more, if there is none "G", the patients would suffer severe side effect.

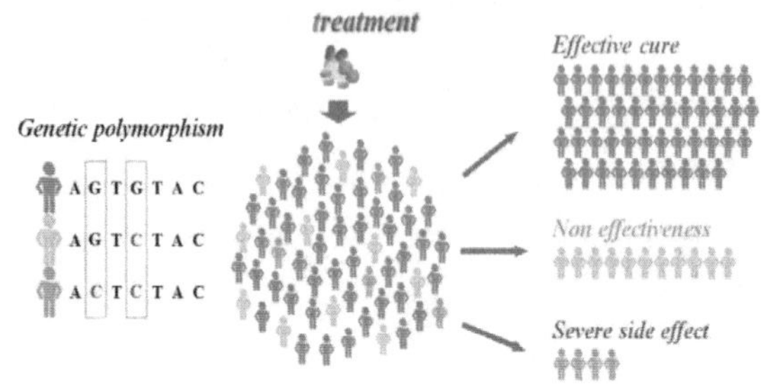

Figure 2. Treatment effect prediction

The evidence-based method of traditional medicine in our country is watch ,hear, ask and touch, even though the birth of medical image provides a deeper basis for doctors' diagnosis, it is still a sampling method. Doctors can get information only from the surface of individual patients, thus the experience is likely to be more important on the accuracy of disease judgment. Furthermore, the existing technology accurate medical image resolution to 3mm, but it is hard for human eyes to extract more widely distributed information. In other hand, the big data techniques can realize the same homogenous disease affect data reconstruction, such as low resolution reconstruction, 3D reconstruction, feature (texture, histogram, image entropy) analysis, then obtain more accurate information of the focus.

We take cancer treatment as an example; doctors could only see the institutional information from CT films, while this information reflected a little. And the accuracy rate is about 30%. But if we use big data according to the clinical pathology and image data of more than 500 cases, extraction characteristics, modelling analysis, the accuracy of front-end data prediction can reach 70 %. In other words, the doctor can reduce the past mistakes from 70 % to 30 %. At the same time, big data can aid doctor's select which is the most effective method for cancer treatment.

3.3 Pharmaceutical R & D

Using data from a group of people with a particular disease can quickly identify biomarkers associated with the occurrence, prognosis, or therapeutic effects of the disease. Big data makes the pathogenesis of ethology and disease more in-depth understanding, full use and is able to accelerate drug screening process.

The prediction model of biological processes and drugs becomes more complex and widely used. By using molecular and clinical data, predictive modelling can help identify potential new molecules that are highly likely to be developed successfully as drugs. Meanwhile there are more channels to recruit accuracy patients into clinical trials, such as social media. Screening criteria for clinical trials will also take into account more factors such as genetic information to target specific populations, so that clinical trials can be smaller, shorter, and less costly and more effective.

4 The problem of medical big data

The research and application of medical big data in medical treatment is very necessary, while at the same time, there are some problems in the application, which can be summarized as follows:

4.1 Data sharing

Data sharing is the basic of the application of medical big data, it should be paid attention that how to break the data island and avoid data use for only a few people or organization. It is necessary to realize the standardization of medical data, which is the premise of data sharing. Data sharing can effectively carry on data integration and data fusion, and obtain more valuable information.

4.2 Data security

How to store and manage data effectively and safely. The volume of medical data is large, the update speed is fast, and because of individual differences, the data is not repeatable, and involves the patient privacy, data security and proper management is strongly demanded.

4.3 Data analysis

How to effectively analyse, integrate and mine data, especially the semi-structured and unstructured image data are the difficulties and challenges of big data analysis. Big data applications require team collaboration, besides technology, data sources. It needs the inter-disciplinary talent who can not only master data mining, parallel computing algorithms, but also understand of biomedical knowledge. Thus, to promote the development of the interdisciplinary of computer science and biomedicine is conducive to the future development of medical big data application that

5. Conclusion

The arrival of big data era has penetrated into varies industries of life. There are a huge amount of data in medical field, its significance not only lies in the amount of data, but also in the deeper value obtained through the processing of these data. The development of medical treatment is also constantly shifting to data-driven, to obtain the optimal decision and program. In general, the development of medical big data is still in the early stage, how to share, standardize, manage and develop these valuable data is the key. Medical big data will change the medical practice mode, improve the quality of medical and health service, and ultimately benefit the medical purpose of individualized treatment and group prevention.

References

1. Snijders, C.; Matzat, U., Reips, U.-D... 'Big Data': Big gaps of knowledge in the field of Internet. International Journal of Internet Science(2012)
2. Viktor Mayer-Schonberger, Kenneth Cukier. *Big Data: A Revolution That Will Transform How We Live, Work and Think.* John Murray Publishers, London (2012)
3. Zhao Guodong, Yi Huanhuan, Mi Wanjun. *Big Data Revolution: How Data Science Changes the World* Tsinghua university press , Beijing.(2013)
4. Groves P, Kayyali B, Knott D, et al.. *The big data revolution in healthcare.* Accelerating value and innovation. Mckinsey & Company.(2013)
5. Inmon W..*Building the data warehouse.* John Wile y & Sons Inc, New York (2002)
6. Eric J. Topol *The Creative Destruction of Medicine Basic Books*,New York (2012)
7. Laney, Douglas. *3D Data Management: Controlling Data Volume, Velocity and Variety* . Gartner.
8. De Mauro, Andrea; Greco, Marco;.Grimaldi, Michele. "A Formal definition of Big Data based on its essential Features". Library Review.(2016)
9. Glasser, M. F. et al. Nature (2016) http://dx.doi.org/10.1038/nature18933 .
10. National Research Council, Toward Precision Medicine: Building a Knowledge Network for Biomedical Research and a New Taxonomy of Disease (NRC,2011)

MATEC Web of Conferences **176**, 04001 (2018) https://doi.org/10.1051/matecconf/201817604001
IFID 2018

Research on the application of color semantics in the human-computer interaction design of smartphones

Bao Xiaoxiao[1] and Liu Wenming[1, a]

[1]School of Design and Art, Shenyang Jianzhu University, 110168 Shenyang, Liao Ning, China

Abstract. To evaluate the user experience in the human-computer interaction design of intelligent products, the quality of color design is a key factor. The purpose of this article is to design the human-computer interaction in smart phones through the study of color semantics, which is one of the branches of product semantics. In particular, the application of color semantics in UI design would help designers better meet user's needs and improve user's experience in the human-computer interaction design of smart products.

1 Introduction

Nowadays, smart phones have become one of the most important terminals for people to receive information, and the use of smart phones has also become indispensable as a forward position. How can we capture users better and faster and give users more perfect user's experience? Human-computer interaction design has become the key to this problem. In the human-computer interaction and UI design, what does the user first feel ? It must be one of the most important elements in visual information--color. The purpose of this paper is to study one of the branches of product semantics--the application of color semantics in smart phone UI design, so as to help designers to better meet user's needs in human-computer interaction design and improve user's experience. [1]

2 The concept of color semantics

"Semanteme" originally refers to the meaning contained in the language, "Semantics" is the discipline that studies the meaning of language, and "Product Semantics" refers specifically to the study of the language meaning of a product. It was the designers who combined the knowledge of the study of language and product design. [2] Product Semantics believes that products should not only have physical functions, but also be able to explain or instruct how to use them. At the same time, products should also have a symbolic meaning and can constitute a symbolic environment in people's lives. In other words, product semantics considers not only physical and physiological functions but also psychological, social, and cultural contexts. Its purpose is to make the product a medium for communication and expression, conveying meaning through the use of styling, texture, material, and color.

In the product semantic system, it contains many elements such as form, color, material and technology. Among these elements, color is the most perceptual element of human visual perception. Color itself is a combination of matter and spirit. It is a perception, a real feeling, not an abstract idea or concept.[3] The color experience begins with the psychological response brought about by the stimulation of light. Therefore, color is a very complex combination of physical and psychological. The process of human perception of color has to go through three phases - physically, psychologically, and culturally, or it is going through three levels -- feeling level, association level, symbol level. Different colors will give people different stimuli, which will lead to different psychological feelings and visual sensations, it may be passionate, depressed, may be warm like in spring or cold like in winter, may be grand and solemn, or light and small; People's life experience will also lead to different emotional associations driven by different colors. Under different cultural backgrounds, colors will also have different cultural symbols.

Color semantics, as the name implies, is to study the significance of color, its core content is: how to accurately convey color information with specific meanings to users in the design, and let users have intuitive and accurate understanding of products through the design colors. Make products not only meet the functional requirements of users, but also meet their psychological needs.

3 Status of smartphone UI design

Interaction design is the field of design that defines and designs artificial system behavior. It defines the content and structure of the interaction between two or more interacting individuals so that they can work together to achieve a certain purpose. The goal of interactive system design can be analyzed from two levels ——"usability" and "user's experience", focusing on people-oriented user's needs. UI design is one of the most important

Corresponding author: [a] Liu Wenming:83373734@qq.com

aspects of human-computer interaction design. UI design means the design of user interface. It refers to the overall design of the software's human-computer interaction, operation logic, and interface aesthetics [4]. It is mainly divided into hardware UI design and software UI design. The scope of the discussion in this paper is smartphone software UI design.

The UI design of smart phones has begun its journey since the invention of the world's first commercial mobile phone in 1973, in the United States, by Martin Coupe, the Motorola engineer. After continuous innovation and development, UI design has gradually become a specialized cross-discipline through comprehensive research on visual experience, psychological experience and erconomics. The style of design has also been gradually transformed from the early "skeuomorphism" design to the "flat" design. [5]It has transformed the human-machine interaction style that simulates natural texture into a simpler color combination style that is more modernistic, which can better improve user's experience and understanding.

4 Combinations in Design Practice

In the smartphone UI design, colors are more prominently and intuitively perceived by the user than texts and images. After experiencing different color experiences in daily life, users will accumulate corresponding color semantics, and will also have different physiological and psychological responses to different color stimuli. Therefore, in the UI design of smartphone, it is not only possible to simply stay in the color and aesthetic point of view to design, but to more deeply combine the relationship between color and the product itself and the experience it brings to the user. Then it will achieve the unity of form and function. This paper have divided the application of color semantics in smartphone UI design into three aspects: functional, emotional, and cultural. Through these three different aspects of research and discussion, we hope to help designers more clearly understand the relationship between color semantics and smartphone UI design practices.

4.1 Functional aspect

Functional aspect is a top priority in smartphone UI design. When facd with a group of interfaces, how can users find the required information in the first time, learn the direction of the next operation step, and understand what the designer wants to express. All these visual information that users want to understand and designers want to convey is the most important manifestation of functionality in color design. The excellent smartphone UI design can timely convey visual information, accurately express functional semantics, reduce the user's learning cost, and make the interface easier to operate, so that let user feel comfortable and free. The specific requirements mainly include the following points:

First, the interface style must be unified, designers should choose the main color for different products. For example, shopping software usually uses red and orange for their main color, because the color semantics of them are bright, exciting and happy, it can stimulate the user's excitement, so as to achieve the purpose of promotion.

Second, the function partition must be clear, designers should colorize the interface according to the software's different functional groups. In the case of figure 1, the designer divided different functional areas with color patches of different hue, while the high light area is used for prompting user information, and the low lightness is used for displaying general information.

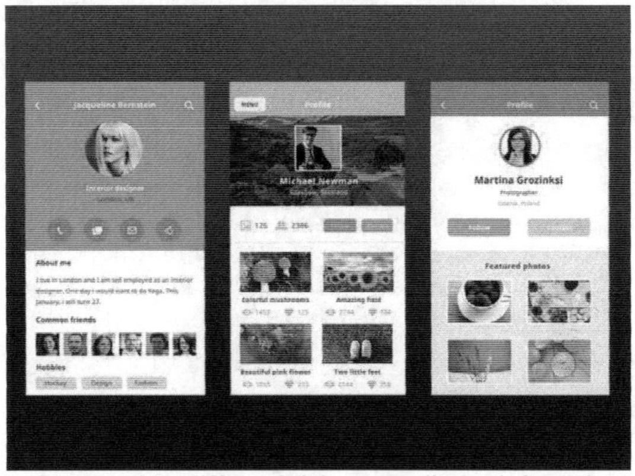

Figure 1. Use different brightness to display information.

Third, the information must be explicitly graded, designers should distinguish colors based on the primary and secondary information content. For instance , in a news and language software with a large amount of information, you can use the repetition, contrast and gradient color changes to mark, distinguish and emphasize information, which enables users to navigate the interface more logically.

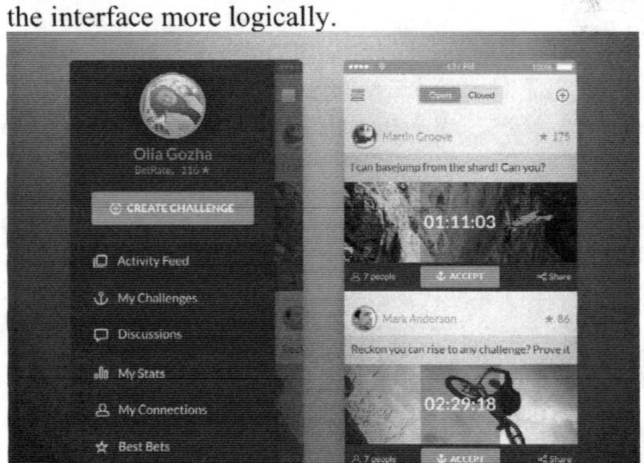

Figure 2. Use color changes to highlight

Fourth, highlight the key modules, according to the color changes the software needs to use. As is shown in figure 2, buttons, guide keys and other modules can be emphasized using contrasting colors, giving the user a visual sensation of jumping to achieve an immediate effect.

4.2 Emotional aspect

"Color evoke emotions, express emotions, and even affect our normal physiological feelings." [6] American art psychologist Blumer said. So, in smartphone UI design, color design needs to focus on the user's emotional factors. Users of different ages and genders have different understandings and feelings about colors. For example, most children prefer bright colors such as red and yellow, black is the most unpopular one. When it comes to adults, most people who prefer blue color are introverted, more literary, and calm down; those who love yellow are outgoing and pursuing ideals; those who love green are mostly decisive and self-respecting; those who prefer red are mostly enthusiastic, impulsive, and enterprising. Therefore, according to the software's target population for the corresponding color design, not only can it better display the software content, but also stimulate the user's psychological resonance, winning the user's heart recognition. In addition, color will also give users psychological feelings such as cold, warm, light, strong and weak, hard and soft, etc.; different hue will lead to a difference between gorgeous and simple feelings; changes in lightness will cause differences in lightness and melancholy; different Purity leads to different feelings of comfort and fatigue. These should all be considered in the UI design of smartphone.

4.3 Cultural aspect

According to archeological data, humans in ancient times had already had a certain understanding of color and given different meanings in different colors. With the historical development and accumulation, different colors have gradually become manifestations of different nationalities, regions, and individual lifestyles. That is to say, colors are artificially endowed with nationality, nationality, and regional characteristics, and become an important aspect of human civilization. Components and established a unique color cultural system.

For example, in ancient China, yellow was the exclusive color of the emperor, it represented the center of the azimuth; cyan represented the east of the azimuth and symbolized the righteousness and sacredness; red represented the south and symbolized fiery and happy; black stands for the North, symbolizing righteousness, selflessness; white represents the West, symbolizing killing and silence and so on. But in Western culture, white is a symbol of purity; rose is a representative of passionate love; red represents danger and revolution and war; black even more, represents death and disaster. Therefore, when designers understand the cultural nature of color design, in the UI design of smart phones, it is necessary to select the color of the design according to the user's different cultural attributes.

5 Summary

By combining the inherent properties of color with the inter-organizational structure of colors, and the expression of cultural attributes, the color semantics form the ever-changing language form. These linguistic forms exhibit a variety of color properties based on people's different ways of understanding. Color is the most important visual language in the smartphone UI design. In order to achieve the best results while mastering basic color design capabilities, designers must deeply understand the influence of color semantics on user psychology and brand effect, then comprehensively combine all factors for flexible matching. This would greatly make the theme and content of the software more easily to be recognized and memorized by the user, it also brings a higher artistic appeal and the best visual experience to users.

References:

1. Li Zenhua, Li Xuelin, Li Yuanzhi. J SHENYANG U T, **01**, 8-10(2006)
2. Bao Hong, *Proceedings of the 2007 International Conference on Industrial Design*, **Volume 1/2**, 3 (2007)
3. Luo Qiao, Design , **15**, 36-37(2017)
4. Huang Yafei, J YANGZHOU P C, **15(03)**, 21-23(2011)
5. Sun Minghai, Tan Haoxiang, Design, **07**, 34-35(2016)
6. Liu Minlu, Li Lun, J YILI NORMAL UNIV (Nat Sci Ed), **04**, 77-79(2009)

Research on the impact mechanism of user satisfaction with Software as a Service

Shuwen Li[1,2,a]

[1]Hohai University, 210098, Nanjing, Jiangsu, P.R. China
[2]Jiangsu University of Science and Technology, 212003, Zhenjiang, Jiangsu, P.R. China

Abstract. Software as a Service(SaaS)has become a mainstream way for enterprises and governments to promote informatization. However, it is very easy for users to change their SaaS supplier due to low implementation costs. Improving user satisfaction with SaaS products and ensuring their continued usage by users present practical challenges that SaaS suppliers cannot ignore. The traditional information system success model only pays attention to the quality of products which is known as internal quality. This paper combines the internal quality features of SaaS with the suppliers' quality and environmental quality. These two qualities constitute external quality, which also affect user satisfaction. The study comprehensively explores the impact mechanism of SaaS user satisfaction based on the integrated perspective of internal quality and external quality. We use SPSS23.0 and SmartPLS to examine the hypothesis with data from 212 valid questionnaires. The study finds that system, information, service, supplier, and environmental quality have a significant effect on user satisfaction, and the influence of service quality is the greatest.

1 Introduction

With the emergence of cloud computing technology and the rapid spread of service-oriented thought, software as a service (SaaS) provides a new service mode. This is one of the most widely used applications in cloud computing. SaaS has become a mainstream way for enterprises and governments to promote informatization, but the future of SaaS suppliers' enterprise development is not promising. Many SaaS suppliers' companies such as Yunio and Fleetmatics have either closed down or been acquired. The reason for this is that compared with traditional authorization software, SaaS no longer needs the infrastructure construction and maintenance operation software, users use a very flexible payment model for SaaS services, the start-up costs are very low, and the SaaS deployment cycle is short; hence, it is convenient for users to replace their SaaS provider. SaaS suppliers should therefore understand how to gain a competitive advantage in the fierce market, make users be willing to adopt SaaS services that suppliers provide, and understand the factors influencing user satisfaction with SaaS products.

The information system success model, proposed by Delone and McLean, has been widely used in the field of information management. This model aims to create a comprehensive classification basis to evaluate the success of information systems, including service quality, information quality, and system quality, which are together referred to as internal quality, which affects consumers' intention to use a system, their usage behavior, and satisfaction. However, compared with the traditional information system, the implementation cost of SaaS is very low, thus users can change SaaS suppliers easily. If suppliers want to let users continue to use their SaaS product, only considering internal quality of their SaaS products is not enough, they also need to consider the quality of the SaaS supplier, and environmental quality, which together constitute external quality. The SaaS users, when facing a new SaaS services, will not be familiar with the new SaaS, then the supplier's quality and the environmental quality will directly affect consumers' satisfaction with SaaS.

This article is based on the information system success model considering the internal quality of products, the external supplier quality, and the influence of environment quality on SaaS satisfaction. The employees of three manufacturing companies who use the SaaS service serve as the research subjects. A questionnaire survey was used to collect data, and a partial least squares structural equation model was used to analyze the data. Through the above work, we expect to understand the influencing mechanism of user satisfaction with SaaS, provide corresponding countermeasures for SaaS suppliers, and promote the development of social informatization.

2 Research model and hypothesis

Combining internal quality with external quality,the theoretical model of users' satisfaction with SaaS is

*Corresponding author: [a] 511065089@qq.com

shown in figure 1.

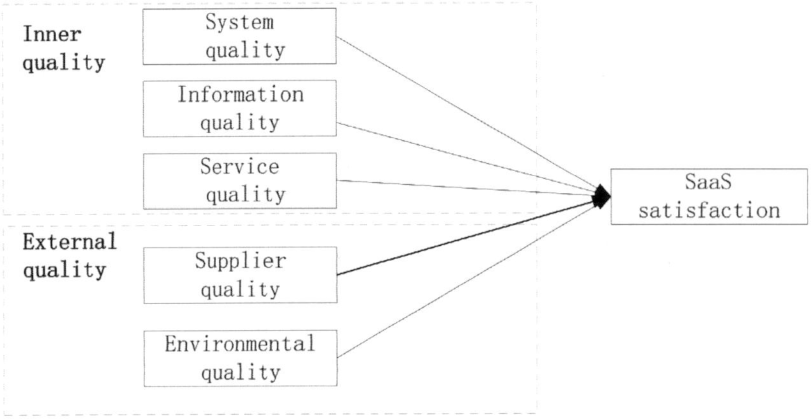

Figure 1. Research model

2.1 Internal quality

System quality refers to the characteristics or the expected performance of information systems, including three indexes: functionality, ease of use, and flexibility[1]. Functionality means the ability for a user to use SaaS to complete tasks, and it is the most basic requirement of SaaS. Ease of use is a vital quality of SaaS software. SaaS is an innovative product for users in the early implementation stage. Easy to use software allows users to quickly master the method of utilizing the software, and improves the work performance. Flexibility embodies the users' personalized configuration requirements of SaaS, how SaaS can fit in with work tasks and users' habits. Thus, the well-designed SaaS systems with high quality are not only simple and practical, but also satisfy users' demand, and are bound to promote users' satisfaction with SaaS. Therefore, we propose the following hypothesis:

H1:System quality has a positive impact on users' satisfaction with SaaS.

Information quality refers to the output of a quality information system[1], which includes three dimensions, they are accuracy, completeness, and timeliness[2]. Specific to SaaS information quality, accurate and complete information can improve users' trust of a system, and users are willing to continue to use the system. Timeliness means the SaaS system can respond to the demands of users in a timely manner. If SaaS systems can not provide persuasive, high quality information to meet the needs of users, the latter will be dissatisfied with the system. Therefore, we suggest the following hypothesis:

H2:Information quality has a positive impact on users' satisfaction with SaaS.

Service quality is defined as the difference in degree between the standardization of service that customers expect and users' perception of service performance. This article selects responsiveness and reliability as SaaS service quality indicators. Responsiveness means the ability of suppliers to ensure a timely response in providing service support[3]. A SaaS service can have multi-tenant architecture; however, If the users' scale is large, the service will possibly be delayed. This results in a decrease of SaaS responsiveness, which affects the service quality. In addition, the users' data is stored at a data center in a SaaS system, which means that the users can not control their data directly. Thus, the users' concern about the SaaS reliability will be higher than traditional licensed software. Therefore, we put forward the following hypothesis:

H3:Service quality has a positive impact on users' satisfaction with SaaS.

2.2 External quality

Supplier quality of SaaS, includes reliability, brand awareness, advertising, etc. SaaS as a commercial product, also has brand awareness, degree of advertising, and other external properties. In fact, as a result of SaaS belonging to the category of information products, users can not determine its quality before consumption, so users tend to use external attributes to determine the value of the products; a higher reliability, brand awareness, and advertising of a SaaS supplier, means a higher supplier quality. Thus, the users' confidence in the supplier will also increase. Users would choose the SaaS products which are provided by trusted suppliers[4-6]. Therefore, we put forward the following hypothesis:

H4:Supplier quality has a positive impact on users' satisfaction with SaaS.

Environmental quality is also a key external quality that will affect users' satisfaction with SaaS. Environmental quality includes network performance, environmental security, and the social effect[7,8]. SaaS services need a higher requirement of network performance. A bad network performance will affect the users' experience of SaaS. In addition, SaaS is an innovative service mode; therefore, for more conservative masses, the safety of the environment has a direct influence on whether they are willing to use SaaS. Finally, users' consumption behavior will also be impacted by other users' consumption behaviors in society; Ajzen defines this impact as a social factor[8]. An increase in the SaaS social effect will promote the users' identification with identity of SaaS. Therefore, we put forward the following hypothesis:

H5:Environmental quality has a positive impact on users' satisfaction with SaaS.

3 Research methods

3.1 The questionnaire design

According to research models, we designed the questionnaires to contain six constructs: system quality(SyQ), information quality(IQ), service quality(SeQ), supplier quality(SuQ), environmental quality(EQ), and SaaS satisfaction(SS). The latent variables and their measurement items are shown in table 1. These items mainly stem from existing literature. Each item is measured on a seven-point Likert scale: 1 represents "strongly disagree" and 7 represents "strongly agree".

Table 1. Variables and measuring items

Construct	Item	Reference
SyQ	①SaaS operation stability	[1]
	② I can use the functions of SaaS easily	
	③SaaS can flexibly adjust to cope with my diverse needs	
IQ	①SaaS can provide accurate information for me	[2]
	②SaaS can provide complete comprehensive information	
	③The information I need can be obtained from SaaS at any time	
SeQ	①SaaS can provide rapid service	[3,9]
	②SaaS can be relied on	
SuQ	①My SaaS service provider can be relied on	[4-6]
	②My SaaS service provider is a big brand	
	③I can often see the SaaS service provider's ads	
EQ	①My network environment can implement SaaS smoothly	[7]
	②Existing regulations of SaaS can protect my interest	
	③The people around me are willing to use SaaS	
SS	① I feel satisfied about the SaaS	[10,11]
	② SaaS satisfies my needs	
	③ I would be happy to use SaaS	

3.2 Data collection

We collected the data from three enterprises which implemented SaaS services. They served as the research subjects. With the help of the human resource management unit of the company, we selected 300 employees and managers who use SaaS to complete the survey questionnaires. A total of 264 complete responses were obtained. We then used SPSS23.0 to delete outliers, and finally obtained a total of 212 valid questionnaires. Basic investigation statistics of this study show that male users accounted for 64.28%, while female users accounted for 35.72%. Additionally, 86.42% of users were aged under 30 while the remaining 13.58% were aged over 30.

3.3 The reliability and validity analysis

The SmartPLS software was used to analyze the collected data. The reliability test results are shown in table 2. All the multi-item factor loadings were greater than 0.7. The structure of Cronbach 's alpha and component reliability (CR) are greater than 0.7; this shows that the reliability of scale is good.

Table 2. Confirmatory factor analysis results

Construct	Item	Factor loading	T Value	CR	Cronbach's alpha	AVE

Construct	Item	Factor loading	T Value	CR	Cronbach's alpha	AVE
SyQ	SyQ1	0.839	22.309	0.834	0.702	0.626
	SyQ2	0.748	9.111			
	SyQ3	0.783	15.343			
IQ	IQ1	0.785	22.488	0.819	0.708	0.601
	IQ2	0.731	16.647			
	IQ3	0.806	24.907			
SeQ	SeQ1	0.746	13.151	0.757	0.701	0.601
	SeQ2	0.813	21.587			
SuQ	SuQ1	0.845	33.328	0.846	0.727	0.648
	SuQ2	0.732	16.861			
	SuQ3	0.833	43.357			
EQ	EQ1	0.853	30.829	0.851	0.742	0.657
	EQ2	0.778	15.805			
	EQ3	0.799	26.064			
SS	SS1	0.871	58.591	0.875	0.786	0.700
	SS2	0.805	16.306			
	SS3	0.834	34.151			

In addition, the structures of the Average Variance Extracted(AVE) were greater than 0.5, which means that the scale has good convergent validity (see table 2). Each structure was greater than the square root of AVE values below it, when compared with other structure correlation coefficients. This shows the discriminant validity of the scale (see table 3) is good.

Table 3. Discriminant validity analysis

Construct	SyQ	IQ	SeQ	SuQ	EQ	SS
SyQ	0.791					
IQ	0.553	0.775				
SeQ	0.358	0.534	0.775			
SuQ	0.570	0.659	0.547	0.805		
EQ	0.339	0.600	0.616	0.534	0.811	
SS	0.602	0.669	0.691	0.723	0.694	0.837

3.4 Structure model analysis

We used the Bootstrap algorithm (N = 1000) to calculate the value of multiple correlation square values (R^2); this estimates the path coefficient of the structural equation and the significance test. The results of this model are shown in figure 2. The results show that this model has a good explanation power ($R^2 = 0.756$), and all the path coefficients between latent variables are effective. The results show that:

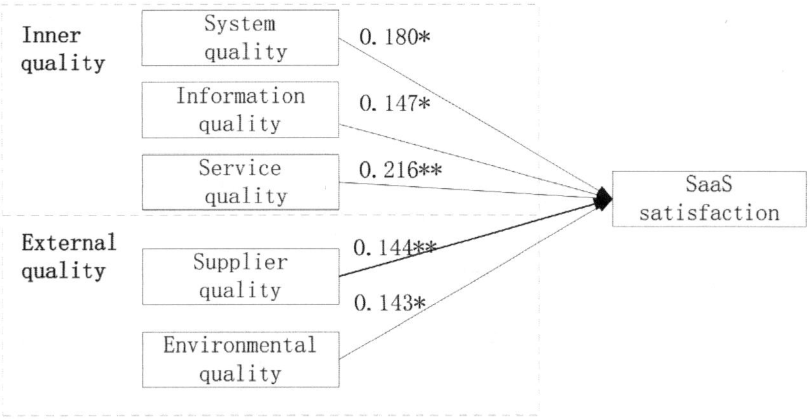

Figure 2. Structure model analysis results

The correlation coefficient between system quality and SaaS satisfaction is significant; therefore, hypothesis H1 was supported;

The correlation coefficient between information quality and SaaS satisfaction is significant; therefore, hypothesis H2 was supported;

The correlation coefficient between service quality and SaaS satisfaction is significant; therefore, hypothesis H3 was supported;

The correlation coefficient between supplier quality and SaaS satisfaction is significant; therefore, hypothesis H4 was supported;

The correlation coefficient between environmental quality and SaaS satisfaction is significant; therefore hypothesis H5 was supported.

4 Conclusion and discussion

Our results show that the proposed five hypotheses of this model are supported, and SaaS service quality is the main factor which influences satisfaction (path coefficient = 0.216); this is because when compared to traditional authorized software, the SaaS mode is delivered over the network, and the multi-tenant feature of SaaS makes it more prone to congestion. Thus for SaaS users, service quality is an important factor that affects their satisfaction. In addition, as SaaS is essentially a software product, users need to use specific functions of SaaS to realize the real true utility of SaaS, therefore, information quality and software quality are also important factors that influence satisfaction. Moreover, supplier quality will also affect users' satisfaction with SaaS. Supplier quality indirectly influences users' perceived quality of SaaS products provided by the respective supplier, and users will choose products sold by well established brands, which they trust. Additionally, the better the external environment for users using SaaS, the higher the user satisfaction with SaaS.

This paper innovatively integrates internal quality and external quality into a whole framework, and explores the mechanism of influencing user satisfaction with SaaS from a comprehensive perspective. According to the results of this study, the implications for management practice are as follows: (1)SaaS providers should pay great attention to service quality, information quality, and software quality of SaaS. SaaS suppliers should meet the needs of users, develop SaaS products that have practical value, and at the same time, pay attention to construct infrastructure with the corresponding quality of service, to ensure that users can enjoy uninterrupted and timely service, and use fluent software. (2)SaaS suppliers need to pay attention to their publicity as well as that of their SaaS products. On the one hand, fully publicizing their ability can improve the perceived quality of suppliers, while on the other hand, enterprises need to take measures to improve the users' security awareness of SaaS, so that users can fully accept SaaS products, and thus improve the quality of the environment.

In this paper, there are a few limitations, which can be addressed in future research. First, we did not distinguish the differences during the whole SaaS life cycle. In fact, in the market at present, most SaaS providers have adopted a strategy of free trial. The life cycle of a user flows through the following stages: watching, trial, buy, use and continued use, so the factors that influence users' satisfaction may have somewhat changed, and future research can focus on the dynamic change of users' satisfaction. Secondly, this paper has not yet considered other external factors such as government support, and how government policy will affect users' adoption of SaaS products, so future research can be integrated with external government policy support to establish a more realistic model.

References

1. Gündoğdu M Ç. Re-thinking Entrepreneurship, Intrapreneurship, and Innovation: A Multi-Concept Perspective[J]. Procedia-Social and Behavioral Sciences, 2012, 41: 296-303.
2. Huh Y, Keller F, Redman T C, et al. Data Quality[J]. Information and Software Technology, 1990, 32(8): 559-565.
3. Benlian A, Koufaris M, Hess T. Service Quality in Software-as-a-Service: Developing the SaaS-Qual Measure and Examining Its Role in Usage

Continuance[J]. Journal of Management Information Systems, 2011, 28(3):85-126.

4. Benlian A, Koufaris M, Hess T. Service Quality in Software-as-a-Service: Developing the SaaS-Qual Measure and Examining Its Role in Usage Continuance[J]. Journal of Management Information Systems, 2011, 28(3):85-126.
5. Walsh G, Kilian T, Buxel H. Assessing the Consumer Perceived Value Scale[J]. Advances in Consumer Research, 2008, (35):688-689.
6. Brodie R J, Whittome J R M, Brush G J. Investigating the ServiceBrand: A Customer Value Perspective[J]. Journal of Business Research, 2009, 62(3): 345-355.
7. Balasubramanian S. Customer Satisfaction in Virtual Environments: A Study of Online Investing[J]. Management Science, 2003, 49(7): 871-889.
8. Ajzen I. The Theory of Planned Behavior[J]. Organizational behavior and human decision processes, 1991, 50(2): 179-211.
9. Alali H, Salim J. Virtual Communities of Practice Success Model to Support Knowledge Sharing Behaviour in Healthcare Sector[J]. Procedia Technology, 2013, 11: 176-183.
10. Urbach N, Smolnik S, Riempp G. An Empirical Investigation of Employee Portal Success[J]. The Journal of Strategic Information Systems, 2010, 19(3): 184-206.
11. Fleischmann M, Amirpur M, Grupp T, et al. The Role of Software Updates in Information Systems Continuance — An Experimental Study from A User Perspective[J]. Decision Support Systems, 2016, 83: 83-96.

https://doi.org/10.1051/matecconf/201817604003

User acceptance of m-banking application: Indonesian cases

Yovita Arifiani[1] and Ari Widyanti[1,a]

[1]Department of Industrial Engineering, Bandung Institute of Technology (ITB), Labtek 3 Ganesa 10 Bandung, Indonesia

Abstract. M-banking is one of the emerging banking facilities lately. Indonesian bank has been offering m-banking services for several years. However, the use of Indonesian m-banking users is still not as expected. This study aims to observe user acceptance of Indonesian m-banking application using the approach of Technology Acceptance Model (TAM). 205 participants are involved in this study voluntarily by filling out the user acceptance questionnaires with regards to two different m-banking application from bank A and bank B. Result shows that Indonesian banks need to give more promotions related to its m-banking, especially about the usefulness, the security system, and the risk that may be faced by the consumers.

1 Introduction

M-banking, or often called m-banking, is a commercial application on smartphones that accommodate the users in doing bank transactions whenever and wherever [1]. The use of m-banking itself is influenced by the development of the latest mobile phone technology, the smartphone. Compared to the internet banking as the previous banking service, the m-banking is superior in terms of its practicality, because m-banking can be accessed anywhere and anytime, without the need of a hard token.

In Indonesia, it was recorded that almost half of 126 banks have initiatives or have already offer m-banking services in 2010 [2]. However, the increasing number of the use of Indonesian m-banking is below the expectation due to several reasons, one of them is the issue of user acceptance.

User acceptance in relation to information technology is defined as the willingness of a user to use certain information technologies [3]. The concept of user acceptance itself emerged upon the increasing competitiveness of innovations in information technology. The user acceptance issue is particularly important since in reality, users are not always accept new technologies, even the new technology is supposed to be more sophisticated and useful than the others [4].

Various models have been proposed to evaluate user acceptance. One of the most widely used models is the Technology Acceptance Model (TAM) developed by Davis [5]. In this model, there are two factors that are most influencing the acceptance and adoption of a technology, namely perceived usefulness and perceived ease of use. Perceived usefulness is defined as the degree to which a person believes that using a particular system would enhance his or her job performance. While perceived ease of use is defined as the degree to which a person believes that using a particular system would be free of effort [5].

In relation to m-banking, Munoz-Leiva et al. [6] modify TAM by adding 3 other factors, namely social image, perceived trust, and perceived risk. The social image is defined as the level of which one can gain the respect of the surrounding environment when using a particular m-banking[7]. The perceived trust is a person's expectation that his with m-banking will not take advantage of him [8]. While perceived risk is defined as risk in relation with the innovations in m-banking [9]. These factors will then affect the attitude, which is the form of acceptance or rejection, and finally led to the intention to use as can be seen in Figure 1.

This study aims to observe user acceptance of Indonesian m-banking using approach of the Technology Acceptance Model (TAM), as an effort to increase the number of m-banking' use in Indonesia.

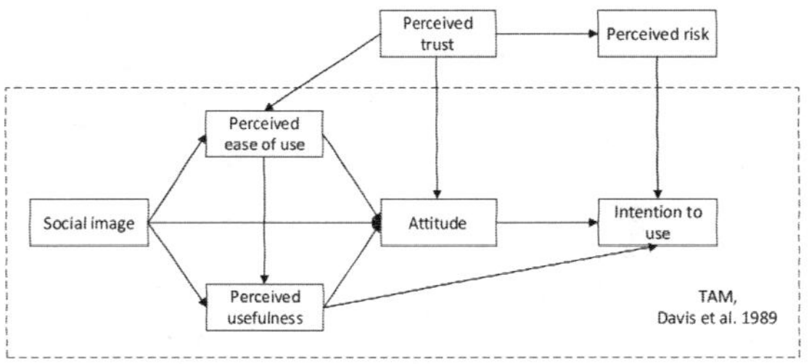

Figure 1. The m-banking acceptance model (source: Munoz-Leiva et al., 2016)

2 Method

205 respondents (mean age = 21.5 years, SD = 3.4 years) are involved in this study voluntarily. The sample of

[a] Corresponding author: widyanti@mail.ti.itb.ac.id

respondents is chosen based on a convenience sampling. The respondents can be classified into 3 groups: the user of m-banking A, the user of m-banking B, and non-m-banking users (new users).

User acceptance data are obtained using a set of questionnaire ([5], [6]), which consists of 21 statement items, with Likert-type scales ranging from 1 (strongly disagree) to 7 (strongly agree). Before user acceptance and usability questionnaires are used, the reliability and validity of the questionnaire have been checked. For the reliability test, a Cronbach's alpha indicator is used with a limit value of 0.7. Meanwhile, for validity test, Spearman correlation coefficient value with 95% confidence level is used.

3 Result and analysis

Since the data is a nominal data, the median value is used for subsequent processing. Participants' responses data to the user acceptance questionnaire are then tested using Mann-Whitney U Test in order to see whether there is a significant difference between the groups of participants. From the results of median calculations and significance tests, there are significant differences in some factors, namely perceived usefulness, attitude, perceived trust, and perceived risk, as can be seen in Table 1.

For social image factor, all three groups of participants give a fairly low score that is in the range from 2 to 3. This can lead to the conclusion that m-banking A has a bad social image. In this case, it means that using m-banking A is not a prestige thing and m-banking A is not a status symbol to participants. This condition can be explained by the fact that various banks in Indonesia have already offered m-banking services, so using m-banking from a particular bank tends not to make someone feel exclusive. To be able to improve and enhance the social image, bank A can offer new features in m-banking applications that do not yet existed and offered by other banks. By being a pioneer in a feature, m-banking A can gain exclusivity and attract target users' attention.

For perceived ease of use factors, there are no significant differences between the responses of all three groups of participants, the median value of participants' responses are in the middle-up scale. This shows that m-banking A is considered quite easy to use, but this condition can be improved. One thing that bank A can do is to create a tutorial on how to use the application, which appears on the first use of the application. This recommendation is proposed based on some participants' difficulties experiences.

Overall, perceived usefulness is also considered good enough by the participants, but significant differences between m-banking A and non-users responses show that non-users participants feel that m-banking A is not as useful as how m-banking B. This condition can be improved by doing marketing activities in the form of campaigns, promotions, and others. From research conducted by [16], it is found that marketing has a significant impact on the adoption of m-banking. Banks that do marketing actively, earn an average adoption rate 2 times higher than banks that do not. Through marketing, a bank can educate potential users about m-banking features, transactions that can be done, and what benefits can be gained.

For perceived trust, the median value of the participants' responses has shown a fairly good level of trust, but significant differences between m-banking A and non-users responses are found. It shows that non-users of m-banking have a low level of trust, compared to both m-bank A and B level of trust. To improve this condition, the bank can also take advantage of marketing activities, e.g. by using testimony from m-banking users.

The same result is also found in the perceived risk. The non-users responses for perceived risk are the highest among 2 other groups of participants, which indicates that non-users participants feel that using m-banking is a risky option. Some participants also stated the reason for not using m-banking is due to security issues, since m-banking applications connected with mobile phones that can be easily lost and misused. Same as previous factors, to improve perceived risk, a bank can explain m-banking's security system, what risks may be faced, and mitigations that can be done.

Median values from three groups of participants for attitude factor are in the range from 5 to 6. These results indicate that the three groups of participants have a good attitude towards m-banking. There is 1 significant difference, that is between m-bank A and m-ban B which indicate that m-bank B feel that using m-banking is not a thoughtful idea compared to using m-banking that is currently being used.

For intention to use, median value of both groups of participants' responses are in the range from 5 to 6. It can be concluded that both groups of participants have a big intention to use m-banking A if they are given access to the bank. However, m-banking A is not the main choice in choosing m-banking.

Factors	**Median value**			**Significance test result (*: significantly different)**		
	Bank A	*Bank B*	*non-users*	*Bank A – Bank B*	*Bank A and non-users*	*Bank B and non-users*
Social image						
The use of m-banking have more prestige than those who do not use them	2	2	3	-	-	-
The use m-banking have a higher status	3	2	3	-	-	-
Using m-banking is a status symbol in my environment	2	2	2	-	-	-
Perceived ease of use						
Using m-banking is clear and understandable	5	5	5	-	-	-
Using m-banking requires mental effort (thinking, making decision, counting, memorizing)	4	3	4	-	-	-
I find that m-banking is easy to use for any need	6	5	5	-	-	-
In general, m-banking is easy to use	6	5	5	-	-	-
Perceived usefulness						
Using m-banking can help my banking transactions	6	6	6	-	*	-
Using m-banking increase the effectiveness of my banking transactions	6	6	6	-	*	-
In general, m-banking can be useful for my banking transactions	6	6	6	-	*	-
Perceived trust						
I think that bank will keep their terms and commitment applied to m-banking application	6	6	5	-	*	-
I think that m-banking is reliable	6	6	6	-	*	-
In general, I trust m-banking	6	5	6	*	*	-
Perceived risk						
Other people might know my online transactions if I use this application	3	3	4	*	*	*
There is a significant risk when making my queries and/or banking transactions through m-banking (R2)	3	3	4	-	*	-
I believe that making queries and/or banking transactions with this application is a risky choice	2	3	4	-	*	*
Attitude						
Using m-banking is a thoughtful idea	6	5	5	*	-	-
Using m-banking is an interesting idea	6	5	5	-	-	-
I am happy to use m-banking	6	5	5	-	-	-
Intention to use						
Assuming you have access to m-banking, you intend to use it	6	6	6	-	-	-
If I have access to m-banking in a few months ahead, I believe that I will use it	6	5	5	-	-	-

Both attitude and intention to use can be improved by improving the five previous factors. This is because based on the research of [5] that 5 other factors will directly affect the attitude and intention to use. Therefore, if other factors have been improved, it can also improve the attitude and intention to use m-banking.

4 Conclusions

M-banking A acceptance level is quite low and can be improved by various factors. Several things can be done to improve this level of acceptance, that are creating new innovative features that can enhance the exclusivity of m-banking A and by doing marketing activities with greater emphasis on the benefit of using m-banking, security factors, and risk factors. This marketing activities also can be used to increase the awareness level of non-users. The marketing activities itself also needs to be done through an appropriate channel such as various kind of social media.

This research has many limitations and can be further developed in the future. User acceptance analysis can be further conducted by finding which factors that are the most influential to user acceptance level. By knowing which factors that are most influencing, the bank can more focus on making improvements and development. In addition, research can also be further developed by reviewing other transaction functions in m-banking or reviewing other banking services such as internet banking, SMS banking, etc., so that the bank can improve overall performance, not only in m-banking.

References

1. S. K. Chitungo and S. Munongo, "Extending the Technology Acceptance Model to m-banking adoption in rural Zimbabwe," *Journal of Business Administration and Education*, vol 3, no. 1, pp. 51-79, 2013.
2. International Finance Corporation. (2010). M-banking in Indonesia. [Online]. Available: http://www.ifc.org/wps/wcm/connect/1a5695804723d0248b21ab2b131bed2a/Mobile%2BBanking%2BFinal%2BReport.pdf?MOD=AJPERES
3. A. Dillon, "User acceptance of information technology," in *Encyclopedia of Human Factors and Ergonomics,* W. Karwowski, Ed. London: Taylor and Francis, 2001.
4. J. Bradley, The technology acceptance model and other user acceptance theories. IGI Global, 2009, pp. 277-294.
5. F. D. Davis, "Perceived usefulness, perceived ease of use, and *user acceptance* of information technology," *MIS Quaterly,* 13, no. 3, pp. 319-340, 1989.
6. F. Munoz-Leiva, S. Climent-Climent, and F. Liebana-Cabanillas, "Determinants of intention to use the m-banking apps: An extension of the classic TAM model," *Spanish Journal of Marketing-ESIC*, vol. 21, no. 1, pp. 25-38, 2017.
7. C. P. Lin and A. Bhattacherjee, "Extending technology usage models to interactive hedonic technologies: A theoritical model and empirical test," *Information System Journal*, vol. 20, no. 2, pp. 163-181, 2010.
8. D. Gefen, E.Karahanna, and D. W. Straub, "Inexperience and experience with online stores: The importance of TAM and trust," *IEE Transactions on Engineering Management,* vol. 50, no. 3, pp. 307-321, 2003.
9. P. Gerrard and J. Cunningham, "The diffusion of internet banking among Singaporean consumers," *International Hournal of Bank Marketing*," vol. 21, no. 1, pp. 16-28, 2003.

Study on Man-machine Design of Armoured Vehicles Operation Space

Du Hemin [a], Wang Ting

Xi'an Technological University, Xi'an, Shaanxi 710021

Abstract. This paper proposes an improved armoured vehicle control room based on ergonomic theory and computer-aided design technology to create efficiency by improving panel layout and seat design. Current design of existing control rooms that do not maximize ergonomics can create operator fatigue and user error. Optimal control room design was created by considering console size, console layout, and user seat dimensions and were entered into JACK software for simulation tests.

1 Analysis of interior design of armored vehicle control room

1.1 Control Room Design Factors

Because the design of the armoured vehicle requires two operators in a limited space, it is critical to design the work area to maximize efficiency, personnel comfort so that the two operators can do their jobs without any impediments to their movements.

The design of the user's console is particularly critical because this space is limited where both of the operators will spend most of their time performing duties.

In response to both operators working long hours in the armoured vehicle performing duties, the console and control panel design in addition to the location of visual displays must be created so that the operators can quickly process information and respond to it while remaining physically comfortable at the same time.

1.2 Manipulator Design Requirements

The purpose of the control room is to observe data and use instruments on the console and visual displays. Console room design can be broken up into three elements: interior structural design, console layout and size, and seating design. All three elements are indispensable and should be considered equally in order to create the most efficient work space in the armoured vehicle.

The ergonomic variables to optimally design the control room are: The instruments and consoles should be within the operators' visual range and require little movement during operation, maximize quick and correct interpretation of the data, and minimize operators' movements and communication in response to the data.

2 Armored car control room design principles

2.1 Visual Domain Design Principles

The range of vision of the seated operator can be divided into four viewing zones according to the speed of recognition of the visual signals by the human eye while the head remains still. The viewing zones include the central viewing zone, the best viewing zone and the effective viewing zone. The optimal design of the control panel should completely fall into the best and effective views.

The range for the best viewing zone is 15° and 20° horizontal in the direction of the plumb bob. The recognition effect of the best range allows the operator to recognize the data quickly and effectively. The range of effective viewing zones is 10° between to 30° in the direction of the plumb bob, and 30° in the horizontal direction. The recognition effect of this range is that the operator needs to concentrate and take more time to recognize the data than the best viewing range

2.2 Panel layout and colour design and design principles

The location of buttons and joysticks on the control panel should be coordinated and prioritized based on operational sequence, importance or frequency of use. In the case where there are many buttons, the arrangement should be consistent with their function and should remain in the operator's best vision range.

Alert mechanisms should be designed to immediately catch the operator's attention so that the operator can identify and react to the threat in a timely and effective manner.

The colour of the buttons on the operation panel should be classified according to the purpose. For example, red indicates danger, Stop, prohibit, Green indicates safety, normal operation, and so on. In addition,

* Corresponding author: [a] author@e-mail.org

the symbols, such as the code numbers used to indicate the functions, are located above or on the sides of the manipulation buttons or joysticks, and white and black are suitable.

2.3 Seat design principles

Ergonomic variables that go into the seat design are appropriate materials and the shape of the seat should conform to the contours of the human body. In addition, various seat designs should take into account the physiological needs of the human body that creates a reasonable spatial distance from the control console.

2.3.1 Seat height analysis

The height of the seat surface refers to the vertical distance between the horizontal surface of the seat to the ground. The height of the seat surface should make the position of the thighs line up with the seat horizontal and be parallel to the ground. The lower leg should remain naturally vertical and the soles of the feet should rest comfortably on the ground, ensuring that the lower body is comfortable and relaxed while the operator is performing tasks. Reducing back Muscle pressure can also be accomplished by making sure, so the chair is not too low to the ground for the operator.

2.3.2 Seat width analysis

The width of the seat surface of the chair is often narrower in front and wider than the width of the seat. The width of the front edge of the seat is wide before sitting, and the width of the back edge is wide after sitting. The width of the seat should allow the hips to be fully supported and have adequate room for movement to facilitate the sitting position of the seated person. In general, the width of the seat surface should be wide enough for the operator to comfortably execute a wide variety motions in performing tasks.

2.3.3 Seat depth analysis

The seat depth mainly refers to the distance from the leading edge to the trailing edge of the chair surface. The depth of the seat surface has a great effect on the sitting posture of the human body. Seat depth should meet three conditions: sufficient support for the buttocks; proper support of the back by the backrest; proper distance between the front edge of the seat and the lower leg to ensure the thigh The muscles are not pressured and the legs are free to move.

Therefore, the chair seat surface depth must be moderate in a seat design. If the chair surface is too deep and exceeds the horizontal length of the thigh, the backrest will cause the position of the back to have a large inclination, causing muscle fatigue in the lower back and thighs. In addition, if the depth of the seat surface is too shallow, a numbness of the leg or knee can result.

2.3.4 Seat lumbar support and inclination analysis

The waist of the seat should fit the waist of the human body perfectly and give the human body good support. It can effectively relieve the fatigue of the waist caused by sitting down for long periods of time. The lumbar support has no pressure point on the human body, which has a positive effect on the lumbar pain.

3 armored vehicle control room design basis

3.1 Console width

As the armoured vehicle control room is subject to space constraints, and the operator is mostly male, the size of the male encompasses 95% of all sizes men and is selected as the numerical basis for the console design.

The overall size of armoured vehicle control room space is: 1482*1427*1320 (mm), and two operator control consoles and access doors are also required. The maximum shoulder width of 95% of men in the horizontal dimension of the human body is 469mm. Sitting width of elbow and shoulder: 489mm, plus or minus 8mm. Based on the above values and combined with the space size and layout design, the widths of the No. 1 operator station and the No. 2 operator station are all calculated to be 489+8*2=505(mm).

3.2 Control console and display device height

3.2.1 Console height

The height of the control console and display equipment in the control room must conform to two variables: the height limitation of the overall space and the height of operator to maximize comfort and range of motion in the limited space.

The measurement of 95% male males knee height while sitting was selected: 532mm with an error of 25-38mm. therefore, the height of the console was determined as: 532+38=570(mm).

3.2.2 Display device height

The operator of the armoured vehicle needs to use two display devices at the same time to complete tasks. Due to the limited space of the control room, the layout of the display devices is set to the up and down layout mode, and the display device uses the 19-inch display.

19-inch screen size is: 376.8 * 301.4mm, the main display height is: 301.4mm * cos10 ° = 296.8mm, the secondary display height: 301.4 * cos20 ° = 282.8mm (Figure 1) Shown), the sum of the two results in a total height of 579.6 mm for both screens.

According to the height of the console and the height of the display device, the total height of the console is: 579.6+570=1149.6 (mm).

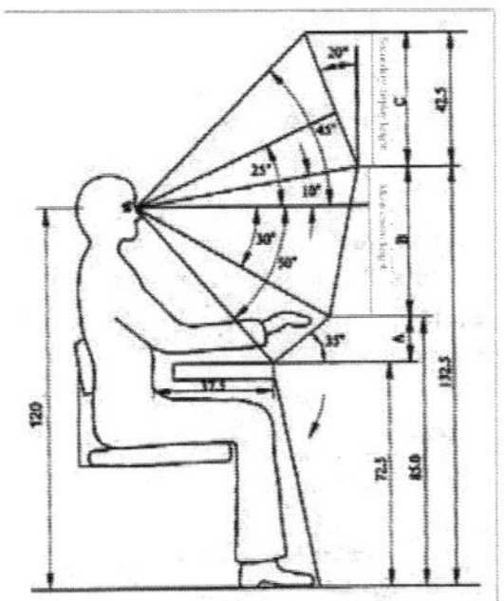

Figure 1. Screen size

3.3 Console seat size

3.3.1 Seat height

The mean length of the 95% male leg is: 403mm. This value of 403mm is. The adjustment of the range of activity and comfortable position of the body parts. The comfort range of the calf to the thigh falls between 95° and 120°. This value is assigned to the variable α. As shown in Figure 2, we will finally get the seat height h. The calculation process is as follows:

Because, β=5°, α∈ (-95° ~ -120°) , So, Ω∈ (-10° ~ -35°)

β=5°, α∈ (-95° ~ -120°) , therefore, Ω∈ (-10° ~ -35°)

L1=403, Ω∈ (-10° ~ -35°) this results in, h1∈ (396.88 ~ -330.12mm)

L1=403, Ω∈ (-10° ~ -35°) , therefore, h1∈ (396.88 ~ -330.12mm)

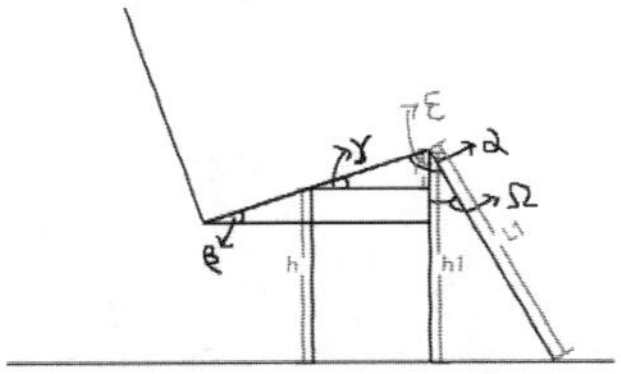

Figure 2. Seat height calculation example

It is known that γ=β=5° and it follows that ε=85°. The seat depth in the main parameters of the work seat ranges from 360 to 390 mm. Finally, the value range of L is 17.06 to 15.75 mm. The seat height range calculation process is:

396.88-17.06=379.82; 330.12-17.06=313.06

396.88-15.75=381.13; 330.12-15.75=314.37

It can be concluded that the seat height of the armoured vehicle control room ranges from 313.06 to 381.13 mm. In addition, if it is a step less adjustment seat, it is a file every 20mm.

3.3.2 Seat width

Male seated hip width (284mm ~ 369mm), 95% of the male seat hip width correction value is: 13mm, obtained: seat width ∈ (297mm ~ 382mm)

Because the seat width (370mm-420mm) is the main parameter of the seat, the width of the seat should not be too wide. The width of the shoulder should be the comfortable posture of the natural arm. Therefore, the seat width in the armoured vehicle should be: 395mm.

3.3.3 Seat depth

The main parameters of the work seat in the seat squat (360mm ~ 390mm), seat inclination ∈ (0 ° ~ 5 °), obtained, armoured vehicle seat depth calculation process for the seat range: 360 * cos 5 ° = 31.5mm, 390*cos5 ° = 34.12mm, seat depth ∈ (31.5mm - 34.12mm).

3.3.4 Seat lumbar support and inclination

The main parameters of the work seat in the lumbar long range: 320 ~ 340 mm, take the recommended value of 330 mm;

Waist width range: 200 ~ 300 mm, take the recommended value of 250 mm;

Lumbar thickness range: 35 ~ 50 mm, taking the recommended value of 40 mm;

The height of lumbar support is: 165-210 mm;

Waist radius of the arc is in the range of 400-700 mm, taking the recommended value of 550 mm;

The lumbar inclination angle ranges from 95° to 115° and the recommended value is 110°.

4 Design and Simulation Analysis of Armored Vehicle Control Room

4.1 Design scheme

Based on the data obtained from the above calculations on the dimensions of the control console, a control room model was established, shown in Figures 3, 4, and 5. Because the height of the operator has a certain variance, so the seat is adjustable (Figure 4) to account for the height difference between the operator and the height of the sitting position.

Figure 3. Manipulation room interior overall display

Figure 4. Control room left area display

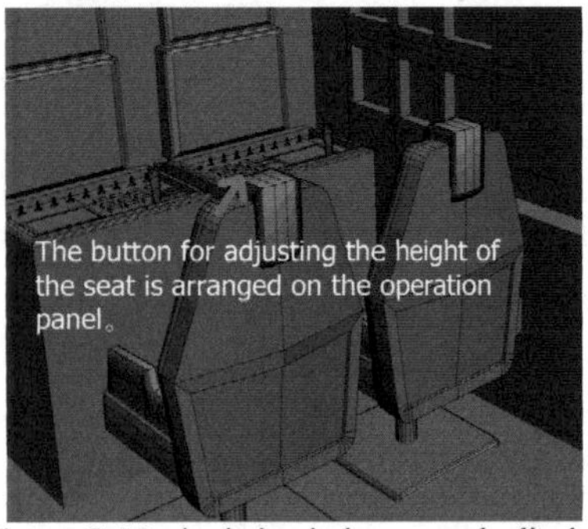

Figure 5. Manipulating indoor console display

4.2 Human Machine Simulation

(1) Armoured Vehicle Operator Visual Field

The visibility of the displays and control panels in the armoured vehicle control room must be considered. In order for the visual displays to be effective, they must be clearly seen by the operator. However, the speed and accuracy with which the armoured vehicle operator reacts to the display varies depending on the position of the display device in the operator's field of vision.

Figure 6 shows the visual field of the operator sitting on the left, where the purple area is the operator's right-eye viewable area and yellow is the operator's left-eye viewable area. As shown in FIG. 6, the left operator's visual range can cover the operation panel and the display device it controls.

Figure 7 shows the visual field of the right operator, where the pink area is the operator's right eye viewable area and purple is the operator's left eye viewable area. As shown in the figure, the visual range of the right operator can also cover the operation panel and display device it controls.

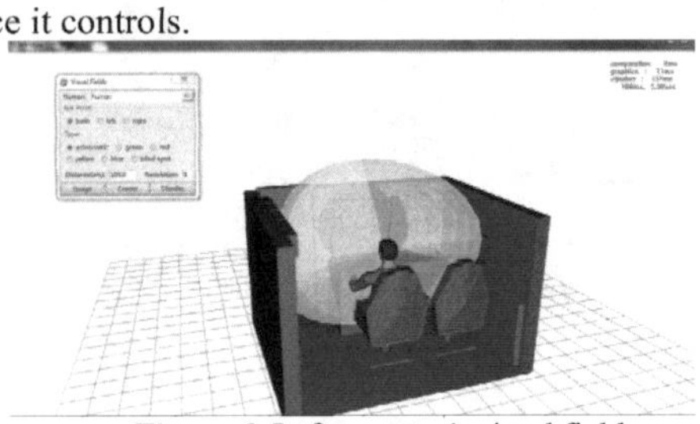

Figure 6. Left operator's visual field

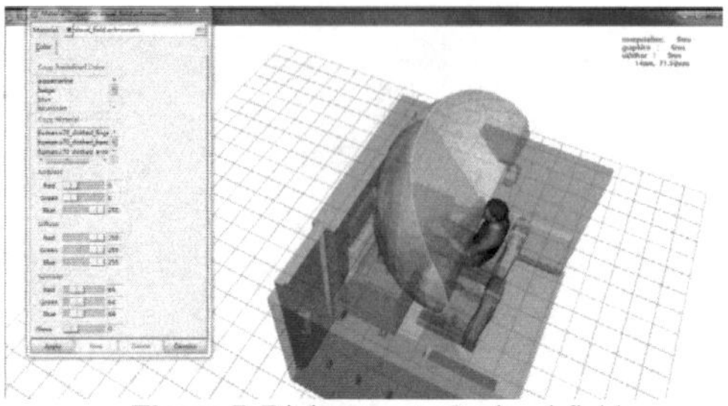

Figure 7. Right operator's visual field

Achievable accessibility of armoured vehicle operators

Figure 8 The coverage of the green area is the reachable domain of the left-hand operator's left hand. As shown in the figure, based on the above table, the operator's left-hand reachable domain is within reach.

Figure 9 The coverage area of the blue area is the reachable domain of the right operator's right hand. As shown in the figure, based on the above calculation data, the operator's right hand reachable domain is within reach.

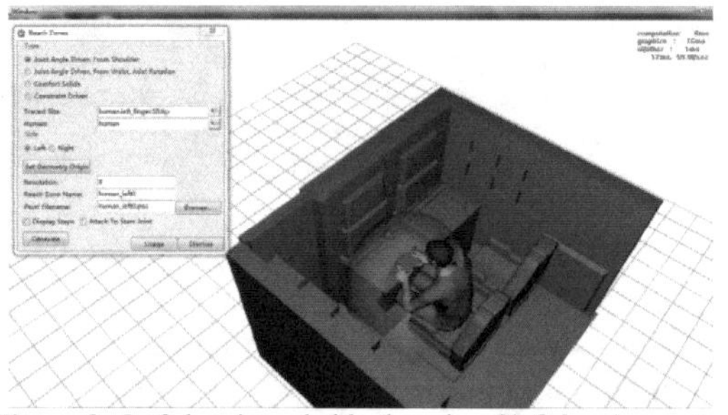

Figure 8. Left-hand reachable domain of left-hand operator

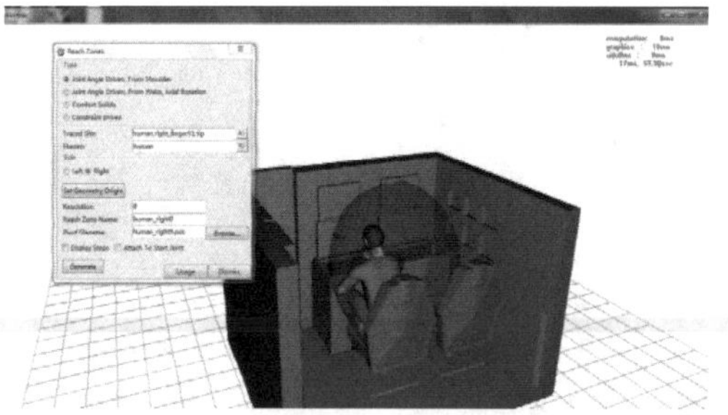

Figure 9. Right-hand reachable domain of left-hand operator

Figure 10 The coverage area of the red area is the reachable domain of the right-hand operator's left hand. As shown in the figure, the left-hand reachable domain of the right-hand operator is within the reachable range based on the above-mentioned measured data.

Figure 11. The coverage area of the red zone is the right-hand operator's right-hand reachable domain. As shown in the figure, the right-hand reachable domain of the right-hand operator is within the reach of the operator station based on the above measured data.

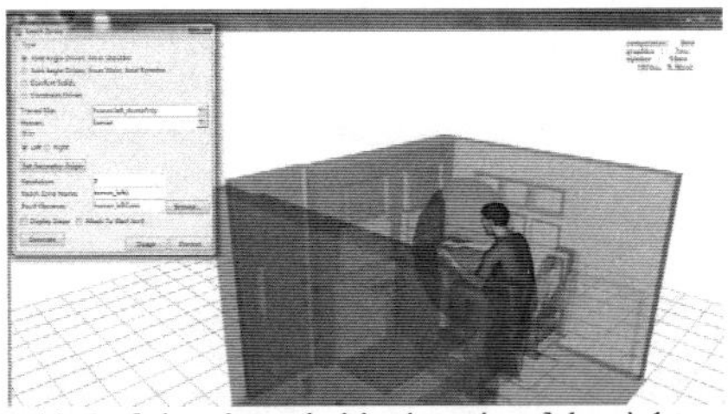

Figure 10. Left-hand reachable domain of the right operator

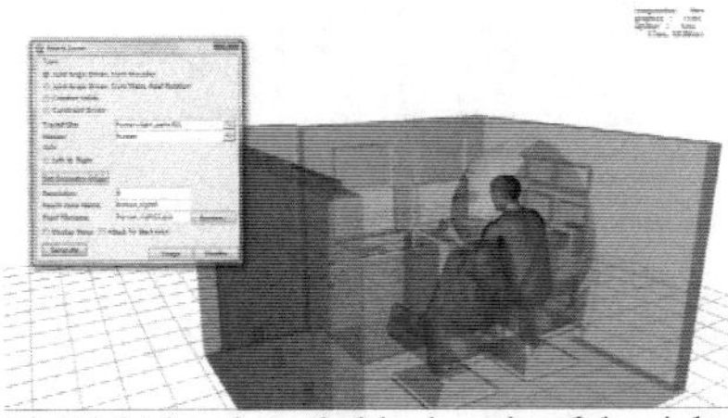

Figure 11. Right-hand reachable domain of the right operator

The comfort of armoured vehicle operators

In Figures 12 and 13, the High and Low values in the message box are the end points of the interval satisfying the operator's comfort requirements; the values shown by Value indicate the comfort calculated according to the position of a certain position; The numerical value indicates the theoretical optimum value of operator comfort in the same posture. When the Mode value goes to Low or High, comfort deteriorates.

Figure 12 shows the comfort level of the left-side operator. As shown in the figure, according to the above-mentioned calculation data, the comfort level of the left-side operator during the normal operation is within the comfortable range.

Figure 13 shows the right operator's comfort test results. Due to the limited space of the control room, the comfort level of the left and right arms of the operator sitting on the right side is displayed in yellow, that is, the operator's right and left arm's comfort is only at the comfortable edge during normal operation.

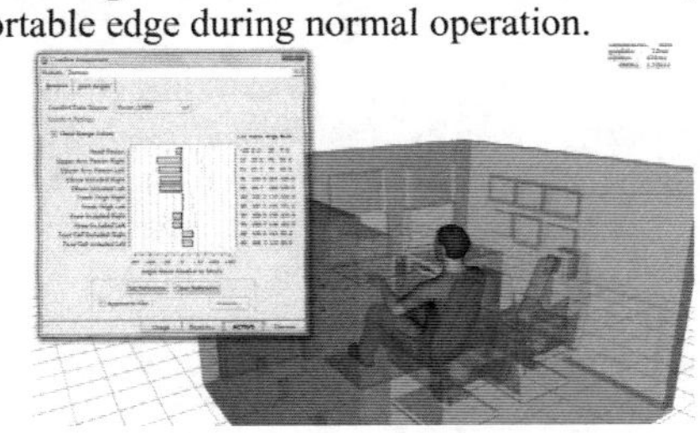

Figure 12. Left Operator Comfort

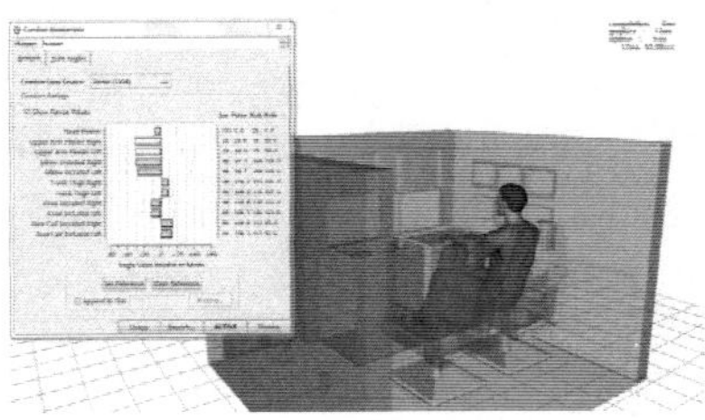

Figure 13. Right Operator Comfort

5 Conclusion

The control room inside the armoured vehicle is an organically interconnected microcosm of two separate components: the structure of the control room and the control platform. Included in the control platform component is the size and orientation of the control panel and ergonomic seat design. Based on objective data, the dimensions of the control console, the layout of the console panel, the colour of components on the console, and the dimensions of the seats on the control console were calculated to establish the model control room. In future designs of armoured vehicles an effort must be made to make the design and layout of the control room both comfortable and efficient for the operators.

Here are some examples:

Reference

1. Ding Yu-Lan. Ergonomics [M]. Beijing: Beijing institute of technology press, 2006.
2. Xiang Ying-Hua. Ergonomics [M]. Beijing: Beijing institute of technology press,2008.
3. Tong Shi-Zhong. Man-machine engineering design and application manual [M]. Beijing: China standard press, 2007.
4. Ruan Bao-Xiang, Shao Xiang-Hua. Industrial design ergonomics [M]. Beijing: mechanical industry press, 2005.
5. Ma Zhi, Xue Hong-Jun, Su Run-E. Analysis of human body modeling and ergonomics based on JACK [J]. Aviation computing technology,2008, 38(1):97-100.
6. Dong Ai-Hua. Modelling and structural design of the console [J]. Electronic mechanical engineering.2010, 3:21-23.
7. Song Xiao-Qing, Shen Xi. Research on control panel design based on ergonomics [J]. Equipment manufacturing technology.2006, 4: 67-69.
8. Li Le-Shan. Arts and design [M]. Xi 'an: xi 'an jiaotong university press,2010.

Design of Service Framework Based on the Trip Experience of the Elderly – Take the cultural and historical scenic spot as an example

Ying Meng[1,a], Kaining Meng[1] and Jiahao Liu[1]

[1] Xihua University, School of Art and Design, Chengdu, China

Abstract. The tourism market that serves the aged is already being paid more and more attention to with the trend of population aging, but there is still no suitable mode for the tourism of the old in the view of sightseeing, visiting, nostalgia and other qualities. Based on existing relevant research, the author adopts questionnaire and interview survey, this paper analyzes the present travel intention and pain point of the elderly and then investigates the historical and cultural sights of the city with large passenger flow through field investigation method. By summarizing the common characteristics of individual cases, this paper analyzes the common problems existing in our country's humanistic and historical tourist attractions and constructs a service framework suitable for the elderly to visit the cultural and historical scenic spots to improve the existing deficiencies.

1 The introduction

1.1 The analysis of the present situation of the elderly

The aging of the population has developed into a global problem. According to the survey data, by 2050, the population over 60 of age will increase from nearly 600 million in 2000 to nearly 2 billion, and the proportion of the population aged 60 or over is expected to double, from 10% to 21%.[1] The fastest-growing rate of the population is the developing countries. As for our country, we are at the stage of the rapid development of population aging. At the end of 2015, the population of aged 60 and over has reached 212 million, accounting for 15.5% of the total population.[2] It is expected that in 2025, it will break through 300 million and the proportion of the elderly population in China will reach 30% of the total population by 2050. Compared with the past, the elderly have higher incomes, more leisure time and more willingness to travel. Many elderly people are very active. They often travel, compared with young people, they spend more time on vacation and spend more on leisure activities. [3]

1.2 Characteristics of the tourism market of the elderly

With the increasing number of elderly social groups, the elderly industry that meets the needs of older people's goods and services has shown unprecedented opportunities for development. The "silver hair economy" promotes the vigorous development of the elderly tourism industry, and promotes the reform of the domestic tourism consumption market structure in a certain way. However, as a sunrise industry, the development of aged tourism market is not satisfactory.

According to the statistics of the National Tourism Administration, the number of elderly tourists aged 65 and above increased from 8 million in 2000 to 15 million in 2010. Although the growth rate was rapid, it still accounted for only 14% of the whole elderly group and less than 20% of the total tourism market. In the developed countries, the proportion of old tourism in the whole tourism market has reached 40%-50% 20 years ago.[4] Therefore, the tourism market for the elderly in China is still not fully developed and has unprecedented opportunities. The research on domestic aged tourism is carried out under the hypothesis of "broad prospects for the aged tourism market", which largely ignores the research on tourism restriction factors. Therefore, it is of great significance to improve level of involvement of the elderly through studying the various restrictive factors in tourism.

1.3 The present situation of the tourism of the elderly

1.3.1 High attention of tourism enterprises and society

Most of the elderly travel rely on travel agencies. More and more travel agencies also attach more importance to

*Corresponding author: [a] Ying Meng: 437361971@qq.com

the tourism market for the elderly. Tourism enterprises will tailor their travel routes for the elderly to ensure that the elderly consumers get more safe, comfortable and high-quality tourism services. For example, in Shanghai, 1/6 travel agencies have launched activities with the theme of "silver hair Tour", and some travel agencies set up "department of the elderly", and some travel agencies are dedicated to serving for the elderly. At the same time, the industry association also attached great importance to the tourism of the aged, and gave greater support, set up all kinds of associations of the elderly, the elderly tourism association, the old university and so on have been all over the country.

1.3.2 The number of elderly people who want to travel is increasing

According to Maslow's Hierarchy of Needs, when people's physiological needs, security requirements and other lower level demands are satisfied, they will gradually pursue high-level spiritual needs. According to a survey by the Chinese Consumer Association in 2014, 45.2% of the elderly are willing to travel. This proportion has risen than in previous years, with 13.8% of its elderly people saying they are going to travel often, and 31.4% of the elderly saying they are going to travel occasionally. Therefore, with the increasing economic income and social security of the elderly gradually improved, more and more elderly people have not been satisfied with play in the scenery of living city,and going out with their friends to see the outside world becomes a kind of social needs and life fashion.[5]

1.3.3 The safety of the elder people is much lower

Along with the growth of age, the physiological function of the elderly has degenerated, causing inconvenience. Many elderly people suffer from varying degrees of hypertension, hyperlipidemia, hyperglycemia, or some heart diseases. Therefore, the elderly tourists have higher requirements for travel safety and quality of service. But at present, the travel agencies in the market are far from enough in terms of the safety and security of the elderly. For example, there is no accompanying doctor during the tour. If there is any danger or difficulty on the way, they cannot get timely assistance. At the same time, some travel agencies in order to save costs and attract more elderly tourists, in the transportation, accommodation, catering arrangements and other aspects of low standard, resulting in a lot of elderly people are too tired or previous disease recurrence after traveling back, and they lose interest and desire to travel again.

2 Research method

This study aims to understand the difficulties and needs when the elderly have been the willingness to travel, and during the journey, after the trip. As well as the existing service mode and software and hardware facilities of the cultural and historical scenic spots, and propose and build the scenic spot service framework.

2.1 The early research

We can draw a conclusion by studying the current situation of the tourism market of the aged that their travel willingness increase with time passing by, more and more elderly people wish to travel. And now the tourism market do not have specific service system that is fully suitable for the elderly, and that some scenic spots exist certain problems and imperfections for the elderly, so lots of elderly people are still hesitant and wait-and-see in travel, which leads the travel market for the elderly is not as desirable. In view of this phenomenon, the author conducted further investigation and research on the aged over 60 in the way of questionnaire.

The 60-70 year old accounted for 74.07% of the total number of questionnaires, 71-80 years old accounted for 23.46%, and the elderly over 81 accounted for 2.47%. From the results of the questionnaire that the elder people get the travel information mainly from the children, books, newspapers, and conversation between the elderly. As a result, we can see that the way for the elderly to obtain tourism information is relatively backward, and the current promotion of the service for the elderly still needs to be strengthened. The purpose of old people travel is very diverse, in addition to enriching life to relax body and mind, also to the nostalgia. In the area of hardware facilities, elderly people pay more attention to the improvement of public facilities.

The author makes a detailed inquiry, after learning that the elderly had an unhappy experience, 67.9% of the elderly had expectations about their next trip. 32.1% of them said the previous unpleasant experience will affect the mood of the next trip. The results of the survey once again confirmed that it is necessary to improve the tourism service system of the elderly.

2.2 Stage of development

After the preliminary questionnaire survey, the author conducted fieldwork in the cultural and historical scenic spot in Chengdu by simulating the travel habits of the elderly. The survey found that there are several common problems in most of the scenic spots: 1)In the aspect of hardware facilities, many scenic spots are not up to standard. for the elderly to visit. Figure 1 is a live shot of the Qingyang Palace and Cultural Park in Chengdu. As shown in the figure, the number of public rest areas on both sides of the hard road is clearly insufficient, and many narrow roads have no seats on either side, resulting in so many tourists take a piece of paper to sitting on the ground for rest. 2)Later tracking on the signs of drinking water and medical service point, the number of drinking water points in the scenic area is low, or the drinking water point cannot be used; Following the instruction path of the medical service point, it was found that there was no corresponding medical facility at the end. The setting point did not play a corresponding role. 3)There

https://doi.org/10.1051/matecconf/201817604005

are few barrier-free channels for public facilities in the scenic area. Through these phenomena indicated that the present scenic spot does not have a complete service system for the elderly, and many facilities fail to meet the standards that the elderly are willing to travel. This is a very important reason why the elderly tourist market has not achieved the expected effect.

Figure 1. Cultural Park Qingyang Palace

Combined with questionnaire survey and field survey results, and then the author have a user interview with three old people, as follows.

Interview content	Interviewee 1	Interviewee 2	Interviewee 3
How old are you?	Sixty-four	Seventy-two	Seventy-five
Would you like to travel?	Yes, I' d like to very much. I like traveling.	Yes, if there are no things to do in my family.	Yes, I like traveling before. But now I cannot go to some places because I'm in a low state of health.
How many times do you travel in a year?	Maybe four places or so.	Maybe two times if I have nothing to do.	Maybe one. It depends on my physical condition.
Trip purpose/The reason that restrict your journey	I have nothing to do, so I travel to places that I' ve never been.	It' s hard to plan a trip because my children are too busy.	I have some trouble with walking, therefore I cannot bear too long walking.
If the tourism spots do some improvements to the existing hardwarfacilities (increasing the number of drinking spots, seats, and ramps) and improve the medical service system, will it be a factor that will attract you to travel?	Yes, it would be best if this can be improved. Especially the increase of seats, I can not find a place to take a rest in many places after walking a long distance.	Yes, of course. It would be better to add these facilities. The idea of the drinking point is also very good because the water in the scenic spot is very expensive.	Yes, this medical service system will reassure me a lot when I go out (play) .The increase of ramps and seats will bring a bit crippled people like me much convenience.
If the scenic spot provides services for picking up and arranging accommodation, will it be convenient for you to travel?	Arrangement for pick-up and drop-offs is very convenient, and I expect the accommodation arrangements can provide different standards.	Arranging accommodation is convenient because it takes a lot of time for children to find accommodation. But I still have some concerns about prices.	I hope there is a pick-up service. Accommodation is usually arranged by my children.
Do you need to add online (WeChat) customer service to help you solve problems encountered in the scenic area.	Yes, it' s very convenient and worry-free.	Children may like it, I am not very skilled in operating WeChat.	Maybe, but my children will definitely like it.

Figure 2. User interview chart

We can see from the table that the degree of concern of the elderly for the change of facilities in scenic spots is high, such as adding the drinking water point, increasing the quantity of seat and rest area. For the elderly with recessive disease, improving the medical assistance points in the scenic area becomes their focus. And they also are interested in the upgrade of soft service, such as scenic spots arrange vehicles to pick up the elderly, arrange hotel in advance for the elderly come from afar etc.

3 Build the service framework

Based on the above comprehensive survey on the tourism market of the elderly, the author simulates a storyboard from the start of the journey to the end of the tour. 1)Before the trip. The elderly can contact the scenic spot by themselves (old people who are not proficient in the Internet can use the phone to contact the customer service), to discuss travel arrangements. For tourists who are planning to travel for days, the scenic spot can arrange accommodation and transport for the elderly in advance; For local visitors, they can choose to go to the scenic spot by taking the nearest scenic spot bus. The entrance of the scenic spot will set up a special window for the reserved visitors — After buying a ticket, the elderly can enter the scenic spot directly. 2)After entering the scenic spot, rental services are provided for old people(or disabilities), such as alpenstocks, crutch chairs, etc, there also have umbrellas, rain capes, kneecap and so on everyday goods. The scenic spot is set up to serve the elderly's guidance system and guide their travel route. At the same time, medical assistance station has medical staff on duty during the opening hours of the scenic spot, and the scenic spot provides medical drugs for the elderly

Stage	Actions	Content
Inquire customer servic		Uncle Li and Aunt Li have recently planned to visit the X site. They have seen a special service customer service at the X site, so they call the service personnel of the site to book travel itinerary, including prices,transportation, accommodation and other related matters.
Pick-up service		Visitors from both the city and outside the city can enjoy the pick-up service provided by the tourist attractions by making appointments with scenic spots in advance, visitors from both the city and the city can enjoy this service. ·City - the nearest pick-up point from home ·Outside the city - transportation hubs like airports and railway stations.
Pick-up service		The scenic spot provides services for tourists to arrange accommodation. (for tourists outside the city) ·Received tourists from the city and sent them directly to the attractions. ·Received tourists from outside the city and arranged for visitors to leave luggage at the hotel.
Enter the attraction		At the entrance of the attraction, a special window is set up for Uncle Li and Aunt Li (order through this reservation service in advance). They do not need to wait in line to buy the ticket again and can enter the park directly.
Leasing service		After entering the area, there is a rental service for the elderly (motor barriers)such as walking aids like trekking poles and crutch chairs and daily necessities like umbrellas, ponchos and knee pads.
Guide System	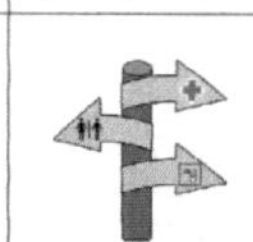	In the interior of the scenic spot, a series of camera guide systems are made for the elderly to guide them to the proper attractions. The guide system will point to the nearest drinking point and medical aid point.
Rest area		The interior of the scenic spot is equipped with a proper number of public seats and rest areas for the temporary rest of the tired old people or others tourists.
Accessible Channel		Set up standards-compliant ramps at places with height differences, such as public toilets, pavilions and some paths to the landscape to provide services to elderly people with limited mobility.
Leave the attraction		After the tour, the elderly can take the pre-arranged vehicles to the next destination at the scenic exit
Customer service return visit		After the play, we will make a timely return visit to the service system and the quality of the scenic area, listen to the elderly's suggestions for improvement, and convey to them that we will offer the corresponding preferential treatment if the elderly are willing to come again.

Figure 3. Trip storyboard

with the possibility of sudden illness. The scenic area is equipped with sufficient seats in the public rest area to provide temporary rest for the tired tourists; In public toilets, pavilions and other buildings to set up a standard ramp, for the mobility of the elderly convenience. 3)At the exit of the scenic spot, the elderly can go home or go back to the hotel by courtesy bus. 4)Last but not least. The service personnel of the scenic spot will play a timely return visit for this service system and the quality of the scenic spot, the aim is to listen to the old man's suggestions for improvement. This system of service hope to truly serve the old man. To pave the way for more complete service design in the future. See figure 3.

After building the service framework, the flow chart of the elderly was simulated, which shows more intuitively that the elderly have begun to make contact point with scenic spots when they have a travel plan. Each contact point will affect the satisfaction of the old people to the scenic spots and the overall trip, and even it will produce positive or negative radiation towards the subsequent travel.

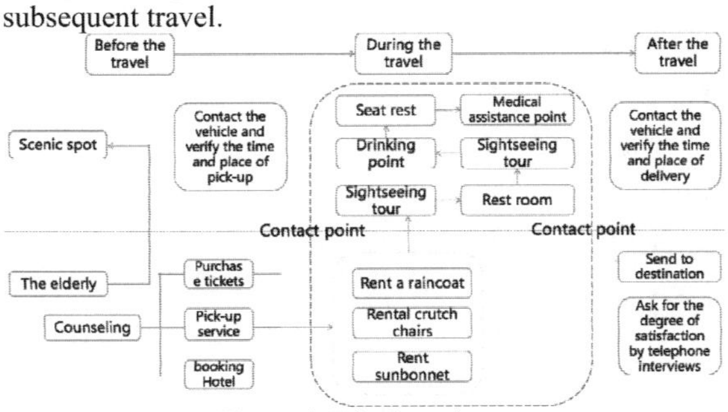

Figure 4. Trip flow chart

4 Brief summary

Through the analysis of the current situation of the elderly tourism market, the investigation and analysis of the elderly's willingness to travel and the actual travel situation, we can see that there are still large vacancies in the tourist market of the elderly. A complete set of elderly tourism service system will greatly improve the current tourism situation. Under the trend of aging, the Chinese government attaches great importance the problem of population aging, and actively develops the cause of aging. It has initially formed a working pattern of government leading, social participation and the concern of the whole people for the aging industry. The tourism service of the elderly is still in the embryonic stage. There will be much research space in the future. We hope this paper can make a preliminary guidance to the tourism service industry of the elderly and improve the elderly's experience of traveling through service design.

Acknowledgment

Fund project. Major projects in Sichuan education department.(Item number:W171300); University-level graduate innovation fund project of Xihua University.(Item number:ycjj2017110).

References

1. Liyan Yu. Research on the protection system of tourism rights for the elderly in China. MBBS, (2012)
2. Huan Ren. Ministry of civil affairs released *the 2015 social service development statistics bulletin*, (2015)
3. KAZEMINIA A, et al. Seniors'travel constraints and their coping strategies. JOTR, **54**(2015)
4. Runlian Zhang. Analysis on the quantitative analysis of elderly tourism in China. JOLNU, (2013)
5. Haiying Yang. A review of the research on elderly tourism at home and abroad. JOBLSVC,(2014)

MATEC Web of Conferences **176**, 04006 (2018) https://doi.org/10.1051/matecconf/201817604006
IFID 2018

Research on the Development Law of Smart Phone Screen based on User Experience

Pei Xuesheng[1, 2, a], Wang Yang[2]

[1]School of Mechatronic Engineering and Automation, Shanghai University, Shanghai, China
[2]School of Art and Design, Henan University of Science and Technology, Luoyang, China

Abstract. Modern electronic products are changing with each passing day, and the most prominent one is the smart phone. Screen is the key part for people to extract and exchange information through mobile phones, and its development is very rapid. This article summarize the development laws of screen size, screen occupation ratio, resolution and shape from the perspective of user experience, and analyze the reasons for its development law. According to the research, the optimal size of the mobile phone screen suitable for the users is summed up and verified through the questionnaire, which provides a reliable basis for the developer of mobile phone to design smart phone screen and improve the satisfaction of the user experience.

1 Introduction

With the advancement of technology, smart phones have become an essential product in people's lives. The screen technology is also rapidly developing, and the screen of the mobile phone has undergone great changes in materials, modeling, size, and resolution. Mobile developers constantly adjust the screen size and screen occupation ratio to bring better visual experience and interactive experience to users.

But what exactly happened to the evolution of the mobile phone screen, what kind of screen size can most meet the needs and comfort of users, this article summarizes the development law of the screen through data collection and collation, and analyze the reasons for the formation of this rule in order to get the best screen size which is suitable for people. This study will provide a theoretical basis for mobile phone developers to design and improve products, help them grasp the future development direction of mobile screens, and then improve the satisfaction of user experience.

2 Development status of mobile phone screen

In recent years, the replacement of mobile phones has largely been related to the improvement of the screen. Companies such as Apple, Samsung, HUAWEI and MI have continued to compete in the screen occupation ratio, big screen and high screen ratio become the goals pursued by big enterprises. But while improving the user experience, there are some problems and hazards.

For the user experience of mobile phone and the development of the screen, user experience refers to people's cognitive impressions and responses to products, systems or services that are used or expected to be used. It is a truly extended and distinct perspective on quality of interactive technology[1].Si Yaqing and others collected the satisfaction factors and dissatisfaction factors in the experience of the smart phone users, and put forward the results of the user experience in terms of emotions, satisfaction, continuous use intentions, etc., and elaborated the user's psychological changes when there is a difference between the user's psychological expectations and the actual use of the feelings [2].Tian Meiling and Zhao Xinjun analyzed the development of mobile phone screen based on TRIZ, and proposed that the mobile phone screen will adapt to the high intelligence requirements of the mobile phone, make its resolution higher, the material is more advanced, and the size is more consistent with ergonomics requirements [3]. Wang Songpei and others studied the future development direction of the mobile phone screen and proposed that the mobile phone screen will become more beautiful, durable, stylish and portable [4]. Xin Yizhong and others proposed that smart phones with large size screen provide more information display space for users, and also bring difficulties to the target selection operation of single hand operation[5]. Karlson and others used experiments to evaluate how the size of the device, the target position, and the direction of movement affect the mobility of the thumb when handheld device interacts with one hand [6].

Therefore, study the trends and laws of mobile phone screen, and analyze the negative impact of excessive mobile phone screen to users, comprehensive data to summarize the best screen size for people to use, which will help mobile phone developers understand user demands, target optimization of improved products,

*Corresponding author: [a] Pei Xuesheng: pxsh12@126.com

improve competitive advantage of brand.

3 Research on the development of mobile phone screen and its laws

This study summarizes the indicators and data of smart phone screens of Samsung, Apple, and HUAWEI mobile phone enterprises in recent years, reveal their development rules, and analyze the specific reasons for the formation of laws.

The research object selected Samsung Galaxy S Series, Apple iPhone Series and HUAWEI P Series, including two large-screen series of Samsung Galaxy S+ and iPhone plus. The content of the study is the release year, screen size, screen occupation ratio, resolution, and screen shape. The different series of specific information are shown in Table 1, table 2, table 3, table 4, and table 5.

Table 1. Galaxy S Series

Mobile phone models	The release year/year	Screen size/Inches	Screen occupation ratio/%	Resolution	Screen shape
Galaxy S	2010	4.0	58.1	480×800	Straight screen
Galaxy S2	2011	4.3	61.3	480×800	Straight screen
Galaxy S3	2012	4.8	65.9	1280×720	Straight screen
Galaxy S4	2013	5.0	72.3	1920×1080	Straight screen
Galaxy S5	2014	5.1	70.0	1920×1080	Straight screen
Galaxy S6	2015	5.1	70.9	2560×1440	Straight screen
Galaxy S7	2016	5.1	73.9	2560×1440	Straight screen
Galaxy S8	2017	5.8	84.0	2960×1440	Hyperboloid
Galaxy S9	2018	5.8	89.5	2960×1440	Hyperboloid

Table 2. Galaxy S+ Series

Mobile phone models	The release year/year	Screen size/Inches	Screen occupation ratio/%	Resolution	Screen shape
Galaxy S6 edge	2015	5.1	72.0	2560×1440	Hyperboloid
Galaxy S7 edge	2016	5.5	76.1	2560×1440	Hyperboloid
Galaxy S8+	2017	6.2	83.3	2960×1440	Hyperboloid
Galaxy S9+	2018	6.2	83.6	2960×1440	Hyperboloid

Table3. HUAWEI P Series

Mobile phone models	The release year/year	Screen size/Inches	Screen occupation ratio/%	Resolution	Screen shape
HUAWEI P1	2012	4.3	61.0	960×540	Straight screen
HUAWEI P2	2013	4.7	67.0	1280×720	Straight screen
HUAWEI P6	2013	4.7	70.1	1280×720	Straight screen
HUAWEI P7	2014	5.0	71.6	1920×1080	Straight screen
HUAWEI P8	2015	5.2	78.3	1920×1080	Straight screen
HUAWEI P9	2016	5.2	72.5	1920×1080	Straight screen
HUAWEI P10	2017	5.4	71.2	1920×1080	Straight screen
HUAWEI P20	2017	5.8	80.3	2244×1080	Straight screen

Table4. iPhone Series

Mobile phone models	The release year/year	Screen size/Inches	Screen occupation ratio/%	Resolution	Screen shape
iPhone 4	2010	3.5	54.0	960×640	Straight screen
iPhone 4s	2011	3.5	54.0	960×640	Straight screen
iPhone 5	2012	4.0	60.9	1136×640	Straight screen
iPhone 5s	2013	4.0	60.9	1136×640	Straight screen
iPhone 6	2014	4.7	65.8	1334×750	Straight screen
iPhone 6s	2015	4.7	65.8	1334×750	Straight screen
iPhone 7	2016	4.7	65.6	1334×750	Straight screen
iPhone 8	2017	4.7	65.4	1334×750	Straight screen
iPhone X	2017	5.8	81.2	2346×1125	Straight screen

Table5. iPhone plus Series

Mobile phone models	The release year/year	Screen size/Inches	Screen occupation ratio/%	Resolution	Screen shape
iPhone 6 plus	2014	5.5	67.7	1920×1080	Straight screen
iPhone 6s plus	2015	5.5	67.7	1920×1080	Straight screen
iPhone 7 plus	2016	5.5	67.7	1920×1080	Straight screen
iPhone 8 plus	2017	5.5	67.4	1920×1080	Straight screen

3.1 Analysis of the overall change of mobile phone screen.

The screen size, screen occupation ratio, resolution, and screen form of the mobile phone have all undergone great changes. The screen size increases gradually in a certain range and then tends to be stable. The screen occupation ratio continues to increase, and it develops in the direction of a full screen. Screen resolution has also been greatly improved to meet users' requirements for screen quality and color. The screen shape also has a new breakthrough. In 2015, Samsung first launched the hyperboloid screen phone, making the mobile phone more rounded and have a wider viewing angle, and improving the user's touch and visual experience.

In general, with the development of science and technology, the upgrading of mobile phone screens continues to meet the needs of users and brings better experience to users. This article will focus on the mobile phone screen size and screen occupation ratio, analyze the law of change and explore its causes, and then speculate the development trend of the mobile phone screen.

3.2 Analysis of change law of mobile phone screen size

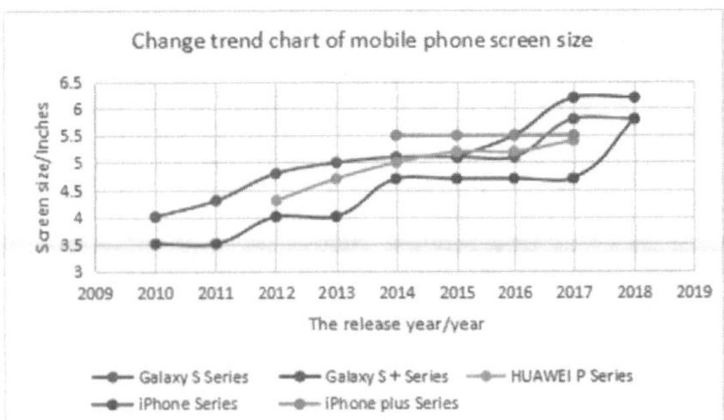

Figure 1. Change trend chart of mobile phone screen size

According to the Figure 1, we can see that since 2010, the size of the mobile phone screens of each brand has been rising, and there are some regularities in the process of rising. It is worth noting that between 2010 and 2014, the overall change in screen size was large and it rose rapidly. However, from 2014 to 2017, the size changes of the Samsung Galaxy S series, the HUAWEI P series, the iPhone series and the iPhone plus series were minimal or even unchanged, showing a basic stable state, with a stable value of 5.1 inches, 5.2 inches, 4.7 inches, and 5.5 inches.

The phenomenon reflects that the screen size of mobile phones will not increase infinitely, the size of the mobile phone screen, and the size of the mobile phone will develop steadily in a suitable area, which is determined by the user's needs and the satisfaction of the user experience.

In order to further confirm the optimal screen size suitable for people's use, this study conducted a single-questionnaire survey on "What size do you think is the most comfortable screen size to use?" The way to answer the questions is to fill in the numbers. The respondents included students, teachers, and the public, among whom 82 were males and 76 were females. Finally, 160 data were retrieved. The effective data was 158. The effective recovery rate was 98.75%, which met the research requirements.

According to statistics, the mean value of data filled by men is 5.30 inches, and the mean value of data filled by women is 5.01 inches. People choose 4.7 inches, 5.5 inches, and 5.1 inches for the best screen size of mobile phone, which is in complete agreement the stable value of three surveyed brands above and verified the value range of the best screen size of mobile phone.

3.3 Analysis of change law of mobile phone screen occupation ratio

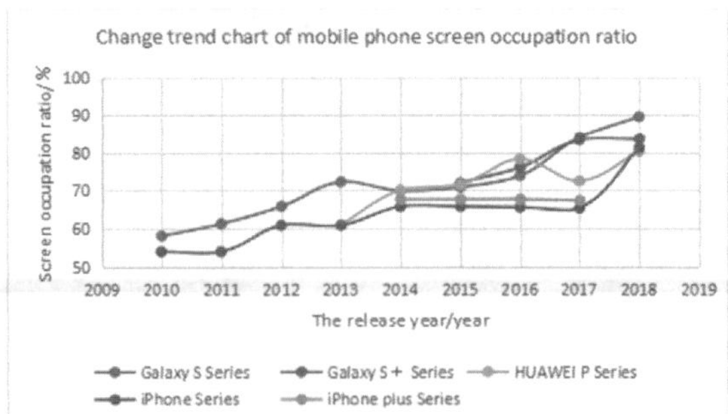

Figure 2. Change trend chart of mobile phone screen occupation ratio

According to the Figure 2, it can be seen that since 2010, the proportion of mobile phone screens of each brand series has been steadily rising, except for the iPhone series and iPhone plus series which have no change in screen occupation ratio and screen size from 2014 to 2017. In addition, the percentage of other mobile phone screens has gradually increased in the past nine years.

According to the above analysis, the mobile phone screen size cannot be infinitely large, but in order to further increase the utilization rate of the frontal area of the mobile phone and enhance the user experience, all major manufacturers have chosen to develop and introduce products with a higher proportion of screens and enhance brand competitiveness. Since the mobile phone products have been developed relatively well so far, we have continuously increased the proportion of screens, developed full-screen technology, and met the development trend of the mobile phone market to meet the specific needs of mobile phone users.

3.4 The negative effect caused by the oversized cell phone screen

Although mobile phone with large-screen enhances the user's visual experience, it brings many inconveniences and is harmful to people. This article will propose three negative effects that the screen is too large to users after investigation and study, then analyze the reason why the screen size of the mobile phone tends to be stable, finally infer the optimal screen size value.

The first impact: Excessive screen size is harmful to human health

While large-screen mobile phones provide users with more information, they gradually make it difficult to operate the screen with one hand. According to the physiological structure of the human hand, the main activity finger in the single-handed operation of the mobile phone is the thumb, but due to the limitation of the knuckle length, the reach of the thumb is very limited, so long-term single-handed operation of the large-screen mobile phone may cause hand joints, muscle and ligament injuries [7]. If operators use both hands for a long time, fatigue of the hand muscles and inflexible hand movements may be caused, causing stenosis tenosynovitis [8]. In addition, due to the small viewing distance when using a mobile phone, excessive screens cause eye fatigue and decreased vision.

The second impact: Excessive screen size is not convenient for daily carrying.

According to people's habits, especially for male users, it is more convenient to carry a mobile phone into a pocket of clothes every day to conveniently view information at any time. However, as mobile phone screens become larger and larger, this type of carrying method will inevitably cause inconveniences. Especially when the clothes are thin in summer, the large-screen mobile phones are difficult to be fully loaded into pockets, which not only makes the user feel uncomfortable, but also can easily fall or be stolen. It can be seen that the screen is too large to a certain extent, does not meet the requirements of humanized design.

The third impact: Excessive screen size increases screen breakage.

As the screen of smart phones continues to develop toward the full-display, the chance of screen breakage increases as the proportion of screens increases. The damage of the screen will greatly reduce the user's satisfaction with the product, and replace the screen will also cost a lot of money. Therefore, the reinforcement of the screen will also become the focus of future research for major manufacturers. However, the screen is fragile and the service life reduction is the key negative effect caused by the large screen size.

3.5 Suggestions

Through the analysis of the screen size and screen occupation ratio of the mobile phone, and the summary of the negative impact on the screen, it can be concluded that the screen size should be within a benign range, while the screen occupation ratio can be continuously improved with the progress of technology.

According to the law analysis and questionnaire survey, the best values for the screen size are 4.7 inches, 5.5 inches and 5.1 inches. Therefore, this study can conclude that the best range of screen size is 4.7-5.5 inches. Mobile phone manufacturers can make different choices according to the brand development status. In addition, the questionnaire survey found that the difference between male and female needs is not significant, but there are still some differences. Therefore, mobile phone manufacturers can launch a series of targeted products by dividing the user population. For example, launching iPhone and iPhone plus with different screen sizes is an excellent strategy.

4 Conclusion

This study summarizes the development status of mobile phone screens of Samsung, Apple, and HUAWEI in recent years. Based on the user experience, this paper summarizes the best screen size and the development direction of the screen, which can provide theoretical support for manufacturers to design mobile phone, help them adjust the direction of research and development, and develop new product development strategies.

At the same time, there are still some shortcomings in this study. For example, the purpose of this paper is to analyze only part of the information in the form, the other parts still have high research value, and may have a little impact on the results of the study. Secondly, the questionnaire survey content is single and the number of samples is less. Due to the large number of mobile phone users, 160 valid questionnaires are not sufficient to accurately represent all users. In light of these deficiencies, this research will continue in the future to obtain more accurate and complete research results.

References

1. Hassenzahl M. *International Conference on Association Francophone d'Interaction Homme -Machine*, **339**, 11(2008)
2. Si Yaqing, Liu Lei, *Software*, **3**, 111(2015)
3. Tian Meiling, Zhao Xinjun, *Science Innovation and Brand*, **6**, 52(2013)
4. Wang Songpei, Wang Wei, Xu Shanshan, Zhang Qi, *Enterprise Guide*, **3**, 44(2015)
5. Xin Yizhong, Li Yang, Li Yan, Jiang Xinhui, *Journal of Computer-Aided Design & Computer Graphics*, **28**, 1750 (2016)
6. Karlson A, Bederson B, Contreras J, *USA:IGI Global Press*, 86(2006)

7. YS Park, SH Han, *International Journal of Industrial Ergonomics*, **1**, 68 (2010)
8. Zhu Shenbo, Cui Lanhai, Chen Zhengnan, Wu Jiaqian, Shen Zhongzhou, Zhang Jiyong, *Health Medicine Research and Practice*, **13**, 24 (2016)

Constructing a framework of user experience for museum based on gamification and service design

Shunli Liu[1] and Muhammad Zaffwan Idris[2,a]

[1]Universiti Pendidikan Sultan Idris, 35900 Tanjong Malim, Perak, Malaysia
[2]Universiti Pendidikan Sultan Idris, 35900 Tanjong Malim, Perak, Malaysia

Abstract. Museum plays an integral part in modern society. For nearly four decades, museums around the world have experienced a shift in their focus from "object" to "people", and attempted to enhance the visitors' experience through various means. In the context of museum open to the public, however, the museum has not become a place frequently visited by people in China. This paper focuses on exploring a method of constructing a model to achieve a desirable user experience (UX) in museum through adapting the role of Gamification and Service Design. The purpose of this study is to inspire potential visitors, specifically the young generation, to have their own motivations to constantly visiting the museum.

1 Introduction

In the history of development urbanization, the museum has been thought of as a key factor in effectively expanding the space for cultural sharing, enhancing the cultivation of populace, and shaping humanistic spirit [1]. In the column Front Line of the journal "Art & Design", the expert demonstrated that the largest core driving force of a country's culture is the museum, which is the top of the cultural pyramid [2]. However, research have shown that both virtual and physical museum tend to focus on the representation of information [3], they cannot stimulate potential visitors to be motivated enough to visit the museum continuously.

Essentially, assortment of artefacts is not the only mission of the museum, the issue of exhibition, education, interpretation and commitment to community has received considerable critical attention in the twentieth century [4]. Over the past century, museums have shown an increased interest in attracting visitors, which is a shift of service concept from the exhibits to the audience, and put more emphasis on the relationship between the museum and the public. People can be seen as both rational and emotional, and often pursue the User Experience (UX) of fantasies, feelings, and fun [5]. It can be seen from a recent study involving a questionnaire that 'entertainment' accounts for the highest proportion (80%) of the audience's motivation to visit the museum [6].

In order to achieve better museum UX, identifying users' different experience needs is prerequisite. Next, museum needs to investigate what services should museum provides to users throughout the process of Pre-Visit, During-Visit, and Post-Visit. Fortunately, the using of interdisciplinary design strategies such as Gamification and Service Design is expected to help to achieve the aims. Hence, this paper focuses on exploring a method of constructing a model to achieve a desirable museum UX through the role of Gamification and Service Design.

2 Museum

In recent years, the interest in redefining the function of museum has increased. For example, in 2007 the International Council of Museums (ICOM) emphasized in the latest museum definition that museum functions include education, study, and enjoyment. Historically from definitions proposed by ICOM, education, study, and enjoyment are the most cited in the purpose of the museum since the 1960s. Moreover, the educational function is becoming more and more important today. The mission of the new era museum is that not only concerned about the collection, but also concerned about how to use the collection; not only concerned about the arts, but also the people [7] .

In the context of museum open to the public, one may presume that the museum has become a place that regularly visit by people, but in China, this is not the case. In 2015, China Youth Daily survey showed that only 17.3% of respondents frequented the museum and 61.1% of the respondents occasionally visited, due to lack of affinity for the museum, inconvenient access to information, and weakness of interactive visit [8]. Compared with the average frequency of visiting museums in developed countries that is three to five times per year, every citizen in China enters the museum about every two years on average [9]. Museums should

*Corresponding author: [a] zaffwan@fskik.upsi.edu.my
[1] Shunli Liu also serves as a lecturer at the Art & Culture College of Tianjin University of Sport.

 https://doi.org/10.1051/matecconf/201817604007

learn to interact with their visitors specifically the young generation who are not passionate about ancient art such as paintings [3, 10]. Today, museums are often overlooked by young people [11]. To a certain extent, the participation of the young generation could determines the museum's future audience [3].

In order to attract more young people to participate in museums, a study has been conducted and proved the complementary relationship between physical museum and virtual museum [12]. It can be seen that the physical museum is mainly related to the 'During-Visit', and the virtual museum is mostly related to the 'Pre-Visit' as well as 'Post-Visit'. However, there are some deficiencies in previous studies. First of all, there has been less discussion about the issue on how the museum systematically connects virtual museums and physical museums throughout 'Pre-Visit', 'During-Visit', and 'Post-Visit'. In addition, previous studies ignored the different needs from UX. It may be feasible that a new method to increase the audience's experience is needed. In particularly through gathering insight into the psychology of young people, categorizing museum audiences based on their intrinsic motivation and identifying users' different experience needs.

3 User experience (UX)

For the definition of UX, scholars highly recommend the definition that proposed by Nielsen, a well-known UX designer and researcher. The definition is as follow: "'User Experience' encompasses all aspects of the end-user's interaction with the company, its service, and its products." [13-14]. There are other opinions believes that the UX is a feeling of strong excitement [15]. In other words, feelings beyond expectations can be called user experience.

Consumer or visitor should be able to obtain three different levels as shown in figure 1. The progressive relationship from low to high for: Functionality, Usability and Pleasure. (1) Functionality: no function, no use. What the product be used for, as well as the context or environment in which it will be used must be understood; (2) Usability: users expect the product easy to use; (3) Pleasure: according to the theory 'hierarchy of human needs', higher level needs always follow the prior satisfaction has been achieved, that is why after the Usability is satisfied, the user is inevitable to pursue more, such as emotional experience.

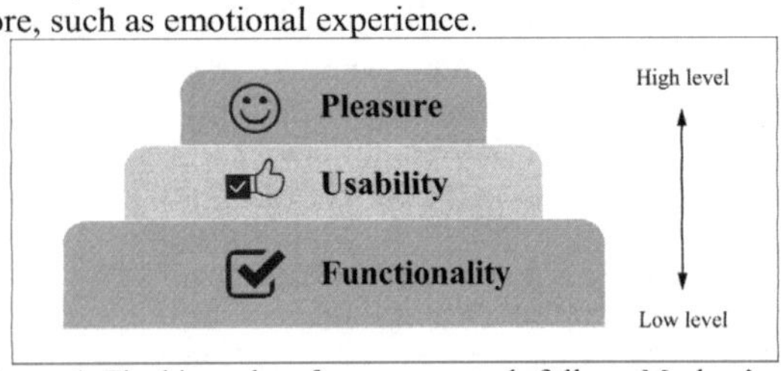

Figure 1. The hierarchy of consumer needs follows Maslow's theory

4 Gamification

4.1 Game

Maroney defined the game as: "a game is a form of play with goals and structure." [16] The author defined the game by four shared traits: a goal, rules, a feedback system, and voluntary participation [17]. Gaming elements increase the visitor engagement because of the 'Edutainment', which is a solution that combines education and entertainment to enhance learning experiences [18]. Gamers can achieve more in online worlds than they can in real life. They can have stronger social relationships in games than they can have in real life, they get better feedback and feel more rewarded in games than they do in real life. The broken reality needs to use the game to repair [17]. Players do believe that they are capable of changing virtual worlds and not the real world. Hence, we have to start making the real world work more like a game [19].

4.2 Understanding Gamification

The term Gamification was defined as follows: "Gamification is the use of elements of game design in non-game contexts." [20] This definition helps distinguish 'Gamification' from 'Game'. The term 'non-game contexts' tends to mean that the purpose of using game elements is to help accomplish other things. The figure 2 presents more detailed explanation of the Gamification definition mentioned above [21].

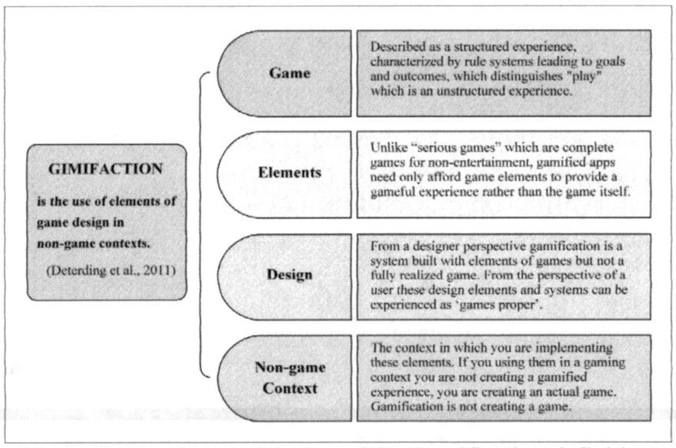

Figure 2. Detailed explanation of the Gamification definition

In recent years, there has been an increasing amount of literature on Gamification. Deterding et al. said: "Origins Gamification as a term originated in the digital media industry. The first documented use dates back to 2008." [20] The authors further pointed out the use of the term Gamification was widely adopted by some industry participants and conferences in the second half of 2010. Additionally, although Gamification originated in the digital media industry, it does not need to focus only on digital form since the distinction between digital and non-digital artefacts is increasingly blurred.

As a non-game environment, the museum is expected to introduce Gamification concepts to enhance the UX. In order to attract new target groups, especially young people, Gamification is one of the ways to solve the problem of museum audience reduction [11]. Specifically, the same study provided new insights into another potential problem: "How can potential visitors be motivated to visit the museum continuously and how can knowledge of the artwork be transferred?" The Gamification is a better scientific solution since it is a way to increase user engagement by adding game mechanism.

5 Service Design

Like any product, services need to be designed. As early as 2005, the International Council of Societies of Industrial Design (ICSID) included services in the definition of design [22]. In 2006, with the arrival of The First Nordic Conference on Service Design and Service Innovation, the Service Design began to be concerned [23]. In the 1990s, the traditional service industry was growing and design still focused on physical and tangible production. During this decade, the main task of the Service Design was to let the idea of 'design could and should work on services' be accepted by society [24].

5.1 Definition of Service Design

The term Service Design was defined as: "The process of planning and organizing people, infrastructure, communication and material components of a service, with the goal of improving the service's quality, the interactions between a provider and its customers, and the customers' experiences." [25] In the article entitled *Building A Service Design Explanation*, the authors hold the point that Service Design is the design of how a service delivers an experience to their customers over time [26].

5.2 Time concept of Service Design

According to the time, the touchpoints in Service Design can be divided into three stages: 'Pre-Service', 'During Service', and 'Post-Service' [22]. The figure 3 shows these three stages concisely: (1) Pre-Service: The contact before customers got service such as advertising, website, promotion, the main purpose is marketing; (2) During Service: Each touchpoint in the service process, such as the services provided by the airport (registration procedures, security procedures, shopping, rest, internet, catering, smoking, prayer rooms, children's play area); (3) Post-Service: Customer contact after leaving the service such as maintenance and management, after-sales service, customer loyalty management. Further, Service design enables users to enjoy aesthetics, escape from reality, enjoy entertainment or be educated.

Public places such as museums and airports will increasingly be transformed into complexes of services, which are closely related to the visitors' lifestyle. In the column Front Line of the journal "Art & Design", Chen Nan, the deputy director of Visual Communication Design Department, Academy of Fine Arts, Tsinghua University, mentioned: "the purpose of people going to the museum not necessarily for the exhibition, but a way of life on weekends." [2]. Consistent with the concept of Service Design, museums also have the concept of time flow. The Service Design can help enhance the museum experience through the organization of traditional and virtual during 'Pre-Visit', 'During-Visit', and 'Post-Visit'.

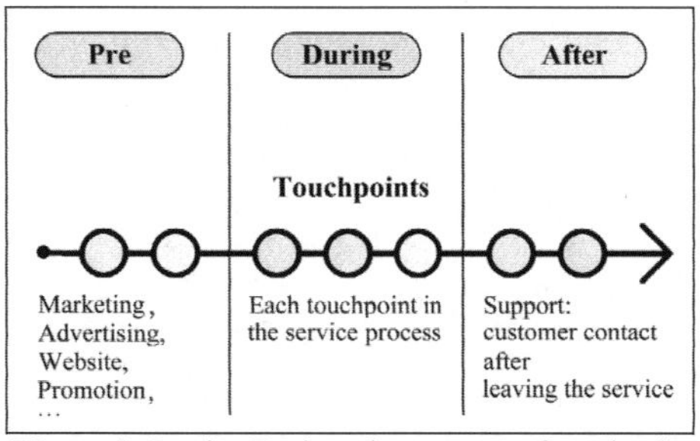

Figure 3. Service Design: three stages of touchpoints

6 Application of Gamification and Service Design in improving the UX of museum

6.1 Application of meaningful Gamification

Incorporating Gamification concept into the process of enhancing UX in museums is not a simple use of game elements because most Gamification that offering rewards is only suitable for the short-term purpose instead of the long-term change.

6.1.1 Meaningful Gamification based on intrinsic motivations

It is undeniable that rewards can help players to enter the system. For example, the use of badges and points can guide players and lead people to engage with a system. Over time, however, the role of rewards should be gradually reduced and replaced by ongoing meaningful engagement since intrinsic motivations are more motivated than external motivation [27]. The concept of meaningful Gamification was introduced by Nicholson to achieve the long-term change [28], which emphasizes intrinsic or internalized motivations for people's engagement in activities. The author pointed out: "removing the scoring elements from a Gamification context encourages a focus on the integration of play". That is to say, meaningful Gamification encourages a deeper integration of game mechanisms into non-game contexts.

6.1.2 Player needs based on SDT

The Self-Determination Theory (SDT) proposed by Deci and Ryan shows how to make systems that help users find their own reasons for engagement through constructing intrinsic motivation [27].

Using Gamification thinking, players in game can be identified into four types: achievers, socializers, explorers, and attackers [29]. This theory can be applied to the classification of museum audience's visit motivation. By analyzing types of player, Nicholson connected the player types to the three basic needs in SDT [27], and the conclusion is shown in the figure 4: (1) Using Gamification systems, Socializers tend to meet and engage with others, they are interested in the Relatedness concept; (2) Try to break the boundaries of the Gamification system, Explorers desire to participate in broadness, they value the concept of Play and pay special attention to the Autonomy element; (3) Achievers are looking for a feeling of accomplishment, they highly value the Competence (Mastery) element; (4) Attackers expect competition and conquest, and value the Mastery element of SDT.

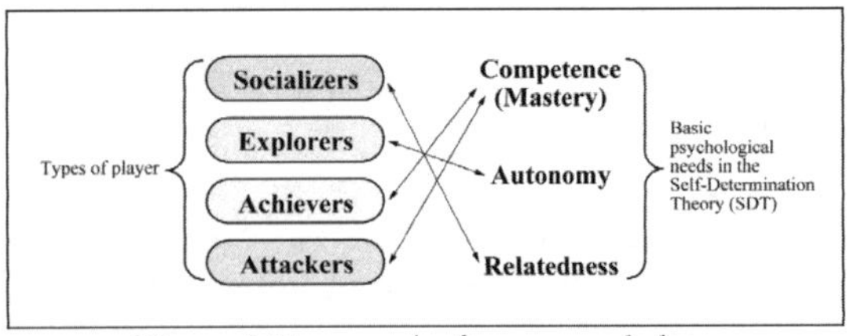

Figure 4. Framework of gamer psychology

6.2 Application of Service Design

According to the principle of touchpoints in Service Design, the touchpoints of service design can be divided into three stages: 'Pre-Service', 'During-Service', and 'Post-Service'. In the same vein, the audience experience of the museum can be divided into 'Pre-Visit', 'During-Visit', and 'Post-Visit' [30]. In general, the Pre-Visiting stage is mainly information and ticket service; the During Visiting stage is mainly based on deep excursions and knowledge services, including watching, listening and touching; the Post-Visiting stage is mainly for sharing exchanges, souvenir buying, and entertainment services.

Although most of the studies focus on 'During-Visit' of the museum, existing research has recognized the critical role played by 'Pre-Visit' and 'Post-Visit'. After researching several groups of people, the researchers found 57% of people visiting museum websites before and after they visit the physical museum [31]. Therefore, the introduction of the concept of Service Design will help the museum enhance its UX throughout the entire process of 'Pre-Visit', 'During-Visit', and 'Post-Visit'.

6.3 Exploring a model to achieve a desirable museum UX

When exploring a model for museum UX, the designer can classify the audience based on the above player types to find out their respective motivations to go to the museum. The process of classifying the audience must be combined with the various services the museum should provide. After that, in conjunction with the concept of 'Pre-Visit', 'During-Visit', and 'Post-Visit', Service Design concepts helping to enhance museum UX can be explored. This process connects virtual museums with physical museums, inspiring potential visitors motivated to constantly visit the museum. To clarify and propose relationships among the concepts, the framework for this study was established and presented in figure 5.

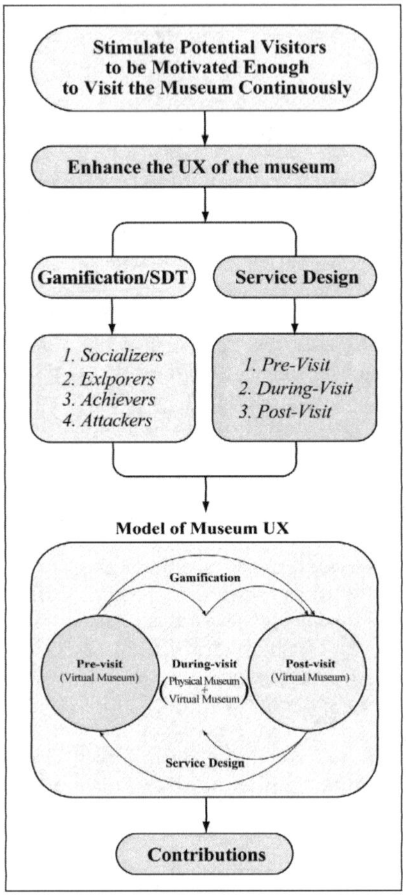

Figure 5. The framework of research

7 Conclusion

In general, this paper focuses on exploring a method of constructing a model to achieve a desirable museum UX through the application of Gamification and Service Design. As a cross-disposing study, this work use different perspectives to help the museum to better understand its audiences so as meeting the experience demand by different types of users. Through this research, it is expected that the participation of the young generation will be highly achievable for the museum's future main audience.

References

1. P. Jian, S. Q. Li. Social Education and the Development of the Museum. In S. H. M. Secretariat of CAMOC-CSM (Ed.), *Variation of City Memory: Proceeding of CAMOC-CSM (2013-2014)* (pp. 618–622). Guang'an, Sichuan; Xiamen, Fujian: Shanghai Jiao Tong University Press. (2014)

2. Z. Zhou. Discussion on Cultural Products of Museums. Art & Design, (4), 46–51(2016)
3. F. Izzo. Museum Customer Experience and Virtual Reality: H.BOSCH Exhibition Case Study. Modern Economy, **8**(4), 531–536 (2017)
4. E. P. Alexander, M. Alexander, J. Decker. *Museums in Motion: An Introduction to the History and Functions of Museums*. Rowman & Littlefield. (2017)
5. M. B. Holbrook, E. C. Hirschman. The Experiential Aspects of Consumption: Consumer Fantasies, Feelings, and Fun. Journal of Consumer Research. (1982)
6. S. Y. Li. The Development of Museum APPs and its Solutions. Journal of Huizhou University, **37**(4) (2017)
7. P. W. Jordan. *Designing Pleasurable Products An Introduction to the New Human Factors*. Boca Raton, Florida: CRC Press, Taylor & Francis Group. (2002)
8. J. Liu, F. L. Liu. Public Service Design of Internet+ Museum Based on Role Cognition: Taking the Palace Museum as an Example. Art & Design, (11), 118–119 (2017)
9. J. McGonigal. *Reality is Broken: Why Games Make Us Better and How They Can Change the World*. New York: The Penguin Press. (2011)
10. W. Hürst, B. de Boer, W. Florijn, X. J. Tan. Creating New Museum Experiences for Virtual Reality. In *Multimedia & Expo Workshops (ICMEW), 2016 IEEE International Conference* (pp. 1–6). IEEE. (2016)
11. A. Döpker, T. Brockmann, S.Stieglitz. Use Cases for Gamification in Virtual Museums. *Informatik 2013, Informatik Angepasst an Mensch, Organisation Und Umwelt: Tagung Vom 16. - 20. September 2013 in Koblenz; 43rd Meeting of the German Informatics Society*, (September 2013), 2308–2321 (2013)
12. P. F. Marty. Museum Websites and Museum Visitors: Before and After the Museum Visit. *Museum* Management and Curatorship, **22**(4), 337–360(2007)
13. L. Miller. *The Practitioner's Guide to User Experience Design: Top Practitioners Share Lessons Learned on the Journey from Beginner to Expert*. UK: Hachette. (2015)
14. D. Norman, J. Nielsen. The Definition of User Experience (UX) (n.d.). Retrieved December 1, 2017, from https://www.nngroup.com/articles/definition-user-experience/
15. H. Y. Zhou. *Zhou Hongyi's Own Statement: My Internet Methodology*. Beijing: China CITIC Press. (2014)
16. K. Maroney. My Entire Waking Life. The Games Journal, **5**(2001). Retrieved from http://www.thegamesjournal.com/articles/MyEntireWakingLife.shtml
17. J. McGonigal. *Reality is Broken: Why Games Make Us Better and How They Can Change the World*. New York: The Penguin Press. (2011)
18. L. Van Der Lans, E. L. Ansems, V.-J. Khan. BrainChain App: A Fully Crowdsourced Design Process for Museums. Eindhoven University of Technology, (May). (2016)
19. J. McGonigal. Gaming Can Make A Better World. (2010). Retrieved from https://www.ted.com/talks/jane_mcgonigal_gaming_can_make_a_better_world#t-737987
20. S. Deterding, R. Khaled, L. Nacke, D. Dixon. Gamification: Toward a Definition. *CHI 2011 Gamification Workshop Proceedings*, (January 2011), 12–15(2011)
21. J. Charalambous. S Health Redesign. (n.d.). Retrieved January 9, 2018, from https://jasoncharalambous.myportfolio.com/s-health-redesign
22. Z. Qin. To Enhance Service Experience Through Service Touchpoints Design. Package & Design, (3), 103–105 (2014)
23. S. Holmlid. Participative, Co-Operative, Emancipatory: From Participatory Design to Service Design. In *First Nordic Conference on Service Design and Service Innovation* (p. 14) (2009)
24. D. Sangiorgi. Building Up A Framework for Service Design Research. In *8th European Academy Of Design Conference 1st 2nd 3rd April 2009* (pp. 415–420). Aberdeen, Scotland: The Robert Gordon University. (2009). Retrieved from http://ead09.org.uk/Papers/037.pdf
25. M. Steen, M. Manschot, N. De. Koning. Benefits of Co-Design in Service Design Projects. International Journal of Design, **5**(2), 53–61 (2011). Retrieved from uuid:eefaaa3c-cc7d-408e-9e00-883c6f2ccb03
26. S. Sandoval, O. Sortland. Building A Service Design Explanation. (2013). Retrieved from http://odasortland.com/service-design-explanation/
27. S. Nicholson. *A RECIPE for Meaningful Gamification*. (T. Reiners & L. C. Wood, Eds.), *Gamification in Education and Business*. New York. (2015)
28. S. Nicholson. A User-Centered Theoretical Framework for Meaningful Gamification. In Games+ Learning+ Society (Vol. **8**, pp. 223–230). Madison, WI. (2012)
29. R. A. Bartle. *Designing Virtual Worlds*. US: New Riders. (2004)
30. J. Liu, F. L. Liu, Public Service Design of Internet+ Museum Based on Role Cognition: Taking the Palace Museum as an Example. Art & Design, (11), 118–119(2017)
31. V. Kravchyna, S. K. Hastings. Informational Value of Museum Web Sites. First Monday, **7**(2) (2002)

https://doi.org/10.1051/matecconf/201817604008

Research on Form Design of New Generation Upgrade Products Based on Brand Identity

JN Su[1,a], Y Lv[1], P Wang[1] and RS Bai[1]

[1]School of Design Art, Lanzhou University of Technology, 730050 Lanzhou Gansu, China

Abstract. The form design of new generation upgrade products based on the brand identity was studied in this paper, and the regional cultural symbols was integrated into it creatively, which provided a new way of thinking for the design of new generation upgrade products. Taking the AC contactor of Tianshui 213 as an example, firstly the consumer ' s perceptual demand and the brand identity of the products was analyzed, secondly kansei engineering theory was used to deconstruct the form of products, and then design format analysis was used to deconstruct the regional cultural symbols. Finally, the relevant design elements were combined to create a new product with regional culture and era characteristics.

1 Brand identity and product form design under the background of regeneration

Under the condition of economic globalization and the information network, product regeneration has become a common phenomenon in the commodity market. The iPhone has been updated to the eighth generation in just a few years since its launch. The purpose of upgrading products is to better meet the needs of the times. Under different times background, people's aesthetics and preferences often present certain differences, and also social trend style will be different. At the time when the market competition is becoming increasingly competitive, if the product is blindly conservative and do not know innovation and flexibility, it will be eliminated by the times[1].

Under the background of product regeneration, the development of each product is a process of repeated inheritance and continuous innovation. The new and old products not only have certain connections, but also have differences. Famous companies such as Mercedes-Benz, BMW, Volvo, Danish B & O, Apple, Sony, IBM, Philips, Italian Alessi, have always maintained a certain degree of inheritance in their products' styles during the continuous innovations. No matter how many times their products have been updated, consumers are adept at identifying them from a wide range of brands, such as Lamborghini's angular bodywork, BMW's double kidney grille and Hofmeister kink, MINI's round headlight and so on, as shown in figure 1. In the process of product regeneration, the product form design plays an important role, it is the important content and the most obvious result of product regeneration.The form design of new generation upgrade products should not only retain the brand identity, but also conform to the trend of the times, and seek variation in the inheritance to meet the material and spiritual needs of consumers. In this paper, based on brand identity, the form design of new generation upgrade products was studied with the example of AC contactor in Tianshui 213 Electrical Apparatus Co., Ltd.

Figure 1. Brand identity of BMW Series.

2 Positioning analysis on form design of new generation upgrade products

The form of new generation upgrade products will change with the development of the times, which is the objective law of the evolution of new generation upgrade products. The accuracy of design positioning will directly affect the success or failure of the design and development of new generation upgrade products[2]. In the early stage of new products design, the designers need to specify the design direction through detailed positioning analysis of social demands and brand identity.

2.1 Positioning analysis on social demand

Social demand, which is the demand of consumer group. It is the original motivation to promote product regeneration. It can be divided into functional demand and emotional demand. Functional demand, which is the rational demand of consumers. It is the basis of product regeneration. While emotional demand refers to consumers' perceptual demand and is the orientation of

*Corresponding author: [a] sujn@lut.cn

product regeneration, as shown in figure 2. Baxter has pointed out that the users' needs and preferences are the main determinants of product success[3,4].

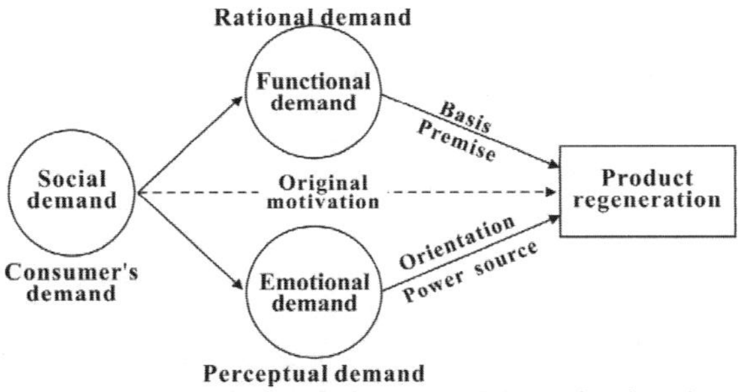

Figure 2. The relationship between social demand and product regeneration.

As far as AC contactors are concerned, consumers not only consider the functional demands of their new generation upgrade products, but also have a certain preference for their style images. Consumer's image preference vocabulary for AC contactors were obtained through previous market research, as shown in table 1.

Table 1. Vocabulary database of kansei image for AC contactors.

Vocabulary database of kansei image for AC contactors			
Quality	Technology	Safety	Designability
Precision	Novelty	Internationalism	Innovativeness
Integrity	Flatness	Uniqueness	Mechanical
Conciseness	Regularity	Progressiveness	Humanism
Delicacy	Fashion	Harmony	Practicability
Contemporaneity	Aesthetic	...	Creation

Through similarity analysis, four representative kansei image words were obtained: integrity, quality, technology and humanism. At the same time, consumers also have a certain demand for the cultural connotation of products. So, in the form design of regeneration for AC contactors, we can introduce regional cultural symbols to achieve the purpose of increasing the cultural connotation of new products.

2.2 Positioning analysis on brand identity of new generation upgrade products

In the process of form design of new generation upgrade products, only by clearly grasping the brand identity of product, can we make clear the direction of new generation upgrade products. Tianshui 213 Electrical Apparatus, which is China well-known trademark and one of the top ten brands of Chinese architectural electric. It has always been adhering to the enterprise spirit of 'harmony, loyalty, professionalism, innovation', practicing the values of 'humanity, fraternity, justice, rigor', and carrying out the business philosophy of 'quality first, customer first, law first, mutual benefit'. It also has always been dedicating to use innovation and quality to build the great wall of the safe operation of electrical system and creating a world-class electrician electrical R & D manufacturing group. As far as the Tianshui 213 AC contactors are concerned, consumers are impressed by its military quality and humanism. Compared with other products of the same kind, its arc shoulder shape and little curved and multi-straight form are the most obvious form features and the key to distinguish its from other brands, as shown in figure 3. Therefore, in the later regeneration design, it is necessary to extend its arc shoulder shape, little curved and multi-straight form to guarantee the brand identity.

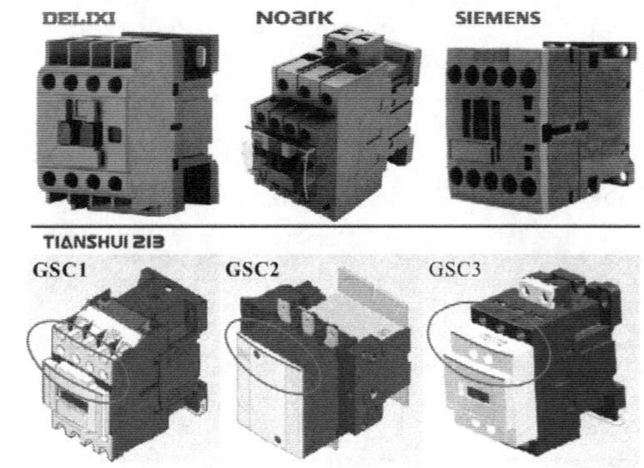

Figure 3. Brand identity of Tianshui 213 AC contactors.

3 Form deconstruction of new generation upgrade products

The form of the new generation upgrade products directly influences the consumers' sensory impression of it. It is an important factor for the success of the product regeneration[5]. Based on the kansei engineering theory[6], the form deconstruction of new generation upgrade products should be started from three aspects. Firstly, through market investigation and analysis, the overall form features can be obtained. Secondly, the visual control elements of contactors' form can be obtained by using morphological analysis[7]. Thirdly, the consumers' qualitative perceptual cognition was quantified by using the quantification-I theory[8], and the mapping relationship between the target images and the visual control elements of form was obtained to guide the development and design of new products.

3.1 Analysis on form features of new generation upgrade products

Different products have different functional characteristics and form features, whose functional characteristics determine the form features, and the form features reflect the functional characteristics. In the form design stage of new generation upgrade products, it is necessary for us to deeply understand the existing products and analyze the forms of them to define their form features. As far as AC contactor is concerned, it is different from other consumer products in the market. As a safety appliance for controlling load, its form features must meet certain functional requirements. By visiting the architecture electrical market, using the contactor catalogue and contactor introduction leaflet, browsing the network and other channels, we can collect the pictures of AC contactors at home and abroad to establish the sample library. The sample library was screened to remove the samples with high similarity and 26 representative samples were obtained and treated uniformly. The angle of AC contactor was to choose the squint angle (left squint / right squint), so as to show the form details of AC contactor as much as possible. At the same time, due to the color matching, nameplate, sticker and brand logo will affect the visual effect of product form in a certain extent, the AC contactor pictures were de-colored and information-processed, only gray space was used to indicate the difference of color matching between AC contactors. And we numbered them as shown in table 2.

Table 2. Sample library of representative AC contactors.

Sample library of representative AC contactors				
Sample 1	Sample 2	Sample 3	Sample 4	Sample 5
	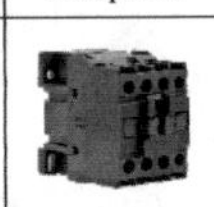	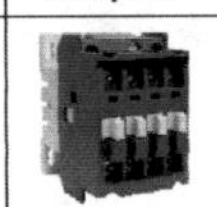	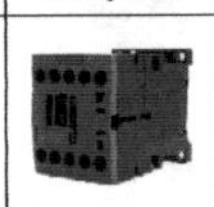	
Sample 6	Sample 7	Sample 8	Sample 9	Sample 10
			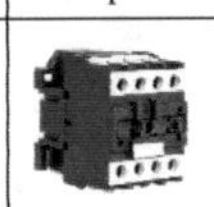	
Sample 11	Sample 12	Sample 13	Sample 14	Sample 15
		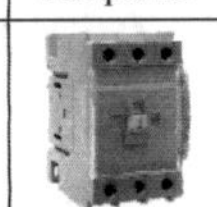	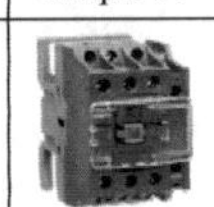	
Sample 16	Sample 17	Sample 18	Sample 19	Sample 20
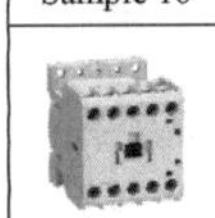		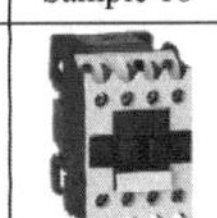	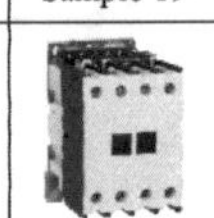	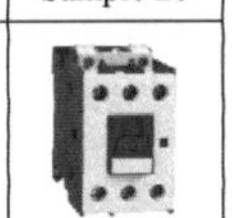
Sample 21	Sample 22	Sample 23	Sample 24	Sample 25
		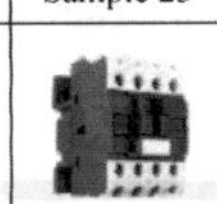		
Sample 26				

By analyzing the representative samples, we can see that the integral shape of AC contactors was mostly square and straight, and occasionally there were contrastive changes between small arc and large straight. But on the whole, they were biased toward square and uniform, in line with its function characteristics of high performance, high efficiency, high precision and high quality.

3.2 Analysis on form visual control elements of new generation upgrade products

The form visual control elements of the new generation upgrade products determine the overall form of the new generation upgrade products. Morphological analysis was used to decompose 26 representative samples, and the visual control elements (items) and classifications (catagories) of AC contactors were summarized, as shown in table 3.

Table 3. Items and categories of AC contactor form.

Items	Categories	Shapes
Dust cover	No dust cover	
	Transparent dust cover	
	Dust cover with observation window	
Coil hole	No countersink	
	Round countersink	
	Square countersink	
Parting line	Straight line	
	Broken line	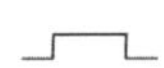
Contact slot	No penetration type	
	Arc penetration type	
	Square penetration type	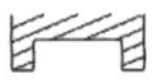
Side slot	Square	
	Arc	

3.3 Brand identity on form visual control elements of new generation upgrade products

3.3.1 Making a questionnaire

Consumers' 4 kansei image preferences for AC contactors and 26 representative AC contactor samples in table 2 were combined. A 5-level SD questionnaire was made by using the semantic differential method[9]. Fourteen AC contactor designers and users were invited to fill out the questionnaire.

3.3.2 Calculating the mean values of the images

The 14 valid questionnaires were statistically analyzed to calculate the mean values of the target images of each sample. The results were shown in Table 4.

Table 4. Mean values of target image of representative samples.

Samples Images	Integrity	Quality	Technology	Humanism
Sample 1	2.64	2.79	2.07	3.07

Sample 2	3.71	3.36	3.50	3.00
Sample 3	2.79	3.00	3.14	2.21
Sample 4	2.50	2.21	1.71	3.29
Sample 5	2.07	2.07	1.64	2.86
Sample 6	2.79	2.93	2.64	2.64
Sample 7	2.00	2.36	2.29	2.21
Sample 8	2.64	2.36	2.93	2.93
Sample 9	3.07	2.79	3.36	3.14
Sample 10	3.21	2.93	2.71	3.29
Sample 11	3.07	2.50	2.93	2.71
Sample 12	3.86	3.71	3.79	3.79
Sample 13	3.00	3.14	2.71	3.21
Sample 14	2.79	2.86	2.57	2.07
Sample 15	3.14	2.86	2.79	2.86
Sample 16	3.21	2.57	2.50	3.64
Sample 17	2.86	2.71	2.71	2.21
Sample 18	2.64	2.21	2.29	1.79
Sample 19	2.79	2.07	1.71	3.36
Sample 20	2.00	1.79	1.64	2.93
Sample 21	2.43	2.29	2.00	1.93
Sample 22	3.79	3.29	3.86	2.71
Sample 23	2.29	2.00	1.79	1.93
Sample 24	4.21	3.79	4.07	3.64
Sample 25	3.79	2.64	2.71	3.36
Sample 26	2.21	2.14	1.50	2.43

3.3.3 Quantifying visual control elements

Based on the quantification-I theory, the form visual control elements of contactors were quantized, and the binary category response values were compiled, as shown in table 5.

Table 5. Binary category response values of samples.

Samples Categories	Dust cover a			Coil hole b			Parti-ng line c		Contact slot d			Side slot e	
	a 1	a 2	a 3	b 2	b 2	b 3	c 1	c 2	d 1	d 2	d 3	e 1	e 2
Sample 1	0	0	1	1	0	0	0	1	1	0	0	1	0
Sample 2	1	0	0	1	0	0	0	1	0	0	1	0	1
Sample 3	1	0	0	0	0	1	0	1	0	1	0	1	0
Sample 4	1	0	0	1	0	0	1	0	1	0	0	1	0
Sample 5	1	0	0	1	0	0	1	0	0	0	1	1	0
Sample 6	0	0	1	1	0	0	0	1	0	0	1	1	0
Sample 7	1	0	0	0	0	1	1	0	0	0	1	1	0
Sample 8	1	0	0	1	0	0	1	0	0	0	1	1	0
Sample 9	1	0	0	1	0	0	1	0	0	0	1	0	1
Sample 10	1	0	0	1	0	0	1	0	0	0	1	0	1
Sample 11	0	1	0	1	0	0	1	0	0	1	0	0	1
Sample 12	0	1	0	0	1	0	0	1	0	0	1	0	1
Sample 13	0	1	0	0	1	0	1	0	0	0	1	0	1
Sample 14	0	1	0	1	0	0	0	1	0	0	1	1	0
Sample 15	1	0	0	0	0	1	1	0	0	0	1	1	0
Sample 16	1	0	0	1	0	0	0	1	0	0	1	0	1
Sample 17	0	0	1	1	0	0	0	1	0	1	0	0	1
Sample 18	1	0	0	1	0	0	1	0	0	1	0	0	1
Sample 19	1	0	0	1	0	0	0	1	0	1	0	0	1
Sample 20	1	0	0	1	0	0	1	0	0	0	1	1	0
Sample 21	1	0	0	0	1	0	1	0	0	0	1	0	1
Sample 22	0	1	0	1	0	0	0	1	0	1	0	0	1
Sample 23	1	0	0	1	0	0	1	0	0	1	0	1	0
Sample 24	1	0	0	0	1	0	0	1	0	0	1	1	0
Sample 25	1	0	0	1	0	0	0	1	1	0	0	1	0
Sample 26	1	0	0	1	0	0	0	1	1	0	0	1	0

3.3.4 Establishing the mapping relationship between images and visual control elements

A computer-assisted analysis system on visual control element of product form was developed. The mapping relationships between target images and contactor visual control elements were established by using the quantification-I theory. Thus, the visual control elements of contactor form under the target images were identified, as shown in Table 6.

In the data， the multiple correlation coefficient indicated the precision of the model, the partial correlation coefficient indicated the importance of element, the standard coefficient indicated the category's contribution value to the image. Finally, the predictions of the target images were realized, the form design of contactor's new generation upgrade products were guided.

In table 6, the multiple correlation coefficients of integrity, quality, technology and humanism were 0.70, 0.80, 0.67 and 0.62 respectively, and their values were generally large. The results showed that the accuracy of the models is relatively high. For 'integrity', the partial correlation coefficients between parting line and side slot were 0.60 and 0.38 respectively, and the values were relatively large, which indicated that they have a great influence on the 'integrity' image of the contactors. However, the partial correlation coefficients of dust cover, coil hole and contact slot were 0.29, 0.20 and 0.16 respectively, and the values were relatively small, which indicated that these items have less influence on the 'integrity' image of the contactors. According to the standard coefficients, when the parting line was a broken line and the side slot was arc, the product image tended to 'integrity'. In view of 'quality', the parting line and coil hole had great influences on it, and the parting line should choose the broken line, and the coil hole should select the round countersink. In the view of 'technology', the parting line had great influences on it, and the parting line should be a broken line. In view of 'humanism', contact slot and parting line had great influences on it, the contact slot should be non-penetrating, and the parting line should be a broken line. In summary, when the coils hole had a round countersink, the parting line was a broken line, the contact slot was non-penetrating and the side slot was arc, the integral shape of AC contactors tended to integrity, quality, technology and humanism.

Table 6. Image analysis of visual control elements in contactor form.

Items	Categories	Integrity		Quality		Technology		Humanism	
		Standard coefficients	Partial correlation coefficients	Standard coefficients	Partial correlation coefficients	Standard coefficients	Partial correlation coefficients	Standard coefficients	Partial correlation coefficients
Dust cover	No dust cover	0.73		0.62		0.48		0.89	
	Transparent	2.04	0.29	1.92	0.32	1.61	0.29	2.31	0.22
	Observation window	1.77		1.94		1.30		2.24	
Coil hole	No countersink	0.00		0.00		0.00		0.00	
	Round countersink	0.23	0.20	0.34	0.50	0.22	0.27	0.05	0.13
	Square countersink	0.05		0.09		0.40		-0.16	
Parting line	Straight line	0.00	0.60	0.00	0.62	0.00	0.48	0.00	0.32
	Broken line	0.33		0.26		0.30		0.16	
Contact slot	No penetration	0.00		0.00		0.00		0.00	
	Arc penetration	-0.10	0.16	-0.08	0.40	0.25	0.33	-0.57	0.50
	Square penetration	0.02		0.09		0.25		-0.07	
Side slot	Square	0.00	0.38	0.00	0.30	0.00	0.23	0.00	0.27
	Arc	0.20		0.11		0.15		0.17	
Multiple correlation coefficients		0.70		0.80		0.67		0.62	

4 Deconstruction of regional cultural symbols

Symbols are the identifies with representative meaning and the carriers of informations. It can not only refer to things, but also express feelings and ideas[10]. Regional cultural symbols are the precious wealth of human beings, and it is also a very useful design resource in the process of form design of new generation upgrade products. If the regional cultural symbols are integrated into the form design of new generation upgrade products, it can embody the cultural connotation of the new generation upgrade products on the basis of satisfying its functions.

Tianshui 213 Electrical Apparatus is located in Tianshui, Gansu province. Tainshui Maiji Mountain Grottoes and Fuxi Temple are most well known. So the regional cultural symbols of Tianshui were deconstructed from Maiji Mountain Grottoes and Fuxi Temple. Firstly, the representative forms were integrated from of Maiji Mountain Grottoes and Fuxi Temple. Secondly, the representative forms were interpreted, and four form factors were obtained and numbered, as shown in figure 4. Finally, by using the design format analysis[11], as shown in figure 5, the kansei image features of form factors were extracted, and the synthetic values of the kansei images of form factors were obtained, as shown in table 7. The synthetic value ordering of kansei images of form factor 2, form factor 3 and form factor 4 were high, so it was suitable to integrate the cultural elements into the new generation upgrade products form design of Tianshui 213 AC contractor.

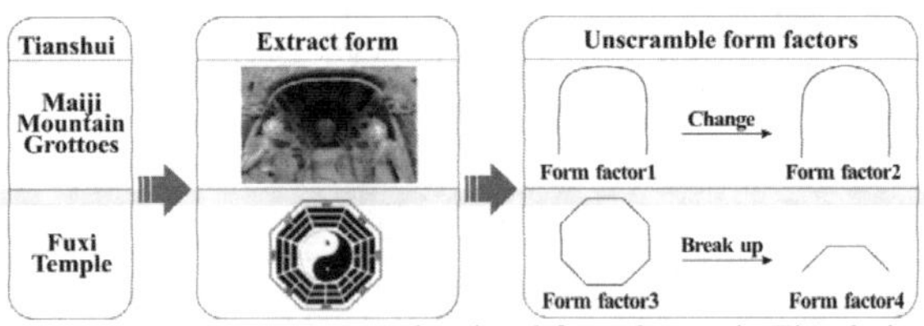

Figure 4. Capture process of regional form factors in Tianshui.

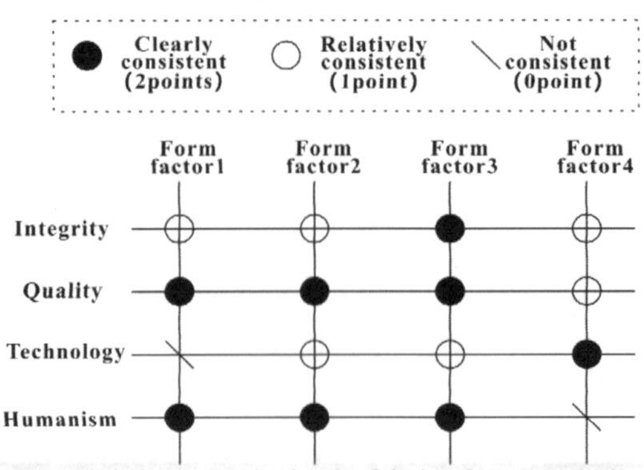

Figure 5. Diagrammatic sketch of design format analysis.

Table 7. Mean values and synthetic values ordering of form factors to images.

Images Form factors	Form factor1	Form factor2	Form factor3	Form factor4
Integrity	1.08	1.08	1.62	1.31
Quality	1.23	1.46	1.46	0.92
Technology	0.85	1.31	1.54	1.46
Humanism	1.31	1.85	0.92	1.38
Synthetic values	4.46	5.69	5.54	5.08
Ordering	Form factor 2>Form factor 3>Form factor 4>Form factor 1			

5 Innovative form design of new generation upgrade products

By deconstructing the form of AC contactors, we can see that the form design of the 213 new generation upgrade AC contactor need to embody integrity, quality, technology, and humanism, and should give priority to the selection of coil hole with round countersink, broken parting line, non-penetrating contact slot and arc side slot. The form factor 2 obtained by regional cultural symbols meeted the needs of coil hole with round countersink and arc side slot. The form factor 4 meeted the form requirement of broken parting line. In summary, based on the brand identity of the 213 AC contactor, the obvious arc shoulder form was retained. Form factor 2 and form factor 4 were selectively incorporated into its form design of new generation by using the aesthetic principles, while ensuring that the integral shape was square and straight, with less curve and more straight. The new generation upgrade design was shown in figure 6. The new product was not only brand identifiable, but also reflected the functional characteristics of AC contactors, and meeted the consumers' perceptual needs and cultural connotations. In addition, it also satisfied consumers' perceptual needs.

Figure 6. New generation upgrade design of 213 AC contactor.

6 Conclusion

The product regeneration conforms to the pace of the development of the times, and it overcomes the restriction of the product life cycle. Under the circumstance of the decline of the previous generation products, the new product will go back to the starting point of the life cycle. Based on brand identity, this study integrated regional cultural symbols into the form design of new generation upgrade product. It endowed the new product with certain cultural connotation, and made the new generation upgrade product form design have rules to follow. Designers should firmly grasp the pulse of the times and timely transform the functions, ideas, emotions and connotations of the brand into the form elements of the new products, to communicate the specific images for users and creat the new products which accord with the trend of the times and have national characteristics. The new products will make consumers get the aesthetic experience and spiritual satisfaction, so as to ultimately obtain design recognition, which can not only deepen the impression of the brand, but also guarantee the long-term heritage of the brand.

Acknowledgments

The authors would like to extend our sincere thanks to all those who contributed to this study, especially the participants who took the trouble to respond to the questionnaires. The project is sponsored by National Natural Science Foundation of China (51465037), Hongliu Outstanding Talent Development Program of Lanzhou University of Technology (J201406) and New Generation Series Products Appearance Industrial Design of Tianshui 213 Electrical Apparatus (H1707cc006).

References

1. M Xu, JC Lv, W Li, YK Wu. Strategies and Methods of Car Form Design in the Background of Cars Regeneration. South Agricultural Machinery, **48**, 15, 138+145 (2017)
2. JH Hu. Orientation Views of Product Design. Packaging Engineering, **22**, 6, 77-78 (2001)
3. M Baxter. *Product design-practical methods for the systematic development of new products* (Stanley Thornes Ltd, Cheltenham, 1995)
4. JN Su, HQ Li, FQ Li. Investigation of kansei image direction for product design. Journal of Lanzhou University of Technology, **30**, 2, 40-43 (2004)
5. XW Li. Strategies and Methods of Car Styling Design in the Background of Cars Regeneration. Journal of Wuhan University of Technology (Social Sciences Edition), **29**, 2, 308-313 (2016)
6. K Yamamoto. *Kansei Engineering: The Art of Automotive Development at Mazda* (The University of Michigan, Ann Arbor, 1986)
7. DY Li. Introduction of Design Format Analysis in Product Design. Tianjin Textile Science & Technology, **41**, 2, 26-28 (2004)
8. JN Su, HQ Li. Investigation of relationship of form design elements to kansei image by means of

quantification-I theory. Journal of Lanzhou University of Technology, **31**, 2, 36-39 (2005)

9. CE Osgood, CJ Suci, PH Tannenbaum. *The measurement of meaning* (University of Minoes Press, Urbana, 1957)
10. SJ Luo, WJ Li. *Product Family Design DNA* (China Architecture & Building Press, Beijing, 2016)
11. P Oscar, S Jan, S Dirk. Should new products looks imilar or different? The influence of the Market environment on strategic product styling. Design Studies, **29**, 1, 30-48 (2008)

MATEC Web of Conferences **176**, 04009 (2018) https://doi.org/10.1051/matecconf/201817604009
IFID 2018

FBS framework application based on user requirement analysis

ZHANG Qing, CHEN Deng-kai

Shaanxi Engineering Laboratory for Industrial Design, Northwestern Polytechnic University, Xian 710072

Abstract. Users' requirements are key factor for optimizing the design of products. It could be classified into two groups: qualitative research work and quantitative research work. Wireless internet terminal equipment could be used as one example to further study the qualitative research work of requirements. FBS guided by users' requirements was discussed. The users centered service designing process model was established through the analysis of users' needs (Ra) in the function of design, use-pattern, delivery and transformation. Based on this work, the relation between users' needs and requirements of the design was set up. The completely research work about transformation of users' needs to design requirements was discussed in this study, and finally a wireless terminal equipment was used as a case study to verify this method.

1 Introduction

In the era of large-scale industrial data, with diversified products and complicated functions, the requirements of customers have increasingly become the focus of designs. First of all, industrial design needs to study the requirements of people, and then to solve the problem of how to make products effectively serve users. Industrial design is based on user-centered. The purpose of product design is to improve people's quality of life. Only the designer accurately grasps the user's requirements, the user is likely to buy and have good feedback on the product. User research has long been considered an important stage of design, and it plays an important role in a complete design process. However, the design process deviates from the expected results because subjective factors affect the accuracy of user researches. At present, there are many design methods that can guide user research to play an even greater role. The function-behavior-structure model (FBS model) was proposed by Gero in 1990. After continuous in-depth research by Gero and other scholars, this model has now formed a complete process of design [1] [2]. This article focuses on how to incorporate user research information into the model so that designers can obtain accurate conclusions that reflect real needs in the process of design.

2 User research

Taking wireless Internet access products as an example: When we were doing user research, in order to understand the research object, we selected 100 research subjects and let them describe the concept of wireless internet terminal and choose the products they approve. There are simple and complicated products. Different understanding of product concepts will make different choices. We can get 100 different answers from 100 research subjects, which is mainly because everyone has a different understanding of things. Research subjects need to pick out products that they approve from many electronic products. Basically, they can all find out smoothly. The research object undoubtedly understands the concept of a wireless internet terminal. But their understanding of the concept extension is uncertain. Therefore, we require the research subjects to classify the products according to their shapes, which will cause various deviations. This is part of the research which is difficult to research accurately.

2.1 Definition of user requirements

User requirements refer to the user's desire to solve the problem, which are in work or life and cannot be effectively resolved, and need to be resolved by product, technology, or business methods. In terms of the design process, the designer understands what the user really wants through these requirements, so the design will have a direction. But understanding these needs accurately requires a lot of work. Taking a wireless Internet access terminal as an example, the designer should do research to determine whether the user really needs this product and avoid the "detour" in the design. In addition to the normal product background and user questionnaires, we also conducted in-depth analysis of user needs through scene analysis and shooting with follow.

2.2 Process of user survey

There are two types of user survey, qualitative research and quantitative research. Qualitative research is an exploratory research with a free form of research, which

*Corresponding author: [a] zhangqing@e-mail.org

uses special methods and techniques to investigate the deep information of the target's perceptions, reasons, motivations, etc. Its commonly used methods include user interviews, field survey, usability testing, focus groups, and photo diaries. Quantitative research is a scientific research that investigates the attributes of things and their movement. Accurate data-based research can select more users than qualitative research, analyze big data, and prioritize more important tasks [3]. Figure 1 is the research process of wireless mobile internet terminals, combining qualitative research and quantitative research.

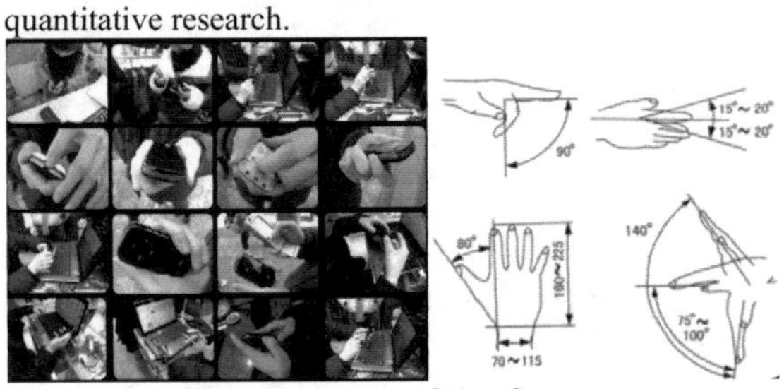

Figure 1. Process of User Survey.

2.3 Analysis of user requirements

We need to calculate, analyze semantics and integrate information in order to derive the core requirements from the large amount of information and data obtained from research. The data and information obtained during the research process can be fed back into the design process, as shown in Figure 2

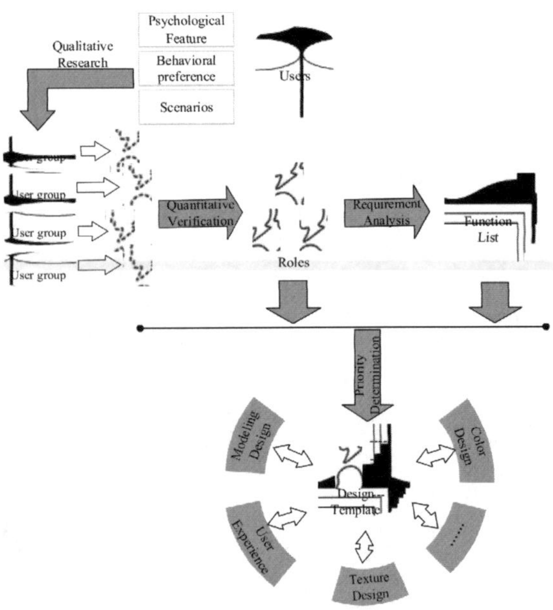

Figure 2. Flow chart of user analysis.

3 FBS Theory

The FBS model is a classic model used to describe the process of product design. It transforms the behavioral system (B) to create a corresponding relation between the functional system (F) and the structural system (S). This model contains three variables of function, behavior, and structure, as well as the basic process in the design process. The needs and requirements of the design were originally non-reference variables of the FBS model. However, the needs of users undoubtedly have a dominant role in design in the actual design process. In the previous study, what the first step in the design of any product was designers think about how to translate "function" into "behavior" of product. Gero has proposed a solution to the design in the early stages of FBS theory. That is, four strategies to solve problems that can be used on the basis of the prototype. See Figure 3.

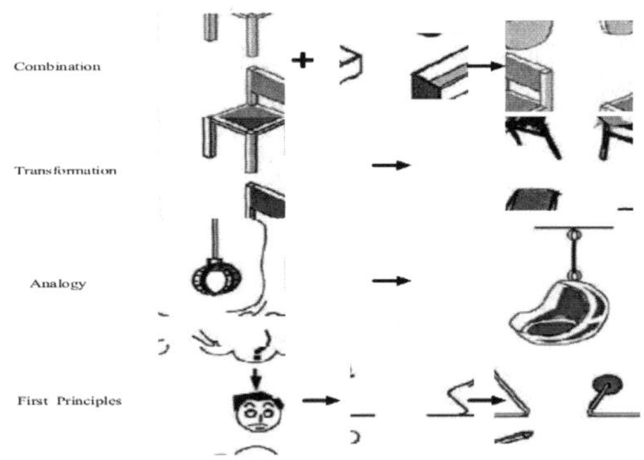

Figure 3. The solution to the design proposed by Gero.

Combination: A recombination or rearrangement of the design scheme. Mutation: This strategy mainly modifies the inadequacy of certain attributes and makes changes to the design scheme. Analogy: This strategy focuses on innovation by selecting similar features and extracting similarities. The first principle: This strategy focuses on getting the proper form and results[4] from the original requirements or functions of the design.

In 2004, Gero continued to refine the FBS model and introduced a new variable: Requirements. This study interprets the world-wide concepts Fi, Bi, and i through design models. Therefore, the demand R[5] is also well-interpreted. By summarizing these model methods and combining Gero's strategy for solving the four problems, we can obtain the other corresponding three strategies:1.In order to extract the key elements of user needs, we can use the strategies of "mutation" or "first principle" to amend or get rid of the unreasonable aspects of the design scheme. It applies to the development stage of the design scheme. We can continue to modify the design to form a collection of design schemes. In the end we will get a satisfactory scheme.2. At the stage of generating the scheme, we need to use the strategy of "combination" to merge all the demand points, thereby motivating new innovations of design.3. The strategy of "analogy" will motivate more innovations. We use this strategy at the generation and development stage of scheme. The strategy of "analogy" can bend the brain in new directions by integrating new elements. In the case of wireless internet terminals, the most numerous design schemes were created by using the strategy of analogy.

4 Research on the combination of user requirements and FBS Model

Based on the cognitive structure of semantic features and strategies for solving problems, we can determine that analysis (Ra) and behavior (B) are key variables in product design issues. According to requirements of design, designers can use the Ra-FBS model to classify complex and decentralized design issues and then analyze the functional characteristics of the results to solve problems. This will help designers make reasonable choices in the design process that follows.

Throughout the whole design process, the designer first needs to transform user requirements into analysis of user requirements (R-Ra) and transform the product functions into expected behaviors that can achieve the functions. Expected behavior can be a structural scheme through requirements' analysis of design strategy. The designer then obtains structure-driven behavior from the structural scheme, and then makes comparisons and evaluations. If the evaluated scheme is incomplete, the designer can repeat the above steps, which can make the step of transforming requirements into functions more clear. When designers analyze user requirements, they can use this method, overall structure, details of simple mechanical structure, calculation of similarity of space conversion function, variation of functional combination, to transform requirements into structural functions. Designers are not satisfied with the function of the optimized structure scheme and can then modify the function. After the structural scheme is redesigned, the designer can finally obtain a more complete design scheme which is based on the user's needs through the description of the structural scheme. Model see Figure 4.The meaning of each variable in the model is described in Table 1.

Table 1. The meaning of the parameters in the model.

R_a-FBS Variable Definition	
Variable symbol	Definition
R	Requirement
F	Function
A	Analogy
B_e	Expected Behavior
B_s	Behavior Derived from Structure
S	Structure
R_a	User requirementanalogy result

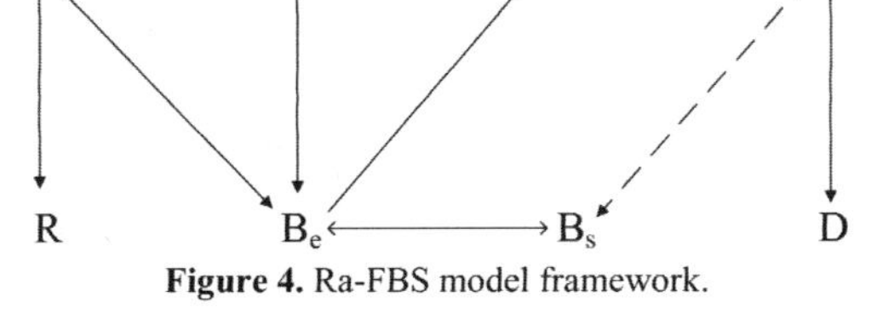

Figure 4. Ra-FBS model framework.

The transformation from behavior to structure, Be—Ra—S, in the FBS model can be seen as a change of turn. It clearly shows the structural changes under the influence of different behavioral patterns. User requirements analysis is a variable in this process. A preliminary program set can be combined and formed by various structural changes. In terms of style, color, and human-computer interaction, we can generate and optimize a set of design schemes by strategies of combining, classifying, and mutating, which will ultimately result in a set of diverse and understandable design schemes.

5 Real design case about system verification

With various functions and shapes, the wireless internet terminal products are typical and complex products. The product is designed using the analysis model of user requirements, Ra-FBS. The analysis of different types of requirements is the basis for the development of enterprise products. The designer transforms uncertain user requirements into points in the design, so that the design requirements are clear, resulting in innovative products that have both real consumer needs and product design quality.

The Ra-FBS design process shown in Figure 5 applies to industrial products which are based on requirements analysis. However, in the actual design process, there are many uncertain factors. Because of the expansion of designer's thinking, the design process is not fixed, and some design steps are neglected in different stages. This is directly related to the differentiation of the selected objects, and they can all be flexibly adjusted. The design of the wireless internet terminal equipment adopts the model framework, Ra-FBS, and the corresponding design process is as follows:

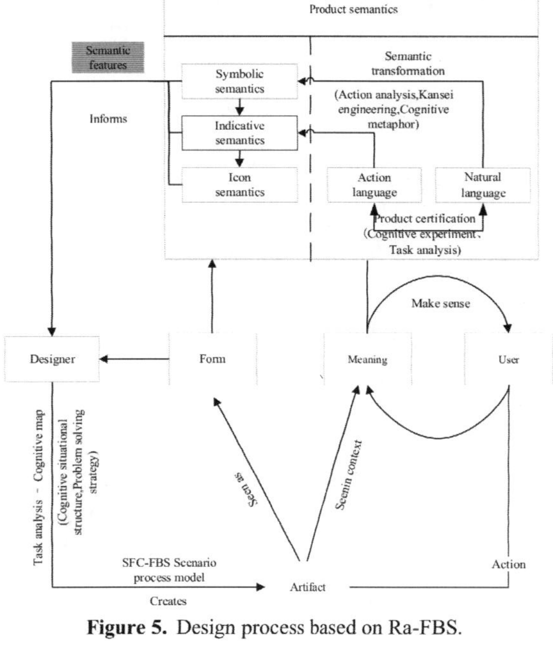

Figure 5. Design process based on Ra-FBS.

Step 1: R→Ra→F. We transform user requirements into product functions through Ra, and then analyze the qualitative structure and functions of this case to divide the wireless internet terminal equipment into various combinations. The core part of the design is the main function of the product. We analyze the usage to get the product's usage habits. Step 2: F→Be. We transform product functions based on different user requirements into expected behavior, and then compare and analyze similar products. Step 3: Be→Ra→S. Based on the analysis of different user requirements, designers integrate to form a design scheme. We combine product shapes, colors and patterns under the guidance of style features, in the horizontal dimension of the paradigmatic axis. We extract design elements from features and use strategies of analogy and mutation for these elements and pattern features. Finally we got three series with a total of 8 design schemes. Step 4: S→Bs→Be→Ra→S. We need to re-evaluate and modify the design i n this step. The step of S→Bs is to evaluate whether the design scheme satisfies the rationality of the structure through relevant theory. In the step of Bs → Be, the designer compares and evaluates the design scheme and the initial design in order to select a more complete scheme and remodify. In the step of Be → Ra → S, the designer selects the morphological changes of the core product mainly through strategies such as combination, inheritance, and first principles, and finally produces a series of wireless internet terminal products. Figure 6 shows the case.

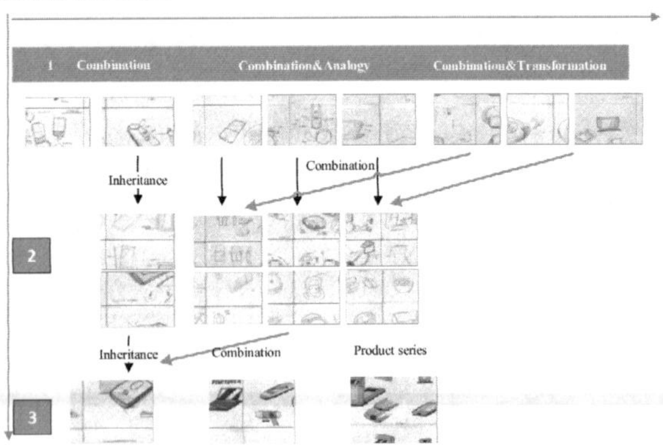

Figure 6. Design process based on Ra-FBS.

6 Conclusion

Based on user requirements, this article systematically constructs the function-behavior-structure feedback model (Ra-FBS), which forms a complete method for designing industrial products from user requirements to designers' requirements. With this method, the user's needs are clearly reflected in the actual function of the product in the design process. This article only studies the combination of user requirements and the FBS model, ignoring the impact of other design processes on the product. In further research we should pay attention to the impact of behavior and structure on the product.

References

1. Gero J S. Design Prototypes: A Knowledge Representation Schema for Design[J]. Ai Magazine, 1990, 11(4):26--36.
2. Gero J S, Kannengiesser U. Representational affordances in design, with examples from analogy making and optimization[J]. Research in Engineering Design, 2012, 23(3):235-249.
3. Galle P. The ontology of Gero's FBS model of designing[J]. Design Studies, 2009, 30(4):321-339.
4. Gero, J. S., Kannengiesser, U. The situated function – behavior - structure framework[J]. Design Studies, 2014, 25(4): 373-391.
5. Gero, J S., Kannengiesser, U. The Function – Behaviour - Structure Ontology of Design[M]. An Anthology of Theories and Models of Design. Springer London, 2014:263 -283.

AUTHOR INDEX

AUTHOR INDEX

AUTHOR INDEX

EDP Sciences – Web of Conferences
17, Avenue du Hoggar
Parc d'Activité de Courtabouf
BP 112
F-91944 Les Ulis Cedex A
France

ISBN 978-1-5108-6599-0

9 781510 865990

CURRAN ASSOCIATES INC.
proceedings.com